Changing Global Media Landscapes:
Convergence, Fragmentation, and Polarization

Jabbar A. Al-Obaidi
Bridgewater State University, USA

A volume in the Advances in Media, Entertainment, and the Arts (AMEA) Book Series

Published in the United States of America by
IGI Global
Information Science Reference (an imprint of IGI Global)
701 E. Chocolate Avenue
Hershey PA, USA 17033
Tel: 717-533-8845
Fax: 717-533-8661
E-mail: cust@igi-global.com
Web site: http://www.igi-global.com

Copyright © 2024 by IGI Global. All rights reserved. No part of this publication may be reproduced, stored or distributed in any form or by any means, electronic or mechanical, including photocopying, without written permission from the publisher. Product or company names used in this set are for identification purposes only. Inclusion of the names of the products or companies does not indicate a claim of ownership by IGI Global of the trademark or registered trademark.

Library of Congress Cataloging-in-Publication Data

CIP DATA PROCESSING

2024 Information Science Reference

ISBN(hc): 9798369337677
ISBN(sc): 9798369348994
eISBN: 9798369337684

British Cataloguing in Publication Data
A Cataloguing in Publication record for this book is available from the British Library.

The views expressed in this book are those of the authors, but not necessarily of the publisher.

For electronic access to this publication, please contact: eresources@igi-global.com.

Advances in Media, Entertainment, and the Arts (AMEA) Book Series

Giuseppe Amoruso
Politecnico di Milano, Italy

ISSN:2475-6814
EISSN:2475-6830

Mission

Throughout time, technical and artistic cultures have integrated creative expression and innovation into industrial and craft processes. Art, entertainment and the media have provided means for societal self-expression and for economic and technical growth through creative processes.

The **Advances in Media, Entertainment, and the Arts (AMEA)** book series aims to explore current academic research in the field of artistic and design methodologies, applied arts, music, film, television, and news industries, as well as popular culture. Encompassing titles which focus on the latest research surrounding different design areas, services and strategies for communication and social innovation, cultural heritage, digital and print media, journalism, data visualization, gaming, design representation, television and film, as well as both the fine applied and performing arts, the AMEA book series is ideally suited for researchers, students, cultural theorists, and media professionals.

Coverage

- Products, Strategies and Services
- Popular Culture
- Fine Arts
- Traditional Arts
- Communication Design
- Digital Media
- Drawing
- Print Media
- Cross-Media Studies
- Design Tools

IGI Global is currently accepting manuscripts for publication within this series. To submit a proposal for a volume in this series, please contact our Acquisition Editors at Acquisitions@igi-global.com or visit: http://www.igi-global.com/publish/.

The Advances in Media, Entertainment, and the Arts (AMEA) Book Series (ISSN 2475-6814) is published by IGI Global, 701 E. Chocolate Avenue, Hershey, PA 17033-1240, USA, www.igi-global.com. This series is composed of titles available for purchase individually; each title is edited to be contextually exclusive from any other title within the series. For pricing and ordering information please visit http://www.igi-global.com/book-series/advances-media-entertainment-arts/102257. Postmaster: Send all address changes to above address. Copyright © 2024 IGI Global. All rights, including translation in other languages reserved by the publisher. No part of this series may be reproduced or used in any form or by any means – graphics, electronic, or mechanical, including photocopying, recording, taping, or information and retrieval systems – without written permission from the publisher, except for non commercial, educational use, including classroom teaching purposes. The views expressed in this series are those of the authors, but not necessarily of IGI Global.

Titles in this Series

For a list of additional titles in this series, please visit: www.igi-global.com/book-series

Media Representation of Migrants and Refugees
Serpil Kir Elitaş (Hatay Mustafa Kemal University, Turkey)
Information Science Reference • copyright 2024 • 338pp • H/C (ISBN: 9798369334591) • US $245.00 (our price)

Making Art With Generative AI Tools
Shalin Hai-Jew (Hutchinson Community College, USA)
Information Science Reference • copyright 2024 • 300pp • H/C (ISBN: 9798369319505) • US $265.00 (our price)

Exploring the Impact of OTT Media on Global Societies
Nithin Kalorth (Mahindra University, India)
Information Science Reference • copyright 2024 • 332pp • H/C (ISBN: 9798369335260) • US $295.00 (our price)

Advancements in Socialized and Digital Media Communications
Gülbuğ Erol (Iğdır University, Turkey) and Michael Kuyucu (Alanya University, Turkey)
Information Science Reference • copyright 2024 • 364pp • H/C (ISBN: 9798369308554) • US $230.00 (our price)

Using Traditional Design Methods to Enhance AI-Driven Decision Making
Tien V. T. Nguyen (Industrial University of Ho Chi Minh City, Vietnam) and Nhut T. M. Vo (National Kaohsiung University of Science and Technology, Taiwan)
Information Science Reference • copyright 2024 • 503pp • H/C (ISBN: 9798369306390) • US $245.00 (our price)

News Media and Hate Speech Promotion in Mediterranean Countries
Elias Said Hung (Universidad Internacional de la Rioja, Spain) and Julio Montero Diaz (Universidad Internacional de la Rioja, Spain)
Information Science Reference • copyright 2023 • 364pp • H/C (ISBN: 9781668484272) • US $215.00 (our price)

701 East Chocolate Avenue, Hershey, PA 17033, USA
Tel: 717-533-8845 x100 • Fax: 717-533-8661
E-Mail: cust@igi-global.com • www.igi-global.com

Table of Contents

Preface xvii

Acknowledgment xxv

Chapter 1
Agenda-Setting and Framing Theories: Perspectives on Digital and Social Media Fragmentation
and Convergence 1
    Jabbar A. Al-Obaidi, Bridgewater State University, USA

Chapter 2
Revocation of Article 370 Changing Global Media Landscapes in India: Media Framing of
Conflict Types in Dawn, The Hindu, and the New York Times 16
    Keerthana Thankachan, Bharathiar University, India
    Thomas Peedikayil Eapen, Bharathiar University, India
    Vishnu Achutha Menon, Central University of Tamil Nadu, India

Chapter 3
Crises Determine Preference and Media Credibility: Case Study of Mass Protest in Iraq 38
    Haitham Hadi Numan, University of Exeter, UK

Chapter 4
Media and Contemporary African Society: Constructing an Environment Sensitive
Communication Theory of Media Effect 55
    Desmond Onyemechi Okocha, Bingham University, Nigeria
    Maureen Chigbo, Bingham University, Nigeria

Chapter 5
Navigating the Social Media Maze: Strategies for Effective Digital Marketing in a Fragmented
Landscape 84
    Surjit Singha, Kristu Jayanti College (Autonomous), India

Chapter 6
Global Media Changes and Digital Advertising: Impact of Digital Advertising on Consumer
Behavior 107
    Kevser Zeynep Meral, İstanbul Bahçeşehir University, Turkey

Chapter 7
Beyond Goodwill: The Interplay of CSR Communication, Individual Beliefs, and Corporate
Reputation 128
    Stefania Romenti, IULM University, Italy

Chiara Esposito, IULM University, Italy
Elanor Colleoni, IULM University, Italy
Grazia Murtarelli, IULM University, Italy

Chapter 8
Understanding Health Communication in the Era of Media Convergence 149
B. K. Ravi, Koppal University, India

Chapter 9
Engaging With the News: Applying the 5Cs Model of News Literacy to Young Audiences............. 160
Sameera Tahira Ahmed, UAE University, UAE

Chapter 10
Social Media Landscape in Africa: Mobilising and Engineering Youths for Socio-Political Change in Sub-Saharan Africa... 179
Desmond Onyemechi Okocha, Bingham University, Nigeria
Maureen Chigbo, Bingham University, Nigeria

Chapter 11
The Disinformation Divide: Understanding the Impact of Social Media on Polarization................. 199
Tasnim Jahan, School of Law, Ramaiah University of Applied Sciences, Bengaluru, India
Shashikant Saurav, Symbiosis International University (Deemed), India
Shabnam Jahan, Leisure Byte, India

Chapter 12
Entertainment and Persuasion in Online Politics: A Qualitative Study of Young Voters' Approach in Turkey's 2023 Elections 215
Emine Nazlı Aytuna, Galatasaray University, Turkey
Zindan Çakıcı, Üsküdar University, Turkey
Alparslan Ergün Özkaya, Galatasaray University, Turkey

Chapter 13
Exploring the Dark Side of Social Media and Digital Consumer With a Dystopian Perspective 234
Aysegul Sagkaya Gungor, Istanbul Medeniyet University, Turkey

Chapter 14
Visual Media in Light of the Challenges of Generative Artificial Intelligence in Egypt 258
Hanan Elshibiny, Cairo University, Egypt

Chapter 15
Artificial Intelligence in the Spanish Media: New Uses and Tools in the Production and Distribution of Content 283
Marta Sánchez Esparza, UNIE Universidad, Spain
Santa Palella Stracuzzi, EAE Business School, Spain

About the Contributors 346

Index 349

Detailed Table of Contents

Preface xvii

Acknowledgment xxv

Chapter 1
Agenda-Setting and Framing Theories: Perspectives on Digital and Social Media Fragmentation
and Convergence 1
    Jabbar A. Al-Obaidi, Bridgewater State University, USA

Recent media literature shows that agenda-setting theory has faced several critical challenges, including information processing, identity and affiliation, cultural connection, and environment. The foundational premise for agenda-setting is that the media play a major role in setting and deciding the issues for consumers. On the other side, the framing theory creates a shape or a frame for issues to be presented to the audience. This research proposes that despite the many changes and challenges in the media environment, both theories are still able to influence the choices the consumers make about gathering and processing media content. As a historical reference, the 1968 study by McCombs and Shaw in 1972 laid the ground for the application of the agenda-setting theory and its effect on media messages. The scope of this chapter sheds light on the "distinguish genuine agenda setting" and the "pseudo agenda setting" in digital and social media fragmentation and convergence environment. An analytical discussion of the main components of media convergence is discussed.

Chapter 2
Revocation of Article 370 Changing Global Media Landscapes in India: Media Framing of
Conflict Types in Dawn, The Hindu, and the New York Times 16
    Keerthana Thankachan, Bharathiar University, India
    Thomas Peedikayil Eapen, Bharathiar University, India
    Vishnu Achutha Menon, Central University of Tamil Nadu, India

In this study, the authors investigate how the revocation of Article 370 is framed in the media and how the newspapers frame the types of conflicts by examining the coverage in three prominent newspapers: *The Hindu, Dawn*, and *The New York Times*. Employing a non-experimental ex-post facto research design, we utilize a qualitative content analysis to categorize and analyze the various frames used in media coverage. The analysis encompasses a total of 1,117 stories published over the course of one month, from August 5, 2019, to September 5, 2019, spanning different formats such as news reports, articles, feature stories, editorials, opinions, and cartoons.

Chapter 3
Crises Determine Preference and Media Credibility: Case Study of Mass Protest in Iraq 38
    Haitham Hadi Numan, University of Exeter, UK

This study examines how university students in Iraq perceive credibility and their media preferences during the protests. The research found that the students' political views influenced their choices and perceptions, leading them to shift from traditional media like television, radio, and newspapers to social media platforms like Twitter and Facebook used by the protesters. The study used Cede Gaziano and Kristin McGrath's credibility analysis factors, which include importance, fairness, bias, accuracy, completeness, and trust, to survey a sample of Iraqi undergraduate students before and after the protests. The results showed a significant change in students' perceptions of credibility and their reliance on traditional media versus social media after the start of the protests.

Chapter 4
Media and Contemporary African Society: Constructing an Environment Sensitive
Communication Theory of Media Effect 55
    Desmond Onyemechi Okocha, Bingham University, Nigeria
    Maureen Chigbo, Bingham University, Nigeria

This research proposes a theory that ameliorates the deficiencies of agenda-setting, two-step flow, and third-person effect theories that are linear in explaining the influence of mass media on their audience. Whereas postmodernism abhors universality because, in reality, different groupings of individuals in different societies receive and respond to media messages differently depending on the influence of both internal and exogenous variables in the society in any communication process. These lacunas in the theories birthed the environment dynamo theory which does not intend to replace but to capture the idea that science, psychology, ethnography, and technology have broadened the understanding of the nuances that determine the relationship between the media and audience, and vice versa. The environment dynamo theory cumulatively created a web to explain media effects in society based on three components that are intricately interwoven - the audience, media, and environment.

Chapter 5
Navigating the Social Media Maze: Strategies for Effective Digital Marketing in a Fragmented
Landscape 84
    Surjit Singha, Kristu Jayanti College (Autonomous), India

Integrating digital marketing and social media is crucial for organizations to navigate the ever-changing global media environment. Amidst polarization, fragmentation, and convergence, marketers can utilize social media's potential to foster connections, increase brand recognition, and involve communities. Attainment requires manoeuvring through the digital environment, adjusting to shifting consumer preferences and imbibing novel ideas. Methods encompass data analytics to obtain valuable insights, develop engaging content experiences, and emphasize genuineness and adaptability. Anticipating forthcoming developments and adopting novel strategies will be essential for optimizing the influence of marketing efforts. In our interconnected world, social media marketing presents various opportunities and challenges that necessitate a strategic, audience-focused, and data-driven approach to achieve success.

Chapter 6
Global Media Changes and Digital Advertising: Impact of Digital Advertising on Consumer
Behavior 107
    Kevser Zeynep Meral, İstanbul Bahçeşehir University, Turkey

This study aims to review digital advertising literature, to identify and define different aspects of 'digital advertising' role in consumers' behavior. Researchers investigated the role of digital advertising on consumers' behavior while online shopping, exposed to digital ads. Research showed that although new digital advertising legislation, rules, regulations, and self-regulations by voluntary initiatives came into force, it could not stop unethical practices in digital advertising. Mainly, due to controlling difficulties in digital world and advised policy makers and governmental bodies to develop new control techniques and applications of digital ads control along with supporting media literacy and family education about effects of digital ads. In conclusion, as the digital world is constantly changing, policy makers and governments must adopt to changes, and must revise legislation and using new controlling techniques without delay. Developing countries must also implement related protective rules of digital advertising and changes which are in force in developed countries.

Chapter 7
Beyond Goodwill: The Interplay of CSR Communication, Individual Beliefs, and Corporate Reputation 128
    Stefania Romenti, IULM University, Italy
    Chiara Esposito, IULM University, Italy
    Elanor Colleoni, IULM University, Italy
    Grazia Murtarelli, IULM University, Italy

This chapter investigates the interplay between consumer activism, corporate social responsibility communication (CSR), and corporate reputation. Using IKEA as a case study, the present study investigates the relationship between CSR communication, CSR-fit, CSR credibility, individual beliefs and corporate reputation using a quantitative design to quantitatively assess the role of CSR-fit and CSR credibility in mediating the role of CSR communication on corporate reputation and the influence of individual beliefs as a moderator of corporate reputation. Results confirm that a strong alignment between a company's CSR initiatives and its core activities positively enhances the credibility of its CSR engagement, consequently contributing to a favorable corporate reputation. By synthesizing academic theories and real-world insights, this research contributes to the understanding of the relationship between individual beliefs, CSR, and corporate reputation, offering valuable implications for companies navigating the complex realm of consumer activism and reputation management.

Chapter 8
Understanding Health Communication in the Era of Media Convergence 149
    B. K. Ravi, Koppal University, India

Today the media landscape is undergoing rapid transformations, driven by technological advancements. The rapid advancements in technology have led to the convergence of various media platforms, resulting in a paradigm shift in the way health information is communicated. The convergence of media platforms and technologies has transformed the media landscape, bringing about significant changes in the way information is accessed, consumed, and shared. The dynamic interplay between traditional and digital media platforms has created new opportunities and challenges in the realm of health communication, shaping the way individuals receive and engage with health information. In this context of media convergence, it is crucial to understand how the changing media landscape affects the delivery and reception of health messages. The integration of multiple media platforms, such as television, radio, print, online platforms, and social media, has led to an unprecedented availability of health information.

Chapter 9
Engaging With the News: Applying the 5Cs Model of News Literacy to Young Audiences............. 160
    Sameera Tahira Ahmed, UAE University, UAE

News literacy (NL) is an increasingly important aspect of media literacy as it emphasises the role that news plays in our daily lives and asks questions about production, consumption, understanding and impact of information garnered from news in contemporary digital media environments. The news consumption of young people is of great interest for both academic and industry sectors as it is often misunderstood or stereotyped yet is key in helping understand future trends. This chapter seeks to apply the 5Cs model of NL to examine the news consumption of university students in a Gulf state. Using data obtained from an online survey (n = 435), it examines context, creation, content, circulation and consumption. In doing so it demonstrates that young people are aware of and practice news literacy behaviours (NLB) which are critical for operating in today's global digital news media environments.

Chapter 10
Social Media Landscape in Africa: Mobilising and Engineering Youths for Socio-Political Change in Sub-Saharan Africa.. 179
    Desmond Onyemechi Okocha, Bingham University, Nigeria
    Maureen Chigbo, Bingham University, Nigeria

Since the Arab Spring pro-democracy riots and upheavals that shook the Middle East and North African authoritarian regimes in 2010 and 2011 and the EndSARS protest against police brutality in Nigeria in 2020, the debate on the influence of social media in galvanizing youth to action has raged. The research was done to establish how social media has advanced the mobilization of youths for social-political change in sub-Saharan Africa in the last five years that countries in the region have witnessed successful general elections. Premised on the theoretical frameworks of media ecology and agenda-setting, the study explained how social media through improved affordable technology and democratization of media have aided and abetted the participation of young people in the transformation of society.

Chapter 11
The Disinformation Divide: Understanding the Impact of Social Media on Polarization.................. 199
    Tasnim Jahan, School of Law, Ramaiah University of Applied Sciences, Bengaluru, India
    Shashikant Saurav, Symbiosis International University (Deemed), India
    Shabnam Jahan, Leisure Byte, India

Communication is one of the oldest tools that have been utilized in all the possible sectors/institutions that can have a positive impact on a developing society. There are no doubts about the role and importance of the same but at the same time, all such instruments can have negative connotations as well. Since time immemorial, vocabulary, conversations, and other forms of communication were given high regard with respect to the impact that any such instrument can have and were used for different purposes other than friendly and informal discussions. With time and tech-advancements, the world witnessed the expansion and blooming of the communication methods and also the impact, both positive and negative, it brought along with. This chapter deals with one of such issues that misuse of communication can cause, that is 'the disinformation divide' and their impact on society. This study firstly conceptualizes the problem in order to understand the origin of the same, secondly it explores all the mediums that are responsible for the above defined problem.

Chapter 12
Entertainment and Persuasion in Online Politics: A Qualitative Study of Young Voters' Approach in Turkey's 2023 Elections 215
    Emine Nazlı Aytuna, Galatasaray University, Turkey

Zindan Çakıcı, Üsküdar University, Turkey
Alparslan Ergün Özkaya, Galatasaray University, Turkey

This study investigates the influence of entertainment elements on political persuasion among young Turkish voters during the 2023 General Elections. Conducting 31 semi-structured interviews with demographically diverse participants aged 18-30 from various locales, it elucidates the nuanced interplay of cultural factors in shaping political attitudes. While participants exhibit a propensity for incorporating entertainment into political discourse, discernible reservations exist regarding the potential propagation of misinformation and the oversimplification of complex political issues. Ultimately, the findings underscore the primary function of entertainment elements in capturing attention rather than effecting substantive shifts in political decision-making processes.

Chapter 13
Exploring the Dark Side of Social Media and Digital Consumer With a Dystopian Perspective 234
Aysegul Sagkaya Gungor, Istanbul Medeniyet University, Turkey

Social media has emerged as a central focus of consumer research, with marketers recognizing its ongoing significance in their field. While previous research has primarily explored consumer behavior and its outcomes through the lens of social media opportunities, it is now apparent that social media carries inherent risks for individuals, companies, and society at large. This chapter delves into the darker aspects of social media, shedding light on its multifaceted nature within the marketing context. By adopting the honeycomb model, the author elucidates the contributions of various parties—individuals, social network owners, and collaborating companies—to the emergence of these dark phenomena. Through careful reflection, the author put forth a series of propositions throughout the article, highlighting avenues for future research and unveiling theoretical implications in this domain.

Chapter 14
Visual Media in Light of the Challenges of Generative Artificial Intelligence in Egypt 258
Hanan Elshibiny, Cairo University, Egypt

The research focuses on the possible changes in the basic foundations of the media message industry in light of the data of artificial intelligence and its applications such as writing the media material, preparing its executive text and presenting it to the recipient from designing clips of images, designing graphics, and sound effects. It also highlights the importance of the tremendous development in aspects of artificial intelligence and its implications for developing the media message, and the performance of visual media in particular, and contributing to the creation of a specialized field in media forms. In light of the tremendous technical developments that have included the media, they are positive that contribute to advancing media progress or negative loses its value.

Chapter 15
Artificial Intelligence in the Spanish Media: New Uses and Tools in the Production and
Distribution of Content 283
Marta Sánchez Esparza, UNIE Universidad, Spain
Santa Palella Stracuzzi, EAE Business School, Spain

In Spain, the media have been exploring artificial intelligence tools for some time. This study investigates which tools are used and in which processes, as well as their impact on the generation of content and the transformation of professional profiles. The methodology has a quantitative approach, through a survey of 35 journalists from the Association of Investigative Journalists (API), made up of media professionals from all over Spain. Among the main uses of AI are the processing and conversion of oral language into writing, the analysis of large amounts of data, the automation of tasks, and the relationship with audiences. A significant segment of respondents use AI tools in their work and believe that it will eventually be used for all automated tasks. However, most of them are not afraid of losing their jobs, as they value the importance of the human and creative component in their work performance.

About the Contributors 346

Index 349

To my current and former students in the U.S., Iraq, Jordan, Yemen, the United Arab Emirates, and China

Foreword

Today we live in a world that no longer believes in the limits of relativity in everything, or even the idea of the end of humanity at the crossroads of the atom, neutrons, and silicon fibers, as that expected progress has exceeded the limits of small human dreams and aspirations in the era of supercomputers and intercontinental globalization, to cause this technological revolution. Digital and industrial technology has led to the occurrence of the most dangerous intellectual shift in human history, which is the explosion of the human fabric, or the arrival of human progress to the limits of the "single point," a point that could not have been discussed and imagined 100 years ago except in science fiction films.

Although today's talk revolves around the impact of the scientific revolution on the environment, thought, and human life, the debate of influence and influence, polarization and repulsion, and the promises and challenges it holds, many researchers agree with the American thinker (Alvin Toffler) in his famous book (Future Shock), that Science and technology have turned into a tool for striking the old and traditional foundations prevailing in human society, reshaping them according to new concepts and systems. As a result, human society will face radical, shock-like changes in many areas of its life and the prevailing relationships between its components.

Therefore, we do not know exactly how this information revolution will end, just as the ancient world was ignorant of what the discovery of nuclear energy meant. Opinions were that the world had discovered a way to generate energy and move factories for the benefit of humanity, only to discover later that it had opened the door to massive destructive wars to destroy the world and spread fear and anxiety. Today, we cannot determine specifically the future of humanity in the era of the flood of information flowing through new media channels, which increases anxiety, frustration and despair for humanity.

It is clear that technology alone is not a decisive cure for the world's ills, but it can create a positive world that is in the interest of humanity, just as it creates a negative world of collision, difference, and disharmony between people, and creates Complications in the field of value behavior, as it contains a lot of brainwashing, falls, and exaggerations. Choking texts and news, distorting facts, exaggerating errors, exaggerating failures, fabrication and distortion, belittlement and distortion, deception, deception and falsification, and obfuscation and demonization of the opponent. It is a media that can be described as the contradiction that creates the contradiction!

in our time, paradoxes abound, and contradictions combine, so that white becomes black and black becomes white, and truths become lies and lies are truths, and the rules of wisdom and the foundations of reason and logic disappear in shame. Let (power) remain logic, and it is the first and last rule, and it is the only one sitting on the throne of thinking, and on its basis everything that emerges in this turbulent world is evaluated and dealt with.

On the other hand, humanity faces the challenges of the gradual collapse of values, due to the storms of life's complexities and the toxins of the media, which played a stimulating role in devoting it to the system of social and cultural values, which helped create new patterns of relationship with reference and identity, and contributed to creating contradictory value equations, some positive and others. Negative. The weak developing environments, contaminated with the values of tyranny, oppression and deprivation, including Arabic, produced the opposite values that produced racist subcultures and societal problems in which the values declined to a low level of effectiveness and innovation, so that the values of fanaticism, hatred and violence spread.

Where there is a culture of incorrect use, the way values are expressed, and the value secretions presented by these means. The spread of communication and smartphones around the world has become more powerful among citizens than at any other time in human history, which will be accompanied by costs, especially at the level of values, privacy and security. Technology will collect and store a lot of personal information in the present, past, and future, and it can be used against the individual, society, and countries against individuals. As well as individuals interacting with each other, which contributes to spreading chaos and cracking social values.

The most serious problem is that most people suffer from fatal class disparities, terrifying gaps in the right to communication, and devastating hunger. This is a crisis of inverted values that was formed due to faulty human upbringing and the culture of "inevitability" established by globalization and the means of communication, through blind acceptance of these values. The most dangerous thing is to believe that these sick values are the reality and there is no alternative to them.

It is clear that the corruption of life in our contemporary societies is increasing at rapid rates, and with it is increasing violence, the destruction of the planet and people, and indifference to the catastrophe of loss of history, as the levels of lying to oneself regarding the role one plays in value crises reach astonishing rates, and they rise with the deterioration of reality. According to the opinion of the German sociologist Max Weber, the advancement of the mind, instead of leading to its mastery, led to its abandonment. The victory of rationalism, instead of being accompanied by its prosperity, was accompanied by its dissolution, and this laxity, or dissolution, was represented in the emergence of multiple, clashing values.

Without a doubt, the three elements: law, freedom, and media ethics, are not the same in importance, but the absence of one of them threatens the media's message and its proper functioning. Without freedom, the content of the media becomes official data, without laws the profession becomes open, unprotected and vulnerable to conflict, and without ethics the media becomes corrupt, controls decline and the role of the main media as observer and critic is threatened.

As a result, we need media that does not mix the rope of difference with the arrows of disagreement, and does not be irritating, divisive, and opposing, but rather reflects the values of rapprochement, tolerance, and attraction, and does not invert the reversed values and make them level with the surface of the earth, and does not create for us worlds of jagged and clashing value planes that make our world burn with death and racism. And hate. Humanity cannot bear more pressures, value clashes, and media discourses that issue evil inverted values. The world we know will head, due to inverted media values, into a terrifying abyss during the next few years!

Yas Al-Bayati
Alnoor University, Nineveh, Iraq

Preface

The central theme of this book focuses on the idea of global interconnectedness and the evolving media environment, which includes convergence and fragmentation. The media landscape has undergone significant changes, with an explosion in the quantity of content. The quality of information is now influenced by ideologies, special interests, political agendas, financial influences, and intensive competition.

The idea for this volume originated from my involvement in the Arab-U.S. Association for Communication Educators (AUSACE). The 27th Annual Conference was organized by AUSACE and took place from October 28th to 30th, 2023 at Kuwait University, Kuwait. The central theme for the annual conference was "changing media landscapes: convergence and fragmentation". I was intrigued by the theme and the subthemes of the conference. The committee of the 27th Annual Conference captured the essence of the dilemma encountered by today's media: "The phenomena of digitization, media convergence, media fragmentation, and consumption of media and user-generated content set the agenda of interests and concerns for educators, scholars, and practitioners". Furthermore, the AUSACE has posted a call for research papers on its website. The call focuses on the rapid development of media platforms, which has disrupted traditional models for publishing, broadcasting, and advertising, and has created a need for identifying new models. As media become more fragmented and at the same time converge, implications can be seen across several different areas, such as the way people access media, how media are marketed, and how the media industry is changing. The 27th Annual International Conference was a success and provided me with the opportunity to interact with world-class scholars.

Precisely, the broader horizon of research reflects the evolving media landscape in the United States and around the world. The conference was attended by representatives from about 12 countries. Among the topics discussed were fake news, artificial and generated content and international law, theories and applications in media technology, literacy and new media, and agenda-setting and framing theories. The editor of this volume raised the question of power: who owns it? Is it the media corporations, the governments, the users, or the big cartels of communication and media technologies? There is no easy answer to this complex question as in the words of Noam Chomsky (2006): It is no easy task to gain an understanding of human affairs". He added "It is necessary to dismantle the structures of deception erected by doctrinal systems, which adopt a range of devices that flow very naturally from ways in which power is concentrated" (p. 103). The ultimate power, however, appears to be held by the big media and communication technologies on the one hand, and by manipulative political leaders, and digital media owners on the other. The fake news and disinformation are threatening democracy, the flow of true information, and the well-being of communities around the world. It is the attack from within as Barbara McQuade describes the power of disinformation. She wrote: "Disinformation is the deliberate use of lies to manipulate people, whether to extract profit or to advance a political agenda. Its unwitting accomplice, misinformation, is spread by unknowing dupes who repeat lies they believe to be true" (McQuade, 2024, p.5). In this sense, media content, whether it is generated by cable television, radio, other digital outlets,

Preface

or social media could be fragmented, while digital media and communication technologies are always open to convergence.

This book offers well-searched global perspectives on the status of media, its digital technologies, the rise of social media, and the danger of fragmentation, and tribalism in news coverage, for example. It emphasizes the importance of adhering to truthful media that aims to inform and educate the audience, rather than misinform or provoke.

As a comprehensive book, it addresses six fundamental educational goals:

- Describe media theories and global perspectives.
- Compare the state of the international media landscape.
- Investigate the rise of social media and its impact.
- Demonstrate the importance of media ethics and law.
- Explore the utilization of artificial intelligence (AI) and the media industry.
- Inspire future media and communication research based on the recommendations offered in the various chapters.

ORGANIZING OF THE BOOK

Section 1: Global Theoretical Perspectives

Chapter 1: Agenda-Setting and Framing Theories: Perspectives on Digital and Social Media Fragmentation and Convergence

The foundational premise for agenda-setting is that the media play a major role in setting and deciding the issues for consumers. On the other side, the framing theory creates a shape or a frame for issues to be presented to the audience. This paper proposes that despite the many changes and challenges in the media environment, both theories are still able to influence the choices the consumers make about gathering and processing media content. As a historical reference, the 1968 study by McCombs and Shaw in 1972 laid the ground for the application of the agenda-setting theory and its effect on media messages. The scope of this paper sheds light on the "distinguish genuine agenda setting" and the "pseudo agenda setting" in digital and social media fragmentation and convergence environment. An analytical discussion of the main components of media convergence (industrial, cultural, social, technical, and textual) is provided.

Chapter 2: Revocation of Article 370 Changing Global Media Landscapes in India: Media Framing of Conflict Types in Dawn, the Hindu, and the New York Times

Media representation of conflicts and its portrayal of Kashmir is mediated (M. et.al, 2020; Graber, D. Appel, MacCombs, M. E, & Weaver, D. H, 1981) thereby resulting in an escalation of the conflict. Media's eyes are the eyes of the public which sets the background and context for the perceptualizing of a situation. Thus, framing the images is equivalent to the framing of public perception and understanding the media language of framing Kashmir in revocation is necessary to understand the media role of portraying the conflict. This book chapter studies how the media covers the revocation of Article 370, revealing various conflict types and the impact of framing techniques on public perception. Comparative analysis of media from affected and third-party nations offers insight into Kashmir's long-term crisis.

Chapter 3: Crises Determine Preference & Media Credibility: Case Study of Mass Protest in Iraq

This chapter explores the issue of credibility and media preferences during crises, using the Iraqi demonstrations that occurred in October 2019 as a case study. It examines the nature of variable credibility and preference in light of the decline of traditional means of communication, such as television and radio, in exchange for social media platforms such as Facebook and Twitter. Despite the extensive literature that discusses misleading information and the unfiltered nature of social media, public perceptions towards them differ from scientific theories. Our study shows that credibility and media preference changed dramatically after the demonstrations began, with social media becoming a voice for the voiceless.

Chapter 4: Media and Contemporary African Society Constructing an Environment-Sensitive Communication Theory of Media Effect

The environment dynamo theory cumulatively created a web to explain media effects in society based on three components that are intricately interwoven - the audience, media, and environment. The study is a quantitative study that deployed a multi-stage sampling technique to select 493 respondents comprising lecturers and students from the Mass Communication Departments of the Alex Ekwueme Federal University, Ndufu-Alike, Abakiliki, Ebonyi State; Bayero University, Kano State and Lagos State University, Lagos State. The findings show that variables such as demography, psychology, socio-political, cultural, ethnoreligious, and technology combine to determine the effects of the media in society. Consequently, the study recommends further empirical testing of the new theory.

Section 2: Media Landscape

Chapter 5: Navigating the Social Media Maze: Strategies for Effective Digital Marketing in a Fragmented Landscape

This chapter explores the critical strategies necessary to navigate the complex world of social media in the context of evolving global media environments. This analysis will explore how convergence has transformed conventional and digital media platforms into one another, thereby presenting marketers with novel prospects to engage with consumers through various channels. Simultaneously, the proliferation of niche communities and micro-audiences has resulted from fragmentation, presenting targeted messaging with challenges and opportunities. Furthermore, due to the polarized nature of online discourse, brands are compelled to adopt a nuanced content creation and engagement strategy. It entails the skillful handling of delicate subjects while upholding their credibility and honesty. It aims to give marketers the requisite understanding and resources to flourish in this ever-changing landscape by integrating theoretical perspectives and pragmatic case studies. By leveraging the potential of data analytics and comprehending the psyche of social media users, we shall reveal tried and true approaches to optimizing reach, engagement, and, ultimately, business outcomes.

Preface

Chapter 7: Beyond Goodwill: The Interplay of CSR Communication, Individual Beliefs and Corporate Reputation

This chapter aims to explore the influence of consumers' individual beliefs in shaping corporate reputation. More specifically, the goal is to address a gap in the current academic literature shifting the focus from the macro-level of analysis of CSR to the micro-level, that of the individual perceptions of CSR information dissemination practices by consumers to explore if the level of knowledge and interest that consumers hold about CSR affect their advocacy behaviours and their activism in favour or against a company, ultimately shaping the company's reputation. By examining the role of individual beliefs in shaping perceptions of CSR and its impact on corporate reputation, this study contributes to the growing body of research on the effectiveness of CSR communication in the evolving media landscape.

Chapter 8: Understanding Health Communication in the Era of Media Convergence

With the advent of the digital age, the health communication scenario in India has witnessed significant transformation. This transformation was accelerated especially during the COVID-19 pandemic times, when the effective health communication was the utmost priority. During the pandemic it was crucial to disseminate accurate health information to the citizens. In such challenging times, the Indian Government utilized digital technologies, including websites, social media, health apps, and telemedicine platforms, to reach a wide range of audiences and create awareness about health issues. The people were constantly given updates about the preventive measures. India today has a health-conscious generation that has facilitated the use of health and fitness apps, along with wearable devices. To complement this trend, the Indian Government initiated campaigns such as the "Fit India Movement," which seeks to propagate health and wellness through multimedia strategies.

Section 3: Social Media

Chapter 9: Engaging with the news: Applying the 5Cs model of news literacy to young audiences

Understanding and applying media literacy skills are becoming increasingly vital in our information saturated societies. On par with reading and writing in traditional literacy, these new literacy skills are indispensable for people to function effectively in both their personal and professional lives in societies where information and communication technologies are widely available. Within the broad spectrum of literacies that exist today, news literacy (NL) commands a prominent role for several significant reasons. The first of these is that the definition of news itself is changing along with an increase in what is deemed newsworthy content. Secondly, what was available to audiences from legacy media, with TV, radio and newspapers as the purveyors of news, was clearer and easier to identify. Now however, the choices available in fragmented news environments in many parts of the world have altered the relationship between producers and consumers as well as disrupting the flows of news and information.

Chapter 10: Social Media Landscape in Africa: Mobilising and Engineering Youths for Socio-Political Change in Sub-Saharan Africa

The chapter establishes how social media has advanced the mobilization of youths for social-political change in countries in sub-Saharan Africa that have witnessed successful general elections in the last five years. Premised on the theoretical frameworks of media ecology and agenda-setting, the study explained how social media through improved affordable technology and democratization of media have aided and abetted the participation of young people in the transformation of society. The qualitative research used secondary data to show the significance of social media in engineering youths for social change in socio-political, economic, or cultural activities in the countries in the region.

Chapter 11: The Disinformation and Divide Understanding: The Impact of Social Media on Polarization

The present era witnessed and has been in trap of Contagion of disgrace which is the spread of fake news and disinformation through tech-related products and services. This has been facilitated more by the sharp rise in social media by people of all ages. India, the second most populous democracy globally, is facing a significant challenge from false news due to the proliferation of divisive propaganda and low literacy rates, which hinder the implementation of democratic decision-making and threaten its democratic fabric. The target audience for this study is not restricted to any particular age group or any specific gender though, it emphasizes youth ranging from aged 13 to the late 20's. The chapter delves into detail by data representation of the age groups that are exposed to any media first of all, moving to a smartphone and then to social media, exploring the most used media to disseminate news and also investigating the major reasons people are using social media in the recent years.

Chapter 12: Entertainment and Persuasion in Online Politics: A Qualitative Study of Young Voters' Approach in Turkey's 2023 Elections

This study was conducted during the campaign period of Turkey's 2023 General Elections, utilizes a qualitative approach based on semi-structured interviews with young voters to examine the incorporation of entertainment aspects into political communication. Specifically, it examines the ways in which these elements are perceived by voters, with a focus on the strategic use of dance videos, social media challenges, storytelling, humor, edits, captions, and memes. Through focused interviews with young voters, the study sheds light on the employment of these entertainment elements to shape political messages, attitudes, and values. This research aims to fill a notable gap in the literature by examining the perceptions and interactions of young Turkish voters with entertainment elements in political communication during the 2023 General Elections. Although the body of research exploring the evolution of political discourse and politician-voter communication on social media is expanding, there is a limited qualitative study in the domain. This is particularly evident in research centered on the incorporation of entertainment elements in social media strategies during election campaigns.

Preface

Chapter 13: Exploring the Dark Side of Social Media and Digital Consumer with a Dystopian Perspective

Polarization refers to divisions or schisms among different groups in the field of social science. It can refer to a situation where divisions have already reached a significant magnitude or a process in which divisions are growing over time, even if they are still relatively small. Polarization can manifest in various ways and is not necessarily problematic. Despite evidence to the contrary, many people believe that echo chambers are widespread and filter bubbles are real. This has led to significant public and political concerns about polarization in numerous countries. Several surveys indicate that a significant portion of the general population believes that the United Kingdom is currently more fragmented than it was in previous times.

Section 4: Artificial Intelligence (AI) and Media

Chapter 14: Visual Media in Light of the Challenges of Generative Artificial Intelligence in Egypt

In the Arab world and Egypt, the newly developed artificial intelligence (AI) systems are still in their early experimental stages. Automating the media sector is something in the near future, but media experts disagree about the ability of artificial intelligence. AI can't replace a journalist, as it is unable to interact live and directly or collect information from sources, and even the issue of objectivity and accuracy, disagreement still exists about the ability of AI to ensure adherence to professional values and ethics, and the press and media move the world and are the two sectors that are among the most technologically advanced in the world. The world and the news determine the priorities of dialogue and public debate to identify what problems should be focused on.

Chapter 15: Artificial Intelligence in the Spanish Media: New Uses and Tools in the Production and Distribution of Content

Artificial Intelligence (AI) has revolutionized the way media outlets operate and deliver content to their audiences. With the advancement of this technology, media has found new ways to collect, analyze, and present information in a more efficient and personalized way. Machine learning algorithms can analyze large amounts of information in a short amount of time, making it easier to identify patterns and trends in data. This has led to an improvement in the accuracy and speed of news delivery, allowing publishers to provide up-to-date and relevant information to their audience more quickly. The arrival of AI in the media is not completely replacing human work, but for the time being, it complements it and streamlines certain processes. Media professionals play a crucial role in monitoring, making decisions, and ensuring the quality of AI-generated content. AI has the potential to help journalists craft new and original content, engage with audiences, verify online media content, and more, making media processes more efficient and impacting yet to be determined.

LAST WORDS

The wide disparity between entertainment, news stories, investigative reports, and interviews reflects the ever-changing landscape of audience expectations and the evolving trends in media consumption. For instance, news reporters and journalists strive to stick to factual information with credible and verifiable sources, while most hosts of late-night talk shows skillfully blend entertainment with the delivery of serious news in a light-hearted and comical manner. However, the impact of personal relationships on news reporting shows the importance of objectivity and truthfulness in journalism, especially in light of sensitive topics such as the economy, race, gender, class, laws, immigration, and politics.

Media organizations and journalists must adhere to solid ethical guidelines and high standards. Loyalty in the business of media whether locally, regionally, and globally should be dedicated to the pursuit of truth.

The expansion of social media and social networks (WhatsApp, YouTube, Facebook, Instagram, WeChat, TikTok, Telegram, X, and Snapchat), and the involvement of users to act as information producers and distributors show how complex the new digital age has become. Spreading false information on social media may harm and be detrimental to community members of communities and may cause a serious problem for their physical safety and mental health.

Jabbar A. Al-Obaidi

REFERENCES

Chomsky, M. (20026). *Failed States: The Abuse of Power and the Assault on Democracy*. A Metropolitan//Owl Book, Henry Holt and Company, New York.

McQuade, B. (2024). *How Disinformation is Sabotaging America: Attack From Within*. Seven Stories Press.

Acknowledgment

I am grateful to my highly esteemed colleague Nina Eddinger, *Assistant Book Development* Editor IGI Global, for her commitment and valuable insights. Nina's encouragement and sufficient communication were fundamental in making this educational project possible.

I am truly grateful to all my colleagues and friends who contributed to this book. Their work will be appreciated by students, scholars, international, reginal and local media organizations, decision-makers, and the international audience.

My special thanks and appreciation to my friend Dr. Yas Al-Bayati, who is a Writer, Journalist, and Professor of Media at Alnoor University, Nineveh, Iraq for dedicating some of his busy time to write a foreword to this book.

I would like to express my gratitude to my beloved wife, Wafaa Al-Hassan. Her persistent support of my academic and educational journey has been truly incredible.

I thank my family members Sarah, Ghalyah, Erika, Reggie, Ayah Nooriah, Amani, and Gravity Alaia for their unwavering support.

Section 1
Global Theoretical Perspectives

Chapter 1
Agenda-Setting and Framing Theories:
Perspectives on Digital and Social Media Fragmentation and Convergence

Jabbar A. Al-Obaidi
http://orcid.org/0009-0008-9588-7535
Bridgewater State University, USA

ABSTRACT

Recent media literature shows that agenda-setting theory has faced several critical challenges, including information processing, identity and affiliation, cultural connection, and environment. The foundational premise for agenda-setting is that the media play a major role in setting and deciding the issues for consumers. On the other side, the framing theory creates a shape or a frame for issues to be presented to the audience. This research proposes that despite the many changes and challenges in the media environment, both theories are still able to influence the choices the consumers make about gathering and processing media content. As a historical reference, the 1968 study by McCombs and Shaw in 1972 laid the ground for the application of the agenda-setting theory and its effect on media messages. The scope of this chapter sheds light on the "distinguish genuine agenda setting" and the "pseudo agenda setting" in digital and social media fragmentation and convergence environment. An analytical discussion of the main components of media convergence is discussed.

INTRODUCTION

Technology and its functionality are subject to stages of Recent media literature showing that agenda-setting theory has faced several critical challenges, including information processing, identity and affiliation, cultural connection, and environment.

The foundational premise for agenda-setting is that the media play a major role in setting and deciding the issues for consumers. On the other side, the framing theory creates a shape or a frame for issues to be presented to the audience. This paper proposes that despite the many changes and challenges in the media environment, both theories are still able to influence the choices the consumers make about gathering and processing media content. As a historical reference, the 1968 study by McCombs and Shaw in 1972 laid

DOI: 10.4018/979-8-3693-3767-7.ch001

the ground for the application of the agenda-setting theory and its effect on media messages. The scope of this paper sheds light on the "distinguish genuine agenda setting" and the "pseudo agenda setting" in digital and social media fragmentation and convergence environment. An analytical discussion of the main components of media convergence (industrial, cultural, social, technical, and textual) is provided.

In reviewing an international book "Communication and Democracy" edited by Maxwell McCombs, Donald L. Shaw, and David Weaver (1997), James W. Dearing highlighted that the theoretical relationship between the historically construed "agenda-setting effect," in which "media set the agenda for what audience members consider important, and media framing, the meanings that characterize mass media news content. The task is ambitious, the chapters by and large interesting, and, for scholars interested in agenda setting, the book is an important contribution" (p. 126).

The argument focuses on the public agenda setting and the influence of the media agenda on the public agenda. It goes a full circle. For example, the public agenda pushes by policymakers, the media highlights what it thinks is important, and pushes back to the audience with specific focus and framing. The aim here is a more" expansive understanding of how the mass media affect their audiences" (Dearing, 1998, p. 126). James Dearing added "The process of framing is conceptualized not just as closely related to agenda setting, but within the agenda-setting paradigm (p. 126).

BACKGROUND

For any society to grow steadily, it needs the full participation and contribution of its citizens. Traditional outlet media and social media could play a major role in creating a participatory environment for the audience. However, media corporations prioritize the bottom line, focusing on profitability and financial returns. They aim to create content and distribution channels that will generate profits. In doing so, media corporations have inadvertently fostered division among their audiences, leading to uncontrollable competition, fragmentation, and tribalism. They have their agenda, and they frame a news story, an event, or a public or private occurrence as they see fit. In the words of veteran journalist and anchor Carol Marin "As long as I've been a reporter people have accused the media of having an agenda" (Uiaa.org. para 25). She also said "I'm not an advocate reporter. My job is to tell a story and let the people get outraged" (Uiaa.org. para 25). The public experience with the media is a mix of mistrust, offense, and indifference. Global media and communication technologies are the highlights of the 21st Century. The central concern for professionals and scholars has been how digital media and social media content and delivery systems are significantly impacted by the ever-fast-changing communication technologies to the extent that media organizations are continually searching for creative ways to stay in business and to remain competitive (Al-Obaidi &Covington, 2007).

Historically, students of the media were studying what is known as Frederick S. Siebert's four theories of the press. Siebert's four theories include authoritarian, totalitarian, libertarian, and social responsibility. Along this side, other cultural theories were considered including social cognitive theory, uses and gratification theory, and media democracy. The uses and gratification theory examines the media from a humanistic perspective. Meanwhile, the modern media ecology theory examines how media influence human perception, understanding, interpretation, and social values. Sieber's and other media theories are still applicable to digital media and social media. However, the politicization of media is not healthy for the sustainability of the democratic process. Hence, it becomes essential to study the most effective theories, such the Agenda Setting and Framing. It's the purpose of this chapter. The study of media ecology involves investigating media environments, the structures, regulations, ethics, content, and their impact on people in the United States and around the globe.

METHODOLOGY

This research applies historical, analytical, and descriptive methods. The historical descriptive approach enables this research to trace the history of agenda-setting and framing theories. It also facilitates the analysis of the components of these two theories. In addition, a network analysis is used to investigate the main components of media convergence, including industrial, cultural, social, technical, and documented aspects. This way the research avoids discussing a highly segmented marketplace of ideas generated by the media and social media. Webster and Ksiazek (2012) suggested that "One problem with the media-centric studies on fragmentation that buttress many of these commentaries is that they provide no direct evidence of the more relevant user- or audience-centric behaviors in question. This leaves analysts free to speculate about the relationship between niche media and audience loyalties" (p.50).

The methodology is informed by the work of sociologist Anthony Giddens (1984), who coined the "theory of structuration" which provides a framework and has been adapted to describe the operation of the media environment (Webster and Ksiazek, 2012; Webster, 2008, 2011). Applying this methodology is based on the following procedures and the research. Questions.

PROCEDURES

1. Examine the history of Agenda Theory and the theory of framing.
2. Define with illustration the development of the two theories.
3. Provide evidence for the application of Agenda Theory and the theory of framing.

RESEARCH QUESTIONS

The following questions are addressed in this paper:
1. What is the current situation regarding agenda-setting and framing theories and digital programming and content?
2. How does framing theory shape issues presented to the audience?
3. How do social media contribute to the fragmentation and polarization of society?
4. Do stakeholders (Corporations, employees, customers) have differing views on the usefulness of social media marketing?

THEORETICAL PERSPECTIVES

The rationale behind a theory is to understand the process and to identify the purpose of a particular theory. The analytical discussion concerning digital and social media fragmentation and convergence is informed by agenda-setting and framing theories. It is known that "Framing is a process in which a perceived reality is organized in such a way that certain aspects of the reality are stressed, while others are de-emphasized, leading to a particular to a particular definition or understanding of the social world" (Luther et al, 2018, p. 12). The availability of digital information accompanied by the massive use of social media allows every user to significantly "identify and interpret the information" differently (Gofman, 1974 & Luther et al, 2018, p.12). Hence, news, opinions, and views are put in certain framing and conveyed by traditional media (cable TV and the like) and social media users. Luther et al, 2018 argued "Journalists have also been found to rely on framing in their work" (p. 12). Robert Entman describes framing as "the process of culling a few elements of perceived reality and assembling a narrative that highlights connections among them to promote a particular interpretation" (Entman, 2007, p. 164; Luther et al, 2018, p. 12-3). Entman proposed through this interpretation process the receivers are motivated to "think, feel, and decide in a particular way" Entman, 2007. Media researchers pointed out that "frames tend to echo the perspectives of those who hold political and economic power in society" (Gitlen 2003; Ryan, Carragee, and Meinhofer, 2001; Luther et al, 2018, p.14). It's critical to understand the framing approach and its influence on the audience. Another theory that demonstrates how messages might influence people's perceptions is the agenda-setting theory. Figure one below demonstrates the levels of public agenda setting about media purpose.

Figure 1. Levels of agenda setting

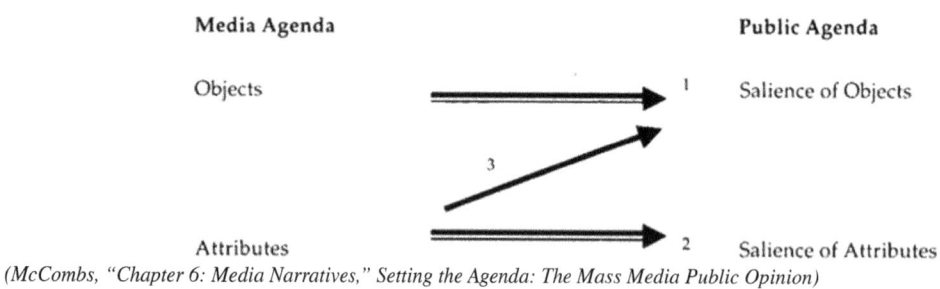

(McCombs, "Chapter 6: Media Narratives," Setting the Agenda: The Mass Media Public Opinion)

Many studies have discussed the similarities between agenda setting and framing. These studies concluded that *"Both processes are psycho-social in nature and involve the construction of media messages by journalists and reporters. The terminology used to define these concepts is similar and often interchangeable. Two key components of framing, selection and salience, are also key components of agenda setting. Media selects certain aspects, "frames" or "attributes" and highlights them through coverage, thus increasing their salience among the audience"* (Yioutas &Segvic, 2003).

FRAGMENTATION AND CONVERGENCE

According to Theorist Henry Jenkins "Media convergence is the flow of content across multiple media platforms, the cooperation between multiple media industries, and the migratory behavior of media audiences who will go almost anywhere in search of the kinds of entertainment experiences they want" (Jenkins, 2006, pp. 2-4, 17-18, 258-260). Jenkins cautioned convergence does not occur through media applications, but it occurs within the brains of consumers and through their social and cultural interactions with other people who may or may not know them (Jenkins, 2006). Convergence also describes the cultural and technological processes that "Affect how meaning is made, how ideas "spread," and how taste cultures take shape in society" (Jenkins, 2006).

In today's digital age, we live in a participatory culture and social environment. The abundance of information has led to the rapid growth and prominence of fragmentation. Media consumers enjoy having more choices, "As more offerings are delivered on broadband networks and more choices are available "on-demand," patterns of consumption become more widely distributed" (Webster& Ksiazek, 2012, p.39). Media critics and scholars are divided into two factions.

The larger faction celebrates this digital development Still others are very critical and even skeptical with deep concerns. They argued that "Fragmentation spells the end of a common cultural forum, or worse, the birth of media enclaves and "sphericules" that scarcely interact (Webster& Ksiazek, 2012, p.39, Gitlin, 1998; Katz, 1996; Sunstein, 2007). Webster and Ksiazek (2012) explain the relationship between senders and receivers in a toxic environment as follows: "In a nutshell, we see media as providing resources (media providers) that agents (media users) appropriate to accomplish their purposes. To do this effectively, both parties rely heavily on information regimes (media measures) to monitor consumption" (p.40). It's a duality as characterized by sociologist Anthony Giddens (1984). Simply, the media environment is jointly assembled from the interaction of structures and agents (Webster& Ksiazek, 2012, p. 40). The media environment prior to the development of cable television consisted of basic television and FM and AM radio broadcasting but satellite television changed the landscape of news reporting and news coverage in the world. According to Napoli (2003) and Webster and Ksiazek (2012) that:

"The most obvious cause of fragmentation is a steady growth in the number of media outlets and products competing for public attention. This happens when established media, such as television, expand or when newer media, such as the Internet, enter the competition. These are sometimes categorized as intra- and intermedia fragmentation, respectively" (p.40).

Fragmentation is also caused by: First, the availability of social media (X, Facebook, Instagram, YouTube, TikTok, Pinterest, Snapchat, LinkedIn, etc.) as digital tools, they represent complex domains, enterprises, ideologies, social and cultural groups, entities, and individuals. Second, the abundance of valued and unhinged content of social media, and third, the loose regulations and policies. The production of media, especially social media, by professional organizations and networks and the armature will continue and expand. Audiences will certainly spread across media networks searching for what they see as the most relevant offerings (Webster &Ksiazek, 2012). Professional media (traditional and digital) relates to media convergence through transmedia storytelling, in which stories are told across multiple platforms.

The media coverage in the United States is characterized by polarization and fragmentation. A large number of voters, for example, are willing to travel long distances to attend a rally or a political campaign that "stir the emotions to a high pitch, like a nineteenth-century revival meeting or a Beatles concert" (Kagan, 2024, p. 196).

Media networks rely on the proven service of Nielsen Cross Media Measurement (Nielsen ONE), which "tackles the fragmentation of cross-media measurement head-on with comprehensive coverage of TV networks, streaming services, connected TV providers and digital publishers—including many direct, walled garden integrations"(www.nielsen.com, para 6). Encountering the issues of fragmentation, cross-media measurement provides media platforms and networks accurate data to know who is watching what and when and empower media clients to plan and measure their actions accordingly.

LITERATURE REVIEW

Understanding the meaning of the word frame is essential as it demonstrates the complexity both in language and in practice. Merriam-Webster dictionary defines frame as a verb as follows: To form or make, as by fitting and uniting parts together, construct. to contrive, devise, or compose a plan, law, or poem--to frame a new constitution" (para 1). Framing definition in American English-Collins Dictionary means "to shape or form according to a pattern; design". As a transitive verb, "If an object is framed by a particular thing, it is surrounded by that thing in a way that makes the object more striking or attractive to look at "(Collins, dictionary/english/frame.com". Some examples on the web read as follows: "But that's like one art thief stealing the Mona Lisa and then blaming another for wanting the frame" (Gordon Monson, The Salt. Lake Tribune, 3 Aug 2023). Nathan Ruiz, Baltimore Sun provided another example from the baseball match "After pitching prospect Cade Povich allowed a run on one hit and one walk over six innings, Akin pitched a scoreless seventh with a walk, and Givens worked for the nest two frames with the only base runner being a hit better" (3 Aug 2023). Here is how Toyota describes a frame "The steel ladder frame is 50 percent more rigid overall than its predecessor" (Don Schroeder, Car and Driver, 2 Aug 2023). Kriston Capps, Washington Post wrote: Yet the artist has also framed her floral arrangements as an act of political protest or collective action" (Capps, 1 Aug 2023).

Research on media framing suggests that the manner in which a news story is presented in an article, radio, or television report, or in any digital media can influence how the audience perceives and understands that story. Hence, it is argued that "in this way, a journalist has the power to evoke a specific reaction (Caroll & Engel 2021, p. 412; Scheufele 1999). Further, Robert Entman (1993) defined framing as fellow: "To frame is to select some aspects of a perceived reality and make them more salient in a communicating text, in such a way as to promote a particular problem definition, causal interpretation, moral evaluation, and/or treatment recommendation for the item described" (Entman, 1993. P.1; Caroll & Engel 2021).

Applying agenda setting and framing theories on everyday social media practices and to some extent traditional media outlets like print media, cable television, a podcast (digital audio programs), and radio shows demonstrate the degrees of alienation, fragmentation, polarization, and tribalism among the audience. Robert Kagan (2024) argued that in the U.S. when the founders' established checks and balances, they thought of a way to prevent the rise of tyrannical demagogues, they did not envision national parties and their media uniting broad coalitions of interregional interests" (p 186). A gifted demagogue could influence ordinary people by appealing to their emotions, unsatisfied desires, and prejudices. Agenda-setting and framing approaches feed into more divisions among people locally, regionally, and globally. Speaking of American exceptionalism in terms of liberalism and democracy, "The founders also hoped the checks and balances they established in the Constitution would be sufficient to contain the ambitions of a demagogue" (Kagan, 2024, p. 187).

In short, the digital revolution and the expansion of social media defeated distances and geographical boundaries. Fareed Zakaria (2024) summarized this revolution this way: "For millennia, messages could only be sent via a courier on foot or horseback, or in mailbags carried on boats. But in the 1840s and 1850s, the telegraph allowed news to spread among world capitals faster than ever before" (p. 173). Furthermore, Fareed Zakaria framed the issue of the information unbound technology this way:

> *"Today, with the digital revolution that has unfolded since the 1970s (the Third Industrial Revolution) and the rise of artificial intelligence and biotechnology in the 2020s (what some are calling the Fourth Industrial Revolution), the world is again changing faster than ever--and many people feel like they'll be the ones stuck on the tracks"*(p.203)

ANALYTICAL DISCUSSION

This section is designed to address the research questions.

Q. 1. What is the current situation regarding theories of agenda setting and framing in relation to digital programming and content?

Q. 2. How does framing theory shape issues presented to the audience?

Agenda setting and framing theories are widely used in traditional (print, radio, and television), cable television, and professional digital media. Mostly, traditional media adhere to ethics and what's good and useful for the individual and society. Additionally, the content and programming are governed by professional code and rationality for different choices. The ability to explain the ways agenda and framing theories are applied is "an important one for journalists." (Patterson and Wilkins, 2002, p.3). However, the same measure is not necessarily applied in the case of public users of social media. According to Jack Rosenberry and Lauren A. Vicker (2009) priming, obtrusiveness of issues, and framing are the central factors for agenda setting theory (p.151-152). CNN applies these three factors by emailing viewers a daily prompt followed by a leading line "Here's what else you need to know to start your day". As an illustration, on August 8, 2023, CNN sent this prompt *"An American nurse and her daughter have been released in Haiti after being kidnapped around two weeks ago"* followed by five top headlines, which CNN wants viewers to know about and to start their day. The following are the 5 top headlines that the researcher received on August 10, 2023:

1. Maui fires *At least 36 people have been killed in catastrophic wildfires that are raging across the Hawaiian island of Maui.*
2. Trump *Two employees of President Donald Trump are set to be arraigned today on new charges brought by the special counsel in the case regarding the alleged mishandling of classified documents.*
3. Ecuador *A candidate in Ecuador's upcoming presidential election was assassinated at a rally in the country's capital Wednesday as a deadly escalation of violence grips the South American nation.*
4. Boat dock brawl *Two men charged in connection with a brawl at a Montgomery riverfront dock are in police custody, Alabama authorities say.*
5. Artificial intelligence *The Biden administration announced new rules Wednesday banning some US investments in advanced technology industries in China.*

The above randomly selected prompts and the headlines illustrate the main three factors for agenda setting priming, obtrusiveness of issues, and framing. The process of priming is in effect when the network focuses on some issues and overlooks other problems. The obtrusiveness of issues occurs with issues that "the public has not directly experienced" (Rosenberry & Vicker, 2002, p. 151-152). At the same time, framing of the above headlines is applied through the use of "selection, emphasis, exclusion, and elaboration" (Rosenberry & Vicker, 2002, p. 151-152). The analysis shows that the agenda setting and framing theories are intertwined.

Table 1 shows how the media has the power to influence what issues and problems the public pays attention to. This is often done intentionally or unintentionally, under the guise of "the public's need to know". News outlets, such as newspapers and television programs, investigate and report on issues and problems with the goal of bringing them to the public's attention. This helps to shape the public agenda and determine what issues are considered important (Rosenberry & Vicker, 2002). Closely relating to this analysis is Walter Lippmann's argument (1922) that the press contributed to "The World Outside and Pictures in our Heads" (Rosenberry & Vicker, 2002, p. 150).

Table 1. CNN Here's "what else you need to know to start your day"

Date	Headlines	Agenda Setting	Framing
8/11/2023	Maui Fires The death toll from the wildfires burning through Hawaii's Maui island has risen to at least 55 officials said late Thursday night, as the number of missing remains unclear.		X
	Presidential Race Nearly all GOP presidential candidates are converging at the Iowa State Fair this weekend as they seek to connect with voters ahead of the first Republican debate in two weeks.	X	X
	Ukraine President Joe Biden is asking Congress for more than $24 billion in aid for Ukraine and other international needs as he works to sustain support for the war amid signs of softening support among Americans.	X	X
	Hollywood Strikes The Writers Guild of America and Hollywood studios have agreed to meet today to resume negotiation for the first time since the writers went on strike more than 100 days ago.	X X	X
	Space Missions For the first time in 47 years, Russia launched a lunar lander today.		
8/14/2023	Maui Fires The death toll from the Maui wildfires has reached 96 and there are warnings it could climb further as people remain unaccounted for.	X	X
	Trump Former President Donald Trump may be facing this fourth indictment in the coming days. Atlanta-area prosecutor Fani Willis, a Democrat, is expected to seek charges against more than a dozen individuals when her team presents its case before a grand jury this week.	X	X
	Ukraine Ukrainian President Volodymyr Zelensky vowed to respond with "completely fair retaliation" after Russian shelling on Sunday killed at least two dozen people, including a newborn baby, in the Kherson region.	X	X
	Eiffel Tower The Eiffel Tower was evacuated for several hours Saturday over a bomb threat. Traffic was diverted and a large security perimeter was established so a team of deminers could assess the situation.		X
	Toyota Recall Toyota has announced a voluntary recall for more than 168,000 vehicles — the automaker's largest recall of the year.	X	X

Table 2. CNN Here's "what else you need to know to start your day"

Date	Headlines	Agenda Setting	Framing
9/29/2023	Government Shutdown The House is expected to take up a Republican stopgap bill to extend government funding today — but House Speaker Kevin McCarthy appears to lack the votes to pass it, and Congress is still on track to trigger a government shutdown.	X	
	Autoworkers strike The United Auto Workers union is preparing to announce a possible expansion of its strike against General Motors, Stellantis and maybe Ford today if there isn't more progress in talks, according to a union source familiar with the plans.	X	X
	A Flood threat high-impact flood event is targeting millions in New York City and the Northeast today as heavy rain threatens to flood subways and roads.	X	X
	Ukraine Moscow said it will boost its military spending by almost 70% in 2024, with Russia's finance minister calling the war in Ukraine "a significant strain on our budget" but "our priority."	X	X
	College admissions The Department of Education on Thursday released new recommendations for colleges to promote diversity in the wake of a Supreme Court ruling that gutted affirmative action. For the first time in 47 years, Russia launched a lunar lander today.	X	X
9/18/2023	Lee aftermath Post-tropical cyclone Lee is forecast to gradually weaken early this week before moving back out into the Atlantic Ocean.		X
	Government shutdown Congress is facing a spending deadline at the end of the month and lawmakers are acknowledging that a government shutdown may be inevitable.		X
	Strikes The United Auto Workers' strike against General Motors, Ford and Stellantis has entered its fourth day.	X	X
	United Nations World leaders are meeting in New York City starting today for the UN General Assembly.	X	X
	Libya floods The UN has revised its previous death toll from the floods in Libya as crews race to provide aid to thousands of those impacted.		X

What is shown in Tables 1 and 2 illustrates the complexity of the use of agenda-setting and the framing of theoretical and practical applications. However, it should not be interpreted as a judgmental call on the quality of the headlines that the network is proposing to its audience.

SOCIAL MEDIA STATUS

Is social media dead? The answer is not yet. However, "it has become less social and more media" as Insider Intelligence reported (insiderintelligence.com. parg. 1). Insider Intelligence added that: 1) Users are posting less every day as polished influencer marketing campaigns and algorithm-curated social feeds make the stakes of posting feel too high. 2) More time is being spent on most platforms, with the exception of Facebook and X (parg. 2). Relevant to this perspective analyst Debra Aho from Inside Intelligence wrote "I still log in multiple times a day to my social media accounts. And that's true for Gen Z as well. analyst Debra Aho Williamson added that "They're still checking their feeds, watching Stories, exchanging DMs, and consuming short videos"((insiderintelligence.com. parg. 3). Figure 2. Illustrate how TikTok surpasses Instagram in total daily minutes in 2022 and it's projected to overwhelm Facebook in 2025.

Figure 2. TikTok v. Instagram

TikTok Passed Instagram in Total Daily Minutes in 2022 and Will Pass Facebook in 2025
millions of minutes per day among the US adult population

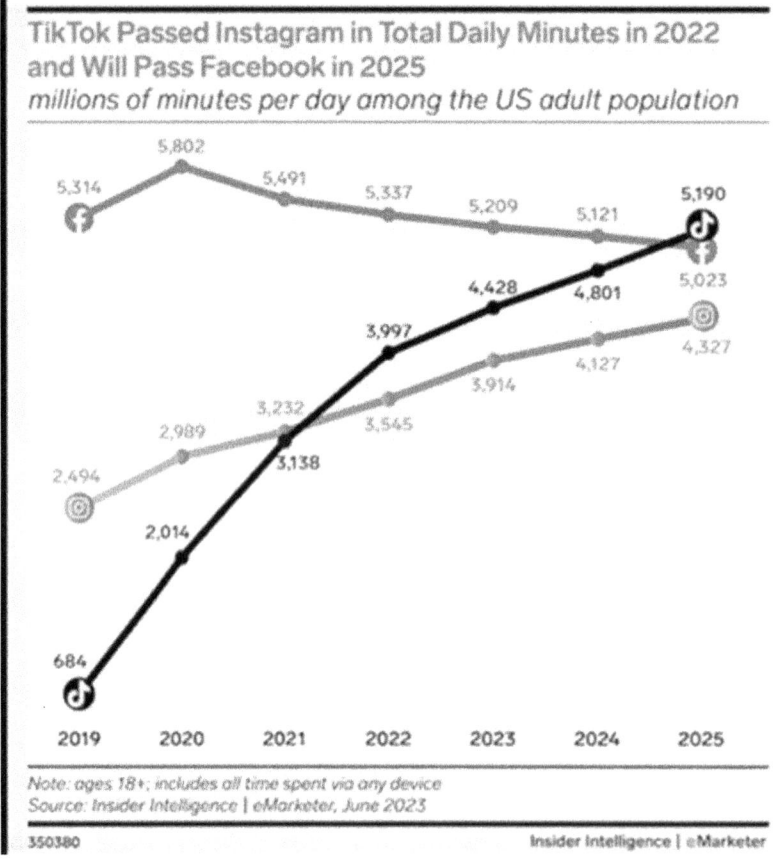

Year	Facebook	Instagram	TikTok
2019	5,314	2,494	684
2020	5,802	2,989	2,014
2021	5,491	3,232	3,138
2022	5,337	3,545	3,997
2023	5,209	3,914	4,428
2024	5,121	4,127	4,801
2025	5,190	4,327	5,023

Note: ages 18+; includes all time spent via any device
Source: Insider Intelligence | eMarketer, June 2023

(350380 Insider Intelligence eMarketer)

Williamson explained the reasons why consumers appeared to prefer TikTok and Instagram "Posting is hard work. Watching a few videos to kill some time is way easier," as it is more interesting to spend time watching videos than posting. On September 5, 2023, Williamson added, "Posting is hard work. Watching a few videos to kill some time is way easier" (www.insiderintelligence.com). Adam Mosseri, the head of Instagram declared "If you look at how teens spend their time on Instagram, they spend more time in DMs than they do in Stories, and they spend more time in Stories than they do in-feed" (20VC" episode podcast, Sep 5, 2023). According to Axios "TikTok may be moving toward messaging and other social media engagement features" (https://www.axios.com/). Media convergence impacted social media as a process and content. Britannica outlined the five elements of media convergence—the technological, the industrial, the social, the textual, and the political (parg1, www.britannica.com).

FINDINGS

The concept of agenda-setting highlights the enormous influence of the media in shaping public priorities and preferences. By selectively emphasizing certain issues and making predictions, the media can direct public attention and shape public opinion. The Framing approach continues to be applied to how the media's coverage of selected issues is spined off in certain ways and how the public receives and interprets them. Additionally, unverified information and digital content conveyed by social media cause a level of confusion and fragmentation.

Yet, factual information and data set the stage for social, cultural, and economic development (Al-Obaidi, 2019). Social media has contributed a great deal to the bank of information that every user may benefit from and get virtually connected with other people throughout the world but at the same time, people feel lonely and isolated. The revolution of information does not necessarily strengthen social ties between people or build a new web of social and cultural relationships among users. The seriousness of the public health crisis of loneliness is alarming.

Fragmentation has resulted from a mix of media providers, various content formats, and diverse consumers. As more offerings are delivered by various media networks and platforms including social media, the audience fragmentation is widened. The media industry has transformed drastically and so have the media consumers. In other words, media convergence reflected the changes in technology, the industry, the cultural, the social, the political, and the financial.

The answers to the research questions are positive. Media corporations and professional social media intentionally or otherwise apply the aspects of the agenda-setting and framing theories. The content of digital and social media provides plenty of evidence.

The media environment is created through the interaction of structures and agents, which Giddens referred to as a 'duality.' The research outlined the main components of the agenda and framing theories, emphasizing the factors that contribute to audience fragmentation.

CONCLUSION

This research raised the question of how social media contributes to the fragmentation and polarization of both local and global societies. It also discusses media-centric fragmentation and how far the process can go. Anderson's research (2006) corresponds with the findings of this research by raising a similar critical question: "Will future audiences distribute themselves evenly across all media choices, or will popular offerings continue to dominate the marketplace?" (p. 181). The various markets media in the United States, Canada, Europe, and Asian countries are highly divided and "segmented with little in common" (Webster &Ksiazek, p. 51).

The social and cultural dimensions of media consumption also lead to concentration of attendance due to social desirability and individual and group preferability. Media have long served as a ''coin-of-exchange'' in social and political situations" (Levy & Windahl, 1984). It should be understood that analyzing the applications of theories of agenda-setting and framing tends to leave room for interpretation and speculation.

These are sometimes classified as intra- and intermedia fragmentation, respectively (Napoli, 2003). However, with digital technologies making it easier for both content and users to move across platforms, such distinctions seem less important. It's interesting to observe the emergence and reemerging of the process of fragmentation and convergence. Whatever their means of delivery, media organizations strive to attract the attention of consumers. Grabbing the attention has typically been monetized in a "dual-product" marketplace, digital media and social media providers sell content to users and "eyeballs" to advertisers (Napoli, 2003, p. 40).

This descriptive and analytical research concludes that agenda-setting and framing effects could influence the audience and lead them to making attitudinal and behavioral changes because of exposing them to certain content by digital and social media exposure. Historically socially, and culturally, the media and now the social and digital media are powerful and influential. Hence, it is highly recommended to enforce the teaching of media, information, and technology literacy.

RECOMMENDATIONS AND FUTURE RESEARCH

The applications of agenda setting and framing are significantly important and require more research. Fragmentations of media providers and content professional and amateur producers are ever-expanding, which calls on researchers to offer more analytical studies in the future.

Audience studies are needed as well to ascertain the needs and interests of users across broader media networks.

Further, the critical importance of the theories of agenda setting and framing in various media applications requires further descriptive and analytical research. The increasing fragmentation of media providers and the expansion of content from both professional and online amateur contributors highlight the need for more in-depth analytical studies. Additionally, there is a need for audience research to understand the interests of media consumers across broader media networks.

REFERENCES

Al-Obaidi, A. (20027). *Broadcast, Internet, and TV Media in the Arab World and Small Nations.* The Edwin Mellen Press, Lewiston.

Al-Obaidi, J. (2019). Information, Data, and Intelligence: Global Digital Media Polarization, Democratization, and Participation. In *Global Perspectives on Media, Politics, Immigration, Advertising, and Social Networking.* Cambridge Scholars Publishing.

Anderson, C. (2006). *The long tail: Why the future of business is selling less of more.* Hyperion. Britannica. https://www.britannica.com/topic/media-convergence

Carroll, L. & Engel, S. (2021). Framing basic income in Australia: how the media is shaping the debate. *Australian Journal of Political Science, 56,* 410–427 10.1080/10361146.2021.1998344

Chung, K. & Kim, J. (2021). Multi-modal emotion prediction system using convergence media and active contents. *Personal and Ubiquitous Computing (2023), 27,* 1245– 1255. 10.1007/s00779-021-01602-8

Dearling, W. J. (1998). *Communication and Democracy: Exploring the Intellectual Frontiers in Agenda-Setting Theory.* Mahwah, NJ: Lawrence Erlbaum Associates.

Dodd, S. (2016, April 1). Learning from HGTV: Media Convergence and Design Branding in America. *Design Issues*, 32(2), 53–63. 10.1162/DESI_a_00382

Entman, R. (1993). Framing: Toward Clarification of a Fractured Paradigm. *Journal of Communication*, 43(4), 51–58. 10.1111/j.1460-2466.1993.tb01304.x

Goffman, E. (1974). *Frame Analysis: An Essay on the Organization of Experience.* Harpor & Row.

Jenkins, H. (2006). *Convergence Culture: Where Old and New Media Collide.* New York University Press.

Kagan, R. (2024). *Rebellion: How Antiliteralism is Tearing America Apart-Again.* Alfred A.

Levy, M. R., & Windahl, S. (1984). Audience activity and gratifications: A conceptual clarification and exploration. *Communication Research*, 11(1), 51–78. 10.1177/009365084011001003

Luther, A. (2018). *Diversity in US Mass Media.* 2nd (ed). Wiley Blackwell.

McCombs, M., Shaw, L. D., & Weaver, D. (1997). *Communication and Democracy: Exploring the Intellectual Frontiers in Agenda-Setting Theory.* Mahwah, NJ: Lawrence Erlbaum Associates, 1997.

Mosseri, A. (2023). *Head of Instagram. During an episode of the "20VC" podcast.*

Napoli, P. M. (2003). *Audience economics: Media institutions and the audience marketplace.* Columbia University Press.

Napoli, P. M. (2003). *Audience economics: Media institutions and the audience marketplace.* Columbia University Press.

Napoli, P. M. (2011). *Audience evolution: New technologies and the transformation of media audiences.* Columbia University Press.

Rosenberry, J., & Vicker, L. A.(2002). *Applied Mass Communication Theory: A Guide for Media Practitioners*. Pearson, Boston and New York.

Scheufele, D. (1999). Framing as a Theory of Media Effects. *Journal of Communication*, 49(1), 103–122. 10.1111/j.1460-2466.1999.tb02784.x

Webster, J. G.& Ksiazek, T. B. (2012). The Dynamics of Audience Fragmentation: Public Attention in an Age of Digital Media. *Journal of Communication.*

Yioutas, J., & Segvic, I. (2003). Revisiting the Clinton/Lewinsky Scandal: The Convergence of Agenda Setting and Framing. September 2003. *Journalism & Mass Communication Quarterly*, 80(3), 567–588. 10.1177/107769900308000306

Zakaria, F. (2024). *Age of Revolutions: Progress and Backlash from 1600 to the Present*. W.W. Norton & Company.

ADDITIONAL READING

Boorstin, D. (1961). Setting the Polling Agenda for the Issue of AIDS. *Public Opinion Quarterly*, 53(3), 309–329.

Dearing, J. W., & Rogers, E. M. (1996). *Agenda-Setting*. Sage. 10.4135/9781452243283

Lippmann, W. (1922). *Public Opinion*. Harcourt Brace.

McCombs, M. (1997). *New Frontiers in Agenda Setting: Agendas of Attributes and Frames*. Paper presented to the annual meeting of the Association for Education in Journalism and Mass Communication, Chicago.

Trumbo, C. (1995). Longitudinal Modeling of Public Issues: An Application of the Agenda-Setting Process to the Issue of Global Warming. *Journalism Monographs, 152*.

Yankelovich, D. (1991). *Coming to Public Judgment: Making Democracy Work in a Complex World*. Syracuse University Press.

KEY TERMS AND DEFINITIONS

Agenda Setting Theory: Researchers Maxwell McCombs and Donald Lewis Shaw embarked on a study of the presidential election in 1968. The theory proposes that the media can identify and promote certain issues that impact public opinion.

Factual Information: It refers to truthful, actual, and accurate information that media conveys to the public.

Framing Theory: It is a conceptual method that frames a message, an issue, or an event in a specific way. It can reorient the audience's way of thinking or seeing things around them.

Media Convergence: The process by which a single media and separate communication technologies are interconnected and begin to offer various services to their users.

Media Fragmentation: It refers to the increasing of communication technologies and media content that enable the audience to choose from hundreds of media channels and content.

Pseudo Agenda Setting: A pseudo is something incredible or fake **that** aims to catch the attention of the media and consequently the audience.

Social Media Fragmentation: This means the availability of numerous digital social media that compete with one another to gain more users at the expense of content quality.

Chapter 2
Revocation of Article 370 Changing Global Media Landscapes in India:
Media Framing of Conflict Types in Dawn, The Hindu, and the New York Times

Keerthana Thankachan
Bharathiar University, India

Thomas Peedikayil Eapen
Bharathiar University, India

Vishnu Achutha Menon
Central University of Tamil Nadu, India

ABSTRACT

In this study, the authors investigate how the revocation of Article 370 is framed in the media and how the newspapers frame the types of conflicts by examining the coverage in three prominent newspapers: The Hindu, Dawn, and The New York Times. Employing a non-experimental ex-post facto research design, we utilize a qualitative content analysis to categorize and analyze the various frames used in media coverage. The analysis encompasses a total of 1,117 stories published over the course of one month, from August 5, 2019, to September 5, 2019, spanning different formats such as news reports, articles, feature stories, editorials, opinions, and cartoons.

INTRODUCTION

Media is the primary source during conflicts for the public to gather information. Therefore, the need to understand conflict's nature, form, structure, and intensity is important to understand the power of conflict in portraying the context and content of the crisis. The conflict theories from different dimensions need to be configured to comprehensive the reasons and the possible ways for analysis in media coverage. Authors confirm that framing techniques are used for high invulnerability identity (Idoiaga,et.al, 2016)

DOI: 10.4018/979-8-3693-3767-7.ch002

and multiple frames can be operated (McInnes and Lee, 2012) at the same time for desired outcomes. Framing is a well-established concept in public relations as explained by a number of authors (Kuan, D. et.al, 2021; Yousaf, M. et.al, 2020). Media representation of conflicts and its portrayal of Kashmir is mediated (M. et.al, 2020; Graber, D. Appel, MacCombs, M. E, & Weaver, D. H, 1981) thereby resulting in an escalation of the conflict. Media's eyes are the eyes of the public which sets the background and context for the perceptualizing of a situation. Thus, framing the images is equivalent to the framing of public perception and understanding the media language of framing Kashmir in revocation is necessary to understand the media role of portraying the conflict. This book chapter studies how the media covers the revocation of Article 370, revealing various conflict types and the impact of framing techniques on public perception. Comparative analysis of media from affected and third-party nations offers insight into Kashmir's long-term crisis.

Conceptualization from the Reviews

Oberschall's (1978) coordination of theories is used in the study to analyze conflict dimensions and thus it is treated as 5 conflict types in the current research. Ancient Hatred, the first conflict type deals with the memories of past events and patterns of previous generations. Media therefore provide a strong connection between the present events from the segments of previous conflicts in a case or discourse (Williams, 1994; Schelling, 1963; Kaplan, 1994; Huntington 2000). Manipulative Elites (ME) examines the interventions of those who are interested to stir up conflicts in nationalistic passions through fear, threat, or insecurity. The frames involved in such contents either benefit an idea or vested interest fr intended outcomes. This conflict type can lead to the next step instigating the components for Identity Politics which becomes the next type of conflict dimension. Both the types work well for politicians or religious leaders to point at an identity or to gain profit out of the targeted motives in conflict. Therefore, both these types can go hand-in-hand in national and international conflicts that have religious and political contexts (Bates, 1983; Horowitz, 1985; Fearon and Laitin, 2000; Lynch, 2011; Kaufman, 1999; Taylor 1992; Mills, 1956; Nadel, 1956).

One of the major factors that is questioned during conflicts is the economy during the crisis. Trade relations or a failed economy is a major title of discussions during conflicts or the Economic Roots itself can be a reason for the emergence of a conflict. The retarded developments of conflicts wreck the economy resulting in the escalation or development of a next conflict. The factors of economic crisis which are often portrayed during the conflicts are treated as the fourth type of conflict in the study (Collier and Hoeffler 1998; Lewis, 1985; Easterly and Levine 1997). Along with the above four factors, a major conflict type that associates the concepts of Tilly (1991) about power transitions is considered as the fifth type of conflict in framing the supremacy of control. Contention for Power is different from all the four concepts since power becomes the only means in this context to conceptualise goals and satisfy needs. The status of the nation or a state is under pressure during a conflict and hence power is equated with influence and status in national and international conflicts at emergency. The power of such content in framing is destructive since the discourse is a combination of acute ideologies that can affect the progress of a state or a country (Morgenthau, 1948; Waltz, 1979; Mearsheimer, 2001). Conceptual dimensions of conflict framing while comparing media platforms are discussed by several new researchers globally. The study explained by Chong and Druckman (2007) points out that the frames put forth by the stakeholders consider citizen's opinions and attitudes. Journalists provide the opportunity for politicians and other opinion-holders to reach the audience in both traditional, as well as social media. Studies from Western media analysis reveal that journalists greatly value objective reporting in conflict framing (Schudson, 2001) and frame fair and unbiased accounts of a story (McManus, 1994). This is a major concern for the Indian scenario to understand how conflict framing is conceptualized and whether the media routine contributes to the emergence of conflict frames in the media for objectivity or prejudice.

Approaches to Conflict Framing

Several frames appear in media platforms to contextualize the contents of conflicts. The approaches to framing in conflict are also segmented and divided according to researchers. Framing in conflict reports is a communicative agent for perpetual judgments (O'Regan, 2007). Therefore, to analyse a case like Revocation of Article 370, which has historical, political, and religious backgrounds, 8 particular frames are adopted from the classification of an extensive type of frames from the reviews collected. The frames that are endorsed in this study are used as a means of control and communication. Entman's (1993) concept of characteristics of media frames from a socially constructed outlook is also considered since conflict coverage can play along with human 'common sense'. An intentional or non-objective viewpoint usually adopted for political intentions can be marked under the genre of intended frames and the outcome of such frames is pre-intended or previously known. Routine frames often consist of a set of schemata where the journalists prefer to act as agents of information transmission and a link in the knowledge circuit. Compared with a neutral-text condition, an indicative frame can hide a perceived risk, emotions, and symbols within itself that often become indicators for decision-making. Identity frames address the question, "Who are you"? and "Where do you belong to"? The basic human tendency of protecting self-identity and creating a sense of self is exploited (Wondolldeck, Gray, and Bryan, 2003) in identity frames.

A manipulative frame is a collective combination of logical fallacies, psychological manipulations, propaganda, and agendas inbuilt in the contents of the text. When we mix feelings with conventional social movements by large-scale ubiquitous and univocal framing of a particular issue (Johnston, Hank, and John, 2005) the extracted product will be a motivational frame of reference (as like religion –a primary source of emotion in India). Frames under the peace category will shape public opinion and perception of the root cause and seek solutions for them (Hoffmann, and Virgil, 2015). The language and the angles covered by dispute frames with uncertainty in reporting create an environment of terror and isolation. As applied to politics and religion, dispute frames are cavernous to explain why an issue matters and what might be the responsibility rather than what should be done. The detailed analysis and the characteristics of each of the frames are discussed and debated in the literature section to understand how each frame is conceptualized by different researchers over the period.

Framing of Types of Conflicts: From the Overview of Studies

Media's powerful influence in setting the frames of agenda is well researched by scholars across the globe. Salwen and Matera (1992) studied the influence of media and analysed that specific information in the form of media messages (frames) are transferred to people. In a more recent study, Noakes and Wilkins (2002) reviewed US media coverage of the first Palestinian intifada and the results pointed a sympathetic approach taken towards the Palestinians. Conflict frames in war focus political issues and can provide "hard" information (Hänggli and Kriesi, 2010) since journalists can easily intervene in conflict frame-building process (Bartholomé, Lecheler, and de Vreese, 2015). Even though there are a lot of research focus on media contents, most content analyses towards conflict frames (Semetko and Valkenburg, 2000) does not focus on the types of conflict and frames along with their characteristics.

Conflict frame building is associated with the interventions (Bartholomé, Lecheler, and de Vreese, 2015) and in a case like Kashmir; this intervention determines the degree to which journalists opinions are converted as contents. The interpretative frame method in the reports thus takes a further step beyond facts and statements of sources (Falasca, 2014) for perpetual judgements. The game frame or horse-race coverage studied by the researchers (Takens et al., 2013) points the level of substantive ideological clash in the contents of conflict frames. Therefore, it is important to study the distinction in conflict framing beyond the context of conflict framing as scholars have expressed. In an increased political cynicism like Kashmir issue, strategic game frames take roles in (Jackson, 2011) to create context for targeted motives.

The epistemic or moral principles in the formation of conflict frames analysed in the reviews point to how our beliefs are formed (De Ridder, 2021; Kappel, 2018) and the level of journalistic intervention in a news message. The interventionism in the contents from various levels in conflict frames helps to incorporate different theoretical concepts which results in creating a focus on concepts such as strategy (Gross and Brewer, 2007). Therefore studies also confirm the positive relationship between conflict frames and journalistic interventionism in the frame-building process resulting in a formative role in shaping the agenda. Thus, the following objectives are formed as per the nature and characteristics of the frames and conflict types to facilitate innovative approaches in future research.

Objectives

- To understand the type of conflicts addressed in the revocation of article 370 by Indian, Pakistani and American print media to frame a conflict.
- To analyse the different types of frames adopted by Dawn, The Hindu and The New York Times in the revocation of article 370
- To examine the dominant and deviant frames used by Indian, Pakistani and American print media to portray revocation of Article 370
- To dissect how a type of conflict is associated with the type of frames in the coverage of revocation of article 370 by Dawn, The Hindu and The New York Times

Conceptual Framework

The approaches of conflict coverage which are considered as the types of conflicts in the research are listed as Ancient Hatred, Identity Politics, Manipulative Elites, Economic Roots, and Contention for Power. As the theories of conflict trace out the elements that constitute a major part of the conflict, the intensity and manipulation of media exerted in these types to frame a conflict are identified by treating the concepts with frame analysis. The theory of frame analysis attributed to Erving Goffman, (1974) provides the core of framing research in conflict communication. The process of framing worked as it started to make a focus point to certain aspects of an issue. This was the instance where political figures identified the long-term effects of framing (Reese et al. 2011) to mobilize public opinion and to design communication in a way to motivate people for active political participation.

Conceptual framing is designed by coordinating the theories of conflicts and frame analysis by different theoreticians. The five theories of conflicts in politics namely the ancient hatred, identity politics, contention for power, manipulative elites, and economic roots are coordinated with the framing theory in media by considering the contents in which a frame is developed. The eight selected frames from the theories of framing as a result of the collaboration of frames identified from the reviews are categorized based on their positivity, negativity, and neutrality in dispersing the contents. The conceptual framework is the combination of the five theories of conflicts and the framing effects of media by adding the variables to test the valence of the contents delivered through print media during conflict situations. The theories adopted for the study are a combination of political and social scenarios to explain the case as it is a continuity of events from the independence to till date. Adding up the concept of framing along with the practice of political communication in conflict situations, it is easy to understand the ability of a news story the manipulate words and symbols (Edelman, 1985) in communication. Apart from agenda-setting, priming, and propaganda that work on ideological acts (Shaw, 1979), frames differ in their inherent ability to communicate and control a story in their ability to play along with human 'common sense'. Understanding these frames and categorizing them based on particular context and content helps to identify framing as an effect of political and religious manipulation. All the conflicts, (especially religious and importantly political) that we witness in modern conflict reports can be classified under these eight major frames–Intended, Routine, Indicative, Identity, Manipulative, Motivational, Peace, and Dispute Frames.

Along with the theories, the application of the contents from the select newspapers provides the contents to analyse for indicating the media language in which frames are distributed to its readers. The theories from contexts reveal the effects of contents by operating and analysing the contents using the codes to understand the level of objectivity and reality in delivering the contents. This level of subjectivity or objectiveness is directly linked to the concepts of journalistic intervention that creates the reality of frames leading to solutions or further insurgencies. Thus the framework is linked with the series of contents collected from three various newspapers of India, Pakistan, and America (Dawn, The Hindu, and The New York Times) to understand the framing aspects of India-Pakistan issues. The results of the treatment of framing give the output of the reality of frames following the nature, presentation, and characteristics of the stories. The creation of this abstract or concrete reality in media frames works among the readers to form their perpetual judgments. Therefore the formation of reality through the process of blending the concepts of types of conflicts through the treatment of frames is coherent to explain the print medium interventions of media in conflict situations during and after the conflict reports.

The framework is a combination of the theories of conflicts which is treated as the types of conflicts along with the theory of framing stated by different researchers . The framework incorporated Entman's concept of selection and salience catchphrases as the context for the formulation of the framework. Smetko's and Valkernburg's approaches to framing is also a reference to conceptualise the contents for analysis and segregation of contents selected . Prevalence of the frames and the sequence of contexts forms the basis for identification of the end reality of frames. All the concepts adopted are placed based on the background of framing theory in media content analysis.

METHODOLOGY

Research Design

The study demands a systematic process as per the characteristics of the media outlets to understand the nature of the contents and the way its reflections of framing. The design of this study is conceptualized as a non-experimental ex-post facto research design, as described by Kothari (2004). In this approach, the samples are grouped together based on the characteristics and traits of media frames in coverage. The design helps to compare the sets of contents based on their independent and dependent nature.

Method: A combination of three concepts (Kerlinger, 1986) of content analysis is pertinent to use in this study to perform a scientific analysis. An empirical study from the direct facts in reports published by the newspapers and indirect observations from reviews or experiences of people (in the form of articles, comments, opinions, etc.) are analysed. Content analysis of the published reports in The Hindu (Indian newspaper), Dawn (Pakistani newspaper), and The New York Times (American newspaper) of particular cases is used to endorse the comparison in the next stage. The selection of the newspapers is based on a pilot study conducted before the analysis with some select samples of relevant international conflicts between India and Pakistan. To understand the presence of conflict frames in the select newspapers is conducted and the stories are retrieved from the newspapers published on the select dates from the date of the issue to one month. Those stories and articles which contain a minimum of one reference to the case either in the headline are selected. All such samples are collected for a month and are divided for analysis for all three newspapers.

Variables: Types of conflicts and types of frames are the major variables selected for the extraction of contents. Using the sub variables of each variable a qualitative content analysis of extraction of words from reports is employed to extract the content and media portrayal related to the Revocation of Article 370, using coding sheets. The frames and its characteristics (words that represent the frames) are treated as subjects and grouped based on codes, considering them as exclusive clusters. Data collection is conducted from August 5, 2019, to September 5, 2019 (till one month), using archives from the respective newspapers. All forms of published stories, including news, articles, feature stories, editorials, opinions, and cartoons, are considered for analysis.

Data Collection procedure: Access to the newspaper archives of foreign newspapers for references and cross-checks is taken care of by snowball sampling with the help of journalists and from the support of international forums like UMISARC (Centre for South Asian Studies). Contacts of an international journalist and local reporters of Kashmir are also collected from cross references with the help of media and academic personnel from conferences and summits.

Data Collection Tools: In the construction of techniques for content analysis, conceptual and relational types of content analysis are taken into consideration. To examine the conceptual content analysis, frequency constructs are infused in the text. In relational analysis, the comparative conceptual relationship is adopted in the text. For creating the codes for content analysis, conventional, direct, and summative methods of approaches have been relied up on. The shift in sentences, the themes detected, reasons, encouragements, and observations of the text from the pilot study helped to strengthen the tool. Through selection and salience model proposed by Entman, four framing functions is identified from the selected sample namely, problem, cause, judgements and remedies if any. Also, the frame identification is done using deductive approach put forth by Smetko and Valkernburg by considering the conflict frames, economic consequences and the eight pre-defined frames.

Coding Sheets: Selected words, phrases, contexts, and tone of the contents are the criteria for analysing the above variables. These codes are determined before the analysis from the reviews that studied the contents of international and national conflicts. Each word count is recorded and the frequency of each of the identified words forms the overall set for analysis of a story. Each of the variables is coded in a coding sheet for labelling the numbers according to the presence of the words to determine the characteristics of the contents. The coded variables are categorised based on the contexts and the frequency of occurrence is measured to calculate the effect of the frames. The codes are grouped and the valence is determined based on its frequency of occurrences. The codes for the types of conflicts are assigned a range from 1 to 5 based on the presence of specific words, which helps determine the characteristics of the content. Conflict frame codes are determined by the frequency of occurrences, ranging from 0 to more than 25 times in the same story.

Coding Procedure: The researcher developed a codebook to measure the conflict framing contents from the variables collected from the review based on the conflict theories and frame analysis. The coders are asked to identify and indicate whether an article or news story contained a conflict frame from the list of fifty-two frames listed from the reviews. The codes are represented by the selected words from these fifty-two conflict frames such as opposing dialogues, conflicting perspectives, attacks (personal and institutional), disagreements, criticisms, cynicisms, etc (purely on the usage of words and verbs). Those items that are selected by the coders with the presence of a conflict frame are analyzed in more detail (word to word) by the researcher. Each news story, article, editorial, feature, etc with a reference is treated as a separate unit of analysis

Scaling: Nominal and ordinal scales are applied to the values, considering the magnitude, and frames are treated as items to compare their relationship with the nature of the conflicts. The frequency of occurrence is considered as a comparative rating scale and a six-point scale is adopted for the frames.

Sampling: A total of 1,117 stories (482 from The Hindu, 616 from Dawn, and 19 from The New York Times) related to the revocation of Article 370 from these three newspapers are collected and analyzed.

Validity and Reliability: Inter-rater reliability is ensured through coding by two separate individuals, and inter-coder reliability, as described by Tinsley and Weiss (2000), is calculated to provide reliable computable values. Additionally, face, content, and construct validity are tested to assess the overall appropriateness of the scale.

Data Analysis: To facilitate comparison, content analysis of published reports in The Hindu (an Indian newspaper), Dawn (a Pakistani newspaper), and The New York Times (an American newspaper) related to this particular case is conducted for one month from the issue date. To assess the valence of these frames, the frame clusters are subjected to a positive, negative, and neutral scale. Data analysis is conducted using a deductive approach with predetermined variables for conflicts and frames. Statistical analyses are employed for data analysis, including descriptive and correlational tests to examine the relationship between the variables."

Research Questions

1. RQ1: What are the types of conflicts addressed in the revocation of article 370 by Indian, Pakistani and American print media to frame a conflict?
2. RQ2: Is there a difference in the types of frames adopted by Dawn, The Hindu and The New York Times in reporting the case 'revocation of article 370'?

3. RQ3: Are there any dominant and deviant frames used by Indian, Pakistani and American print media to portray revocation of Article 370?
4. RQ4: How a type of conflict is associated with the type of frames in the coverage of revocation of article 370 by Dawn, The Hindu and The New York Times?

Results

Table 1. Types of conflicts

	Dawn		The Hindu		The New York Times	
	n	%	n	%	n	%
Ancient Hatred	173	28.1	63	13.1	3	15.8
Identity Politics	283	45.9	269	55.8	9	47.4
Manipulative Elites	104	16.9	87	18	2	10.5
Economic Roots	21	3.4	14	2.9	1	5.3
Contention for Power	35	5.7	49	10.2	4	21.1
Total	616	100.0	482	100	19	100

The presented results in the table (Table 1) illuminate noteworthy patterns in the representation of various conflict typologies within the reporting of three prominent newspapers: Dawn, The Hindu, and The New York Times. It is conspicuous that "Identity Politics" emerges as the preeminent type of conflict across all three publications, with The Hindu demonstrating the highest prevalence at 55.8%. This finding underscores the pronounced emphasis placed on issues related to identity, encompassing dimensions such as ethnicity, race, religion, and cultural affiliations, within the contemporary media discourse. However, the data also reveals substantial disparities in the coverage of "Ancient Hatred" and "Manipulative Elites" amongst the three newspapers, ostensibly attributed to editorial choices, geographical foci, and regional contextual variations. In contrast, "Economic Roots" and "Contention for Power" receive relatively limited attention, indicating the media's inclination to prioritize topics deemed more sensational.

Types of Frames

Table 2. Intended frames

Occurrences	Dawn		The Hindu		The New York Times	
	n	%	n	%	n	%
0-5	495	80.4	433	89.8	7	36.8
6-10	96	15.6	38	7.9	4	21.1
11-15	23	3.7	9	1.9	7	36.8
16-20	1	0.2	2	0.4	1	5.3

continued on following page

Table 2. Continued

Occurrences	Dawn		The Hindu		The New York Times	
	n	%	*n*	%	*n*	%
21-25	1	0.2				
Total	**616**	100.0	482	100	**19**	**100**

The data is categorized into five ranges, each denoting the number of occurrences of intended frames (Table number 2). In the 0-5 Intended Frames category, the predominant observation is that the majority of frames fall within this range for all three newspapers. Dawn and The Hindu exhibit a relatively high percentage of frames in this range, indicating a prevailing tendency to rely on a limited set of thematic frames to frame their news stories. In contrast, The New York Times has a lower percentage, suggesting a somewhat broader range of intended frames, although it remains relatively constrained in diversity. Moving on to the 6-10 Intended Frames category, we find a moderate level of diversity in thematic framing. Dawn and The Hindu allocate a smaller percentage of frames to this category, indicating a relatively more restricted range of themes or narratives. Conversely, The New York Times displays a comparatively higher percentage within this range, signifying a slightly broader spectrum of intended frames. The categories of 11-15 and 16-20 Intended Frames represent frames with even higher diversity. However, it's important to note that their occurrences are notably low across all three newspapers. Dawn and The Hindu have only a minimal percentage of frames in these categories, implying that a limited number of news stories are structured around more diverse frames. On the contrary, The New York Times exhibits a higher percentage in these ranges, suggesting a somewhat more multifaceted approach in their framing strategies.

Table 3. Routine frames

Occurrences	Dawn		The Hindu		The New York Times	
	n	%	*n*	%	*n*	%
0-5	616	100	482	100	19	100
Total	**616**	**100**	482	100	**19**	**100**

The analysis of routine frames within the three newspapers reveals a consistent and prevalent usage pattern (Table number 3). Specifically, routine frames characterized by their occurrence within the range of 0-5 times are the predominant choice in all three newspapers. This observation is underscored by the fact that the percentage of these routine frames in each newspaper is uniformly 100%, indicating that a substantial majority of thematic or narrative frames applied in their respective news reports adhere to this range. This consistent reliance on routine frames suggests a marked preference for a constrained and frequently employed set of thematic or narrative structures when configuring and presenting news stories within these publications. Such a preference may reflect the newspapers' editorial orientations, priorities, and conventions.

Table 4. Indicative frames

Occurrences	Dawn		The Hindu		The New York Times	
	n	%	n	%	n	%
0-5	15	2.4	53	11	2	10.5
6-10	34	5.5	86	17.8		
11-15	64	10.4	98	20.3		
16-20	101	16.4	107	22.2		
21-25	109	17.7	57	11.8		
Above 25	293	47.6	81	16.8	17	89.5
Total	616	100	482	100	19	100

The analysis of "Indicative Frames", (Table number 4) categorizes frames into different ranges, indicating the frequency with which such frames are employed in each publication. In the "0-5 Occurrences" range, Dawn exhibits 15 indicative frames, constituting 2.4% of its total frames, while The Hindu features 53 frames in this category, making up 11% of its overall frames. On the other hand, The New York Times displays a mere 2 frames in this range, accounting for 10.5% of its total frames. This range underscores the presence of indicative frames in all three newspapers, albeit to varying degrees, suggesting a moderate reliance on such frames in their reportage. Expanding upon the analysis, the "6-10, 11-15, 16-20, 21-25 Occurrences" categories denote increasing occurrences of indicative frames, reflecting greater diversity in thematic and narrative framing. Notably, The Hindu and The New York Times exhibit a notable abundance of indicative frames within these ranges, with percentages amplifying as the range broadens. The "Above 25 Occurrences" category spotlights the pronounced prevalence of indicative frames that surpass 25 occurrences. This is particularly discernible in Dawn and The New York Times, where these frames constitute a substantial proportion, representing 47.6% and 89.5% of their total frames, respectively.

Table 5. Identity frames

Occurrences	Dawn		The Hindu		The New York Times	
	n	%	n	%	n	%
0-5	613	99.5	479	99.4	18	94.7
6-10	2	0.3	2	0.4		
11-15					1	5.3
16-20						
21-25						
Above 25	1	0.2	1	0.2		
Total	616	100	482	100	19	100

The above table (Table 5) reveals distinct patterns in the prevalence and diversity of Identity Frames. Specifically, the data underscores that the overwhelming majority of identity frames, primarily falling within the 0-5 occurrences range, are the dominant choice across all three newspapers. To be precise, 99.5% of identity frames in Dawn, 99.4% in The Hindu, and 94.7% in The New York Times are clustered within this range, implying a pronounced reliance on identity frames with relatively limited thematic or narrative diversity within this context. However, when considering the 6-10, 11-15, 16-20, and 21-25 occurrences categories, which signify increased occurrences of identity frames and theoretically reflect greater thematic diversity, the data reveals a striking scarcity of such frames across all three newspapers. The limited presence of identity frames in these categories suggests a marked editorial focus on the utilization of relatively few thematic or narrative frames in addressing identity-related issues. The "Above 25 Occurrences" category unveils that identity frames occurring more than 25 times are remarkably rare in the newspapers, with a solitary occurrence in each publication. This rarity underscores a notably low frequency of frequently employed identity frames, highlighting a degree of uniformity and consistency in how identity issues are framed in these newspapers' reporting.

Table 6. Manipulative frames

Occurrences	Dawn		The Hindu		The New York Times	
	n	%	n	%	n	%
0-5	596	96.8	466	96.7	11	57.9
6-10	16	2.6	13	2.7	4	21.1
11-15	4	0.6	2	0.4	3	15.8
16-20					1	5.3
21-25						
Above 25			1	0.2		
Total	616	100	482	100	19	100

Table 6 reveals distinctive patterns in the utilization and diversity of Manipulative Frames. Most manipulative frames appear 0-5 times, with Dawn at 96.8%, The Hindu at 96.7%, and The New York Times at 57.9%. This indicates a heavy reliance on low-frequency manipulative techniques. Categories of 6-10 and 11-15 occurrences show limited diversity in manipulative frames, suggesting such techniques are not commonly varied. Frames in the 16-20, 21-25, and above 25 occurrences categories are rare or absent, indicating a strong preference for lower-frequency manipulative strategies across all three newspapers.

Table 7. Motivational frames

Occurrences	Dawn		The Hindu		The New York Times	
	n	%	n	%	n	%
0-5	215	34.9	306	63.5	3	15.8
6-10	186	30.2	113	23.4		
11-15	125	20.3	39	8.1	4	21.1
16-20	44	7.1	13	2.7	4	21.1
21-25	22	3.6	7	1.5	4	21.1
Above 25	24	3.9	4	0.8	4	21.1
Total	616	100	482	100	19	100

This classification delineates the frequency of motivational frames across different ranges, signifying the degree to which these newspapers employ narrative techniques aimed at inspiring or motivating their readership (Table 7). Specifically, the "0-5 Occurrences" category highlights the prevalence of motivational frames across all three newspapers. In Dawn, this range constitutes 34.9% of its total motivational frames, indicating a substantial reliance on motivational framing. Remarkably, The Hindu places a pronounced emphasis on this narrative technique, with 63.5% of its motivational frames falling within this range, signifying a particularly robust use of motivational frames in their news reporting. In contrast, The New York Times exhibits a notably lower percentage at 15.8% within this category, suggesting a relatively less frequent utilization of motivational frames. Turning to the "6-10, 11-15, 16-20, and 21-25 Occurrences" categories, which theoretically denote an increased diversity in motivational framing techniques and their frequency, the data reveals a comparatively limited presence of motivational frames in these categories across all three newspapers. Dawn displays the highest percentages in these categories, with figures ranging from 3.6% to 30.2%, indicating that motivational frames with moderate to higher occurrences are relatively infrequent in their reporting. Meanwhile, The Hindu presents lower percentages in these categories, suggesting that motivational frames with higher occurrences are relatively scarce in their coverage. The New York Times consistently utilizes 21.1% in these categories, demonstrating a notable consistency in their application of motivational frames. In the "Above 25 Occurrences" category, the data underscores that highly frequent motivational frames are rare in all three newspapers, with minimal occurrences, each featuring four frames. This highlights the infrequent use of motivational frames that occur with significant frequency within these newspapers.

Table 8. Peace frames

Occurrences	Dawn		The Hindu		The New York Times	
	n	%	*n*	%	*n*	%
0-5	560	90.9	453	94.0	16	84.2
6-10	47	7.6	28	5.8	2	10.5
11-15	7	1.1				
16-20			1	0.2	1	5.3
21-25	2	0.3				
Above 25						
Total	616	100	482	100	19	100

The analysis of "Peace Frames" likely encapsulate narrative elements that accentuate or endorse themes related to peace, reconciliation, or conflict resolution. The data underscores the extent to which these newspapers employ such narrative techniques (Table 8). The "0-5 Occurrences" category emerges as the most prominent range for the utilization of peace frames across all three newspapers. Dawn, in particular, demonstrates a substantial reliance on peace frames in this range, accounting for 90.9% of its total peace frames. The Hindu follows closely with 94.0%, while The New York Times employs these frames to a slightly lesser extent, with 84.2% of its peace frames falling within this category. This indicates that all three newspapers incorporate peace frames in their reporting to varying degrees, with a noteworthy concentration in the 0-5 occurrences range. This concentration suggests a relatively limited thematic diversity in the depiction of peace and conflict resolution within their narratives. In contrast, when considering the "6-10, 11-15, 16-20, and 21-25 Occurrences" categories, which theoretically imply a greater diversity in the use of peace frames and their frequency, the data reveals a relatively limited presence of peace frames in these categories across all three newspapers. For instance, The Hindu employs 5.8% of its peace frames in the 6-10 range and 0.2% in the 16-20 range. The New York Times exhibits 10.5% in the 6-10 range and 5.3% in the 16-20 range. Interestingly, there is no mention of peace frames in the 11-15 range in any of the newspapers, and in the 21-25 range, there is minimal representation, comprising 0.3% in Dawn and 0.2% in The Hindu. Moreover, the "Above 25 Occurrences" category indicates the use of peace frames occurring more than 25 times. However, the data underscores that these frames are exceedingly rare or non-existent in the newspapers, with minimal occurrences.

Table 9. Dispute frames

Occurrences	Dawn		The Hindu		The New York Times	
	n	%	n	%	n	%
0-5	380	61.7	426	88.4	2	10.5
6-10	169	27.4	43	8.9	2	10.5
11-15	48	7.8	9	1.9	2	10.5
16-20	14	2.3	3	0.6	4	21.1
21-25	2	0.3			7	36.8
Above 25	3	0.5	1	0.2	2	10.5
Total	**616**	**100**	**482**	**100**	**19**	**100**

The analysis of "Dispute Frames" reveals distinct patterns in the prevalence and diversity of such narrative techniques (Table 9). The dataset allows for an examination of the extent to which these newspapers employ such narrative techniques. Firstly, in the "0-5 Occurrences" category, it is evident that dispute frames are a recurring feature in all three newspapers. In Dawn, a notable 61.7% of its total dispute frames are found within this range, indicating a significant incorporation of dispute framing techniques. The Hindu, while employing dispute frames to a slightly lesser extent in this range, still dedicates a substantial 88.4% of its total dispute frames to this category. In contrast, The New York Times employs dispute frames to a significantly lesser degree, with only 10.5% falling within this range. This suggests that all three newspapers integrate dispute frames, but there is considerable variability in the intensity of their utilization, with The Hindu demonstrating a pronounced reliance on this narrative technique within the 0-5 occurrences range. Moving to the "6-10, 11-15, 16-20, and 21-25 Occurrences" categories, which theoretically signify a broader thematic diversity in the use of dispute frames and their frequency, the data reveals that the prevalence of dispute frames in these categories is comparatively less prominent. For instance, Dawn allocates 27.4% of its dispute frames to the 6-10 range and 7.8% to the 11-15 range. The New York Times consistently maintains 10.5% in these categories, while The Hindu's utilization of dispute frames in these ranges is notably more limited. In the "Above 25 Occurrences" category, it is evident that dispute frames occurring more than 25 times are relatively rare, with minimal occurrences found in all three newspapers. This highlights the infrequent use of highly frequent dispute frames within these newspapers.

continued on following page

Table 10. Continued

Table 10. Descriptive statistics (dawn)

	N	Minimum	Maximum	Mean	Std. Deviation
Intended Frames	616	1	5	1.24	.536
Routine Frames	616	1	1	1.00	.000
Indicative Frames	616	1	6	4.84	1.385
Identity Frames	616	1	6	1.01	.209
Manipulative Frames	616	1	3	1.04	.225
Motivational Frames	616	1	6	2.26	1.311
Peace Frames	616	1	5	1.11	.402
Dispute Frames	616	1	6	1.54	.824
Types of Conflicts	616	1	5	2.13	1.041

Table 10 presents descriptive statistics for various frame categories within the news reporting of the Dawn newspaper. In the context of "Intended Frames," the data shows that these frames generally exhibit a range between 1 and 5, with an average occurrence of approximately 1.24 and a standard deviation of around 0.536. This indicates that, on average, Dawn's articles tend to incorporate approximately 1.24 intended frames, displaying a moderate level of variability around this mean. Conversely, the category of "Routine Frames" demonstrates a consistent value of 1, with no discernible variability, as indicated by a standard deviation of 0.000. This suggests that "Routine Frames" represent a constant and unchanging feature within Dawn's news reporting, consistently present in every article. The "Indicative Frames" category displays a more extensive range, spanning from 1 to 6, with an average occurrence of approximately 4.84 and a standard deviation of around 1.385. This implies that Dawn's articles, on average, encompass roughly 4.84 indicative frames, while simultaneously exhibiting substantial variability in their utilization. In the "Identity Frames" category, the range extends from 1 to 6, with an average occurrence of approximately 1.01 and a minimal standard deviation of around 0.209. This signifies that Dawn's articles tend to incorporate a relatively limited number of identity frames, with relatively low variability in their frequency. Within the "Manipulative Frames" category, the range spans from 1 to 3, with an average occurrence of approximately 1.04 and a standard deviation of about 0.225. This suggests that Dawn's articles typically employ an average of 1.04 manipulative frames, with limited variability in their frequency. In the realm of "Motivational Frames," the range varies from 1 to 6, with an average occurrence of approximately 2.26 and a standard deviation of around 1.311. This indicates that Dawn's articles tend to incorporate an average of about 2.26 motivational frames, with a relatively higher degree of variability in their use. In the context of "Peace Frames," the range spans from 1 to 5, with an average occurrence of approximately 1.11 and a standard deviation of around 0.402. Dawn's articles typically include an average of 1.11 peace frames, while simultaneously displaying moderate variability in their utilization. The "Dispute Frames" category encompasses a range from 1 to 6, with an average occurrence of approximately 1.54 and a standard deviation of around 0.824. This suggests that Dawn's articles tend to incorporate an average of approximately 1.54 dispute frames, with a degree of variability in their frequency. Lastly, the "Types of Conflicts" category spans a range from 1 to 5, with an average occurrence of approximately 2.13 and a standard deviation of around 1.041. This signifies that, on average, Dawn's news articles encompass approximately 2.13 different types of conflicts, with some variability in the range of conflict types discussed.

Table 11. Descriptive statistics (the hindu)

	N	Minimum	Maximum	Mean	Std. Deviation
Intended Frames	482	1	4	1.13	.418
Routine Frames	482	1	1	1.00	.000
Indicative Frames	482	1	6	3.56	1.585
Identity Frames	482	1	6	1.01	.236
Manipulative Frames	482	1	6	1.05	.306
Motivational Frames	482	1	6	1.58	.954
Peace Frames	482	1	4	1.06	.270
Dispute Frames	482	1	6	1.16	.498
Types of Conflicts	482	1	5	2.41	1.084

The Hindu newspaper's news reporting, an analysis of descriptive statistics reveals pertinent insights into the frequency and variability of various frame categories (Table 11). These statistics provide a comprehensive overview of the framing techniques employed in their articles. "Intended Frames," which reflect the core themes and messages of the news, are generally employed moderately, with a mean occurrence of approximately 1.13 and a standard deviation of around 0.418. This suggests that, on average, articles in The Hindu incorporate about 1.13 intended frames, and there is a moderate degree of variability in their utilization. In contrast, "Routine Frames" consistently exhibit a fixed value of 1, with a standard deviation of 0.000, indicating no variability. This implies that "Routine Frames" are a constant and invariant feature in The Hindu's news reporting, uniformly present in every article. The category of "Indicative Frames" showcases wider variability, spanning from 1 to 6, with an average occurrence of approximately 3.56 and a standard deviation of about 1.585. This indicates that articles in The Hindu encompass around 3.56 indicative frames on average, and the notable standard deviation underscores a substantial level of variability in their inclusion. "Identity Frames" tend to integrate a limited number of identity frames, with a relatively low standard deviation of around 0.236, suggesting relatively low variability in their frequency. "Manipulative Frames" typically have an average occurrence of approximately 1.05, and there is limited variability with a standard deviation of about 0.306 in their frequency. In the "Motivational Frames" category, articles in The Hindu tend to include around 1.58 motivational frames on average, but there is a relatively higher degree of variability with a standard deviation of approximately 0.954 in their utilization. Within the "Peace Frames" category, articles encompass an average of 1.06 peace frames, with a moderate level of variability indicated by a standard deviation of approximately 0.270. "Dispute Frames" cover a range of values from 1 to 6, with an average occurrence of approximately 1.16 and a standard deviation of around 0.498. This suggests that, on average, articles in The Hindu incorporate about 1.16 dispute frames, and there is some variability in their frequency. In the category related to "Types of Conflicts," articles cover around 2.41 different types of conflicts on average, with a degree of variability in the range of conflict types discussed, as indicated by a standard deviation of approximately 1.084.

Table 12. Descriptive statistics (The New York Times)

	N	Minimum	Maximum	Mean	Std. Deviation
Intended Frames	19	1	4	2.11	.994
Routine Frames	19	1	1	1.00	.000
Indicative Frames	19	1	6	5.47	1.577
Identity Frames	19	1	3	1.11	.459
Manipulative Frames	19	1	4	1.68	.946
Motivational Frames	19	1	6	3.95	1.682
Peace Frames	19	1	4	1.26	.733
Dispute Frames	19	1	6	3.95	1.545
Types of Conflicts	19	1	5	2.68	1.416

The tabulated data provides a comprehensive analysis of descriptive statistics related to distinct frame categories within news reporting by The New York Times (Table 12). Drawing from a sample of 19 articles, it is evident that each frame category exhibits unique patterns in terms of occurrence and variability. For "Intended Frames," the data reveals a moderate range with a mean occurrence of 2.11 and a standard deviation of 0.994. This suggests that, on average, articles encompass around 2.11 intended frames, with a noticeable degree of variability. In stark contrast, "Routine Frames" exhibit a fixed value of 1 across all 19 articles, reflecting no variability with a standard deviation of 0.000, indicating their consistent presence in every article. "Indicative Frames," however, display a wider range, with a mean occurrence of 5.47 and a substantial standard deviation of 1.577, suggesting notable variability. "Identity Frames" tend to integrate a limited number of frames, showing relatively low variability with a mean occurrence of 1.11 and a standard deviation of 0.459. "Manipulative Frames" show moderate variability with a standard deviation of approximately 0.946, while "Motivational Frames" exhibit a relatively higher degree of variability, as indicated by a standard deviation of approximately 1.682.

Table 13. Correlation table

Dawn				The Hindu	The New York Times	
		Manipulative Frames	Peace Frames	Peace Frames	Indicative Frames	Motivational Frames
Types of Conflicts	Pearson Correlation	.104**	-.127**	-.141 **	-.576**	-.497*
	Sig. (2-tailed)	.010	.002	.002	.010	.030
	N	616	616	482	19	19

In the analysis of the "Dawn" newspaper's reporting on conflicts (Table 13), it is noteworthy that Manipulative Frames and Peace Frames exhibit positive correlations with types of Conflicts, with correlation coefficients of 0.104** and -0.127**, respectively. These results are statistically significant, as evidenced by their low p-values of 0.010 and 0.002. In parallel, "The Hindu" and "The New York Times" demonstrate analogous trends in their correlations between types of conflicts and the utilization of different frames. On the contrary, a compelling pattern emerges across all three newspapers in the form of a robust negative correlation between motivational frames and types of conflicts, characterized by correlation coefficients of -0.576**, -0.497*, and -0.141**, respectively. While Indicative Frames also display a negative correlation with Types of Conflicts, it is notably weaker in comparison to the correlations involving Motivational Frame.

DISCUSSIONS

The prominence of identity politics within the analyzed conflicts is a central point of critical research discussion, shedding light on the intricate intersections of political and religious contexts. This thematic underpinning underscores the pivotal role of identity in shaping the narratives surrounding the conflicts in question. These narratives are deeply entwined with issues of political sovereignty, cultural heritage, and religious affiliations. The interplay of identity politics within these conflicts serves as a critical lens through which we can understand the multifaceted dynamics at play. One of the key findings in the analysis pertains to the portrayal of identity-related threats in the context of Kashmir, with a particular focus on the legacy of partition. Dawn, the Pakistani newspaper, underscores the conflict in Kashmir as primarily a matter of identity. It highlights how the region's historical and cultural identity is a central point of contention, with significant implications for the Kashmiri population's self-perception and self-determination. This perspective emphasizes the enduring resonance of historical identity within the conflict and its impact on the broader socio-political landscape in the region.

Conversely, in the Indian daily, Kashmir is portrayed as a site of conflict primarily driven by issues of interest and political manoeuvring. The narrative here revolves around the strategic and economic significance of the region, casting it as a territorial dispute driven by geopolitical calculations. This perspective underscores the complex geopolitical factors that have contributed to the ongoing tensions in Kashmir. The American daily offers yet another dimension by framing the issue as a recurrence of ancient hostilities, devoid of any significant manipulation or economic motives. Instead, it is characterized as a protracted historical conflict characterized by deep-seated animosities. This perspective underscores the enduring nature of the India-Pakistan conflict, with a focus on the cyclical nature of tensions, drawing attention to the historic roots of the conflict as a primary driver. The American daily places considerable emphasis on the central concept of partition in the India-Pakistan issue. It recognizes partition as a foundational event that has shaped the region's political landscape, often leading to new outbreaks of tension. The concept of partition remains a recurring theme in the American newspaper's coverage, drawing attention to how the legacy of this historical event continues to influence contemporary conflicts and relationships in the subcontinent. The relationship conflict between India and Pakistan is another noteworthy dimension that the newspapers target through their content. This perspective highlights the intricate dynamics between the two nations, including diplomatic exchanges, military posturing, and cross-border skirmishes. The portrayal of this relationship conflict serves as a crucial aspect of the analysis, as it underscores the ongoing complexities and interactions between these two major South Asian powers.

The dynamics of framing in Indian and Pakistani newspapers offer intriguing insights into the portrayal of conflicts and the influence of various frames on public perception and policy decisions. These critical research discussions delve deeper into these dynamics:
1. Emotion-Fuelled Frames vs. Defensive Postures: The Indian newspapers prominently feature frames driven by emotions such as hatred, often in the pursuit of perceived opportunities. In contrast, Pakistani newspapers adopt a more defensive stance, seeking to deflect accusations against their side. This contrast highlights the differing emotional undercurrents in the narratives presented by the two nations. Dawn, in particular, incorporates frames of diplomacy as the case comes under

global scrutiny. This research discussion underscores the role of emotions and defensive strategies in shaping the narrative and public sentiment.
2. Complex Confluence of Frames in Dawn: Dawn, the Pakistani newspaper, intricately combines frames of dispute and power contention while infusing elements of manipulation and motivation. This amalgamation of frames, alongside the presence of ancient hatred, underscores the multifaceted nature of the narratives presented by newspapers in this conflict. The scarcity of frames promoting meaningful discussions and bilateral engagement is a noteworthy concern, with broken relationships dominating the discourse. The role of these frames in influencing public opinion and the perpetuation of disputes is a critical area of research interest.
3. Fairness and Objectivity in Frame Balancing: The distant dream of fairness and objectivity in frame balancing becomes evident, as dominant frames in The Hindu and Dawn continue to revolve around the question of identity. The motivational frames are directed toward shaping public opinion, often steering the narrative in a more positive direction that sustains the fires of dispute. This raises questions about the role of newspapers in either perpetuating or mitigating conflicts through their framing choices.
4. The Observer Role of the American Daily: The American daily assumes a distinct role as an observer, conducting surveillance over the disparities between the nations. It refrains from actively promoting peace or instigating disputes, adopting an objective stance that reflects historical animosities without actively engaging with the conflict. This approach underscores the contrast between the American newspaper's framing and those of the Indian and Pakistani newspapers, emphasizing the influence of external factors in framing choices.
5. Dominance of Dispute Frames: Dispute frames eclipse peace frames in both The Hindu and Dawn, with occasional shifts toward motivation or manipulation frames. The analysis of these frames unveils the type of control exercised in shaping news stories and their relevance in specific contexts. This discussion highlights the persistent influence of frames on the narratives of conflicts and their impact on audience perceptions.
6. External Factors in Framing: It is crucial to recognize the integral role of external factors in the framing process, from the formation of initial frames to the development of follow-up stories. These external factors, including the nature of the conflict, its characteristics, features, and the involvement of various stakeholders, play a substantial role in uniting frames to convey the emotional and contextual aspects of a story. This research discussion underscores the complexity of the framing process and the interplay of diverse factors that shape news narratives.

CONCLUSION

In conclusion, the discussions stemming from the analysis of conflicts and their associated contents underscore the profound influence of identity politics, particularly within political and religious contexts. The narratives within the analyzed cases reflect the complex interplay of identity-related dynamics, often portraying the existential threat to identity that has persisted in Kashmir since its partition. Notably, these narratives take distinct forms in the examined newspapers, with The Hindu emphasizing the notion of a conflict of interest, Dawn highlighting a conflict of identity, and The New York Times characterizing the issue as a recurrence of historical animosities rather than manipulation or economic crisis. The central theme of India-Pakistan relations, shaped by the spectre of partition and periodic eruptions of tension, remains a focal point in the American daily's coverage.

The newspapers also convey elements of a relationship conflict between the two nations, reflecting the ongoing dynamics between India and Pakistan. These dynamics manifest differently in Indian and Pakistani newspapers, where hatred emotions and defensive stances are prominent in Indian papers, while Dawn combines dispute frames with power contention, intertwined with manipulation and motivation, all amidst the backdrop of historical animosities. It is evident that both Indian and Pakistani news contents analyzed in this study have limited frames that encourage meaningful discussions, with peace frames taking a backseat to themes focused on fractured relationships. Fairness and objectivity in frame balancing appear elusive, as dominant frames continue to revolve around questions of identity, motivation for public opinion, and maintaining a positive social context that sustains discord. Conversely, the American daily assumes the role of a detached observer, maintaining an objective stance, merely reflecting the historical crisis without actively promoting peace or exacerbating disputes. Here, dispute frames eclipse peace frames, occasionally giving way to motivation or manipulation frames. The analysis underscores the critical role played by frame selection in shaping the narrative and defining the relevance of the context in which a news story unfolds, catering to the expectations and emotions of the audience. In summary, it is evident that external factors, such as the inherent nature of the conflict, its characteristics, features, and the interventions of various stakeholders, significantly influence the framing process, from the initial formation of frames to the subsequent development of stories. The disposition of newspapers, along with their engagement with external factors, plays a pivotal role in uniting frames and effectively conveying the emotional undercurrents of the story. This complex interplay of factors shapes the narratives surrounding conflicts and their portrayal in the media.

ACKNOWLEDGMENTS

The authors would like to acknowledge Indian Council of Social Science Research (ICSSR) for their support.

REFERENCES

Bartholomé, G., Lecheler, S., & de Vreese, C. (2015). Manufacturing Conflict? How Journalists Intervene in the Conflict Frame Building Process. *The International Journal of Press/Politics*, 20(4), 438–457. 10.1177/1940161215595514

Bates, R. H. (1983). Modernization, Ethnic Competition, and the Rationality of Politics in Contemporary Africa. *State versus Ethnic Claims: African Policy Dilemmas*. Westview Press.

Chong, D., & Druckman, J. N. (2007). A Theory of Framing and Opinion Formation in Competitive Elite Environments. *Journal of Communication*, 57(1), 99–118. 10.1111/j.1460-2466.2006.00331.x

Collier, P., & Hoeffler, A. (1998). On economic causes of civil war. *Oxford Economic Papers*, 50(4), 563–573. 10.1093/oep/50.4.563

Easterly, W., & Levine, R. (1997). Africa's growth tragedy: Policies and ethnic divisions. *The Quarterly Journal of Economics*, 112(4), 1203–1250. 10.1162/003355300555466

Edelman, M. W. (1985). The sea is so wide and my boat is so small: Problems facing Black children today. In McAdoo, H. P., & McAdoo, J. L. (Eds.), *Black children: Social, educational, and parental environments* (pp. 72–82). Sage Publications, Inc.

Entman, R. M. (1993). Framing: Toward clarification of a fractured paradigm. *Journal of Communication*, 43(4), 51–58. 10.1111/j.1460-2466.1993.tb01304.x

Falasca, K. (2014). Political News Journalism: Mediatization across Three News Reporting Contexts. *European Journal of Communication*, 29(5), 583–597. 10.1177/0267323114538853

Fearon, J. D., & Laitin, D. D. (2000). Violence and the Social Construction of Ethnic Identity. *International Organization*, 54(4), 4. 10.1162/002081800551398

Goffman, E. (1974). *Frame Analysis: An Essay on the Organization of Experience*. Harvard University Press.

Graber, D. (1981). Media agenda-setting in a presidential election: issues, images, and interest. New York (N.Y.): Praeger.

Gross, K., & Brewer, P. R. (2007). Sore Losers: News Frames, Policy Debates, and Emotions. *The Harvard International Journal of Press/Politics*, 12(1), 122–133. 10.1177/1081180X06297231

Hänggli, R., & Kriesi, H. (2012). Frame Construction and Frame Promotion (Strategic Framing Choices). *The American Behavioral Scientist*, 56(3), 260–278. 10.1177/0002764211426325

Hoffmann, J., & Hawkins, V. (Eds.). (2015). *Communication and Peace: Mapping an emerging field* (1st ed.). Routledge., 10.4324/9781315773124

Horowitz, D. (1985). *Ethnic Groups in Conflict*. University of California Press.

Huntington, S. P. (2000). *The clash of civilizations? In Culture and politics* (pp. 99-118). Palgrave Macmillan, New York.

Jackson, D. (2011). Strategic Media, Cynical Public? Examining the Contingent Effects of Strategic News Frames on Political Cynicism in the United Kingdom. *The International Journal of Press/Politics*, 16(1), 157–175. 10.1177/1940161210381647

Johnston, H., & Noakes, J. A. (Eds.). (2005). *Frames of protest: Social movements and the framing perspective*. Rowman & Littlefield Publishers.

Kaplan, R. D. (1994). *The coming anarchy: how scarcity, crime, overpopulation, tribalism, and disease are rapidly destroying the social fabric of our planet.*

Kaufman, S., & Smith, J. (1999). Framing and reframing in land use change conflicts. *Journal of Architectural and Planning Research*, 16, 164–180.

Kerlinger, F. N. (1986). *Foundations of Behavioral Research* (3rd ed.). Holt, Rinehart and Winston.

Kothari, C. R. (2004). *Research Methodology: Methods and Techniques* (2nd ed.). New Age International Publishers.

Kuan, D., Hasan, N. A. M., Zawawi, J. W. M., & Abdullah, Z. (2021). Framing Theory Application in Public Relations: The Lack of Dynamic Framing Analysis in Competitive Context. *Media Watch*, 12(2), 333–351. 10.15655/mw_2021_v12i2_160155

Lewis, W. A. (1985). *Racial Conflict and Economic Development*. Harvard University Press. 10.4159/harvard.9780674424654

Lynch, G. (2011). *I Say to You: Ethnic Politics and the Kalenjin in Kenya*. University of Chicago Press. 10.7208/chicago/9780226498096.001.0001

McManus, J. H. (1994). *Market-driven Journalism: Let the Citizen Beware?* Sage.

Mearsheimer, J. J. (2001). *The Tragedy of Great Power Politics*. W. W. Norton.

Mills, C. W. (1956). *The power elite*. Oxford University Press.

Morgenthau, H. J. (1948). World politics in the mid-twentieth century. *The Review of Politics*, 10(2), 154–173. 10.1017/S0034670500042236

Nadel, S. F. (1956). Understanding primitive peoples. *Oceania*, 26(3), 159–173. 10.1002/j.1834-4461.1956.tb00676.x

Noakes, J. A., & Wilkins, K. G. (2002). Shifting frames of the Palestinian movement in US news. *Media Culture & Society*, 24(5), 649–671. 10.1177/016344370202400506

O'Regan, M. (2007). Explaining Media Frames of Contested Foreign Conflicts: Irish National "Opinion Leader" Newspapers. Frames of the Israeli-Palestinian Conflict (July 2000 to July 2004)'. *Networking Knowledge*, 1(2), 1–25. 10.31165/nk.2007.12.27

Oberschall, A. (1978). Theories of social conflict. *Annual Review of Sociology*, 4(1), 291–315. 10.1146/annurev.so.04.080178.001451

Reese, E., Haden, C. A., Baker-Ward, L., Bauer, P., Fivush, R., & Ornstein, P. A. (2011). Coherence of Personal Narratives across the Lifespan: A Multidimensional Model and Coding Method. *Journal of cognition and development: official journal of the Cognitive Development Society, 12*(4), 424–462. 10.1080/15248372.2011.587854

Salwen, M. B., & Matera, F. R. (1992). Public Salience of Foreign Nations. *The Journalism Quarterly*, 69(3), 623–632. 10.1177/107769909206900310

Schelling, T. C. (1963). War without Pain, and other Models. *World Politics*, 15(3), 465–487. 10.2307/2009474

Schudson, M. (2001). The Objectivity Norm in American Journalism*. *Journalism*, 2(2), 149–170. 10.1177/146488490100200201

Semetko, H. (2000). Framing European Politics: A Content Analysis of Press and Television News. *Journal of Communication, 50*(2), 93–109. doi:. 1460-2466.2000.tb02843.x.10.1111/j

Shaw, E. F. (1979). Agenda-Setting and Mass Communication Theory. *Gazette (Leiden, Netherlands)*, 25(2), 96–105. 10.1177/001654927902500203

Takens, J., van Atteveldt, W., van Hoof, A., & Kleinnijenhuis, J. (2013). Media Logic in Election Campaign Coverage. *European Journal of Communication*, 28(3), 277–293. 10.1177/0267323113478522

Taylor, P. M. (1992). *War and the media: Propaganda and persuasion in the Gulf War*. Manchester University press.

Tilly, C. (1991, September). Domination, resistance, compliance... discourse. In *Sociological forum* (pp. 593–602). Eastern Sociological Society.

Waltz, K. N. (1979). *Theory of International Politics*. Addison-Wesley Publishing Company.

Williams, R. M.Jr. (1994). The sociology of ethnic conflicts: Comparative international perspectives. *Annual Review of Sociology*, 20(1), 49–79. 10.1146/annurev.so.20.080194.000405

Wondolleck, J. M., Gray, B., & Bryan, T. (2003). Us versus them: How identities and characterizations influence conflict. *Environmental Practice*, 5(3), 207–213. 10.1017/S1466046603035592

Yousaf, M., Rahman, B. H., & Yousaf, Z. (2020). Constructing Reality: Framing of the Kashmir Conflict in Dictatorial and Democratic Regimes in the Pakistani English Press. *Media Watch*, 11(3), 401–415. 10.15655/mw_2020_v11i3_203045

Chapter 3
Crises Determine Preference and Media Credibility:
Case Study of Mass Protest in Iraq

Haitham Hadi Numan
http://orcid.org/0000-0001-9115-1792
University of Exeter, UK

ABSTRACT

This study examines how university students in Iraq perceive credibility and their media preferences during the protests. The research found that the students' political views influenced their choices and perceptions, leading them to shift from traditional media like television, radio, and newspapers to social media platforms like Twitter and Facebook used by the protesters. The study used Cede Gaziano and Kristin McGrath's credibility analysis factors, which include importance, fairness, bias, accuracy, completeness, and trust, to survey a sample of Iraqi undergraduate students before and after the protests. The results showed a significant change in students' perceptions of credibility and their reliance on traditional media versus social media after the start of the protests.

INTRODUCTION

In October 2019, Pictures, and videos of protesters at Tahrir Square, which is situated in the center of the Iraqi capital, Baghdad, went viral on social media during the first two days of the protest movement. This protesting movement called Tishreen uprising. The hashtag "#I_came_taking_my_right" (I want my rights) was launched to garner support for the protests. Muhannad Al-Ghazi, a journalist, and the editor-in-chief of a local news agency revealed that during the first two days of the demonstrations, television channels barely covered the events. Only three stations were interested in airing breaking news and some pictures of the demonstration squares. Meanwhile, the TV channels that were affiliated with the government such as the Iraqi Media Network and the religious party TV channels, did not show any interest in covering the protests Odeh. (2019).

The Iraqi government began controlling Facebook, and the Iraqi protesters secretly downloaded virtual private network (VPN) applications (a virtual network that allows communication with servers outside the country). Others began to publish details about the upcoming demonstrations. The Tahrir

DOI: 10.4018/979-8-3693-3767-7.ch003

Copyright ©2024, IGI Global. Copying or distributing in print or electronic forms without written permission of IGI Global is prohibited.

Square protests showed that social media, especially Facebook and Twitter, provided new sources of information that the political regime could not easily manage. These were crucial in convincing citizens to participate in the demonstrations. (Arraf & Lonsdorf, 2020). The massive protests occurred in early October 2019, when protesters massed in Baghdad's streets and cities in southern Iraq to demand the government's ouster, an end to corruption, and a halt to the overwhelming influence of Iran. The Iraqi government sent 70% of the country offline, unable to access the internet. Internet freedom monitor Netblocks blocked social media, including Facebook, Twitter, WhatsApp, and Instagram, to quell protests sweeping through significant cities (Bostock, 2019). However, the traditional press, which consists of newspapers, radio, and television, continued to broadcast news.

Most traditional media in Iraq receives private funding from "parties, political and religious institutions, state officials, and businessmen, in addition to foreign entities that come from Arab, regional, or neighboring states, such as Iran, Turkey, and Saudi Arabia" (Salim, 2021). Ownership of current media is either public, private, or partisan. The government owns and finances the public press. Partisan channels compete for space. For example, Sunni and Shi'ite stations compete over viewers. Kurdistan runs several Kurdish channels (Salim, 2021).

The Journalistic Freedoms Observatory in Iraq (JFOI) conducted a study in 2016 that explored the impact of financial uncertainty on journalism's independence in Iraq. In Iraq, media freedom has been declining (Awad, and Eaton, 2013). The JFOI study found that more than 50 local media organizations, including TV and radio stations, daily print publications, and news websites, received funding from unknown sources. Several local media institutions also received technical and financial support from political movements (Bennett, Lawrence, and Livingston, 2008).

A few crises may have motivated the Tishreen uprising. Iraqis had spent weeks peacefully protesting unemployment and a lack of job opportunities outside some of Baghdad's government buildings. Then, in late September, a video of demonstrators being dispersed by water cannons drew much attention to the government's aggressive tactics (D.L.B., DSA's, 2021). Anti-government protests, therefore, erupted in Iraq when Iraqi citizens vented their anger at the endemic corruption, high unemployment, limited public services, and foreign interference. The youth-dominated demonstrations called for an overhaul of the country's corrupt political system, in addition to changes that addressed the influence of Iran in Iraq's politics, measures to address high unemployment, particularly among the country's younger generations, where it stood at 25%, and improvements to public services (Tung, 2020). Additionally, more than 450 people were killed after these protests (Idris, 2020).

Protesters used social media to document the demonstrations, which prompted the Iraqi government to shut down the Internet for hours every day to prevent the events surrounding the protests among Iraqis and the international community (Lovotti, and Proserpio, 2021).

The research in this study surveyed Iraqi college students' perceptions about the media credibility and preferences of social and traditional media sources before and after the uprising. It measured any significant differences in media perceptions by students in Iraq by using a survey that treated credibility as a multidimensional concept and looked at gender differences in their perceptions and their political attitudes.

LITERATURE REVIEW

Otlan, Kuzmina, Rumiantseva, and Tertytchnaya (2023) point out that censoring news about protests in other countries may cause audiences to turn to alternative news sources; covering such events could motivate citizens to participate in protests at home. For instance, the media coverage of foreign protests reduces on days of significant protests in Russia when there are potentially higher costs of encouraging mobilization.

In 2023, a study by Masullo, Brown, & Harlow showed that a new approach to writing protest stories challenges press patterns among underrepresented groups. News articles that elucidate a protest's objectives and historical context employing the strategy of legitimizing and humanizing the individual whose demise triggered the protest rather than portraying them as a criminal resulted in news consumers attaining a more comprehensive comprehension of the protest and the associated social movement. The researchers discovered that people with conservative political ideas saw these articles as less trustworthy than those adhering to the journalistic standards commonly observed in the United States, which often negatively portray demonstrators and their causes. Conversely, people with liberal ideas experienced the opposite outcome.

Onuch, Mateo, and Waller (2021) Examine inquiries to gain a deeper comprehension of the factors that attract large groups of people to protest, the influences on public opinion, and the spread of false information during mass mobilization. Onuch, Mateo, and Waller examine assumptions prevalent in contemporary protest literature regarding the impact of "new" media (social media and online news) and "old" media (television) on protest behavior and attitudes. They compared supporters of the demonstrations with non-supporters and found that supporters consumed more news related to the demonstrators. Furthermore, it is a more reliable indicator of accepting misinformation compared to consuming modern media sources.

Besalú and Pont-Sorribes (2021) have highlighted the importance of credible digital news in today's democracies, especially considering the spread of fake news and the decline of traditional media outlets. Four news formats were evaluated to assess the credibility of digital news: digital newspapers, digital television, Facebook, and WhatsApp. The participants were divided into four experimental groups and given a credibility score and a probability of sharing score for four different political news items presented in these formats. The mean credibility scores assigned to the same news item presented in various formats showed significant differences among groups, as did the likelihood of sharing the news. News items presented in traditional media formats, mainly digital television, were considered more credible than those offered in social media formats, and participants were more likely to share the former. This indicates a more cautious attitude towards social media as a news source.

Pearce and Rodgers (2020) have reviewed recent research on the role of social media platforms in activists' reporting of street protests. The review raises questions about whether social media platforms can be considered a cultural source for protest movements. The "many-to-many" dynamic of alternative journalism via social media has implications for the incursion of more democratic and participatory cultures and structures compared to traditional media's traditional "one-to-many" approach. Existing literature suggests that user-generated content via social media has the potential to replace traditional journalism in protest situations due to advantages such as first-hand access.

In conclusion, Otlan, Kuzmina, Rumiantseva, and Tertytchnaya (2023), Masullo, Brown, & Harlow (2023), Onuch, Mateo, and Waller (2021), Besalú and Pont-Sorribes (2021) and Pearce and Rodgers (2020), agreed on specific differences between traditional media's credibility and social media's in terms of monitoring coverage and writing styles, the consumption of news by demonstration supporters and non-supporters, and traditional media's dynamism in motivating protesters. Therefore, the study seeks to fill the gap by determining if credibility and media preferences towards social and traditional media are stable or changeable variables. Credibility and media preferences can be affected by changing circumstances and events. Consequently, this study considers whether the perception of credibility and media preferences remain constant or if they change in response to political events by examining our hypothesis that the credibility of young people in Iraq has changed from traditional to social media since the outbreak of demonstrations, and that related with a change in their political stance on the events of demonstration.

Hypothesis

This research study on media credibility hypothesizes that 1) audiences prioritize news that is free from government interference over media professionalism, and 2) audiences lean toward news that is consistent with the masses' political attitude. Consequently, the credibility of social media increased after revolutionary events and popular movements. Therefore, the research question is: How much has credibility shifted from traditional media to social media pre- and post-protest? Do gender and political attitudes play a role in this change?

THEORETICAL FRAMEWORK

Media Credibility

Aristotle first introduced the idea of source credibility by referring to the image of a source that recipients have in their minds as ethos. McCroskey & Teven (1999) described source credibility as a perceiver's attitude toward a source. Gunther (2020) argued that perceived source credibility was more related to the audience's responses than message source attributes. Bracken (2006) points out that source credibility is "the amount of believability attributed to a source of information (either a medium or an individual) by receivers." Credibility was initially studied as an attribute of the source. (Hovland, Janis, & Kelley, 1953). Gunther (1992) also defined credibility as a relational variable based on the audience's perception of the source. Finally, McQuail (2010) stated, "Source credibility is how people find a source credible, and it contributes to news learning effects." Some trust is essential for a news source to be valid. However, plenty of evidence shows that people habitually pay attention to media sources they do not trust. (Hu, 2015).

Media Preference Theory

Media preference theory explains how people become reliant on media as a resource. This theory describes how the relationship between the media and social systems shapes the media's impact on its audience. The theory is based on two elements: sources and goals. According to DeFleur & Rokeach (1976), different individuals, groups, and organizations must rely on media resources controlled by other people, groups, or organizations to achieve their personal and social goals. To understand the social world, individuals seek to accomplish these goals by learning and obtaining news and information through direct contact with the social system (Wainner, 2018). Media preference mainly aims to provide information; media serves as an information system through which people seek news to achieve their goals (Ball & Rokeach, 1985). The media perform four tasks: collecting information through delegates and correspondents assigned to do so, coordinating information, revising the information gathered, and disseminating knowledge by distributing previously organized and coordinated information to the public (Cho, 2009).

Media preferences theory proposes three hypotheses regarding the reliance on media. The first hypothesis suggests that as a society becomes more unstable, its members depend more on the media (Loveless, 2008). The second hypothesis states that the more effectively the media can fulfill the public's goals and satisfy its needs, the more the media will be relied upon. The third hypothesis posits that media dependence varies depending on users' circumstances, characteristics, and goals (Carillo, Scornavacca, and S, 2017).

Building on these three hypotheses, the author suggests that individuals shift their reliance on media after crises by seeking credible information and news that align with their goals. If a person perceives a lack of credibility in their sources, they will attempt to find alternative sources to get what they perceive to be credible news and information.

After the Iraqi protests, the students were closely aligned with the protesters because many were university students (Lovotti and Proserpio, 2021). They turned to social media because it provided unfiltered coverage of the events without any restrictions (Belair-Gagnon, 2015). Political parties or individuals with ties to the political elite owned most traditional media outlets, including television and radio (Amos, 2010). Therefore, media credibility is a form of media preference (Rahman, 2014).

Political attitudes

Political attitudes refer to the opinions and values that individuals hold about political issues, events, and personalities. Social scientists started studying these attitudes systematically in the 1930s and 1940s. While surveys had been used occasionally prior to this, it wasn't until the publication of "The People's Choice" in 1944 that scholars began examining the impact of media exposure and campaign-related events on evaluations of major party presidential candidates (Lazarsfeld, Paul, Bernard Berelson, and Helen Gaudet. 1944). Attitudes are long-lasting perspectives towards things like concepts, ideas, or others, which help us understand the world around us. Attitudes are different from beliefs in that they are less focused on the individual's personality, less specific in opinions, and only useful for analysis, even though they can be used as descriptive statistics (Hennessy, 1970).

Gaziano and McGrath Credibility Scale

The study used factor meta-analysis to measure media credibility and shift in preference theory. The study also used survey research to measure credibility perceptions and the change in students' media preference after the protests. Gaziano and McGrath (1986), Hellmueller, and Trilling, (2012) developed a credibility scale factor to assess the reliability of news sources among the masses. This factor considers various aspects such as fairness or bias, accuracy and completeness of the news, respect for people's privacy, consideration of audience interests, concern for the community's well-being, separation of fact from opinion, trustworthiness, prioritization of public interest over profits, factual reporting versus opinionated reporting, quality of reporters and their social concerns, and adherence to moral standards instead of sensationalism. Theoretically, to operationalize media credibility and independence in surveys, the design survey questionnaire was based on the assumptions of media preference theory, as well as the meta-analysis of the credibility scale. The first two researchers applied meta-analysis in communication studies to examine media preference (Dillard, Hunter, & Burgoon, 1984). Later, scholars gradually increased the use of this approach as a significant potential methodology to summarize findings quantitatively. (Glass, 1976; Schmidt & Hunter, 2014). Meta-analytic outcomes can flash empirically and theoretically central developments for large swaths of media credibility and preference in communication studies. The instrument is designed to rate credibility factor meta-analysis characteristics from 1 to 3 on a three-point scale, making comparisons. The credibility scale questions included six key topics: importance, fairness, bias, accuracy, story completion, and trust. This research forms the factor analysis of credibility scores and analyzes the audience's preference on social versus traditional media.

In conclusion, this theoretical framework relies on our proposed four concepts: credibility, media preference, political attitude, and political events. Hence, the theoretical framework conceptualizes credibility and media preference as dependent variables. In contrast, the independent variables are political events that match or differ with the political tendencies of the public. The study defined it as the time that preceded the protests and the times before and after the protests began, and the second variable is traditional and social media. Further, by comparing perceptions of credibility and media preferences before and after the protest toward social media and traditional means, we can conclude whether credibility and media preference are constant factors or whether they change with changing circumstances in the audience perceptions that change their political attitude. (See Table 1).

To operationalize these variables, the theoretical framework was applied Gaziano and McGrath Credibility Scale, and Loveless, (2008) and Carillo, Scornavacca, and S, (2017) hypothesis of Media Preference Theory in a field survey on a random sample in frame of university students in universities in Baghdad. The author chose universities as sample farms because they are the best way for reaching the young generation, which was the grassroots of the protesters in the October 2019 protests in Iraq.

Table 1. Independent and dependent variables

Dependent Variable	Independent Variables	
Credibility And Preference	**Male Audience**	**Female Audience**
	Pre-Protest	Pre-Protest
	Post - protest	Post - protest
	Traditional media Traditional media	
	Social media Social media	
	Political Attitude Political Attitude	

METHODOLOGY

Data Collection

Participants comprised 212 college students from five universities in Baghdad (125 male and 87 female). Interviews were an average of 11 minutes long. The daily interview completion rate was four to six interviews. To ensure the reliability of the data, 10% of the data was reentered. The data were analyzed using SPSS version 17.0. The statistical cross-tabulation technique was employed to test perception differences to see if they existed.

Sample Plan

In sociology and statistics research, there is snowball sampling (Goodman, 1961), chain sampling, chain-referral sampling, or referral sampling (Masullo, Brown, & Harlow, 2023). Snowball sampling is a nonprobability sampling technique where existing study subjects recruit future subjects from among their acquaintances. Thus, the sample group will grow like a rolling snowball. As the sample builds up, enough data is gathered to be useful for research (Given, ed., 2008). Therefore, the study used a snowball sample of college students in this survey, and the fieldwork was conducted between November 16, 2022, and January 19, 2023.

The researcher selected a sample of students from two governmental universities and three private universities in Baghdad. Randomly recruit diverse snowball seeds of student numbers, resulting in 8 to 14 interviews at several colleges. Two students, male and female students were recruited in each department. Therefore, a round of 40 interviews was conducted at each university (i.e., 212 total interviews). The author also ensured that the starting seeds of our sample were diversified in terms of college students' gender and the type of college program.

Findings

According to the survey, 82% of college students showed their support for the protests, while only 18% were against them. The survey also found that of the female respondents, 46% supported the demonstrations, compared to only 4% who were against them. Meanwhile, for male students, 36% endorsed the protests, while 10% were against them. Thus, it appears that women were more supportive of the movement than men, (Figure 1).

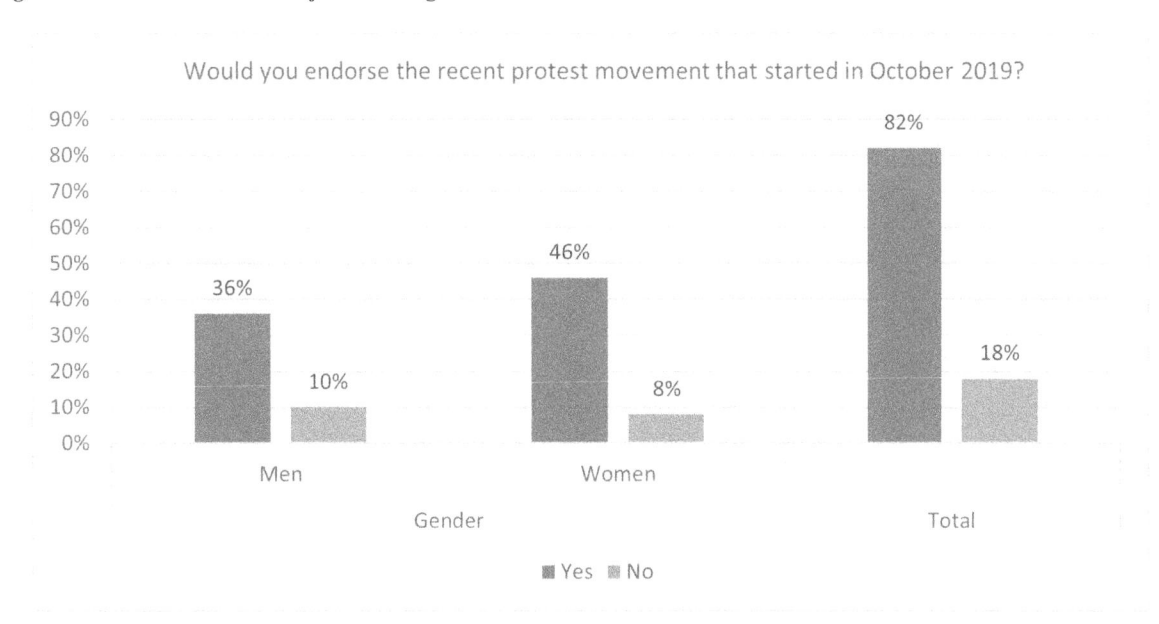

Figure 1. Political attitude of the college students

Would you endorse the recent protest movement that started in October 2019?

Gender	Yes	No
Men	36%	10%
Women	46%	8%
Total	82%	18%

Using traditional and social media among undergraduate students

According to a study, 43% of college students relied on social media for news about the protests, while only 21% used traditional media such as TV, radio, and newspapers to stay updated. Another 36% depended on both traditional and social media for news.

When it comes to gender, 47% of female students relied on social media for news, while 29% used traditional media and 24% relied on a combination of both. For male students, 40% depended on social media, 24% on traditional media, and 36% on a mix of both. (Figure 2).

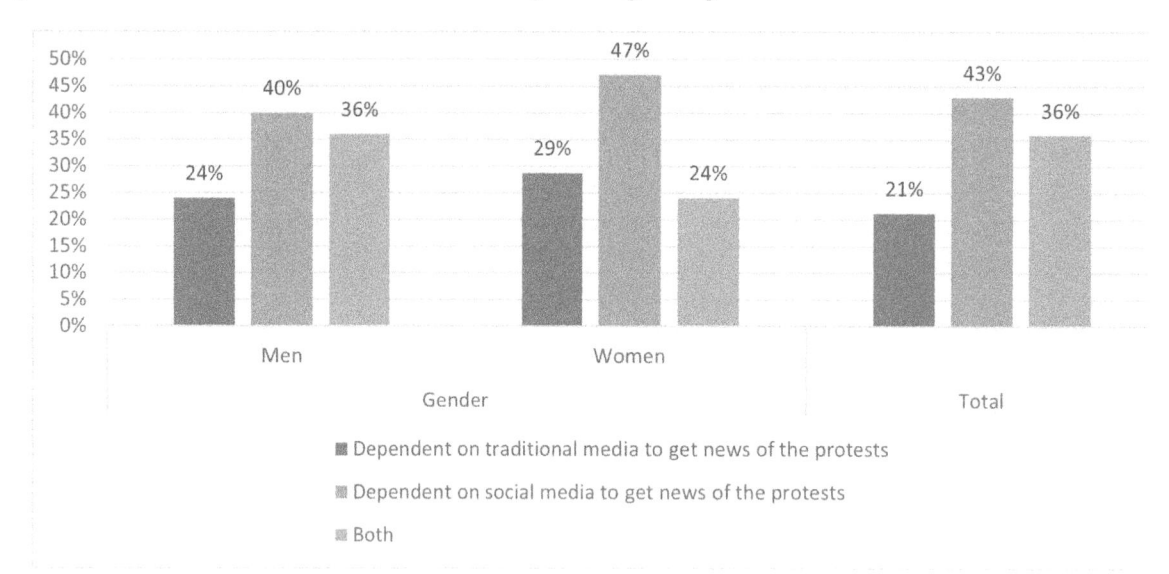

Figure 2. Traditional media vs social media usage among college students

[Bar chart showing percentages by Gender (Men, Women) and Total:
- Men: Dependent on traditional media 24%, Dependent on social media 40%, Both 36%
- Women: Dependent on traditional media 29%, Dependent on social media 47%, Both 24%
- Total: Dependent on traditional media 21%, Dependent on social media 43%, Both 36%]

Students' preference, and media usages

First, according to a survey, 21% of college students agreed that social media provide them with a better understanding of the events happening after protests compared to traditional media. Out of all the students, 11% believed that they turned to social media because they found traditional media news ambiguous after protests. Additionally, 22% of the students believed that social media provided them with more information about the events after the protests. 25% of the college students perceived social media as a platform where they could express their opinions and views on current events. Finally, 22% of the college students believed that social media could help them find news about topics they are interested in or need information about. (*Figure 3*).

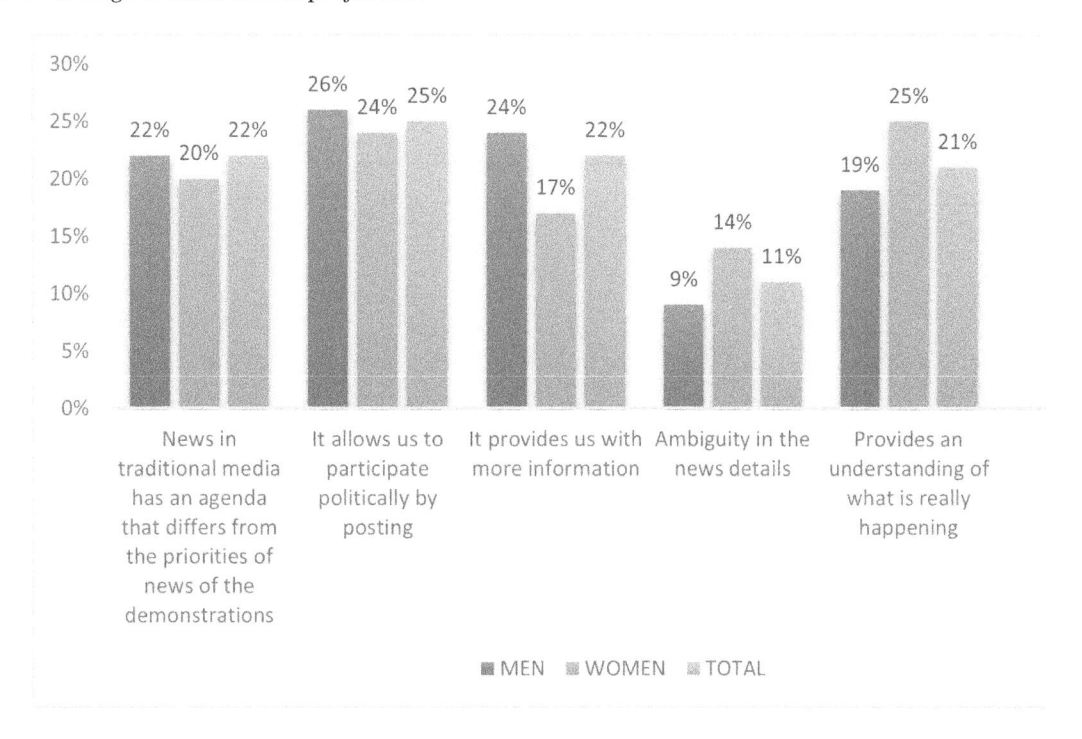

Figure 3. College student media preference

[Bar chart showing percentages by Men, Women, and Total across five categories:
- News in traditional media has an agenda that differs from the priorities of news of the demonstrations: Men 22%, Women 20%, Total 22%
- It allows us to participate politically by posting: Men 26%, Women 24%, Total 25%
- It provides us with more information: Men 24%, Women 17%, Total 22%
- Ambiguity in the news details: Men 9%, Women 14%, Total 11%
- Provides an understanding of what is really happening: Men 19%, Women 25%, Total 21%]

Secondly, 50% of college students believe that traditional media sources like television, radio, and newspapers are associated with groups that have certain ideologies. Additionally, 39% of college students perceive that partisan groups fund these traditional media sources. However, only 7% of college students believe that traditional media does not uphold democratic values and freedom, while 4% believe that they have a political agenda. (*Figure 4).*

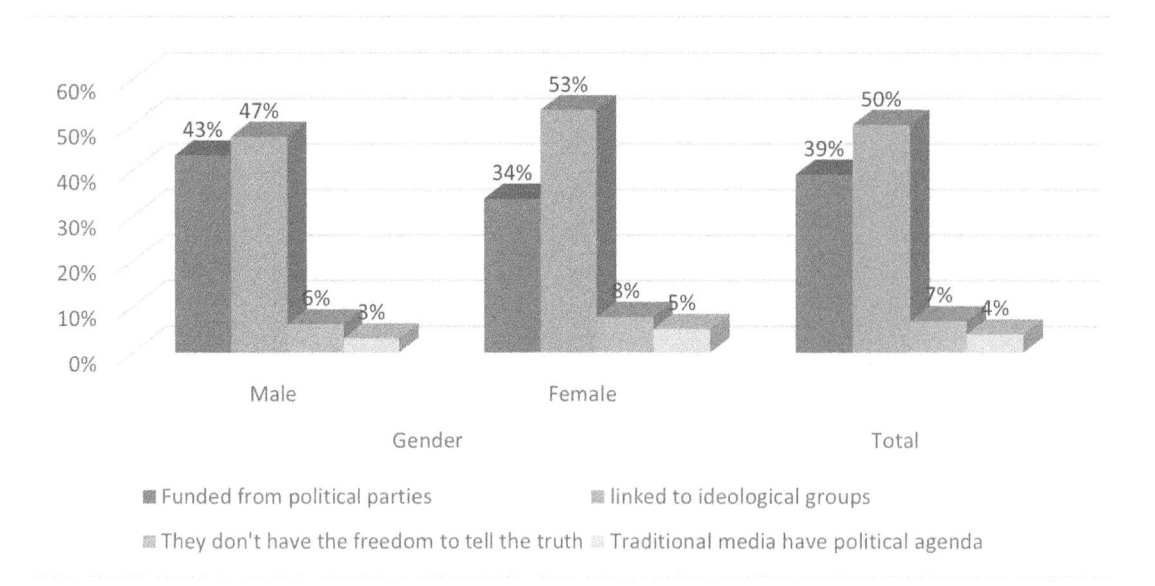

Figure 4. Partisan agenda in traditional media

MEASURING MEDIA CREDIBILITY PRE AND POST PROTESTS

Using meta-analysis factors in survey research to measure media credibility according to the scale of following themes: (Importance, Fairness, Bias, Accuracy, Completed Story, and Trust).

- Importance Scale

Traditional media's credibility was considered important by 29% of people before the protests, while 27% considered it unnecessary. After the protests, the credibility scale for traditional media ranged from 32% (important) to 26% (unimportant). Before the protests, 32% of people considered social media's credibility important, while 22% considered it unimportant. After the protests, the scale for social media credibility ranged from 44.2% (important) to 15.3% (unimportant). There was a significant shift in social media's perceived importance After the protests.

- Fairness Scale

Before the protests, traditional media's fairness was seen as fair by 20.3% of people, while 25.4% saw it as unfair. After the protests, the fairness scale for traditional media ranged from 11% (fair) to 41.5% (unfair). Before the protests, social media's fairness was seen as fair by 27.6% of people, while 22.3% saw it as one-sided. After the protests, the fairness scale for social media ranged from 44.9% (fair) to 16.9% (unfair). There was a significant change in students' perceptions of social media outlets' fairness After the protests.

- Biased Scale

After the protests, the traditional media's credibility was found to be biased 38.7% of the time, whereas only 15.1% of the time it was unbiased. The bias scale ranged from 2.5% unbiased to 63.6% biased. As for social media, the credibility was biased 27.8% of the time and unbiased 28% of the time. The bias scale ranged from 22% biased to 41.6% unbiased. Social media's biased-unbiased ranking changed after the protests.

- Accuracy Scale

Before the protests, traditional media's credibility was found to be accurate 22.4% of the time and inaccurate 26.3% of the time. The scale for accuracy ranged from 10.2% accurate to 54.2% inaccurate. On the other hand, social media's credibility was accurate 23.6% of the time and inaccurate 25.1% of the time before the protests. The scale for accuracy ranged from 42.6% accurate to 22% inaccurate. There was a significant change in students' perceptions of social media's accuracy after the protests.

- Completed Story Scale

The completed story scale for traditional media's credibility before the protests was 29.6% (completed-story) compared to 24.6% (incomplete-story). The scale ranged from 20.3% (completed-story) to 42.4% (incomplete-story) after the protests. Meanwhile, the completed story scale for social media's credibility before the protests was 30% (completed-story) compared to 23.7% (incomplete-story). The scale ranged from 43% (completed-story) to 21.2% (incomplete-story) after the protests. There was a significant change in students' perceptions of social media's credibility (completed-story to incomplete-story after the demonstrations.

- Trustworthy Scale

The trusted scale for traditional media's credibility before the protests was 34.1% (trusted) compared to 21.9% (untrusted). The scale ranged from 17.8% (trusted) to 56.8% (untrusted) after the protests. Meanwhile, the trust scale for social media's credibility before the protests was 21.3% (trusted) compared to 36% (untrusted). The scale ranged from 58.5% (trusted) to 11.5% (untrusted)

after the protests. There was a significant change in the social media scale (trusted-untrusted) after the protests.

- Balance Scale

The balance scale for traditional media's credibility was 27.2% balanced and 16.9% unbalanced before the protests. After the protests, the scale ranged from 15.2% balanced to 56.8% unbalanced. On the other hand, the balance scale for social media's credibility was 21% balanced and 31% unbalanced before the protests, but after the protests, the scale ranged from 47.5% balanced to 18.5% unbalanced. Social media's ranking (balanced-unbalanced) underwent a significant change after the protests.

DISCUSSION

This study explores the impact of critical factors on the credibility of media among students and the changing trends in their use of social media after political crises like protests. The first factor is the political orientation of students. The study found that most students backed the protests and their demands, and their political views aligned with those of the protesters. Additionally, most students shifted from traditional media like television, radio, and newspapers to social media after the protests. They viewed social media as representing their political orientation and opinions, while traditional media symbolized the political elite, parties, and their agendas.

The second factor is gender. The study found no significant difference between male and female students in their views of social media versus traditional media. Both genders were equally supportive of the protests and relied more on social media than traditional media after protests.

The third factor is the situation that media users find themselves in. There is a difference between traditional and social media use in times of political stability. However, after protests, most students turned to social media as they considered it the best way to get a reliable, unbiased, and fair portrayal of events.

According to a meta-analysis, college students heavily relied on social media to voice their opinions after protests. Social media became the primary means of expressing their dissent. Several factors explain this trend. Firstly, social media provides access to unfiltered news and real-time communication. Secondly, social media platforms are instrumental in raising awareness and sustaining movements. Thirdly, the study found that this was due to the inability of the government to control the information shared on social media. As a result, protesters could freely post updates from the demonstration sites and express their opinions on these updates.

Furthermore, the recent protests in Iraq have shed light on the concept of digital democracy, where social media is used to challenge government barriers against individual rights and freedom of expression. This shift towards social media use after the demonstrations has impacted Iraqis' views on supporting protests. The analysis found that college students who previously relied on traditional media such as television, radio, and newspapers before the protests now prefer social media platforms to follow the events.

This result is consistent with one of the critical hypotheses of media preference theory, which suggests that the more unstable a society is, the more its members depend on the media.

Additionally, the findings align with the Media preferences theory in the literature on how active selectors use media to attain their objectives and, in the process, become reliant on the media. The undergraduate students' goals or needs are to understand the situation, prevent ambiguity, obtain information, participate in politics, and follow a political agenda. Besides, Media preference theory highlights understanding as one of its objectives.

Moreover, Ambiguity is the second goal that media preference theory has identified. The college students preferred social media because they perceived traditional media, such as television, radio, and newspapers, to be ambiguous in their coverage of the protests. Women were more likely to depend on social media to avoid ambiguity in news about the protests.

Another goal of media preference theory is to obtain information. The sample changed to prefer social media to provide them with information about the protests since they felt that traditional media were not offering comprehensive coverage of the demonstrations. Men were more likely to depend on social media for this purpose.

Regarding political participation, media preference theory also highlights political participation as a goal. The study found that people prefer social media after the protests as an outlet for political participation, which is impossible with traditional media. Women were more likely to participate by sharing their opinions. In addition, the political agenda was another factor in changing the public's attitudes toward credibility and preference after the protests. A study found that college students refrained from relying on traditional media due to their perception that these outlets have a political agenda and do not prioritize the protesters' news. Men were more likely to use social media to learn about the protesters' priorities.

In conclusion, media preferences and credibility are changeable variables that depend on the events and political attitudes of media users. Beyond that, traditional media has become a tool for expressing the opinions of the ruling authority, governments, and politicians, while social media has become a tool for the masses to express their opinions.

REFERENCES

Amos, D. (2010). Confusion, contradiction, and irony: The Iraqi media in 2010. *Shorenstein Center Discussion Paper Series.*

Arraf, J., & Lonsdorf, K. (2020). Iraqi security forces storm Tahrir Square, clash with protesters. *NPR News.*

Ball-Rokeach, S. J. (1985). The origins of individual media-system preference: A sociological framework. *Communication Research*, 12(4), 485–510. 10.1177/009365085012004003

Ball-Rokeach, S. J., & DeFleur, M. L. (1976). A preference model of mass-media effects. *Communication Research*, 3(1), 3–21. 10.1177/009365027600300101

Belair-Gagnon, V. (2015). *Social media at BBC news: The re-making of crisis reporting*. Routledge. 10.4324/9781315742052

Bennett, W. L., Lawrence, R. G., & Livingston, S. (2008). *When the press fails: Political power and the news media from Iraq to Katrina*. University of Chicago Press.

Besalú, R., & Pont-Sorribes, C. (2021). Credibility of digital political news in Spain: Comparison between traditional media and social media. *Social Sciences (Basel, Switzerland)*, 10(5), 170. 10.3390/socsci10050170

Bostock, B. (2019). Iraq blacked out the internet for 70% of the country and blocked social media to quell deadly anti-corruption protests. *Business Insider.* <https://www.businessinsider.com/iraq-blocks-facebook-whatsapp-cuts-internet-protests-2019-10>

Bracken, C. (2006). Perceived source credibility of local television news: The impact of television form and presence. *Journal of Broadcasting & Electronic Media*, 50(4), 723–741. 10.1207/s15506878jobem5004_9

Carillo, K., Scornavacca, E., & Za, S. (2017). The role of media dependency in predicting continuance intention to use ubiquitous media systems. *Information & Management*, 54(3), 317–335. 10.1016/j.im.2016.09.002

Cho, Y. (2009). *New media uses and preference effect model: Exploring the relationship between new media use habit, preference relation, and possible outcomes* [Doctoral dissertation, Rutgers University-Graduate School-New Brunswick]

Dillard, J. P., Hunter, J. E., & Burgoon, M. (1984). Sequential-request persuasive strategies: Meta-analysis of foot-in-the-door and door-in-the-face. *Human Communication Research*, 10(4), 461–488. 10.1111/j.1468-2958.1984.tb00028.x

Gaziano & McGrath. (1986). Measuring the concept of credibility. *Journalism Quarterly, 63*(3), 451-462.

Glass, G. V. (1976). Primary, secondary, and meta-analysis of research. *Educational Researcher*, 5(10), 3–8. 10.2307/1174772

Goodman, L. A. (1961). Snowball sampling. *Annals of Mathematical Statistics*, 32(1), 148–170. 10.1214/aoms/1177705148

Gunther, A. C. (1992). Biased press or biased public? Attitudes toward media coverage of social groups. *Public Opinion Quarterly*, 56(2), 147–167. 10.1086/269308

Hellmueller. (2012). *The credibility of credibility measures: A meta-analysis in leading communication journals, 1951 to 2011*. In WAPOR 65th Annual Conference, Hong Kong.

Hennessy, B. (1970). A headnote on the existence and study of political attitudes. *Social Science Quarterly*, 463–476.

Hovland, I., Janis, L., & Kelley, H. (1953). *Communication and persuasion; Psychological studies of opinion change*. Yale University Press.

Hu, X. (2015). *Assessing source credibility on social media—An electronic word-of-mouth communication perspective*. [Doctoral Dissertation, Bowling Green State University].

Hunter, J. E., & Schmidt, F. L. (2004). Methods of meta-analysis: *Correcting errors and bias in research findings.Sage (Atlanta, Ga.)*.

Idris, I. (2020). *Responding to popular protests in the MENA region*.

July, D.L.B., DSA's. (2021). Flawed International Outlook: The Appeal of the Mass Party and its. *Contradictions*.

Lazarsfeld, P., Berelson, B., & Gaudet, H. (1944). *The People's Choice: How the Voter Makes Up His Mind in a Presidential Campaign*. Duell, Sloane, and Pearce.

Loveless, M. (2008). Media dependency: Mass media as sources of information in the democratizing countries of Central and Eastern Europe. *Democratization*, 15(1), 162–183. 10.1080/13510340701770030

Lovotti, C. and Proserpio, L. (2021). The October 2019 Protest Movement in Iraq. An Analysis of the'Early Moments of the Mobilization. *Partecipazione e conflict,14*(2) .644-662.

Masullo, G. M., Brown, D. K., & Harlow, S. (2023). Shifting the protest paradigm? Legitimizing and humanizing protest coverage lead to more positive attitudes toward protest, mixed results on news credibility. *Journalism*, 0(0). 10.1177/14648849231200135

Masullo, G. M., Brown, D. K., & Harlow, S. (2023). Shifting the protest paradigm? Legitimizing and humanizing protest coverage lead to more positive attitudes toward protest, mixed results on news credibility. *Journalism*, 0(0). 10.1177/14648849231200135

McCroskey, J. C., & Teven, J. J. (1999). Goodwill: A reexamination of the construct and its scale. *Communication Monographs*, 66(1), 90–103. 10.1080/03637759909376464

McQuail, D. (2010). *McQuail's mass communication theory*. Sage publications.

Netblocks. (2016). *Iraq shuts down the internet again as protests intensify*. Netblocks. https://netblocks.org/reports/iraq-shuts-down-internet-again-as-protests-intensify-Q8oOWz8n>

Odeh. S. (2019). *al-ilam al-araqi pen al-taghtiyya "al-babghaiya" lalaslata wagma fadaiyat (Iraqi media between "parrot" coverage of the authority and the repression of satellite channels)'*. Independent Arbaya.

Onuch, O., Mateo, E., & Waller, J. G. (2021). Mobilization, Mass Perceptions, and (Dis)information: "New" and "Old" Media Consumption Patterns and Protest. *Social Media + Society*, 7(2). 10.1177/2056305121999656

Otlan, Y., Kuzmina, Y., Rumiantseva, A., & Tertytchnaya, K. (2023). Authoritarian media and foreign protests: Evidence from a decade of Russian news. *Post-Soviet Affairs*, 39(6), 391–405. 10.1080/1060586X.2023.2264079

Pearce, S. C., & Rodgers, J. (2020). Social media as public journalism? Protest reporting in the digital era. *Sociology Compass*, 14(12), 1–14. 10.1111/soc4.12823

Rahman, B. H. (2014). Conditional influence of media: Media credibility and opinion formation. *Journal of Political Studies*, 21(1), 299.

Salim, S.K. (2021). 5. Iraq: Media between Democratic Freedom and Security Pressures. *Arab media systems,3*.

Tung, N. (2020). A fragile inheritance. *VQR Online*.https://www.vqronline.org/photography/2020/09/fragile-inheritance

Wainner, C. N. (2018). *Social media addiction and its implications for communication.*

Chapter 4
Media and Contemporary African Society:
Constructing an Environment Sensitive Communication Theory of Media Effect

Desmond Onyemechi Okocha
http://orcid.org/0000-0001-5070-280X
Bingham University, Nigeria

Maureen Chigbo
Bingham University, Nigeria

ABSTRACT

This research proposes a theory that ameliorates the deficiencies of agenda-setting, two-step flow, and third-person effect theories that are linear in explaining the influence of mass media on their audience. Whereas postmodernism abhors universality because, in reality, different groupings of individuals in different societies receive and respond to media messages differently depending on the influence of both internal and exogenous variables in the society in any communication process. These lacunas in the theories birthed the environment dynamo theory which does not intend to replace but to capture the idea that science, psychology, ethnography, and technology have broadened the understanding of the nuances that determine the relationship between the media and audience, and vice versa. The environment dynamo theory cumulatively created a web to explain media effects in society based on three components that are intricately interwoven - the audience, media, and environment.

INTRODUCTION

In a postmodern world, truth and reality are shaped by both internal and exogenous variables such as personal history, social class, gender, culture and religion, individuality, and technology all of which combine to define the narratives and meanings of our lives which are locally constructed without universal applications (Cornell, 2006). These variables could not be sufficiently explained with linear theories of the media as postulated in agenda-setting, two-step and third-person effect. In this era, major changes in the characteristics of the media, audience, and environment have occasioned varied responses to mass

DOI: 10.4018/979-8-3693-3767-7.ch004

media messages. Unlike in the past when media analyses and effects were monolithic in explaining the effects of the media on audience and environment, advancements in science and technology have pushed the frontiers of knowledge and awakened the consciousness that different variables – demography, psychology, ethno-religious, culture, politics, socio-economy - all combine to influence the outcome of the media content; who is communicating what to whom, and with what effect in a spiral of news source (Musa, 2011; Imoh, 2013; Oludele, 2020).

This development has pushed to the fringes the era when a single story defined an explanation of an all-powerful media effect on society. At present, science and technology have shown that different narratives combine to influence audience reaction to media content. As Cornell (2006) posited, the pre-modern era marked the period religion was the source of truth and reality while science characterized truth and reality in the modern era as against the postmodern era where there is no single defining source for truth and reality beyond the individual. This can be seen in the different reactions that greeted the recent Pope's Fiducia Supplicans on the blessing of couples in irregular situations and of couples of the same sex. (Francis, Fernandez & Matteo, 2023) observed that previously, it would have been a fait accompli for an imprimatur from the hierarchy of the Catholics Church without dissent. Arnold (2024) observed that there is a growing resistance in Africa to the Fiducia Supplicans while globally, bishops are divided as to its acceptance or rejection.

Apart from the clerics, the faithful have voiced their opinions which was either contrary or supported the Pontiff's declaration based on their different individualism, laws, and cultural peculiarities. The stance was predicated on how the media in different countries interpreted and communicated the declaration on Fiducia Supplicans. This is obvious in the position of the Catholic Bishops' Conference of Nigeria (CBCN) that assured there would be no possibility of blessing same-sex unions and activities in the church as that would go against God's law, the teachings of the Church, the laws of our nation and the cultural sensibilities of our people (Ugorji & Ogun, 2023). Contrary to that, Argentina, the home country of the Pontiff while in support, states that Fiducia Supplicans does not give rise to confusion and that confusing the blessings with approval or permission would be reductionism (Arnold, 2024).

Closely allied to this is Strinati's (1995) view on post-modernism and mass media delineated culture and society where social environment appears different from ordinary life. For instance, Koskei (undated) observed that we now have TV, radio and computers in our sitting rooms, bedrooms and places of work where cultural representations such as music, videos, news etc., are part of our everyday life. In the 1970s and 1980s in Nigeria, many homes did not have television sets so, many people in the neighbourhood would converge at a viewing centre or in the house of the wealthy individual in the community to watch Nigeria Television Authority (NTA), the only TV station in Nigeria that boasted of 30 million viewers then. But this has changed as 740 television stations (Okamgba, 2023) now beam different programmes to varied audiences. There is, however, no guarantee that the signals received in different homes of people with different backgrounds will have the same universal effect as envisaged by the agenda setting, two-step and third person effect theories in a pre-modern and modern era. This dovetails into Jean Bauldrillard's 1920 - 2007 narrative on hyperreality and simulation by the media in a postmodern era that sees the stages of communication as being more real than the real communication; hence, the real is abolished. The mass communication is under pressure of information; it pursues enticing disruption of the society and culture (Standard Encyclopedia of Philosophy, 2020). For instance, the media unravelled a cross- dresser popularly called Bobrisky after propping up his celebrity status which many in the conservative world had believed would have a negative influence on the youth. Bobrisky was arrested after spraying money at a social event, a cultural practice that is prevalent in the country. At the court, the media dramatized his admission that he is a male so, he was kept in a male detention cell until he was sentenced to prison by the court. The fact remains that Bobrisky can only happen in premodernism when the receivers of media messages battle with other vicissitudes of life that made them immune to the cross-dresser's imprisonment to the extent that the civil society organisation did not protest against his prison sentence despite the spiralling messages the mainstream media and social media conveyed. Apparently, the attitude of the people to Bobrisky's case was explained by Koskei (undated) whose comment on Jean Bauldrillard (1929 - 2007) explained that we all live by the passionate idealism of meaning and communication; an ideal is a wish, an unreality which when internalised, becomes our reality; which in essence is a non-reality or hyperreality. He also viewed television as the biggest contributor to the hyperreality, regulating everything from a distance. This resonates with the NTA's coverage of the 2019 elections campaigns that did not focus on protesters who pelted former President Muhammadu Buhari with sachets of water but featured the story as if all went well until reports of the incident surfaced on the social media and other TV stations. By not showing exactly what transpired, the TV station concealed the process of simulation which restricts our vision of reality, said Bauldrillard. The obfuscation of reality has worsened in an era of infodemic occasioned by the internet and new media when receivers are also content creators and cannot be easily influenced by messages from the mainstream media unless self-mediated content. As Koskei (undated) wrote, post modernism has tried to reject the existence of objective reality or realism and refers to a school of thought that denies the existence of an objective realism that is independent of media creation and influence.

Agreeing, Valkenberg and Peter (2013) postulated that new media technology enabled reception and creation of messages is important for media effect theory and research as it results in self-generated media effects which can be direct or indirect. Participation in a development process and feedback from the recipients of self-generated content media effects could be either benign or toxic, depending on the proclivity of the recipients as well as environmental and psychological factors which influence the reception that stimulates response to mediated content. An example of this manifested in Nigeria during the 2023 general election when the older political parties such as the ruling All Progressives Congress (APC) and Peoples Democratic Party (PDP) which had structures and funding that outpaced the advertisements and publicity of the Labour party. They were, however, shocked at the performance of the little-known Labour Party which was backed by youths mobilised through the *Obidients* movement. New media or social media messages which were created individually and collectively among members were shared to the larger society and this caused the bigger parties to lose election in their strongholds dramatically. There was no/an? omnibus effect on the populace; the messages of APC and PDP was passed through to the traditional media to toe the old pattern of voting them.

Furthermore, Cornell (2006) posited that post-modernism extremized relativism and individualism and then applied them to all provinces of knowledge including science and media. In a post-modern world, media effects are individually shaped by personal history, social class, culture, religion, and gender which combine to influence responses to stimuli and narratives that give meaning to our lives (Cornell, 2006; Rotaru et al., 2010, Jameson, 1997). This implies that the variables are culturally embedded, localized social constructs without any universal application; there is no single defining source for truth and reality beyond the individual (Cornell, 2006). Unlike the narratives of theories of two-step flow, agenda-setting, and third-person effect, the limitations in explaining media effects on society because of the linear, omnibus and unidirectional assumptions is based on homogeneity. The three theories are anchored on a universal truth of a linear media effect on society as against post-modernism which abhors totalizing ways of viewing any dimension of life and rejects any single defining source for truth and reality albeit the effects of media on society (Cornell, 2006).

Supporting, Valkenberg and Peter (2013) opined that the vast majority of media-effects studies conceptualised it as a unidirectional influence of a given medium on an outcome of interest, which is transactional. Empirical studies that ignore transaction effects, Valkenberg and Peter (2013) said are not consistent with contemporary media effect theories. Thus, the Environmental Dynamo theory falls under recent media effect theories that propose transactional and symbiotic relationships between media use and outcome variables. This is prevalent in these days when spiral news circles that can source content from mainstream media and mainstream media can equally source content from new media particularly where the content producer also uses the same media. In transactional media relationships, Valkenberg and Peter (2013), affirmed that media use and effects are seen as part of a reciprocal influence process in which media outcomes are the reason for disruptions in media use. For instance, in Nigeria, there was a time, in the 1970s and 1980s, when many people were glued to the NTA 9 O'clock news as a major source of information but now owing to avalanche of 740 broadcast stations, most people have switched their loyalty to other television stations. The result is that NTA which once claimed that about 30 million viewers watching its programmes can no longer do so. They can no longer lay claims to having an omnibus and unidirectional influence on how Nigerians think and behave as advanced by the agenda setting, two-step and third person effect theories.

Conversely, the Environmental Dynamo model takes cognisance of the entire media environment variables to explain media outcome on the audience. In other words, Environmental Dynamo falls within the ambit of transactional models of complementary media influence process. Valkenburg and Peter (2013) recognised this when they stressed the appropriateness of complementary media effect models that explain studies in behavioural genetics and development where traits variables (personality factors such as extroversion, neuroticism temperament - shyness, emotionality, sociability) show less heritability than was previously assumed. Another variability - environmental influence on individual from peers, friends, parental treatment, and illness can change over time. These unpredictable exogenous variables have to be factored in media effect theories due to their influence on content outcomes (Valkenberg & Peter, 2013). For instance, despite the media messages on Child Rights Act over the years, Abdulmalik Sarkindaji, Speaker of Niger State House of Assembly under his Mariga Constituency project in the Muslim dominated Northern Nigeria, undertook to finance the mass wedding of 100 girls some of whom are under-aged (Igwe, 2024). To the Muslim and those from the North, not much emotion ought to be dissipated over what they consider normal. But the minister of Women Affairs from the South East where such customs and traditions are rare, appealed to the Inspector General of Police who has yet to join the fray to stop the wedding. The fact remains that the Speaker's action will be a welcome development to the people who are likely to view the actions of the minister negatively for challenging their religion and custom in the North despite her offer to send the under-aged girls to school. Another illustration of how religion influences content outcomes can be seen in Mauritania, where divorce is treated as a normal way of life and female divorcees can easily remarry. The scenario also obtains in the Muslim communities In Northern Nigeria where divorce is also common. But in the Christian dominated South East Nigeria, divorce is frowned upon and divorcees find it difficult to remarry.

Another cultural practice, in most parts of South Eastern Nigeria, with the exception of few communities in Abia State, which will make media messages on DNA test irrelevant is because traditionally, the man who paid the bride price inherits all the children from a marriage and whether he is the biological father or not is immaterial. These influence media effect from content beamed on audience in different parts of the world who will respond based on religious, cultural, and educational norms in their society without an omnibus outcome. Hence, this research aims to correct the flaws by proposing the environment dynamo theory that recognizes the differences and plurality in society about media and its effect based on Borah (2016) who observed that communication research on media effects includes theories that explain how the mass media influences attitudes and perception of audience members. For Borah (2016), the history of media effects remains a contested space, especially as new theories and methods interrogate the findings of earlier researchers. Also, theorists have increasingly propounded alternative models of media effect theory to expand and examine the various iterations of the phase model. Lang and Lang (1993) argued against the phase model and instead proposed a model that emphasizes investigations of cumulative effects. Perse (2001) proposes an alternative model based on four types of media effects: direct, conditional, cumulative, and cognitive transactional. Perse's model seeks to demonstrate a more nuanced understanding of the interplay of media content variables and audience variables regardless of time or media. Postelnicu (2016) posited that mass communication researchers cannot, therefore, treat the public as a homogenous mass audience that actively processes and responds to media messages uniformly, as had been postulated by initial theories of mass communication which assumed that audiences respond to media messages directly.

Similarly, Rotaru et al. (2010) (citing Featherstone, 1988, 203-205; Bauman, 1988, 225-226) opined that post-modernism narrows the borders between art and everyday life, high culture and mass culture; the pluralism of cultures and knowledge, radicalism, realism, and fundamentalism which are influenced by technology, globalization, capitalism, and socialization which affects the ways messages communicated in the media are received and interpreted by different people of the world. Hence, the research is targeted at proffering a solution for the inadequacies of agenda-setting, two-step, and third-person effect theories in explaining media effect on society in post-modernism.

RESEARCH OBJECTIVES

The objectives of the research are to:
1. establish the limitations of demography, ethno-religious, culture, politics, socio-economy - all combine to influence media outcome using the linear-based theories of agenda-setting, two-step flow, and third person in explaining media effects on society in a postmodern era;
2. examine who is communicating what to whom and the public perception of the Environmental Dynamo theory; and
3. illustrate how the spiral of news source in an inclusive environment dynamo theory can remedy the inadequacies in the theories of agenda-setting, two-step flow, and third person.

METHODOLOGY

The quantitative study deployed a multistage sampling technique to select 493 respondents comprising lecturers and students from the Mass Communication Departments of the Alex Ekwueme Federal University, Ndufu-Alike, Abakiliki, Ebonyi State; Bayero University, Kano State, and Lagos State University, Lagos State. Apart from the lecturers, the students selected were 400 level students who have been exposed to communication theories over the years; so, it is believed that they are conversant with the assumptions of the agenda setting, two-step flow and third person effect stories. Two hundred questionnaires were given to the Mass Communication department of each university to fill. Distribution and collection of the questionnaire lasted for two months from September to October 2023. The universities were selected to reflect the three major regions in Northern, Western, and Eastern Nigeria. This method is justified since the research is based on Yarahmadi's (2020) argument that the multistage sampling technique divides large populations into smaller groups to make the selection process more practical. Also, he stated that this technique is used when the population is spread over a wide geographical region and it is difficult to procure a representative sample with only one technique.

Similarly, McCombes (2022) said the technique is good for exploratory and qualitative research in order to have an initial understanding of a large, small, or under-researched population. Dudovskiy (2022) stated that although multistage sampling is more complex, it helps to divide large clusters of population into smaller groups in several stages and this makes primary data collection more manageable. He also argued that multistage sampling is not as effective as true random sampling though it is not overly expensive or time-consuming. This method fits this research because, as recommended by Dudovskiy (2022), the multistage sampling technique is effective in primary data collection from the geographically dispersed population; it is cost and time effective with high-level flexibility.

Against this background, the three-stage sampling used considered geographical areas of North, East and West regions in Nigeria. It then narrowed on the universities that offer Mass Communication as a course and picked one university each from the regions and finally determined that the questionnaire can only be administered to level four students and lecturers in Mass Communication departments of the universities who have been exposed to mass media theories in their four-year study and understand issues raised in the questionnaire. It is pertinent to state that the students and lecturers are of different demography, ethno-religious, culture, politics, socio-economy status that influence their perception of media content and the impact such will have on them. Therefore, this sampling method is in line with Bhat (2024) that described multistage sampling as a method that splits selected population into sub-groups at various stages to make it simpler for primary data collection and is considered the best option for this study.

LIMITATIONS OF STUDY

The environmental dynamo theory is envisaged as a complementary model to older models of mass media in explaining media content outcomes in postmodernism where individualism is the basis for ascertaining truth, and elasticity of meanings of ideas influenced by advancement in technological innovations. As with all previous research, the study notes some delimitations. Firstly, the findings were limited to the framework of the categories and definitions used in the investigation. The limitations of the study lie in the fact that only three Departments of Mass Communication in three different universities located in the three regions (East, West and North) of Nigeria were used for the study. The focus was on the final year (400-level) students of these universities who are believed to have been exposed to lectures in mass communication theories for at least 3 years prior to this study. Some Mass Communication lecturers were equally selected for participation. Although the 400-level students before graduation are expected to conduct their seminars and research projects based on any of the mass communication theories, there is a lingering doubt about their capacity to fully understand theoretical arguments advanced in the study on environmental dynamo theory. This limitation can be remedied by further empirical studies to expand the scope of the sample population to include more schools of mass communication where research instrument can only be tested on only lecturers of mass communication or only those teaching theories of mass communication in order to validate the findings of the research. This, of course, will require more resources of time and funding to accomplish. Nevertheless, this study made a contribution in questioning the efficacies of the existing theories and their postulations on the relationships between the media and their audience using scientific research methods.

LITERATURE REVIEW

Synthesis of Agenda-Setting, Two-Step Flow and Third-Person Effect Theories

In its expose on media effects and environment, Klinger and Metag (2021) listed three levels of influences - the micro (individual's cognition, emotion, or action), meso (relationships between groups of individuals or organizations), and macro (relationships within social systems). These pervade Brubaker's (2008) thoughts on agenda-setting by Maxwell McCombs and Donald Shaw in 1968 that mass audiences determine the salient issues covered by media; Paul Lazarsfeld, Bernard Berelson, and Hazel Gaudet's expose in 1948 about the two-step theory of information flow from media to certain persons who wield influence and Phillips Davison's third-person effect theory that mass media messages have more impact on others than on themselves. Hence, in Africa, communication takes place among diverse communal age groups, town unions, institutions, and the larger society. For instance, Nigeria's 200 million population has 371 ethnic groups with diverse religious, cultural, educational, economic, and political inclinations, and at the various levels, information on government economic programs transmitted through the media elicits different stimuli that could not be explained fully with theories of agenda setting, two-step flow and third-person effect in post-modernism. Thus, the theories whittle in significance given Takov and Balanjo's (2021) and Adebumiti and Ofomegbe's (2021) postulation that post-modernism drastically modified human beliefs, attitudes, and behaviors in social relationships: sexuality, ethics, morality, religion, education, and politics. Ezaka (2022) expressed the need for the era to exert more intellectual energy on media landscape trends in order to unravel their influence on content production and consumption. Given that science and technology expanded the frontiers of knowledge on media and society (Brubaker, 2008) with television and internet users, the public possesses agendas that differed significantly from that of the media and this failed to support agenda-setting. The implication is that the media is not powerful in setting the public agenda in post-modernism (Brubaker, 2008).

Furthermore, Messner and Distaso (2008) established that sources have the power to influence the news agenda of the media and that media, under certain circumstances can act as sources for each other with weblogs serving as sources for the traditional media and the use of sources in weblogs in general. Through content analysis of 2059 articles over a six-year-period from the New York Times and the Washington Post, it found that the newspapers increasingly legitimized weblogs as credible sources. They separately content-analyzed 120 weblogs and found that they relied heavily on traditional media as sources. By mutually influencing their news agendas, the traditional media and weblogs create what the researchers introduce and define as a news source cycle through which news content can be passed back and forth from media to media (Messner & Distaso, 2008).

Consequently, Brubaker (2008) agreed that the changed role of traditional media has turned agenda-setting theory from its "offensive" posture of placing items on the public agenda, to a "defensive" one requiring report or coverage on certain issues in a certain way because those issues were first placed on the agenda by the political blogosphere (Messner & DiStaso, 2008) and expanded the traditional agenda-building process by sending traditional media content into the digital universe (Brubaker, 2008). Hence, agenda-setting occurs because of how frequently issues are discussed in the mass media and not how they are treated (Borah, 2016; Cappella & Jamieson, 1977).

Similarly, Weimann (2015) viewed the two-step flow of communication theory as the flow of information and influence from the mass media to certain individuals (i.e., the opinion leaders) and from them to the public. However, the cycle of news sources (Borah 2016) implies that changes in new frontiers of communication sources show a growing trend of a spiral web of information flow and the decline in popularity of the two-step flow (Weimann, 2015).

Agreeing, Postelnicu (2016) opined that two-step flow oversimplified the actual flow of information from mass media to consumers which has more than two steps as additional research revealed that conversations based on media content are more frequent among opinion leaders themselves and not just between them and less-informed individuals. This creates the extra step of opinion sharing among equally informed individuals, compared with only a vertical flow of information from opinion leaders to followers (Postelnicu, 2016).

Allied to Postelnicu's argument is the third-person effect theory by Davison (1983), which is limited in determining media influence in society given that a person exposed to persuasive communication in the mass media believes the effect will be greater on others than himself as each individual believes he will not be influenced, but others may well be persuaded by media messages. In some cases, communication leads to action not because of its impact on those to whom it is ostensibly directed, but because others (third persons) think that it will have an impact on its audience. Contrarily, Sun, Shen and Pan (2008) through web-based survey data results established that the third-person perception was a robust and significant predictor across all three messages, although the directions of such effects differed across messages with desirable or undesirable presumed influence.

Postmodernism and Media Effects on Society

What is common among the linear theories is that the agenda-setting, two-step flow, and third-person effect explained media effects majorly based on the truth and reality, not on individualism (Bazargani & Larsari, 2015). They do not take into account the individual psychology, philosophy, and environmental factors that can derail or amplify messages to make them acceptable or not. For instance, in Nigeria, COVID-19 vaccination messages that conveyed via traditional media were received with great suspicion nationwide because of fake information and half-truths that were spread on social media despite mass media messages to the contrary.

Consequently, many people failed to take the vaccination which resulted in some deaths that could have been prevented had the media truly set the agenda on the health issue in the country then. The rejection of the COVID-19 vaccine demonstrates that, variables such as: demographics, culture, religion, education, technology, politics, and socio-economic and environmental conditions in the society to a large extent determine audience response to the media messages. The defects of the sequenced theories of agenda-setting, two-step flow, and third-person in explaining media effects in society birthed the

Environmental Dynamo model to holistically appraise the dynamics of the plural audience, media, and environment and the interplay that determines the effects of the media on the society in a postmodern era.

Furthermore, in a postmodern world, major changes in the characteristics of the media, audience, and environment elicit varied responses to media messages. Unlike in the past when the media analysis and effects were centered on dominant values of truth, religion, and cultural beliefs on audience and environment, advancements in technology and science have pushed the frontiers of knowledge and awakened the consciousness that demography, psychology, ethno-religious, culture, politics, and economy influence the media content and its effect on society (Hariharasudan, Pandeeswari & Hassan, 2022). The reactions across continents to the recent visit of Prince Harry and Megan Markle to Nigeria to promote the Invictus game which the Prince founded 10 years ago at the instance of Nigeria's Chief of Defence Staff, General Christopher Gwabin Musa, vividly illustrates the need for a complementary model to explain the outcome of media content. Sequel to the visit, Christopher Wilson, a British Journalist, tweeted on May 14, 2024, that Nigeria's human rights record is not far short of Nazi German with a picture of Prince Harry and Megan and that of Duke of Windsor and his wife, Wallis, in Germany in 1937. Trolled by swift negative reactions of netizens, Wilson deleted the tweet because of what he described as "the unintended consequences". This can only be possible in postmodernism that the internet and social media has expanded the frontiers of communication and not the era when BBC and CNN controlled narrative of global events. In addition, technology innovation has inspired the growth of other media such as Arise Television and Al Jazeera that provide counter narrative to the Western media.

This development reinforces the fact that a single variable cannot explain fully the media's effect on society. Whereas, Hariharasudan, Pandeeswari and Hassan (2022) emphasized technological influence in a postmodern era, Cornell (2006) characterized the pre-modern as truth and reality while science is the hallmark of modernity as against the postmodern era where there is no single defining source for truth and reality beyond the individual. Cornell's (2006) notion is that post-modernism extremized relativism and individualism and then applied them to all provinces of knowledge and even to science and media. In a postmodern world, media effects are individually shaped by personal history, social class, culture, religion, and gender, which combine to influence the narratives and meanings of our lives (Cornell, 2006). This implies the variables are culturally embedded, localized social constructions without any universal application, unlike the single-story explanation of theories of agenda setting, two-step flow, and third-person effect in their perspective of media effects on a homogenous society. As Cornell (2006) stated, the most important value of postmodernity is the inadmissibility of generalizations of any dimension of life. Post-modernity, he said, rejects any single defining source for truth and reality while emphasizing difference, plurality, and selective forms of tolerance.

Postmodernism's Influence on Audience, Environment, and Mass Media

In post-modernism era, Luedecke and Boykoff (2017) posited that media bridge different ways of knowing about the environment, and often mediate public perceptions, attitudes, perspectives, and behaviors related to environmental issues. For instance, people from different cultural backgrounds in Nigeria and Africa get to know about one another's festivals, religious practices, and culinary practices through the media and this may facilitate acculturation and assimilation. Understanding these practices helps in coaching media content that will be acceptable to different communities with different religious practices and cultures. The mindset is that there is no universality to the realities and truth of audience peculiarities; for example, Northern Nigeria is made up of predominantly Muslims while the Southern part is predominantly Christian and more educationally advantaged. Even within the Southern region, some areas which are more educationally advanced than others, are bound to receive media content differently. For instance, according to UNDP Nigeria/Nigeria Bureau of Statistics (NBS), Human Development Indicators showed that at state levels all the North East States scored below the national level of 0.521, with Taraba, and Bauchi having 0.4286 and 0.6515, respectively, while Lagos (Southern Nigeria) had the highest score of 0.6515. This implies that even though they are in the country, media messages to the states will most likely not have the same media effect because of their peculiarities and this also applies to African countries with different human development indexes.

Allied to this reality is that in Africa, the rich geodiversity is underreported among earth's geo-heritage, prompting the need for policy initiatives to identify geo-sites, promote and increase the awareness among policymakers and the general public, especially local communities which need to protect geo-parks set aside for sustainable socio-economic development (Neto & Henriques, 2022). It throws up the need to formulate appropriate messages to sensitize the local population on how to conserve and protect geo-heritage (Neto & Henriques, 2022). As Luedecke and Boykoff (2017) posited, from entertainment and economy to news, the media including television, films, books, flyers, newspapers, magazines, radio, and the Internet, provide critical links between formal environmental change science and policy decision-making, and the realities of how people experience and interact with their environments on the ground.

Another happenstance that characterizes post-modernism is what Reichard (2011) wrote about Alvin Toffler's prediction of a move by developed nations from mass industrial societies to demassified information communities. Tofler talked about how masses receive the same messages while small de-massified groups receive and send large amounts of their evocation to one another disrupting consensus with the only challenge being economic disparities between regions and people and not the whole countries of the world have equal access to technologies. As explained earlier, the reaction of netizens to Christopher Wilson's Nazi comment about Nigeria would not have been possible in a pre-modern or modern world where the world media and technology was dominated by the Western world. With advancement in technology, the world has become a global village as predicted by Marshal McLuhan. Hence the immediacy of reaction and counterreaction that followed Wilson's tweet.

Against the foregoing, the Environmental Dynamo theory is strengthened by the need to review the notions that underlie the theories studied in the research as contemplated by Barry (2002) that many of the notions previously regarded as universal and fixed (gender identity, individual selfhood) are actually fluid and unstable as they are socially constructed or contingent categories rather than absolute or essential ones. All thinking and investigation are affected by prior ideological commitments. There is no disinterested inquiry. Language itself conditions, limits, and predetermines what we see. Language does not record reality but constructs it (Barry, 2002). Meaning in texts is jointly constructed by the reader and writer. Stating that theorists distrust all totalizing notions (great books, human nature) Barry (2002) sums these ideas up in five key points: - politics is pervasive - language is constitutive - truth is provincial - meaning is contingent - human nature is a myth.

Insight into the Environmental Dynamo Theory

Over the years, many mass media scholars have debated the relationship between theory to understanding communication behaviour. As far back as 1976, P.R.R Sinha said that it was difficult to think any practice without a theory and cited Kurt Lewin as saying: "There is nothing so practical as good theory" and that practitioners lethargy and negative dispositions to theory was caused by poor theories over a long period of time and a basic misunderstanding about meaning and ramifications of a theory (Sinha, 1976) According to him, the quality of a good theory is measured not on its applicability at the individual (personal level alone, but at the society and community levels while scholars must be conscious of shortcoming in the absence of the practical base as communication as a field of study has emerged from practical life situations. Communication provides the impetus for actual decoding of the economic, sociological, psychological, political, cultural and religious spheres of the individual and society. Similarly, Kreft (2011) affirmed that communication theories help in explaining communication behaviour notwithstanding the debate as to the practicability of theories which help to discern the causes and effects in a communication process. For Kreft (2011), the challenge for non practicalism of a theory is to state what value might be and that without any substantial account of the value of a true impractical theory, it becomes easier for practicalists to bite the bullet and accept counter-intuitive consequence of his position.

Deviating slightly, Ramirez (2024), a biopsychologist, who wrote in this era of postmodernism, the basis for proposing a new contemporary theory that will complement agenda setting, two step flow and third person theories in explaining mass media outcome, opined that most theories about the behaviour of large numbers of people are untestable even when they are reasonable. By Ramirez's view, sociologists, political scientists, and economists all have the same problem, adding that "Their most common tool is correlation, showing that two things happen together. But showing that two things go together isn't the same as showing that one causes the other. Proper experiments could settle the issue but, for these fields, they are usually too difficult to conduct."

However, a new theory is only likely to be required if there is a fundamental change in the forms of social organization of media technologies, in the social relations that are promoted, or in what is seen as the 'dominant structures of taste and feeling' (McQuail, 2010). The mass media have already changed very much, starting from the early-twentieth-century days of one-way, one-directional and undifferentiated flow to an undifferentiated mass. There are social and economic as well as technological reasons for this shift, but it is real enough (McQuail, 2010).

In this regard and for a proper understanding of the environmental dynamo theory in explaining media effect in a contemporary African society, there is need for a historical background on the continent.

Historically, the media environment in Africa has been characterized by the struggle for existence and freedom from oppression by the ruling class typified by colonialism, military dictatorship and the current wave of mixed democratic practices. The media, in order to survive, have leaned towards partisanship, becoming highly politicized and militant in informing the populace (Nyamnjoh, 2010, Chigbo & Okocha, 2023). In the fight against colonialism, military dictators and civilian administration, the media as Nyamnjoh stated, divided citizens into righteous and wicked, depending on their party-political leanings, ideologies, regional, cultural, ethnic and religious inclinations. During colonial, military (pre-modern and modern era) and civilian rule postmodernism) in Africa, the state has remained the major source of patronage of resources. In addition, economic institutions, are used to detract the flow of resources, employment at all levels of governance and in the case of Nigeria this operates at the federal, state and local government levels from which heterogeneous urban initially derive (Nyamnjoh, 2010). This is contrary to what obtains in the Western economies that are based on capitalism and resources are controlled by the private individuals. For instance, in Cameroun, citizens look towards the elites including journalists and media owners wade into modern centers of accruement as newbie big men and women. These people manage and redistribute their personal wealth to those back home in the villages in exchange for neo-traditional titles while taking advantage of economic and political opportunities in the cities to participate actively in the cultural and religious affairs, government and development of their hinterland. In these places, the customary laws and local opinion influence the outcome of national policy making decision at the federal, state and local government levels (Nyamnjoh, 2010). As African transitioned from old traditional to modernism and postmodernism, it has witnessed sustained changes in social values, norms, personal, institutions, relationships and stratifications that influence media outcomes which cannot rely only on linear based media theories to be explained (Oludele, 2020). These changes are occasioned by internal and external and forces like climate change and small-scale structural rearrangements with far reaching influence on the demography of the society. For instance, apart from colonial inherited structures that split indigenous ethnic people into different countries, the military in Nigeria bequeathed civilian administration with 36 states. The split resulted in ethnic groups that became the minority and this has resulted in constant agitations of marginalization and tension in the society which in turn affects how media content is perceived from primordial sentiments that has negative effects on national cohesion and the consequent effect on media ownership. In addition, some of the countries in Africa have witnessed civil wars - Nigeria (1967 -1970), Liberia (1989 to 1997 and 1999 to 2003) and Sierra Leone (1991 - 2002) - that left indelible marks on the defeated even though the governments in peace agreements vouched to ensure there was no victor and no vanquished, they have continued to implement skewed political, economic and development programs that marginalize the defeated leading to tension and agitations in the society. These are reflected in media content outcomes that impact differently on various segments of the society with different individual and collective realities that shape their existence in other localities. Hence, social change in Nigeria emanates from unresolved social challenges of continuous social structures, social relationships and social institutions that requires understanding of the driving forces of social change and the eventual global integration of socio-cultural, economic and political environment that shapes media content outcomes in postmodernism (Oludele, 2020).

Furthermore, the past 41 years saw the masses in Africa alienated by their rulers and elites as they navigated through military dictatorship to democracy with neocolonialism powers still controlling instruments of political and economic powers stealthily. The flapping from ineffectual political apologists, civil society groups dancing to the piper of foreign funders; pseudo-intellectual apologists and the impoverished and disenchanted masses who have suffered egregiously from bad governance, deification of power and numbed acquiescence of shared misery and pain are palpable (Imoh, 2013). The worrisome aspect is that African leaders consumed by corrupt absolute power mentality continue to see the State as the sole source of personal aggrandizement and flourish (Imoh, 2013). Unlike their counterparts in the Western world, leaders are elected to serve the people; they cannot deviate from century old institutionalized norms and values. A case in point was in 2019 when former President Donald Trump was forced to leave office and hand over to President Joe Biden who was declared winner amidst the claim of election rigging.

In Africa, leaders have been known to perpetuate themselves in office by thwarting the wishes of the people in electoral processes. Imoh (2013), observed that African leaders cleverly use political powers for private ends, and guided by mercenary ethos or kleptocratic instincts become reticent upholding popular democracy. They prefer to hold onto power by conducting fraudulent and violent elections as exemplified by the 2023 general elections in Nigeria, an election that was grossly condemned by national and international civil society organizations, European Union and National Democratic Institute. It is against these realities in Africa context that the agenda setting, two-step flow and third person theories is deemed insufficient in explaining media outcomes especially given that new media and internet have changed media landscape. Hence the complementary environmental dynamo model below proposed to capture all the dynamics in a mass communication process in a postmodernism era where truth is elastic and individualistic. The above is depicted by the diagram below:

Figure 1. Model of environmental dynamo of mass communication effect

Media audience

Personal history, gender, culture, cognition, intellect, experiences, perception, economy, age, religion, income etc.

Broader/Macro-environment: Internet access, Economy, Nationality, International politics, Imperialism, Neocolonialism, Human rights, Diplomacy, Closed/open society, Standard of living

Media Environment: News Framing, censorship, media regime, media freedom, cyber space and digital integration, language, media ownership, gate keepers, media philosophy, media economy

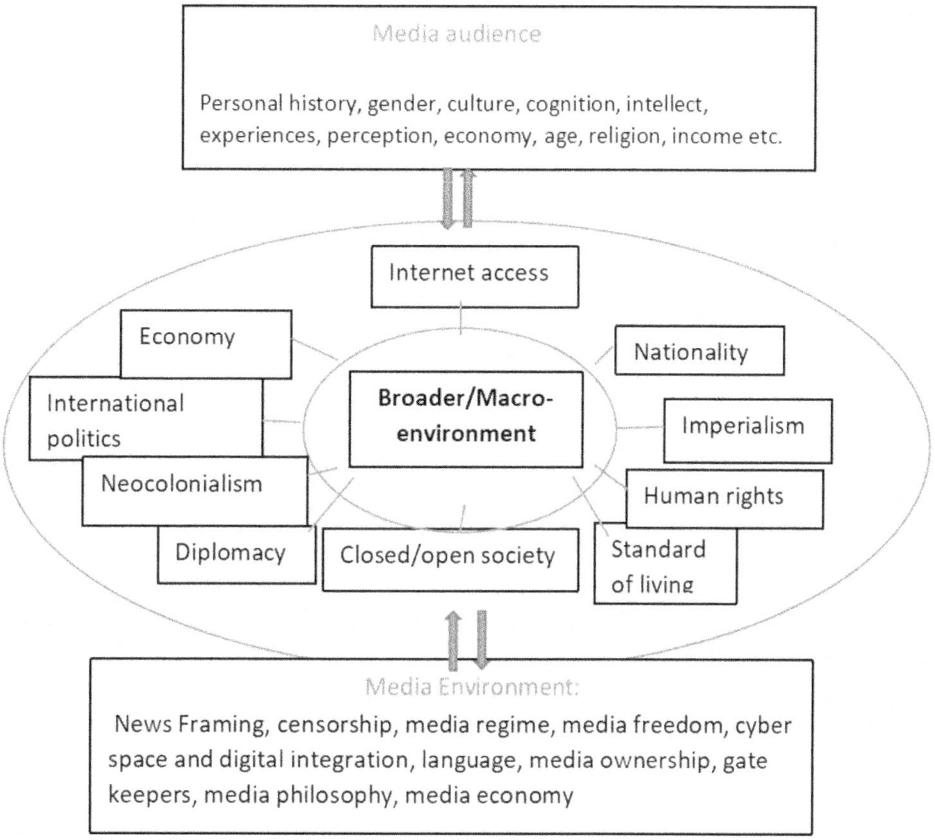

Researchers' Construct, (2023)

The above model of the Environmental Dynamo of mass communication effect shows variables that could act individually or collectively to influence media effects on society at the meso, micro, and macro media environment. The variables include personal history, gender, culture, cognition, intellect, experiences, perception, economy, age, religion, and income. That these variables disrupt the communication process as in the case of technology on social media and traditional media of print and broadcast media can be seen in the argument of Cornell (2006) on postmodernism which asserts that there is no one definition of truth and reality beyond the individual as the media audience.

Corroborating, O'Shaughnessy and O'Shaughnessy (2002) posit that so long as the influence of post-modernism has been benign or progressive, results from being dramatized and intensified criticism that only the physical sciences represent the gateway to certain knowledge. Thus, the disadvantage of post-modernism is the indefensible addition of this awareness that would, if taken by marketing, be highly disruptive. In effect, there is an attempt to bring back aesthetic approaches to human discourse, elevate linguistic and symbolic spheres of life, project visuals and scenes to levels of critical discourse, the recognition of subjective experience as meaningful part of human practices, and the redefinition of the human subject as both a cognitive and aesthetic subject. O'Shaughnessy and O'Shaughnessy (2002) cited Friedrich Nietzsche from 1844 -1900 as associating postmodernism with the fact that reality is too complex to be encompassed by a single perspective, and a multi-perspective is needed. This, if accepted, may lead to undermining the claims of absolute truth. In other words, postmodernism encompasses a pot-pourri of ideas and languages and meanings which determine media behaviour and outcomes that will be based on principally jaundiced assumptions. Embedded, in these assumptions is social class which vary in different societies. In Nigeria, the determination of social class differs from what is obtainable in England, its colonial master. In England, social class is determined at birth though this has been rejected in the United States since the American revolution. This practice varies in Nigeria: it is accepted in Northern Nigeria, rejected in South East Nigeria while the South West Nigeria is neutral. The social class syndrome explains one of the raging outcomes of the recent visit Prince Harry and Megan Markle to Nigeria as discussed earlier and this can only happen in a postmodern world. This is contrary to the assumptions of agenda-setting, two-step flow, and third-person theory that rely on stage-by-stage transmission of information based on variables that are constant to explain the outcome. This tallies with Valkenburg and Peter's (2013) postulation that hardly any contemporary media model assumes that media exert a direct influence on a passive audience. At present, media effect theories posit that outcomes of media use on certain effects are explained by the way in which media are processed (Valkenberg & Perter, 2013). Also, this resonates with Mcleod et al. (2009) communication mediation model: Changes in media systems, political environments, and electoral campaign demand that these influences, and the communication mediation model be revised to account for the growing convergence of media and conversation, heightened partisan polarization, and deepening social contentiousness in media politics (Shah, et al, 2017).

Also, the model resonates with the meso, micro, and macro levels of Klinger and Metag's (2021) theory on media effects and environment. In the model, the communication process in a broader/macro environment is affected by internet access, nationality, imperialism, human rights, standard of living, economy, neocolonialism, international politics, diplomacy, and closed /open society. The model echoed the thoughts of Luedecke and Boykoff (2017) on the interplay of variables in content production in a given media environment and submitted that media bridge different ways of knowing about the environment, and often mediate public perceptions, attitudes, perspectives, and behaviors related to environmental issues.

Also, in a media environment, variables such as news framing, censorship, media regime, media freedom, cyberspace and digital integration, language, media ownership, gatekeepers, media philosophy, and media economy work to determine the effects of the media in society. This implies that a combination of the variables dispels the idea that the media can simply set the agenda for the society; or that leaders wield total influence on media impact and that the media will influence others other than the originator or bearer of the information.

DATA ANALYSIS AND PRESENTATION

Table 1. Demographic data of respondents

	Frequency	Percentage (%)
Gender		
Males	229	46.45
Females	264	53.55
Age		
18-30	468	94.93
31-50	18	3.65
51-60	5	1.01
Above	2	0.41
Participating Universities		
Alex Ekwueme University	158	
Bayero University	152	
Lagos State University	183	
Occupation		
Students	469	95.13
Lecturers	24	4.87
Educational Qualification		
Ph. D	17	3.45
Masters	7	1.42
HND/BSc	63	12.78
OND	3	0.61
Undergraduate	403	81.74

Source: Field Data, 2023

The demographic data in Table 1 showed that there were more female respondents 264 (53.55 percent) as against the males numbering 229 (46.45 percent) out of a total of 493. The majority of the respondents were within the age bracket of 18 - 30 numbering 468 (94.93 percent); This age group were mostly undergraduates who were optimistic about the Environmental Dynamo theory in explaining media effects on society in postmodern era. This age groups are avid users of technological innovations that have pushed the frontiers of knowledge and are more individualistic in determining the reality of their environment unlike those in the age bracket of 51 and above whose truth and reality are not fluid.

Table 2. Respondents' perception of agenda-setting, two-step flow, and third-person effect

Variables	Strongly Agree	Agree	Neutral	Disagree	Strongly Disagree
1. The limitation of agenda-setting theory in explaining media effects in society is that they are based on the concept of a homogenous society and the same universal reactions of audiences to a stimulus.	116(24%)	251(51%)	95(19%)	26(5%)	5(1%)
2. The limitation of the two-step theory in explaining media effects in society is that they are primarily based on the concept of a homogenous society and the same universal reactions of audiences to a stimulus.	83(17%)	236(47.8%)	94(19.1%)	69(13.9%)	11(2.2%)
3. The limitation of third-person effect theory in explaining media effects in society is that they are primarily based on the concept of a homogenous society and the same universal reactions of audiences to a stimulus.	74(15%)	200(40.6%)	130(26.4%)	70(14.2%)	19(3.8%)
4. Inadequacies of the agenda-setting theory in explaining media effects in a postmodern era could be remedied with a new media theory that accommodates all variables that show societies are not homogenous and respond to media messages differently.	116(23.5%)	220(45%)	114(23.1%)	31(6%)	12(2.4%)
5. Inadequacies of the two-step theory in explaining media effects in a postmodern era could be remedied with a new media theory that accommodates all variables that show societies are not homogenous and respond to media messages differently.	95((19.3%)	203(41%)	127(26%)	57(11.5%)	11(2.2%)
6. Inadequacies of the third-person theory in explaining media effects in a postmodern era could be remedied with a new media theory that accommodates all variables that show societies are not homogenous and respond to media messages differently.	93(19%)	201(41%)	137(28%)	49(10%)	13(2%)
7. A new media theory that takes cognizance of both covert and overt variables akin to the audiences, environment, and media is needed to properly understand the whole ramifications of media effects in society.	117(24%)	175(35.5%)	157(32%)	32(6.5%)	12(2%)
8. The media effect is complex and multi-dimensional and the interaction between the media and audience is dynamic as many variables are involved that affect the way communication stimuli are received hence the need for an integrated theory to explain those dynamics and complexity.	132(27%)	198(40%)	113(23%)	33(7%)	17(3%)

Source: Field Data, 2023

Table 2 shows that 487(98.8 percent) of the respondents agreed that the limitations of the agenda setting, two-step flow, and third-person effect theories are based on the concept of homogenous society and universal reactions of audiences. Significantly, 67 percent of respondents affirmed that media effect is complex and multi-dimensional and the interaction between the media and audience is dynamic as many variables are involved that affect the way communication stimuli are received hence the need for an integrated theory to explain those dynamics and complexity. Corroborating, respondents agreed that theories under study are limited in explaining media effects in a postmodern era based on the concept of a homogenous society with the same universal reactions of audiences to a stimulus.

Table 3. Audience factors in relations to media effect

Variables	Strongly Agree	Agree	Neutral	Disagree	Strongly Disagree
1. The educational level of the audience influences their responses to media messages with the result that those with higher education could respond differently to stimuli compared to those with lower qualifications or no education at all.	195(39%)	182(37%)	79(16.0%)	28(6%)	9(2%)
2. The psychological disposition of audiences from different backgrounds is certain to have different influences on the reception of media content.	171((35%)	180(36%)	105(21%)	28(6%)	9(2%)
3. The level of economic empowerment of varying audiences will elicit different levels of understanding of media messages.	125(25%)	221(45%)	101(20%)	38(8%)	8(2%)
4. People of different age groups will not have a universal way of reacting to media content and will need different theories to accommodate these differences.	162(33%)	189(38%)	83(17%)	50(10%)	9(2%)

Source: Field Data, 2023

Table 3 shows the belief of the respondents on the fact that educational, psychological, economic empowerment, and age groups influence their response to media messages. 410 (83%) respondents agreed to this, while 88(18%) of the respondents disagreed that the above factors do not influence audience responses to media messages. This implies that not just one reality or truth can determine how an audience reacts to media messages but the fluidity of variables shape media effects in society. This is reinforced by majority of the respondents (68 percent) who believe that people of different age groups will not have a universal way of reacting to media content and will need different theories to accommodate these differences compared to 12 percent who disagreed.

Table 4. Technology and environmental influence on the media space

Variables	Strongly Agree	Agree	Neutral	Disagree	Strongly Disagree
1. Technological innovation has democratized the media space and has created a news source cycle whose influence on media effect on society cannot be explained with agenda-setting theory.	135(27.4%)	184(37.3%)	120(24.3%)	49(10%)	6(1%)
2. Technological innovation has democratized the media space and has created a news source cycle whose influence on media effect on society cannot be explained with the two-step flow theory	92(19%)	188(38%)	142(29%)	62(12%)	9(2%)
3. Technological innovation has democratized the media space and has created a news source cycle whose influence on media effect on society cannot be explained with third-person effect theories under study.	94(19.0%)	197(39.9%)	146(29.6%)	49(9.9%)	8(1.6%)
4. Technology advancement and innovation influence audience response to media messages and are accommodated in the Environmental Dynamo theory in understanding media's effect on society.	112(22.7%)	214(43.4%)	120(24.3%)	40(8.2%)	7(1.4%)

Source: Field Data, 2023

Table 4 shows that the influence of technological innovation on media effect cannot be explained with agenda-setting, two-step flow, and third-person effect theory. This showed in the majority of respondents 411(83percent) who confirmed that technological advancement and innovation influence audience response to media messages and are accommodated in the Environmental Dynamo in understanding media effects compared to only 9.6 percent who disagreed.

Table 5. International environment and the impact on the media space

Variables	Strongly Agree	Agree	Neutral	Disagree	Strongly Disagree
1. The international environment is a complex network of economic, legal, and cultural forces that can influence the outcome of media messages on society.	142(29%)	213(43.2%)	99(20%)	26(5.2%)	13(2.6%)
2. The international environment is not homogenous and this affects the way media messages on issues are received in different societies in the United States and Africa.	129(26.1%)	196(39.8%)	108(22%)	48(9.7%)	12(2.4%)
3. Different political systems in different societies will influence audience reaction to media messages and this cannot be explained with agenda-setting theory.	95(19.3%)	190(38.5%)	136(27.6%)	65(13.2%)	7(1.4%)
4. Different political systems in different societies will influence audience reaction to media messages and this cannot be explained with two-step theory.	88(18%)	193(39.1%)	126(25.5)	70(14.2%)	16(3.2%)
5. Different political systems in different societies will influence audience reaction to media messages and this cannot be explained with the third-person effect theory	84(17%)	200(40.6%)	129(26.1%)	55(11.2%)	25(5.1%)

Source: Field Data, 2023

Table 5 shows that the international environment is not homogenous and different political systems in different societies influence audience reaction to media messages. Significantly, 413(83.8%) respondents agreed while 264(53.5%) disagreed, implying that in a broader macro media environment prevailing political systems must be factored in to fully explain media effect on society as espoused in the integrated Environmental Dynamo theory that takes cognizant of complex network of economic, legal, and cultural forces that can influence the outcome of media messages on society in a broader international media environment.

Table 6. The place of culture and religion on media effect

Variables	Strongly Agree	Agree	Neutral	Disagree	Strongly Disagree
1. Culture and religion are instrumental to audience reaction to media messages	187(38%)	202(41%)	73(15%)	25(5%)	6(1%)
2. A very religious society will respond to media messages on gender differently from a very liberal society and the agenda-setting theory will not fully explain the underlying factors determining how people respond to the content.	154(31%)	204(41%)	87(18%)	38(8%)	10(2%)
3. A very religious society will respond to media messages on gender differently from a very liberal society and the two-step flow theory will not fully explain the underlying factors determining how people from the different societies respond to the content.	122(24.7%)	204(41.4%)	113(23%)	42(8.5%)	12(2.4%)
4. A very religious society will respond to media messages on gender differently from a very liberal society and the third-person effect theory will not fully explain the underlying factors determining how people in the two societies will respond to the content.	91(18%)	193(39%)	132(27%)	64(13%)	13(3%)
5. Environmental Dynamo theory can help to understand how a very religious society will respond to media messages on gender differently from a very liberal society.	126(25%)	207(42%)	117(24%)	34(7%)	9(2%)
6. Environmental Dynamo theory can help to fully explain the underlying factors determining how people in religious and liberal societies will respond to media messages.	103(20.9%)	224(45.4%)	122(24.8%)	33(6.7%)	11(2.2%)

Source: Field Data, 2023

Table 6 shows that 406(82 percent) of the respondents agree that the culture and religion of the people are instrumental to audience reaction to media messages. 431(87.4 percent) also agreed that Environmental Dynamo theory can help to understand a religious society. While 236(48.2 percent) respondents disagree with the fact that religion and culture cannot influence audience media messages. Significantly, the majority of the respondents numbering 103 (20.9 percent) and 224 (45.4 percent) strongly agree and agree, respectively, that Environmental Dynamo theory can help to fully explain the underlying factors determining how people in religious and liberal societies will respond to media messages.

Table 7. The media ecosystem and nature of content

Variables	Strongly Agree	Agree	Neutral	Disagree	Strongly Disagree
1. Media and the way they are consumed are changing so rapidly that it can be overwhelming to easily explain all its ramifications in society by agenda-setting theory.	129(26.1%)	228(46.2%)	99(20%)	23(4.7%)	14(3%)
2. Media and the way they are consumed are changing so rapidly that it can be overwhelming to easily explain all its ramifications in society with a two-step theory.	90(18.2%)	232(47.1%)	123(25%)	32(6.5%)	16(3.2%)
3. Media and the way they are consumed are changing so rapidly that it can be overwhelming to easily explain all its ramifications in the society with third-person effect theory.	101(20.5%)	188(38.1%)	133(27%)	58(11.8%)	13(2.6%)
4. Environmental Dynamo theory anchored on post-modernism can explain the media and the way it is consumed in a rapidly changing society.	96(19.5%)	204(41.4%)	142(29%)	35(7.1%)	16(3%)

Source: Field Data, 2023

Table 7 shows affirmation by the majority of the respondents 357 (72.3 percent) that media consumptions are changing rapidly that it cannot fully be explained by agenda-setting, two-step flow and third-person effect theories. However, lesser number of respondents, 300, representing 60.9 percent, also concur that an Environmental Dynamo theory anchored on post-modernism is required to explain the media and the way it is consumed in a rapidly changing society.

Table 8. Psychological disposition of audience and media outcomes

Variables	Strongly Agree	Agree	Neutral	Disagree	Strongly Disagree
1. In a plural society, the psychological disposition of people affects media outcomes which the agenda-setting theory will not capture in explaining media effects on society.	114(23.1%)	209(42%)	113(23%)	47(9.5%)	10(2%)
2. In a plural society, the psychological disposition of people affects media outcomes which the two-step theory will not capture in explaining media effects on society.	84(17%)	222(45%)	131(27%)	46(9%)	10(2%)
3. In a plural society, the psychological disposition of people affects media outcomes which the third-person effect theory will not capture in explaining media effects on society.	81(16.4%)	197(40%)	148(30%)	55(11.2%)	12(2.4%)
4. In a plural society, the psychological disposition of people affects media outcomes which the Environmental Dynamo theory will capture in explaining media effects on society.	97(20%)	200(40%)	134(27%)	44(9%)	18(4%)
5. The proposed diagram/model effectively explains the media's effect on society based on the integrated Environmental Dynamo theory that accommodates the plurality of variables in the postmodern era.	101(20.5%)	220(44.6%)	133(27%)	28(5.7%)	11(2.2%)

Source: Field Data, 2023

Table 8 shows affirmation by the majority of the respondents, 279 (56.5 percent) of the psychological disposition of the audience and media outcomes which the agenda-setting, two-step, and third-person effect theory will not capture in explaining media effects in a plural society. More importantly, 200 (40 percent) of the respondents concur that in a plural society, the psychological disposition of people affects media outcomes which the Environmental Dynamo theory will capture in explaining media effects on society. Also, 220(44.6 percent) of respondents agreed that the proposed diagram/model effectively explains the media's effects on society based on the integrated Environmental Dynamo theory that accommodates the plurality of variables in the postmodern era.

DISCUSSION OF FINDINGS

The quantitative and qualitative data obtained from the literature review and field data from respondents met the objectives of the study to establish that demography, psychology, ethno-religious, culture, politics, socio-economy - all combine to influence the outcome of the media content, who is communicating what to whom and with what effect and vice versa in a spiral of news source (Musa, 2011; Imoh, 2013, Oludele, 2020).

They were used to establish the limitations of the agenda-setting, two-step flow, and third-person effect; examine public perception of the Environmental Dynamo theory, and illustrate that it can remedy the defects the three theories studied. Based on analysis of field data from respondents, the research established the inadequacy of the theories in explaining media effects in a postmodern world as different variables act individually or combine to influence media effects on society. For instance, 487 (98.8 percent) of the respondents affirmed their limitations based on the concept of a homogenous society and no universal reactions of audiences in a plural society.

The literature review corroborated the finding of Bazargani and Larsari's (2015) that the theories studied do not capture pluralism and variables such as the individual psychology, philosophy, and environmental variables in both micro, meso, and macro levels that influence mass media messages in society. Again, the model of the Environmental Dynamo theories showed there are three levels at which different variables can have varying media effects – the media audience, the broader/macro environment, and the media environment. This is in line with Klinger and Metag's (2021) three levels of viewing media effect - the micro, meso, and macro. That is why the Environmental Dynamo model listed variables interfacing at the level of media audiences as personal history, gender, culture, cognition, intellect, experiences, perception, economy, age, religion, and income. Other elements in the broader/macro environment include internet access, economics, international politics, nationality, imperialism, neocolonialism, diplomacy, closed/open society, human rights, and standards of living. In the media environment, variables such as news framing, censorship, media regime, media freedom, cyberspace and digital integration, language, media ownership, gatekeepers, media philosophy, and media economy influence the communication process.

The implication is that the intricately interwoven interplay of variables ensure fluidity of media effects in a postmodern era that centers on what is real to the individual as against a predetermined truth that defined media effects in a pre-modern era when the theories of agenda-setting, two-person flow, and third-person effect were propounded.

It is instructive that 487 (98.8 percent) of the respondents agreed that the limitations of the agenda setting, two-step flow, and third-person effect theories are based on the concept of a homogenous society and the universal reactions of audiences while the reverse is so in post-modernism. Also, 378 (77.1

percent) of the respondents affirmed that the defects of the theories can be cured with a new media theory that accommodates all the variables; while 65(13.5 percent) rejected the idea that there is no need for the assumption that a new media theory with certain variables is needed to properly understand the ramifications of media effects in society while overwhelming majority (98.8 percent) concur that agenda-setting has limitations in explaining media effects and reinforces the need for an inclusive Environmental Dynamo model to establish the influence of media on society in a post-modern era.

The study established that the majority of respondents believed that educational, psychological, economic empowerment, and age groups influence their response to media messages. Also, the majority of respondents strongly agree that the educational level of the audience influences their responses to media messages with the result that those with higher education could respond differently to stimuli compared to those with lower qualifications or no education. Field data also showed that many of the respondents believe that the psychological disposition of audiences from different backgrounds is certain to have different influences on the reception of media content. Responding to the statement that the level of economic empowerment of varying audiences will elicit different levels of understanding of media messages, the majority of the respondents agreed with a few disagreeing. This feedback from respondents tallies with the views of Luedecke and Boykoff (2017) that media bridge different ways of knowing about the environment, and often mediate public perceptions, attitudes, perspectives, and behaviors related to environmental issues.

The same goes for the influence of technological innovation on media effect that respondents said could not be explained with agenda-setting, two-step flow, and third-person effect theory. The field data showed that the majority of respondents numbering 214 (43.4 percent) agreed that technological advancement and innovation influence audience response to media messages and is accommodated in the Environmental Dynamo theory in understanding media effect on society. Comparatively, 197 (39.9 percent) agreed that technological innovation has democratized the media space and has created a news source cycle whose influence on media effect on society cannot be explained with third-person effect theories under study; two-step theory, 188 (38percent); while agenda-setting is 184(37.3%). This synchronizes with the postulation of Hariharasudan, Pandeeswari and Hassan (2022), and Cornell (2006) emphasis on technological influences on media effects in a postmodern where there is no single defining source for truth and reality beyond the individual. The implication is that researchers studying media effect in a plural postmodern society should consider testing their hypotheses not only with the theories of agenda-setting, two-step flow, and third-person effect but also with the Environmental Dynamo theory for a much more reliable explanation of media messages and their effects on society.

CONCLUSION

The fulcrum of this research is to construct a theory that will complement other theories such as agenda-setting, two-step flow, and third-person effect to sufficiently explain media effects in Africa, in a postmodern era media. This is an era in which different variables such as cultural values, religion, and technology among others act individually or combine to influence the outcome of media messages in society based on the truth and reality the individual faces as against a predetermined truth and reality of the pre-modern era, and scientific-based realism of modernity. Based on quantitative and qualitative data from field data, the study established that at the different levels of media audience, broader or macro-environment, and media environment, variables are intricately interwoven to influence the process of communication and its effect on society, especially in a postmodern African society as can be seen in the example of how messages on COVID-19 were received on the continent. Hence, the proposition of the Environmental Dynamo theory is sufficient to remedy the inadequacies and also complement other theories in explaining media effects in society.

RECOMMENDATIONS

Based on the conclusions, the study recommends:
1. Further empirical testing of the Environmental Dynamo theory on a much larger audience in different countries and institutions of mass communication.
2. The Environmental Dynamo theory should be used to understand the media ecosystem and the nature of content for different audiences.
3. The study recommends the use of Environmental Dynamo theory in explaining complex media consumption patterns among different meso, micro, and macro media audiences and environments.

REFERENCES

Arnold, T. (2024, January 3). Resistance to same-sex blessings grows in Africa, but bishops are divided globally. *Catholic News Agency*. https://www.catholicnewsagency.com/news/256435/resistance-to-same-sex-blessings-grows-in-africa-but-bishops-are-divided-globally.

Banning, S. A. (2007). Factors affecting the marketing of a public safety message: The third-person effect and uscs and gratifications theory in public reaction to a crime reduction program. *Atlantic Journal of Communication*, 15(1), 1–18. 10.1080/15456870701212716

Bhat, A. (2024). Multistage sampling: Definitions, steps, applications +example. *QuestionPro* https://www.questionpro.com/blog/multistage-sampling-advantages-and-application/

Borah, P. (2016). *Media effects theory*. .10.1002/9781118541555.wbiepc156

Brubaker, J. (2008). The freedom to choose a personal agenda: Removing our reliance on the media agenda. *American Communication Journal, 10*(3). http://ac-journal.org/journal/pub/2008/fall%200820%20Defining%20Digital%20Freedom/ Article1.pdf

Chigbo, M., & Okocha, D. O. (2023). A self-discourse narrative on survival of the media in Africa. *The NOUN Scholar Journal of Arts and Humanities.*, 3(1), 148–164.

Cornell, S. (2006). What does post-modern mean. *Summit Ministries*. https://www.summit.org/resources/articles/what-does-postmodern-mean/

Davison, W. P. (1983). The Third-Person Effect in Communication. *Public Opinion Quarterly*, 47(1), 1–15. https://www.jstor.org/stable/2748702. 10.1086/268763

De Vreese. (2003, September). The spiral of cynicism reconsidered. *European Journal of Communication*. 10.1177/0267323105055259

Dudovskiy, J. (2022, January). Multi-stage sampling. In *The Ultimate Guide to Writing a Dissertation in Business Studies: A step-by-step assistance* (6th ed.). Business Research Methodology. https://research-methodology.net/sampling-in-primary-data-collection/multi-stage-sampling/

Ezaka, S. (2022, August). Postmodernism and Broadcasting in Nigeria. *International Journal of Innovative Science and Research Technology*, 7(8), 577. https://www.ijisrt.com/assets/upload/files/IJISRT22AUG063_(1).pdf

Francis. (2023). Declaration Fiducia Supplicans on the Pastoral Meaning of blessings. *Vatican*. https://www.vatican.va/roman_curia/congregations/cfaith/documents/ rc_ddf_doc_20231218_fiducia-supplicans_en.html

Hariharasudan, A., Pandeeswari, D., & Hassan, A. (2022, March 16). Research Trends in Post Modernism: A Bibliometric Analysis. *World Journal of English Language*, 12(2), 148–149. 10.5430/wjel.v12n2p148

Igwe, I. (2024). Minister petitions IGP, asks court to stop Niger mass wedding of 100 orphans. *Channels TV*. https://www.channelstv.com/2024/05/14/minister-petitions-igp- asks-court-to-stop-niger-mass-wedding-of-100-orphans/

Imoh, G. O. (2013). Mass media and democratic consolidation in Africa: Problems, challenges and prospects. *New Media and Mass Communication.* 16, https://core.ac.uk/download/pdf/234652401.pdf

Jameson, F. (1997). *Post modernism, or, the cultural logic of late capitalism.* Duke University Press Durham. https://is.muni.cz/el/fss/jaro2016/SOC757/um/61816962/Jameson_The_cultural_ logic.pdf

Kellner, D. (2020). Jean Baudrillard. *The Stanford Encyclopedia of Philosophy.*https://plato.stanford.edu/archives/win2020/entries/baudrillard/>

Klinger, K., & Metag, J. (2021). Media efects in the context of environmental issues. In the *Handbook of International Ttrends in Environmental Communication.* Routledge. https://www.taylorfrancis.com/chapters/edit/10.4324/9780367275204-5/media- effects-context-environmental-issues-kira-klinger-julia-metag.

Koskei, M. K. (n.d.). *Post modernism and hyperreality.* Academa. https://www.academia.edu/10747720/POST_MODERNISM_AND_HYPERREA LITY_AND_THE_MEDIA?email_work_card=title

Kreft, N. (2011). Comment on David Estlund. What good Is it?—Unrealistic political theory and the value of intellectual work. *Analyse & Kritik*, 33(2), 417–422. 10.1515/auk-2011-0205

Luedecke, G. & Boykoff, M. (2017, March 6). *Environment and the media.* Springer. .10.1002/9781118786352.wbieg0464

McCombes, S. (2022). *Sampling Methods | Types, Techniques, & Examples.* Scribbr. https://www.scribbr.co.uk/research-methods/sampling/

McLeod, D. M., Kosicki, G. M., & McLeod, J. M. (2009). Political communication effects. In *J. Media effects: Advances in theory and research.* 228–251. Routledge.

McQuail, D. (2010). *McQuail's mass communication theory.* Sage. https://nibmehub.com/opac- service/pdf/read/McQuail's%20Mass%20communication%20theory.pdf

Messner, M., & Distaso, M. W. (2008). The source cycle. *Journalism Studies*, 9(3), 447–463. 10.1080/14616700801999287

Musa, A. O. (2011). *The role of political, socio-economic factors and the media in Nigeria's Inter-religious conflict.* [Thesis, University of Liverpool]. https://livrepository.liverpool.ac.uk/5335/4/Musa_Ali_Oct2011_5335.pdf

National Bureau of Statistics-Nigeria. (2023). *Nigeria-human development indices general household survey 2017, first round.* National Bureau of Statistics. https://www.nigerianstat.gov.ng/nada/index.php/catalog/72

Neto, K. A., & Hernriques, M. H. (2022). Geoconservation in Africa: State of the art and future challenges. *Gondwana Research*, 110, 107–113. 10.1016/j.gr.2022.05.022

Nyamnjoh, F. B. (2010). *Africa's media: Between professional ethics and cultural belonging.* Fredrich Ebert Stifung. https://library.fes.de/pdf-files/bueros/africa-media/07366.pdf

O'Shaughnessy, J., & O'Shaughnessy, N. J. (2002). Postmodernism and marketing: Separating the wheat from the chaff. *Journal of Macromarketing.* https://www.academia.edu/20497686/Postmodernism_and_Marketing_Separating_ the_Wheat_from_the_Chaff?email_work_card=thumbnail

Okamgba, J. G. (2023). Nigeria has 740 operational broadcast stations, newly approved 67, says NBC. *Techeconomy*. https://techeconomy.ng/nigeria-has-740-operational- broadcast-stations-newly-approved-67-says-nbc/

Oludele, S. M. (2020). Social change in contemporary Nigeria: A theoretical discourse. *RSC, 12*(1), https://www.fuds.si/wp- content/uploads/2020/09/solaja_mayowa_oludele_57-82.pdf

Postelnicu, M. (2016). Two-step flow model of communication. *Encyclopedia Britannica*. https://www.britannica.com/topic/two-step-flow-model-of- communication.

Ramirez, I. (2024). What are some theories about human nature that you believe are true, compatible with scientific understanding, but difficult or impractical to prove? *Quora*https://www.quora.com/What-are-some-theories-about-human-nature-that-you-believe-are-true-compatible-with-scientific-understanding-but-difficult-or-impractical-to-prove

Reichard, J. D. (2011). Demassifying Religion: Futurist Interpretations of American Socioeconomic and Religious Change. *International Review of Social Sciences and Humanities.*, 2(1), 222–229. https://www.academia.edu/2227219/Demassifying_Religion_Futurist_Interpretations_of_American_Socioeconomic_and_Religious_Change

Rotaru, I., Nitulescu, L., & Rudolf, C. (2010). The post-modern paradigm–a framework of today's media impact in cultural space. *Procedia: Social and Behavioral Sciences*, 5, 328–330. 10.1016/j.sbspro.2010.07.098

Strinati, D. (1995). *An introduction to theories of popular culture.* Routledge https://api.pageplace.de/preview/DT0400.9781134565085_A25033634/preview- 9781134565085_A25033634.pdf

Sun, Y. (2008, April). On Behavioral component of the third-person effect. *Communication Research*, 35(2), 257–278. 10.1177/0093650207313167

Takov, P., & Banlanjo, N. M. (2021). Postmodernism vis-a-vis African Traditional Cultures: Rethinking the Pathways to Authenticity. *Global Journal of Human-Social Science: Arts & Humanities-Psychology*, 21(2), 33. https://globaljournals.org/GJHSS_Volume21/5-Postmodernism-Vis-a-Vis- African.pdf

Turner, , Baker, R., & Kellner, F. (2018). Theoretical Literature Review: Tracing the Life Cycle of a Theory and Its Verified and Falsified Statement. *Human Resource Development Review*, 17(1), 34–61. 10.1177/1534484317749680

Ugorji, L.I. & Ogun D. A. (2023, December 20) *Concerning fiducia supplicans: A declaration for the propagation of the faith on the pastoral meaning of blessings in the church.* A statement issued by the Catholic Bishops Conference of Nigeria.

Weimann, G. (2015). Communication, twostep flow of. In *International Encyclopedia of the Social & Behavioral Sciences* (Second Edition). 10.1016/B978-0-08-097086-8.95051-7

Yarahmadi, F. (2020, January 6). *Multistage Sampling Technique and Estimating Sample Size for a Descriptive Study on Viewers' Perception of TV Commercials.* Sage Research Method. https://doi.org/10.4135/9781529713961

ADDITIONAL READING

Alexander, S. (2000). Marshal McLuhan is back from the dustbin of history; with the interest; his ideas again seem ahead of their time. *New York Times.* https://www.nytimes.com/2000/10/14arts/marshal-mcluhanback-dustbin. history-with-internet-his-ideas-again-seem-ahead

Anaeto, S., Onabajo, O., & Osifeso, J. (2008). *Models and theories of mass communication.* African Renaissance Book Incorporated.

Anderson, M. L., & Taylor, H. F. (2009). *Sociology: The essentials.* Thomson Wadsworth.

Nicotera, A. M. (2009). Constitutive view of communication. In Littlejohn, S. W., & Foss, K. A. (Eds.), *Encyclopedia of communication theory* (pp. 175–179). Sage.

Torp, S. M. (2015). The strategic turn in communication science: On the history and role of strategy in communication science from ancient Greece until the present day. In Holtzhausen, D. R., & Zerfass, A. (Eds.), *The Routledge handbook of strategic communication* (pp. 34–52). Routledge.

West, R., & Turner, L. H. (2010). *Introducing communication theory: analysis and application* (4th ed.). McGraw-Hill.

KEY TERMS AND DEFINITIONS

Agenda-Setting Theory: In a nutshell, agenda setting refers to the process by which mass media — including journalistic media — present certain issues (e.g., gun violence) frequently and prominently, with the result being that large segments of the public come to perceive those issues as being more important than others.

Communication: The exchange of information, ideas, or thoughts between individuals or groups.

Culture: Culture is a term that refers to a large and diverse set of mostly intangible aspects of social life. According to sociologists, culture consists of the values, beliefs, systems of language, communication, and practices that people share in common and that can be used to define them as a collective.

Environmental Dynamo Theory: This is a postmodern mass communication theory propounded in the year 2024 by Dr. Desmond Onyemechi Okocha and Maureen Chigbo from Bingham University, Nigeria. Aside principally factoring the social-cultural dynamics of the African media ecosystem, the theory sought to remedy the deficiencies of selected linear theories such as the agenda-setting, two-step flow and third-person theories. Its central argument is that the nature and elements defining three major environments (1. the physiological, psychological and sociological make-up of media audience, 2. The external economic and political environments of the audience, and 3. The media, ownership structure, contents and the environment within which the media exist and operate) are responsible for the dynamics and interactions between the media and their audience.

Mass Media: refers to the technologies used as channels for a small group of people to communicate with a larger number of people. The concept was first addressed during the Progressive Era of the 1920s, as a response to new opportunities for elites to reach large audiences via the mass media of the time: newspapers, radio, and film. Indeed, the three forms of traditional mass media today are still the same: print (newspapers, books, magazines), broadcast (television, radio), and cinema (movies and documentaries).

Media Ecosystem: It is the study of media environments, the idea that technology and techniques, modes of information and codes of communication play a leading role in human affairs.

Third-Person Effect Theory: Audience perceptions regarding media influence have been extensively studied since the 1980s. Originating with a landmark article by W. Phillip Davison, the term "the third-person effect" (TPE, later on also referred to in the literature as the "third-person perception," or TPP) relates to people's tendency to perceive that mass-media messages have only minimal influence on them but greater influence on other people—the "third persons." Much research has been dedicated to documenting such perceptions in various contexts and to exploring the psychological mechanisms behind them.

Two-Step Flow Theory: The concept of the 'two-step flow of communication' suggests that the flow of information and influence from the mass media to their audiences involves two steps: from the media to certain individuals (i.e., the opinion leaders) and from them to the public.

Section 2
Media Landscape

Chapter 5
Navigating the Social Media Maze:
Strategies for Effective Digital Marketing in a Fragmented Landscape

Surjit Singha
http://orcid.org/0000-0002-5730-8677
Kristu Jayanti College (Autonomous), India

ABSTRACT

Integrating digital marketing and social media is crucial for organizations to navigate the ever-changing global media environment. Amidst polarization, fragmentation, and convergence, marketers can utilize social media's potential to foster connections, increase brand recognition, and involve communities. Attainment requires manoeuvring through the digital environment, adjusting to shifting consumer preferences and imbibing novel ideas. Methods encompass data analytics to obtain valuable insights, develop engaging content experiences, and emphasize genuineness and adaptability. Anticipating forthcoming developments and adopting novel strategies will be essential for optimizing the influence of marketing efforts. In our interconnected world, social media marketing presents various opportunities and challenges that necessitate a strategic, audience-focused, and data-driven approach to achieve success.

INTRODUCTION

Within the ever-evolving domain of digital marketing, attaining proficiency in the complexities of social media has evolved into a dual-sport endeavour. In an ever-changing digital environment characterized by fragmentation, polarization, and convergence, marketers face the formidable task of establishing meaningful connections with their target audiences amidst the inundation of online content. In the contemporary era of interconnectivity, social media has emerged as a formidable influencer of consumer behaviour and worldwide communication. In an era characterized by the widespread adoption of digital platforms and varied media consumption patterns, marketers are confronted with the challenge of operating in a fragmented environment where the attention of their target audience is scattered across multiple channels

DOI: 10.4018/979-8-3693-3767-7.ch005

Copyright ©2024, IGI Global. Copying or distributing in print or electronic forms without written permission of IGI Global is prohibited.

(Zhang, 2023). This chapter examines the convergence, fragmentation, and polarization of evolving global media environments about the intersection of social media and digital marketing strategies.

This chapter explores the critical strategies necessary to navigate the complex world of social media in the context of evolving global media environments. This analysis will explore how convergence has transformed conventional and digital media platforms into one another, thereby presenting marketers with novel prospects to engage with consumers through various channels. Simultaneously, the proliferation of niche communities and micro-audiences has resulted from fragmentation, presenting targeted messaging with challenges and opportunities. Furthermore, due to the polarized nature of online discourse, brands are compelled to adopt a nuanced content creation and engagement strategy. It entails skilful handling of delicate subjects while upholding their credibility and honesty.

This chapter aims to give marketers the requisite understanding and resources to flourish in this ever-changing landscape by integrating theoretical perspectives and pragmatic case studies. By leveraging the potential of data analytics and comprehending the psyche of social media users, we shall reveal tried and true approaches to optimizing reach, engagement, and, ultimately, business outcomes. In navigating the complex realm of social media, it is critical to acknowledge the fundamental value of flexibility and ingenuity. By remaining updated on emerging trends and consistently honing our strategies, we can successfully exploit the dynamic media environment to establish significant connections with our intended audiences.

METHODOLOGY

This chapter comprehensively examines multiple facets of social media marketing, encompassing performance measurement, audience segmentation, content creation, and community management. By utilizing theoretical frameworks and concrete illustrations, this chapter examines significant subjects, including the psychological aspects of social media users, the ramifications of algorithmic modifications on organic reach, and the influence of influencer marketing on consumer conduct. Furthermore, the chapter analyzes developing trends and technologies influencing the trajectory of digital marketing. It gives readers an anticipatory outlook on maintaining a competitive edge in a swiftly changing environment.

OBJECTIVES OF THE STUDY

The Objectives of this Chapter

- To thoroughly examine successful digital marketing strategies amid the diverse and fragmented global media environment.
- To analyze the obstacles and prospects that social media platforms present.
- To effectively furnish marketers with the information and resources to manoeuvre this intricate landscape.
- To foster substantial interaction with intended demographics.

THEORETICAL FRAMEWORK

Theoretical frameworks offer a structured approach to comprehending various facets of social media marketing. In the context of the provided chapter, several theoretical frameworks prove pertinent. Social Cognitive Theory elucidates how individuals learn and behave via observation, imitation, and reinforcement (Bandura, 2012), offering insights into how social media users interact with content and how marketers can leverage this to influence consumer conduct. Diffusion of Innovation Theory explores the spread of new ideas, products, or technologies within a society or social group (Rogers et al. 2014), aiding marketers in understanding the adoption process of new digital strategies and technologies. Social Identity Theory examines how individuals define themselves through group affiliations (Islam, 2014). It guides marketers in understanding how social media users engage with online communities and enables effective audience segmentation and community management. The Elaboration Likelihood Model elucidates how individuals process persuasive messages based on involvement and motivation levels, assisting marketers to tailor content creation and messaging strategies to engage different audience segments effectively. Network Theory explores the structure and dynamics of social networks (Gamper, 2022), facilitating analysis of how relationships and interactions shape information flow and behaviour on social media platforms. Lastly, the Uses and Gratifications Theory explores motivations behind media consumption (Chaney, 1972), aiding marketers in understanding why people engage with social media and how to create content that meets their needs and desires. By employing these frameworks, marketers can gain profound insights into social media users' psychological, social, and behavioural dimensions and the broader dynamics of digital marketing trends and technologies.

CONCEPTUAL FRAMEWORK

The conceptual framework of this chapter is derived from marketing psychology, communication theory, and media studies, among others. By integrating audience reception, network effects, and persuasion theories, this chapter offers a more comprehensive comprehension of the fundamental mechanisms that propel consumer behaviour on social media platforms. In addition, to shed light on the intricate dynamics among brands, individuals, and digital technologies in the delivery and circulation of marketing messages, the theoretical framework will integrate findings from studies concerning digital culture, online communities, and brand identity. The conceptual framework of this chapter draws from various disciplines, including marketing psychology, communication theory, and media studies. This chapter aims to comprehensively understand the underlying mechanisms driving consumer behaviour on social media platforms by integrating theories such as audience reception, network effects, and persuasion. Additionally, to illuminate the complex dynamics between brands, individuals, and digital technologies in disseminating marketing messages, the theoretical framework will incorporate findings from research on digital culture, online communities, and brand identity. This multi-faceted approach enables a deeper exploration of the interactions and influences shaping social media marketing practices.

The chapter is organized around strategic social media marketing, which systematically organizes, implements, and assesses marketing endeavours on various social media platforms. Phenomena such as audience analysis, content strategy, engagement tactics, and performance metrics are interdependent and bolster one another within this conceptual structure, constituting a unified methodology for attaining marketing goals in the digital domain. The chapter's objective is to furnish readers with a pragmatic guide for resolving quantifiable challenges and attaining tangible outcomes in a constantly evolving social media environment by conceptualizing social media marketing as a dynamic and iterative process.

BACKGROUND

The dynamic nature of the global media environment is influenced by technological progress, cultural transformations, and changing consumer preferences. The consumption, sharing, and monetization of information have been profoundly transformed in recent years due to the proliferation of digital technologies, which have ushered in an age of unparalleled interconnectivity and interactivity. In addition to democratizing information access, this digital revolution has also democratized production and distribution methods, granting organizations and individuals the ability to generate and distribute content independently (Knell, 2021).

At the heart of this paradigm shift lies the proliferation of social media platforms, which have become the predominant means of exchanging information, communicating, expressing themselves, and interacting with content. Platforms such as Facebook, X, Instagram, and TikTok have become indispensable components of the daily lives of billions of individuals across the globe. They function as virtual communities where users congregate to exchange information, viewpoints, and personal encounters (Ostic et al., 2021). Nevertheless, in addition to social media's prospects, marketers encounter many obstacles that arise from the disjointed structure of the online environment. Audience fragmentation has resulted from the proliferation of platforms and channels; consequently, brands need help capturing and retaining attention amidst the cacophony.

Furthermore, brands must navigate the minefields created by the polarization of online discourse to avoid backlash and reputational harm (Gupta et al., 2021; Webster & Ksiazek, 2012). In light of this context, to be successful, digital marketing strategies must exhibit agility, adaptability, and a profound comprehension of the technological and sociocultural dynamics in operation. Through data analytics, market research, and consumer insights, marketers can discern nascent trends, predict changes in consumer behaviour, and customize their communications to connect with their intended audiences effectively.

Moreover, brands can nurture advocacy and loyal communities in an increasingly competitive market by encouraging genuine, significant customer interactions (Moi & Cabiddu, 2020). The subsequent chapters comprehensively examine social media marketing, encompassing case studies, emerging trends, and optimal strategies. This equips marketers with the information and resources to effectively maneuver the complex digital environment and accomplish their organizational goals amidst a perpetually shifting worldwide media panorama.

LITERATURE REVIEW

In the era of rapidly changing global media landscapes characterized by convergence, fragmentation, and polarization, navigating the social media maze presents a formidable challenge for marketers seeking to implement effective digital marketing strategies. This literature review examines critical research findings and theoretical frameworks pertinent to understanding and addressing the complexities of social media marketing in today's fragmented landscape. Convergence underscores the integration of various media forms and technologies, blurring traditional boundaries between platforms and reshaping audience behaviours and consumption patterns (Sîrbu et al., 2019; Zotto & Lugmayr, 2016). However, alongside convergence, fragmentation has emerged as a defining characteristic of contemporary media landscapes, fueled by the proliferation of niche content and platforms catering to diverse audience interests (Webster & Ksiazek, 2012). This fragmentation challenges marketers to reach and engage fragmented audiences across multiple channels (Liu & Gu, 2019).

In response to the challenges posed by fragmentation, marketers have increasingly turned to social media platforms as critical channels for engaging audiences and disseminating marketing messages. Audience segmentation, content personalization, and community management have emerged as core strategies for effective social media marketing (Li et al., 2020). Marketers can enhance engagement and foster brand loyalty by leveraging audience insights and employing tailored content strategies. Top of Form Understanding social media users' psychological and behavioural dynamics is crucial for devising effective marketing strategies. Audience reception theories, such as Uses and Gratifications, shed light on the motivations behind social media use and consumption patterns (Hossain, 2019).

Network effects theories highlight the influence of social connections and interactions on information dissemination and user engagement (Liu & Gu, 2019). Persuasion theories provide insights into how marketing messages influence consumer behaviour (Eisend & Tarrahi, 2021). Integrating these theoretical frameworks enables a deeper comprehension of the underlying mechanisms driving consumer behaviour on social media platforms. In social media marketing, understanding digital culture and online communities is essential for building authentic brand identities and fostering meaningful connections with audiences (Tang & Chan, 2020). Research on brand identity in digital environments emphasizes the importance of authenticity, transparency, and community engagement in shaping brand perceptions and loyalty (Safeer et al., 2021). As marketers navigate the social media maze in today's fragmented landscape, a nuanced understanding of audience behaviours, platform dynamics, and brand-consumer interactions is essential. By integrating insights from the literature on convergence, fragmentation, social media marketing strategies, psychological dynamics, and digital culture, marketers can develop effective strategies for engaging fragmented audiences and driving meaningful interactions in an increasingly complex media environment.

UNDERSTANDING THE EVOLVING SOCIAL MEDIA LANDSCAPE

Social media's evolution intertwines technology, culture, and behaviour, reshaping communication, information consumption, and societal interaction through innovations and accessibility (Bik & Goldstein, 2013; Joshi et al., 2023). For example, Clubhouse is used for audio-based discussions, and TikTok is used for short films. The evolving social media landscape reflects shifts in socioeconomic and cultural trends. Platforms serve as mirrors of public discourse and, at times, fuel them, thereby stimulating social movements and cultural phenomena. Illustratively, social media platforms facilitated the spread of activism and transformative discourse using #MeToo and other similar movements that gained momentum through these channels. The influence of human behaviour on the dynamics of social media is crucial. Individuals are driven to engage with platforms through diverse means due to their aspirations for social connection, validation, and personal expression. Behavioural phenomena, including the inclination towards seeking approbation via likes and shares and FOMO (fear of missing out), have significantly impacted individuals' self-perception and perception of others in the digital realm. Regrettably, this transformation frequently poses challenges such as online harassment and self-comparison (Hsu et al., 2015; Joshi et al., 2023).

Social media-influenced business environments are undergoing profound transformations. Brands and influencers utilize these channels to expand their reach to a broader audience and intensify user engagement. The advent of targeted advertising and influencer marketing has brought about a significant transformation in social media, transforming it into a formidable marketplace where the boundaries between personal content and business promotion are becoming less distinct. To fully grasp the evolving landscape of social media, it is imperative to remain vigilant regarding its ramifications on individuals and society. Regulation and scrutiny are necessary to address privacy concerns, misinformation, and algorithmic biases (Goanta & Ranchordas, 2019). As social media develops, users must diligently navigate the delicate equilibrium between technological advancement and ethical standards. These platforms must facilitate a constructive revolution instead of sowing discord and damage. To comprehensively understand the dynamic social media landscape, employing a holistic approach that considers technological progress, cultural patterns, human behaviour, and ethical ramifications is imperative. By acknowledging the complex intricacies of social media, we can effectively utilize its capabilities to foster meaningful connections, magnify diverse viewpoints, and responsibly navigate the challenges that emerge from its ongoing evolution.

EMERGENCE OF NEW PLATFORMS

New social media platforms arise due to technology, changing preferences, and innovation, altering how people connect and share information (Dwivedi et al., 2021; Joshi et al., 2023; Kapoor et al., 2017; Soares & Jóia, 2015). The emergence of these innovative platforms reflects the evolving preferences and behaviour of users, who are in search of experiences that are more personalized, interactive, and captivating.

Due to users increasingly seeking platforms that align with their specific interests, values, and modes of communication, the social media environment is becoming increasingly fragmented. There exists a close relationship between technological progress and the emergence of social media platforms. Technological advancements in mobile devices, artificial intelligence (AI), and augmented reality (AR) have enabled the development of innovative approaches to content creation, distribution, and interaction. As an illustration, Snapchat's implementation of augmented reality (AR) lenses and filters transformed photographs into engaging and interactive experiences (Du et al., 2022; Ryan et al., 2017). An additional noteworthy advancement pertains to the growing convergence of social media platforms with other digital ecosystems. E-commerce incorporation on prominent social media platforms (e.g., Instagram and Facebook) has shifted significantly, transforming them into influential marketplaces that enable seamless purchasing experiences and generate direct revenue for content creators and businesses (Attar et al., 2022).

Furthermore, the emergence of innovative platforms gives rise to substantial apprehensions regarding privacy, content regulation, and digital welfare. Stakeholders and regulators are conducting a thorough analysis of the societal impact of social media, advocating for platforms to be managed transparently and responsibly (Larasati et al., 2022; Soares & Jóia, 2015). The emergence of novel social media platforms in a rapidly evolving digital landscape indicates ongoing innovation and shifting consumer demands. While these platforms offer unique opportunities for individuals to connect, express themselves, and foster innovation, they also present challenges that require careful consideration and ethical inquiry. Changes in technology will inevitably impact the social media environment, thereby shaping the trajectory of digital engagement and communication in the coming years.

SHIFTING USER DEMOGRAPHICS AND BEHAVIORS

User patterns and demographics shape content trends and platform characteristics, influencing digital culture and brand engagement strategies. Furthermore, this practice has enhanced the attractiveness of mobile-first platforms that prioritize visual content and immediate user engagement, such as Instagram and TikTok (Brandt et al., 2020; Larasati et al., 2022). The rise in popularity of social media has led to an increased consciousness among consumers regarding privacy and data safeguarding. In response to this shift in user behaviour, platforms have implemented measures to enhance privacy configurations, enforce stricter data policies, and increase transparency regarding data utilization. Users, especially younger demographics, are growing aware of the recipients and the nature of the information they divulge on the Internet. The visibility of materials and the level of user confidence in online platforms are being impacted by this. No longer do a handful of significant networks monopolizes social media. There is a growing trend among individuals to prefer small groups and specialized platforms that appeal to their distinct identities and areas of interest (Cremer et al., 2022). The fragmentation described above can be attributed to the increasing desire for personalized experiences and meaningful connections within communities that share common interests. This has given rise to various platforms, including the professional networking site LinkedIn, the discussion forum Reddit, and the gaming platform Twitch. The increasing prevalence of transient content on social media platforms like Snapchat and Instagram Stories underscores the transformation in user conduct toward impromptu and authentic dissemination. Users desire immediate and interactive engagement and value current and unaltered content. As a result, services such as live broadcasts and disappearing messages have become increasingly popular. There is a growing trend among users to utilize social media platforms as a means of activism, raising awareness, and advocating for social issues. This conduct signifies an inclination towards substantial engagement that transcends interpersonal relationships (Villaespesa & Wowkowych, 2020). Companies and influencers consequently align themselves with societal causes and beliefs to establish an authentic rapport with their audiences. Social media users are adopting meditative practices as a reaction to concerns regarding mental health and digital addiction. This entails establishing screen time limits, refraining from viewing detrimental content, and proactively identifying platforms that encourage constructive engagements. The transition has impacted the design of platforms, resulting in the integration of functionalities such as content control settings and time management tools intended to enhance digital well-being. Dynamic shifts in user demographics and behaviours drive innovation and transformation within social media. By recognizing and adapting to these changes, platforms and organizations can improve their capacity to interact with their intended audiences, foster genuine dialogue, and effectively influence the perpetually evolving digital culture.

IMPACT OF ALGORITHMIC CHANGES AND CONTENT TRENDS

Algorithmic changes on social media platforms influence user interactions, content strategies, and business marketing approaches, requiring adaptation for engagement. Algorithms enhance the prominence of viral trends and popular topics by expanding their reach and visibility. This may inspire content providers to capitalize on prevailing trends to augment their audience's engagement and outreach. Rapidly shifting content trends on social media are determined by societal shifts, user preferences, and the platforms' capabilities. Social media platforms such as TikTok, Instagram, and Pinterest emphasize visual narratives through graphics, videos, and photographs (Li et al., 2022).

The proliferation of short-form videos has significantly contributed to the growth and progress of platforms like TikTok and Instagram Reels. Users highly value the authenticity and transparency of the material. There is an increasing trend among companies and influencers to reveal unannounced experiences, user-generated content, and behind-the-scenes insights to cultivate trust and establish a rapport with their audience. Forms of interactive content, including surveys, polls, and augmented reality filters, increase user engagement and participation (Heiss et al., 2024).

Platforms give precedence to content that fosters substantive engagements and motivates active involvement from the community. Individuals prefer educational and informational material that improves their overall well-being. The popularity of instructional videos, tutorials, and do-it-yourself guides suggests a need for applicable and practical content (Barry et al., 2024). Content creators adapt to algorithmic changes by experimenting with formats, schedules, and interaction methods, prioritizing engagement and cross-promotion (Lops et al., 2019). Consistently participating in discussions, fostering substantial exchanges of ideas, and conscientiously incorporating audience feedback are essential for sustaining long-lasting success. Content trends and algorithmic modifications impact businesses and marketing, propelling digital marketing strategies. Organizations employ algorithms to target specific audience segments strategically, considering their demographics, interests, and behaviours. It increases the frequency with which users perform the intended actions and improves the relevance of advertisements. Influencer marketing can establish a rapport with contemporary content trends by leveraging producers' credibility and extensive viewership. Brands form strategic alliances with influencers to enter specific communities and increase brand awareness. Organizations improve their content strategies by applying platform analytics and data-driven insights (Ziakis & Vlachopoulou, 2023). It involves implementing A/B testing, content scheduling, and performance monitoring to maximize return on investment (ROI). The dynamics of social media are profoundly impacted by algorithmic adjustments and changes in content patterns, shaping how users obtain information, artists engage with their audiences, and businesses implement digital marketing strategies. Staying informed about these modifications and adapting one's approach accordingly is imperative for successfully navigating the competitive landscape of social media.

FRAGMENTATION AND ITS IMPLICATIONS FOR DIGITAL MARKETING

Digital fragmentation encompasses diverse platforms and channels, requiring marketers to tailor content to specific audience segments and preferences (Cioppi et al., 2023). It facilitates enhanced precision in targeting and personalized communication. Marketers must adapt their content's formats, tones, and styles to ensure successful engagement across multiple platforms and demographics. The success of content demonstrating strong performance on one platform may not consistently translate to another due to user routines and preferences variations. To each platform's unique audience and objective, marketers ought to deliver contextually suitable content that utilizes platform-specific attributes and current trends. Due to fragmentation, resources must be allocated with care across numerous platforms and channels. Marketers should prioritize platforms with the greatest return on investment (ROI), considering audience engagement, conversion rates, and company objectives (Koob, 2021). Budgetary and resource allocation must be executed efficiently to maintain a consistent presence on pertinent platforms and optimize performance metrics. Consistency across multiple platforms is essential in establishing brand recognition and trust. To establish a strong connection with audiences across multiple channels, marketers must develop a cohesive and consistent message and visual aesthetic that also adapts to the unique attributes of each platform (Ritter, 2020). Organizations can guarantee users a unified brand experience across various touchpoints by employing cross-platform marketing strategies, including collaborative narratives and integrated campaigns. Fragmentation results from using multiple sources for performance measurements and audience insights, complicating data collection and analysis. It is recommended that marketers employ analytics platforms and data integration tools in order to aggregate data from diverse sources and derive actionable insights. The effective utilization of data is critical in optimizing marketing campaigns, ascertaining cross-channel attribution, and enhancing targeting techniques through analyzing comprehensive audience profiles. Fragmentation necessitates the capacity to modify digital marketing strategies rapidly and effectively. Marketers are required to be able to adjust and react swiftly to market dynamics due to the swift progressions in platform prominence, emerging trends, and technological advancements (Cosentino, 2022). Marketers can surmount fragmentation challenges and capitalize on novel prospects through the consistent application of experimentation, analysis of industry developments, and adaptability in executing strategies.

DIVERSIFICATION OF AUDIENCE SEGMENTS

Approaches to mitigating fragmentation emphasize the process of audience segmentation and the construction of comprehensive profiles to discern distinct inclinations and behaviours across various media platforms. Customize content and messaging to captivate specific audience segments by capitalizing on platform-specific characteristics and contemporary trends. By analyzing audience demographics, engagement metrics, and corporate objectives, one can determine the most important platforms to prioritize. Enhance the efficacy of content across various platforms by considering factors such as the specific format, timing, and user interaction patterns (Deane et al., 2023). Maintaining a consistent representation of the brand across all points of contact is crucial for increasing brand recognition and fostering client trust. Cohesive strategies should be implemented to engage diverse media platforms through integrated narrative and messaging techniques. Invest in analytics systems and data integration tools to aggregate and evaluate performance indicators from multiple channels to enhance targeting, attribution, and resource allocation and implement data-driven analysis. It is imperative to maintain a comprehensive understanding of the most recent advancements in your industry, such as platform modifications and the introduction of novel technologies (Ren et al., 2023; Webster & Ksiazek, 2012). This will empower you to modify your digital marketing strategies efficiently. Encourage the development of a culture that values experimentation and ongoing progress to leverage emergent opportunities and address challenges arising from fragmentation effectively. The digital domain's fragmentation gives marketers various challenges and prospects. Effectively managing fragmentation and carrying out influential digital marketing campaigns across multiple platforms and channels can be accomplished by applying audience-centric approaches, platform-specific optimization, brand consistency, data integration, and agility.

CHALLENGES IN TARGETING AND ENGAGEMENT

Digital marketing faces challenges in targeting and engagement due to evolving consumer behaviours and data privacy regulations. Adaptation is necessary (Ullah et al., 2022). Marketers must develop inventive approaches to circumvent ad blockers and deliver effective, seamless content that engages the audience. Attribution challenges manifest as a result of complex client journeys incorporating numerous touchpoints and technologies—precisely quantifying campaign performance and attributing conversions to specific marketing endeavours present difficulties for marketers. The saturation of content and the decline in engagement rates are consequences of the abundance of content competing for audience attention. In marketing, creating compelling and unique content that effectively differentiates itself from the sea of information and establishes a profound connection with the target audiences is an absolute necessity (Sabherwal et al., 2019). The evolving trends in consumer behaviour, including diminished attention spans and a growing preference for interactive content, pose challenges for traditional approaches to consumer engagement. Marketers should adopt agile methodologies and investigate innovative engagement strategies to adapt to changing consumer behaviours. Algorithmic modifications implemented on social media platforms directly impact the prominence and dissemination of content, thereby influencing engagement metrics. Marketers must adapt their content strategies to increase engagement and organic reach in response to algorithmic modifications. To maintain consistent engagement across multiple channels and platforms, employing a cohesive message and customizing interactions is imperative (Salminen et al., 2023). Marketers face challenges coordinating cross-channel campaigns to deliver consistent brand experiences and foster long-lasting connections with viewers. To surmount challenges, one may utilize data analytics to understand the target audience's behaviours, preferences, and demographics. Leverage machine learning and predictive analytics techniques to optimize audience targeting and tailor engagement strategies to individual preferences (Diehl et al., 2022). Develop content that is relevant to distinct target demographics and suitable for a variety of channels. Engage in examining interactive content formats, including polls, surveys, and live videos, to increase participation and encourage two-way communication. Incorporate an omnichannel marketing strategy into your operations to ensure that all points of contact deliver consistent messages and insights. Leverage marketing automation technologies to orchestrate customized experiences and support potential customers throughout every stage of the customer lifecycle. Constantly monitor the campaign's advancement and modify strategies in response to accurate and expeditious observations. Incorporate agile methodologies to facilitate rapid iteration, enable empirical exploration of innovative ideas, and improve engagement strategies by utilizing insights derived from data analysis (Appel et al., 2019). Promote brand loyalty and community engagement through immersive brand interactions, partnerships with influential individuals, and user participation in content creation. Emphasize fostering connections instead of solely focusing on transactional interactions to cultivate brand loyalty and advocacy. To address the complexities associated with targeting and engagement, it is critical to employ a strategic amalgamation of relationship-oriented marketing tactics, omnichannel methodologies, personalized content initiatives, and agile optimization (Messaoudi & Loukili, 2024). To adequately confront these obstacles and adjust to changing consumer patterns, marketers may employ novel strategies to improve the accuracy of audience segmentation, stimulate greater user participation, and facilitate substantial engagements that yield quantifiable business advantages.

STRATEGIES FOR REACHING NICHE AUDIENCES

It is essential for businesses seeking to engage with specific, highly focused market segments to target niche audiences. Narrow audiences, while relatively lesser in scale when compared to more general demographics, generally comprise engaged and valuable communities with specific interests and needs (Dalgic & Leeuw, 2014; Saqib, 2020). Tailor strategic approaches to unique audience characteristics and preferences through comprehensive research, persona development, targeted content creation, and influencer collaboration (Joshi et al., 2023; Widaman et al., 2013). Create or participate in online forums, organizations, or communities devoted to particular interests to foster community engagement. Encourage user-generated content, facilitate dialogues, and offer channels for select groups to share information and network.

Tailor products and services to the preferences and requirements of the target audience. By delivering outstanding value and tailored experiences, the brand can position itself as a frontrunner in the market. Audience segmentation and data analytics can be utilized to enhance targeting and messaging. Construct a system that provides information per user preferences and behaviour to enhance pertinence and input. Preserve integrity and transparency in brand communications directed at specialized audiences. Establish trust by demonstrating expertise, disclosing accomplishments, and exhibiting an authentic comprehension of the target market. Use engagement, conversion, and customer lifetime value metrics to evaluate the efficacy of a campaign. Effectively reach the intended audience by refining targeting criteria, content strategies, and campaign iterations in light of the new information.

CONVERGENCE IN CONTENT CREATION AND DISTRIBUTION

Understanding convergence is crucial for content creators, marketers, and organizations navigating the interconnected digital landscape. Utilizing the distinctive functionalities of various platforms such as websites, social media, video streaming services, podcasts, and mobile applications, content creators and publishers customize their material to augment engagement and expand their target audience (Joshi et al., 2023; Martinez-Caro et al., 2018). By integrating text, voice, video, and graphics, this convergence enhances the allure of the content, facilitates audience engagement, and improves the narrative, ultimately leading to greater brand participation. By repurposing content, such as transforming articles into videos, podcasts into blog entries, or infographics into social media excerpts, the value and longevity of the content are increased across multiple platforms and among consumers. Integrated with marketing communications, personalized content concepts, targeted communication, and adaptable distribution strategies increase user engagement and conversion rates. Technology advancements facilitate the seamless dissemination of content across various platforms and devices (Safeer et al., 2021).

Conversely, convergence integrates user-generated content (UGC) derived from contests, testimonials, and co-creation initiatives, which aids organizations in establishing authentic connections with their target audience. By prioritizing viewer interaction via social media, live broadcasting, and interactive content, convergence leverages real-time feedback to personalize content, foster strong relationships, and cultivate brand loyalty. Convergence possesses profound and far-reaching consequences. Convergence enhances engagement and reaches by enabling content to reach a wider audience across multiple touchpoints and platforms (Shetu, 2023).

Convergence optimizes resource utilization by repurposing content, ensuring brand coherence and channel competitiveness. Data-driven analytics inform adjustments, enhancing customer engagement and loyalty and fostering favourable outcomes in the digital marketplace. Integrating social media with traditional marketing optimizes outreach by expanding audiences and enhancing engagement across multiple touchpoints (Joshi et al., 2023; Kumar et al., 2016). Social media enhances consumer engagement and communication, complementing conventional marketing methods, fostering trust, and providing valuable data for refining strategies. Al-Hooti et al. (2024) affirm that data-driven strategies enhance campaign efficacy, integrating social media with traditional channels for cohesive cross-promotion.

Organizations integrate social media's reach and interactivity with traditional channels to expand business, fortify relationships, and boost brand recognition (Kumar et al., 2016). Organizations enhance marketing efforts by integrating user-generated content (UGC) and partnering with influencers, fostering brand credibility and genuine audience engagement (Jain, 2024). UGC promotes authenticity, while influencer collaborations establish connections with targeted audiences, expanding brand reach and reputation through relatable content creation and promotion (Chen et al., 2024). Integrating user-generated content with influencer collaborations yields a dynamic and captivating marketing approach. By amplifying authentic user-generated content (UGC), influencers can expand their reach and bolster the source's credibility.

Similarly, influencers can inspire and encourage their followers to participate in user-generated content (UGC) endeavours, fostering a sense of community and shared experiences around the brand. Integrating influencer collaborations with user-generated content can significantly enhance brand exposure, interaction, and overall marketing efficacy (Zhang & Choi, 2022). By capitalizing on trusted individuals' influence and user-generated content's potency, businesses can successfully engage their target audiences by forming partnerships with influencers. By adopting these tactics, organizations can strengthen their customer relationships, cultivate brand allegiance, and effectively achieve their marketing objectives in the fiercely competitive digital landscape of the present day.

MULTI-CHANNEL CAMPAIGN APPROACHES

Multi-channel campaigns integrate various platforms for effective audience engagement, ensuring consistent messaging and tailored content for enhanced interaction (Brown & Dant, 2013; Jha & Verma, 2023). Understanding the customer journey informs timely messaging and optimization efforts, facilitating personalized campaigns across diverse audiences (Pantouvakis & Gerou, 2022; Smith, 2017). Adapting strategies to societal shifts fosters understanding and unity while mitigating crises, empowering brand supporters and promoting inclusivity (Gómez-Rico et al., 2022). It is crucial to comprehensively understand various perspectives, respect different opinions, and avoid taking strong political positions that could isolate specific customer segments. Brands can prioritize fostering understanding, promoting unity, and appealing to shared values beyond political or cultural differences. With a thoughtful and considerate approach, brands can effectively navigate these differences and cultivate strong connections with various consumers. Shin (2024) discussed the relationship between misinformation and algorithmic bias. Ensuring the integrity and reliability of information dissemination is crucial in today's digital age, where addressing misinformation and algorithmic biases is paramount. In today's digital age, the rapid dissemination of information through online platforms and social media has become a double-edged sword. While it allows for easy access to a wealth of knowledge, it also opens the floodgates for the rapid spread of misinformation. This, in turn, can cause widespread confusion and erode trust in the information we consume. Ensuring the accuracy of the information and empowering users to differentiate between reliable sources and false information is crucial. In addition, biases in algorithms used by online platforms can perpetuate discrimination and inequality by favouring specific perspectives while marginalizing others. Transparency and accountability in algorithm design and implementation are crucial for addressing these biases. By proactively tackling misinformation and addressing algorithmic biases, we can ensure that the digital space upholds the values of truthfulness, fairness, and inclusivity, thereby promoting a more knowledgeable and fair society.

BUILDING TRUST AND AUTHENTICITY IN BRAND MESSAGING

Building trust and authenticity in brand messaging through consistent values, transparent communication, and fulfilling commitments fosters enduring consumer loyalty (Ilicic & Webster, 2014). Gaining a comprehensive comprehension of one's audience is crucial in the ever-evolving realm of social media marketing (Priya & Kesavraj, 2022). Practical audience analysis involves utilizing various social media analytics tools at one's disposal. These tools provide abundant data points, ranging from third-party analytics platforms to native platform insights, comprising demographic data, engagement metrics, and content performance (Bashar et al., 2024; Batrinca & Treleaven, 2014). These tools can provide marketers with invaluable information regarding their target audience, content engagement patterns, and the most effective channels for eliciting responses.

In addition to superficial metrics, data analytics empowers marketers to gain a more profound understanding of audience sentiment and preferences. By analyzing social media conversations, sentiment analysis tools can discern patterns, themes, and emotional reactions linked to a particular brand or marketing initiative (Singh et al., 2024). Through a comprehensive comprehension of audience sentiment, marketers can customize their communications to establish a connection with distinct audience segments while minimizing potential public relations hazards.

Data-driven decisions drive social media marketing success, optimizing campaigns through performance analysis, audience insights, and A (control) /B(variant) testing (Szukits & Móricz, 2023). Gamification and interactive storytelling captivate audiences, converting spectators into engaged participants through competition, reward, and challenge elements (Daineko et al., 2023). Consumers have elevated expectations beyond mere products and services during the digital era. They now demand personally engaging, fully immersive brand experiences. Interactive content allows brands to generate impactful, all-encompassing experiences that surpass the boundaries of conventional advertising. By utilizing interactive microsites, virtual reality (AR), or augmented reality (VR), brands can transport their target audience to unexplored realms, elicit intense emotions, and establish more profound connections (Zeng et al., 2023). The fundamental tenet of compelling interactive content experiences is user participation and community engagement. Through the implementation of audience co-creation initiatives, story sharing, and community interaction, brands can cultivate a sense of ownership and affiliation that surpasses the boundaries of conventional marketing strategies. User-generated content enhances brand visibility and credibility by utilizing brand advocates' combined ingenuity and impact and functioning as genuine social validation (Simon, 2016).

DISCUSSION

Social media marketing is an ever-changing environment, influenced by technological advancements, consumer behaviour modifications, and platform algorithm adjustments. A fundamental motif that surfaced from our investigation is the intricacy of the digital environment. Due to the widespread adoption of social media platforms, the division of audiences, and the divisive atmosphere of online discussions, marketers encounter many obstacles when attempting to connect with and captivate their intended audience effectively. Nevertheless, these obstacles present prospects for ingenuity and originality. By capitalizing on the opportunities presented by data analytics, embracing genuineness, and maintaining flexibility and adaptability, marketers can effectively manoeuvre through the intricacies of the digital environment and discover fresh paths to expansion and interaction.

Data analytics' crucial function in informing and optimizing social media marketing strategies is a recurring theme in our discourse. Through social media analytics tools, marketers can acquire significant knowledge regarding their target audience's behaviours, preferences, and trends. This empowers them to formulate well-informed decisions and execute campaigns that have a profound effect. Furthermore, data analytics empowers marketers to assess the efficacy of their endeavours, pinpoint areas that require enhancement, and refine their approaches in real-time, thus optimizing their return on investment and fostering ongoing progress.

Using interactive content experiences has become potent in captivating audiences and cultivating more profound connections. Through gamification, interactive narrative, and user-generated content, marketers can engross audiences, incite dialogues, and foster dynamic virtual communities. Furthermore, interactive content allows brands to distinguish themselves in a saturated market by providing consumers with immersive and memorable experiences that deeply connect with them individually.

Anticipating the future, it is evident that social media marketing will persistently undergo swift transformations, propelled by the advent of novel technologies, changing consumer inclinations, and evolving platform dynamics. Marketers must remain informed about these developments and trends, preempting changes in platform algorithms and consumer inclinations and adjusting their approaches correspondingly. To thrive in a progressively dynamic and competitive environment, marketers can establish a favourable position by adopting and prioritizing authenticity, transparency, and community engagement while embracing emergent technologies such as artificial intelligence, virtual reality, and blockchain.

For brands aiming to interact with their target demographic in the digital era, social media marketing grants both obstacles and prospects. Through the utilization of data analytics, the promotion of genuineness, the cultivation of community involvement, and the maintenance of flexibility and adaptability, marketers can effectively manoeuvre through the intricacies of the digital terrain, stimulate significant interaction, and accomplish their organizational goals amidst a perpetually shifting milieu.

FINDINGS

Key findings in the realm of social media marketing:

1. **Convergence of Social Media and Digital Marketing**: Social media remains a crucial aspect of digital marketing strategies, offering opportunities for businesses to engage diverse consumers and cultivate significant connections.
2. **Navigating Complexity**: Marketers must confront the complexities of fragmentation, convergence, and polarization in the media landscape to utilize social media as a marketing tool effectively.
3. **Adaptability and Innovation**: Success in social media marketing requires adaptability to changing consumer behaviours, platform dynamics, and emergent trends. Marketers must embrace innovation and adjust strategies accordingly.
4. **Audience-Focused Strategy**: An effective social media marketing campaign necessitates a methodical, audience-focused, and data-driven approach. Emphasizing authenticity, transparency, and community involvement can foster trust and credibility among the target audience.
5. **Continuous Vigilance**: Marketers must maintain constant vigilance, remain aware of emergent technologies and shifting market dynamics, and actively pursue opportunities to innovate and refine their strategies.
6. **Opportunities and Challenges**: Social media marketing presents opportunities and challenges for brands seeking to interact with their target audience. By leveraging data analytics, authenticity, and innovation, marketers can navigate the intricacies of the digital environment and accomplish organizational goals.

SOLUTION AND RECOMMENDATION

Solutions

- Leverage data analytics to gain deeper insights into audience trends, preferences, and behaviours.
- Utilize social media analytics tools to monitor key performance indicators and refine campaign strategies based on data-driven insights.
- Prioritize authenticity and transparency in social media marketing initiatives to establish credibility and trust with the audience.
- Develop relevant, high-quality content tailored to audience preferences and interests, experimenting with various formats to keep them engaged.
- Stay flexible and adaptable in social media marketing strategy, closely monitoring industry trends and consumer behaviours to adjust tactics accordingly.
- Foster a dedicated community of brand advocates through active involvement, collaboration, and engagement on social media platforms.
- Invest in ongoing training and professional development to ensure continuous learning and stay abreast of emerging technologies and best practices.

Recommendations

- Emphasize authenticity and openness in all social media interactions to build trust and credibility with the audience.
- Adapt content to audience preferences and interests, experimenting with different formats like video and interactive experiences.
- Stay updated on industry trends and platform algorithms to adjust strategies and tactics proactively.
- Encourage user-generated content and timely responses to audience interactions to foster a sense of community and brand loyalty.
- Invest in continuous training and development so the team can advance in social media marketing innovation.

By implementing these solutions and recommendations, marketers can effectively navigate the dynamic and competitive landscape of social media marketing and achieve their organizational goals.

FUTURE TRENDS AND INNOVATIONS IN SOCIAL MEDIA MARKETING

In the dynamic realm of social media, marketers must remain at the forefront of emergent trends and innovations to sustain their relevance and achieve success amidst a perpetually shifting environment.

An assortment of nascent technologies, including blockchain technology, virtual reality (VR), and artificial intelligence (AI), are positioned to fundamentally transform how brands interact with their target audiences on social media. Virtual reality (VR) experiences transport users to immersive brand worlds, while blockchain technology enables secure and transparent transactions. AI-powered chatbots provide personalized customer service. By capitalizing on these technologies, progressive marketers can gain access to fresh prospects for ingenuity, effectiveness, and novelty in their endeavors related to social media marketing.

It is imperative to comprehend the dynamic nature of consumer behaviours and platform preferences to maintain a competitive edge in social media marketing. In light of evolving platforms and the emergence of novel ones, marketers are compelled to modify their strategies to align with shifting consumer preferences and expectations. It is critical to remain informed about changes in consumer behaviour, such as the increasing significance of social commerce on platforms like Instagram and Facebook and the rise of short-form video content on platforms like TikTok, to maintain relevance and foster engagement in a progressively competitive environment.

Amidst the perpetual flux of circumstances, agility and adaptability are pivotal qualities determining triumph in social media marketing. To remain competitive, marketers must adopt an attitude of perpetual learning and experimentation, regularly testing new strategies, tactics, and technologies. By cultivating an environment that promotes collaboration and innovation, brands can discern nascent prospects, alleviate potential hazards, and adapt rapidly to changing market conditions. Moreover, in an ever-evolving digital landscape, brands can ensure that their social media marketing efforts remain pertinent, genuine, and influential by maintaining audience engagement and soliciting feedback. To ensure their success in the ever-changing and competitive social media environment, brands must adopt emergent technologies, proactively anticipate changes in consumer behaviour, and foster a culture that values flexibility and responsiveness.

CONCLUSION

As the global media landscape evolves, convergence of social media and digital marketing remains pivotal for engaging diverse consumers. Marketers must navigate the complexities of fragmentation, convergence, and polarization to effectively utilize social media to build connections, enhance brand recognition, and foster community engagement. To succeed, they must employ methodical, audience-focused, and data-driven strategies while prioritizing authenticity, transparency, and community involvement to build trust and brand loyalty. Remaining flexible and responsive to changing consumer behaviours and market dynamics is essential. Marketers should anticipate emerging trends, embrace innovations, and refine strategies accordingly. Success in this ever-changing digital environment hinges on vigilance, adaptability, and innovation. By leveraging data analytics, authenticity, and innovation, brands can navigate the challenges and opportunities of social media marketing, fostering meaningful user engagement and achieving organizational goals in a digitally-driven era.

REFERENCES

Al-Hooti, Z., Alawi, A. A., Ahmed, Z., & Al-Busaidi, T. (2024). Impact of social media marketing, innovation, and effective management on SMEs performance: A conceptual study. In *Communications in computer and information science* (pp. 222–232). Springer. 10.1007/978-3-031-50518-8_17

Appel, G., Grewal, L., Hadi, R., & Stephen, A. T. (2019). The future of social media in marketing. *Journal of the Academy of Marketing Science*, 48(1), 79–95. 10.1007/s11747-019-00695-132431463

Attar, R. W., Almusharraf, A., Alfawaz, A., & Hajli, N. (2022). New trends in e-commerce research: Linking social commerce and sharing commerce: A systematic literature review. *Sustainability (Basel)*, 14(23), 16024. 10.3390/su142316024

Bandura, A. (2012). Social cognitive theory. In Van Lange, P. A. M., Kruglanski, A. W., & Higgins, E. T. (Eds.), *Handbook of theories of social psychology* (pp. 349–373). Sage Publications. 10.4135/9781446249215.n18

Barry, C. T., Berbano, M., Anderson, A., & Levy, S. (2024). Psychology TOK: Use of TikTok, mood, and self-perception in a sample of college students. *Journal of Technology in Behavioral Science*. 10.1007/s41347-024-00390-1

Bashar, A., Wasiq, M., Nyagadza, B., & Maziriri, E. T. (2024). Emerging trends in social media marketing: A retrospective review using data mining and bibliometric analysis. *Future Business Journal*, 10(1), 23. 10.1186/s43093-024-00308-6

Batrinca, B., & Treleaven, P. (2014). Social media analytics: A survey of techniques, tools and platforms. *AI & Society*, 30(1), 89–116. 10.1007/s00146-014-0549-4

Bik, H., & Goldstein, M. (2013). An introduction to social media for scientists. *PLoS Biology*, 11(4), e1001535. 10.1371/journal.pbio.100153523630451

Brandt, J., Buckingham, K., Buntain, C., Anderson, W., Ray, S., Pool, J., & Ferrari, N. (2020). Identifying social media user demographics and topic diversity with computational social science: A case study of a major international policy forum. *Journal of Computational Social Science*, 3(1), 167–188. 10.1007/s42001-019-00061-9

Brown, J. R., & Dant, R. P. (2013). The role of e-commerce in multi-channel marketing strategy. In *Progress in IS* (pp. 467–487). 10.1007/978-3-642-39747-9_20

Chaney, D. (1972). The Theory of 'Uses and Gratifications'. In: *Processes of Mass Communication. New Perspectives in Sociology*. Palgrave, London. 10.1007/978-1-349-00684-7_3

Chen, J., Zhang, Y., Han, C., Liu, L., Liao, M., & Fang, J. (2024). A comprehensive overview of micro-influencer marketing: Decoding the current landscape, impacts, and trends. *Behavioral Sciences (Basel, Switzerland)*, 14(3), 243. 10.3390/bs1403024338540546

Cioppi, M., Curina, I., Francioni, B., & Savelli, E. (2023). Digital transformation and marketing: A systematic and thematic literature review. *Italian Journal of Marketing*, 2023(2), 207–288. 10.1007/s43039-023-00067-2

Cosentino, C. (2022). Data fragmentation and data linking: A threat and an opportunity. *Harvard Data Science Review*. 10.1162/99608f92.946ef791

Cremer, F., Sheehan, B., Fortmann, M., Kia, A. N., Mullins, M., Murphy, F., & Materne, S. (2022). Cyber risk and cybersecurity: A systematic review of data availability. *The Geneva Papers on Risk and Insurance. Issues and Practice*, 47(3), 698–736. 10.1057/s41288-022-00266-635194352

Daineko, L., Гончарова, H. B., Zaitseva, E., Гончарова, H., & Dyachkova, I. A. (2023). Gamification in education: A literature review. In *Lecture notes in networks and systems* (pp. 319–343). Springer. 10.1007/978-3-031-48020-1_25

Dalgic, T., & Leeuw, M. (2014). Niche marketing revisited: Theoretical and practical issues. In *Developments in marketing science:Proceedings of the Academy of Marketing Science* (pp. 137–145). Springer. 10.1007/978-3-319-13159-7_32

Deane, F., Woolmer, E., Cao, S., & Tranter, K. (2023). Trade in the digital age: Agreements to mitigate fragmentation. *Asian Journal of International Law*, 14(1), 154–179. 10.1017/S204425132300036X

Diehl, S., Koinig, I., & Scheiber, R. (2022). *Cross-media advertising in times of changing media environments and media consumption patterns*. Springer eBooks. 10.1007/978-3-030-86680-8_11

Du, Z., Liu, J., & Wang, T. (2022). Augmented reality marketing: A systematic literature review and an agenda for future inquiry. *Frontiers in Psychology*, 13, 925963. 10.3389/fpsyg.2022.92596335783783

Dwivedi, Y. K., Ismagilova, E., Rana, N. P., & Raman, R. (2021). Social media adoption, usage and impact in business-to-business (B2B) context: A state-of-the-art literature review. *Information Systems Frontiers*, 25(3), 971–993. 10.1007/s10796-021-10106-y

Eisend, M., & Tarrahi, F. (2021). Persuasion knowledge in the marketplace: A meta-analysis. *Journal of Consumer Psychology*, 32(1), 3–22. 10.1002/jcpy.1258

Gamper, M. (2022). Social Network Theories: An Overview. In Klärner, A., Gamper, M., Keim-Klärner, S., Moor, I., von der Lippe, H., & Vonneilich, N. (Eds.), *Social Networks and Health Inequalities*. Springer. 10.1007/978-3-030-97722-1_3

Goanta, C., & Ranchordas, S. (2019). The regulation of social media influencers: An introduction. *Social Science Research Network*. 10.2139/ssrn.3457197

Gómez-Rico, M., Collado, A. M., Vijande, M. L. S., Molina-Collado, M. V., & Imhoff, B. (2022). The role of novel instruments of brand communication and brand image in building consumers' brand preference and intention to visit wineries. *Current Psychology (New Brunswick, N.J.)*, 42(15), 12711–12727. 10.1007/s12144-021-02656-w35035183

Gupta, S., Jain, G., & Tiwari, A. A. (2021). Investigating the dynamics of polarization in online discourse during the COVID-19 pandemic. In *Lecture notes in computer science* (pp. 704–709). Springer. 10.1007/978-3-030-85447-8_58

Heiss, R., Bode, L., Adisuryo, Z. M., Brito, L., Cuadra, A., Gao, P., Han, Y., Hearst, M., Huang, K., Kinyua, A., Lin, T., Ma, Y., Manion, T. O., Roh, Y., Salazar, A., Yue, S., & Zhang, P. (2024). Debunking mental health misperceptions in short-form social media videos: An experimental test of scientific credibility cues. *Health Communication*, 1–13. 10.1080/10410236.2023.230120138389200

Hossain, M. A. (2019). Effects of uses and gratifications on social media use. *PSU Research Review*, 3(1), 16–28. 10.1108/PRR-07-2018-0023

Hsu, M., Tien, S., Lin, H., & Chang, C. (2015). Understanding the roles of cultural differences and socioeconomic status in social media continuance intention. *Information Technology & People*, 28(1), 224–241. 10.1108/ITP-01-2014-0007

Ilicic, J., & Webster, C. (2014). Investigating consumer–brand relational authenticity. *Journal of Brand Management*, 21(4), 342–363. 10.1057/bm.2014.11

Islam, G. (2014). Social Identity Theory. In Teo, T. (Ed.), *Encyclopedia of Critical Psychology*. Springer. 10.1007/978-1-4614-5583-7_289

Jain, S. (2024). An analysis of the influence of user generated content (UGC) on brand perception and consumer engagement in digital marketing strategies. *Social Science Research Network*. 10.2139/ssrn.4781464

Jha, A. K., & Verma, N. K. (2023). Social media platforms and user engagement: A multi-platform study on one-way firm sustainability communication. *Information Systems Frontiers*, 26(1), 177–194. 10.1007/s10796-023-10376-8

Joshi, Y., Lim, W. M., Jagani, K., & Kumar, S. (2023). Social media influencer marketing: Foundations, trends, and ways forward. *Electronic Commerce Research*. 10.1007/s10660-023-09719-z

Kapoor, K. K., Tamilmani, K., Rana, N. P., Patil, P. P., Dwivedi, Y. K., & Nerur, S. P. (2017). Advances in social media research: Past, present and future. *Information Systems Frontiers*, 20(3), 531–558. 10.1007/s10796-017-9810-y

Knell, M. (2021). The digital revolution and digitalized network society. *Review of Evolutionary Political Economy*, 2(1), 9–25. 10.1007/s43253-021-00037-4

Koob, C. (2021). Determinants of content marketing effectiveness: Conceptual framework and empirical findings from a managerial perspective. *PLoS One*, 16(4), e0249457. 10.1371/journal.pone.024945733793631

Kumar, V., Choi, J., & Greene, M. (2016). Synergistic effects of social media and traditional marketing on brand sales: Capturing the time-varying effects. *Journal of the Academy of Marketing Science*, 45(2), 268–288. 10.1007/s11747-016-0484-7

Larasati, Z. W., Yuda, T. K., & Syafa'at, A. R. (2022). The digital welfare state and the problem arising: An exploration and future research agenda. *The International Journal of Sociology and Social Policy*, 43(5/6), 537–549. 10.1108/IJSSP-05-2022-0122

Li, C. H., Chan, O. L. K., Chow, Y. T., Zhang, X., Tong, P. S., Li, S. P., Ng, H. Y., & Keung, K. L. (2022). Evaluating the effectiveness of digital content marketing under mixed reality training platform on the online purchase intention. *Frontiers in Psychology*. 10.3389/fpsyg.2022.881019

Liu, Y., & Gu, X. (2019). Media multitasking, attention, and comprehension: A deep investigation into fragmented reading. *Educational Technology Research and Development*, 68(1), 67–87. 10.1007/s11423-019-09667-2

Lops, P., Jannach, D., Musto, C., Bogers, T., & Koolen, M. (2019). Trends in content-based recommendation. *User Modeling and User-Adapted Interaction*, 29(2), 239–249. 10.1007/s11257-019-09231-w

Martinez-Caro, J., Aledo-Hernandez, A., Guillen-Perez, A., Sanchez-Iborra, R., & Cano, M. (2018). A comparative study of web content management systems. *Information (Basel)*, 9(2), 27. 10.3390/info9020027

Messaoudi, F., & Loukili, M. (2024). E-commerce personalized recommendations: A deep neural collaborative filtering approach. *SN Operations Research Forum, 5*(1). 10.1007/s43069-023-00286-5

Ostic, D., Qalati, S. A., Barbosa, B., Shah, S. M. M., Vela, E. G., Herzallah, A. M., & Liu, F. (2021). Effects of social media use on psychological well-being: A mediated model. *Frontiers in Psychology*, 12, 678766. 10.3389/fpsyg.2021.67876634234717

Priya, C. I., & Kesavraj, G. (2022). Social media—A key pathway to marketing analytics. In *Cognitive Science and Technology* (pp. 263–275). 10.1007/978-981-19-2350-0_26

Ren, P., Wang, Y., & Zhao, F. (2023). Re-understanding of data storytelling tools from a narrative perspective. *Visual Intelligence/Visual Intelligence, 1*(1). 10.1007/s44267-023-00011-0

Ritter, T. (2020). Reclaiming or rebranding marketing: Implications beyond digital. *AMS Review*, 10(3–4), 311–314. 10.1007/s13162-020-00178-5

Rogers, E. M., Singhal, A., & Quinlan, M. M. (2014). Diffusion of innovations. In *An integrated approach to communication theory and research* (pp. 432–448). Routledge.

Ryan, T., Allen, K., Gray, D. L. L., & McInerney, D. M. (2017). How social are social media? A review of online social behaviour and connectedness. *Journal of Relationships Research*, 8, e8. Advance online publication. 10.1017/jrr.2017.13

Sabherwal, R., Sabherwal, S., Havakhor, T., & Steelman, Z. R. (2019). How does strategic alignment affect firm performance? The roles of information technology investment and environmental uncertainty. *Management Information Systems Quarterly*, 43(2), 453–474. https://api.semanticscholar.org/CorpusID:167222033. 10.25300/MISQ/2019/13626

Safeer, A. A., He, Y., Lin, Y., Abrar, M., & Nawaz, Z. (2021). Impact of perceived brand authenticity on consumer behaviour: Evidence from generation Y an Asian perspective. *International Journal of Emerging Markets*, 18(3), 685–704. 10.1108/IJOEM-09-2020-1128

Salminen, J., Mustak, M., Sufyan, M., & Jansen, B. J. (2023). How can algorithms help in segmenting users and customers? A systematic review and research agenda for algorithmic customer segmentation. *Journal of Marketing Analytics*, 11(4), 677–692. 10.1057/s41270-023-00235-5

Saqib, N. (2020). Positioning – A literature review. *PSU Research Review*, 5(2), 141–169. 10.1108/PRR-06-2019-0016

Shetu, S. N. (2023). Do user-generated content and micro-celebrity posts encourage generation Z users to search online shopping behaviour on social networking sites—The moderating role of sponsored ads? *Future Business Journal*, 9(1), 100. 10.1186/s43093-023-00276-3

Shin, D. (2024). Misinformation and Algorithmic Bias. In Smith, M. R. (Ed.), *Artificial Misinformation* (pp. 15–31). Palgrave Macmillan. 10.1007/978-3-031-52569-8_2

Simon, J. P. (2016). User-generated content – Users, a community of users and firms: Toward new sources of co-innovation? *Info*, 18(6), 4–25. 10.1108/info-04-2016-0015

Singh, K. U., Kumar, A., Kumar, G., Choudhury, T., Singh, T., & Kotecha, K. (2024). Sentiment analysis in social media marketing: Leveraging natural language processing for customer insights. In *Lecture notes in networks and systems* (pp. 457–467). 10.1007/978-981-99-9489-2_40

Sîrbu, A., Pedreschi, D., Giannotti, F., & Kertész, J. (2019). Algorithmic bias amplifies opinion fragmentation and polarization: A bounded confidence model. *PLoS One*, 14(3), e0213246. 10.1371/journal.pone.021324630835742

Smith, R. A. (2017). *Audience segmentation techniques*. Oxford Research Encyclopedia of Communication. 10.1093/acrefore/9780190228613.013.321

Soares, C. D. M., & Jóia, L. A. (2015). The influence of social media on social movements: An exploratory conceptual model. In *Lecture notes in computer science* (pp. 27–38). Springer. 10.1007/978-3-319-22500-5_3

Szukits, Á., & Móricz, P. (2023). Towards data-driven decision making: The role of analytical culture and centralization efforts. *Review of Managerial Science*. 10.1007/s11846-023-00694-1

Tang, M. J., & Chan, E. T. (2020). Social media: Influences and impacts on culture. In *Advances in intelligent systems and computing* (pp. 491–501). 10.1007/978-3-030-52249-0_33

Ullah, I., Borelli, R., & Kanhere, S. S. (2022). Privacy in targeted advertising on mobile devices: A survey. *International Journal of Information Security*, 22(3), 647–678. 10.1007/s10207-022-00655-x36589145

Villaespesa, E., & Wowkowych, S. (2020). Ephemeral storytelling with social media: Snapchat and instagram stories at the Brooklyn Museum. *Social Media + Society*, 6(1), 205630511989877. 10.1177/2056305119898776

Webster, J. G., & Ksiazek, T. B. (2012). The dynamics of audience fragmentation: Public attention in an age of digital media. *Journal of Communication*, 62(1), 39–56. 10.1111/j.1460-2466.2011.01616.x

Widaman, K. F., Early, D. R., & Conger, R. D. (2013). *Special populations*. In Oxford University Press eBooks. 10.1093/oxfordhb/9780199934874.013.0004

Zeng, J., Xing, Y., & Jin, C. (2023). The impact of VR/AR-based consumers' brand experience on consumer–Brand relationships. *Sustainability (Basel)*, 15(9), 7278. 10.3390/su15097278

Zhang, G. (2023). The influence of social media marketing on consumers' behaviour. *Advances in Economics. Management and Political Sciences*, 20(1), 119–124. 10.54254/2754-1169/20/20230181

Zhang, X., & Choi, J. (2022). The importance of social influencer-generated contents for user cognition and emotional attachment: An information relevance perspective. *Sustainability (Basel)*, 14(11), 6676. 10.3390/su14116676

Ziakis, C., & Vlachopoulou, M. (2023). Artificial intelligence in digital marketing: Insights from a comprehensive review. *Information (Basel)*, 14(12), 664. 10.3390/info14120664

ADDITIONAL READING

Al-Obaidi, J. (2012). Social media and political changes in Al-Alam Al-Arabi. *Bridgewater Review, 31*(2), 25-28. https://vc.bridgew.edu/br_rev/vol31/iss2/10

Al-Obaidi, J. A. (2007). Satellite television in the Middle East: Evaluation of quality programming in the 1990s: Al-Jazeera, Dubai, LBC, MBC, Future and Egypt space channel. *International Journal of Instructional Media, 34*(4), 375+. link.gale.com/apps/doc/A273359014/AONE?u=anon~4948ba28&sid=googleScholar&xid=6645a9ec

Al-Obaidi, J. A. (2008). Hajj tabouz and media censorship in the Middle East. *Bridgewater Review, 27*(1), 8-11. https://vc.bridgew.edu/br_rev/vol27/iss1/6

KEY TERMS AND DEFINITIONS

Audience Engagement: The interaction, participation, and involvement of individuals with content, brands, or communities, reflecting the level of connection and interest between users and media.

Brand Visibility: The extent to which a brand is seen, recognized, and remembered by target audiences across various media channels, influencing brand awareness, perception, and recall.

Convergence: Integrating different media technologies, platforms, and content formats, blurring the boundaries between traditional and digital media and enabling seamless cross-platform experiences.

Digital Marketing: Strategies and tactics leveraging digital channels, such as websites, email, and social media, to promote products or services, engage audiences, and drive business objectives.

Fragmentation: The division of audiences, content, and channels into smaller, specialized segments or niches, resulting in diverse media consumption patterns and communication channels.

Global Media Landscape: The interconnected network of media platforms, channels, and audiences on a global scale, shaped by technological advancements, cultural dynamics, and geopolitical factors.

Social Media: Online platforms facilitate user-generated content, interactions, and networking, enabling individuals and businesses to share information, engage with audiences, and build communities.

Chapter 6
Global Media Changes and Digital Advertising:
Impact of Digital Advertising on Consumer Behavior

Kevser Zeynep Meral
http://orcid.org/0000-0002-2514-8744
İstanbul Bahçeşehir University, Turkey

ABSTRACT

This study aims to review digital advertising literature, to identify and define different aspects of 'digital advertising' role in consumers' behavior. Researchers investigated the role of digital advertising on consumers' behavior while online shopping, exposed to digital ads. Research showed that although new digital advertising legislation, rules, regulations, and self-regulations by voluntary initiatives came into force, it could not stop unethical practices in digital advertising. Mainly, due to controlling difficulties in digital world and advised policy makers and governmental bodies to develop new control techniques and applications of digital ads control along with supporting media literacy and family education about effects of digital ads. In conclusion, as the digital world is constantly changing, policy makers and governments must adopt to changes, and must revise legislation and using new controlling techniques without delay. Developing countries must also implement related protective rules of digital advertising and changes which are in force in developed countries.

INTRODUCTION

Digital advertising or display advertising subject itself is novel because the definition of 'digital advertising or display advertising" is defined by Marketing Accountability Standards Board in 2018 (MASB, 2018) as advertising or other marketing communications which are visually based via websites. It can have different formats like video, text, image, audio, movement, of which digital advertising is delivered to whom visit the website. If the website is the retail website, digital advertising purpose is to influence the customer for shopping stage. Online behavioral advertising and interest-based advertising is using data from a specific computer/device to find out internet user's interests/preferences via users' internet viewing behavior, to send ads to that computer/device based on the data from previous interest/

DOI: 10.4018/979-8-3693-3767-7.ch006

preferences (Interactive Advertising Bureau, 2011). Although Marketing Accountability Standards Board has used the term 'digital advertising' and 'display advertising' at the same time, 'digital advertising' term will be used throughout the text.

Internet users have reached 5,1 billion and in parallel to this increase, digital advertising and digital advertising revenue has also increased. Pandemic has speeded up digitalization and digital consumption via online shopping. Digital advertising revenue is 601,8 billion in 2023 with 9.5% percent increase. According to Internet Advertising Bureau (IAB) report digital advertising revenue has increased 35,4 percent to 189,3 billion dollars in 2021 from 139,8 billion dollars in 2020, with pandemic effect in digitalization, which was 8,09 billion dollars only in 2000 in US.

Digital marketing is growing because life has changed from offline to online. Internet users which were 2,3 billion in 2012 increased to 5,1 billion users in 2022, of whom 4,7 billion are at the same time use social media in July 2022 (Statista.com, 2022). Digital advertisement revenues increased accordingly. In parallel with increase in online, traditional advertising has been taken over by digital advertising. Total (digital and traditional) advertising media revenue which was 759 billion revenue and total digital advertising was 522,5 billion dollars in 2021. Digital advertising is expected to be 681 billion dollars in 2023 (Statista.com, 2023). It is expected to exceed one trillion dollars by 2026 (Guttmann, 2022).

There are different forecasts about amount of digital advertising revenue. Digital marketing expenditure is increasing because it is cheaper compared to TV ads however more affective via digital, mobile, and social media. Faria (2022) suggested that digital advertising total expenditure worldwide in 2021 was 455 billion dollars and expected to exceed 645 billion dollars within three years, stating that only Google's digital advertising revenue was 146 billion dollars in 2020. The maximum increase rate is expected to be in mobile internet advertising from approximately 288 billion dollars in 2021 to be increased to 412 billion dollars in 2024, and 69 percent of digital advertising will be affected via mobile within five years, by 2027. Consistently leading digital companies' revenues have increased as for only Meta platforms (Facebook, Instagram, WhatsApp, and Messenger) to nearly 118 billion dollars, Microsoft Corp to 11,5 billion dollars from global search advertising and TikTok to 38,6 billion dollars advertising revenue for the year 2021 (Weibo.com, 2022).

BACKGROUND

This review is about digital advertising and the role of digital advertising which has entered into our lives via internet which is an integral part of our daily internet life, in digitalization era which is accelerated by pandemic, digital advertising is in our pockets with our mobile internet accessed phones, while in social media, online games, online news, online tv, even while searching anything we are all exposed to digital ads at the same time.

This chapter covers role of digital advertising in consumers' behavior literature review, followed with digital advertisement rules, voluntary self-regulations about digital ads and unethical practice of digital advertisement. Literature review is followed with discussion, recommendation and finally conclusion.

Digital Advertising Effects on Consumer Behavior summary results in Table 1 followed with Rules, Regulations, and Voluntary Initiatives Self-Regulations in Digital Advertising (Table 2) and Unethical Practices in Digital Advertising (Table 3) and Recommendations of Institutions/Specialists (Table 4) can be found in Appendix.

METHODOLOGY AND PROCEDURES

Research method used in this study is narrative literature review. The main reason for literature review using as a research method is that the subject digital advertising (digital displaying) itself is novel. Digital advertising literature compared to other subjects of business is relatively few. Therefore, by conducting narrative literature review method specifically on 'digital advertising' topic and by searching and reviewing the previous research with the main key word 'digital advertising', this study aims to discuss the subject and find out gaps and suggest future research areas where more research is required. At the same time, aims to provide guidelines based on the review results.

LITERATURE REVIEW

Digital Advertising Effects on Consumer Behavior

Digital advertising is very important in consumer behavior and how consumers respond to digital ads is a major aspect of marketing literature. Literature results on how digital advertising affect consumer behavior have different aspects, interaction with customers have a positive impact on purchase intent of consumers. Tiago and Veríssimo (2014) found that relationship-based interactions with customers is a very important factor in digital marketing and demonstrated how they accomplished. Hwang and Zhang (2018) in their study with celebrities, showed that parasocial relationships influenced purchase intentions and eWOM positively. Murphy and Sashi (2018) found that face-to-face communication influenced social interaction, mutual feedback, and number of contacts, where digital communication has weaker effect on them. Bart et al. (2014) found that products with higher involvement increased purchased intention.

Too much exposure of digital ads effects may differ like can have a negative effect than positive, might decrease purchase intention. In other words, exposure choices are important, in their experimental study of Nettelhorst, Jeter, Brannon, & Entringer (2017) found that too much choice requires more effort comparing to no choice. Therefore, they suggest limiting advertising choice or elimination advertising exposure in online marketing. On the other hand, Haryani & Motwani, (2015) argue that consumers' buying intention is affected by too much emphasize, escalated brand factors and professed security in their study WOM. Likewise, Hoeck and Spann's (2020) research on multi-screen advertising also demonstrated that multi-screen decreases advertising effectiveness. Another interesting result was found by Sharma et al (2022) where advertising irritation affect advertising effectiveness negatively with 272 participants research. However, on the contrary, another research demonstrated that digital video advertising through television, mobile TV, and the Internet research show that being exposed to repetitive ads on different media platforms are perceived more brand, ad, message credibility than a single ad (Lim and et al, 2015). In another research about digital advertising effect on shopping cart abandonment behavior and ad avoidance behavior in social media platforms is found by Khan et al (2022) as receiving a futile/useless message.

Different platforms like mobile internet, Facebook, games, and other platforms are used for digital advertisements. Mobile internet users have exceeded five billion in 2022 (Statista.com, 2023). Research on consumer behavior in mobile advertising conducted by Izquierdo-Yusta, Olarte-Pascual and Reinares-Lara (2015) demonstrated that mobiles with internet access influence consumers' receiving ads intention positively but not their positive attitudes. There are studies about SMS and MMS in mobile digital advertising, of which Gavilan, Avello, and Abril (2014) compared SMS (short text message) ads and MMS (multimedia message) with videos, photos ads and suggested that although multimedia messages had greater impact on vividness and elaboration where mental imagery mediates ad type effect on ad trust and has a positive influence on purchase intention but SMS mobile ads had greater impact on quantity in mobile marketing. Mobile devices are very important in terms of online shopping. Brasel and Gips (2014) found that online shopping via mobile devices compared to mouse clicking increase feelings of owner ship and endowment and product valuations in tablets might be higher than traditional computers.

Facebook advertising, according to Leong et al (2018) marital status and hours spent in internet effects impulse purchasing in Facebook commerce. In another research about Facebook advertising Celebi (2015) demonstrated that activities using social media influence internet advertising positively, and privacy security also influence Facebook groups attitudes positively. Wilcox and Stephen (2013) found how an individual uses Facebook affects self-control, and with closer friends' exposure in Facebook, they showed less self-control in healthy behaviors like choosing a healthy meal instead of not healthy with closer friends.

Research about in-game advertising, Ghosh (2016) argued that outcome and performance feedback game messages are important in players' motivation which affect their attitude and memory in in-game advertising (IGA). Oliveira et al (2014) illustrated that interactive digital marketing via playing games in gaming platforms enable consumers to create independently. Even format of digital advertising in digital world has been changed to attract children, converted to gaming or advergames, according to An, Jin, Park, (2014) "gaming" is rising however the children playing these games are at the same time exposed to different advertising techniques like pop-up and unlock to play and they do not understand that it is an ad, they need advertising literacy education. Meyer et al, (2019) demonstrated that hidden adds are found in educational apps for children under-age of 5. Parents must be aware of advergames as children are influenced negatively and that they are found to be more influential than tv commercials (Neyens, Smits, Boyland, 2017), (Norman et al, 2018). Therefore, parents must be aware of this and must enable their children to have advertising literacy education.

Previous literature reviews related to digital marketing show that different classification of digital marketing/advertising in terms of platforms. For example, Stephen's (2016) review is based on four main journals covering 2013-2015 reviewed 29 articles published and three preview review articles about digital marketing and social media marketing, found how consumers are influenced by digital ads and argued that researchers mainly focus on WOM and grouped under five themes as customers' digital culture, response to digital ads, how digital environments affect consumers, mobile environments and online WOM.

Review of Kim (2021) covering 698 papers presented in 2018 Tokyo Global Marketing Conference grouped presented articles in four groups as SNS (Social Networking Service) Marketing, Digital Service Marketing, Digital Marketing Communication and Digital Marketing and Consumer Behavior.

Krishen et al (2021) review, covering 1990-2019, about interactive digital marketing, mobile and marketing literature argued that using interactive digital marketing via digital platforms and Information and Communication Technology (ICT) created more empowered, connected groups of customers. In their bibliometric network analysis with Citation Network Analysis (CNA) which is a technology forecasting tool that acts as an alternative to an expert-based approach, they found that digital marketing (DM) triggered the creation of more informed, empowered, and connected groups of customers in both the real and virtual worlds.

Other digital advertising tools like self-endorsing is a new persuasion instrument in digital media, in their experimental study of using virtual selves to persuade physical selves, Ahn, Phua, Shan (2017) suggest that unfamiliar brands, self-endorsed advertisements (SEAs) were more effective in favorable brand attitudes and found that self-created self-endorsed advertisements (SEAs) elicited greater self-referencing for existing brands than other-created self-endorsed advertisements (SEAs). The effects of digital advertising on consumer behavior research details are detailed in Table 1 given in Appendix.

Rules, Regulations, and Voluntary Initiatives
Self-Regulations in Digital Advertising

Previous sections cover literature reviews about digital ads role on consumers behavior and on children and adolescents' behavior. This section is about rules, regulations set by several governments including banning, restricting digital advertisements. Self-regulating rules initiated by voluntary initiatives are also used in practice to protect and help consumers. However, regulations, rules in force, and self-regulations by voluntary initiatives could not stop unethical practice in digital advertising. Therefore, along with governments, researchers, universities, schools, must try to avoid digital advertising negative effects.

In United States, Interactive Advising Bureau has developed self-regulatory principles and practices for Online Behavioral Advertising / Interest-based Advertising (OBA) (Interactive Advertising Bureau, 2011) and Federal Trade Commission (FTC, 2013) revised guidance about 'Dot.com Disclosures' in 2000 for digital advertisement to avoid deception by making disclosures clear including bloggers in United States. Taber et al (2016) suggested that policies can be extended to restrict sales of all sugary drinks as in compliance with Institute of Medicine recommendations. Beverage companies having realized unhealthy effects of sugary drinks and to increase low-calorie sales voluntarily initiated to advertise alternative beverages which are healthier to children under 12 years old (Wolstein, Babey, 2018). United States has banned sugary drinks and snacks at schools and implemented new standards as of July 2014 (American Dental Education Association, 2013).

United Kingdom, Advertising Standards Authority (ASA) banned foods with high fat, salt and free sugars, if 25% of advertisement's audience is children in non-broadcast media environments, including celebrities and characters in ads targeting younger children (Advertising Standards Authority, 2017) in 2017, and digital (online) advertisements like advergames in 2018 (BBC News, 2018) and Ireland Broadcasting Authority Broadcasting Authority of Ireland (2013) established limits on advertising to protect children from unhealthy lifestyle or unhealthy eating or drinking habits.

France has regulated alcohol and tobacco advertisement in 1991 by prohibiting young people and the law required health warning on the products (Friant-Perrot, and Garde,2022). France published self-regulatory body published a guide in 2018 forbidding all modes of marketing under 12 including social media (Béjot, and Doittau, 2004).

Canada, to avoid unhealthy food and beverage consumption increase, self-regulatory initiative groups established like Canadian Children's Food and Beverage Advertising Initiative (CAI) to limit such advertising (Canadian Ad Standards, 2016). Canadian government started to restrict unhealthy food and beverages to children as well (Heart and Stroke Foundation of Canada, 2017).

Burkhalter et al (2014) argued that policy makers, regulatory bodies published guidelines of disclosure for marketing endorsements and testimonials in social media platforms and that consumers might be motivated to buy if they think endorsements are by independent bodies in social media. Rules, Regulations, and Voluntary Initiatives Self-Regulations in Digital Advertising literature review details are given in Table 2 in appendix.

Unethical Practices in Digital Advertising

Although there are governmental rules, voluntary initiatives are already in use, ethical practices are very important in digital advertising as Behera et al (2022) in their study of ethical principles demonstrated that digital marketing mistakes damage reputation, therefore good ethical practices are necessary for reputation of the company. Ethics codes, based on voluntarily acceptance of honesty, integrity, fairness for practitioners by Academy of Nutrition and Dietetics (2018), these ethics characteristics can be applied to all types of marketing including digital marketing (Helm, 2013).

However, this is not so in practice, researchers show that unethical practice in digital advertising practice did not stop and that there are non-ethical applications in digital advertising to children. Kent and Pauze, (2018) found out that Canadian Children's Food and Beverage Advertising Initiative (CAI) self-regulatory failed in reducing exposure of unhealthy foods advertisement to children, on the contrary, companies who have signed Canadian Ad Standards self-regulation rules were found to have advertised 2,2 times more foods with excessive fat, salt or free sugars. Furthermore, the signatory companies' advertisements had higher sugar, salt, energy per serving than the other companies who did not sign self-regulation of Canadian Ad Standards self-regulation.

In European Union countries namely Belgium and Netherlands research results show that signatory companies' majority i.e., 88,5 percent of them provided unhealthy foods advertisements to children under 12 years (Neyens, Smits, 2017). Children Advertising Initiatives (CAI) findings were that only one in 45 brand exposure had a healthful message in CAI (Boyland, Whalen, 2015). In France, Gallopel-Morvan et al, (2017) found that French Évin law does not appear to protect young people effectively from exposure to alcohol advertising in France. Spain has amended co-regulatory code in 2012 banning all internet marketing to children under 15 (León-Flández, 2017).

Research results show that digital advertisement affect consumers' purchase behavior via advertisements, whether digital or traditional, main aim is to increase consumption, to change purchase behavior via triggering purchase intention. Advertisements affect not only adults' behavior change, but they also affect children and adolescents' purchase behavior as well. They do not only affect consumption behavior of goods like clothes, toys etc. they also affect children's and adolescents' behavior in terms of health issues, like increase in alcohol consumption, in smoking and in sugary beverage/food consumption. Research also shows that digital ads targeting children and adolescents are more effective but less controllable. Children cannot even differentiate that they are exposed to digital ads embedded in games and even in educational web sites, hidden ads affect children and adolescents' behavior. Therefore, children and including adolescents under age 18 are to be protected from these effects which result in behavior changes in terms of health.

'Exposure Time Limitation' are recommended for children and adolescents, researchers advise that fast/junk food and beverage with sugar advertisements must be limited addressing to children and youth (Harris et al, 2009) and exposure of children to digital media and advertising must be limited (Pearson, 2020), (Rasmussen et al. 2020). Council on Communications and Media (2016) recommended that children younger than 18 months must be avoided any type of screen media except video chatting and for children between 18-24 months, and that parents must interact with children, for children 2-5 must not exceed 1 hour and screen time of media use must be arranged with the family, furthermore bedrooms must be clear of screen media including iPads, cell phones tv etc., recommend parents to watch together with children and that content must be discussed with children. According to Royal College of Pediatrics and Child Health report, families are recommended to negotiate time limitation with their children (Viner, Davie, Firth, 2019). Published guidelines about screen exposure for children aged under 5, school aged and adolescents advise parents to minimize exposure to advertising and ensure that there is no advertising of which children are exposed, parents are also advised to talk about online use and issues like not only advergames etc. and are recommended to watch together with their children whenever possible and encourage digital media literacy, by questioning advertising messages (Ponti et al, 2013).

SOLUTIONS AND RECOMMENDATIONS

Public education especially family education is very important in digital literacy. To avoid negative effects and influence on young people about substance use related behaviors, young people are advised media literacy- educating young people about media to be able and encourage them to process media messages critically. Government must provide funding for media education and for positive media content which shows and encourages healthy lifestyles and choices. Harvard University guides parents with their new Center on Media and Child Health at Harvard, (2022) and AAP has established a parent-oriented web site providing parents to deal with cyberbullying, food ads and media education (American Academy of Pediatrics, 2022). Popkin, argued that education would not be enough as sugary and sugary beverage sectors of billions of dollars would not be able to be controlled and that governmental actions are required (Popkin, 2009).

Governments, policy makers, health institutions, universities, voluntary self-regulation initiatives have taken action to protect children under age 18 and legislation are set into force. However new legislation could not stop digital advertisement effects on children (including adolescents) under age 18 due to unethical digital advertisement practice and difficulty in controlling digital advertisements. Even signed companies who are in voluntary self-regulation initiatives are not in compliance with rules and regulations. Further steps have been taken by governments like United States not only published rules restricting ads to children and adolescents, banned selling fast food and sugary drinks at public schools. United Kingdom banned ads of high fat, salt and free sugar food and drinks to children. Ireland limited advertising of unhealthy eating and drinking to children.

Countries all over the world are trying to take necessary precautions to decrease high calorie food and beverages (high in fat, sugars, or salt) consumption by implementing mandatory policies and voluntary policies for advertising to children and adolescents under age 18. According to World Health Organization (WHO, 2022) in Euroland, 34 countries have implemented mandatory policies and 17 countries have implemented voluntary policies.

These policies must be implemented by all countries including developing countries as obesity in the long term creates health issues, and health expenditure of countries increase and becomes a major cost to the society, and developed countries are limiting or banning ads to children and adolescents under 18, to stop or reduce consumption of fast food and sugary drinks. Self-regulations of voluntary initiatives are not enough to avoid unethical application in digital marketing as even signed companies do not comply with the voluntary rules. Recommendations of institutions and specialists' details are given in detail in Table 4 in appendix.

EMERGING TRENDS

Data risk with social media and interactive digital advertising is one of the most trending topics as (Meral, 2021) has pointed out in her study, nowadays resulted by official precautions taken by governments including banning Tik-Tok in some countries, at the same time a gap for future research (MIT Technology Review, 2023), (Euronews, 2024), (European Commission, 2024), (TNW-The Next Web, 2024), and (Reuters, 2024).

Along with data risk, another aspect is that lack of digital control or not sufficient digital control is another trending topic (New York Times, 2023) and at the same time a gap of digital advertising for future researchers, especially considering risks not only data risk, but like other effects of digital advertising embedded in games advertising etc. especially on consumers of different demographic groups, like children, adolescents.

FUTURE RESEARCH DIRECTIONS

Future researchers can investigate negative effects in longitudinal studies, other risk factors which affect youth's behaviors via internet exposure, digital advertisements, including individual, environmental, and social risks, along with health issues due to increase in unhealthy food and sugary drinks, alcohol, and smoking consumption behavior. Social networking sites and game platforms on mobile phones with peers are widely used. Therefore, future research must cover these new virtual game platforms and new platforms like TikTok and impacts on children and adolescents' as well. Future researchers are recommended longitudinal studies for long term effects and new methods for measuring digital advertising effects on consumers behavior. Future researchers are recommended to conduct studies about new platforms like TikTok. Furthermore, in their review (Kaya and Bayat, 2022) advised researchers to be held in different sectors. In another research (Tariq et al, 2023) advised cross-public and other cultures' research.

CONCLUSION

Internet or the 'online' concept has become an integral part of our daily lives with more than 5 billion internet users, especially with the pandemic triggering effect everybody is familiar with online working, online school/studying, online meeting, online socializing, online reading/watching, online banking, online health and online shopping via mobiles, laptops, tablets, and electronic watches. With this tremendous increase in shift to online, advertising has also shifted from traditional advertising to digital advertising. Digital advertising messages are so active and penetrating in digital world that consumers are familiar with receiving digital ads via sms marketing messages, artificial intelligence used pop up ads nearly from every platform of social media like Instagram, Facebook, twitter etc.

Advertising companies are targeting different groups of consumers in digital world. Their main goal is to sell their products by triggering purchase intent via digital world. Literature review of digital advertising role on consumers show that digital advertisements have an important role in consumers' behavior to trigger purchase intention. Advertising companies use interaction methods to affect consumers, however too much exposure to digital advertising might decrease this effect. These companies use all digital platforms to reach their target including social media users, in-game players, mobile internet users as well.

Research show that one of target groups of digital advertisement are children's and adolescents under age 18. Research found that digital ads affect children and adolescent group behavior and health negatively, like increase in smoking consumption, in problematic alcohol consumption and due to unhealthy foods and sugary beverage consumption increase via digital ads obesity and obesity related health problems increase.

Considering the risks of digital advertising, new strategies, governmental rules, practices and self-regulatory initiative activities and ethical codes for digital ads are developed by various official bodies and self-regulated i7nitiatives. However, although implemented rules and polices come into force, it is not easy to follow up especially with big players (like Google, Facebook, Amazon etc.) of whom have a closed system, and do not share information. Even self-regulated initiatives are not successful as signed companies do not change their digital advertisement on children. Furthermore, although it is cheaper, it is more difficult to control digital advertisements due to methods used like up pop ups in social media or embedded in advergames so that children might not be aware that they are exposed to ads.

Close monitoring of digital advertisements to children and adolescents about alcohol, smoking and unhealthy food and sugary drinks is required. Governments must develop new digital control and monitoring techniques to follow up digital advertisements. This is such a problem that governments must work with parents, families, schools, academicians, policy makers, academician, public health staff, they all must act together to avoid negative effects on children and adolescents' consumption behavior. Governments must provide funds for digital advertisement literacy to educate parents and children. Children and youth face the risk of obesity due to unhealthy foods and sugary beverage ads which will lead to serious illnesses in future along with smoking and alcohol consumption increase in youth.

REFERENCES

Academy of Nutrition and Dietetics. (2018). *Code of Ethics for the Nutrition and Dietetics Profession.* AND. https://www.eatrightpro.org/-/media/files/eatrightpro/practice/code-of-ethics/codeofethicshandout.pdf

Adam, B. S., & Gips, J. (2014). Tablets, touchscreens, and touchpads: How varying touch interfaces trigger psychological ownership and endowment. *Journal of Consumer Psychology*, 24(2), 226–233. 10.1016/j.jcps.2013.10.003

Advertising Standards Authority. (2017). *Advice online. Children: Food.* ASA. https://www.asa.org.uk/advice-online/children-food.html

American Academy of Pediatrics. (2022). *Family Life/Power of Play.* AAP. https://www.healthychildren.org/English/family-life/Pages/default.aspx

American Dental Education Association. (2013). *The U.S. Department of Agriculture Issues Rule Banning Sugary Drinks and Snacks in Schools.* ADEA. https://www.adea.org/ADEA/Blogs/ADEA_State_Update/The_U_S__Department_of_Agriculture_Issues_Rule_Banning_Sugary_Drinks_and_Snacks_in_Schools.html

An, S., Jin, H. S., & Park, E. H. (2014). Children's advertising literacy for advergames: Perception of the game as advertising. *Journal of Advertising*, 43(1), 63–72. 10.1080/00913367.2013.795123

Bart, Y., Stephen, A. T., & Sarvary, M. (2014). Which products are best suited to mobile advertising? A field study of mobile display advertising effects on consumer attitudes and intentions. *JMR, Journal of Marketing Research*, 51(3), 270–285. 10.1509/jmr.13.0503

BBC News. (2018). *First ads banned under new junk food rules.* BBC News. https://www.bbc.com/news/uk-44706755

Béjot, M., & Doittau, B. (2004). Advertising to children in France. *Young Consumers*, 5(3), 69–72. 10.1108/17473610410814274

Boyland, E. J., & Whalen, R. (2015). Food advertising to children and its effects on diet: Review of recent prevalence and impact data. *Pediatric Diabetes*, 16(5), 331–337. 10.1111/pedi.1227825899654

Broadcasting Authority of Ireland. (2013). *Policy - BAI Children's Commercial Communication Code.* WHO. https://extranet.who.int/nutrition/gina/en/node/22970

Burkhalter, J. N., Wood, N. T., & Tryce, S. A. (2014). Clear, conspicuous, and concise: Disclosures and Twitter word-of-mouth. *Business Horizons*, 57(3), 319–328. 10.1016/j.bushor.2014.02.001

Canadian Ad Standards. (2016). *About the Initiative.* Canadian Ad Standards. https://adstandards.ca/wp-content/uploads/2018/03/2016ComplianceReport-2.pdf

Celebi, S. I. (2015). How do motives affect attitudes and behaviors toward internet advertising and Facebook advertising? *Computers in Human Behavior*, 51, 312–324. 10.1016/j.chb.2015.05.011

de Bruijn, A., Engels, R., Anderson, P., Bujalski, M., Gosselt, J., Schreckenberg, D., Wohtge, J., & de Leeuw, R. (2016). Exposure to online alcohol marketing and adolescents' drinking: A cross-sectional study in four European countries. *Alcohol and Alcoholism (Oxford, Oxfordshire)*, 51(5), 615–621. 10.1093/alcalc/agw02027151968

Euronews (2024). Which countries have banned TikTok and why? *Euronews.*

European Commission Press Release. (2024) *Commission opens proceedings against TikTok under the DSA regarding the launch of TikTok Lite in France and Spain, and communicates its intention to suspend the reward programme in the EU.* EC. https://ec.europa.eu/commission/presscorner/detail/en/ip_24_2227

Faria. (2022) *Advertising worldwide, statistics and facts.* Statista. https://www.statista.com/topics/990/global-advertising-market/#topicOverview

Federal Trade Commission. (2013). *"Dot Com Disclosures" Guidance Updated to Address Current Online and Mobile Advertising Environment.* FTC. https://www.ftc.gov/news-events/news/press-releases/2013/03/ftc-staff-revises-online-advertising-disclosure-guidelines

Friant-Perrot, M., & Garde, A. (2022). The regulation of alcohol marketing in France: The Loi Evin at thirty. *The Journal of Law, Medicine & Ethics*, 50(2), 312–316. 10.1017/jme.2022.5735894563

Gallopel-Morvan, K., Spilka, S., Mutatayi, C., Rigaud, A., Lecas, F., & Beck, F. (2017). France's Evin law on the control of alcohol advertising: Content, effectiveness and limitations. *Addiction (Abingdon, England)*, 112(S1), 86–93. 10.1111/add.1343127188432

Gavilan, D., Avello, M., & Abril, C. (2014). The mediating role of mental imagery in mobile advertising. *International Journal of Information Management*, 34(4), 457–464. 10.1016/j.ijinfomgt.2014.04.004

Ghosh, T. (2016). Winning versus not losing: Exploring the effects of in-game advertising outcome on its effectiveness. *Journal of Interactive Marketing*, 36(1), 134–147. 10.1016/j.intmar.2016.05.003

Harris, J. L., Pomeranz, J. L., Lobstein, T., & Brownell, K. D. (2009). A crisis in the marketplace: How food marketing contributes to childhood obesity and what can be done. *Annual Review of Public Health*, 30(1), 211–225. 10.1146/annurev.publhealth.031308.10030418976142

Haryani, S., & Motwani, B. (2015). Discriminant model for online viral marketing influencing consumers behavioural intention. *Pacific science review B: Humanities and social sciences*, 1(1), 49-56.

Helm, J. (2013). Ethical and legal issues related to blogging and social media. *Journal of the Academy of Nutrition and Dietetics*, 113(5), 688–690. 10.1016/j.jand.2013.02.008

Hoeck, L., & Spann, M. (2020). An experimental analysis of the effectiveness of multi-screen advertising. *Journal of Interactive Marketing*, 50(1), 81–99. 10.1016/j.intmar.2020.01.002

Hwang, K., & Zhang, Q. (2018). Influence of parasocial relationship between digital celebrities and their followers on followers' purchase and electronic word-of-mouth intentions, and persuasion knowledge. *Computers in Human Behavior*, 87, 155–173. 10.1016/j.chb.2018.05.029

Interactive Advertising Bureau. (2011). *Self-Regulatory Program For Online Behavioral Advertising Factsheet.* IAB. OBA_OneSheet_Final.pdf (iab.com)

Interactive Advertising Bureau. (2011). *Self-Regulatory Program For Online Behavioral Advertising Factsheet.* IAB. https://www.iab.com/wp-content/uploads/2015/06/OBA_OneSheet_Final.pdf

Izquierdo-Yusta, A., Olarte-Pascual, C., & Reinares-Lara, E. (2015). Attitudes toward mobile advertising among users versus non-users of the mobile Internet. *Telematics and Informatics*, 32(2), 355–366. 10.1016/j.tele.2014.10.001

Jernigan, D. H., Ross, C. S., Ostroff, J., McKnight-Eily, L. R., & Brewer, R. D. (2013). Youth exposure to alcohol advertising on television—25 markets, United States, 2010. *Morbidity and Mortality Weekly Report, 62*(44), 877. https://www.cdc.gov/mmwr/preview/mmwrhtml/mm6244a3.htm

Kaya, R., & Bayat, M. (2022). Çevrimiçi dünyada yükselen bir trend: Display (görüntülü) reklamlar. *Elektronik Sosyal Bilimler Dergisi*, 21(82), 759–770. 10.17755/esosder.1031584

Kent, M. P., & Pauzé, E. (2018). The effectiveness of self-regulation in limiting the advertising of unhealthy foods and beverages on children's preferred websites in Canada. *Public Health Nutrition*, 21(9), 1608–1617. 10.1017/S1368980017004177729433594

Khan, A., Rezaei, S., & Valaei, N. (2022). Social commerce advertising avoidance and shopping cart abandonment: A fs/QCA analysis of German consumers. *Journal of Retailing and Consumer Services*, 67, 102976. 10.1016/j.jretconser.2022.102976

Kim, K. H. (2021). Digital and social media marketing in global business environment. *Journal of Business Research*, 131, 627–629. 10.1016/j.jbusres.2021.02.052

Krishen, A. S., Dwivedi, Y. K., Bindu, N., & Kumar, K. S. (2021). A broad overview of interactive digital marketing: A bibliometric network analysis. *Journal of Business Research*, 131, 183–195. 10.1016/j.jbusres.2021.03.061

León-Flández, K., Rico-Gómez, A., Moya-Geromin, M. Á., Romero-Fernández, M., Bosqued-Estefania, M. J., Damian, J., López-Jurado, L., & Royo-Bordonada, M. Á. (2017). Evaluation of compliance with the Spanish Code of self-regulation of food and drinks advertising directed at children under the age of 12 years in Spain, 2012. *Public Health*, 150, 121–129. 10.1016/j.puhe.2017.05.01328675833

Leong, L. Y., Jaafar, N. I., & Ainin, S. (2018). The effects of Facebook browsing and usage intensity on impulse purchase in f-commerce. *Computers in Human Behavior*, 78, 160–173. 10.1016/j.chb.2017.09.033

Lim, J. S., Ri, S. Y., Egan, B. D., & Biocca, F. A. (2015). The cross-platform synergies of digital video advertising: Implications for cross-media campaigns in television, Internet and mobile TV. *Computers in Human Behavior*, 48, 463–472. 10.1016/j.chb.2015.02.001

Marketing Accountability Standards Board. (2018). *Common Language in Marketing Project Team, 2018. Display Advertising (Digital) Definition.* Marketing Dictionary. https://marketing-dictionary.org/d/display-advertising-digital/

Meral, K. Z. (2021). Social media short video-sharing TikTok application and ethics: data privacy and addiction issues. In *Multidisciplinary approaches to ethics in the digital era* (pp. 147–165). IGI Global. 10.4018/978-1-7998-4117-3.ch010

Meyer, M., Adkins, V., Yuan, N., Weeks, H. M., Chang, Y. J., & Radesky, J. (2019). Advertising in young children's apps: A content analysis. *Journal of Developmental and Behavioral Pediatrics*, 40(1), 32–39. 10.1097/DBP.0000000000000062230371646

Murphy, M., & Sashi, C. M. (2018). Communication, interactivity, and satisfaction in B2B relationships. *Industrial Marketing Management*, 68, 1–12. 10.1016/j.indmarman.2017.08.020

Nettelhorst, S. C., Jeter, W. K., Brannon, L. A., & Entringer, A. (2017). Can there be too much of a good thing? The effect of option number on cognitive effort toward online advertisements. *Computers in Human Behavior*, 75, 320–328. 10.1016/j.chb.2017.04.061

Neyens, E., & Smits, T. (2017). Empty pledges: A content analysis of Belgian and Dutch child-targeting food websites. *International Journal of Health Promotion and Education*, 55(1), 42–52. 10.1080/14635240.2016.1218295

Neyens, E., Smits, T., & Boyland, E. (2017). Transferring game attitudes to the brand: Persuasion from age 6 to 14. *International Journal of Advertising*, 36(5), 724–742. 10.1080/02650487.2017.1349029

Norman, J., Kelly, B., McMahon, A. T., Boyland, E., Baur, L. A., Chapman, K., King, L., Hughes, C., & Bauman, A. (2018). Sustained impact of energy-dense TV and online food advertising on children's dietary intake: A within-subject, randomised, crossover, counter-balanced trial. *The International Journal of Behavioral Nutrition and Physical Activity*, 15(1), 1–11. 10.1186/s12966-018-0672-629650023

Oliveira, F., Santos, A., Aguiar, B., & Sousa, J. (2014). GameFoundry: Social gaming platform for digital marketing, user profiling and collective behavior. *Procedia: Social and Behavioral Sciences*, 148, 58–66. 10.1016/j.sbspro.2014.07.017

Pearson, N., Biddle, S. J., Griffiths, P., Sherar, L. B., McGeorge, S., & Haycraft, E. (2020). Reducing screen-time and unhealthy snacking in 9–11 year old children: The Kids FIRST pilot randomised controlled trial. *BMC Public Health*, 20(1), 1–14. 10.1186/s12889-020-8232-931996192

Ponti, M., Bélanger, S., Grimes, R., Heard, J., Johnson, M., Moreau, E., & Williams, R. (2017). Screen time and young children: Promoting health and development in a digital world. *Paediatrics & Child Health*.29601064

Popkin, B. M. (2009). Global dimensions of sugary beverages and programmatic and policy solutions. *Official Journal of the International Chair on Cardio Metabolic Risk*, 2(2), 6–9.

Rasmussen, M. G. B., Pedersen, J., Olesen, L. G., Brage, S., Klakk, H., Kristensen, P. L., Brønd, J. C., & Grøntved, A. (2020). Short-term efficacy of reducing screen media use on physical activity, sleep, and physiological stress in families with children aged 4–14: Study protocol for the SCREENS randomized controlled trial. *BMC Public Health*, 20(1), 1–18. 10.1186/s12889-020-8458-632293374

Reuters. (2024). *EU opens formal investigation into TikTok over possible online content breaches*. Reuters. https://www.reuters.com/technology/eu-opens-formal-proceedings-against-tiktok-under-digital-services-act-2024-02-19/

Sharma, A., Dwivedi, R., Mariani, M. M., & Islam, T. (2022). Investigating the effect of advertising irritation on digital advertising effectiveness: A moderated mediation model. *Technological Forecasting and Social Change*, 180, 121731. 10.1016/j.techfore.2022.121731

Statista.com. (2020). *Number of internet and social media users worldwide as of July 2022*. Statista. https://www.statista.com/statistics/617136/digital-population-worldwide/#:~:text=As%20of%20April%202022%2C%20there,population%20were%20social%20media%20users

Statista.com. (2022). *Global advertising revenue 2014-2027*. Statista.com https://www.statista.com/statistics/236943/global-advertising-spending/

Statista.com. (2023). *Digital advertising worldwide - statistics & facts*. Statista. https://www.statista.com/outlook/dmo/digital-advertising/worldwide (May,2023).

Statista.com. (2023). *Mobile internet users worldwide*. Statista. https://www.statista.com/topics/779/mobile-internet/#topicOverview

Stephen, A. T. (2016). The role of digital and social media marketing in consumer behavior. *Current Opinion in Psychology*, 10, 17–21. 10.1016/j.copsyc.2015.10.016

Taber, D. R., Chriqui, J. F., Vuillaume, R., Kelder, S. H., & Chaloupka, F. J. (2015). The association between state bans on soda only and adolescent substitution with other sugar-sweetened beverages: A cross-sectional study. *The International Journal of Behavioral Nutrition and Physical Activity*, 12(1), 1–9. 10.1186/1479-5868-12-S1-S726221969

Tariq, S., Tariq, A., Raweem, A., Tahira, H., Amjad, J., & Nauman, K. (2023). Impact of Social Media Advertisement on Customer Purchase Intention: A Sequential Mediation Analysis. *Abasyn University Journal of Social Sciences, 16*(1).

The Next Web (TNW). (2024). What it'd take for the EU to ban TikTok. *The Next Web*.https://thenextweb.com/news/would-eu-us-ban-tiktok

Tiago, M. T. P. M. B., & Veríssimo, J. M. C. (2014). Digital marketing and social media: Why bother? *Business Horizons*, 57(6), 703–708. 10.1016/j.bushor.2014.07.002

Viner, R., Davie, M., & Firth, A. (2019). *The health impacts of screen time: a guide for clinicians and parents*. Royal College of Paediatrics and Child Health. https://www.rcpch.ac.uk/sites/default/files/2018-12/rcpch_screen_time_guide_-_final.pdf

Wilcox, K., & Stephen, A. T. (2013). Are close friends the enemy? Online social networks, self-esteem, and self-control. *The Journal of Consumer Research*, 40(1), 90–103. 10.1086/668794

Wolstein, J., & Babey, S. H. (2018). Sugary Beverage Consumption Among California Children and Adolescents. *Policy Brief (UCLA Center for Health Policy Research)*, 2018(2), 1–8.29999284

World Health Organization. (2022). *WHO European regional obesity report*. WHO. https://www.euro.who.int/en/publications/abstracts/who-european-regional-obesity-report-2022

KEY TERMS AND DEFINITIONS

Consumers Behavior: Consumers' behavior are affected by digital advertisements, their purchase intention or consumption might change by digital ads. Behavioral advertising is used based on specific interest of internet user, based on previous interests and preferences.

Digital Advertisement (Display Advertising): Advertising based via websites, like video, text, image, audio, movement format to website visitors.

Digital Control: Digital control over digital ads is important however it is not as easy as traditional ads, due to difficulties of digital ad control, because sometimes digital ads are embedded in websites, especially children may not even be aware of ads therefore digital control is vital for digital ads.

Regulations and Self-Regulation Rules: Regulation are set by state officials rules in force but self-regulations are set by voluntary initiatives and they are voluntarily accepted, there is no force.

Unethical Practice: Unethical practice in digital advertising are like exposure of unhealthy foods advertisement to children are violeted by companies who themselves signed the voluntary initiatives.

APPENDIX ONE

Table 1. Digital advertisement effects on consumers behavior

Author / Year	Methodology	Results/key Findings	Sample	Research Area
Tiago and Veríssimo (2014).	survey-multidimensional scale analysis with the synthetic indicators	found that relationship-based interactions with their customers is very important in improving digital marketing, demonstrate how they have accomplished.	170 marketing managers	interactive marketing in Portuguese companies
Hwang and Zhang (2018).	survey/SEM-structural equation model	results indicate that para-social relationship moderates the paths between followers' persuasion knowledge and purchase intentions and between followers' persuasion knowledge and eWOM intentions	389 Chinese SNS (Social Network Sites) users survey of digital celebrities' followers, valid data were analyzed using structural equation modeling.	interactive marketing via Chinese celebrities
Murphy and Sashi (2018).	survey/SEM-structural equation model	found that dyadic contact has a negative association with relationship satisfaction.	308 managers	commercial printing and graphic design industry
Bart, Stephen, and Sarvary (2014).	field experiment - large-scale test-control field experiment data provided by agency	found that MDA (Mobile Display Ads) campaigns when advertised products with higher (vs. lower) involvement increased consumers' purchase intentions.	54 U.S. large campaigns of MDA (Mobile Display Ads) (2007-2010) with 39,946 consumers,	MDA (Mobile Display Advertisement) campaigns effects on consumers in US
Nettelhorst, Jeter, Brannon and Entringer (2017).	experimental -university students were randomly assigned	found that too much choice of online advertising needs more effort compared to no choice, suggests limiting or eliminating advertising exposure.	208 students	university students' exposure to too much choice of online ads
Haryani and Motwani (2015).	survey results were analyzed with discriminate analysis by using statistical software SPSS 16.0.	found that consumer's buying intention is affected by immense efficacy, professed security and escalating brand factors.	201 respondents-self-structured questionnaires	prediction of eWOM effects on consumers' buying intention
Hoeck and Spann (2020).	experimental analysis of multi-screen advertising	Multiscreen decreases effectiveness of advertising.	233 workers of Amazon Mechanical Turk (MTurk) platform	product ice-cream
Sharma et al. (2022).	survey-multi-analytic approach of moderated mediation, necessary condition analysis (NCA) and partial least squares structural equation with modeling (PLS-SEM)	advertising irritation affect advertising effectiveness negatively	272 university students	advertising irritation effect on UAE university students

continued on following page

Table 1. Continued

Author / Year	Methodology	Results/key Findings	Sample	Research Area
Lim et al. (2015).	experimental	Effect of digital video advertising through television, mobile TV, and the Internet research show that being exposed to repetitive ads on different media platforms are perceived more brand, ad, message credibility than single ad.	282 undergraduate students	university students of Korea
Khan, Rezaei and Valaei (2022).	Fuzzy sets/Qualitative Comparative Analysis (fs/QCA) is used to find out outcome of shopping cart abandonment.	found that consumers who have ad avoidance in social media create a learning mechanism about shopping cart abandonment about a brand or a product if they are interrupted by a futile message or content.	191 online questionnaire responses	individuals from Germany/online consumer behavior
Izquierdo-Yusta, Olarte-Pascual and Reinares-Lara (2015).	empirical study with a representative sample of 612 recipients of mobile advertising in Spain, featuring both users of mobile Internet and consumers who choose not to access this service	found that mobiles which has internet access influence consumers' intention to receive ads positively but not contribute to positive attitudes	612 respondents who receive ads via mobile phones	consumers who receive ads via mobile phones
Gavilan, Avello and Abril (2014).	experimental-influence of the type of message – SMS vs. MMS – content type – informational vs. transformational – on the three dimensions of mental imagery: vividness, quantity and elaboration is examined by using a 2 × 2 factorial experimental design	shows MMS mobile ads have greater impact on vividness and elaboration, where SMS mobile advertisements have a greater impact on the quantity and argued that ad trust can be improved by mobile ads using rich mental imagery. Vivid and elaborate mental imagery mediates affect ad type on ad trust and has a positive influence on purchase intention.	169 undergraduate students	Spanish university students receiving MMS mobile ads
Brasel and Gips (2014).	experimental-2 lab studies	found that touch-based devices like tablets can lead to higher product valuations when compared to traditional computers.	experimental-2 lab studies-Two laboratory studies using a variety of touch technologies explore how touchscreen interfaces can increase perceived psychological ownership, and this in turn magnifies the endowment effect.	lab studies
Leong, Jaafar and Ainin (2018)	data collected using mall-intercept technique and analyzed with Smart PLS 3, after the Stimulus-Organism-Response framework.	found that marital status and hours spent in internet have moderating effects on impulse purchasing, however no effect of income.	800 questionnaires	Facebook commerce

continued on following page

Table 1. Continued

Author / Year	Methodology	Results/key Findings	Sample	Research Area
Celebi (2015).	survey	found that activities using social media influence attitudes towards internet advertising positively,	140 undergraduate students-survey research	particular characteristics of Turkish Internet and Facebook users in İzmir
Wilcox, Stephen (2013).	experimental-five experiments	findings by demonstrating that social networks primarily enhance self-esteem for those focused on strong ties during social network use. Additionally, this research has implications for policy makers because self-control is an important mechanism for maintaining social order and well-being.	Study1-100 Facebook users study2-108 Facebook users study3- 84 Facebook user study4- 88 undergraduates study5-541 Facebook users	Facebook users
Ghosh, (2016).	involvement scale of Beatty and Talpade (1994)'s four-item product used to measure involvement with each of products	found that In-game Advertising (IGA) outcome and performance feedback in the form of game messages plays a major role in explaining players' motivation which in turn also affects their memory and attitude.	25 post-graduates in first, and 30 different group of students in second phase.	in game advertising
Oliveira, Santos, Aguiar and Sousa (2014).	gaming platform	digital marketing with interactivity via playing games in platforms, social networks and environments enables clients to create independently.	524 users	gaming
An, Jin and Park (2014).	experimental	found that children need advertising literacy education, otherwise do not recognize advergames as a type of advertising.	129 children	gaming
Meyer et al. (2019).	exploratory-coding scheme created by playing with a pilot study of 39 apps for children	found that high rates of mobile advertising through manipulative and disruptive methods, which might require advertising regulation, parent media choices, and apps' educational value.	135 downloaded apps for children 5 and under age	gaming and children apps
Neyens, Smits and Boyland (2017).	experimental	argued that children playing advergame reported positive brand attitudes compared to children who had watched the TV ad and children in the no advertising exposure control group.	940 children	games
Norman et al. (2018).	trial-within-subject, randomized, crossover, counterbalanced trial	showed that online ('advergame') advertising with TV ads influenced children's food consumption more than TV advertising alone.	160 children	games

continued on following page

Table 1. Continued

Author / Year	Methodology	Results/key Findings	Sample	Research Area
Ahn, Phua and Shan (2017).	experimental	self-endorsed advertisements (SEAs) are more effective in brand attitudes	study 1 (N-63) and study 2 n75	Self-endorsed ads (SEA)
Stephen (2016).	Literature review-2013-2015 September of four main journals on digital marketing, social media marketing	shows how consumers are influenced by digital	29 articles published and three review articles	review
Kim, (2021).	review of 698 papers presented in 2018 Tokyo Global Marketing Conference- Digital and Social Media Marketing in Global Business Environment Theme	are grouped in four groups as 1-SNS (social networking service) Marketing 2-Digital Service Marketing 3-Digital Marketing Communication 4-Digital Marketing and Consumer Behavior	698 accepted papers	review
Krishen et al. (2021).	literature review- A bibliometric network analysis	Using interactive digital marketing via digital platforms and Information and Communication Technology (ICT) created more empowered, connected groups of customers. Digital marketing (DM) triggered the creation of more informed, empowered, and connected groups of customers in both the real and virtual worlds.	A bibliometric network analysis-Citation network analysis (CNA) is a technology forecasting tool that acts as an alternative to an expert-based approach.	review

Table 2. Digital advertising regulation, rules, and voluntary initiatives self-regulations

Author / Year	Methodology	Results/key Findings	Sample	Research Area
American Dental Education Association (2013).	Banning rules	United States has banned sugary drinks and snacks at schools and implented new standards as of July, 2014.	na	US banned sugary food and drink at schools
Advertising Standards Authority, (2017).	ad standarts	UK published advertising standards	na	UK-restricted children ads
BBC news. (2018)	banning rules	UK published-banning junk food ads in advergames	na	UK banned ads in advergames
Friant-Perrot, Garde. (2022).	review	France legislative amendments of banning alcohol advertisement	review	France banned alcohol ads
Heart and Stroke Foundation of Canada (2017)	guidance principles	Canada guidance principles-recommended four principles to minimine, mitigate, mindfully using, modeling healthy use of screens to children	na	Canada guidance principles
Broadcasting Authority of Ireland. (2013).	ad limitation rules	limits on advertising of HFSS--High in saturated Fat, Salt and Sugar-food as no more than one in four advertisements and no more than 25% of sold advertising time "across the broadcast day".	na	Ireland voluntary code of practice

continued on following page

Table 2. Continued

Author / Year	Methodology	Results/key Findings	Sample	Research Area
Taber et al. (2015).	student data of National Youth Physical Activity and Nutrition Study	sugary drinks must be restricted	8,696 students	children and sugary drinks
Federal Trade Commission (2013)	online ad disclosure rules	Published online advertising disclosure rules	na	US disclosure guidelines
Béjot, M., & Doittau, B. (2004).	self-regulation ads control	authorized to control and withdraw ads institution in France is Bureau de Vérification de la Publicité (BVP).	na	France-self regulation
Canadian Ad Standards. (2016).	Canada Ad Standards	Advertising Standards Canada (Ad Standards) is the national, independent, not-for profit advertising self-regulatory body.	na	Canada advertising initiative
Burkhalter, et al. (2014).	survey	Policy makers, regulatory bodies published guidelines of disclosure for marketing endorsements and testimonials in social media platforms.	167 students	Disclosure practise in twitter

Table 3. Unethical practices in digital advertising

Author / Year	Methodology	Results/key Findings	Sample	Research Area
Behera et al. (2022).	Exploratory Factor Analysis (EFA) with IBM SPSS Modeler and Confirmatory Factor Analysis (CFA), Structural Equation Modelling (SEM) with IBM AMOS to test validity	found that ethical based practices are important for effectiveness and organizational reputation.	300 participants	ethical practice-disclosure
Academy of Nutrition and Dietetics. (2018).	Code of ethics rules	The updated Code of Ethics approved by the Academy Board of Directors and the Commission on Dietetic Registration, effective June 1, 2018	published code of ethics	voluntarily acceptance-ethics rule
Helm, J. (2013).	Code of ethics rules can be applied and found in social media ethical rules as well.	Code of ethics approved by Academy of Nutrition and Dietetics can be applied to all types and digital marketing.	code of ethics	codes of ethics-social media
Kent & Pauzé (2018).	Internet advertising exposure data of children's websites to determine the frequency of food ads (June 2015-May 2016). Nutrition content was assessed using the Pan American Health Organization (PAHO) and UK Nutrient Profile Models (NPM)	found that self-regulation in limiting the advertising did not help, compulsory rules necessary, as CAI-company ads were 2,2 times more likely to be excessive and 2,5 times more likely to be less healthy than non-CAI ads. CAI-company product ads also contained more energy, sugar and Na per 100 g serving than non-CAI ads on average.	54 million food/ beverage ads	Canada internet ads in children web sites
Neyens & Smits (2017).	49 Belgian and Dutch child-targeting food websites	found that 88,5 pct of signatory companies used unhealthy ads to children, ad-break reminders were completely absent, therefore children had unlimited access to websites promoting unhealthy food.	49 Belgian and Dutch food content in children websites	Belgium and Dutch internet ads of children web sites
Boyland, E. J., & Whalen, R. (2015).	Review literature (2009–2014) food advertising, food marketing, children,	found food advertising promotes largely energy dense, nutrient poor foods to increase food consumption. Policy makers must change rules to support healthier choices and reduce the incidence of obesity and related diseases.	review literature of 2009-2014	review of food marketing to children in 2009–2014

continued on following page

Table 3. Continued

Author / Year	Methodology	Results/key Findings	Sample	Research Area
Gallopel-Morvan et al. (2017)	survey	found that French Évin law does not appear to protect young people effectively from exposure to alcohol advertising in France.	6642 students survey	France rule banning alcohol
León-Flández, et al. (2017).	Cross sectional (2008 and 2012)	found that non-compliance with the Spanish Code of self-regulation (PAOS Code) in 2012 is higher than 2008.	2582 ads	Spain self-regulation ads to children evaluation

Table 4. Recommendations of institutions/specialists

Author / Year	Methodology	Results/key Findings	Sample	Research Area
Pearson et al. (2020).	trial with children and parents	show that reductions in children's computer game use were found after intervention in the groups, while self-reported smartphone use increased in these groups.	75 children and 64 parents	recommended time limitation
Rasmussen et al. (2020).	randomized controlled trial	advised limiting screen time	95 families and 186 children	recommended time limitation
Harris, et al. (2009).	review	suggested to reduce food marketing	review	recommended time limitation (reduce food marketing)
Council on Communications and Media, (2016).	statement guidance	advised time limits and to take part with the children in healthy activities	statement / guidance	recommended 18 months avoid any type of screen
Viner, R., Davie, M., & Firth, A. (2019).	education guidance web site for parents	suggested families to set screen time with children together	parents	recommended time limitation with families
Harvard University, Center on Media and Child Health. (2021)	education guidance web site for parents	stated that screens are integrated to daily life via-smart phones, in classes, as watches, in cars and even in the hands of babies, therefore family digital wellness website is established	families	parents educaton/recommendation
American Academy of Pediatrics. (2022).	education guidance web site for parents	recommended parents to play with their kids	parents	parents educaton/recommendation

Chapter 7
Beyond Goodwill:
The Interplay of CSR Communication, Individual Beliefs, and Corporate Reputation

Stefania Romenti
IULM University, Italy

Chiara Esposito
IULM University, Italy

Elanor Colleoni
http://orcid.org/0000-0001-7176-0638
IULM University, Italy

Grazia Murtarelli
http://orcid.org/0000-0002-6602-8503
IULM University, Italy

ABSTRACT

This chapter investigates the interplay between consumer activism, corporate social responsibility communication (CSR), and corporate reputation. Using IKEA as a case study, the present study investigates the relationship between CSR communication, CSR-fit, CSR credibility, individual beliefs and corporate reputation using a quantitative design to quantitatively assess the role of CSR-fit and CSR credibility in mediating the role of CSR communication on corporate reputation and the influence of individual beliefs as a moderator of corporate reputation. Results confirm that a strong alignment between a company's CSR initiatives and its core activities positively enhances the credibility of its CSR engagement, consequently contributing to a favorable corporate reputation. By synthesizing academic theories and real-world insights, this research contributes to the understanding of the relationship between individual beliefs, CSR, and corporate reputation, offering valuable implications for companies navigating the complex realm of consumer activism and reputation management.

DOI: 10.4018/979-8-3693-3767-7.ch007

Copyright ©2024, IGI Global. Copying or distributing in print or electronic forms without written permission of IGI Global is prohibited.

INTRODUCTION

In a context where societal fears are on the rise, trust in government and media is declining, and institutions are failing to address existential challenges such as the pandemic and climate change, businesses are pressured to take on societal problems.

The increasing importance of Corporate Social Responsibility (CSR) in this context has led to a growing body of research exploring the relationship between CSR and corporate reputation (e.g., Brammer et al., 2007; Sen et al., 2006; Chen, 2010). However, the role of individual beliefs in shaping perceptions of CSR and its impact on corporate reputation remains underexplored.

In recent years, the landscape of corporate social responsibility (CSR) has witnessed a profound shift, where all stakeholders hold business accountable. According to the 2023 Edelman Trust Barometer, among more than 36.000 respondents in 28 countries, 58% buy or advocate for brands based on their beliefs and values, 60% choose a place to work according to their belief and values, 64% invest following their beliefs and values and 88% of institutional investors subject ESG to the same scrutiny as operational and financial considerations. These findings highlight the growing importance of understanding how individual beliefs shape perceptions of CSR and its impact on corporate reputation.

This changing panorama reflects a transformation in consumer behavior, where individuals increasingly consider a company's social and environmental practices when making purchasing decisions (Maignan & Ferrell, 2004; Du et al., 2010). Simultaneously, companies have been adapting their CSR strategies and their communication activities to align with consumer expectations and societal concerns (Brammer et al., 2007; Sen et al., 2006; Chen, 2010). Despite these efforts, the effectiveness of CSR communication in enhancing corporate reputation remains a subject of debate, particularly in the context of the evolving media landscape (Castelló et al., 2013). The evolving media landscape, characterized by the rise of digital platforms and social media, has significantly impacted the dynamics of CSR communication and consumer activism (Verk et al., 2021). Consumers are no longer passive recipients of corporate messages but active participants in shaping the narrative around CSR (Castelló et al., 2013). The ease of information sharing and the ability to mobilize support through digital channels have empowered consumers to hold companies accountable for their social and environmental impact (Glozer et al., 2019). This shift in power dynamics has intensified the need for companies to engage in authentic and transparent CSR communication, as any perceived inconsistencies can quickly lead to consumer backlash and reputational damage (Rim & Song, 2016). The proliferation of digital media and online platforms has significantly amplified consumer voices, enabling them to express their opinions, share experiences, and mobilize support for causes they care about (Glozer et al., 2019). Social media, in particular, has become a powerful tool for consumers to engage in activism and hold companies accountable for their actions (Rim & Song, 2016). The viral nature of social media allows consumer concerns and criticisms to spread rapidly, putting pressure on companies to address issues and communicate their CSR efforts effectively (Verk et al., 2021).

In this scenario, the topic of Corporate Social Responsibility (CSR) garners mixed reactions, becoming particularly polarizing in the context of the evolving media landscape (Castelló et al., 2013; Kim & Rim, 2024; Park, 2022;). According to Castelló et al., (2013) for instance, social media speed up and widen communication, inviting a range of perspectives that can intensify debates around CSR. The authors point out that CSR's narrative is becoming richer and more complex, pushing companies to adeptly manage a broader and more varied conversation with their stakeholders. This has led, for example, to a growing interest in audiences with different attitudes towards CSR communication, such as skeptics (Kim & Rim, 2024; Park, 2022) or advocates (Kent & Taylor, 2016; Shah & Khan, 2021). CSR advocates for instance argue that businesses have a broader obligation than just profit-making; they should consider their impact on society, the environment, and all stakeholders (Shah & Khan, 2021). This view is increasingly amplified through digital platforms, where stories of corporate good deeds can quickly enhance a brand's reputation and foster customer loyalty, suggesting a potential pathway to long-term profitability (Kent & Taylor, 2016).

Amidst this evolving scenario, understanding how individual beliefs shape CSR and CSR communication initiatives perceptions and influence corporate reputation has become paramount. While the relationship between CSR, its communication, and corporate reputation is recognized, the detailed investigation of how individual beliefs affect the perception of CSR and in turn influence corporate reputation is still not fully explored. This chapter aims to fill this gap by examining the role of individual beliefs in shaping perceptions of CSR and its impact on corporate reputation. The challenge lies in unraveling the intricate interplay between individual beliefs, the alignment of CSR with a company's core activities (CSR-fit), and the resultant effects on corporate reputation. Bridging this gap is critical to providing companies with insights into managing their CSR disclosure initiatives in the face of rising consumers expectations and the consequent increase in consumer activism.

This chapter aims to explore the influence of consumers' individual beliefs in shaping corporate reputation. More specifically, the goal is to address a gap in the current academic literature shifting the focus from the macro-level of analysis of CSR to the micro-level, that of the individual perceptions of CSR information dissemination practices by consumers to explore if the level of knowledge and interest that consumers hold about CSR affect their advocacy behaviours and their activism in favour or against a company, ultimately shaping the company's reputation. By examining the role of individual beliefs in shaping perceptions of CSR and its impact on corporate reputation, this study contributes to the growing body of research on the effectiveness of CSR communication in the evolving media landscape.

In order to do so, the present study investigates the relationship between CSR perception, CSR-fit, CSR credibility, individual beliefs and corporate reputation using a quantitative design to quantitatively assess the role of CSR-fit and CSR credibility in mediating the role of CSR perception on corporate reputation and the influence of individual beliefs as a moderator of corporate reputation.

This chapter contributes to both academia and industry. Academically, it advances our understanding of how individual beliefs shape CSR perception and how this perception, in turn, impacts corporate reputation. Practically, the findings offer valuable insights for companies aiming to strategically navigate the evolving media landscape, guiding them in aligning their CSR communication initiatives with their core activities and enhancing their corporate reputation.

THEORETICAL BACKGROUND

CSR Communication as a Driver for Corporate Reputation

Corporate reputation plays a crucial role in the success and sustainability of businesses in today's competitive and interconnected world. It refers to the overall perception, evaluation, and assessment of a company's character, actions, and behavior by its stakeholders, including consumers, employees, investors, and the public (Fombrun, 1996). It represents the collective beliefs, opinions, and judgments formed about a company based on its past actions, performance, and communication.

The significance of corporate reputation cannot be overstated. It serves as **a** valuable intangible asset that can have a significant impact on a company's success and competitiveness in the marketplace (Dowling, 2006).

Reputation forms through signaling: companies send out signals about their actions and individuals evaluate them. The reputational judgement of a company is thus based on a set of attributes ascribed to a firm, inferred from firm's past actions (Weigelt & Camerer, 1988).

A strong reputation can contribute to increased customer loyalty, positive brand perception, stakeholder trust, and enhanced financial performance (Fombrun & Shanley, 1990). On the other hand, a damaged or negative reputation can result in lost sales, reduced employee morale, investor skepticism, and difficulties in attracting and retaining talent (Barnett et al., 2006).

Numerous factors influence corporate reputation, including the company's financial performance, product quality, customer service, stakeholder engagement, organizational culture and corporate governance (Fombrun, 1996).

Consistency in delivering on promises and meeting stakeholder expectations is crucial in forming a positive reputation. In recent years, corporate social responsibility (CSR) has emerged as a significant driver of corporate reputation (Sen & Bhattacharya, 2001).

CSR refers to an organization's commitment to balancing its economic, social, and environmental responsibilities while addressing societal concerns (Carroll, 1979). By voluntarily engaging in CSR activities, companies demonstrate their commitment to social and environmental causes, contributing to societal well-being and considering the interests of multiple stakeholders (Carroll, 1999). Linked to CSR management, CSR communication has been increasingly explored in recent years. CSR communication is a complex and dynamic process through which businesses share their commitment and actions towards social responsibility with a broad audience. This process involves a wide range of activities designed to communicate a company's initiatives in CSR, their societal and environmental impact, and their alignment with the company's core values and objectives. Recent developments in CSR communication and in the media landscape indicate a trend towards more engaged and dialogic methods (Song & Tao, 2022). This approach prioritizes active engagement and dialogue with stakeholders over merely broadcasting information, signifying a departure from viewing communication solely as a tool for achieving business goals (Verk et al., 2021). Instead, there is a growing recognition of CSR communication as a foundational element in the creation and negotiation of CSR's meaning and its role within society (O'Connor & Ihlen, 2018).

One of the prominent concerns related to the increasing attention to CSR communication is the emergence of conflicting expectations among diverse stakeholder groups about the contents of CSR disclosures (Verk et al., 2021). Given the unique interests of diverse stakeholder groups, these conflicts can create suspicion and mistrust when CSR communications are perceived as excessive, thereby deterring companies from achieving a favorable CSR image (Verk et al., 2021).

In the digital age, the role of media platforms in shaping CSR communication and corporate reputation has become increasingly significant. The rise of social media, online forums, and influencer marketing has transformed the way companies interact with their stakeholders and communicate their CSR initiatives (Colleoni, 2013; Etter et al., 2018). Digital platforms have amplified the reach and impact of CSR messages, allowing companies to engage directly with consumers, share compelling stories, and demonstrate their commitment to social and environmental causes (Cho et al., 2017). However, the digital landscape has also empowered consumers to hold companies accountable for their actions, with online activism and viral campaigns putting pressure on organizations to address societal concerns and maintain a positive reputation (Rim & Song, 2016). In this context, companies must develop proactive and responsive CSR communication strategies that leverage the power of digital media while navigating the challenges of a rapidly evolving and increasingly scrutinized business environment (Glozer et al., 2019). By effectively utilizing digital platforms and engaging in authentic, transparent, and stakeholder-centric communication, companies can build trust, strengthen their reputation, and foster meaningful relationships with their consumers in the digital era (Verk et al., 2021).

In this section, we explore the relationship between CSR and corporate reputation, shedding light on how CSR initiatives can shape stakeholder perceptions and enhance a company's reputation.

CSR communication initiatives that address societal concerns, such as environmental sustainability, community development, and ethical business practices, are seen as indicators of a company's commitment to responsible behavior (Bhattacharya et al., 2008). Positive perceptions of a company's CSR efforts can translate into favorable reputational outcomes, including increased trust, loyalty, and positive word-of-mouth (Du et al., 2010; Chen, 2010).

Research has shown that organizations engaging in socially responsible practices tend to enjoy enhanced reputation among stakeholders, including consumers, investors, and employees (Brammer et al., 2007; Sen et al., 2006).

Consumers are increasingly considering CSR information and disclosure practices when making purchasing choices, particularly among socially conscious and environmentally aware segments of the population (Maignan & Ferrell, 2004; Chen, 2010). By aligning their purchasing decisions with companies that demonstrate social responsibility, consumers aim to contribute to positive social change and feel a sense of ethical consumption. This consumer behavior not only supports CSR initiatives but also strengthens the reputation of socially responsible companies.

CSR communication initiatives also provide companies with an opportunity to differentiate themselves in a competitive marketplace (Porter & Kramer, 2006). In industries where products and services are largely commoditized, a strong CSR reputation can serve as a unique selling proposition, attracting socially conscious consumers and investors (Sen & Bhattacharya, 2001). CSR can also contribute to building brand equity, as consumers increasingly associate socially responsible behavior with positive brand attributes (Creyer & Ross, 1997).

Corporate CSR communication activities have a positive impact on internal stakeholders as well. Companies with robust CSR practices tend to attract and retain top talent, as employees are more likely to be motivated and committed to organizations that demonstrate a genuine commitment to societal welfare (Bhattacharya et al., 2008). Moreover, CSR activities enhance employee morale, job satisfaction, and overall organizational commitment (Brammer et al., 2007). This internal positive perception of the company's CSR initiatives can lead to increased productivity, reduced turnover, and a more engaged workforce.

Finally, CSR communication practices can also attract investors who increasingly prioritize environmental, social, and governance (ESG) factors in their investment decisions. Companies with a strong CSR reputation are more likely to gain investor trust and access to sustainable investment capital, contributing to long-term financial stability and growth. Furthermore, research has shown that CSR communication can have a positive impact on consumer attitudes and behaviors, such as brand loyalty, purchase intentions, and advocacy (Du et al., 2010; Bhattacharya & Sen, 2004). However, the effectiveness of CSR communication is influenced by various factors, including the perceived fit between the company's

CSR initiatives and its core business (Becker-Olsen et al., 2006), the credibility of the communication (Yoon et al., 2006), and the individual beliefs and values of the consumers (Bhattacharya et al., 2009).

It is important to note that the impact of CSR on corporate reputation is contingent upon the authenticity and credibility of CSR initiatives. Companies that engage in greenwashing or implement CSR activities without genuine commitment and integration into their core business practices risk damaging their reputation (Porter & Kramer, 2006). Stakeholders are becoming more and more skeptical and demand transparency and accountability in CSR efforts. Hence, it is crucial for companies to ensure the alignment of CSR activities with their core values, strategy, and operations (Kim & Fergusson, 2019; Gilal et. al., 2021).

In addition to enhancing corporate reputation, CSR practices also contribute to financial performance and long-term business sustainability. Numerous studies have demonstrated a positive relationship between CSR and financial performance, refuting the notion that organizations must prioritize profit at the expense of social and environmental considerations (Orlitzky et al., 2003).

Furthermore, CSR communication activities have been proven to act as a buffer and insure firms against reputational risks and crisis situations, saving the firm money, avoiding regulatory scrutiny, and preserving the value of its brand (Minor & Morgan, 2011).

In conclusion, CSR plays a vital role as a driver for corporate reputation, and it is increasingly crucial for companies to understand the relationship between CSR and corporate reputation to navigate the evolving expectations and demands of stakeholders.

The Role of CSR-Fit: The Link Between a Company's CSR Activities and its Core Business

CSR activities and CSR communication practices are being increasingly adopted by companies based on growing evidence that appealing CSR activities bring many benefits to the firm and that consumers are willing to give incentives to socially responsible corporations (Ellen et al., 2000; Sen & Bhattacharya, 2001; Nelson, 2004; Moon, 2014; Zhang et al., 2017).

However, stakeholders are becoming more and more skeptical and demand transparency and accountability in CSR efforts. Hence, it is crucial for companies to ensure the alignment of CSR activities with their core values, strategy, and operations (Kim & Fergusson, 2019; Gilal et. al., 2021).

To create better consumer perceptions towards CSR communication activities, firms need to have strategic CSR activities (Moon, 2014). To take full advantage of CSR activities, the firms need to consider not only what they do, but also how those activities are recognized by consumers taking into account CSR-brand fit (Kemp & Owen, 2013). The CSR-brand fit is defined as the CSR activities which align with the companies' core business. Core business activities refer to representative aspects of the companies which can be their products or services (Kemp & Owen, 2013).

According to the findings by Austin and Gaither (2018) and Alhouti, Johnson and Holloway (2016), the CSR-brand fit can be divided into four dimensions, which are high/low fit, and positive/negative fit. The first two dimensions (high/low fit) describes how much the CSR communication activities are aligned with the companies' core business, and the latter two (positive/negative fit) indicate how the CSR practices influence the brand image through the congruence of companies' CSR activities and their core business.

As claimed by Austin and Gaither (2018), CSR-brand fit has a positive effect on companies' reputation only when it is high, and the goal of CSR activities aligns positively with companies' image.

Studies have shown that when CSR activities are closely aligned with a company's core business, they can generate various benefits. CSR-fit can lead to strategic advantages such as improved brand reputation, enhanced customer loyalty, and increased market value (Margolis & Walsh, 2003). Consumers tend to perceive CSR disclosure activities that are consistent with a company's core business as more genuine and authentic, which can positively impact their purchasing decisions (Sen & Bhattacharya, 2001).

Another study by Fatma and Khan (2020) also highlighted that when CSR communication initiatives are harmonized with company's core business, the consumers tend to have more credibility and sincerity towards not only the activities but the brand itself, positively affecting corporate reputation. Similarly, Gilal et al. (2021) stated that well-structured CSR-brand fit leads to consumers to have a higher positive image and loyalty to the brand.

It is critical to mention that consumers rely heavily on companies' prior reputation to make inference on attribution of CSR motives (Song et al., 2018; Kim & Fergusson, 2019).

Schema theory argues that high-fit CSR programs have a positive impact (Rifon et al. 2004; Seok et al., 2012), as a good fit between prior expectations, knowledge, associations, actions, and competencies of a company and a specific social initiative can more easily be incorporated into the consumer's pre-existing cognitive structure, i.e. schema, strengthening the link between the company and the social initiative. Information processing will be more fluid and lead to less skepticism when the new CSR information is consistent with customers' pre-existing schema associated with the brand.

In addition to that, according to image transfer theory, consumers transfer the company's prior image to its CSR programs (Hoeffler & Keller 2002; Meenaghan 2001). Therefore, companies with negative associations benefit from implementing low-fit CSR programs, because a low-fit CSR program attenuates the transferability of bad associations from the company itself to its CSR programs.

Under a bad prior reputation condition, it has been proven that high-fit CSR elicits significantly higher skeptical attribution than low-fit CSR, and the escalated skepticism leads to worsened attitudes toward the company, weaker supportive communication intent and weaker purchase intent (Aksak et al., 2016; Kim & Ferguson, 2019).

Authenticity of CSR-brand fit plays an important role in terms of corporate hypocrisy (Kim & Lee, 2019). The concept of CSR-fit has been extensively studied in the literature, with numerous studies highlighting its importance in shaping consumer perceptions and attitudes towards CSR initiatives (e.g., Sen & Bhattacharya, 2001; Becker-Olsen et al., 2006; Simmons & Becker-Olsen, 2006). When CSR activities are perceived as congruent with a company's core business, consumers are more likely to view them as authentic and credible, leading to more positive evaluations of the company (Becker-Olsen et al., 2006). howWhen CSR communication activities are perceived as disconnected or incongruent with a company's core business, it can lead to skepticism and accusations of greenwashing (Brammer & Millington, 2008). The results of the study by Alhouti et al. (2016) show that firms must consider not only filling the gap between their core business and CSR disclosure activities, but also not having "wrong" CSR activities which is defined as CSR-brand misfit.

Stakeholders, including consumers, investors, and advocacy groups, may question the authenticity of a company's CSR claims and its commitment to social and environmental responsibility (Brammer et al., 2012). As stakeholders do not blindly believe companies' stated motives to be true, being honest about the business interests behind CSR has been proven to increase the credibility of the communicated messages. (Song & Wen, 2019). Finally, the same study highlighted that the motives also interact with other factors, like reputation and CSR-fit to influence the CSR outcome.

The Role of Individual Beliefs in Shaping Corporate Reputation

Although CSR encompasses policies and actions undertaken by organizations, it is important to note that these policies and actions are influenced and implemented by actors operating at various levels, including institutional, organizational, and individual (Aguinis & Glavas, 2012). However, Aguinis and Glavas (2012) stressed how existing literature exhibits a high degree of fragmentation, with scholars approaching the subject from various disciplinary and conceptual perspectives. This fragmentation is also visible at the levels of analysis employed: typically, there is a predominant focus on the macro level (institutional or organizational) rather than the micro level (individual).

Given the existing gap in individual level analysis within the CSR literature, this study aims to address this limitation by specifically focusing on the individual level of analysis, providing valuable insights into the role of individual beliefs and its impact on corporate reputation.

As pointed out by Bhattacharya et al. (2009), people's beliefs, values, and ideologies influence their expectations and judgments regarding a company's CSR communication practices. For example, individuals with strong environmental beliefs may evaluate a company's environmental sustainability initiatives more favorably, while those prioritizing social justice may focus on a company's labor practices and community engagement. Understanding how individual beliefs interact with CSR perception, company's credibility, and ultimately corporate reputation, can provide insights into the diverse responses of consumers and other stakeholders to a company's CSR activities. Individual beliefs and values play a crucial role in shaping consumer perceptions and responses to CSR communication (Bhattacharya et al., 2009). Consumers with strong pro-social or pro-environmental beliefs are more likely to engage with and support companies that demonstrate a commitment to social and environmental responsibility (Sen & Bhattacharya, 2001). On the other hand, consumers who prioritize economic value or have more conservative beliefs may be less receptive to CSR initiatives (Bhattacharya & Sen, 2004).

The rise of consumer social responsibility (CnSR) has expanded the scope of factors influencing consumer decisions beyond traditional considerations such as price, reliability, and availability (Caruana & Chatzidakis, 2014). It now encompasses social issues related to justice, fairness, rights, virtue, and sustainability. CnSR refers to the conscious and deliberate choice to make consumption decisions based on personal and moral beliefs (Devinney et al., 2006).

As a result, the relationship between corporations and consumers has evolved from one primarily focused on utility maximization and product efficiency to a more complex socio-moral and political connection. Consumers now extend their "moral gaze" (Crane, 2005) to scrutinize corporations and expect them to demonstrate corporate social responsibility (Bhattacharya & Sen, 2004; Vogel, 2005).

Hypotheses Development

Based on the foregoing discussion, this study proposes the following theoretical framework:

Figure 1. Theoretical framework

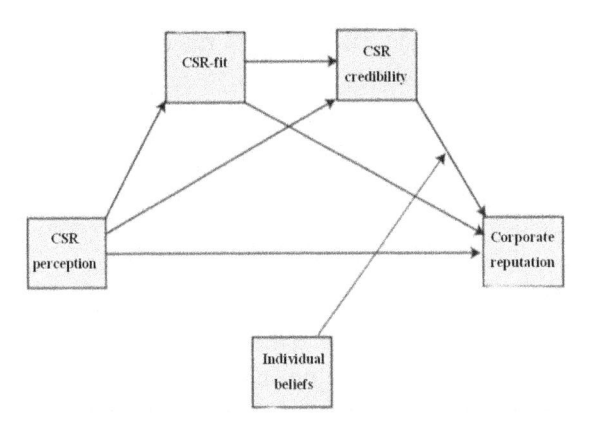

Taking the theoretical model as a reference, the hypotheses that will guide this study have been formulated as follows:

H1. CSR perception has a direct relationship/significant positive impact on corporate reputation.

H2. CSR perception has an indirect significant positive impact on corporate reputation, mediated by CSR-fit and the credibility towards a company's CSR actions.

H3. Individual beliefs act as a moderator between credibility and reputation, ultimately shaping the relationship between CSR perception and corporate reputation.

These hypotheses will serve as a foundation for the subsequent section, where a case study of IKEA will be conducted to examine the influence of individual beliefs and CSR-fit on corporate reputation in the context of consumer activism.

METHODOLOGY

In order to test our hypothesis, we asked carried out a survey asking respondents to express their opinions about the CSR actions and corporate reputation of the company IKEA, a multinational furniture and home furnishings retailer known for its functional and affordable products.

IKEA has been chosen for this case study due to several compelling reasons. Firstly, IKEA is a globally recognized company renowned for its commitment to sustainability and corporate social responsibility (Ambrose, 2021; IKEA, 2021a; IKEA, 2022a). The company has a strong reputation for its efforts in environmental conservation, responsible sourcing, and social initiatives, making it an ideal subject for exploring the relationship between individual beliefs, CSR-fit, and corporate reputation. Furthermore, IKEA's emphasis on transparency and accountability in its sustainability practices makes it an excellent case study candidate. The company's sustainability report provides detailed information about its goals, progress, and challenges in various sustainability areas. This transparency enables to gain deeper insights into the alignment between IKEA's CSR activities and its core business.

Data Collection Methods

The data have been collected through a self-administered questionnaire, designed through Google Forms and distributed with a snowball sample of 120 respondents. The data collection process took place during June 2023. The survey provided valuable insights into the respondents' beliefs, perceptions, and experiences regarding IKEA's CSR initiatives and its impact on corporate reputation.

Variables

To develop the questionnaire, each set of questions corresponding to the different variables in the theoretical model has been retrieved from pre-existing batteries, backed by sounding theory.

The first variable taken into consideration is the overall CSR perception of IKEA, which captures individuals' general perception of a company's commitment to corporate social responsibility. The battery included in the questionnaire comprises four questions and investigates the respondents' beliefs about IKEA's social role, environmental efforts, and commitment beyond profit generation (Chaudary et. al, 2016).

The second variable is CSR-Fit, and it is set to measure the extent to which a IKEA's CSR initiatives align with its core business activities. It assesses the congruence between the company's CSR programs and its overall mission and values (Joo et al., 2019, cited in Fatma & Khan, 2020).

Then, the third variable is CSR credibility (Joo et al., 2019, cited in Fatma & Khan, 2020) and its battery includes three questions aimed at assessing the respondents' perception of the authenticity and genuineness of IKEA's CSR engagement. It captures their beliefs about whether the CSR initiatives reflect the company's values and beliefs.

Then, prior individual beliefs towards IKEA were captured using a battery with two questions about their affective commitment (Mowday et al.,1979, cited in Fatma & Khan, 2020), and then another two questions about their attachment to the company based on positive CSR perceptions (Thomson et al., 2005, cited in Chaudary et al., 2016).

Finally, the likelihood of the respondents to actively engage in a series of advocacy behaviors such as for example positive word of mouth, mentioning CSR activities to other people, posting on social media in favor of the company or taking part in a protest against IKEA in favor of a cause that is relevant to the respondents (Romani et al., 2013), was captured through a series of six general questions and five questions specifically related to IKEA,.

All these variables are expected to influence the last battery included in the theoretical model, that is corporate reputation. The battery used to investigate this item, according to Fombrun, Ponzi, Gardberg (2011), captures the overall perception and evaluation that individuals hold about a company, including their feelings, trust, admiration, and respect towards the company.

Statistical Analysis

In order to test the statistical validity of the theoretical model, the moderated mediation model 87 of PROCESS model was used following Hayes SPSS syntax.

The variables previously outlined for this study (Image 1), have been included in model 87 (Image 4) as follows:

Y: dependent/outcome variable → corporate reputation

X: independent/predictor variable → CSR perception
M_1: first mediator → CSR-fit
M_2: second mediator → CSR credibility
W: moderator → individual beliefs (individual advocacy)

The output tables of the statistical analysis contain all the relevant information to determine if the hypotheses have been met or not.

Figure 2. Statistical framework

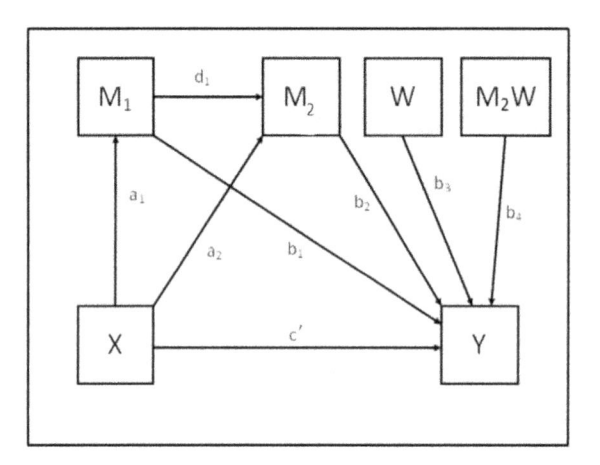

FINDINGS

The aim of the present analysis is to explore if the three hypotheses, previously outlined in this study, are confirmed. The single steps of the statistical analysis all have the objective of determining whether firstly the mediations M_1, M_2 (CSR-fit and CSR credibility) are present and secondly finding out whether the moderator W (individual advocacy) is changing the strength of the indirect effect of X (CSR perception) on Y (corporate reputation).

The results of the individual sections are presented in Table 1 and Table 2.

Table 1. Summary table direct relationships

Direct Relationships	Unstandardised Coefficient	T values
csr_perc → csr_fit (path a_1)	1.1702**	18.3756
csr_fit → csr_cred (path d_1)	0.5442**	12.0573
csr_perc → csr_cred (path a_2)	0.5398**	8.8082
csr_fit → rep (path b_1)	0.1457	1.4574
csr_cred → rep (path b_2)	- 0.0651	- 0.3102
csr_perc → rep (path c')	0.3049**	2.6044

continued on following page

Table 1. Continued

Direct Relationships	Unstandardised Coefficient	T values
ind_adv → rep (path b_3)	- 0.6365**	- 3.6449
cred*ind_adv → rep (path b_4)	0.0988**	2.8720

Table 2. Summary table indirect relationships

Indirect Relationship	Direct Effect	Indirect Effect (SE)	Confidence Interval Low/High
csr_perc → csr_fit → csr_cred → cred rep	0.3049**	0.2104(0.0995)**	0.0060/0.4032
Probing Moderated Indirect Relationships	*Effect*	*SE*	*Confidence Interval Low/High*
Low Level of ind_adv	0.1474	0.1051	-0.0742/0.3393
High Level of ind_adv	0.3048**	0.1028	0.1077/0.5121
Index of Moderated Mediation	0.0629**	0.0253	0.0197/0.1192

The first output is the one for the outcome variable M_1 (CSR fit). There is only one predictor, which is the variable specified as X (CSR perception). The results show that path a_1 is significant, which means that CSR perception has a significant impact on CSR-fit (b=1.1702, t=18.3756, p<0.001).

The output for the second mediator M_2 (CSR credibility) has two predictors, the X variable (CSR perception) and the first mediator (CSR fit). The results show that both the a_2 and the d_1 paths are significant. The a_2 path shows that CSR perception has a significant impact on CSR-credibility (b = 0.5398, t = 8.8082, p < 0.001), while the d_1 path indicates that CSR-fit has a significant impact on CSR credibility (b = 0.5442, t = 12.0573, p < 0.001).

Then, the output for the Y variable (corporate reputation) is presented. This output gives the b_1, b_2, b_3, b_4 and c' paths. Path c' shows that CSR perception has a significant impact on corporate reputation (b = 0.3049, t = 2.6044, p = 0.0104). While path b_3 shows that individual advocacy has a significant negative impact on corporate reputation (b = -0.6365, t = -3.6449, p = 0.0004). Also path b_4, called the interaction effect, is significant (b = 0.0988, t = 2.8720, p = 0.0049) which means that the interaction between CSR credibility and individual advocacy has a significant effect on corporate reputation.

The moderator (individual advocacy) negativity affects the relationship between CSR credibility and reputation, meaning that it weakens the relationship. Furthermore, the R2-chng (0.0119) for the interaction effect between CSR credibility and individual advocacy is statistically significant (p = 0.0049) which means that the interaction is causing a significant change in the outcome variable (corporate reputation).

On the contrary, paths b_1 and b_2 are not significant. This means that CSR-fit and CSR credibility do not have a significant direct impact on corporate reputation.

The Johnson-Neyman analysis for individual advocacy, the table indicates that for low levels of individual advocacy, the variable has no significant effect (ind_adv = 3.0000, b = 0.2315, t = 1.5413, p = 0.1261), but it has a significant and higher effect at higher levels (ind_adv = 4.0000, b = 0.3303, t = 2.3269, p = 0.0218; ind_adv = 5.5000, b = 0.4786, t = 3.3037, p = 0.0013).

The model also confirms that the direct impact of CSR on corporate reputation (path c') is significant (b = 0.3049, t = 2.6044, p = 0.0104). The conditional indirect effects show that the indirect effect in presence of the mediators CSR-fit and CSR credibility is lower and non-significant at low levels of individual advocacy, higher and significant at higher individual advocacy.

The indirect effect in presence of the moderator individual advocacy (At Mean Level) is 0.2104, and per the bootstrap, that is within the confidence interval at p < 0.05.

Finally, the results show that individual advocacy moderates the indirect effect of CSR perception on corporate reputation which means that the strength from X (CSR perception) to Y (corporate reputation) through the mediators M1 and M2 (CSR-fit, CSR credibility) changes with the changes in individual advocacy.

It also shows that the index of moderated mediation is significant. Thus, we can conclude that the indirect effect is moderated by individual advocacy.

At the conclusion of this analysis, it is now possible to assess whether or not the initial hypotheses are confirmed.

Hypothesis H1 suggested that CSR perception had a significant positive impact on corporate reputation. H1 was supported as the direct effect of CSR perception on corporate reputation (b = 0.3049, t = 2.6044, p = 0.0104) is positive and significant.

Hypothesis H2 suggested that the indirect effect of CSR perception on corporate reputation will be mediated by CSR-fit and the credibility towards a company's CSR actions. H2 was supported as the indirect effect of CSR perception on corporate reputation (b = 0.2104, 95% CI = [0.0060/0.4032]) is positive and significant since 95% CI does not include 0.

Finally, Hypotheses 3 suggested that the indirect effect of CSR perception on corporate reputation through CSR-fit and the credibility towards a company's CSR actions will be moderated by individual beliefs, especially advocacy. H3 was supported as the index of moderated mediation (index = 0.0629, 95% CI = [0.0197/0.1192]) is significant since 95% CI does not include 0.

CONCLUSION

The goal of this chapter was to investigate how consumers perceive and react to corporate CSR communication initiatives by looking into the interplay between CSR perception, CSR-fit, credibility, individual beliefs, and corporate reputation within the context of IKEA.

Through a comprehensive analysis of the perception of IKEA, this study unraveled significant insights. The statistical analysis demonstrated how CSR-fit and credibility act as mediating factors in the relationships between CSR perception and corporate reputation, and additionally the moderator role of individual advocacy on corporate reputation.

Importantly the research confirms that a strong alignment between a company's CSR communication initiatives and its core activities positively enhances the credibility of its CSR engagement, consequently contributing to a favorable corporate reputation.

This study's theoretical significance lies in its contribution to the broader understanding of CSR and CSR communication by highlighting the pivotal role of individual beliefs as a driving force behind consumers' perceptions of CSR disclosure initiatives and their subsequent influence on corporate reputation. This aligns with studies such as Bhattacharya and Sen (2004), who emphasized the connection between consumer responses and CSR initiatives, thus extending the theoretical foundation of the field.

From a managerial standpoint, the findings offer valuable insights for organizations seeking to enhance their CSR communication strategies in response to the rise in consumer suspicion and mistrust towards corporate CSR and the subsequent surge of consumer activism. The study underscores the importance of aligning CSR communication initiatives with a company's core activities (CSR-fit) to foster credibility and positively influence corporate reputation. This echoes the findings of Du et al. (2010), who stressed the significance of effective CSR communication in shaping consumer perceptions. As underlined by Verk et al. (2021), the digital landscape poses significant challenges for firms used to more structured communication practices. According to the authors, the blurred lines between content consumers and creators in the realm of social media complicate established communication strategies, making CSR communication efforts even more complex.

The findings of this study also shed light on the intersection of CSR communication, consumer activism, and media dynamics. The rise of digital platforms and social media has transformed the way consumers engage with CSR information and express their support or dissatisfaction with corporate practices (Rim & Song, 2016). The real-time nature of social media has accelerated the spread of information and amplified the impact of consumer activism on corporate reputation (Glozer et al., 2019). Companies must adapt their CSR communication strategies to effectively navigate this dynamic landscape, leveraging the power of digital channels to engage in authentic dialogues with consumers while remaining vigilant to potential reputational risks (Verk et al., 2021). To effectively communicate CSR initiatives in the digital age, companies must adopt a multi-channel approach that leverages various media strategies and communication channels (Glozer et al., 2019). Social media platforms, such as Facebook, Twitter, and Instagram, provide opportunities for companies to engage directly with consumers, share CSR stories, and respond to feedback and concerns (Rim & Song, 2016). Influencer partnerships can also be a powerful tool for CSR communication, as influencers can help amplify CSR messages and lend credibility to a company's efforts (Verk et al., 2021). Additionally, digital storytelling techniques, such as videos, infographics, and interactive content, can help bring CSR initiatives to life and make them more engaging and memorable for consumers (Glozer et al., 2019). By leveraging these media strategies and communication channels, companies can effectively communicate their CSR efforts, build trust with consumers, and mitigate the risks associated with consumer activism in the digital age.

By examining the role of individual beliefs in shaping perceptions of CSR and its impact on corporate reputation, this study contributes to the broader understanding of how the changing media landscape influences the relationship between companies and consumers. The insights gained from this research can guide companies in developing CSR communication strategies that are responsive to the evolving expectations and activism of consumers in the digital age.

The insights derived from this study offer a roadmap for companies navigating the complex landscape of consumer activism and reputation management. By leveraging the theoretical foundations of this research and aligning them with practical strategies, companies can position themselves strategically to thrive in an era characterized by heightened consumer consciousness and changing expectations.

REFERENCES

Aguinis, H., & Glavas, A. (2012). What we know and don't know about corporate social responsibility: A review and research agenda. *Journal of Management*, 38(4), 932–968. 10.1177/0149206311436079

Aksak, E. O., Ferguson, M. A., & Duman, S. A. (2016). Corporate social responsibility and CSR fit as predictors of corporate reputation: A global perspective. *Public Relations Review*, 42(1), 79–81. 10.1016/j.pubrev.2015.11.004

Alhouti, S., Johnson, C., & Holloway, B. (2016). Corporate social responsibility authenticity: Investigating its antecedents and outcomes. *Journal of Business Research*, 69(3), 1242–1249. 10.1016/j.jbusres.2015.09.007

Ambrose, J. (2021, April 21). Ikea to invest £3.4bn in renewable energy by 2030. *The Guardian*. https://www.theguardian.com/business/2021/apr/21/ikea-to-invest-34bn-by-2030-in-renewable-energy

Austin, L., & Gaither, B. (2018). Redefining fit: Examining CSR company-issue fit in stigmatized industries. *Journal of Brand Management*, 26(1), 9–20. 10.1057/s41262-018-0107-3

Barnett, M. L., Jermier, J. M., & Lafferty, B. A. (2006). Corporate reputation: The definitional landscape. *Corporate Reputation Review*, 9(1), 26–38. 10.1057/palgrave.crr.1550012

Baxter, P., & Jack, S. (2008). Qualitative case study methodology: Study design and implementation for novice researchers. *The Qualitative Report*, 13(4), 544–559.

Bhattacharya, C. B., Korschun, D., & Sen, S. (2009). Strengthening stakeholder–company relationships through mutually beneficial corporate social responsibility initiatives. *Journal of Business Ethics*, 85(2), 257–272. 10.1007/s10551-008-9730-3

Bhattacharya, C. B., & Sen, S. (2004). Doing better at doing good: When, why, and how consumers respond to corporate social initiatives. *California Management Review*, 47(1), 9–24. 10.2307/41166284

Bhattacharya, C. B., Sen, S., & Korschun, D. (2008). Using corporate social responsibility to win the war for talent. *MIT Sloan Management Review*, 49(2), 37–44.

Birtchnell, T., Devinney, T. M., Auger, P., & Eckhardt, G. (2006). The other CSR. *Stanford Social Innovation Review*, 4(3), 30–37.

Boutilier, R. G., Thomson, I. H., & Geall, V. (2018). Greenwashing and the problem of legitimacy: Creating credibility in sustainability reporting. *Journal of Business Ethics*, 147(2), 349–362.

Brammer, S., Jackson, G., & Matten, D. (2012). Corporate social responsibility and institutional theory: New perspectives on private governance. *Socio-economic Review*, 10(1), 3–28. 10.1093/ser/mwr030

Brammer, S., & Millington, A. (2008). Does it pay to be different? An analysis of the relationship between corporate social and financial performance. *Strategic Management Journal*, 29(12), 1325–1343. 10.1002/smj.714

Brammer, S., Millington, A., & Rayton, B. (2007). The contribution of corporate social responsibility to organizational commitment. *International Journal of Human Resource Management*, 18(10), 1701–1719. 10.1080/09585190701570866

Brunk, K. H. (2010). Reputation building: Beyond our control? Inferences in consumers' ethical perception formation. *Journal of Consumer Behaviour*, 9(4), 275–292. 10.1002/cb.317

Carroll, A. B. (1979). A three-dimensional conceptual model of corporate performance. *Academy of Management Review*, 4(4), 497–505. 10.2307/257850

Carroll, A. B. (1999). Corporate social responsibility: Evolution of a definitional construct. *Business & Society*, 38(3), 268–295. 10.1177/000765039903800303

Caruana, R., & Chatzidakis, A. (2014). Consumer social responsibility (CnSR): Toward a multi-level, multi-agent conceptualization of the "other CSR". *Journal of Business Ethics*, 121(4), 577–592. 10.1007/s10551-013-1739-6

Castelló, I., Morsing, M., & Schultz, F. (2013). Communicative dynamics and the polyphony of corporate social responsibility in the network society. *Journal of Business Ethics*, 118(4), 683–694. 10.1007/s10551-013-1954-1

CDP. (n.d.). *Carbon Disclosure Project (CDP)*. CDP. https://www.cdp.net/

Chaudary, S., Zahid, Z., Shahid, S., Khan, S. N., & Azar, S. (2016). Customer perception of CSR initiatives: Its antecedents and consequences. *Social Responsibility Journal*, 12(2), 263–279. 10.1108/SRJ-04-2015-0056

Chen, H. S. (2010). Towards green loyalty: Driving from green perceived value, green satisfaction, and green trust. *Sustainable Development (Bradford)*, 21(5), 294–308. 10.1002/sd.500

Crane, A. (2005). Meeting the ethical gaze: Challenges for orienting to the ethical market. In Harrison, R., Newholm, T., & Shaw, D. (Eds.), *The ethical consumer* (pp. 421–432). Sage. 10.4135/9781446211991.n15

Creyer, E. H., & Ross, W. T. (1997). The influence of firm behavior on purchase intention: Do consumers really care about business ethics? *Journal of Consumer Marketing*, 14(6), 421–432. 10.1108/07363769710185999

Delmas, M., & Burbano, V. C. (2011). The drivers of greenwashing. *California Management Review*, 54(1), 64–87. 10.1525/cmr.2011.54.1.64

Deloitte. (2020). *#GetOutInFront - Global research report*. Deloitte..

Dowling, G. R. (2006). *Creating corporate reputation: Identity, image, and performance*. Oxford University Press.

Du, S., Bhattacharya, C. B., & Sen, S. (2010). Maximizing business returns to corporate social responsibility (CSR): The role of CSR communication. *International Journal of Management Reviews*, 12(1), 8–19. 10.1111/j.1468-2370.2009.00276.x

Edelman. (2023). *2023 Edelman Trust Barometer – Global report*. Edelman. https://www.edelman.com/trust/2023/trust-barometer

Ellen, P. S., Mohr, L. A., & Webb, D. J. (2000). Charitable programs and the retailer: Do they mix? *Journal of Retailing*, 76(3), 393–406. 10.1016/S0022-4359(00)00032-4

European Parliament and the Council of the European Union. (2014). *Directive 2014/95/EU of the European Parliament and of the Council of 22 October 2014 amending Directive 2013/34/EU as regards disclosure of non-financial and diversity information by certain large undertakings and groups*. Europea. https://data.europa.eu/eli/dir/2014/95/oj

European Parliament and the Council of the European Union. (2019). *Regulation (EU) 2019/2088 of the European Parliament and of the Council of 27 November 2019 on sustainability-related disclosures in the financial services sector*. Europea. https://data.europa.eu/eli/reg/2019/2088/oj

European Parliament and the Council of the European Union. (2022). *Directive (EU) 2022/2464 of the European Parliament and of the Council of 14 December 2022 amending Regulation (EU) No 537/2014, Directive 2004/109/EC, Directive 2006/43/EC and Directive 2013/34/EU, as regards corporate sustainability reporting*. Europa. https://data.europa.eu/eli/dir/2022/2464/oj

Fairtrade International. (n.d.). *Standards for businesses*. FTI. https://www.fairtrade.net/act/fairtrade-for-business

Fatma, M., & Khan, I. (2020). An investigation of consumer evaluation of authenticity of their company's CSR engagement. *Total Quality Management & Business Excellence*. 10.1080/14783363.2020.1791068

Fombrun, C. J. (1996). *Reputation: Realizing value from the corporate image*. Harvard Business School Press.

Fombrun, C. J., & Shanley, M. (1990). What's in a name? Reputation building and corporate strategy. *Academy of Management Journal*, 33(2), 233–258. 10.2307/256324

FSC. (n.d.). *What is FSC?* FSC. https://www.fsc.org/en/what-is-fsc

Gilal, F. G., Paul, J., Gilal, N. G., & Gilal, R. G. (2021). Strategic CSR-brand fit and customers' brand passion: Theoretical extension and analysis. *Psychology and Marketing*, 38(5), 759–773. 10.1002/mar.21464

GRI. (n.d.). *About GRI*. GRI. https://www.globalreporting.org/standards/

Hayes, A. F. (2022). *Introduction to mediation, moderation, and conditional process analysis: A regression-based approach*. Guilford Publications.

Hoeffler, S., & Keller, K. L. (2002). Building brand equity through corporate societal marketing. *Journal of Public Policy & Marketing*, 21(1), 78–89. 10.1509/jppm.21.1.78.17600

IKEA. (2021a). *IKEA continues commitment to climate action by joining COP26 as a partner*. IKEA. https://www.ikea.com/us/en/newsroom/corporate-news/ikea-joins-cop26-as-a-partner

IKEA. (2021b). *Insights from new global study*. IKEA. https://about.ikea.com/en/newsroom/2021/10/25/globescan-study-2021

IKEA. (2022a). *Sustainability – caring for people and the planet*. IKEA. https://about.ikea.com/en/sustainability

IKEA. (2022b). *People & Planet Positive - IKEA sustainability strategy*. IKEA. https://ikea-sustainability-strategy

IKEA. (2022c). We want to make healthy and sustainable living affordable for everyone. IKEA. https://about.ikea.com/en/sustainability/healthy-and-sustainable-living

IKEA. (2022d). *IKEA Sustainability Report FY2022*. IKEA. https://https://ikea-sustainability-report-fy22

ISO. (2018). *26000 Guidance on social responsibility*. ISO. https://www.iso.org/iso-26000-social-responsibility.html

Jackson, G., Bartosch, J., Avetisyan, E., Kinderman, D., & Knudsen, J. S. (2020). Mandatory non-financial disclosure and its influence on CSR: An international comparison. *Journal of Business Ethics*, 162(2), 323–342. 10.1007/s10551-019-04200-0

Kemp, D., & Owen, J. R. (2013). Community relations and mining: Core to business but not "core business.". *Resources Policy*, 38(4), 523–531. 10.1016/j.resourpol.2013.08.003

Kent, M. L., & Taylor, M. (2016). From Homo economicus to Homo dialogicus: Rethinking social media use in CSR communication. *Public Relations Review*, 42(1), 60–67. 10.1016/j.pubrev.2015.11.003

Kim, S., & Lee, H. (2019). The effect of CSR fit and CSR authenticity on the brand attitude. *Sustainability (Basel)*, 12(1), 275. 10.3390/su12010275

Kim, S., & Rim, H. (2024). The role of public skepticism and distrust in the process of CSR communication. *International Journal of Business Communication*, 61(2), 198–218. 10.1177/2329488419866888

Kim, Y., & Ferguson, M. A. (2019). Are high-fit CSR programs always better? The effects of corporate reputation and CSR fit on stakeholder responses. *Corporate Communications*, 24(3), 471–498. 10.1108/CCIJ-05-2018-0061

King, B. G. (2015). Reputation, risk, and anti-corporate activism: How social movements influence corporate outcomes. In L. Bosi, M. Giugni & K. Uba (2016), *The consequences of social movements* (pp. 215–236). Cambridge University Press.

Luo, X., & Bhattacharya, C. B. (2006). Corporate social responsibility, customer satisfaction, and market value. *Journal of Marketing*, 70(4), 1–18. 10.1509/jmkg.70.4.001

Maignan, I., & Ferrell, O. C. (2004). Corporate social responsibility and marketing: An integrative framework. *Journal of the Academy of Marketing Science*, 32(1), 3–19. 10.1177/0092070303258971

Margolis, J. D., & Walsh, J. P. (2003). Misery loves companies: Rethinking social initiatives by business. *Administrative Science Quarterly*, 48(2), 268–305. 10.2307/3556659

Matten, D., & Moon, J. (2008). "Implicit" and "explicit" CSR: A conceptual framework for a comparative understanding of corporate social responsibility. *Academy of Management Review*, 33(2), 404–424. 10.5465/amr.2008.31193458

Meenaghan, T. (2001). Understanding sponsorship effects. *Psychology and Marketing*, 18(2), 95–122. 10.1002/1520-6793(200102)18:2<95::AID-MAR1001>3.0.CO;2-H

Michelon, G., Pilonato, S., & Ricceri, F. (2015). CSR reporting practices and the quality of disclosure: An empirical analysis. *Critical Perspectives on Accounting*, 33, 59–78. 10.1016/j.cpa.2014.10.003

Minor, D., & Morgan, J. (2011). CSR as reputation insurance: Primum non nocere. *California Management Review*, 53(3), 40–59. 10.1525/cmr.2011.53.3.40

Moon, J. (2014). *Corporate social responsibility: A very short introduction*. Oxford University Press. 10.1093/actrade/9780199671816.001.0001

Mudrack, P. (2007). Individual personality factors that affect normative beliefs about the rightness of corporate social responsibility. *Business & Society*, 46(1), 33–62. 10.1177/0007650306290312

Nelson, K. A. (2004). Consumer decision making and image theory: Understanding value-laden decisions. *Journal of Consumer Psychology*, 14(1-2), 28–40. 10.1207/s15327663jcp1401&2_5

O'Connor, A., & Ihlen, Ø. (2018). Corporate social responsibility and rhetoric: Conceptualization, construction, and negotiation. In *The handbook of organizational rhetoric and communication* (pp. 401–415).

Orlitzky, M., Schmidt, F. L., & Rynes, S. L. (2003). Corporate social and financial performance: A meta-analysis. *Organization Studies*, 24(3), 403–441. 10.1177/0170840603024003910

Pallant, J. (2010). *SPSS survival manual: A step by step guide to data analysis using SPSS*. McGraw-Hill Education.

Park, K. (2022). The mediating role of skepticism: How corporate social advocacy builds quality relationships with publics. *Journal of Marketing Communications*, 28(8), 821–839. 10.1080/13527266.2021.1964580

Peloza, J., & Shang, J. (2011). How can corporate social responsibility activities create value for stakeholders? A systematic review. *Journal of the Academy of Marketing Science*, 39(1), 117–135. 10.1007/s11747-010-0213-6

Ponzi, L., Fombrun, C., & Gardberg, N. (2011). RepTrak Pulse: Conceptualizing and validating a short-form measure of corporate reputation. *Corporate Reputation Review*, 14(1), 15–35. 10.1057/crr.2011.5

Porter, M. E., & Kramer, M. R. (2006). Strategy and society: The link between competitive advantage and corporate social responsibility. *Harvard Business Review*, 84(12), 78–92.17183795

Rifon, N. J., Choi, S. M., Trimble, C. S., & Li, H. (2004). Congruence effects in sponsorship: The mediating role of sponsor credibility and consumer attributions of sponsor motive. *Journal of Advertising*, 33(1), 30–42. 10.1080/00913367.2004.10639151

Romani, S., Grappi, S., & Bagozzi, R. P. (2013). Explaining consumer reactions to corporate social responsibility: The role of gratitude and altruistic values. *Journal of Business Ethics*, 114(2), 193–206. 10.1007/s10551-012-1337-z

SASB. (n.d.). *About SASB*. SASB. https://www.sasb.org/about/

Scholz, R. W., & Tietje, O. (2002). *Embedded case study methods: Integrating quantitative and qualitative knowledge*. SAGE Publications. 10.4135/9781412984027

Schuler, D. A., & Cording, M. (2017). Corporate social responsibility. In Wright, P. M., & McMahan, G. M. (Eds.), *The Oxford handbook of strategic human resource management* (pp. 451–469). Oxford University Press.

Sen, S., Bhattacharya, C. B., & Korschun, D. (2006). The role of corporate social responsibility in strengthening multiple stakeholder relationships: A field experiment. *Journal of the Academy of Marketing Science*, 34(2), 158–166. 10.1177/0092070305284978

Seok Sohn, Y., Han, J. K., & Lee, S. H. (2012). Communication strategies for enhancing perceived fit in the CSR sponsorship context. *International Journal of Advertising*, 31(1), 133–146. 10.2501/IJA-31-1-133-146

Shah, S. S. A., & Khan, Z. (2021). Creating advocates: Understanding the roles of CSR and firm innovativeness. *Journal of Financial Services Marketing*, 26(2), 95–106. 10.1057/s41264-020-00084-8

Song, B., & Tao, W. (2022). Unpack the relational and behavioral outcomes of internal CSR: Highlighting dialogic communication and managerial facilitation. *Public Relations Review*, 48(1), 102153. 10.1016/j.pubrev.2022.102153

Song, B., & Wen, T. J. (2019). Online corporate social responsibility communication strategies and stakeholder engagements: A comparison of controversial versus noncontroversial industries. *Corporate Social Responsibility and Environmental Management*, 27(2), 881–896. Advance online publication. 10.1002/csr.1852

United Nations. (n.d.). *Sustainable Development Goals*. UN. https://sdgs.un.org/goals

Verk, N., Golob, U., & Podnar, K. (2021). A dynamic review of the emergence of corporate social responsibility communication. *Journal of Business Ethics*, 168(3), 491–515. 10.1007/s10551-019-04232-6

Vogel, D. (2005). Is there a market for virtue? The business case for corporate social responsibility. *California Management Review*, 47(4), 19–45.

Weigelt, K., & Camerer, C. (1988). Reputation and corporate strategy: A review of recent theory and applications. *Strategic Management Journal*, 9(5), 443–454. 10.1002/smj.4250090505

Yin, R. K. (2018). *Case study research and applications: Design and methods*. SAGE Publications.

Zhang, D., Morse, S., & Kambhampati, U. (2017). *Sustainable development and corporate social responsibility*. Routledge. 10.4324/9781315749495

KEY TERMS AND DEFINITIONS

Consumer Activism: Consumer activism involves actions taken by consumers to express their preferences about social issues through their purchasing decisions and other market choices. This activism can manifest in boycotting products from companies perceived as socially irresponsible or supporting companies considered socially responsible. Consumer activism is driven by a desire to effect change in corporate or governmental policies or practices.

Corporate Reputation: Corporate reputation is a perceptual representation of a company's past actions and future prospects that describes the firm's appeal to all of its key constituents when compared with other leading rivals. The reputation of a company is built over time through consistent performance, credible communications, and stakeholders' ongoing evaluations.

Corporate Social Responsibility (CSR): Corporate Social Responsibility refers to the practices and policies undertaken by corporations that are intended to have a positive influence on the world. The concept of CSR goes beyond compliance with regulatory requirements and engages in actions that further some social good, beyond the interests of the firm and that which is required by law. CSR activities may include efforts to reduce carbon footprints, improve labor policies, contribute to educational and social programs, or engage in activities that promote environmental conservation and sustainability.

CSR Communication: CSR Communication involves the methods and processes through which a company informs and engages with its stakeholders about its CSR activities. This communication can be internal or external and utilizes various platforms such as reports, advertisements, press releases, social media, and corporate websites. CSR communication aims not only to inform but also to influence perception and build a company's reputation as socially responsible.

CSR Credibility: CSR credibility refers to the degree to which a company's CSR efforts are perceived as genuine and effective by its stakeholders. Credibility is influenced by factors such as the consistency between communicated messages and business practices, the company's history of CSR activities, and the degree to which the company's CSR efforts exceed standard practices.

CSR-fit: CSR-fit refers to the alignment between a company's CSR activities and its core business operations, values, and competencies. A high CSR-fit means that the social or environmental initiatives a company engages in are closely related to its business model, which can lead to greater stakeholder acceptance and enhanced effectiveness of the CSR efforts.

Individual Beliefs: Individual beliefs can be defined as the personal convictions or accepted truths held by an individual, which guide their behavior and decision-making processes. These beliefs are subjective, deeply ingrained, and influence how individuals perceive and react to various situations, including those involving moral and ethical considerations.

Chapter 8
Understanding Health Communication in the Era of Media Convergence

B. K. Ravi
Koppal University, India

ABSTRACT

Today the media landscape is undergoing rapid transformations, driven by technological advancements. The rapid advancements in technology have led to the convergence of various media platforms, resulting in a paradigm shift in the way health information is communicated. The convergence of media platforms and technologies has transformed the media landscape, bringing about significant changes in the way information is accessed, consumed, and shared. The dynamic interplay between traditional and digital media platforms has created new opportunities and challenges in the realm of health communication, shaping the way individuals receive and engage with health information. In this context of media convergence, it is crucial to understand how the changing media landscape affects the delivery and reception of health messages. The integration of multiple media platforms, such as television, radio, print, online platforms, and social media, has led to an unprecedented availability of health information.

INTRODUCTION

Today the world is characterized by unprecedented technological advancements. In the present times, the media convergence and technological advancements has transformed the way information is generated, transmitted, and consumed across various domains. The rapid evolution of technology has not only facilitated the amalgamation of diverse media channels but has also ushered in a new paradigm in the sphere of health communication. The interplay between media convergence and technological innovations has redefined how individuals engage with health information. From traditional media outlets to digital platforms, this convergence has led to the seamless integration of various communication channels, ensuring that health-related messages are not confined to a single medium but are delivered holistical-

DOI: 10.4018/979-8-3693-3767-7.ch008

Copyright ©2024, IGI Global. Copying or distributing in print or electronic forms without written permission of IGI Global is prohibited.

ly through an array of interconnected sources. This interweaving of media forms has transcended the barriers of time and geography, enabling health information to reach wider audiences instantaneously.

The converged media technologies have also enabled the individuals to access interactive and personalized health communication. From telemedicine applications that offer real-time medical consultations to interactive health websites equipped with Chabots and self-assessment tools, individuals can now access health information at their fingertips.

HEALTH COMMUNICATION

Health communication includes the exchange of information, ideas, and messages related to health between various individuals, groups, organizations, and communities is part of health communication. Health communication utilises various communication channels to convey health information and plays a significant role in creating public awareness. The health communication can be in any forms such as:

1. Educational Campaigns: The Public health organizations and Government develop campaigns to raise awareness about specific health information, such as vaccination, tobacco usage, or healthy eating. They use all the media channels to popularise these campaigns and disseminate information.
2. Community Outreach: The workshops, seminars, and health fairs are organised to provide opportunities for healthcare professionals to interact directly with the public, sharing information and answering questions is also form of health communication,
3. Digital Health: Today with the rise of technology, health communication has extended to digital platforms, including health-related websites, mobile applications, wearable devices, and online support groups. During the pandemic these platforms enabled individuals to access health information at their convenience and connect with others.
4. Policy Advocacy: Health communication becomes a potent tool for driving transformations in public health initiatives and regulations, aiming to bring about tangible improvements on a larger scale. Health communication can also influence policy changes by advocating for public health initiatives or regulations. By advocating for public health initiatives or regulations, health communication efforts strive to raise awareness, mobilize public support, and engage with policymakers, thereby impacting broader societal health outcomes.
5. Crisis Communication: During crisis or public health emergencies or outbreaks, the health communication becomes paramount in clear and transparent communication . It not only provides the public with vital safety information but also nurtures a sense of trust and confidence which is crucial to manage public perceptions, minimize panic, and provide accurate updates on the situation.

HEALTH COMMUNICATION SCENARIO IN INDIA

The emergence of the digital age has brought about a notable shift in India's health communication landscape. Effective health communication was of the biggest importance during the COVID-19 pandemic, which expedited this transition. It was essential to provide residents with appropriate health information during the pandemic. The Indian government used digital technologies, such as websites, social media, health applications, and telemedicine platforms, to raise awareness about health issues and reach a wide audience during these difficult times. The public received regular updates regarding the precautionary actions.

The country today has health-conscious generation which has facilitated the use of health and fitness apps, along with wearable devices. To complement this trend, the Indian Government initiated campaigns such as the "Fit India Movement," which seeks to propagate health and wellness through multimedia strategies. This campaign effectively uses a media mix of traditional media platforms like television and radio with digital platforms, ensuring engagement with a individual across the platforms.

Despite these advancements there are several challenges in the country. The main challenge is digital divide, while urban areas have constantly utilized digital health communication, the rural India still struggles with unequal access to digital infrastructure lack of digital literacy limiting them the reach of digital health services. The Indian Government is continuously striving to bridge this gap and promote equitable access to health information across the country.

This profound digital revolution has reshaped health communication in India, amalgamating traditional and digital mediums to convey vital health information. The COVID-19 pandemic facilitated this transformation by ensuring that health information reaches every corner of the country, ultimately contributing to a healthier and more informed society.Top of Form

THEORETICAL FRAMEWORK

The thesis of technological determinism, which holds that a society's technological advancements are what propel its transition, serves as the foundation for this investigation. The renowned scholar Karl Marx is considered as one of the earliest proponents of this theory, asserting that technological progress triggers the change in a society influencing its cultural, political, and economic dimensions Bimber, B. (1990). Karl Marx and the Three Faces of Technological Determinism. *Social Studies of Science*.

In contemporary times, numerous media scholars attribute the theory of Technological Determinism theory to Marshall McLuhan. His contention was that the manner in which communication media were employed held greater significance than the actual conveyed message. McLuhan's renowned phrase, "the medium is the message," underscored the intrinsic impact of communication mediums, Therefore, McLuhan placed more importance on technology than the message itself.

Winner, L. (2014). Technologies as forms of life states that Langdon Winner later expanded upon this theory, proposing the following hypotheses:

- One of the main determinants of the different ways in which a society functions is its technology.
- The main and most significant factor influencing societal transformation is advancements in technology.

UNDERSTANDIND THE SCOPE

The environment for health communication has been completely transformed by media convergence. The quick development of technology has changed how people obtain health-related information. The objective of this study is to examine how media convergence affects how people learn about health issues and engage in personalised health management. The study clarifies how health communication is shaped by media convergence. Researchers and policymakers interested in the junction of media convergence for health communication can find valuable insights from this study.

OBJECTIVES OF THE STUDY

The post pandemic the health communication has undergone unprecedent changes. The media convergence with the integration of various media platforms has made it easy for proliferation of health information.

Therefore, the objectives of this study would be in

- Understanding the process of health communication.
- To assess media convergence's impact on health communication from an analytical standpoint.
- To analyse how media convergence can be used to promote health communication.

METHODOLOGY

The health communication is multifaceted domain that encompasses the interchange of health-related information, concepts, and communications among diverse individuals, communities, organizations, and groups. Hence this study adapts an explorative analysis method. The study analyses the existing literature to draw inferences' present study is confined to only the health communication and hence is trying to look into the various factors that would help in a better understanding.

MEDIA & CONVERGENCE

The term "media convergence" describes how different media technologies and content formats are combined into one platform. It entails the blending of digital and traditional media platforms. Technological developments are always the driving force for convergence. The goal of media convergence is also to adapt to the shifting demands of the consumer. In order to serve a wider audience, media convergence replaces outdated technologies with more modern ones. The three Cs of fusion computing, communication, and content within networked digital media platforms characterise convergence. Schäfer, M. (2011). *Bastard Culture! How User Participation Transforms Cultural Production* says Nicholas Negroponte explored the idea of convergence in media study in his 1995 book "Being Digital." Negroponte predicted that by the year 2000, the print and publishing, computer, and broadcast and motion picture industries would unite as a single entity, explaining that convergence begins with "bits," or the digital DNA of information. In order to illustrate this idea, Negroponte created a model with three intersecting circles, with the common intersection region serving as a representation of convergence.

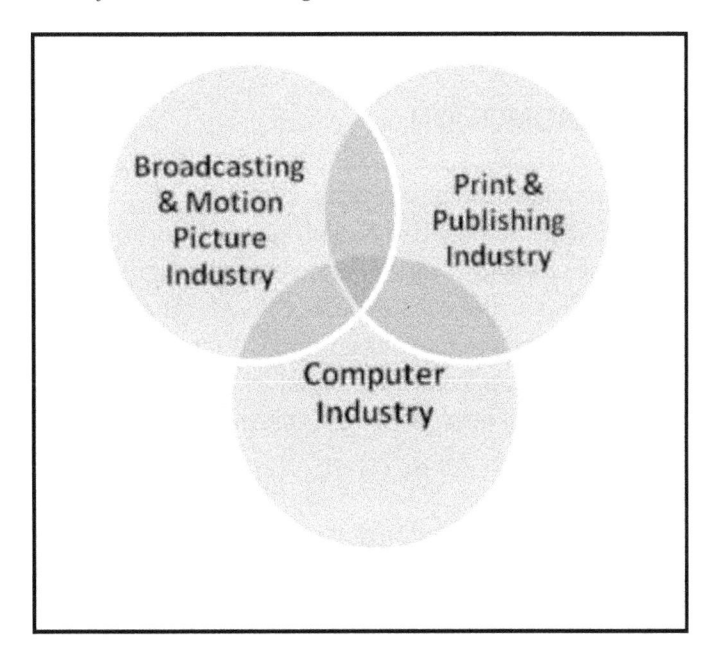

Figure 1. Negroponte model of three intersecting circles

[Venn diagram with three intersecting circles labeled: Broadcasting & Motion Picture Industry, Print & Publishing Industry, Computer Industry]

NEED FOR MEDIA CONVERGENCE IN HEALTH COMMUNICATION

In the globalised world as economies, cultures, and societies become more interconnected, the media convergence has fostered health communication as the convergence created a unified platform with multiple technologies which in turn facilitates to effectively disseminate health information. The media convergence is serving the health communicators and government and non-government organisations to disseminate information easily. In the interconnected world the converged media ensures that health messages are not only efficiently delivered but also reach the vast demographics. During the emergencies and crisis, the converged media plays a significant role as it enables real-time updates. The media convergence thereby effectively addressing the urgency and sensitivity of critical situations. The adoption of a multi-channel approach, ensures that health messages are reinforced across various communication channels, thus heightening the prospects of retention and influence. By harnessing the inherent power of visual storytelling, infographics, videos, and interactive features, media convergence makes health information more relatable, engaging, and memorable.

INFERENCES

Media convergence has facilitated the rapid dissemination of health information with the interconnectedness of various platforms. Media convergence has transformed the health communication sector and fostered the developments in the field of health communication. Media Convergence has potential to cater to the ever-changing health communication needs of citizens. Some examples of media convergence incorporated into health communication include:

HEALTH CAMPAIGNS PROMOTION

The converged media has provided new platforms to promote health campaigns and reach wide demographics easily. The conjunction of traditional media and digital platforms like social media, websites, and streaming services, helps to the reach different demographics and communities. The Indian government has utilized media convergence to amplify the impact of health campaigns. For instance, the "Poshan Abhiyan" (National Nutrition Mission) employs a multifaceted approach, combining television ads, radio programs, social media campaigns, and mobile apps to address malnutrition and promote healthy nutrition practices. With the convergence it helps campaign's message resonates to people across the country.

HEALTH MANAGEMENT

Media Convergence helps in empowering individuals to actively engage in their health management. The availability of digital tools, such as health apps and wearable devices, allows individuals to monitor their health, make informed decisions, and collaborate with healthcare professionals in real time. For example, media convergence was essential in promoting information and countering false information during the COVID-19 pandemic. Millions of Indians now have access to trustworthy and easily available health information thanks to several apps like Arogya Setu and Covid Dashboard, which were created by government agencies and technology partners. These apps combine chatbot technology with real-time information updates.

REDEFINIG HEALTH DISCOURSE

Today's global health discourse has been transformed by the convergence of media. Converged media give people, organisations, and medical experts a forum to talk about and spread awareness about health issues. For example, the convergent media reshaped the nation's health discourse during the COVID-19 pandemic. The platforms of new and social media were vital in the dissemination of information. Public organisations, such as the Centres for Disease Control and Prevention (CDC) and the World Health Organisation (WHO), frequently used social media and convergent media to disseminate updates and preventive guidelines.

TELEMEDICINE

The media convergence has transformed the landscape of telemedicine. The converged media enables two-way communication and interaction. This enables to exchange health information virtually and with the telemedicine remote monitoring of patient's is also possible. The converged media has facilitated better patient-doctor relationship. For instance, the "eSanjeevani" telemedicine initiative in

India connects patients with healthcare providers through video calls, bridging geographical barriers and increasing healthcare access. The private entities like "Practo," Helium health, Air doctor and others enable patients to consult doctors virtually. This is essential in remote areas, where distance can be a barrier to receiving timely medical care.

ONLINE SUPPORT COMMUNITIES

The converged media landscape has made it possible to provide virtual platforms where individuals dealing with similar health challenges come together to share their experiences, exchange advice, and provide emotional support. These virtual communities harness the power of digital technologies to connect people from diverse backgrounds who are dealing with similar health conditions. This enables users to clarify their doubts with posting questions, share their experiences, and engage in conversations related to their health condition. For example the platform "Patients Engage" is an online support community that serves the Indian population, connects patients, caregivers, and healthcare professionals, providing a space to share experiences, stories, and insights about various health conditions. It allows users to discuss, read personal stories, access health educational resources. This kind of platforms shows how media convergence can create a supportive environment for individuals facing health challenges.

PERSONALIZATION

The converged media technologies enable users to access personalized health communication. The converged media platforms enabled with digital technologies analyse and track the user data and provide customised content for users according to their preference based on data analytics. This personalization enhances the relevance of health information and encourages individuals to engage in health communication.

HEALTH GAMIFICATION

A relatively new and well-liked trend in health communication is health gamification. Health gamification incorporates gaming aspects into health-related apps to encourage users to adopt a healthy lifestyle and raise health awareness in an engaging way, thanks to media convergence technology. This technique of incorporating game mechanics such as challenges, rewards, and competition into health apps ensures that individuals adapt positive lifestyle. The "Fit India" app launched by Government of India is an example of health gamification in India. This application gamified approach encourages users to adopt a healthier lifestyle by incorporating physical activity and motivate users to stay active.

MULTIMEDIA HEALTH INFORMATION

Media convergence enables the integration of multimedia elements in health communication. The inclusion of multimedia elements in communication of health-related information makes it more engaging and easier to understand, complex medical topics. For example, the "Anemia Mukt Bharat" campaign incorporates videos, infographics, and animations to raise awareness about anemia prevention and treatment.Top of Form

COLLABRATION BETWEEN PUBLIC AND PRIVATE ENTITIES

The media convergence enables easy collaboration between public health authorities, communication experts, and technology developers which will help to receive different insights related to health. The collaborative interplay between public and private players leads to bridge gaps between medical information and public understanding. This converged media enables to create a blueprint for optimizing health communication strategies. This collaboration enables to deliver the health messages.

SUGGESTIONS FOR FUTURE RESEARCH

The subject of integrated media utilisation for health communication is expanding quickly, offering numerous prospects for further investigation. With the growing availability of converged media, it becomes crucial to analyse the effectiveness of media convergence strategies in promoting health communication among different demographic groups. The further researchers can try to understand the impact of media convergence on health literacy and its role in bridging health disparities. There is a huge scope for potential research in these areas of incorporating virtual reality and augmented reality into health communication strategies enabled by media convergence. The research can also be conducted to explore how media convergence influences individuals' health-related decision-making processes, including treatment choices and preventive measures. The further researchers can study methods to counter health misinformation in the context of media convergence, focusing on accuracy and credibility.

CONCLUSION

The media convergence has a prominent role in health communication as it utilises the single platform integrated with diverse technologies to convey health information to varied audiences. The converged media also enables health communicators to customise health messages based on the user preferences. and encourage positive behaviour changes. This converged media helps to connect with audience digitally with personalised content and foster interactivity with them through comments, likes, and polls. It also enables real-time information dissemination during emergencies The media convergence empowers health communicators to disseminate information and enhance public health outcomes. The different Public and Private players across the world can potentially use the converged media technologies to communicate regarding health and foster health consciousness among the individuals.

REFERENCES

Babrow, A. S., & Mattson, M. (2003). Theorizing about health communication. In Thompson, T. L., Dorsey, A., Miller, K. I., & Parrott, R. (Eds.), *Handbook of health communication* (pp. 263–284). Lawrence Erlbaum Associates.

Berrigan, F. J. (1979). *Community communications. The role of community media in development.* UNESCO.

Bimber, B. (1990). Karl Marx and the Three Faces of Technological Determinism. *Social Studies of Science*, 20(2), 333–351. https://www.jstor.org/stable/285094. 10.1177/030631290020002006

Colle, R. (2003). Threads of development communication. In Servaes, J. (Ed.), *Approaches to development: studies on communication for development* (pp. 22–72). UNESCO.

Cooke-Jackson, A. (2012). Review: Health Communication in the New Media Landscape (2009). *The Journal of Media Literacy Education*. 10.23860/jmle-4-1-10

Dave, A. (2011). Media Convergence: Different Views and Perspectives. *IMS Manthan*, VI(1), 170.

Deglise, C., Suggs, L. S., & Odermatt, P. (2012). Short message service (SMS) applications for disease prevention in developing countries. *Journal of Medical Internet Research*, 14(1), e3. 10.2196/jmir.182322262730

Hu, Y. (2015). Health communication research in the digital age: A systematic review. *Journal of Communication in Healthcare*, 8(4), 260–288. 10.1080/17538068.2015.1107308

Irwin, H. (1989). Health communication: The research agenda. *Media International Australia*, 54(1), 32–40. 10.1177/1329878X8905400110

Lee, K. (2005). Global social change and health. In Lee, K., & Collin, J. (Eds.), *Global change and health* (pp. 13–27). Open University Press/McGraw-Hill Education.

Lupton, D. (1994). Toward the development of critical health communication praxis. *Health Communication*, 6(1), 55–67. 10.1207/s15327027hc0601_4

Maheshwar, M. (2017). *Mass Media and Health Communication in India.*

Mheidly, N., & Fares, J. (2020). Health communication research in the Arab world: A bibliometric analysis. *Integrated Healthcare Journal*, 2, e000011.37441309

Moorhead, S. A., Hazlett, D. E., Harrison, L., Carroll, J. K., Irwin, A., & Hoving, C. (2013). A new dimension of health care: Systematic review of the uses, benefits, and limitations of social media for health communication. *Journal of Medical Internet Research*, 15(4), e85. 10.2196/jmir.193323615206

Parker, J. C., & Thorson, E. (Eds.). (2009). *Health communication in the new media landscape.* Springer Publishing Company.

Pollock, J., Borges, C., & Cook, P. (2020). *Judi.* Converging Innovations in Health Communication and Public Health The Vibrant Role of Social Capital.

Schäfer, M. (2011). *Bastard Culture!* How User Participation Transforms Cultural Production. 10.5117/9789089642561

Scott, S. D., Klassen, T. P., & Hartling, L. (2013). Social media use by health care professionals and trainees: A scoping review. *Academic Medicine*, 88(9), 1376–1383. 10.1097/ACM.0b013e31829eb91c23887004

Winner, L. (2014). *Technologies as forms of life*. Palgrave Macmillan UK eBooks. 10.1057/9781137349088_4

Section 3
Social Media

Chapter 9
Engaging With the News:
Applying the 5Cs Model of News Literacy to Young Audiences

Sameera Tahira Ahmed
UAE University, UAE

ABSTRACT

News literacy (NL) is an increasingly important aspect of media literacy as it emphasises the role that news plays in our daily lives and asks questions about production, consumption, understanding and impact of information garnered from news in contemporary digital media environments. The news consumption of young people is of great interest for both academic and industry sectors as it is often misunderstood or stereotyped yet is key in helping understand future trends. This chapter seeks to apply the 5Cs model of NL to examine the news consumption of university students in a Gulf state. Using data obtained from an online survey (n = 435), it examines context, creation, content, circulation and consumption. In doing so it demonstrates that young people are aware of and practice news literacy behaviours (NLB) which are critical for operating in today's global digital news media environments.

INTRODUCTION

Understanding and applying media literacy skills are becoming increasingly vital in our information saturated societies. On par with reading and writing in traditional literacy, these new literacy skills are indispensable for people to function effectively in both their personal and professional lives in societies where information and communication technologies are widely available (Hobbs, 2013). Within the broad spectrum of literacies that exist today, news literacy (NL) commands a prominent role for several significant reasons. The first of these is that the definition of news itself is changing accompanied by an increase in what is deemed newsworthy content. Secondly, what was available to audiences from legacy media, with TV, radio and newspapers as the purveyors of news, was clearer and easier to identify. Now however, the choices available in fragmented news environments in many parts of the world have altered the relationship between producers and consumers as well as disrupting the flows of news and information. A third key reason is the increasing occurrence of fake news and misinformation (Ahmed, 2023). For audiences to manage in these changing environments, with increasingly diverse communication channels, sources and types of information, and a variety of platforms, an understanding and application of NL becomes essential. Tully (2021) argues that NL matters because it enables consumers to address such challenges in the contemporary news landscape and that researchers, educators, practitioners and professionals need to effectively teach *and* encourage application of NL. This understanding, knowledge and application of NL manifests itself in news literacy behaviours (NLB) whereby people engage with news content in critical and meaningful ways (Potter, 2004, in Vraga et al., 2021). Vraga et al. (2021) have proposed that NL may be conceptualised using 5 domains: context, creation, content, circulation and consumption – the 5Cs. "These domains holistically address the role of news in society and build on existing work that argues to develop NL requires an understanding of both content and contexts of news production and consumption" (Vraga et al., 2021, p. 5).

Young (18-25) peoples' engagement with news has been an area of interest particularly in relation to their use of social media. Whilst many studies have shown that these audience groups are heavy consumers of social media for social and communication purposes, other studies have examined how this use has extended to news consumption (Schäfer, 2023; Vázquez-Herrero et al., 2022). Both academic research and industry data do not identify teenagers and young adults as traditional audiences for news consumption (Frei et al., 2022). However, with the advent of social media as well as recent global events (for example, COVID, geopolitical conflicts, climate crises), it is evident that the attention of young people has turned to news and current affairs. News itself cannot be defined in narrow terms but constitutes a broad spectrum of information, data and knowledge that consumers find 'useful' and therefore define as news (Swart, 2021). A study across Nigeria, India and the USA found that young people define their 'ideal news experience' as being from a trusted source; of personal significance, and; with desired storytelling formats (Itzkowitz et al., 2023). It was undoubtedly the recent pandemic more than any other event that has propelled news to a singularly critical status, with many deeming the situation as an infodemic (WHO, 2023). The necessity of following news and updates for health, policy and even legal reasons has forced an otherwise reluctant readership to interact with news content. This has merged seamlessly with their prior use of social media platforms for non-news related consumption. Popular platforms and applications such as Instagram, Twitter, TikTok, YouTube and Facebook have become access points for news content and updates from government, official and health organisations. The patterns of usage reflect as effortless transfer to pre-existing channels of information that were already functioning for communication and entertainment.

Having been 'forced' to enter the world of news, younger audiences have developed distinct consumption patterns and habits, as well as different perspectives on what news means to them and what purpose it serves in their lives (Itzkowitz et al., 2023). These patterns reflect their high smartphone ownership and usage; average number of social media accounts; and focus on issues they believe deserve their attention because of the impact on current and future generations. In examining these habits and trends it is important to be aware of making assumptions about young peoples' use of ICTs. Being always connected or switched on and spending more hours online does not necessarily render them experts, even with their status as digital or social natives (boyd, 2014). Research studies have shown that quantitative usage does not equate to higher order qualitative engagement and critical media literacy education is recommended from a young age (Yildiz and Keengwe, 2015; Wright et al., 2023). This has been confirmed in education where undergraduates do not always have the skills and competencies in information, digital or media literacies even though they are confident in using technology. What has become evident though is that the skills and knowledge needed to navigate various news media settings are being acquired by younger audiences, even without any formal training. Learning on the job in organic ways is not uncommon, and students have expressed their confidence in engaging with new technologies (Ahmed, 2020). Whilst formal education and training is available to students in higher education, its application is not always systematic or comprehensive but because of their confidence and perceptions of self-efficacy, students and young people are not afraid to experiment and teach themselves new technology and applications. The same attitudes have been transferred to their access and engagement with news content, and these attitudes, experiences and habits are examined in this chapter. Participants were asked to identify and explore their news consumption habits which consisted of basic frequency patterns, usage characteristics, attitudes towards sources, evaluation and verification processes and self-perceptions about levels of NL. The data obtained from the survey is used to understand whether the 5Cs proposed in NL research are applicable in this case study.

THEORETICAL FRAMEWORK

NL has been defined as "knowledge of the personal and social processes by which news is produced, distributed and consumed, and skills that allow users some control over these processes" (Vraga et al., 2021). Whilst forming part of a wider framework of literacies (including media, digital, information and visual), Ashley (2020) argues that NL is distinct because of the relationship that news has with an informed public. NL is the critical evaluation of not only content but of the contexts within which it is produced and how it is shared. We can think of NL as the set of knowledge, skills, and attitudes that a person brings to their personal consumption of information and to their understanding of the structure of the news media landscape (Ashley 2020). The practice or application of these NL skills can therefore be defined as NLB. Furthermore, Ashley et al (2022) state that "while the lines between the various literacies remain blurry, we think news literacy best applies to research focused on how individuals experience media messages that have been created and distributed by content producers aiming to influence public understanding of current events" (p. 7).

Each of the 5Cs proposed by Vraga et al (2021) - context, creation, content, circulation and consumption - can be used to examine patterns of news consumption and identify the application of NLB. Context refers to the social, legal and economic environment in which news is produced. This includes the role of the government and other institutions as well as the legal frameworks within which journalists and news organizations operate. Creation is the process in which journalists and others engage in conceiving, reporting and ultimately creating news stories and journalistic content. Here we can consider both professional and public news content creators and broaden the traditional definition of news to anything considered newsworthy by audiences. Content is defined as the qualitative characteristics of a news story that distinguishes it from other types of media content, including news values, key features, sources and frames. The ability to identify and evaluate news applies here. Circulation is the process through which news is distributed and spread to potential audiences. It is important for consumers to recognise that this process is influenced by various actors in a social system but that they can exercise some control over exposure to news content. Finally, consumption explains the personal factors that contribute to news exposure, attention and evaluation. This would examine personal biases and predispositions that influence choices about news content resulting in a news diet that satisfies individual information needs.

Vraga et al's (2021) emphasis on context needs to be highlighted here. They believe that much of the research about NL has been undertaken in western settings and that it needs to be expanded to include other locations. Whilst there may be certain commonalities between NL and NLB across the globe, the political, economic, social and cultural settings in different geographical areas have an impact on context, that is, the news environment, and understanding this is necessary if NL is to be examined effectively. "NL research needs to explore news defined broadly to reflect audiences' perspectives and changing structures in news production and delivery and to expand beyond the U.S. and Western perspectives often favoured in scholarship" (p 4). Using this recommendation as a stimulus, this chapter aims to study NL in a non-western context by examining empirical data (the two avenues of future research recommended by Vraga et al (2021)).

METHODOLOGY

The data obtained for this research study consists of an online survey (n = 435) completed between April and June 2022 by undergraduate students selected through purposeful sampling across a range of colleges, though predominantly in the Humanities and Social Sciences and within this the Media Department. The survey consisted of a 20-item questionnaire administered and analysed using Qualtrics in which the following sections were included: consuming and evaluating news; verification practices; sharing, communicating, and creating habits; and NL (news production processes, skills, and knowledge; self-perceptions). Survey questions were developed from previous studies (Maksl et al., 2015; Chan et al., 2021; Ofcom 2022) and modified to suit the context of the institution. Most items were closed-ended questions or consisted of statements and employed a 5-point Likert type rating scale to reduce confusion in open-ended questions and increase validity by eliciting accurate answers to measure respondents' attitudes, behaviour, and practices (Wimmer and Dominick 2011). For the survey respondents that answered the question about gender, 325 were female and 110 were male (total 435). Similarly, for age almost 19% (82) were under 20; 79% (345) were between 21-25; about 1% (6) were 25-30, and; 0.6% (3) were over 30. Of the respondents that specified their nationality, 93% were Emirati, around 5% from other GCC and Arab states and almost 2% from other countries. One limitation in a survey such as this is the possible inconsistency between the researcher's and participants' definitions and understanding of terms and concepts. For example, news, news literacy, skills and bias are terms that may have been interpreted in different ways and this needs to be acknowledged when analysing the data.

FINDINGS

To examine the engagement that participants have with news, the findings will be analysed according to the 5Cs noted above using data obtained from the survey. It is worth noting that previous research supports the fact that the 5C domains are distinct but related. This is because in the practice and implementation of NL and NLB, overlap occurs and the boundaries between each of the 5Cs are often blurred. It is for this reason that, for example, context and creation are examined together and answers for the same question can be used to examine more than one of the Cs.

Consumption

The most obvious of the domains that can be applied to the data collected from the study relate to consumption. When respondents were asked why they follow the news, a high percentage strongly agreed or agreed that they do so because they 'like to' and feel it is 'important to be informed about news'

(70% and 85% respectively). Less than 3% disagreed or strongly disagreed that it was important to be informed about news. The percentages for 'because I am supposed to' and 'out of habit' were slightly lower (48% and 54% respectively). This indicates that users are making a concerted effort to consume news because they perceive it to be valuable or a social expectation. Whilst almost 70% (n = 473) said they thought there was 'too much' news, this did not affect their obligation to access and keep up to date about news and current affairs.

About one fifth (21%, n = 472) stated that they did not follow the news (strongly agree 5.7% and agree 15.6%) but amongst the 90 respondents who answered 'strongly disagree' or 'disagree', fewer were male (19) than female (61) indicating a difference in gender attitudes towards news consumption. Overall, most respondents were news consumers and considered the news to be important as the data shows high levels of news engagement. Research examining news consumption amongst young people around the world has often described their levels of engagement and interest as lower than the rest of the population but this study demonstrates younger people are interested in news and are aware that keeping informed and updated about news is an important aspect of their lives.

Frequency

How much and how often news was consumed by participants shows that the majority (63%) consumed less than 1 hour a day, 28% between 1-3 hours and 8% more than 3 hours (Table 1). Within these results males were consuming slightly more news than females (except for the 5 hours + category). Overall, the participants cannot be regarded as heavy news users.

Table 1. How much news is consumed daily (by gender)

Time/%	Males	Females	Total
Less than 1 hour	56.4	66.5	63.9
1-3 hours	35.5	25.5	28.0
3-5 hours	7.3	3.7	4.6
More than 5 hours	0.9	3.4	2.8

Table 2 then looks at how often news was consumed and reflects the data in the above table showing that males were consuming more news, more often than females.

Table 2. How often news is consumed daily (by gender)

Frequency/%	Male	Female	Total
Throughout the day	43.6	37.4	39.0
2-3 times in a day	27.3	22.7	23.9
Once a day	15.5	25.9	23.2
Varies	13.6	14.0	13.9
Total (answering)	110	321	431

Respondents were asked to identify which types of news they were interested in – local, national, regional or international/global. The most cited was international (31.6%, 249/788 as they were asked to select all that applied). However, national and local were also important (28.3% and 27.4% respectively) and regional was the least cited (12.5%). This may relate to the cohort in the survey who were young, university students, most of whom were studying in the College of Humanities and Social Sciences (including media and politics) as well as the increased focus on global issues in all news. In addition, males were more likely to cite international news (62.7%) compared to females (51.2%) within the overall figure of 54.2% (234 of total 788 where gender was given).

When asked which language they consumed the news in, the majority of respondents (53.7%, n = 463) stated both English and Arabic. For Arabic only the figure was 37.5% and for English only it was 7.3%. A gender difference was clear for respondents that selected Arabic only, with females making up 38.4% and males 30% of the total. French, Hindi, Urdu, Pashtu, Russian and Kazakh were also mentioned by a total of 1.3% of respondents. This reflects the survey participants, that is, the student body and the media landscape of the area. The bilingual nature of news consumption may also link to the habit of verification of news from different sources and preference of one language over the other for better understanding of content. It also correlates with the sources that participants are using which include both English-language news organisations such as BBC and CNN as well as national news platforms such as Ameed, UAE Barq and newspaper websites (Table 3).

Table 3. Most named channels for news

Channel	Frequency
UAE Barq	30
AD Net (@net_ad)	13
Emarat Al Youm	11
Abu Dhabi TV	10
CNN	8
Ameed	8
Al Arabiya	7
BBC	6
Dubai TV	6
Sky News	5

Channels and Platforms

A variety of channels and platforms were accessed by participants (Fig 1), ranging from social media (the most popular at 67.3% 'always use') to traditional/legacy platforms (TV 17.2% 'always use'). The messaging app, WhatsApp, was also popular (40% and almost 60% respectively saying they 'always' or 'regularly' use).

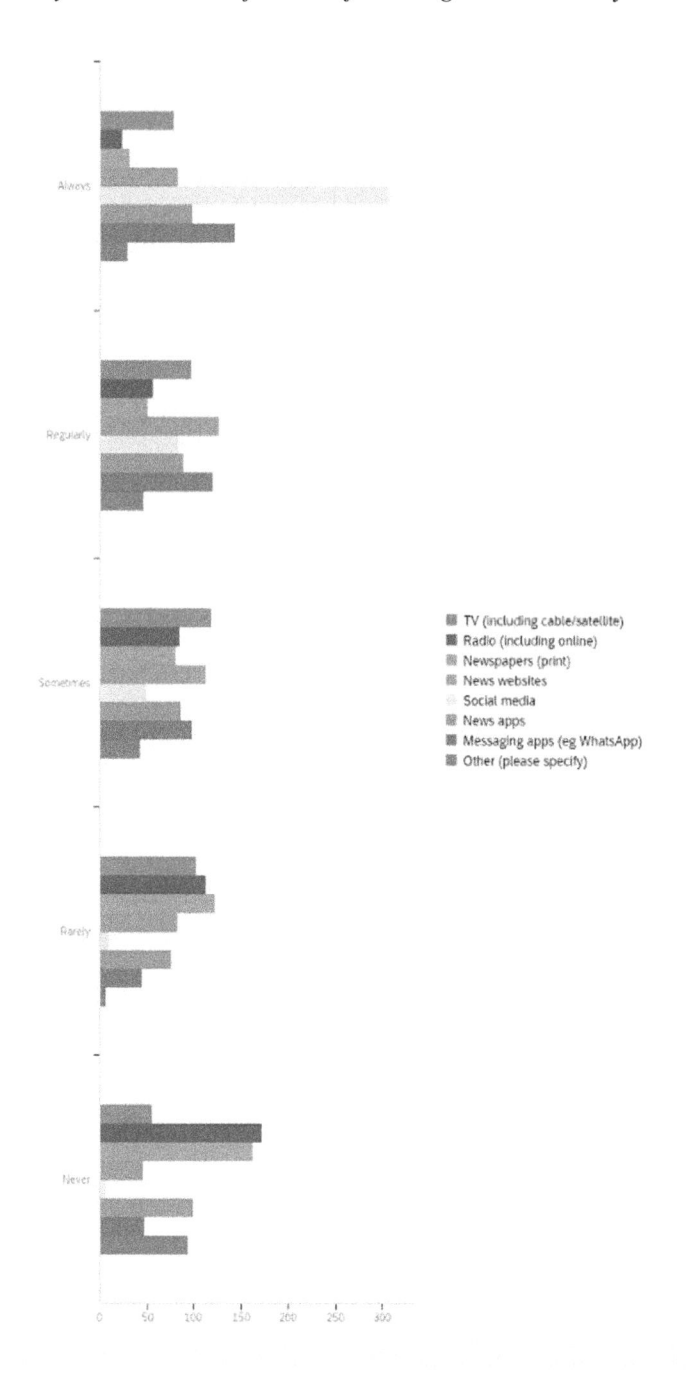

Figure 1. How often do you access news from the following channels daily?

Subsequent questions asked which social media platforms were the most popular/widely used for news consumption and the answer was clearly Instagram (Table 4). This result was confirmed by details in related questions. After Instagram (cited 260 times, 57.1%, as being always used), Snapchat (219, 48%), Twitter (221, 47.9%), WhatsApp (149, 33.1%) and TikTok (147, 32.5%) were the next most popular platforms. Most respondents were not using Facebook for news (71.7%, 325/453 said they never used it) but YouTube and Google+ were cited several times.

Table 4. How often do you use these platforms for news daily?

Platform	A (%)	#	Re (%)	#	S (%)	#	Ra (%)	#	N (%)	#	Total
Facebook	7.06	32	7.95	36	6.84	31	6.40	29	71.74	325	453
YouTube	22.98	105	21.23	97	30.63	140	13.57	62	11.60	53	457
Instagram	57.14	260	22.64	103	14.51	66	2.64	12	3.08	14	455
Twitter	47.94	221	22.34	103	15.40	71	6.51	30	7.81	36	461
Snapchat	48.03	219	16.45	75	15.79	72	7.46	34	12.28	56	456
TikTok	32.59	147	17.07	77	18.18	82	6.65	30	25.50	115	451
Reddit	5.59	25	8.72	39	11.63	52	9.17	41	64.88	290	447
Google+	16.23	74	17.54	80	17.98	82	10.31	47	37.94	173	456
Tumblr	3.56	16	6.89	31	8.67	39	7.11	32	73.78	332	450
Viber	3.33	15	6.22	28	6.22	28	5.11	23	79.11	356	450
LinkedIn	5.33	24	8.22	37	7.78	35	9.56	43	69.11	311	450
WhatsApp	33.11	149	29.33	132	19.56	88	7.33	33	10.67	48	450
Other	10.10	20	12.12	24	12.63	25	7.07	14	58.08	115	198

A – always, Re – regularly, S – sometimes, Ra – rarely, N – never

When looking at gender differences for platform usage, females are using most platforms, more often than males, except for YouTube. Determining which type of news is accessed via YouTube may provide a better understanding of why the percentage is higher for males but as the survey did not ask for this it cannot be explained with certainty. WhatsApp was almost equal for both genders but here it is important to remember that respondents may be defining 'news' differently from each other on a messaging platform which has lots of information shared by family and friends. Whilst TikTok is lower than other platforms, its growing popularity is reflected in global trends (Newman et al., 2022) and as a relative newcomer it has managed to gain significant ground amongst the most popular social media platforms. The Reuters Digital News Report states that "TikTok has become the fastest growing network in this year's survey, reaching 40% of 18-24s, with 15% using the platform for news" (Newman et al., 2022, p 5). They state that usage is much higher in some parts of the world and this can be seen from the data collected here (though the Report does not include the MENA region). In fact, for this cohort, and especially amongst females, the figure is even higher for news consumption.

How much participants felt they were influenced by news varies slightly by gender with males stating they were less influenced than females and that their attitudes were not changed by the news as much as females. Table 5 below shows figures for agreement and disagreement about these statements indicating that male news consumers are more confident about their own opinions and their ability to manage the effects of news.

Table 5. News influence and attitude change

Statement	Agreement	Males (%)	Females (%)
News influences other people more than me	SA	16.4	14.6
	A	44.5	37
	N A/D	32.7	37.6
	D	3.6	10.2
	SD	1.8	0.6
News changes my attitudes	SA	10.9	8.2
	S	28.2	39.2
	N A/D	28.2	33.5
	D	23.6	14.4
	SD	9.1	4.1

SA – strongly agree, A – agree, SD – strongly disagree, D - disagree

Due to the COVID pandemic in recent years, patterns of news consumption have altered considerably (Melki et al., 2021; Veeriah, 2021). The increased focus on news and information during this period was not unexpected but whether this experience has permanently changed people's attitudes towards and habits relating to news needs to be examined. When asked whether their news consumption had changed since COVID began, almost two-thirds of respondents (65.8%, n = 460) said yes, they now consume more news. For males the figure was 56.4% but for females it was higher at 69.3%. This reflects on an important development amongst younger people who may not previously have been interested in news or had relatively low-level news consumption compared to older people but who have become more conscious of the role news plays in their lives (Galan et al., 2021; Madden et al., 2017). Being compelled to engage with information and news content during the pandemic, their news habits have altered and they have become more discerning of sources, platforms and content. In addition to this, the amount of news and information available continues to increase and what people consider to be news is changing (Galan et al., 2021; Newman et al., 2022).

Content

Evaluating news

Fundamental concepts that underpin the profession of journalism such as truth and trust have become increasingly important in recent times. The political economy of media; ownership; role of audiences; fragmentation, and; digitalisation have all impacted on people's relationship with news media. An array of digital platforms offering alternative ways of producing and consuming news has disrupted the dominance of legacy media, especially amongst younger sections of the population. At the same time, the pandemic has put journalism and news reporting under the spotlight. Whereas traditionally people did not question the veracity of news, numerous examples of misinformation in recent years have compelled audiences to scrutinise where news is coming from, who is producing it and what messages it contains (Ashley et al., 2022; Newman et al., 2023). The ability to easily access news from various sources has further eroded mainstream media's dominance. To understand these matters, participants in this study were asked questions about their attitudes and practices of evaluating news. These questions were divided into two broad categories: those about the news itself (truth, trust, bias) and those examining people's

Engaging With the News

habits and practices (fact-checking, comparing, talking). Figure 2 (n = 446) illustrates the opinions of respondents regarding the first set of statements/questions.

Figure 2. Attitudes towards news content

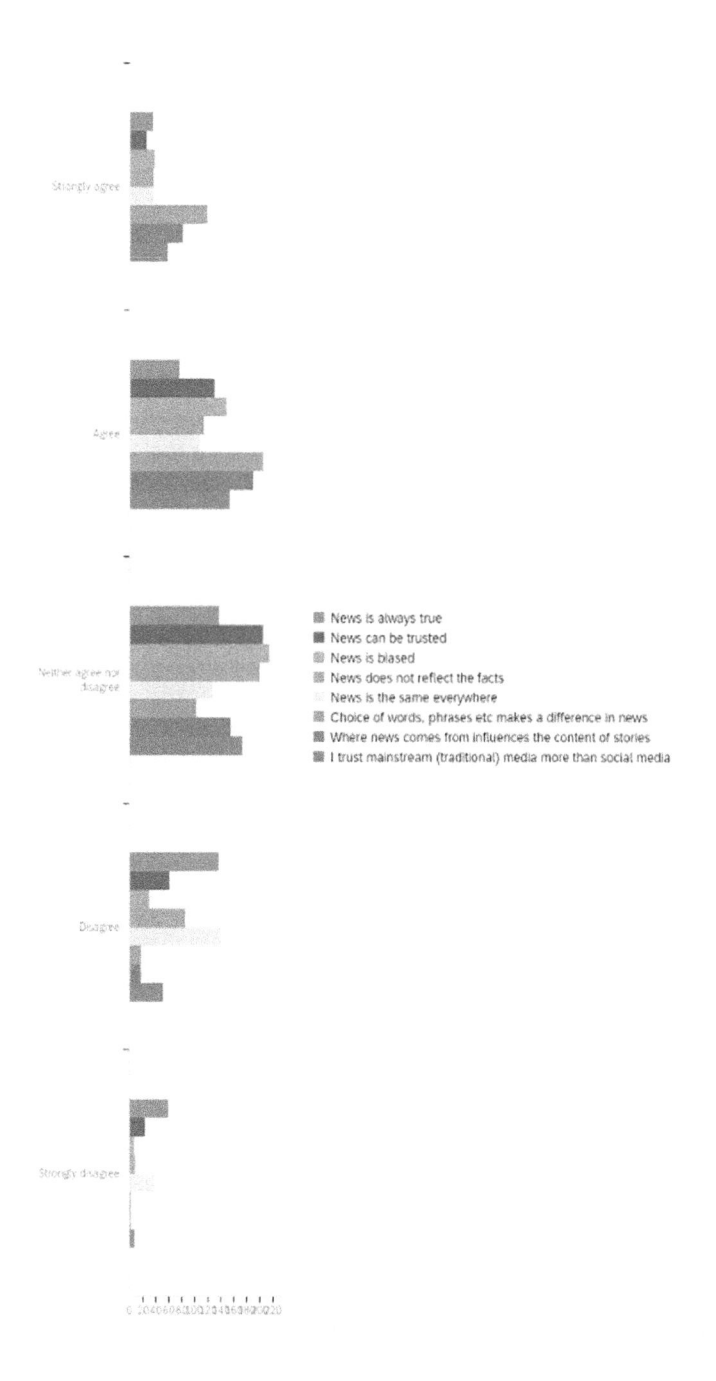

- News is always true
- News can be trusted
- News is biased
- News does not reflect the facts
- News is the same everywhere
- Choice of words, phrases etc makes a difference in news
- Where news comes from influences the content of stories
- I trust mainstream (traditional) media more than social media

Overall, 44% of respondents strongly disagreed (13.4%) or disagreed (30.6%) that news is always true. When considering difference for gender, the figure was 55% (17.4% + 37.6%) for males and 40.8% (12.1% + 28.7%) for females showing that males were more sceptical about news content being true. The percentages for strongly agreeing and agreeing that news was always true were relatively lower at 8% and 17% respectively. Similarly, over 40% of respondents thought that the news was biased (8.8% strongly agree and 33.5% agree) with slightly lower agreement for the statement that the news does not reflect the facts. For males strongly agreeing that news was biased the figure was 11.9% but for females it was 6.6% and 29.6% of females agreed news can be trusted compared to 25.7% of males. Whilst these numbers reflect a certain level of scepticism about news content, the proportion of respondents that said news cannot be trusted was not particularly high (only 13.9% disagreed and 5.1% strongly disagreed that news can be trusted for both genders).

When asked about trust in mainstream or traditional media compared to social media, almost half of respondents agreed (13.3% strongly agreed and 34.4% agreed) that they trusted the former more. The level of trust in mainstream media was considerably higher for females (51.2%) compared to males (35.8%). This is reaffirmed when examining which news sources respondents listed as being more trusted than others (several TV channels and newspapers were named). Gender differences were apparent in this section of the survey. Males showed lower levels of trust (were more sceptical); thought news was biased; had a more global outlook, and; disagreed that news was the same everywhere (46.8% compared to 37.7% for females). This is possibly a reflection of their consumption patterns, that is, more consumption of international news and the diversity of sources. This data then shows NLB are evident in evaluating quality and credibility of news and even in identifying what is to be considered news as opposed to fake news, rumours, misinformation or disinformation.

Context and Creation

Significant global events, starting from the recent pandemic to other current affairs, have brought into focus the role of news and journalism around the world. With this increased attention on the quality and reliability of news and information, many people have become more conscious of the relationship they have with media and news production processes. The survey asked questions relating to news production, sources, motives and media industry ownership and connected this to how media influences audience attitudes and perceptions. The results from these questions show that participants understood news as a product and the political and economic context of the news industry. Almost three quarters (73.7%) strongly agreed or agreed that news was created to attract audiences (with less than 5% strongly disagreeing or disagreeing). Over half (51.2%, strongly agree and agree) stated that news organisations focus on bad/negative news and 40% said the main objective of news organisations is to make money. Whilst the research was conducted in a particular political and economic context, it is worth noting that students were still aware of issues of ownership, diversity, sources and government influence over the media and news production. Furthermore Table 6 shows responses about other issues relating to the political economy of news production covered in the questionnaire.

Table 6. Political economy of news production

Statement	SA %	A %	SA + A %	D + SD %
Governments provide most of the news	14.9	47.7	62.6	8.4
News would be more diverse if other organisations provided it	13.4	47.5	60.9	2.9
Ownership of news organisations affects news content	18.7	49.9	68.6	3.3
I understand how organisations produce news	15.6	42.1	57.7	9.4

SA – strongly agree, A – agree, SD – strongly disagree, D - disagree

Evaluating news is linked to understanding production processes which is then connected to detecting bias. Controlling the information we are consuming relates to another set of skills which include managing, filtering, processing, interpreting and even avoiding news (Ahmed, 2020). Survey respondents were confident about their ability to control information, interpret news and detect bias - skills considered essential for critical thinking and of relevance to NLB. This is shown in Table 7 which also displays interesting variations between males and females. Whether participants are undertaking these practices effectively can only be determined through measurement, but this data indicates perceptions of self-efficacy and ability to engage with news.

Table 7. Relationship with news content

		Total	Male	Female
Total Count (All)/%		435	110	325
I am in control of the information I get from news	SA	19.5	26.4	17.2
	A	40.5	32.7	43.1
	N A/D	29.9	30.9	29.5
	D	6.4	6.4	6.5
	SA	2.1	0.9	2.5
I have the skills and knowledge to interpret news	SA	12.4	10.9	12.9
	A	40.7	50.0	37.5
	N A/D	32.6	24.5	35.4
	D	11.0	10.0	11.4
	SD	1.4	0.9	1.5
I have the skills and knowledge to detect bias in news	SA	12.9	12.7	12.9
	A	42.8	52.7	39.4
	N A/D	31.0	20.9	34.5
	D	9.7	8.2	10.2
	SD	0.9	0.9	0.9

The increased attention given to news during the recent infodemic and the greater awareness that being informed is a social obligation can be seen in the answers to questions about the role news plays in people's lives. Seventy-five percent said they strongly agreed or agreed that they were well informed about the news and only 5.4% disagreed or strongly disagreed (n = 462). If this is gauged against the time spent consuming news (Table 1), it may not correlate quantitatively but it reflects participant's perceptions and self-efficacy in relation to news. It may also relate to their ability to distinguish between and distil news that is important or useful and avoid that which is not, thus, being aware that the *quality* rather than *quantity* of news content matters, especially in an environment where news and other information is so pervasive. In fact, the phenomenon of news avoidance is being experienced by more people recently with consumers perceiving overload of news content, especially relating to conflicts and negative issues (Edgerly, 2017). Newman et al (2023) found that across all markets an all-time high of 36% of respondents are avoiding news, either periodically from *all* sources or restricting consumption at particular times and for certain topics. This finding ties in with their results about trust which has declined by 2% across markets.

Circulation

Sharing, Communicating, and Creating

Considering the typically high rates of social media usage amongst the survey participants, it is conceivable that patterns and habits of sharing will also apply to news accessed through this medium. A number of studies have shown that people prefer to access news through social media for some of the following reasons; it is their first go-to point for news updates, especially first thing in the morning; platform and application convenience; the instant and up to date nature; short form videos; audio-visual content; ease of sharing, and; device usage (smartphones used to access social media) (Dennis et al., 2019). In addition to these factors, newer applications such as TikTok are becoming increasingly popular for obtaining and distributing news content which is adding to the amount of news consumed and shared via social media. These patterns also reflect what is known as incidental news exposure (INE) (Schäfer, 2023) or accidental 'news-finds-me' consumption amongst online and social media users (Park and Kaye, 2021).

Not surprisingly, sharing news via social media was the most popular with 43% saying they do so always (22.8%) or frequently (20.5%). The figure for sharing via a messaging app was 38% (always 15.1% and frequently 23.6%) but for email it was less than 20%, with 50% saying they never shared via email. Sharing or sending news related visual content on social media was more evenly spread with respondents saying always, 17%; frequently, 19.6%; sometimes, 33%, rarely, 13.6% and never, 16.6%. Reasons given for sharing news included 'truth, different perspective, understanding and comparing, check and be sure'.

Generally, the results for rating, commenting, voting, posting, uploading and writing blogs were lower than for sharing. This shows that lower order activities such as sharing are carried out more than higher order ones. Commenting on news on social media was higher (54%) than on news websites (40%) with almost 45% saying they never comment on the latter. Almost 50% said they never write a blog on news or current affairs and about 27% said they never post or upload news related content. About 75% of the responses stated that they deleted news content that they did not trust but fewer (65%) said they warned others about news content. There were no significant differences for gender in this set of questions.

DISCUSSION

Examining NL and news consumption encompasses several aspects of audience behaviour including understanding the importance of being literate; self-perceptions; identifying successful NL practices, and; measuring NL levels. This survey included questions used in previous research to ask respondents if they were aware of the skills and knowledge needed to be news literate; the ability to navigate and control news and information and the importance of NL in their lives. In terms of self-perception, participants showed that they were news literate and aware of news production processes, quality of news, interpretations and detecting bias. For all the statements relating to this topic, about 55-60% strongly agreed or agreed and only around 10% disagreed or strongly disagreed. The only exception to this was the direct statement on defining yourself as being news literate for which 40% strongly agreed or agreed and over 20% disagreed or strongly disagreed (Table 8).

Furthermore, whilst over 60% agreed that being news literate was important, the figure for self-perception was lower at only 40%. This indicates a realistic assessment of individual's skills and abilities to apply NLB, whilst acknowledging that it is important to be news literate. Whilst self-efficacy levels may be higher for specific skills, overall literacy levels were judged to be lower. The gap between these two has been considered in other studies which have shown that having the skills does not necessary mean they are used in practice (Maksl et al., 2015; Vraga et al., 2021). Having identified a discrepancy between the theory and the practice, the next step would be to bridge the gap so that audiences are implementing their literacy skills during news consumption.

Table 8. Being news literate

		Total	Male	Female
Total Count (All)/%		435	110	325
It is important to be news literate (access, evaluate, analyse and create news)	SA	19.3	18.2	19.7
	A	40.5	40.9	40.3
	N A/D	28.7	29.1	28.6
	D	6.9	5.5	7.4
	SD	2.1	1.8	2.2
I am news literate	SA	10.6	9.1	11.1
	A	29.2	30.9	28.6
	N A/D	36.6	33.6	37.5
	D	14.0	16.4	13.2
	SA	7.4	6.4	7.7

Returning to the 5Cs of NL explored in this chapter, it has been shown that the attitudes and behaviour of the survey participants demonstrates NLB that enables them to navigate and negotiate news content in their daily lives. The level of engagement with news varies depending on external factors, namely events and issues on the local, national and international scale that form news agendas and have an impact on audiences. In addition, personal characteristics, predispositions and experiences as well as prior media habits add another layer of influence on individual patterns and diets. In many instances, however, these individual patterns correspond with others in the population that have similar demographics (age, educational level, language, socio-economic status, nationality etc.) to become collective or community patterns.

The overarching media environment and political structures impact on how content is produced, consumed and processed and having an awareness of this enables a better, more critical understanding of news in society. Censorship, government interventions and legal frameworks differ around the world and data from the survey showed that this is recognised by audiences, with issues of truth, trust, bias, interpretation and influence of news relating to this. Consuming news from different sources within and outside the national setting demonstrates how users include multiple sources in a global media landscape.

Thus, choice, access and use reflect the application of NL and confidence in dealing with diverse contexts. Whilst not defining each participant as a sophisticated and critical news consumer, able to discern political agendas, subtleties and narratives in each instance, it indicates an awareness of the framing of news content. Vraga et al (2021) emphasise that having knowledge (NL) and applying that knowledge (NLB) are distinct and there is no guarantee that one will lead to the other. However, where instances of these skills being applied can be seen are in behaviour such as identifying and mitigating fake news; questioning or challenging news content (especially from some sources); choice of credible sources and verifying content by cross referencing with trusted sources.

FUTURE RESEARCH DIRECTIONS

Collecting quantitative data offers one way of understanding the implementation of NL and NLB within news consumption patterns. To supplement this data with more in-depth knowledge, individual or group interviews or media diary methods can be utilised in future research. Longitudinal studies can also facilitate a better understanding of how news diets change over time and are determined by different factors. The current conflict in the Middle East could be used to explore news engagement quantitatively and qualitatively and focus on a critical issue to undertake comparative studies across different audiences and countries. Systematic measurement of NLB is another area of research that can provide data which could inform policy and strategy, at both academic and government levels.

CONCLUSION

The data from this study demonstrates how these young news users' habits and patterns fit into the 5Cs model of conceptualising NL. This study uses empirical evidence to contribute to our knowledge of the application of NL practices and NLB and moves beyond the predominantly western understanding of NL in digital media landscapes. The increasing convergence of globalised media landscapes within which we create, access, consume and share news content has brought about often swift and radical changes in audience attitudes and behaviour. The urgency of certain events and issues has obliged otherwise disinterested audiences to partake in news consumption and altered news diets in a short space of time. These diets may not persist in the long or even medium term but exposure to news; engagement in habitual cycles and an understanding of the processes related to news production and content have certainly affected the attitudes of younger people. Whilst their news consumption may fluctuate depending on external events and their social media usage means news is not always a priority, when they do engage with news, they are demonstrating NL practices and NLB. To develop, enhance and hone these potential or latent skills, higher education institutions can provide formal training and designate courses to improve literacy skills. This would mean progressing from self-taught, perhaps inconsistent, application of NL to an academically rigorous skillset that would result in managing, using and engaging with news content more effectively. This in turn would lead to "active control of one's relationship with news and information" and the implementation of "critical engagement as conscious and thoughtful interrogation of news messages, applying NL (e.g., knowledge and skills) to interpreting their meaning and integrating it into mental schemas" (Vraga et al., 2021, p 8). Furthermore, this type of formal instruction will render measurement of NL more tangible, especially when comparing groups who have and have not completed training or education. Training programmes can be seen as an intervention that would promote successful NLB, raise awareness of the role and importance of news in society and lead to increased engagement with news.

ACKNOWLEDGMENT

I would like to thank the participants who completed the survey.

This research received no specific grant from any funding agency in the public, commercial, or not-for-profit sectors.

REFERENCES

Ahmed, S. T. (2020). Managing News Overload (MNO): The COVID-19 Infodemic. *Information (Basel)*, 11(8), 375–390. 10.3390/info11080375

Ahmed, S. T., & Roche, T. (2021). Making the connection: Examining the relationship between undergraduate students' digital and academic success in an English medium instruction (EMI) university. *Education and Information Technologies*, 26(1), 4601–4620. 10.1007/s10639-021-10443-0

Ashley, S. (2020). *News Literacy and Democracy*. Routledge.

Ashley, S., Craft, S., Maksl, A., Tully, M., & Vraga, E. K. (2022). Can news literacy help reduce belief in COVID misinformation? *Mass Communication & Society*.

Boyd, D. (2014). *It's Complicated: The Social Lives of Networked Teens*. Yale University Press.

Chan, M., Lee, F. L. F., & Chen, H.-T. (2021). Examining the Roles of Multi-Platform Social Media News Use, Engagement, and Connections with News Organizations and Journalists on News Literacy: A Comparison of Seven Democracies. *Digital Journalism (Abingdon, England)*, 9(5), 571–588. 10.1080/21670811.2021.1890168

Dennis, E. E., Martin, J. D., & Wood, R. (2019). *Media use in the Middle East: A six-nation survey*. Northwestern University Qatar.

Edgerly, S. (2017). Seeking out and avoiding the news media: Young adults' proposed strategies for obtaining current events information. *Mass Communication & Society*, 20(3), 358–377. 10.1080/15205436.2016.1262424

Frei, N. K., Wyss, V., Gnach, A., & Weber, W. (2024). 'It's a matter of age': Four dimensions of youths' news consumption. *Journalism*, 25(1), 100–121. 10.1177/14648849221123385

Galan, L., Osserman, J., Parker, T., & Taylor, M. (2021). *How Young People Consume News and The Implications for Mainstream Media (Flamingo Report)*. Oxford University Press.

Hobbs, R. (2013). Media literacy. In Lemish, D. (Ed.), *The Routledge International Handbook of Children, Adolescents and Media* (pp. 417–424). Routledge.

Itzkowitz, A., Whitelaw, B., Donald, D., Montagu, G., Gilbert, J., Germuska, J., Lambertini, L., Fainman-Adelman, L., & Ha, T. (2023). *Next Gen News: Understanding the Audiences of 2030*. FT Strategies & Knight Lab.

Madden, M., Lenhart, A., & Fontaine, C. (2017). *How youth navigate the news landscape: recent qualitative research*. Knight Foundation.

Maksl, A., Ashley, S., & Craft, S. (2015). Measuring News Media Literacy. *The Journal of Media Literacy Education*, 6(3), 29–45.

Melki, J., Tamim, H., Hadid, D., Makki, M., El Amine, J., & Hitti, E. (2021). Mitigating infodemics: The relationship between news exposure and trust and belief in COVID-19 fake news and social media spreading. *PLoS One*, 16(6), 1–13. 10.1371/journal.pone.025283034086813

Newman, N., Fletcher, R., Robertson, C. T., Eddy, K., & Nielsen, R. K. (2022). *Digital Media Report 2022*. Reuters Institute.

Newman, N., Fletcher, R., Eddy, K., Robertson, C. T., & Nielsen, R. K. (2023). *Digital News Report 2023*. Reuters Institute.

Ofcom. (2022). News consumption in the UK: 2022. Ofcom.

Park, C. S., & Kaye, B. K. (2021). What's This? Incidental Exposure to News on Social Media, 'News-Finds-Me' Perception, News Efficacy, and News Consumption. In Shen, F. (Ed.), *Social Media News and Its Impact* (pp. 73–97). Routledge. 10.4324/9781003179580-6

Potter, W. J. (2004). Theory of media literacy: A cognitive approach. *Sage (Atlanta, Ga.)*. 10.4135/9781483328881

Schäfer, S. (2023). Incidental news exposure in a digital media environment: A scoping review of recent research. *Annals of the International Communication Association*, 47(2), 242–260. 10.1080/23808985.2023.2169953

Swart, J. (2021). Tactics of news literacy: How young people access, evaluate, and engage with news on social media. *New Media & Society*, 25(3), 505–521. 10.1177/14614448211011447

Tully, M. (2021). Why News Literacy Matters. In Bélair-Gagnon, V., & Usher, N. (Eds.), *Journalism Research That Matters* (pp. 91–102). Oxford University Press.

Vázquez-Herrero, J., Negreira-Rey, M.-C., & Sixto-García, J. (2022). Mind the Gap! Journalism on Social Media and News Consumption Among Young Audiences. *International Journal of Communication*, 16, 3822–3842.

Vraga, E. K., Tully, M., Maksl, A., Craft, S., & Ashley, S. (2021). Theorizing News Literacy Behaviors. *Communication Theory*, 31(1), 1–21. 10.1093/ct/qtaa005

Veeriah, J. (2021). Young Adult's ability to detect fake news and their new media literacy level in the wake of the COVD-19 pandemic. *Journal of Content. Community & Communication*, 13(7), 372–383.

WHO. (2023). *Infodemic*. WHO. https://www.who.int/health-topics/infodemic#tab=tab_1

Wimmer, R. D., & Dominick, J. R. (2011). *Mass Media Research: An Introduction* (9th ed.). Wadsworth.

Wright, R. R., Sandlin, J. A., & Burdick, J. (2023). What is critical media literacy in an age of disinformation? *New Directions for Adult and Continuing Education*, 178, 11–25.

Yildiz, M. N., & Keengwe, J. (2015). *Handbook of Research on Media Literacy in the Digital Age*. IGI.

ADDITIONAL READING

Bawden, D., & Robinson, L. (2020). *Information Overload: An Introduction*. Oxford University Press.

Head, A. J., Wihbey, J., Metaxas, P. T., MacMillan, M., & Cohen, D. (2018). *How Students Engage with News: Five Takeaways for Educators, Journalists, and Librarians.* Project Information Literacy Research Institute. https://www.projectinfolit.org/uploads/2/7/5/4/27541717/newsreport.pdf

Park, C. S. (2019). Does Too Much News on Social Media Discourage News Seeking? Mediating Role of News Efficacy Between Perceived News Overload and News Avoidance on Social Media. *Social Media + Society*, 5(3), 1–12. 10.1177/2056305119872956

Salem, F. (2017). *The Arab Social Media Report 2017: Social Media and the Internet of Things: Towards Data-Driven Policymaking in the Arab World* (Vol. 7). MBR School of Government.

Vandewater, E. A., & Lee, S. J. (2009). Measuring Children's Media Use in the Digital Age: Issues and Challenges. *The American Behavioral Scientist*, 52(8), 1152–1176. 10.1177/0002764209331539 19763246

Young, E. (2022). *Knowing the News: How Gen Z and Millennials get information on essential topics*. The Media Insight Project. AP-NORC-API. https://apnorc.org/wp-content/uploads/2022/11/MIP-RELEASE-2-Report-Final_v5.pdf

KEY TERMS AND DEFINITIONS

Media Literacy: The ability to access, critically analyse and create content in the mass media and to determine its accuracy or credibility.

News consumption: Being exposed to, accessing, engaging with and sharing content that is regarded as news. This may be created by both formal (news organisations) and informal (citizens) producers.

News Literacy: The ability to understand, evaluate and engage with news content and production.

News Literacy Behaviours (NLB): Behaviours undertaken to enable audiences to engage with news content in critical and thoughtful ways.

5Cs: context, creation, content, circulation and consumption.

Young people: Often defined as being aged between 18 and 25 but in this study referring specifically to university undergraduates.

Chapter 10
Social Media Landscape in Africa:
Mobilising and Engineering Youths for Socio-Political Change in Sub-Saharan Africa

Desmond Onyemechi Okocha
http://orcid.org/0000-0001-5070-280X
Bingham University, Nigeria

Maureen Chigbo
Bingham University, Nigeria

ABSTRACT

Since the Arab Spring pro-democracy riots and upheavals that shook the Middle East and North African authoritarian regimes in 2010 and 2011 and the EndSARS protest against police brutality in Nigeria in 2020, the debate on the influence of social media in galvanizing youth to action has raged. The research was done to establish how social media has advanced the mobilization of youths for social-political change in sub-Saharan Africa in the last five years that countries in the region have witnessed successful general elections. Premised on the theoretical frameworks of media ecology and agenda-setting, the study explained how social media through improved affordable technology and democratization of media have aided and abetted the participation of young people in the transformation of society.

INTRODUCTION

With the advent of the internet and technological innovations including its applications, social media have invaded homes and become a crucial part of man's daily existence (Yan, 2021). Affordable internet services (data) and smartphones owned by the masses in sub-Saharan Africa, especially the youth, have encouraged the use of social media for all forms of communication and content production, and social-political mobilization. Defined by Merriam-Webster dictionary (2023) "as forms of electronic communication (such as websites for social networking and microblogging) through which users create

DOI: 10.4018/979-8-3693-3767-7.ch010

Copyright ©2024, IGI Global. Copying or distributing in print or electronic forms without written permission of IGI Global is prohibited.

online communities to share information, ideas, personal messages, and other content (such as videos)" marketing and business promotions, social media applications including Facebook, Twitter, WhatsApp, Telegram, Instagram, WeChat, blog. In 2023, the projected number of social media users worldwide was 4.89 billion while Africa has 384 million social media users with internet users put at 566 million (Statista, 2023).

Silver and Johnson (2018) wrote that in sub-Saharan Africa most people are gravitating toward social media for social activities over political, religious or commercial ones. In sub-Saharan Africa, most phone owners are use their devices to send text messages and take pictures or video; those who use social media (ranging from 43% in South Africa to 20% in Tanzania) share views on entertainment-related topics such as music, movies, and sports than they post about politics, religion or products they enjoy; they are more are likely to use their mobile devices for social and entertainment purposes than for information-seeking or career and commerce-related activities while around four-in-ten phone owners also use their mobile phones to access social networking sites (Silver and Johnson, 2018). The researchers stated that although mobile phones were responsible for most online presence in Africa, around 19 percent of the total population lived out of reach from mobile connection as of 2020.

However, Sasu (2022) noted that the use of social media increased in recent years, especially in Nigeria where it is deployed to follow friends, family, acquaintances, or actors and people in the art and entertainment industry, with WhatsApp being the most used platform in the country. As of the third quarter of 2021, this instant messaging and voice-over IP platform was used by 92 percent of Nigeria's overall internet users ahead of Facebook and Instagram even though Facebook was the most preferred platform for the majority of individuals accessing the news on social media; men and youth are in the lead in social media usage in Nigeria (Sasu, 2022).

While in 2022, more than 58 percent of the users were men as was reflected across the various platforms. For instance, close to 59 percent of Nigerians on Facebook were men although overall Facebook usage was concentrated among individuals aged 18 – 34 years. The youth and male prevalence remain similar on other social network platforms such as Linkedin and Instagram. Consequently, young people in Nigeria were the most reached by social media advertising compared to people of other age groups (Sasu, 2022). As the Internet is needed for all social media connections, it plays vital roles in the development of social media in Nigeria. In 2020, smartphones and tablets were the most common devices from which the internet was accessed by around 84 percent of Internet users (Sasu, 2022).

Despite the evidence that social media is being used by youths in Africa, of all available data studied for this research none showed how social media has been leveraged for the socio-political mobilization of youths for social change in the 46 countries in sub-Saharan Africa including Nigeria, with the largest population of more than 200 million people and 149.8 million internet users as of August 2020 (Nigerian Communications Commission, 2020). This is the focus of this research to ascertain how social media has influenced the social-political mobilization of the youths, with particular attention on Nigeria, Ghana, Kenya, and The Gambia; all these countries held their general elections recently. The study hinged on media ecology and agenda-setting theories to show how technology innovations has democratized information dissemination through social media to advance human abilities, engineer social progress and make youth active participants and determinants in the socio-economic, electoral processes and governance in sub-Saharan Africa.

SOCIAL MEDIA LANDSCAPE IN AFRICA

The media landscape in sub-Saharan Africa is changing fast from analog to the internet-based dominated social media which is enhanced by affordable data and smartphones that allow people to interact with each other much more than they did in the past (Essoungou, 2010). Worldwide statistics provided by Statista (2023) attests that sub-Saharan African countries are among the leading countries in the usage of social media such as Facebook and WhatsApp. In September 2021, four African countries featured among the countries with the highest social media usage. Brazil topped with 96 percent of the country's digital population engaging with the mobile social messaging platform WhatsApp on a monthly basis, followed by South Africa with 95.4 percent; Argentina, 95.2 percent, Mexico, 94.3 percent, Kenya, 93,5 percent; Nigeria, 91.9 percent; Spain, 91 percent; Italy, 90.8 percent, and Ghana, 89.9 percent. Comparatively, only 29 internet users in the United States used the messaging app, while Japan had the lowest WhatsApp usage rate among the examined markets (Statista, 2023).

Also, in Africa, Northern Africa had the largest number of Facebook users. As of July 2022, there were almost 104 million accounts on the social media platform. Western and Eastern Africa followed with around 58 million and 43 million, respectively, while Central Africa only had 16 million Facebook accounts (Galal, 2022). According to Essoungou (2020), along with regular citizens, African stars, thinkers, political leaders, and companies have rapidly joined the global conversation on social media which has also been used for political campaigns in countries that had elections.

Social media is rewiring the economy and socio-cultural and religious activities to drive developmental changes in the region. Short, Scott, Green, Schoeman, Wapenaar, Ruiters, von Widdern, Choda (2021) wrote that digital technologies have been rewiring the global economy by disrupting ways in which information is generated and shared, production techniques, and the transport of products from producers to consumers. Even seemingly "physical" industries which include tourism, hospitality, food, and transport are being transformed by digital technology. Short et al. (2021) established that the predominant device for accessing the internet in Africa is the mobile phone. In Kenya, 84.1% of the population use mobile devices to access the internet, in Nigeria 87% and in South Africa 73.4%. In sub-Saharan Africa, only 44% of the population have access to a smart phone, and only 26% of the people are able to access the internet with a smart phone. The main barrier is the high cost of smartphones relative to average incomes. The total cost of basic mobile ownership per month (including the handset price, activation and connection price, and 100MB of data) is higher in sub-Saharan Africa than in any other region of the word – users spend on average the equivalent of 6% of income compared to an average of less than 2% in other regions.

However, Silver and Johnson (2019) argued that sub-Saharan Africa has experienced dramatic gains in internet use in recent years. With this rapid growth in connectivity came a host of potential problems, including fake news, political targeting and manipulation, and financial scams, among others. But a Pew Research Center analysis stated that most sub-Saharan Africans feel positive about the role the internet plays in their country. Large majorities say the increasing use of the internet has had a good influence on education in their country, and half or more say the same about the economy, personal relationships and politics (Silver & Johnson, 2019).

SOCIAL MEDIA AND YOUTH MOBILISATION IN SUB-SAHARAN AFRICA

Social media, although a global phenomenon, is extensively used by young people. Numbering 200 million in sub-Saharan Africa, the majority of mobile users, who are under the age of 30 and are among the poor, constitute 70 percent of the population (specifically in Ghana, Malawi, and South Africa) (Ghai et al, 2022). This is not surprising because the youth easily adopt and adapt to technology and innovation which they leverage on to start small and medium enterprises, SMEs. In Nigeria, for instance, social media has proliferated skit-making by young people, who eke out a living from their Youtube, Tiktok, and Instagram posts. This is partly why globally, African youths are recognized as the engine of entrepreneurship and innovation (Executive Office of the US President National Security Council, 2022). They also constitute a disenfranchised group, largely excluded from key socioeconomic institutions and political processes (African Economic Outlook, 2012); but have latched onto the internet to find their groove.

The internet age has seen young people leverage technology to mobilize and engineer socio-political change in sub-Saharan Africa and bring about a non-violent revolution for societal transformation. And also, to address the challenges they face which include unemployment, the search for sustainable livelihoods, the lack of civil liberties, war and the lure of terrorism, political instability, bad governance, failed neo-liberal social and economic policies, longstanding societal problems, lack of financial independence, and therefore the inability to support themselves and (raise) their own families (Eze, 2015).

Corroborating, McGee and Greenhalf (2012) stated that experience so far suggests that some voices, including those of young people, often get left out, just as they do from formal, electoral, and political representation processes. They argued that children and young people, despite their demographic weight, are traditionally, culturally, legally, and structurally marginalized from decision-making processes. Probably, the exclusion led to the spontaneous use of social media by youths to bring about socio-political change which dawned on the world during the Arab Spring pro-democracy riots and upheavals that shook the Middle East and North African authoritarian regimes in 2010 and 2011 and the EndSARS protest against police brutality in Nigeria in 2020.

Eze (2015) chronicled how youth activism and popular protest movements recently deployed in the struggles for economic, political, and social emancipation to include the riot by thousands of young Mozambicans in 2010 forced the government to reverse the price hikes. In Tunisia in 2011, the youth from diverse social strata articulated grievances that ousted the regime of Ben Ali, inspiring similar activism across the continent, even in the Middle East, and in Dakar in June 2011, *Y'eŶ a Marre!* (or We are fed up!) helped to remove Abdoulaye Wade from office. Inn 2012 and in 2014, a similar activism led to the demise of Blaise Compaoré s reign.

These protests showed how the youth used social media to alter political equations in their respective countries as well as to depict their savvy in adapting to technology and innovation for social engineering and entrepreneurship recognized as one of the fundamentals to shape the future of sub-Saharan Africa. This was acknowledged in November, 2021 by the Executive Office of the President National Security Council, EOPNSA, (2022) of the United States that articulated a strategic new vision that recognized the region's youth as an engine of entrepreneurship and innovation. In that EOPNSA document, Anthony Blinken, secretary of State for the United States of America, affirmed that "Africa will shape the future - and not just the future of the African people but of the world" with U.S recasting its traditional policy priorities - democracy and governance, peace and security, trade and investment, and development - as pathways to bolster the region's ability to solve global problems alongside the United States (EOPNSA

2022). Apart from the United States, other global powers of Europe, Russia, and China have realized the import of social media in Africa and its influence in mobilizing the youth for socio-political change in sub-Saharan Africa. Mwakideu (2021) noted that Chinese investment in Kenya's media industry has created 500 jobs — up to 300 of those are journalists on television and radio and also introduced state-of-the-art technology and trained many budding journalists. Chinese investment in sub-Saharan Africa has dramatically increased this century, making the region an arena for strategic power competition with the United States. Acknowledging SMEs as the backbone of the region's economy where youth play, Runde, Savoy, and Staguhn (2021), added that although the United States cannot compete on a dollar-for-dollar basis with China, it has an opportunity to use targeted blended finance and share technology, knowledge, and standards to provide an alternative to the Chinese model and support SMEs in the region.

Also perturbed are the governments of the countries in sub-Saharan Africa which are on edge because young people are not just increasingly embracing technology and innovation but they are also using social media to criticize governance. Empowered by technology and social media, African youths actively engage in a participatory governance cycle in the global public square prompting their leaders to kick back forcefully (Ovuorie, 2022). For instance, in 2022, the government of South Sudan, where an estimated 4 percent of the population in urban areas who use social media, threatened a shutdown of Facebook and Twitter, alleging that users abused it by creating panic. As Ovuorie (2022) observed, those who do have social media access, mainly urban youth, are using it to criticize the government of President Salva Kiir and First Vice President Riek Machar. Ovuorie observed that many governments would not like their citizens to have the power of social activism, hence, Africa is the most censored region of the world with outright bans of social media and laws such as the Cybercrime Act 2011 in Nigeria and the aborted Social Media Law. As Ovuorie said: The continent was responsible for 53% of social media restrictions in 2021, with targeted apps including WhatsApp, Facebook Messenger, Facebook, Twitter, and Instagram. In Nigeria, the government banned Twitter from June 5, 2021, to January 13, 2022.

Nevertheless, youths were galvanized like it had never seen before through social media to participate actively in the 2023 general elections in Nigeria. Dismissed as just four people tweeting in a room, youths used social media to build a revolutionary grassroots movement called the 'Obidients' to mobilize Nigerians of voting age to register so as to obtain the permanent voter card. After eight months of canvassing and campaigning, they propelled Peter Obi, the Labor Party presidential candidate, who was dismissed as having no political structure to emerge as one of the four major presidential candidates. The support they gave resulted in a historic upset in the February 25 presidential election as the Labor Party won 40 national assembly seats. Despite the fact that Obi and Atiku Abubakar are in court challenging the contentious presidential election results announced by the Independent National Electoral Commission (INEC) in which Bola Ahmed Tinubu was declared the winner, the youth are undeterred. They have continued with their unrelenting pressure and through the use of digital technology disseminate information to encourage themselves not to be disoriented by the muddled up electoral process by the INEC. They solicited for a massive turn out in the governorship election in order to oust the old guard politicians in the March 18 governorship and state Assembly elections. It is not certain what would happen until the deed is done. But what is obvious is that social media has permeated the region (Galal, 2022) and the penetration is considerably higher in that Northern and Southern Africa than in other regions.

As of February 2022, some 56 percent of the population in Northern Africa used social media, 45 percent in Southern Africa while Central Africa had only eight percent. In Ghana, Kenya, Nigeria, and South Africa, social media users favored WhatsApp. On the other hand, Egyptian and Moroccan users preferred Facebook (Galal, 2022). Social media is changing the landscape of communication in the sub-Saharan Africa in both formal and informal sectors as more people use it more than radio, television, and print. Thus invariably, because social media is easy to use without much technicalities as it breaks restrictions of time and space, many persons can use it anytime, anywhere and via any online electronic device such as computer, laptop, and cellphones to interact with each other as long as they want (Yan, 2021) and ensures privacy as most messages are encrypted. Yan (2021) posited that social media not only disrupted means of dissemination of information but also has the ability to redistribute power by modifying the relationship between governments and citizens by giving the citizens opportunity to join politics, escalate democracy consciousness, have the power to kick against unfair social events and monitor governance; as well as dispute the position of traditional media and alter media and information diffusion.

Social media in Nigeria provides a "balance of terror" as Gbenga Daniel (2022) explained that anyone who possesses a smartphone and data has the chance of telling their own story as they see it since they are no longer passive recipients of information that is against their interest. It allows anybody who is wrongly portrayed to provide an alternative view unlike in the days when traditional media held sway and people found it difficult to rebut wrong information published about them. For instance, during political campaigns, youth have used social media to project the image of their candidates and swiftly debunk wrong information about the candidate they support. Daniel's opinion is not shared by Wole Soyinka, Nobel Laureate, who described social media users in Nigeria as barbarians (Ogunnaike, 2024). In Nigeria, Soyinka said social media has been dragged down to the lowest common denominator although he believes in the community of the intellect of minds and creativity to rescue us from the monstrosity that the social media has become (Ogunnaike, 2024). Soyinka stretched the truth about social media which is more inclusive of the voiceless who have no access or resources to access the elitist traditional media that are malleable, and can manipulate powers that be to slant or tilt content and dominate dissemination of information in Soyinka's hey days. The social media now is for the long-suffering masses who can now vent their spleen about the bad governance or any societal ills they face.

This dovetails into what Havas Global Comms (2013) described as the single greatest "agents of change" the people empowered by social media". Social media has an effect on the political sphere by shifting who controls information and how to distribute the information and how it can be changed. Social media has also changed the existing media landscape and structure guiding political communication. Besides, social media algorithms have been said to have negative influence on content discovery and diversity (Kulke, 2023). Social media algorithm is a set of guidelines and signals that rates content on a social platform and organises content on social feeds based on how likely each individual social media user is to like and interact with it (Adisa, 2023). Consequently, Kulke (2023) echoed what other social scientists have described as the misalignment between objective of social media algorithms designed to boost user communication, and behavior that can lead to increased polarization and misinformation. According to Kulke (2023), Facebook and Twitter have reputation issues to consider during elections and dissemination of misinformation they can perform better by coding their algorithms to better user experience. Also, of note is Kulke's (2023) argument that algorithms usually select information that boosts user engagement to enhance advertising revenue. Significantly, this amplifies the information from which humans are biased to learn, overload social feeds with "prestigious, ingroup, moral and emotional (PRIME") content, notwithstanding of the content's accuracy or representatives of group's opinion (Kulke, 2023).

Nevertheless, the use of social media for socio-political mobilisation started when former President Barack Obama of the United States became the first one to use it to run for the presidency and got success (Yan, 2021). It also influenced voting patterns in the 2011 presidential election in Nigeria, when two selected presidential candidates were popular because they used social media in their political campaign while former President Goodluck Jonathan emerged winner (Okoro & Tsgyu, 2017).

It reared up between 2014 and 2015 when Muhammadu Buhari, then-presidential candidate of the All-Progressive Congress deployed it to churn out campaign messages, rabid and rancid propaganda against the then-incumbent President Jonathan Gooodluck. As believed, Jonathan lost the social media war because he could not mount an effective counter-attack and also lost his presidential bid for a second tenure. The second tenure bid of President Muhamadu Buhari also witnessed the mobilization of youths and the populace through social media. It was not then surprising that Peter Obi, the Labor Party presidential candidate deployed social media effectively to run his campaign in 2023. Dismissed ignominiously initially as a social media presidential candidate with no structure on the ground to win the election, Obi has emerged as one of the front-runners tipped by many pollsters to win the 2023 presidential race. The highly proactive and mobile youths are the base of his political structure and the largest voting bloc in the country going by statistics from the Independent National Electoral Commission (INEC). Nigerian youths, who constitute about 70 percent of the population, have used and continue to use social media as well as being on the ground to spread messages incessantly to motivate their members to finish their campaign strong, as well as attack aggressively any opponent who throws mud at their candidate or them. Obi's opponents never envisaged the kind of political Tsunami he has unleashed through the 'Obidient' movement which began mostly on social media and is believed to have mutated from the EndSARS youths' nationwide protest against police brutality in 2020. The protest ended disastrously when some of the youths were killed at the Lekki Tollgate, Lagos. This development accords with Morozou (2011) who acknowledged that social media is revolutionary tool for grassroot movement and long-term political mobilisation.

The scale of influence of social media in political mobilization as witnessed in Nigeria is unprecedented and can only match that of Kenya in 2022. The February 25, 2023, presidential election which ended in a fiasco with the gross inefficiency displayed by INEC in addition to the use of thugs by the ruling political party to disenfranchise voters at polling units were captured in viral videos. *Punch* editorial entitled: *Nigeria's electoral show of shame* published March 12, 2023, captured the role social media played thus:

> Evidence on polling day and after bore this out. Online media is replete with videos of security agents, public officials, and thugs tearing ballot papers, massive thumb printing, ballot box snatching, and other irregularities. There are viral videos showing results from polling units were altered and later uploaded to the IReV portal from the original. (p.16)

This is thumbs up for social media which helped record and seamlessly disseminate the heists that took place on election day which would not have been possible if information dissemination on that day was left in the hands of the traditional media of print, radio, and television.

In Ghana, research on new media practices has been described as wide open, with very few studies focusing on youth social media use albeit its use for the socio-political mobilization of young people. Markwei and Appiah (2016) investigated the extent of social media use and the purposes, access, and challenges of its use by the young people of Nima and Maamobi, two suburbs of Accra, Ghana. They found that patterns of youth's social media use appear consistent with similar studies in other countries, with high use among those in economically and educationally disadvantaged communities. Markwei and Appiah (2016) stated the need for young people to have a greater awareness of the risks of social media use and recommended: "nationwide education of youth in Ghana about responsible use of social media, with policy and educational interventions led by multiple stakeholders, including school and public libraries and government agencies, to maximize the benefits and minimize the risks of social media use among Ghanaian". Acknowledging the paucity of research on youth social media use in Ghana, Ocansey, Ametepe and Oduro (2016) stated that young people need to have a great awareness of the risks of social media use and that the majority of Ghanaian youths were using social media on an enormous scale, mainly for communication purposes. Although social media has a positive impact on the youth, quite a large number reported having negative experiences on these online sites.

In Kenya, Ndlela and Mulwo (2017) opined that with the increased accessibility of smartphones and mobile Internet, social media is becoming an integral part of everyday life for young people. The use of new social media tools such as Facebook, Twitter, and WhatsApp are quickly changing in the country. However, previous studies on new media showed socio-demographic differences in the use and access of new technologies that is necessary to understand the multiple ways youth in developing countries such as Kenya appropriate and deploy social media platforms, and how they use these new spaces to connect, interact, and engage on different issues. The new social media configurations are invariably making possible access to alternative spaces for communication relatively 'free' unlike what obtains with traditional media where access is limited and these can lead to social change involving socio-economic and socio-cultural aspects of the society (Ndlela & Mulwo, 2017).

In the Gambia, social media has been a means for agitation for citizens for better governance (Bah, 2022). It has been used to rally people around particular causes to fight for their rights and to topple governments and prep up others more acceptable to the agitators. The Gambia witnessed the use of social media to defenestrate a dictatorship and elect a new government.

The Media Foundation for West Africa (MFWA) (2021) wrote that hours before the 2016 presidential elections President Yahya Jammeh's government shut down the internet including telephone connections. In 2021 in the Gambia, about 430,000 people used social media, representing 16% increase compared to 2020 (MFWA, 2021). Internet penetration in the country has improved to 23%, according to Afrobarometer, which stated that 65% of the citizens use social media as their source of information (MFWA, 2021). Stating that the growth and increasing usage of social media platforms have provided diverse opportunities for popular participation, particularly among the youth, MFWA (2021) noted that it is where political debates take place and political parties that have their own Facebook TV and WhatsApp use it effectively to share videos and voice notes. In the Gambia, social media is a double-edged sword as it facilitates the spread of misinformation and disinformation and the transmission of fake news during elections. Nearly 90% of the citizens believe social media is the foremost purveyor of false news ahead of politicians and political parties, government officials, and the news media and journalists. These issues resurrected concerns about whether the social media platforms should be interrupted ahead of the elections, even though the government did not as many media stakeholders cautioned against it. For instance, Access Now, wrote an open letter to President Adam Barrow, to provide assurance against a shutdown (MFWA, 2021).

PROPENSITY OF SOCIAL MEDIA FOR SOCIETY'S DESTABILIZATION

Social media has become a double-edged sword in the hand of the youth in the sub-Saharan Africa albeit globally, with positive and negative implications on culture, economics, politics, religion, and security (Al Naqbi, Al Momani, & Davies, 2022). The positive is in its unique ability for viral dissemination of information to a vast audience worldwide with the speed of light. Herein lies its major negativity as purveyor of falsehood and fake news that can destabilize an entity if the information equally goes viral and cause collateral damage before it can be retracted. The negative of social media manifest in the form of disinformation and, misinformation. Disinformation and misinformation come in the form of trending stories of past events that are presented as if it is just happening and they are deceptively linked to issues of the moment whereas there is no connection between context and reality. A case in point is a political protest that happened in the Osun State of Nigeria which was presented as the present demonstration by the people of Osun against the outcome of the 2023 controversial presidential election The silver lining is that some fact-checking sites such as Dubawa Fact-Checking Organization have been established to flag false information peddled in the social media. Disinformation is described by the United Nations Higher Commissioner for Refugee Agency (UNCHR) (2022) as an intentional and malevolent content which include hoaxes, spear phishing and propaganda to cause disaffection, instigate fear and chaos among the people. Also, misinformation is seen as incorrect and inaccurate details, rumors, insults, pranks (UNHCR, 2022) peddled in the social media, which also causes disaffection and damage reputation of the affected individual. Furthermore, the UNCHR (2022) listed forms of misinformation and disinformation to include contents that are forged, distorted, and impersonated and used as established brands of an agency. Misinformation contents are also misleading facts under false context or inaccurate or they are factually accurate but presented in a false context to the disadvantage of issues or anyone being targeted. Often times, misinformation can be in the form of headlines that have no relationship with the body of the story. Misinformation comes in form of satire portrayed as true stories in the social media, which can easily deceive the gullible; false connections such as headlines, visuals, captions that do not relate to content; sponsored content, advertising and public relations materials disguised as editorial content. While the youth have used misinformation, it is important to point out that disinformation is mostly done by states at various levels - federal, state and local governments - as propaganda to win public sympathy for their programmes. Political parties also indulge in disinformation to churn out messages to convince the electorate to vote for them during elections. Corroborating, Lin et al. (2022) opined that misinformation on the internet and disinformation effort by government were censured for their role in worsening the corona-virus disease 2019 (COVID-19) pandemic. In Nigeria, disinformation and misinformation on COVID-19 by netizens led to deaths as some members of the gullible public failed to take the vaccine because of information they obtained from the internet (Okocha & Chigbo, 2023).

Furthermore, Mngusuul (2015) established that large a number of youths spend time online to get informed and raise awareness about different issues through e-publicity and demonstrations, thereby promoting good governance and accountability in different ways. He advocated recognizing social media as a veritable tool for aggregating public opinion by public office holders, encouraging free expression therein; that users should move to streets, and office, and get involved more in offline activities; ensuring improved media literacy on the part of avid social media users and activists to enable them to make the best use of the innovation for socio-political participation and reduce incidences of false or, malicious information going viral and affecting the society negatively. Agreeing, Kayode and Omar (2020) opined that the little benefaction of social media to political engagement offline makes the future of democracy in Africa worrisome as youth involvement in online discussion on politics could hinder their articulation of ideas for active engagement in politics offline to strengthen civic participation because basically social media algorithm mechanisms limit information to the needs of users' network.

Consequently, the youth on social media platforms are exposed to a narrow political plan of the society that result in their powerlessness to mingle with other members of the society on important political projects geared towards the well-being of all. This could have negative effect in a country such as Nigeria which has threatening ingrained political divisions that the politicians could exploit. Hence, Kayode and Omar (2020) counselled on the importance of devising ways to get the youth to participate in established political culture other than staying online. This notwithstanding, Akpan and Targema (2022) acknowledged the prospects of social media with millions of subscribers for successful mass mobilisation of different groups to participate in development of the nation. An example of where social media was used effectively for social mobilisation is the 2020 #EndSARS (SARS is an acronym for Special Anti-Robbery Squad), a youth protest to stop all forms of inhuman police action on the public especially the youths who were being targeted in Nigeria. #EndSARS protest showed that social media provided the means for mobilising citizens positively for the development of a nation as it evolved as the media of liberation in an environment dominated by traditional media where the youth access is poor due to limited resources unlike the new media that has become the media for the masses because of its affordability and convenience to use (Akpan & Targema, 2022). Also, the #EndSARS protest symbolizes an incident where the full strength of social media was used for a crusade among the youth to fight societal malaise (Akpan & Targema, (2022). Notwithstanding election seasons and the political sphere, Akpan and Targema, 2022), affirmed that #EndSARS is one of the modern cases where social media's strength was used to champion a social cause in Nigeria similar to what obtained during the Arab Spring riots in 2010. Although there were previous protests in Nigeria such as the #OccupyNigeria in 2012 and Bring Back Our Girls (#BBOG) in 2014, the #EndSARS was more unified and forceful and pushed government to make substantial changes including renaming the police outfit that was associated with brutality. It can also be used for other structural reforms and changes in the society (Akpan & Targema, 2022). This corresponds with Kalyango Jr. and Adu-Kumi (2022) observation that social media platforms are significant in public engagement and cherished as a way of communication as many Ghanaian and Ugandan netizens use the innovation to monitor friends, social-political developments, distant cultures as well get involved with international online forum to post information about their government (Kalyango Jr. & Adu-Kumi, 2022). According to them, netizens from Kenya and Ghana have used social media to demonstrate how to get involved in political conversation and get the governments to respond to their needs the same way ordinary Egyptians and Tunisians did with the movement for social change during the Arab Spring riots.

Similarly, Guanah, Obi, Egbra, and Akumabor (2017) noted that the internet has always had an 'anything goes' atmosphere where harsh language is common and listed among the challenges social media presents to African youths. There is limited internet access because overall internet penetration on the continent is low as internet access is also irregularly distributed, with two-thirds of overall online activity in Africa being generated in South Africa. "This shows that the proportion of the population who do not have access to the internet is high. This population is therefore deprived of all the benefits that social media has to offer" (Guanah, Obi, Egbra, & Akumabor (2017).

Evidently, social media has had some negative effects on the general behavior of some African youth. The general African cultural value of youth demonstrating respect, especially to elders, is being impeded because of how youth exploit social media platforms as users sometimes actually forget that they're speaking out loud when they post a snarky comment-writing something from a smartphone that almost seems like you're talking only to yourself, stated Guanah, Obi, Egbra, and Akumabor (2017), citing the recent abuse of social media by youths as demonstrated in Cote d'Ivoire. Fans of popular Ivorian musician 'DJ Arafat' – known as Les Chinoise – removed the late musician's corpse from his grave to confirm if it was his body. Their abusive use of social media was demonstrated by the posting of pictures and videos of the deceased on social media platforms. Posting of nude pictures, use of slanderous words, and use of social media for character defamation are some of the adverse ways the African youth engage on social media that do not conform with traditional cultural values.

Social media is also throwing up psychological disorders that can lead to a lot of anxiety and depression among the youth (Guanah, Obi, Egbra, & Akumabor, 2017; O'Day and Heimberg, 2021). O'Day and Heimberg (2021) suggested that social media use is related to social anxiety and loneliness, adding: socially anxious and lonely individuals appear to prefer and seek out online social interactions on social media. Another psychological pitfall of social media is that users continually present only their "best selves" online and reap the emotional benefits of lots of "likes" on Facebook for instance, and so, have their self-esteem bloom disproportionately. This, Guanah, Obi, Egbra, and Akumabor (2017) said could negatively impact their self-control with the result that they "feel entitled to be an online meanie".

Agreeing, Al Naqbi, Al Momani, and Davies (2022) also added that social media presents a significant threat to security at the local, regional, national, and global levels. They see social media as a mechanism for seeking to destabilize intellectual convictions, ideological constants, and moral and social virtues to create an imbalance within society, and increase the threat to national security and crisis (Al Naqbi, Al Momani, & Davies, 2022). This double-edged sword nature of social media makes it imperative for all – the youth and all political actors and governments and non-government organizations in the regions to collaborate diligently to sensitize the people on effective and efficient use of the innovative tool to transform and not jeopardize the society for the benefit of all people.

In this wise, what readily comes to mind is the emerging trend of digital activism and role of social media influencer as they commandeer opinion and agenda on conversations on the internet. Castillo-Esparcia et al. (2023) argued that the social media revolution has also profoundly affected activism although its ability to emancipate people or actualise a particular cause is in doubt. This is because of the medialization of all human endeavour which worsened during the corona-virus pandemic isolation forced on the populace worldwide by home governments making more people to seek their information digitally. As Castillo-Esparcia et al. observed, new media has become a haven for socio-political activists to plan both online and offline activism or protest from which they plan to alter news slants and affect political and public agenda. Consequently, activists and their followers use their devises to record and more often than not, stream live any protest or riot or any incident on any trending particular issue in the nation on their social media platform such as WhatsApp, Facebook, Twitter now known as X, Tiktok, etc. There are examples of the #EndSARS (2020); OccupyLagos in Nigeria protest against removal of fuel subsidy in 2014 which forced government to rescind its decision. This is akin to the Arab Spring (2010) in Egypt and Tunisia which led to substantial changes in governance thereby proving the power of new communication technology in bringing about social change. Perhaps, this prompted Castillo-Esparcia et al. (2023) to affirm that digital activism should be seen on the basis of its practices and not as an event borne out of its relations with a specific innovation, which would be seen as digital determinism but also not against idealised vista of traditional protests. Closely associated to digital activism is social media and hashtag activism which trended in Nigeria with the #EndSARS protest. Okocha and Dapoet (2022) affirmed that hashtag activism is now a revolutionary engagement tool for mobilisation, advocacy and creating awareness on development programmes for societal transformation in Nigeria. Hashtag activism in social media is seen by Okocha & Dapoet (2022) as a catalyst that can unleash new norms for governance in Nigeria and elsewhere.

Closely allied to the digital activism is the work of social media influencers (some of who are activists) in determining flow of thoughts, action and opinions of their followers. Kim and Kim (2022) observed that social media influencers such as celebrities, brands and other users in the digital community through symbiotic communication tools like live chats and comments coral millions of loyal fans who they can influence. They found that perceived friendship with social media influencers significantly affected language similarity and self-disclosure, but it did not have important effect on the attitude of their fans. Also, perceived friendship greatly affects the behaviorism and loyalty. Kim and Kim (2022) figured that social media influencers' responsibility determined the pathway from attitudinal well-being to loyalty to those who become famous on television shows and films and their fans feel connected to whatever cause they are involved in. However, of note is that fans of social media influencers select and digest content from them that is in line with their beliefs, customs and traditions (Kim & Kim, 2022), and as such social media influencers can be jettisoned once they are out of tune with their fan based and does not have total control over them and this can blight their influence in mobilisation for social change. For instance, in Nigeria, Reno Omokri, a social media influencer, lost many of his followers that belong to the 'Obidient' movement because he attacked Peter Obi, the presidential candidate of the Labour Party, whom they supported. Recently, Omokri peddled information on X (Twitter) that Obi did not invest in schools contrary to the facts on ground and challenged the 'Obidients' to provide evidence. Of course, the social media was flooded with videos of Obi's achievements in education while he was the Governor of Anambra State, ensuring that the state which was among the last in West African Examination Council became the first consecutively during his tenure, in addition to other posts to denounce and discredit Omokri's falsehood. However, such falsehoods peddled in the social media by the likes of Reno Omokri can be checked with block-chain technology, which ensures accuracy of data or information being circulated on the internet. Block-chain is an immutable advanced technology that ensures information is transparently shared within a business network. Blockchain technology will be useful in archiving social media interactions involving video sharing, photosharing, social networking, blogging and microblogging. These engagements listed happens respectively on YouTube and Vimeo; Facebook, Linkedin and Google; WordPress and Tomblr and Twitter now called X. The platforms are interactive and involve liking and comments with each other and one another and these events have become a major part of the archivists work which blockchain can facilitate. Block-chain technology can also be useful in youth social entrepreneurship (Velte, 2018). According to Velte (2018), modern activist movements use social media platforms as citizen journalists many of who are young people on different platforms and this raises the challenge of archiving posts on the events shared on social media relating to protests like the #ENDSARS. Hence, Velte argued that posts made on social media are catalyst to protests and such accounts on movements would vary without any new media record that viewed events from the perspective of the protesters themselves instead of narratives providing by the traditional media which may have gone through gatekeepers who may have altered the original form. Expatiating on ethical issues about acquiring access to social media's content, Velte (2018) said: when collecting social media as data sets, archivists at present intend to provide moderated access to archives, whereas when dealing with social media accounts, they intend to seek permission to collect from the activists group and provide access online. Presently, she opined that the practice on ethical issues may serve as models for people interested in collecting social media from activists, and that understanding how to reach social media ethically reduces the threat to these important records modern activism faces in not being deleted from history because of the persistent changes in technological innovations that result in data corruption, media and obsolescent software and inadequate metadata and the consequent virtual dark age, a digital gap in historical data as exemplified from the move to Web 2.0 that is more interactive from Web 1.0 that allowed for passive consumption of social media content (Velte, 2018).

The United Nations (2020) stated that a combination of new, emerging and frontier technologies provides opportunities for youth entrepreneurship to transmit and scale-up innovation that can contribute to global welfare by maximising fully the potential of the youth and curb the decline in entrepreneurship of the older generation. The United Nations (2020) listed some of the innovations to include artificial intelligence (AI), cloud technology, autonomous vehicles like drones, synthetic biology, virtual and augmented reality, robotics, block-chain, 3D printing and Internet of things. Acknowledging that the frontiers technology is driving disruptive changes in the society, the United Nations (2020) affirmed that the youth who are digital natives and early adopters of new innovations are better placed to acquire them to engage in social entrepreneurship. However, the youth in developing countries including Africa still lack digital access and digital literacy and that the digital divide extremely affects women and young people in developing countries. Of all those without internal access, 2 billion are women and 9 out of 10 young people who lack access live in Africa or in Asia and Pacific. The solution lies in more investment in education in digital literacy and learning for the youth to ensure they are effectively mobilised to participate in the socio-economic, cultural political affairs of the society digitally.

THEORETICAL FRAMEWORK

The media ecology and agenda-setting theories of mass media were the axles of the study on the social media landscape and socio-political mobilization of youths in sub-Saharan Africa.

The research used media ecology theory (MET) to explain how social media as a technological innovation was embraced by youth to drive the transformation of the socio-political system in sub-Saharan Africa. Propounded by Marshall McLuhan in 1960, the MET as typified in social media messages embodies the sensory balance through hearing, smell, touch, sight, and taste seen in the content creation and dissemination of socio-political messages between and among young netizens in Africa albeit globally in the form of video, audio emoji, cartoon or text messages, etc. Social media is an outcome of technology and as McLuhan stated that technological innovations are development of human abilities and senses that punctuate the perceptible equilibrium bearing a new society that makes new innovations humans can use and the trueness of the relationship between media and the technology used in dissemination and building capacity for digital skills required for the socio-political emancipation of the youth to participate actively in governance.

Moreno and Koff (2016) cited McLuhan (1964) as stating that MET provides an understanding of the social impact of technology and communication as media directly acts to shape and organize culture and processes that influence human perception, feelings, understanding, and value. The proponent of MET understood the influence of technologies including clocks, radios, television, movies, and games. He focused on defining the relationship between technology and members of a specific culture. He noted that electronic media have revolutionized society, and society quickly became reliant on these communication technologies. McLuhan felt that it was almost impossible to find a society unaffected by electronic media. As society has evolved, its technology has also evolved. From the first books published on the internet, society and the media has been affected by the technology. The rules of media set forth by MET – enhancement, obsolescence, retrieval, and reversal – show how technology affects communication through development (Moreno & Koff, 2016). Invariably, young netizens in sub-Saharan Africa have used social media for the exchange of information on a variety of issues but what needs to be explained by the MET is how the technological innovation of social media has been used to bring about socio-political changes and set agenda for the youth of sub-Saharan Africa and society as provided by the agenda setting theory of mass media.

Propounded by Maxwell McCombs and Donald L, Shaw (1968), the crux of agenda-setting theory is that with so much media focus and scrutiny on a single event the mass media is missing or even ignoring other important stories (Alvernia University, 2023). The theory is used to explain how social media determines issues that become the focus of public attention. Its two basic assumptions are that the media filters and shapes what we see rather than just reflecting stories to the audience; and that the more attention social media gives to an issue, the more important the public will consider that issue to be. The agenda-setting theory's downside is that it is difficult to measure if there is a relationship between what is posted and the prominence of issues social media recipients consider important and it may not be for people who already made up their minds. For instance, in Nigeria, the 'Obidents' believe their candidate Peter Obi of the Labour Party won the election and would not accept the result of the contentious presidential election as announced by INEC declaring Bola Ahmed Tinubu as the winner.

This is in line with Feezell (2018) whose study acknowledged that conventional models of agenda setting hold that mainstream media influence the public agenda by leading audience attention, and perceived importance, to certain issues but that increased selectivity and audience fragmentation in today's digital media environment threaten the traditional agenda-setting power of the mass media. However, Feezell (2018) opined that an important development to consider in light of this change is the growing use of social media for entertainment and information. Relying on AGT for the research is supported by Feezell's (2018) work through which he established that participants exposed to political information on Facebook exhibit increased levels of issue salience consistent with the issues shared compared with participants who were not shown political information; these effects are strongest among those with low political interest.

DISCUSSION OF FINDINGS

The findings of this research correspond with the media ecology, and agenda-setting theories used to explain how social media was used to set an agenda for youth to bring about the sociopolitical transformation of sub-Saharan Africa, especially in politics and governance. They also fulfilled the objectives and answered the research questions and established that the youth are positively embracing social media despite the adverse psychological effects that can be handled by balancing the time spent on it (Commey, 2020 & Mngusuul, 2015). This is in agreement with the position of Silver and Johnson (2018) that young people are more likely to use social media than older adults for information, education, economic, cultural, entertainment, and socio-political mobilization and promote causes such as tracking missing members of the family, kidnapped victims, and intervening in governance as can be seen in the 2022 general election in Kenya and that of Nigeria in 2023, where they ran aggressive campaigns, produced and shared contents to either market their candidates or relegate their opponents. This aligns with the objectives of the study which is also supported by the position of the Africa Union (2020), which stated the youth in Africa are at the vanguard of positive innovation and social change that promote prosperity and development. The continent, invariably, faces a double-edged situation: whereas the weight of evidence tilts towards the conclusion that young Africans represent an opportunity, as unique and successful peacebuilders, the popular fixation is still with a small percentage of them that engage in unwholesome activities that contribute to undermining the same peace" (Africa Union, 2020) albeit through social media. In Nigeria, social media was used to pile pressure on the Independent National Electoral Commission after it muddled up the seamless transmission of the presidential election results on its portal and went ahead to announce the winner without reviewing the process as promised. The extent of the effect of the pressure would require another study to find out as it is not within the scope of work.

The study amply established that social media is a double-edged sword (Al Naqbi, Al Momani, & Davies, 2022; MFWA, 2021) that has to be managed well by all stakeholders involved in the socio-political mobilization of the youth to get the desired result. Social media has raised the decibel for information overload and the ability of receivers to differentiate between fake news and real news. There was the contentious February 25, 2023 Nigeria election when INEC delayed uploading of the result in real-time on its portal thus creating the atmosphere for fake news peddlers to circulate all manner of false results much to the chagrin of the recipients.

Another important finding is that managing social media is important to secure sub-Saharan African countries. If not, society will live to rue its mistake as the wrongful use of social media could damage national security and the credibility of a country and its leaders. This means that governments should devise effective ways to engage young people who feel excluded from governance and resort to social media to draw attention and in doing so could divulge information that is injurious to those in government. This dovetails into McGee and Greenhalf's (2012) argument that young peoples' voices often get jettisoned just from formal, electoral, and political representation processes, and suggests understanding how young people perceive and experience engagement with governance processes and structures.

The study established that social media has impacted the socioeconomic well-being of youth and presents several opportunities for employment and swift communication for friends, family, and acquaintances to stay connected always even beyond their geographical environment in sub-Saharan Africa. Unlike the traditional media which include print, television, and broadcasting, social media allow users to participate in the creation of content, and this co-creation of content is the major difference between them (Nwoye & Okafor, 2014). For instance, the tremendous influence of social media was evident in the build-up to the general election in Nigeria. The 18 political parties in the elections, had youth-wing, and leaders, who utilized social media to form groups, especially on WhatsApp to hold meetings, strategize, and plan holistic communications to mobilize and engineer the general public to support and vote during the election. A lot of debates and vicious political battles between, and among members of different political parties, especially the major ones such as the ruling All Progressives Party, APC, Peoples Democratic Party, and Labour Party were fought on social media turf. As Nwoye and Okafor (2014) noted, in sub-Saharan Africa, social media will continue to provide tremendous impetus for political agitation and further create openings for Africans to express and mobilize themselves to change their societies (Nwoye & Okoye, 2014); directly discuss issues of governance using a variety of platforms without intermediaries or mediation.

CONCLUSION

The fulcrum of this research has been the social media landscape in Africa: mobilizing and engineering youths for socio-political change in sub-Saharan Africa. Hinged on the media ecology and agenda-setting theories of the mass media, the research established that the internet and technological innovations increasingly democratized the media, and affordable data and smartphones catalyzed the use of social media by youth to mobilize themselves for socio-political changes in the region. But there is a need for stakeholders to thoroughly manage social media not to jeopardize the security of the nations in sub-Saharan Africa without infringing on the fundamental rights of free speech and dissemination of information.

RECOMMENDATIONS

In view of the conclusions above, the study recommends as follow:
1. There is a need for the government to sensitize the youth and the stakeholders on the efficient and effective use of social media to galvanize them to appropriately use technological innovation like social media responsibly for the transformation of the society in accordance with the rule of law.
2. There is need for government, civil society organisations and international development organisations to collaborate to re-orient the youth on the dangers of social media use that could affect their psychological well-being in addition to enlightening them on the dangers of fake news, misinformation and disinformation.
3. That government and stakeholders should develop policies that will promote and ensure protection of national security without undermining the freedom of the people to engage through the social media.
4. There is need for further empirical research on how social media can be used to mobilise Sub-Saharan African youths to participate in socio-political change.

REFERENCES

Adika, N. (2023). Social media usage trends in Africa: GeoPoll report. *Geopoll.* https://www.geopoll.com/blog/social-media-usage-trends-in-africa-geopoll- report/

Adisa, D. (2023, October 30). Everything you need to know about social media algorithms. *Sproutsocial.* https://sproutsocial.com/insights/social-media-algorithms/

AfDB, OECD, UNDP, UNECA. (2012, May 28) African economic outlook 2012: Promoting youth employment. *African Economic Outlook/OECDiLibrary* OECD. /10.1787/aeo-2012-en

African Union. (2020, June). A *study on the roles of youth to peace and security in Africa: An Independent expert report by the peace and security council of the African Union.* AU. https://www.peaceau.org/uploads/a-study-on-the-roles-and-contributions-of-youth-to-peace-and-security-in-africa-17-sept-2020.pdf

Akpan, E. O. B., & Targema, T. S. (2022). Social media, mass mobilisation, and national development in Nigeria: Lessons from the #EndSARS protest. *ASEAN Journal of Community Engagement.* 2(6), 228-243. https://scholarhub.ui.ac.id/cgi/viewcontent.cgi?article=1166&context=ajce

Al Naqbi, N., Al Momani, N., & Davies, A. (2022, August 30). The Influence of social media on perceived levels of national security and crisis: A case study of youth in the United Arab Emirates. *Sustainability (Basel)*, 14(7), 10785. 10.3390/su141710785

Castillo-Esparcia, A., Caro-Castaño, L., & Almansa-Martínez, A. (2023, May 3). Evolution of digital activism on social media: Opportunities and challenges. *El Profesional de la Información*, 32(3), e320303. 10.3145/epi.2023.may.03

Chigbo, M. (2023, February 6). *Leveraging digital literacy for the economic empowerment of the urban poor in Southwestern Nigeria.* [Thesis, Bingham University, Karu, Nasarawa State, Nigeria]

Commey, G. (2020, February 10). *Impact of social media on African youth.* West African Civil Society Institute. https://wacsi.org/wp-content/uploads/2020/10/Impact-of-Social-Media-on-African-Youth.pdf

Darlington, N. (2022, October 2022). *Blockchain for beginners: What is blockchain technology? A step-by-step guide.* Block Geeks. https://blockgeeks.com/guides/what-is-blockchain- technology/

Essoungou, A. (2010, December). A social media boom begins in Africa. *Africa Renewal.* https://www.un.org/africarenewal/magazine/december-2010/social-media-boom-begins-africa

Eze, K. (2015, August 7 - 8). *Youth participation in governance in Africa* (Discussion paper). The Mandela Institute for Development Studies Youth Dialogue, Victoria Falls. Zimbabwe. file:///C:/Users/MAUREEN%20CHIGBO/Downloads/YOUTH_PARTICIPATION_IN_GOVERNANCE_IN_AFR.pdf

Feezell, J. T. (2018). Agenda setting through social media: The importance of incidental news exposure and social filtering in the digital era. *Political Research Quarterly*, 71(2), 482–494. 10.1177/1065912917744895

Galal, S. (2022, November 17). Social media in Africa – statistics and facts. *Statista.* https://www.statista.com/topics/9922/social-media-in-africa/#topicOverview

Ghai, S., Magis-Weinberg, L., Stoilova, M., Livingstone, S., & Orben, A. (2022, August). Social media and adolescent well-being in the global South. *Current Opinion in Psychology*, 46, 101318. 10.1016/j.copsyc.2022.10131835439684

Guanah, J. S., Obi, J., Egbra, O. S., & Akumabor, N. T. (2017, September). *Social media, youths and agricultural development social media, youths and agricultural development in the Niger Delta region of Nigeria*. Research Gate. https://www.researchgate.net/publication/342716459_Social_media_Youths_and_Agricultural_Development_Social_media_Youths_and_Agricultural_Development_in_the_Niger_Delta_Region_of_Nigeria

Gyimah-Brempong, K., & Kimenyi, M. S. (2013, April). *Youth policy and the future of African development*. (African growth initiative working paper 9). African Growth Initiative at Brookings. https://www.brookings.edu/wp-content/uploads/2016/06/04_youth_policy_african_development_kimenyi.pdf

Hopkins, R. F. (1966). Christianity and sociopolitical change in sub-Saharan Africa. *Social Forces*, 44(4), 555–562. 10.2307/2575091

Kalyango, Y., & Adu-Kumi, B. (2013). Impact of social ledia on political mobilization in East and West Africa. *Global Media Journal*, 12(1).

Kayode, L., & Omar, B. (2020). Do social media matter: Examining social media use and youths' political particiaption during 2019 Nigeria general elections. *The Round Table: The Commonwealth Journal of International Affairs*.

Kim, J., & Kim, M. (2022). Rise of social media influencers as a new marketing channel: Focusing on the roles of psychological well-being and perceived social responsibility among consumers. *International Journal of Environmental Research and Public Health*, 19(4), 2362. 10.3390/ijerph1904236235206553

Lin, T. H., Chang, M.-C., Chang, C.-C., & Chou, Y.-H. (2022). Government-sponsored disinformation and the severity of respiratory infection epidemics including COVID-19: A global analysis, 2001-2020. *Social Science & Medicine*, 29, 114744. 10.1016/j.socscimed.2022.11474435124544

McGee, R., & Greenhalf, J. (2012, December 14). *Young citizens: Youth and participatory governance in Africa*. International Institute for Environment and Development. https://www.comminit.com/la/content/young-citizens-youth-and-participatory-governance-africa

Media Foundation for West Africa. (2021, December 3). *The Gambian elections: the press, social Media and the newfound freedom*. MFWA. https://www.mfwa.org/the-gambian-elections-the-press-social-media-and-the-newfound-freedom/

Merriam-Webster. (2023). Social media. *Merriam-Webster.com dictionary*. https://www.merriam-webster.com/dictionary/social%20media

Mngusuul, U. B. (2015). Social media and the mobilization of youths for socio-political participation. *New Media and Mass Communication,42*. https://core.ac.uk/download/pdf/234652824.pdf

Moreno, M., & Koff, R. (2015). 11. Media theories and the facebook influence model. In the *Psychology of Social Networking, 1*. https://doi.org/10.1515/9783110473780-01

Mwakideu, C. (2021, September 1). China's growing influence on Africa's media. *DW.* https://www.dw.com/en/experts-warn-of-chinas-growing-media-influence-in-africa/a-56385420

Nwoye, K. O., & Okafor, G. O. (2014). New media and political mobilization in Africa: The Nigerian experience. *American Journal of Social Sciences.*, 2(2), 36–42.

Obiora, C., Chiamogu, A. P., & Chiamogu, U. P. (2022). Social media regulation, freedom of expression and civic space in Nigeria: A study based on authoritarian mass communication. *Journal of Government and Political Issues*, 2(3), 126–136. https://papers.ssrn.com/sol3/papers.cfm?abstract_id=4448717. 10.53341/jgpi.v2i3.69

Ogunnaike, J. (2024, January 21). Soyinka laments bastardisation of social media by Nigeria. *Vanguard.* https://www.vanguardngr.com/2024/01/soyinka-laments-bastardization-of-social-media-by-nigerians/#-google_vignette

Okocha, D. O., & Chigbo, M. (2023). Flattening the curve of fake news in the epoch of infodemic in Nigeria news media industry. *Journal of Communication and Media Technology*, 5(1).

Okocha, D. O., & Dapoet, B. A. (2022). *Social media and hashtag activism in Nigeria: A narrative review.* https://www.researchgate.net/publication/364910641_Social_Media_and_Hashtag Activism_in_Nigeria_A_Narrative_Review

Okoro, N., & Santas, T. (2017, February). An appraisal of the utilisation of social media for political communication in the 2011 Nigerian presidential election. *African Research Review.*, 11(1), 115. 10.4314/afrrev.v11i1.9

Olaniran, B., & Williams, I. (2020). Social Media Effects: Hijacking Democracy and Civility in Civic Engagement. *Platforms, Protests, and the Challenge of Networked Democracy*, 77–94. 10.1007/978-3-030-36525-7_5

Olukoshi, A. (2004). Changing patterns of politics in Africa. *Cadernos De Estudos Africanos.* 15 - 38. 10.4000/cea.1045

Ovuorie, T. (2022, April 1). Increased social media use puts African leaders on edge. *DW.* https://corporate.dw.com/en/increased-social-media-use-puts-african-leaders-on-edge/a-61303854

Runde, D. F., Savoy, C. M., & Staguhn, J. (2021, October 15). *China and SMEs in sub-Saharan Africa: A window of opportunity for United States.* Center for Strategic and International Studies. https://www.csis.org/analysis/china-and-smes-sub-saharan-africa-window-opportunity-united-states

Sasu, D. D. (2022, November 15). Social media in Nigeria – statistics & facts. *Statista.* https://www.statista.com/topics/10117/social-media-in-nigeria/#topicOverview

Short, R. (2021, June 22). How social media is empowering small business in Africa, *Genesis.* https://www.wathi.org/how-social-media-is-powering-small-business-in-africa-genesis-june-2021/

Silver, L., & Johnson, C. (2018, October 9). *Internet connectivity seen as having positive impact on life in sub-Saharan Africa.* Pew Research Center. https://www.pewresearch.org/global/2018/10/09/internet-connectivity-seen-as-having-positive-impact-on-life-in-sub-saharan-africa/

United Nations. (2020). *World youth report 2020: Youth social entrepreneurship and the 2020 agenda*. UN-iLibrary. 10.18356/248b499b-en

United Nations High Commissioner for Refugees. (2022). *Factsheet 4: Types of misinformation and disinformation*. UN. https://www.unhcr.org/innovation/wp- content/uploads/2022/02/Factsheet-4.pdf

Van Bavel, J., Rathje, S., Harris, E., Robertson, C., & Sternisko, A. (2021). How social media shapes polarization. *Trends in Cognitive Sciences*, 25(11), 913–916. 10.1016/j.tics.2021.07.01334429255

Velte, A. (2018, March 1). Ethical challenges and current practices in activist social media archives. *The American Archivist*, 81(1), 112–134. 10.17723/0360-9081-81.1.112

Yan, N. (2021, June). Social media is redistributing power. *Open Journal of Social Sciences*, 9(6), 107–118. 10.4236/jss.2021.96010

KEY TERMS AND DEFINITIONS

Activism: This refers to action taken challenging those in power to bring about change in society and benefit the greater good.

Civic Engagement: Participation in activities that improve one's community or address wider social issues. Civic engagement can involve political and non-political activities.

Democracy: A system of government in which state power is vested in the people or the general population of a state.

Digital Citizenship: The ability to navigate our digital environments in a way that's safe and responsible and to actively and respectfully engage in these spaces.

Participatory Governance: A concept that emphasizes democratic engagement, especially through deliberative practices, between the actors of state and society. It is a subset of governance theory that aims to provide high-quality programs and services through the public's collaborative efforts.

Social Disruption: A term used in sociology to describe the alteration, dysfunction or breakdown of social life, often in a community setting. Social disruption implies a radical transformation, in which the old certainties of modern society are falling away and something quite new is emerging.

Social Media Influencers: Social media content creators with expertise in certain niches and who have gained popularity and trust among a growing audience of online followers.

Social Media: Web-based communication tools that enable people to interact with each other by sharing and consuming information.

Sub-Saharan Africa: The term used to describe the area of the African continent which lies south of the Sahara Desert. Geographically, the demarcation line is the southern edge of the Sahara Desert.

Chapter 11
The Disinformation Divide:
Understanding the Impact of Social Media on Polarization

Tasnim Jahan
http://orcid.org/0009-0004-1269-0122
School of Law, Ramaiah University of Applied Sciences, Bengaluru, India

Shashikant Saurav
http://orcid.org/0000-0002-9349-7452
Symbiosis International University (Deemed), India

Shabnam Jahan
Leisure Byte, India

ABSTRACT

Communication is one of the oldest tools that have been utilized in all the possible sectors/institutions that can have a positive impact on a developing society. There are no doubts about the role and importance of the same but at the same time, all such instruments can have negative connotations as well. Since time immemorial, vocabulary, conversations, and other forms of communication were given high regard with respect to the impact that any such instrument can have and were used for different purposes other than friendly and informal discussions. With time and tech-advancements, the world witnessed the expansion and blooming of the communication methods and also the impact, both positive and negative, it brought along with. This chapter deals with one of such issues that misuse of communication can cause, that is 'the disinformation divide' and their impact on society. This study firstly conceptualizes the problem in order to understand the origin of the same, secondly it explores all the mediums that are responsible for the above defined problem.

INTRODUCTION

Tracing back to a couple of decades, the position and usage of smart phones were not the same let alone the data usage. With time, tech-advancements and digitalization, there has been enormous rise in the introduction, manufacture, and sale of mobile phones with over the top facility that enable them to

DOI: 10.4018/979-8-3693-3767-7.ch011

be renamed as smart phones which is used not just for the portable telephonic communication but for almost all the aspect of human lives (Bali, 2022) Today, Smart phones are typically used to stay informed about breaking news and community incidents, as well as to get from one location to another, carrying out day to day activities and navigating transactions such as landing a new job or learning more about a medical condition. This also serves as a means of communication as well as entertainment.

From the very beginning to the end of a person's day, smart phones can be seen used by the internet users which includes all age group people and the major ratio are the youth (Desai, 2023) These phones are currently being used as a clock, calendar, and meeting organizer and are being used to run businesses as well, order food, book tickets, order medications media and file sharing. These alternatives were not always available. At any point of time an average person now uses their phone for an astonishing 3000 times per day meaning thereby every person on the planet has access to a mobile phone thus making it a chaotic experience. The social media revolution began with Google's Orkut in 2004 and quickly spread to Facebook and Instagram. Instagram, initially only available for an iPhone, later became available for Android in 2014. Its unique interface and features, including reels, have attracted users. However, the platform also faces issues like trolls and negative comments, which can lead to suicidal thoughts. Additionally, the lack of fact checking on Instagram allows for the spread of fake news, negatively impacting mental health (Halkot, 2016)

Social media platforms like Facebook, Twitter, Instagram, and LinkedIn have revolutionized communication and business advertising, enabling global connections and real-time engagement. However, they also contribute to the spread of inaccurate information, fake news, anxiety, despair, and low self-esteem. Excessive social media use has been linked to poor physical health outcomes, such as obesity, decreased physical activity, and poor sleep quality, as per (Moorehead et al. 2013). Thus, social media offers communication and knowledge access, but can also spread incorrect information and negatively impact mental and physical health, making responsible use crucial.

PURPOSE OF THE STUDY

Present era witnessed and has been in trap of Contagion of disgrace which is spread of fake news and disinformation through the tech-related products and services. This has been facilitated more by the sharp rise in social media by people of all the age. India, the second most populous democracy globally, is facing a significant challenge from false news due to the proliferation of divisive propaganda and low literacy rates, which hinder the implementation of democratic decision-making and threaten its democratic fabric. The target audience for this study is not restricted to any particular age group or any specific gender though, it emphasizes on youth ranging from aged 13 till late 20's. The study delves into detail by data representation the age groups that are exposed to any media firs of all, moving to a smart phone and then to social media, exploring the most used media to disseminate news and also investigating the major reasons people are using social media in the recent years. Data as available on statista shows that out of 4 variables online news, social media, television and print media, the most number of news consumption is done through online which includes social media platforms, preceded by social media, then television and finally at the lowest level is the print media. Around 72-75% of people agreed to consuming news through social media and accepting it as a fact/trust that can be relied upon and can be shared at the same time. The problem arises when these news are not just shared as a medium but also enables the platform for the creation of content that is shared widely in just few minutes. Moreover, there was always a line between the terminologies 'entertainment' and 'news' which unfortunately has been declining. Today, piece of news is manipulated and circulated for entertainment causing a chain of misinformation and fake news which results in disarming the peace and harmony and ultimately polarizing the views and setting the narratives against a specific or few of the communities at a given point of time. The second-most populous democracy in the world, India, is the focus of this study, which looks into the dissemination of false information. It focuses on how this phenomenon affects democratic processes of decision-making, especially on social media platforms. The study indicates a considerable preference for online news consumption, especially through social media, after analyzing patterns of news consumption using data from Statista and other such reports dealing with this phenomenon. The study does, however, issue a warning because false information circulates quickly through these platforms, making it harder to distinguish between news and entertainment. The goal of the study is to clarify how the manipulation of factual information for entertainment reasons results in a wave of false information and fake news that endangers social harmony and polarization in society. The study attempts to shed light on practical tactics for thwarting misinformation and fake news, defending democratic procedures, and encouraging people to be informed in this digital era and make decision accordingly.

RESEARCH METHODOLOGY

A mixed method is used in this study, integrating empirical and doctrinal research using both quantitative and qualitative data. It looks at existing laws/regulations such as defamation laws, cyber-crime laws, media regulation laws, electoral laws, consumer protection laws, data protection and privacy laws, and regulation of social media platform among others and policies available dealing with the problem statement of this research and find the compliance issue, violations and analyzes quantitative data to determine the type and details of these violations. Measures and scales are used to determine the date and for the qualitative analysis. For the sanctity of the research, three variables has been taken into consideration namely i) News consumption by three set of age groups ii) Social media and user generated content ii) Fact check and sharing of these news and generated content. To increase the credibility of the findings, the research used triangulation, which involves cross-verifying information from both quantitative and qualitative sources. In order to obtain comprehensive insights on news consumption patterns, social media behavior, and fact-checking techniques, it also includes focus groups or interviews. Patterns and trends in the distribution of information can be found with the aid of content analysis. A longitudinal study monitors how people use social media and how they consume news over time. An all-encompassing investigation of the study problem is provided by mixed-methods integration. Ethical consideration have been taken care of and the researcher has followed all the guidelines in order to collect the data without any such infringement. Informed consent was taken while all the data collection including quantitative and qualitative.

INTRODUCTION TO EVOLUTION OF DISINFORMATION

Disinformation is often used alternatively for fake news but till what extent we can actually use both the terminologies interchangeably is the matter of research. Disinformation is a phenomenon where wrong information is passed on to people (Raj, 2020). It is very similar to a game known as 'Chinese

Whisper'. Where a group of people participating is expected to pass on a sentence from one person to another one by one and it is witnessed towards the end of the game that the sentence that was originally passed on went through slight changes at each step leading to different sentence all together by the time it reached to the last person. Spreading disinformation was in existence since time immemorial but slowly and gradually it made its transition to spreading false information as well. Research shows that spreading false and fake news is quite old and can be traced back to the evolution of human societies (Rojecki & Meraz, 2016), but because of technological advancements few things have changed such as the reach of such disinformation beyond a location and even borders (Niklewicz, 2017). This also has added to the complex nature of human communication along with the leading to policy loopholes (Blumler, 2015). With technological advancements there has been sharp rise in digital platform which enables people to commute with people not just staying far away but also share picture, documents and other large files which were not possible earlier.

Digital media is one such way that facilitates the same and also a major reason behind the disinformation and the related issues lately (Benkler et al., 2018). Today's era is also known as 'post-truth era', time where there is a distinction between truth and facts. Moreover the value of truth is lessen and a new phenomenon have arisen which is called by the name 'narratives' which kind of pave way for collective relative concepts that suits the idea of narratives of certain groups at a given point of time (Baptista & Anabela, 2022). There are few such relative terminologies that are being used interchangeably specially in the context of communication and journalism; these are "Misinformation", "fake news", "Disinformation", "false communication", "Post-truth", "Information-Pollution", "bullshit", "Information-Disorder", etc, (Kapantai & ors, 2020). To realize that any consequences of any sort of misinformation is not just limited to the close circle it has been shared to but such information which is not true and contains not just false information but things that are being spread as nothing but truth have all the capabilities of turning into narratives which can have consequences with no end in itself.

Misinformation, deception, and propaganda have been present in human communication since at least the Roman times, when Antony met Cleopatra. Octavian launched a propaganda effort against Antony in an attempt to tarnish his reputation. This manifested as "short, sharp slogans written upon coins in the style of archaic Tweets." These slogans portrayed Antony as a womanizer and an alcoholic, claiming that he had become Cleopatra's puppet, corrupted by his affair with her. Augustus became the first Roman Emperor, and "fake news had allowed Octavian to hack the republican system once and for all." Similarly a lot of such instances are there to back the origin of disinformation or spreading of false news.

Figure 1.

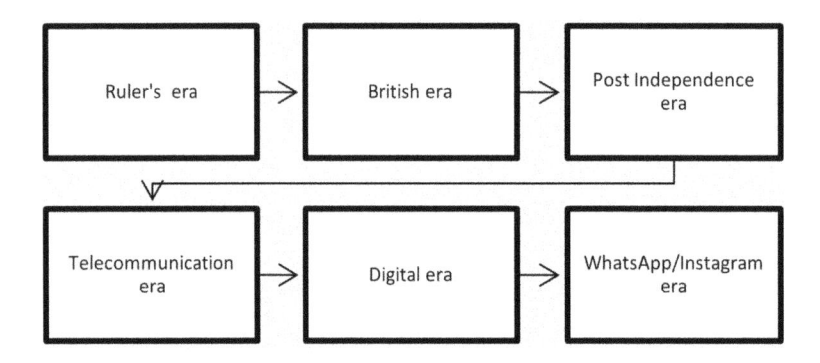

In India evolution of disinformation can be traced back to pre-independence era or the British era. During that time, disinformation was used as a major tool to control as well as manipulate the information, because spread of truth might the fuel enrage within people and endanger their thrown. Efforts were made to stop people gathering at a place at any given point of time so that any kind of planning can be stopped and spread of relevant information can be stopped (Goshwami, 2020). There have been so many instances where violence erupted just because of people gathering at a place to discuss things. Jallianwala Bagh massacre is one such example where gathering of people for meeting/discussions were taken out right of proportion and the repercussion is still clear in our memories till date. Disinformation is not just restricted to spreading false information but also in manipulation of any information/datasets etc and it also extends to stop such information from being spread at all. Even before this, during India's Golden era rulers used to spread fake information in order to be in power and sometimes to protect their reign and people. Fake information has been always used as a tool by the people in power to remain in power and keep the sanctity of their rule (Amire, 2023).

Then we moved to a period with telecommunication and print media and communication became somewhat easy and convenient to what people were going through to pass on single information through series of struggles. And then came the era of mobile phones and communication were made far easier (Pathak, 2020). And with the regular technological advancements and emergence of Internet today, we have fast mode of communications which includes video calls, sharing of images, videos and other large files. The next phase of evolution can be classified into pre and post Internet era. Pre Internet era can be understood as time when most of the information were spread in print media form and later moved to radio station but too were quite few in numbers. And gradually we moved to digital media in form of television first to social media platforms, online news & blogs after the advent of Internet in the early 2000s (Domenico, 2022)

Internet era can be further classified into Google and WhatsApp era which can be understood as period where people initially either relied on print media, television news channels or radio station for news and information about the things going on in the world but lately after digitalisation the transition from the above mentioned news consumption media to the new media such as social media platforms were fast paced and adopted by people too quick as well. *Disinformation become quite well-widespread with the introduction of WhatsApp as this also bridged the gap between the consumption of news as well as provided a platform for sharing the same* (Moravec, Randall K, 2017).

RISE OF SOCIAL MEDIA IN INDIA AND IT'S ACTIVE ROLE IN SPREADING INFORMATION:

Figure 2. Evolution of social media in India

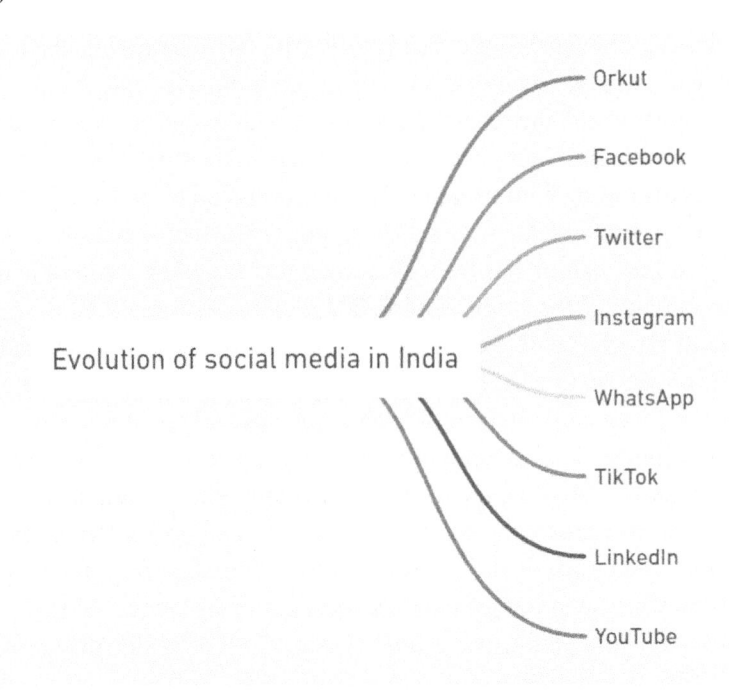

Evolution of social media in India
- Orkut
- Facebook
- Twitter
- Instagram
- WhatsApp
- TikTok
- LinkedIn
- YouTube

Social Media Platforms took the world by storm as it introduced everyone to the idea of being in touch through mediums other than mobile phone or any other telephonic communication. The purpose of social media was to connect people all over the world without sharing the phone numbers or any other details which they don't want to share. The freedom of choice with respect to the material the users wanted to share with the people they chose to connect over a specific social media platform was the key feature of the same. With the rise of social media users, concerns regarding consent and privacy arose and the same was dealt by the concerned authority and similarly any such issues were handles as and when the need arose (Leung, 20121). Today, Social media is often associated with the phenomenon of disinformation and fake news being spread to people at large. Few associations/researchers have disagreed on the point that social media is the reason behind spread of fake news and polarization and that fake news and knowingly/purposefully spreading false news/disinformation was always in existence and was used as tool to create rift and remain in power. Social media is the new age phenomenon and divided by huge time-frame (Gentzkow, 2016). To an extern extent the contention is true but the fact that social media is acting as a catalyst in spreading disinformation and is being used by people in power/influence in order to fulfil their purpose cannot be denied. Like 'Complimentary goods' as we study in economics, where few of the products are so attached to each other that the rise of price of one good/products will most definitely affect the price of the other related goods/products. Similarly social media is such a medium

The Disinformation Divide

without which the spread of disinformation today will not be a cakewalk. Social media is the major catalyst in spread of such fake news and misinformation (Al-Zaman, 2021).

In India, these platforms serve as both a tool for spreading information and a breeding ground for misinformation. Social media accounts such as Tiktok, Instagram and You tube provides opportunity and platform for creating own content and sharing it with the followers. Though there are terms and conditions and the social media team/management take care of the content should be shared or removed but still micro management is not possible as well as the machine learning is not efficient enough to stop the spreading of false information. Also having said that, they can swiftly amplify content, allowing bad actors to promote false narratives with impunity. The anonymity of these sites makes it difficult to track down the source of misinformation. Lack of regulation and monitoring exacerbates the problem. Misinformation distribution is frequently linked to issues about free speech, necessitating a fine balance between combating falsehoods and protecting individual liberties (Pratik, 2019)

Figure 3. Historical internet penetration

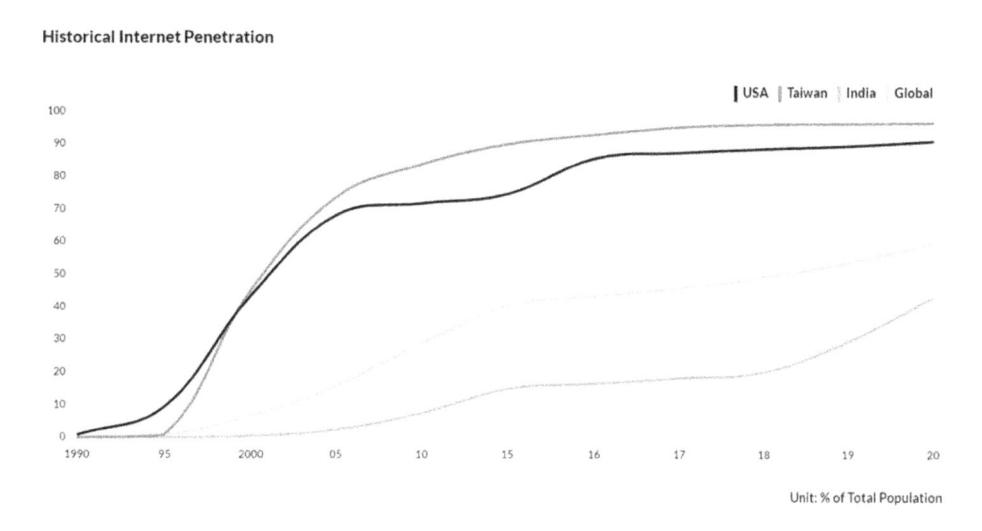

In the first figure (osaga.com, 2023) here gives an insight into the penetration of Internet in these 4 Countries namely USA, India, Taiwan, and China. It can be observed that India definitely was slower in comparison to other variables here in terms of Internet users but in the next figure, it can be seen as not much difference is there in terms of cellular subscription. India more or less are using and subscribing to the need of the hour and going with the flow as well. With such rate of cellular subscription, it is very evident that people were open to the idea of easy communication and there was no hint of hesitance there.

Figure 4. Cellular subscription %

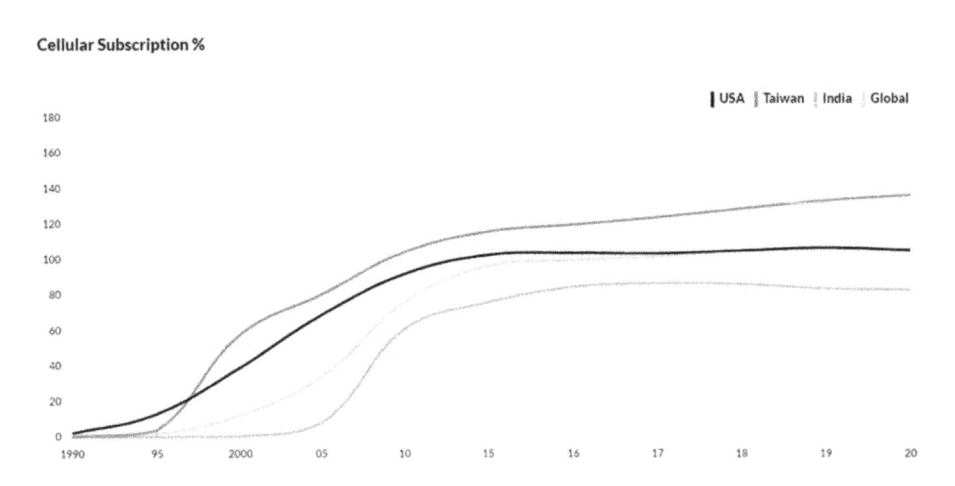

Cellular Subscription %

USA | Taiwan | India | Global

Research provides there has been annual growth of 55-60% of cellular subscription till 2023 and it is highly likely to increase to 70% in next 5 years (World Bank ITU).

Figure 5. Social media user demographics

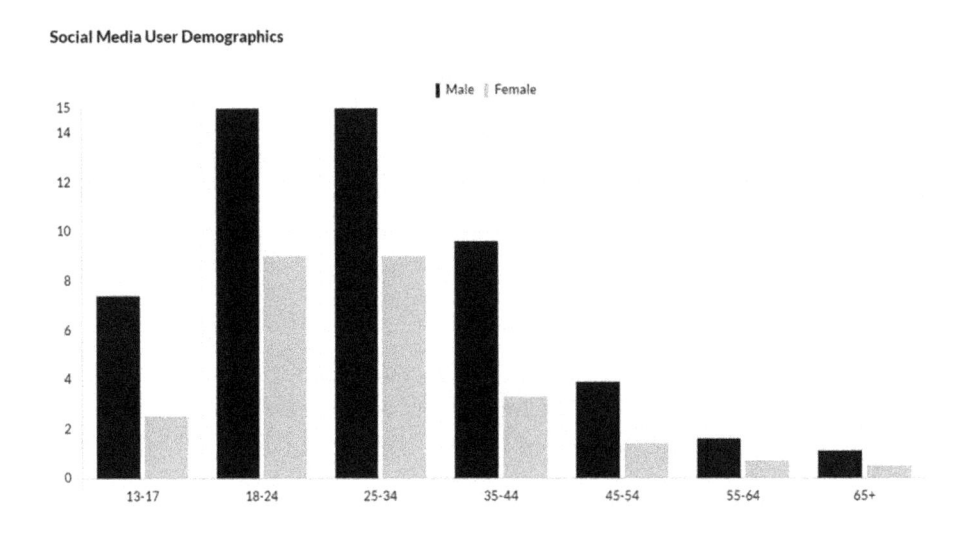

Social Media User Demographics

Male | Female

The above figure provides for the social media user data/demographics which clearly shows how social media platforms are more or less equally prevalent in almost all age groups, though there are some disparity in the gender groups but prevalence is still there and the graph is on the higher note. As per the recent survey (Google data) total number of people using social media in India currently stands at 470 million (approx) till 2022, and with an expected rise by 5-7% by 2025. These data also showed there are people who are not the active users throughout but definitely login at least once a month.

The Disinformation Divide

Figure 6.

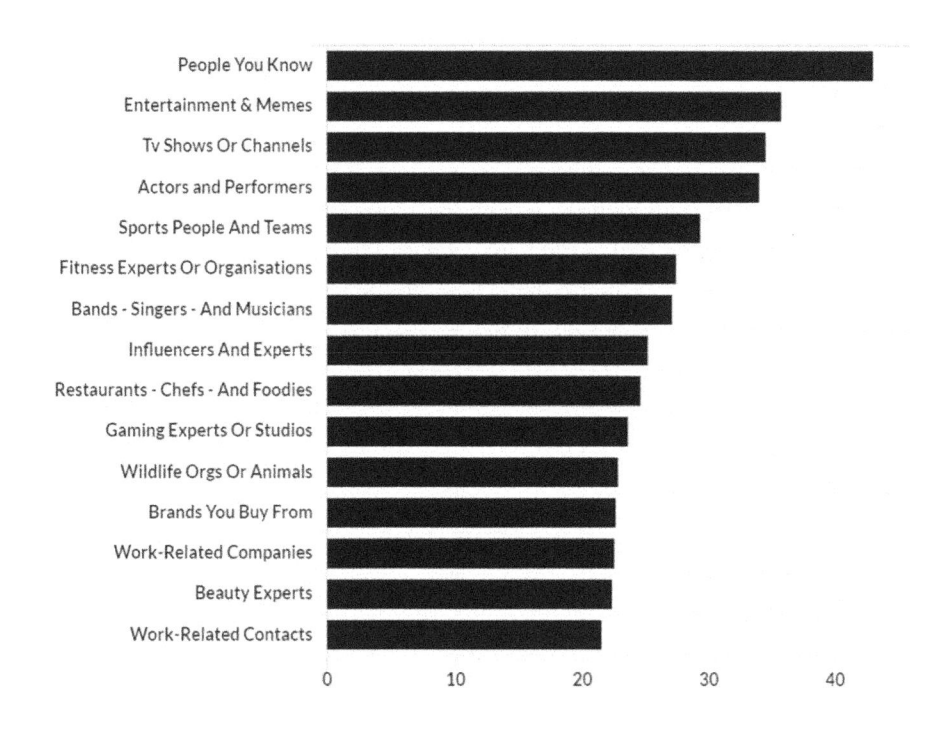

Category	Value
People You Know	~43
Entertainment & Memes	~36
Tv Shows Or Channels	~34
Actors and Performers	~34
Sports People And Teams	~29
Fitness Experts Or Organisations	~27
Bands - Singers - And Musicians	~27
Influencers And Experts	~25
Restaurants - Chefs - And Foodies	~24
Gaming Experts Or Studios	~24
Wildlife Orgs Or Animals	~23
Brands You Buy From	~23
Work-Related Companies	~23
Beauty Experts	~22
Work-Related Contacts	~22

Figure 7.

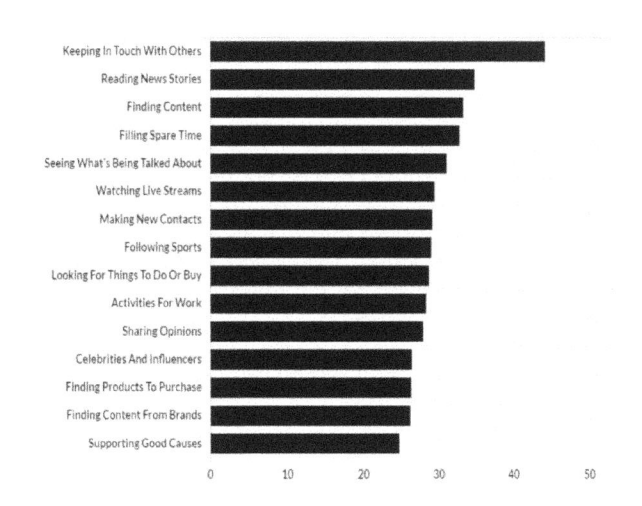

Category	Value
Keeping In Touch With Others	~45
Reading News Stories	~34
Finding Content	~33
Filling Spare Time	~32
Seeing What's Being Talked About	~31
Watching Live Streams	~30
Making New Contacts	~30
Following Sports	~29
Looking For Things To Do Or Buy	~29
Activities For Work	~29
Sharing Opinions	~28
Celebrities And Influencers	~27
Finding Products To Purchase	~27
Finding Content From Brands	~27
Supporting Good Causes	~25

The above two figure shows two most pertinent variables that impacts the social media usage and spread of information for the purpose of this research. The first chart on the left shows who exactly social media users wants to follow mostly on their social media handle. Is it their friends and family or the celebrities or the influencers or content creator etc. Second figure shows the reason why social media users are using the same and which of their purpose are being served.

The above graphs (GWI, 2023) are self explanatory and shows how sharing opinions is one of reason a major bulk of people are actually preferring to use social media and that's where the concern lies in the absence of any regulatory guidelines. Secondly people are following most number of people they already know either personally or are a member of their friends and family circle which again points to the contention that people love to share their views and keep in contact with the other they have been known to. Now, next most important question that arises is which social media is being used by the people at large the most? And the surveys and research suggests it is WhatsApp followed by Instagram, Facebook and so on. During the Pandemic (Covid-19) there was a sharp rise in the usage of social media especially Instagram as this provided with the opportunity to create first hand content for the purpose of entertainment making Instagram the most used app by the youth.

Before moving to the impact of social media platforms on misinformation, there are certain aspects which are correlated to the core concept of this research which can be pointed down by way of negative impact of 'Social Media' on youth as youth population are the major stakeholder of this study.

Negative Impact of Social Media on Mental Health

Social Comparison: Going by this particular theory, people assess their own skills and characteristics by comparing them to those of others (Festinger, 1954). Users of social media sites like Instagram are exposed to a steady stream of photographs of the lives, bodies, and experiences of others that appear to be flawless, which can cause them to feel inadequate, insecure, and low self-worth (Forni & Feeney, 2020; Vogel et al., 2015). For instance, seeing photos of friends enjoying opulent vacations or dining at upscale establishments while one is confined at home may cause envy and discontentment with one's own life (Tiggemann & Slater, 2014). In a similar vein, seeing pictures of influencers with perfect skin and perfect bodies might make people feel self-conscious about their own looks (Forni & Feeney, 2020). It's important to understand that Instagram photographs frequently undergo extensive editing and filtering, which means they might not truly depict reality (Tiggemann & Slater, 2014). Users portray a carefully managed version of themselves, and it's simple to forget that everyone is flawed. People should be aware of how much time they spend on Instagram and carefully select their feed to include accounts that encourage positivity and self-love in order to counteract the detrimental impacts of social comparison there (Forni& Feeney, 2020; Vogel et al., 2015).

Self-Presentation: Self-presentation is a well-known phrase in social psychology that refers to how people present themselves to others and express themselves (Goffman, 1959). Instagram, a popular social networking site, provides users with a variety of options for presenting themselves. However, this operation may have a negative impact on one's mental health. Low self-esteem may result from comparisons and incorrect expectations produced by this (Fardouly et al. 2018).Furthermore, the pressure to sustain a particular image can result in anxiety and tension, and it goes without saying how damaging the impacts can be on mental health (Chua & Chang, 2016).

Unrealistic Beauty Standards: Unrealistic Beauty Standards: According to (Fardouly et al., 2018), Instagram is saturated with images of idealized beauty, such as beautiful skin and perfectly proportioned physique, which can make many individuals feel unattractive and uneasy about their own appearance. The authors believe that celebrities and social media influencers are one of the primary drivers of Instagram's excessive beauty standards. These individuals have a big following on the platform while living opulent or costly lifestyles for the average person. Instagram also provides users with a variety of filters and image-editing tools to let them customize the appearance of their photos.

Evaluating the use of social media by today's youth: Using social media on a regular basis has become a common pastime among today's youth, which has a significant impact on their daily life. It is critical to examine how these platforms have influenced them in order to understand their attitudes, behaviors, and worldviews. A Pew Research Center survey (Lenhart, 2015) found that 71% of American youths use social media on a daily basis. Social media allows young people to interact with friends and communities all around the world, making connections that would not have been possible otherwise. Social media has the unique ability to connect people from all origins and geographies. As a result, today's youth have a stronger sense of empathy and global interconnectedness (Boyd, 2014).

There are few most used and loved social media like "Facebook", "Twitter", "Instagram", and "LinkedIn" that with time, have been offering one or other innovative ways to communicate and share information, and now one cannot imagine their life without the same as it has become important part of our everyday life (Gao, 2020). Social media has significantly facilitated communication, allowing people to connect globally, exchange ideas, and stay updated on current affairs. However, it has also facilitated the spread of inaccurate information and fake news, potentially negatively impacting society. Therefore, while social media has its benefits, it is crucial to use it responsibly and deliberately to avoid negative impacts on mental and physical health.

POLARIZATION IN SOCIETY: THE NARRATIVES ERA

Generally speaking, the term polarization means one-sided or something which does not follow the norm of neutrality and is biased in nature. This also depends on the ideologies that are being followed by the people at large (Singh, 2018). A polarization in society starts paving its way when the people in power, in order to maintain the status quo add such ideologies in their propaganda. Additionally, also cater to the sensitivities of people by mentioning such specific things in the election memorandum (Lenhart, 2015).

Post Truth era is also known as Narratives era, a phenomena in which narratives are modified to support ideologies or objectives rather than being factually accurate. India, with its diverse people and complex history, is an excellent example of this phenomenon. The origins of right- and left-wing information sharing groups/platforms in India may be traced back to the country's colonial history and struggle for independence. Right-wing organizations, such as the Rashtriya Swayamsevak Sangh (RSS), have molded the narrative of Hindutva by emphasizing cultural and religious unity. Left-wing movements, founded on socialist and communist ideals, promote social justice, economic equality, and secularism.

The internet and social media changed information dissemination in the twenty-first century, offering a forum for views across the ideological spectrum to be heard. Right-wing groups took advantage of the digital revolution, using platforms such as Twitter, Facebook, and WhatsApp to communicate their message and rally supporters. Left-wing groups used online tools to organize, mobilize, and oppose right-wing narratives. However, they encountered difficulties in contending with the well-funded and strategically planned right-wing propaganda machine.

The spread of misinformation and disinformation has exacerbated India's post-truth environment, blurring the distinctions between reality and fiction and widening societal divisions. Understanding the roots of these occurrences is critical for navigating the complicated media landscape and cultivating educated, evidence-based conversation in the goal of an equal society.

Press or the News media is considered to be the fourth pillar of the Society but recent instances as well as the survey data shows that it is almost impossible to find a neutral piece of news on mainstream media or independent media as the dissemination of the news by the above mentioned media is highly polarized and cater to the narratives of the people in power. There are several mainstream media which instead of disseminating news, contribute to media trail and declare a person (it includes regular citizen, corporate person, celebrities, government authorities, opposition, etc) to be doing anything right or wrong. And this creates an assumption in the minds of the people coming across these opinions in form of news as to against the person. This consumption of news is one aspect/matter of concern which is current the state of affairs (Singh, 2018). Another, are people who are consuming such news and forming an opinion and then spreading anything that suits their thought process. This is something that has been fed to the public by the fourth pillar of the democracy- the mainstream media and hence people falling for the same are not a difficult deal. Now on the second hand we have the independent media who are either self funded or funded by organisations or association of people who are against the ideologies of the current government in power (Unit survey, 2019).

The authors of this study interviewed the stakeholders from both the above mentioned mediums in order to understand the psychology behind the same. The stakeholders were a) Founder of an independent media b) Newsperson working in mainstream media c) Viewers of mainstream media d) Consumer of Independent media

The brief observations were as follows:

a) People who are consuming mainstream media hardly care about the role of media or press in first place. According to them the media is doing what they are supposed to and help the public by bringing the truth in from of them. Interesting to note here there is clear distinction between the terms trust and facts.
b) The employees of mainstream media talks about the TRP that is again based on viewer's choice. And they show or telecast only that news which is in demand. But the catch is choosing such news based on the demand is not the actual purpose of a press/news company.
c) The Founder of the Independent media agreed to be biased about the kind of news they want showcase but they insisted on the point that the idea or the intention is not profit oriented or to please the government in power but to upheld the constitutional and democratic values. So biasness is still there, leaving no grounds for neutrality.

Given the above discussion, these activities divide the people in groups and they start identifying themselves by the ideology they support and result in forming 'ECHO-CHAMBER'. Eco is formed when any being shouts in oblivion or an empty space most likely to be a hill/mountaintop and the person shouting can hear what they have been shouting in first place. Similarly people identifying themselves by a specific group tends to speak/collaborate, be-in-touch with those people who suits their thought process only, hence giving space for forming echo of their own views and leaving no pace for vocabularies. Digital advertising plays a vital role in consumer behavior, and how consumers respond to digital adverts is a key topic in marketing literature.

The Disinformation Divide

The literature on how digital advertising affects consumer behavior has several features, but engagement with customers has a favorable impact on consumers' purchase-intent. Tiago and (Veríssimo, 2014) concluded that relationship-based contacts with clients are crucial in digital marketing and demonstrated their success. In their study of celebrities, (Hwang and Zhang, 2018) found that para-social interactions had a favorable affect on purchase intentions and eWOM. (Murphy and Sashi, 2018) discovered that face-to-face communication increased social interaction, mutual feedback, and number of contacts, but digital communication had a smaller effect on these. (Bart et al., 2014) discovered that products with higher involvement boosted purchase intention.

LEGAL IMPLICATIONS

In India, false information has serious legal ramifications that affect public safety, politics, and society. The Information Technology (IT) Act of 2000, Sections 66D, 69A, and 153A are among the laws in India that aim to stop the dissemination of misleading information. Sections 505 and 153A of the Indian Penal Code (IPC) are among the provisions that concern the dissemination of false information. Vulnerable groups are shielded from false information under the Scheduled Castes and Scheduled Tribes (Prevention of Atrocities) Act of 1989 and the Protection of Children from Sexual Offenses (POCSO) Act of 2012. In order to control social media sites and online intermediaries, the government has suggested intermediary liability regulations; however, there are still worries that these laws could be abused to stifle dissent and restrict freedom.

The most recent statute dealing with digital data, technology and privacy is 'Digital Personal Data Protection Act' which have taken into consideration the privacy concerns among the online users. Unfortunately, the Act has not included any provisions regarding the fake news, misinformation, AI concerns, deep-fake etc.

Given that social media can sway opinions and intensify ideological disputes, it is imperative to investigate how polarization is impacted by it. Because of the quick transmission of digital content, present law makes it difficult to hold deep-fakes accountable for spreading misleading information. The government has threatened to revoke platform protection under Section 79 of the Information Technology Act of 2000 if they do not cooperate. Deep fakes are governed under Rule 7 of the 2021 Information Technology Rules (Intermediary Guidelines and Digital Media Ethics) Code, as well as Section 66E of the Information Technology Act. Sections 67, 67A, and 67B ban the electronic publication or transmission of pornographic content, sexually explicit behaviours, and content containing children. The Digital India Act is expected to include rigorous measures to combat deep-fakes.

WAY FORWARD

With reference to the last two sections 'Legal Implication and conclusion' further studies shall be done in respect to the ground level mapping that can help the law makers to understand the gap between the statutes and implementations. Few place to start the same can be rural areas and small cities as these places, small circle can help to investigate the reason being easier to locate the origin and cause of such misinformation. Few other suggestions include to explore the fact checking initiative whose track record can verified and proven and to come up with ways to disseminate the same through public awareness programmes. Secondly, technological solution such as AI, Machine learning and Block-chain can be invested upon and utilised for verifications. Transparency can be brought into Algorithms and how the same has been functioning the digital space. Studies can be conducted looking for possible collaboration with the stakeholders and NGOs and the ways the problem can be resolved. Researches and surveys forms the base of the any policy action and this is the best way to explore the legal statutes lacuna and fill the gap accordingly.

CONCLUSION

Even after laws being in place, and a lot of discourses being done to combat the problem of disinformation it can be witnessed that the problem persists because of numerous reasons. One of the major reason that has been the prominent theme of this paper is the deep rooted believe-system in people that also stems out of lack of awareness and education, which is blind faith on narrative set out by people and association having ulterior motives. Secondly, because of the numerous content that is being created on daily basis, no one is having time per se to check for the origin and source of the piece of news that they are consuming and spreading at the same time. None of the laws presently deal with the person that is spreading false information. The differentiation between deliberate offender and unconscious ones are other aspect that has to be dealt with. But, having said that the unconscious offender also stems from the above mentioned reason most of the time as the research suggested. This research investigates the relationship between social media use and societal separation, emphasizing the ways in which these platforms fuel the widening gaps that exist between societies and groups. It looks at the dynamics of false information spreading over social media and looks at possible remedies or mitigating measures. Because more and more people are depending on social media for information, these platforms have emerged as important news sources. According to the preliminary study, social media are the second-most popular news source across a range of demographics, having an effect on public discourse and the formation of opinions. Even after all these years' public awareness and digital literacy is comparatively low in ratio when read together with the graph of digital and technological advancements. Spread of fake news and disinformation is a vicious cycle and each and every person on this planet is directly or indirectly involved in it and for the same reason, every single person has to make an attempt to stop the same and create space for neutrality and bias-free news consumption in addition to the government and legislation attempts. This will ultimately also help in restricting the spread of fake news as well as manipulation of the same.

REFERENCES

Aïmeur, E., Amri, S., & Brassard, G. (2023). Fake news, disinformation and misinformation in social media: A review. *Social Network Analysis and Mining*, 13(1), 30. 10.1007/s13278-023-01028-536789378

Brooks, A. (2018, August 7). 7 Unexpected Ways Instagram Has Changed the World. *Social Media Today* https://www.socialmediatoday.com/news/7-unexpected-ways-instagram-has-changed-the-world/539032/

Cilliers, F. Q. (2013). The role and effect of social media in the workplace. *N. Ky. L. Rev.*, 40, 567.

Cohen, R., Newton-John, T., & Slater, A. (2017). The relationship between Facebook and Instagram appearance-focused activities and body image concerns in young women. *Body Image*, 23, 183–187. 10.1016/j.bodyim.2017.10.00229055773

Edosomwan, S., Prakasan, S. K., Kouame, D., Watson, J., & Seymour, T. (2011). The history of social media and its impact on business. *The Journal of Applied Management and Entrepreneurship*, 16(3), 79.

Engeln, R., Loach, R., Imundo, M. N., & Zola, A. (2020). Compared to Facebook, Instagram use causes more appearance comparison and lower body satisfaction in college women. *Body Image*, 34, 38–45. 10.1016/j.bodyim.2020.04.00732505866

Engeln, R., Loach, R., Imundo, M. N., & Zola, A. (2020). Compared to Facebook, Instagram use causes more appearance comparison and lower body satisfaction in college women. *Body Image*, 34, 38–45. 10.1016/j.bodyim.2020.04.00732505866

Fardouly, J., Diedrichs, P. C., Vartanian, L. R., & Halliwell, E. (2015). Social comparisons on social media: The impact of Facebook on young women's body image concerns and mood. *Body Image*, 13, 38–45. 10.1016/j.bodyim.2014.12.00225615425

Gerson, J. (2020, October 7). Experts Explain Why Instagram's Effects on Mental Health Aren't All Bad. Bustle https://www.bustle.com/wellness/instagram-positive-effects-mental-health-experts

Humphreys, L., Von Pape, T., & Karnowski, V. (2013). Evolving mobile media: Uses and conceptualizations of the mobile internet. *Journal of Computer-Mediated Communication*, 18(4), 491–507. 10.1111/jcc4.12019

Leung, J., Schoultz, M., Chiu, V., Bonsaksen, T., Ruffolo, M., Thygesen, H., Price, D., & Geirdal, A. Ø. Concerns over the Spread of Misinformation and Fake News on Social Media—Challenges Amid the Coronavirus Pandemic. *Med. Sci. Forum, 4*, 39. 10.3390/ECERPH-3-09078

Levinson, A.R. (2016). Solidarity on Social Media. *Colum.Bus. L.Rev.,303*.

Moreton, L., & Greenfield, S. (2022). University students' views on the impact of Instagram on mental wellbeing: A qualitative study. *BMC Psychology*, 10(1), 1–10. 10.1186/s40359-022-00743-635227331

Moreton, L., & Greenfield, S. (2022). University students' views on the impact of Instagram on mental wellbeing: A qualitative study. *BMC Psychology*, 10(1), 1–10. 10.1186/s40359-022-00743-635227331

Number of global social network users 2017–2025. (2022, April 28). Statista. https://www.statista.com/statistics/278414/number-of-worldwide-social-network-users

Olan, F., Jayawickrama, U., Arakpogun, E. O., Suklan, J., & Liu, S. (2024). Fake news on Social Media: The Impact on Society. *Information Systems Frontiers*, 26(2), 443–458. 10.1007/s10796-022-10242-z

Pennycook, G., Binnendyk, J., Newton, C., & Rand, D. G. (2021). A Practical Guide to Doing Behavioral Research on Fake News and Misinformation. *Collabra. Psychology*, 7(1), 25293. 10.1525/collabra.25293

Saxton, G. D., & Wang, L. (2014). The social network effect: The determinants of giving through social media. *Nonprofit and Voluntary Sector Quarterly*, 43(5), 850–868. 10.1177/0899764013485159

Walker, C. E., Krumhuber, E. G., Dayan, S., & Furnham, A. (2021). Effects of social media use on desire for cosmetic surgery among young women. Current Psychology, 40(7), 3355-3364. Tsesis, A. (2017). Terrorist speech on social media. *Vand.L.Rev.*, 70, 651.

Wiederhold, B. K. (2018). The tenuous relationship between Instagram and teen self-identity. *Cyberpsychology, Behavior, and Social Networking*, 21(4), 215–216. 10.1089/cyber.2018.29108.bkw29624448

Wiederhold, B. K. (2019). Instagram: Becoming a worldwide problem? *Cyberpsychology, Behavior, and Social Networking*, 22(9), 567–568. 10.1089/cyber.2019.29160.bkw31526293

Wilson, K., Fornasier, S., & White, K. M. (2010). Psychological predictors of young adults' use of social networking sites. *Cyberpsychology, Behavior, and Social Networking*, 13(2), 173–177. 10.1089/cyber.2009.009420528274

Woods, H. C., & Scott, H. (2016). #Sleepyteens: Social media use in adolescence is associated with poor sleep quality, anxiety, depression and low self-esteem. *Journal of Adolescence*, 51(1), 41–49. 10.1016/j.adolescence.2016.05.00827294324

KEY TERMS AND DEFINITIONS

Disinformation: It is passing of the wrong message to the next person, whether intentional or unintentional.

Polarization: It is concentration of people, communities or societies at two extreme opposing ends because of reasons like political, cultural, economic, religious ideologies.

Social Media: It is basically the platforms where people generate, receive and digest contents of several kinds and share their thought process and ideas over any ongoing issues.

Mental Health: It is the psychological and social well-being of any individual.

Fake News: News created deliberately to deceive or misinform the masses with a hidden agenda.

Chapter 12
Entertainment and Persuasion in Online Politics:
A Qualitative Study of Young Voters' Approach in Turkey's 2023 Elections

Emine Nazlı Aytuna
http://orcid.org/0000-0001-6722-9756
Galatasaray University, Turkey

Zindan Çakıcı
Üsküdar University, Turkey

Alparslan Ergün Özkaya
http://orcid.org/0000-0002-6687-6713
Galatasaray University, Turkey

ABSTRACT

This study investigates the influence of entertainment elements on political persuasion among young Turkish voters during the 2023 General Elections. Conducting 31 semi-structured interviews with demographically diverse participants aged 18-30 from various locales, it elucidates the nuanced interplay of cultural factors in shaping political attitudes. While participants exhibit a propensity for incorporating entertainment into political discourse, discernible reservations exist regarding the potential propagation of misinformation and the oversimplification of complex political issues. Ultimately, the findings underscore the primary function of entertainment elements in capturing attention rather than effecting substantive shifts in political decision-making processes.

INTRODUCTION

The evolution of entertaining content on social media platforms has transformed political communication, making it a new and innovative tool for political figures to engage with the electorate. The term 'entertaining content' encompasses the deliberate incorporation of popular culture, entertainment modalities, and media dynamics by politicians to enhance their public image and persuade the voting population. It has been observed that there is an increasing trend towards the blurring of the boundaries between political action and entertainment, leading to the emergence of "politainment". Otherwise, the combination of "politics" and "entertainment," refers to the transformation of political discourse into a form of political communication. This phenomenon has been the subject of numerous studies in recent years, with researchers examining its impact on political communication (Klinger, Kreiss, & Mutsvairo, 2023; Zamora-Medina, 2023; Salazar, 2023; Cervi, Tejedor, & Blesa, 2023; Gonzalo, Medina, & Rebolledo de la Calle, 2021; Bosshart & Hellmüller, 2009).

Karpf and colleagues (2016) highlight the strategic use of celebrity in the 2012 presidential election, illustrating how political figures leverage popular culture to enhance their appeal and reach a wider audience. This trend is further explored by Berrocal-Gonzalo and Capdevila (2022), who delve into the role of popular culture in shaping political narratives, suggesting that entertainment mediums are not just platforms for political messages but active players in the political discourse. Politicians, facing more media exposure, are starting to act like celebrities, turning politics into a kind of show and blending political talk with entertainment. This trend of mixing politics with entertainment is changing how politicians communicate and interact, ushering in a new wave of 'pop politics' (Mazzoleni & Bracciale, 2019) and politainment (Berrocal et al., 2021).

The present study, conducted during the campaign period of Turkey's 2023 General Elections, utilizes a qualitative approach based on semi-structured interviews with young voters to examine the incorporation of entertainment aspects into political communication. Specifically, it examines the ways in which these elements are perceived by voters, with a focus on the strategic use of dance videos, social media challenges, storytelling, humor, edits, captions, and memes. Through focused interviews with young voters, the study sheds light on the employment of these entertainment elements to shape political messages, attitudes, and values. This research aims to fill a notable gap in the literature by examining the perceptions and interactions of young Turkish voters with entertainment elements in political communication during the 2023 General Elections. Although the body of research exploring the evolution of political discourse and politician-voter communication on social media is expanding, there is a limited qualitative study in the domain. This is particularly evident in research centered on the incorporation of entertainment elements in social media strategies during election campaigns. Considering Turkey's demographic profile, with one of the youngest populations in Europe, this study is positioned to offer a critical perspective in political communication discussion. The aim is to provide a detailed analysis of the Turkish election campaign data, ultimately revealing the distinctive ways in which young voters in Turkey interact with and respond to entertainment-based political content. Based on the literature review, three hypotheses have been established within this scope:

H1: The strategic integration of entertainment elements into political campaigns has been effective in influencing the political participation and voting behavior of young voters in Turkey's 2023 General Elections.

H2: Social media communication is creating forms of political persuasion independent of the socio-political context.

H3: The incorporation of entertainment elements in political messages establishes a strategy of political persuasion that overcomes the resistance of young voters with opposing views.

This research aims to explore the relationship between online entertainment and political persuasion, with a focus on the perspectives and behaviors of young voters in Turkey. The first hypothesis emphasizes the impact of integrating entertainment elements into political campaigns on the engagement and voting behavior of young voters in Turkey. It suggests that merging entertainment with political communication can be effective in persuading this demographic. The second hypothesis focuses on the transformative role of social media in communication processes, questioning the utilization of new communication paradigms created by social media in political discourse, independent of socio-political factors. Finally, the third hypothesis posits that employing entertainment elements in political persuasion can help overcome the barriers young voters construct against opposing views.

This study encompasses a comprehensive literature review spanning three sections to strengthen the theoretical underpinnings, articulate hypotheses, and delineate the research methodology. The initial section establishes a framework for the youth demographics and digital trends in Turkey, elucidating the socio-political context of the 2023 General Elections, and conducting a thorough analysis of the phenomenon of political entertainment. Subsequently, the research methodology devised for testing the hypotheses is detailed, encompassing the research scope, sample selection, and data collection techniques. The findings section rigorously analyzes the acquired data, culminating in the presentation of results pertinent to the confirmation or rejection of the hypotheses. The conclusion section furnishes recommendations for prospective research endeavors, drawing insights from the discerned findings.

Turkey's Youth Demographics and Digital Trends

The May 14, 2023, elections witnessed the participation of 15,709,721 young voters, aged 18-30, accounting for 24.49% of the total 64,145,504 voters (YSK, 2023a). By the second round on May 28, an additional 49,964 young individuals gained voting rights (YSK, 2023b). Turkey's unique demographic, boasting the youngest population in Europe, has resulted in significantly high levels of social media engagement. In 2022, Turkey's total population was recorded at 85,279,553, with youths aged 15-24 numbering 12,949,817, constituting 15.2% of the population. This percentage notably surpasses the average 10.5% youth demographic across the 27 EU member states. A further breakdown reveals 29.7% aged 15-17, 19.1% at 18-19, and 30.2% between 20-22 (TUIK, 2023). Remarkably, 96.9% of the 16-24 age bracket actively uses the Internet (TUIK, 2023).

The "Digital 2023" report by We Are Global (2023) indicates that people in Turkey spend 7 hours and 24 minutes online daily. A significant 83.4% of Turkey's population is online, with 95.4% having mobile internet access. Contrary to global trends, Instagram is the dominant platform in Turkey at 90.6%, followed by WhatsApp and then Facebook. On average, Turkish users are most engaged with Instagram, dedicating 21 hours and 24 minutes monthly, with TikTok close behind at 20 hours and 54 minutes.

These statistics underscore the paramount significance of studying the intersection of digital trends and youth voter dynamics in the context of Turkey's political landscape. They serve as a backdrop to our investigation into the impact of entertainment elements on political persuasion among young voters during the 2023 General Elections, which we believe holds vital implications for understanding modern political engagement and campaign strategies.

The Socio-Political Context of Turkey's 2023 General Elections

The general elections on May 14, 2023, held to determine the 13th President of Turkey and to elect 600 parliamentary members, took place in the aftermath of a profound tragedy. In the second round, Recep Tayyip Erdoğan and Kemal Kılıçdaroğlu emerged as the two leading candidates, and the competition intensified as they sought to secure the majority of votes and claim the presidency. Recep Tayyip Erdoğan secured 52.18% of the votes, becoming the country's 13th President (YSK, 2023a; YSK, 2023b).

Just three months prior to these elections, southern Turkey was struck by a devastating 7.8-magnitude earthquake, resulting in the tragic loss of over 50,000 lives and rendering millions homeless (UNICEF, 2023). This catastrophic event not only gripped the nation with grief but also significantly influenced the electoral landscape, shaping its direction and priorities in unforeseen ways.

In response to this unprecedented tragedy, some political entities chose to approach the 2023 elections with a more somber tone. They choose not to use campaign music and announced that their prepared election songs would not be broadcast on any platform. This unique context provides a distinctive backdrop for our study, which seeks to investigate the persuasive use of entertainment elements in an environment marked by a profound social and psychological impact brought on by the earthquake. Throughout our interviews with the younger demographic, we consistently observed references to this context when discussing their election-related expectations and evaluations. Understanding how this socio-political context shaped their perceptions and responses to entertainment-driven political persuasion is a central focus of our research.

In the 2023 General Elections, the political landscape of Turkey was shaped by the participation of several distinct political alliances, each representing diverse ideologies and identities, contributing to the complex socio-political fabric of the country.

One of these coalitions, known as "The People's Alliance" (Cumhur İttifakı), brought together the Justice and Development Party (AK Party), advocating an Islamist identity (Serdar, 2015, p.12), and the Nationalist Movement Party (MHP), known for its far-right and extreme nationalist orientation (Aslan, 2022, p.223). This alliance was further strengthened by the inclusion of other parties such as the Grand Unity Party (BBP) and the Welfare Party (YRP). In opposition, "The Nation Alliance" (Millet İttifakı) comprised the Republican People's Party (CHP), which embraced a Kemalist, secular, and nationalist identity (Güzel, 2022, p.115), and the Good Party (İYİ Party), which also upheld a nationalist identity (Akçay, 2018, p.2182). The Nation Alliance was formed in direct opposition to the People's Alliance and included parties like the Saadet Party, the Democrat Party, the Future Party, and the Democracy and Progress Party. A third alliance, the "Labor and Freedom Alliance" (Emek ve Özgürlük İttifakı), emerged due to an ongoing closure case against the Peoples' Democratic Party (HDP) at the Constitutional Court. In the 2023 elections, the HDP participated in this alliance under the umbrella of the Green Left Party, which represented a secular and socialist identity (Akkır, 2018, pp.107-108). Additionally, the Turkish Workers' Party (TİP), identified with socialism (Kaymaz-Mert, 2022, p.1), also joined this coalition. Lastly, the "ATA Alliance" (ATA İttifakı) was formed by the Zafer Party and the Justice Party, both of which have a Kemalist and nationalist identity.

Humor in Politics: From Traditional Media to the Digital Age

The relationship between humor and its efficacy in political persuasion has been an enduring topic of academic debate. As social media reshapes political communication, it also transforms the landscape of research in this field. Early studies by Annis (1939) and Brinkman (1968) produced inconclusive results regarding the effectiveness of humor in shaping political discourse. Annis (1939) favored editorials over humorous cartoons as more effective instruments of persuasion, while Brinkman (1968) recognized the value of editorial caricatures. The mid-20th century witnessed the emergence of the concept of a sequential cognitive process model, which was introduced by Hovland et al. (1953) and paved the way for understanding humor-based persuasion which suggests that humor can engage individuals cognitively and emotionally, facilitating the retention of information and making the message more persuasive. Research examining the persuasive power of humor, as highlighted by Sternthal & Craig (1973), Young (2006), Markiewicz (1975), and Fedorikhin & Cole (2004), suggests that humor augments the persuasive efficacy of messages through various mechanisms. It captures attention, enhances cognitive processing, increases the likability of the message source, and establishes a connection between the message and the audience's positive emotional state. Baumgartner (2007) and Becker (2011) demonstrated a mixed impact of humor on political attitudes among young audiences, highlighting its potential to both decrease trust in political institutions and amplify positive evaluations of political candidates.

The advent of the digital age has led to scholarly investigation of how new forms of communication influence political persuasion. Davis et al. (2018) have contributed to this discourse by examining the ways in which digital humor, particularly in the form of memes and online satire, can influence political engagement and participation. Highfield (2017) have insisted on the ways in which digital humor can transcend traditional political communication channels and reach a wider audience, potentially impacting political discourse and civic engagement. Furthermore, Wells et al. (2016) emphasizes the potential of digital platforms to serve as spaces for political expression through humor, thereby influencing individuals' attitudes and behaviors towards political issues and highlighting its potential to both inform and mobilize citizens in the digital era. Shifman et al. (2007) investigated how online humor can shape political discourse. Their study showed that online humor can increase political participation by making political discussions more accessible and engaging.

Tay (2014) coined the term "LOLitics" as a way to make political discourse more entertaining. The study showed that LOLitics can increase political participation by making political issues more accessible and engaging. However, the study also raised concerns that LOLitics can trivialize political issues and make political discussions less serious. Amid the emergence of "pop politics" and "politainment," social media's ascendancy has transformed the entertainment landscape, establishing itself as a predominant influencer among young people. In recent scholarship on politainment, the majority of studies predominantly examine the use of TikTok, Cervi, L., Tejedor, S., & Blesa, F. G. (2023) delved into TikTok's role during the recent Peruvian presidential campaigns. Their findings indicate that candidates mainly employed the platform to spotlight their personal lives and bolster their political images, with a pronounced emphasis on entertainment in most content. The article delves into how Spanish political parties' harness TikTok to captivate younger voters. According to the author, TikTok, with its emphasis on brief videos and visual narrative techniques, aligns perfectly with the concept of politainment—merging politics and entertainment. Such a platform naturally appeals to the youth, who often display a stronger inclination towards entertainment than traditional politics (Zamora-Medina, 2023). Political parties, politicians, and international political institutions alike are progressively leveraging the TikTok platform for the dissemination of their core messages on a daily basis (Meriç & Çakıcı, 2024).

While existing research has provided valuable insights into the impact of humor on political participation, there remains a notable gap in research focusing on the role of entertainment in political communication, especially among the younger demographic in the context of Turkey. A survey conducted with 200 Turkish undergraduate students examined the role of social media in political participation and its impact on democracy and political attitudes (Çildan et al., 2012). Another study conducted at a specific university in Turkey revealed that the use of social media by political party leaders had no significant influence on young voters (Aydın & Gülsoy, 2017). A study based on the March 2014 Local Election explored how the Turkish young generation expressed their use of social media as a political source, political preference, and political action (Mengü et al., 2015). The Ministry of Youth and Sports has published research on young voting behavior in local elections (Karabulut & Önder, 2017). Another recent finding explores the relationship between political knowledge and the use of online sources for news and political information, analyzing original data from the 2015 Turkish Election Study. However, there is still a notable gap in research focusing on entertainment role in political communication, especially among the younger demographic.

In their study, Lee and Yeon (2022) discovered that political entertainment programs utilizing humor can enhance viewers' affinity for the source of oppositional messages. Additionally, viewers perceive the opposing claims as more appealing, even when the content goes against their pre-existing attitudes. In their article, Danielson and Rolandsson (2020) posit that politicians are increasingly tapping into entertainment television to showcase their personal identities, aiming to resonate with voters. They contend that politicians who adeptly harness the power of entertainment television for personal projection stand a better chance of forging connections with the electorate and clinching electoral victories. Greenwood, Sorenson, and Warner (2016) asserted in their article that political comedy remains an influential tool of persuasion, even when disseminated via social media platforms where it's exposed to social pressures. This underscores the idea that political comedy's persuasive power is undiminished outside traditional media environments.

METHOD

Sampling Selection and Description

This research aimed to investigate the effect of entertainment elements on political persuasion through 31 semi-structured interviews conducted with individuals aged between 18 and 30 from various cities in Turkey, including Adana, Diyarbakır, Bursa, Muğla, Aksaray, Kocaeli and Istanbul. These cities were selected to ensure a diverse demographic profile rather than solely representing the national population. The sample consisted of 17 females and 14 males, providing broad representation. The occupational status of the participants comprised 15 employed, 4 unemployed, and 4 students. Educationally, the sample included individuals with varying levels of education, including three who had completed middle school, two high school graduates, five with associate degrees, and 18 who held or were pursuing a bachelor's degree.

In accordance with qualitative sampling strategies, our research prioritized capturing the diversity within the phenomena under study rather than aiming for national representativeness. While our participant selection strategy aimed to capture a diverse demographic profile by including participants from various cities across Turkey, it does not fully encompass the socio-political perspective of Turkey in terms of geographic and demographic representation. Specifically, the regions and demographic groups included in our sample introduce limitations in the generalizability of our findings. Our research is based on the principles of social constructivism, a perspective that asserts reality is shaped through social and cultural processes by individuals and communities. This theoretical approach is critical for understanding how entertainment elements in political content influence individuals' political attitudes. The work of Crotty (1998) is particularly relevant here, as it underscores the substantial impact of cultural influences on the formation of an individual's worldview.

The method of semi-structured interviews we employed for data collection allows participants to express their realities in their own words. This reflects a core aspect of social constructivism, the process by which individuals construct their own experiences and understandings. During the interviews, we asked participants to share examples and experiences related to entertainment elements in political content. This approach helped us to understand how they perceive and construct entertainment elements in the political persuasion process. In selecting our sample, we placed a significant emphasis on achieving demographic diversity, considering specific criteria such as geographical location, gender, age, and educational background. These criteria were deliberately chosen to ensure that our sample encompasses a wide range of perspectives and experiences related to the use of entertainment elements in political persuasion. Geographical location allowed us to capture variations in political dynamics and social media usage habits across different regions of Turkey. Gender and age are also known to influence individuals' interactions with political content and entertainment on social media. Additionally, educational background was a critical factor in our sample selection, as it can impact individuals' digital literacy and engagement with online political discourse. To ensure data saturation, we conducted 31 semi-structured interviews. Given the qualitative nature of our study, the sample size is compatible (Morse, 2015) for the research objectives, and we aimed to attain in-depth insights into the role of entertainment elements in shaping political persuasion Although the inclusion of participants from various Turkish cities aimed to capture a diverse range of perspectives, it is essential to acknowledge that the sample may not fully encompass all demographic, cultural, and political variations. Nonetheless, preliminary observations suggest that the foundational variables of the sample do not exert a pronounced or meaningful impact on the research outcomes.

Table 1. Participant code and demographic profiles in the study

Participant Code	City	Age	Gender	Occupational Status	Education Level
Participant 1	Adana	18	Female	unemployed	High School
Participant 2	Adana	21	Female	student	Bachelor's Degree
Participant 3	Adana	22	Male	student	Bachelor's Degree
Participant 4	Diyarbakır	23	Male	employed	High School
Participant 5	Adana	23	Female	employed	Bachelor's Degree
Participant 6	Muğla	23	Female	student	Bachelor's Degree
Participant 7	Diyarbakır	23	Female	employed	Associate Degree
Participant 8	Aksaray	24	Male	employed	Associate Degree
Participant 9	Diyarbakır	24	Male	employed	Associate Degree
Participant 10	Diyarbakır	24	Male	unemployed	Middle School
Participant 11	Adana	24	Female	employed	Bachelor's Degree
Participant 12	Adana	24	Female	employed	Bachelor's Degree
Participant 13	Kocaeli	25	Male	employed	Bachelor's Degree
Participant 14	Diyarbakır	25	Male	employed	Associate Degree
Participant 15	Bursa	25	Female	employed	Bachelor's Degree
Participant 16	Diyarbakır	25	Male	employed	Bachelor's Degree

continued on following page

Table 1. Continued

Participant Code	City	Age	Gender	Occupational Status	Education Level
Participant 17	Adana	26	Female	student	Bachelor's Degree
Participant 18	Diyarbakır	27	Male	employed	Middle School
Participant 19	Diyarbakır	27	Male	employed	High School
Participant 20	Adana	27	Female	employed	Bachelor's Degree
Participant 21	Diyarbakır	27	Female	unemployed	Associate Degree
Participant 22	Adana	28	Male	employed	Bachelor's Degree
Participant 23	Adana	28	Male	employed	Bachelor's Degree
Participant 24	Adana	28	Male	unemployed	Bachelor's Degree
Participant 25	Diyarbakır	28	Female	employed	Associate Degree
Participant 26	Istanbul	28	Female	employed	Bachelor's Degree
Participant 27	Diyarbakır	29	Male	employed	Middle School
Participant 28	Adana	30	Male	employed	Bachelor's Degree
Participant 29	Adana	30	Male	employed	Bachelor's Degree
Participant 30	Diyarbakır	30	Female	unemployed	Associate Degree
Participant 31	Ankara	27	Male	employed	Bachelor's Degree

Data Collection

The interviews were conducted both in-person and via video conference and lasted between 30 minutes and 50 minutes each. In preparation for the interviews, an interview guide was carefully developed to cover topics such as internet and social media usage habits, political participation, and forms of political persuasion. The participants were also asked questions about the utilization of entertainment elements on social media for political persuasion purposes, specifically within the context of the 2023 election campaign. The interviews were audio-recorded and transcribed verbatim, and thematic analysis was applied to the data. This involved generating initial codes and grouping them into overarching themes through an iterative process of discussion and refinement among the research team.

Our research questions focus on how entertainment elements in political content affect individuals' political perceptions and choices. This aligns how individuals' perceptions and interpretations of political realities are shaped by their social and cultural contexts (Demeritt, 2005; Kukla, 2013; Burr, 2015; Çakıcı, 2023). Particularly through selecting participants from various regions of Turkey, we sought to explore how entertainment elements in political persuasion are perceived and interpreted across different social and cultural environments.

The method of semi-structured interviews we employed for data collection allows participants to express their realities in their own words. During the interviews, we asked participants to share examples and experiences related to entertainment elements in political content.

FINDINGS AND DISCUSSION

In our study, we focused on the use of emerging entertainment elements in social media as a tool for political persuasion. Our findings partially support Hypothesis 1 (H1), which suggests that these elements could significantly influence the political engagement and voting behavior of young voters. The young participants in our study generally viewed the integration of entertainment elements into political communication positively, indicating a trend among youth towards more innovative and interactive methods of political communication.

"I think it's a good thing; it increases likability. It breaks down some barriers" (Participant 3, Adana, 22, Male).

"In my opinion, politicians should share entertaining content. They should laugh with the society. They should create humorous videos. Not everything should be about politics. I really like it when they share such entertaining videos" (Participant 10, Diyarbakır, 24, Male).

"I view it positively; it helps in building more sincerity. Looking at the current government, there is a lack of sincerity among them. Especially, the aides of the opposition, like Ekrem İmamoğlu and Mansur Yavaş, being proficient in internet language brings them closer to the electorate" (Participant 16, Muğla, 23, Female).

Participants have consistently reported that various political figures and parties have drawn their attention on social media through the incorporation of elements from entertainment culture. Illustrative examples of this phenomenon include the dance video of Muharrem İnce, the humorous Twitter posts of Selahattin Demirtaş and Özgür Demirtaş, the kitchen-based video of Kemal Kılıçdaroğlu chopping onions, some joke-related videos of Recep Tayyip Erdoğan, the 'trebuchet' video of the Zafer Party addressing refugees, videos of Mustafa Sarıgül, and videos of Sırrı Süreyya Önder. It should be noted that the specific examples cited vary depending on the city, with participants from Diyarbakır mostly citing Muharrem İnce, Kemal Kılıçdaroğlu, Recep Tayyip Erdoğan, Selahattin Demirtaş, and Sırrı Süreyya Önder, while those from Adana, Aksaray, Bursa, Muğla, Adıyaman, and Ankara mentioned examples excluding Selahattin Demirtaş and Sırrı Süreyya Önder.

"Muharrem İnce's dance video. He was dancing while AK Party members were distributing election papers. The funny posts shared by Selahattin Demirtaş against Özgür Demirtaş. Selahattin Demirtaş can make even those politically distant from him laugh" (Participant 10, Diyarbakır, 24, Male).

"I can give the example of Muharrem İnce's dance. It didn't impress me; I just laughed" (Participant 20, Adana, 27, Female).

However, this support is simultaneously constrained by specific conditions. In other words, while participants endorse the innovative use of humor and other entertainment elements to make politics more accessible and engaging, they also express reservations about the potential consequences of this trend. Participants reported frequently encountering political entertainment elements related to political figures on social networks, especially during election periods, pointing to various social media platforms including Twitter, Instagram, and TikTok. Nevertheless, despite their frequent exposure to such political content, when questioned about the nature of their interactions with it, their responses showed considerable variation. The limitations expressed by participants with respect to the utilization of entertainment elements in political communication extend beyond more interactions. One of the primary concerns is the blurring of distinctions between factual and misleading information, as well as the potential for oversimplifying intricate political matters. These statements suggest a discomfort with the prevalence of ethos over logos in political communication, a phenomenon that Aristotle's rhetorical trilogy (Barthes, 1970) identifies. Moreover, participants have voiced concerns that an excessive reliance on entertainment elements may detract from the gravity and significance of political matters, particularly in the context of decision-making where the credibility and dependability of political actors are of paramount importance.

"The frequent use of such tactics by politicians bothers me to some extent because you expect seriousness in politics" (Participant 11, Adana, 24, Female).

"I think this is a negative situation. Politicians should be serious. In my opinion, they shouldn't share entertaining content. They need to be serious. They shouldn't share so much content with comedic elements" (Participant 16, Diyarbakır, 25, Male).

The study's findings indicate that participants generally have a positive outlook on the incorporation of entertainment elements in political content. However, despite this favorable perspective, participants also highlight several constraints on the function of entertainment elements in shaping political perspectives and choices. These constraints primarily take the form of concerns about disinformation, loss of credibility, restricted interaction due to political apprehensions, and ethical considerations. The study revealed that incorporating entertainment elements in political content can increase its engagement, particularly among young voters. Nonetheless, the influence of such elements on voting choices and political views is not always immediate and direct. Rather, their role appears to be focused on capturing attention and stimulating interest. Therefore, while entertainment may play a crucial role in political communication, its capacity to bring about significant and enduring changes in political decisions and opinions is limited.

In the study, all young participants reported extensive exposure to political content, particularly during election periods. However, when queried about their interactions with such content, significant variations among participants were observed. While some actively engaged through actions like sharing, retweeting, liking, and commenting, others displayed a passive approach, preferring only to review the content. Notably, participants from the Diyarbakır region expressed feeling greater pressure and fear when interacting with political content. Engaging with political content by liking, commenting, or sharing was perceived as carrying personal security risks for these participants, leading to more cautious behaviors.

"I can't comfortably share or comment on political entertainment content. I'm afraid. I can't express my thoughts. For instance, I post a tweet and often have to delete it five minutes later because I feel uneasy. In Turkey, I am constrained by fear from sharing anything. I hesitate. I'm afraid of the government. You could be lynched or face legal consequences if you share something. This situation stems from being Kurdish. I have to think ten times before sharing anything" (Participant 30, Diyarbakır, 30, Female).

"I never like, share, or comment on political entertainment content. If I comment, I might face political troubles. I am not pro-government. If I comment, I could receive a penalty. Therefore, I refrain from commenting on social media" (Participant 21, Diyarbakır, 27, Female).

On the other hand, variations in the use of entertainment elements in politics are observed depending on the differing political participation conditions of various geographic regions. This observation synthesizes with the previous statement, highlighting the nuanced relationship between the context of societal events, like natural disasters, and the appropriateness of employing entertainment elements in political discourse.

The use of entertainment elements in political content on social media elicited mixed responses from participants, who similarly displayed ambivalence when discussing their voting behavior. Most participants indicated that such content did not directly influence their own political beliefs or voting decisions. However, they acknowledged that it could impact the political views or voting preferences of others, particularly young and uncertain voters. While explaining why it might not be effective, participants also highlighted the influence of socio-psychological conditions created by the earthquake disaster. A notable difference was observed within the age group of participants, with those outside the "Z generation" or "younger generation" identifying these younger individuals as the potential target audience for influence.

"I don't think it affected me much. I've seen it influence younger voters than me in my surroundings. The candidate who makes people laugh more might get the votes. I don't think it will change me" (Participant 13, Kocaeli, 25, Male).

"It definitely can't influence my voting choice. We just laugh and move on. We have much bigger problems. People are struggling to make ends meet. There are people dying. There was an earthquake last month. I won't vote for someone just because they produce very funny and nice content under these circumstances" (Participant 15, Bursa, 25, Female).

"Definitely not. I have always been radical since I was born. Humorous content never changes my opinion. It can be influential in society. For example, viral videos can affect the opinions of young people. But it does not affect me. Like, after seeing Muharrem İnce's video, I wouldn't go and vote for him or his party" (Participant 25, Diyarbakır, 28, Female).

Concerns regarding the integration of entertainment culture into political discourse were expressed, including apprehensions about the incorporation of social media influencers into political communication. Participants acknowledged that social media influencers have the capacity to reach extensive audiences and can effectively disseminate their political views. However, there are concerns that influencers' involvement in political content might adversely influence the political preferences of their followers. Despite these reservations, the role of influencers in the political entertainment culture continues to be a subject of diverse opinions among participants.

"Influencers should not share. Influencers should not take a politician's video to different dimensions and share it. Influencers should not talk about politics. They don't know politics. They shouldn't tell their followers 'I support this. You should too.' I find it very wrong for influencers to talk about politics. Influencers can be influential on people. But it's wrong for their followers to vote for a party because of them. Influencers shouldn't change people's opinions." (Participant 10, Diyarbakır, 24)

Our research analyzed the effectiveness of various formats for political messaging with entertainment content. We discovered a significant preference among participants for videos incorporating social media entertainment culture and editing techniques. This preference was attributed to the content's concise nature, visually engaging features, and overall captivating appeal. Participants emphasized that videos, especially those enriched with humor and creative edits, possess a notable capacity to influence viewers, contrasting with the relatively lower impact of written content.

Additionally, the study revealed a strong engagement with humorous memes and witty tweets on social media platforms, indicating their effectiveness in capturing audience attention. Participants suggested that political parties and candidates could leverage these elements for more effective communication on social media. Recommended strategies include the use of short, impactful videos, viral content, engaging video edits, humor-infused messages, and collaborations with social media influencers. These findings imply a paradigm shift in political communication strategies, where visual and interactive elements are becoming increasingly crucial in influencing public opinion and voter behavior.

"Video edits and the memes going around on Twitter. The replies to politicians' tweets are also witty and funny" (Participant 3, Adana, 22, Male).

"Videos about street interviews. I find them very funny and successful. Not just for me, but these videos are successful for everyone. That's what I think. Also, videos are more convincing. Written texts are not very convincing. Videos are more effective" (Participant 16, Diyarbakır, 25, Male).

Participants in this study express differing ethical concerns regarding the utilization of elements of social media entertainment culture in political communication. The rapid dissemination of both true and false information on social media demands heightened vigilance with regard to content selection, and the avoidance of divisive and alienating material. It is also stressed that content should not be used to exploit societal anxieties, should maintain a sense of seriousness, and should be employed in moderation. However, there are also opinions that social media should not be treated with undue seriousness.

Participants deem it imperative that political parties and candidates show sincerity, respect, and adherence to societal values while incorporating elements of entertainment culture on social media. Overstepping the boundaries of humor, using exclusive language, and disregarding the public's sensitivities must be avoided.

"They need to be very careful about their style. No one should be belittled. Others should not be looked down upon. For example, a parliamentary candidate had used negative expressions about Turks and Kurds. It had really upset me." (Participant 30, Diyarbakır, 30, Female)

"They should be careful not to use a discriminatory language. They need to be inclusive." (Participant 2, Adana, 21, Female)

The majority of participants expressed a positive outlook towards the incorporation of entertainment features in political content. They considered these elements to be engaging and effective in rendering political messages more relatable. However, it is worth noting that while these features were well-received, they did not have a significant impact on participants' political views or voting preferences. This observation indicates that while young voters may be receptive to entertainment in political communication, it does not necessarily result in a shift in their political stance or allegiance.

The utilization of entertainment cultural elements in political messaging was noted by participants to increase the attention-grabbing nature of the discourse, often creating a sense of affiliation. However, it was emphasized that such entertaining elements did not necessarily impact their political opinions or decisions. This perspective underscores the distinction between the appeal of entertainment in politics and its perceived ability to influence political viewpoints.

The participants expressed reservations regarding the inclusion of entertainment features in political content, as they believed that it could diminish the gravity of political discourse. While they acknowledged the potential for a more engaging political presentation, they doubted the persuasive power of these elements in shaping their political preferences. This perspective reflects a critical outlook on the utility of entertainment in politics, acknowledging its appeal while challenging its influence on the political decision-making process.

In the field of political communication, the task of persuaders to sway their audience towards a stance contrary to their pre-existing attitudes is particularly challenging. This difficulty arises from individuals' inherent preference for information that confirms their existing beliefs, a tendency leading to the dismissal of opposing views, as noted by Festinger (1957) and Taber & Lodge (2006). Valli and Nai (2023) further highlight that this inclination to resist counter-attitudinal arguments actively works against the acceptance of persuasive efforts. Prior, (2005) show the impact of customizable political information on democratic polarization and media users' exposure to diverse viewpoints.

One of the hypotheses of this study proposes that social media entertainment may serve as a counterbalancing factor capable of overcoming this resistance. This is based on the notion that the emerging culture of entertainment on social media could be instrumental in overcoming the resistance typically encountered in political persuasion efforts. Particularly in the politically dual context of Turkey's 2023 General Elections, the introduction of entertainment elements in political discourse has created a new and effective dynamic among young voters. This phenomenon challenges the 'echo chamber' effect in digital communication, highlighted by Vaccari (2013), Dubois & Blank (2018), and Terren & Borge-Bravo (2021), by enabling users to encounter a diverse range of messages, including those representing opposing viewpoints, thereby mitigating biases and resistance towards contrasting opinions.

"I follow pages and leaders of political parties that don't share my views." (Participant 29, Adana, 30, Male)

"I'm not exactly a cinephile, but I do follow directors and channels that have views opposite to mine, learning from them. I apply this to politics as well." (Participant 23, Adana, 28, Male)

This study's findings provide insights into the validity of the proposed hypotheses concerning the role of entertainment elements in political communication. Hypothesis 1, which suggested that the integration of entertainment elements within political campaigns would significantly influence young voters' political engagement and voting behavior, is partially supported. Participants generally viewed the inclusion of entertainment positively, indicating a shift towards more interactive communication methods. However, the impact on actual voting behavior and political participation varied, suggesting a limited influence on electoral outcomes. Regarding Hypothesis 2, which posited the independent role of social media in political persuasion irrespective of the socio-political context, the evidence is insufficient to fully support this hypothesis. While social media's role in political persuasion is acknowledged, the importance of the socio-political context is highlighted. Regional variations and personal security concerns demonstrate the influence of local dynamics, suggesting that social media's effectiveness in political persuasion is intertwined with socio-political factors. Hypothesis 3, focusing on the ability of entertainment elements in political messages to overcome resistance among young voters, is moderately supported. These elements engage participants and capture attention effectively, but their influence in changing deep-seated political beliefs or voting decisions is limited. This finding indicates that while entertainment plays a role in political persuasion, its impact is more nuanced, primarily serving to engage rather than convert or fundamentally alter political viewpoints.

This study has critically examined the evolving interface between entertainment elements in social media and political communication, with a specific focus on young Turkish voters during the 2023 General Elections. Our findings reveal a complex landscape where the traditional boundaries of political discourse are being reshaped by the infusion of entertainment. Young voters in Turkey are increasingly encountering political content that blends humor, creativity, and media dynamics, a trend that aligns with the global shift towards politainment.

CONCLUSION

The strategic use of entertainment elements, including dance videos, humorous content, and creative social media challenges, has been instrumental in engaging young voters, indicating a significant shift in political communication strategies. While these elements have successfully captured attention and enhanced engagement, their impact on altering deeply ingrained political views and voting preferences appears to be limited. The study underscores the need for a balanced approach in employing entertainment in political discourse, taking into account the ethical implications and potential risks such as disinformation and credibility loss.

In conclusion, the interplay of entertainment and politics on social media platforms presents both opportunities and challenges in the context of political communication. As young voters in Turkey navigate this new terrain, it becomes crucial for political actors to understand the nuances of this medium and its impact on political engagement. This study, while contributing to the broader discourse on politainment, also highlights the necessity of considering the extraordinary socio-political conditions shaped by the pre-campaign earthquake disaster. These unique circumstances in Turkey's political landscape must be factored into the interpretation of the findings, underscoring the importance of context in assessing the impact of entertainment elements in political communication.

For future research endeavors, it is recommended to delve into the intricacies of media consumption patterns among young voters to elucidate their media preferences. Additionally, employing sentiment analysis methodologies would allow for a nuanced understanding of the emotional resonance elicited by political entertainment content. Furthermore, conducting studies focusing on social interaction dynamics would provide valuable insights into the mechanisms underlying social engagement and participation. Integrating neuroscience and biometric analyses could offer a comprehensive examination of the neurological and physiological responses evoked by political entertainment content. Ethnographic inquiries, observing individuals' interactions with political entertainment in real-life contexts, would enrich our understanding of its societal impact. Moreover, conducting diversity-focused investigations would shed light on the varied responses to such content across different demographic strata. In light of recent developments, particularly the outcome of the local elections in Turkey on March 31, 2024, wherein the opposition party secured the highest vote share since 1977, there arises a pressing need for further inquiry into the influence of entertaining political content on voter behavior. Specifically, investigations concentrating on the utilization and ramifications of political entertainment, especially within the context of this seminal election, hold promise for advancing our comprehension of the pivotal role played by young voters in shaping political discourse and decision-making processes.

Ethical Statement

This study has Galatasaray University Scientific Research and Publication Ethics Committee approval (Galatasaray University Ref No: 2023/013 https://gsu.edu.tr/tr/arastirma/etik-kurulu).

Funding

This work was supported by the Galatasaray University, within the scope of the project titled 'Social Media Entertainment Culture and New Forms of Political Persuasion' [grant number SBA-2023-1193].

ACKNOWLEDGEMENTS

The authors express their gratitude; to young people who participated in the work from many cities of Turkey, to thank the students of Galatasaray University Media and Communication Studies Master Program who conducted the interviews with some of the participants, to Research Center for Media Studies (MEDIAR) intern Ulaş Demir, who transcribed the interviews recorded, to the anonymous reviewers for their very careful and beneficial reflections on the paper.

REFERENCES

Annis, W. (1939). The effect of editorial cartoons versus humorous cartoons upon the reader's editorial interpretation. *Journal of Educational Psychology*, 30(7), 513–518.

Baumgartner, J. C. (2007). Humor and political communication: An extension and refinement of political humor typologies. *The Social Science Journal*, 44(1), 177–194.

Becker, A. B. (2011). Laughing matters: Humor's role in persuasion and attitude change. *Human Communication Research*, 37(4), 566–591.

Berrocal-Gonzalo, S., Zamora-Martínez, P., & González-Neira, A. (2023). Politainment on Twitter: Engagement in the Spanish Legislative Elections of April 2019. *Media and Communication*, 11(2), 163–175. 10.17645/mac.v11i2.6292

Brinkman, H. J. (1968). The effects of political cartoons on readers' responses to editorials. *Public Opinion Quarterly*, 32(3), 459–471.

Çakıcı, Z. (2023). Din, Kimlik ve Müzik: Genç Erkeklerin Müzik Dinleme Pratikleri Üzerine Nitel Bir Araştırma. *Etkileşim*, 6(11), 316–337. 10.32739/etkilesim.2023.6.11.199

Cervi, L., Tejedor, S., & Blesa, F. G. (2023). TikTok and political communication: The latest frontier of politainment? A case study. *Media and Communication*, 11(2), 203–217. 10.17645/mac.v11i2.6390

Cervi, L., Tejedor, S., & Blesa, F. G. (2023). TikTok and the Peruvian presidential elections: A new frontier of politainment. *International Journal of Communication*, 17, 4595–4612.

Çildan, M., Erdoğdu, M., & Demirhan, A. (2012). The impact of social media on political participation and political attitudes: The example of Turkey. [IJRTE]. *The International Journal of Research in Teacher Education*, 3(1), 61–78.

Danielson, M., & Rolandsson, B. (2020). Staging authenticity: Personal and political projection in Swedish political entertainment television. *International Journal of Cultural Studies*, 23(5), 690–706.

Davis, R. D., Kitch, S. W., & Kitch, W. (2018). Political jokes and the social cycle: How the era of the weblog remixed humor and news. *Journalism Studies*, 19(12), 1790–1807.

Deuze, M. (2017). Politainment and the transformation of political communication. In Hartley, J., Steemers, J., & Deuze, M. (Eds.), *The Handbook of Global Media and Communication* (pp. 102–113). Wiley-Blackwell.

Dörner, A. (2001). *Politainment: Politics as part of the mediated event society.* Suhrkamp.

Fedorikhin, A., & Cole, C. A. (2004). The effects of humor on memory: Constrained by the pun. *Journal of Memory and Language*, 50(4), 415–429.

Gil-Ramírez, M., de Travesedo-Rojas, R. G., & Almansa-Martínez, A. (2019). Politainment and political personalisation. From television to YouTube. *Revista Latina de Comunicación Social*, 74, 1542–1564. 10.4185/RLCS-2019-1398

Greenwood, S. D., Sorenson, J., & Warner, B. R. (2016). Political satire and the politics of emotion. *The International Journal of Press/Politics*, 21(4), 458–478.

Highfield, T. (2017). Networked humour: Understanding internet memes. In *Digital media, humor and identity* (pp. 59–77). Routledge.

Holbert, R. L., & Young, D. G. (2012). *Exploring relations between political entertainment media and traditional political communication information outlets: A research agenda.* The International Encyclopedia of Media Studies. 10.1002/9781444361506.wbiems127

Hovland, C. I., Janis, I. L., & Kelley, H. H. (1953). *Communication and persuasion: Psychological studies of opinion change.* Yale University Press.

Iyengar, S., & Simon, A. F. (2000). New perspectives and evidence on political communication and campaign effects. *Annual Review of Psychology*, 51(1), 149–169. 10.1146/annurev.psych.51.1.14910751968

Karabulut, N., & Önder, Ç. H. (2017). Determining the factors affecting the voting preferences of young voters in the 2014 local elections. Bilge Adamlar / Wise Men, 16(58), 217-232.

Karpf, D., & Kreiss, D. (2016). The Role of Qualitative Methods in Political Communication Research: Past, Present, and Future. *Political Communication*, 33(3), 343–360.

Lee, M. Y., & Yeon, J. (2022). Humorous entertainment programs and political attitude change: The moderating role of political ideology. *Communication Studies*, 73(2), 257–275.

Lilleker, D., & Cornfield, M. (2011). Politainment: The Use of Entertainment in Political Communication. In McNair, B. (Ed.), *The Routledge Handbook of Political Communication* (pp. 193–204). Routledge.

Markiewicz, D. (1975). Humor as a form of persuasion: A study of some comic elements in political cartoons. *Communication Monographs*, 42(4), 315–326.

Mengü, Y., Sevi, B., Yegen, B. C., & Yilmaz, E. (2015). Usage of social media for political purposes during March 2014 local elections in Turkey. *Social Media + Society*, 1(2), 2056305115614241.

Meriç, E., & Çakıcı, Z. (2024). From TikTok Trends to Pandemic Essentials: A Comparative Analysis of the World Health Organization's Health Communication Strategies on TikTok. In *Transformed Communication Codes in the Mediated World: A Contemporary Perspective* (pp. 1-23). IGI Global.

Nieland, J.-U. (2008). *Politainment.* The International Encyclopedia of Communication. 10.1002/9781405186407.wbiecp047

Riegert, K., & Collins, S. (2016). *Politainment*. The International Encyclopedia of Political Communication. 10.1002/9781118541555.wbiepc157

Ross, K. (2016). *Politainment and the Rise of Celebrity Politicians*. Palgrave Macmillan.

Shifman, L., Thelwall, M., & Wilkerson, I. (2007). With a little help from my friends: A content analysis of the interaction between the UK Independence Party and its online supporters. *Sociological Research Online*, 12(6), 4.

Smith, A. R. (2014). *The politics of popular culture*. Routledge.

Sternthal, B., & Craig, C. S. (1973). Humor in advertising. *Journal of Marketing*, 37(4), 12–18. 10.1177/002224297303700403

Street, J. (2012). *Politainment: When politics and entertainment converge*. Rowman & Littlefield.

Tay, L. (2014). # LOLitics: Analyzing the role of humor in political participation. *The American Behavioral Scientist*, 58(5), 617–634.

Valli, C., & Nai, A. (2023). Let me think about it: Cognitive elaboration and strategies of resistance to political persuasion. *Media Psychology*, 26(2), 89–112. 10.1080/15213269.2022.2098774

Wells, C., Spottswood, E. L., & Marsh, J. C. (2016). Is this the Onion? The humorous potential of internet journalism. *Communication Studies*, 67(5), 551–566.

Young, D. G. (2006). "The Daily Show" and the reinvention of political journalism. *Political Science Quarterly*, 121(2), 293–319.

Zamora-Medina, R. (2023). Politainment as dance: visual storytelling on TikTok among Spanish political parties. In *Research Handbook on Visual Politics* (pp. 228–243). Edward Elgar Publishing. 10.4337/9781800376939.00025

Zamora-Medina, R. (2023). TikTok and its implications for politainment: An analysis of Spanish political parties. *Media Culture & Society*, 45(1), 142–160.

KEY TERMS AND DEFINITIONS

Digital Content: Digital content pertains to the array of textual, auditory, visual, and multimedia materials generated, disseminated, or consumed within electronic milieus.

Political Communication: Political communication denotes the strategic dissemination of policies and messages by political actors to the populace, utilizing various communication channels and methodologies.

Political Entertainment: Political entertainment represents a communicative modality aimed at informing or influencing individuals by accentuating the comedic or engaging facets of political entities or occurrences.

Social Media: Social media delineates the constellation of internet-mediated platforms employed by users to disseminate content, foster interactions, and cultivate virtual communities.

Youth Studies: Youth studies encompass an interdisciplinary domain of inquiry dedicated to comprehending the challenges confronted by adolescents, devising interventions tailored to their exigencies, and fostering their developmental trajectories.

Chapter 13
Exploring the Dark Side of Social Media and Digital Consumer With a Dystopian Perspective

Aysegul Sagkaya Gungor
http://orcid.org/0000-0003-3740-7456
Istanbul Medeniyet University, Turkey

ABSTRACT

Social media has emerged as a central focus of consumer research, with marketers recognizing its ongoing significance in their field. While previous research has primarily explored consumer behavior and its outcomes through the lens of social media opportunities, it is now apparent that social media carries inherent risks for individuals, companies, and society at large. This chapter delves into the darker aspects of social media, shedding light on its multifaceted nature within the marketing context. By adopting the honeycomb model, the author elucidates the contributions of various parties—individuals, social network owners, and collaborating companies—to the emergence of these dark phenomena. Through careful reflection, the author put forth a series of propositions throughout the article, highlighting avenues for future research and unveiling theoretical implications in this domain.

INTRODUCTION

The advent of the Internet and its accompanying technologies, such as internet-connected devices, the Internet of Things (IoT), virtual reality (VR), and artificial intelligence (AI), holds the promise of a profound transformation in consumers' online experiences. For companies, establishing "digital relationships" with consumers has become crucial in this landscape. Consequently, a considerable body of contemporary research has focused on understanding digital consumer behavior within virtual environments, as evidenced by studies by Mathur *et al.* (2022), Kamboj and Sharma (2023), and Ju *et al.* (2022). These researchers sought to uncover the impact of virtual environment characteristics on both consumers and organizations, aiming to maximize the associated benefits. However, it is important to acknowledge that the virtual world also harbors inherent risks for individuals, firms, and society at large.

DOI: 10.4018/979-8-3693-3767-7.ch013

Copyright ©2024, IGI Global. Copying or distributing in print or electronic forms without written permission of IGI Global is prohibited.

While these platforms facilitate collective efforts to promote products and services, it is essential to recognize that collectively generated product reviews and information sharing can inadvertently create a breeding ground for malicious activities, potentially giving rise to a dystopian environment.

The exploration of the negative aspects of digitalization is still in its early stages (Zwass, 2021). Drawing from the dystopian perspective, this study centers its attention on the negative aspects of online social networking services (oSNS). The choice of oSNS as the focal point is driven by two key factors. Firstly, social media platforms inherently possess both positive and negative attributes. oSNS offers genuine advantages in achieving company objectives by serving and engaging with customers, influencing their decision-making processes, and facilitating information exchange among customers and other businesses. However, it is crucial to recognize that alongside these benefits, incidents have increasingly revealed a "dark side" of oSNS. These platforms seem to fuel deviant behaviors at an alarming rate. Examples include provoking compulsive and impulsive buying tendencies among customers, promoting trolling, fostering addictive usage patterns, facilitating destructive interactions, enabling the fabrication of fake news, facilitating privacy violations, and propagating misinformation (Sultan, 2021; Aghakhani and Main, 2019; Wu et al. 2020; Lund et al., 2020; Wansink, 1994). Despite all these studies, the current literature falls short of providing a comprehensive understanding of the breadth and multidimensionality of the dark side of oSNS.

Research Problem

The primary objective of this study is to contribute to the understanding of the dark side of oSNS by elucidating the characteristics of social media platforms that contribute to negative consequences. Furthermore, it aims to identify the roles played by different parties, including consumers, social network owners, and collaborating companies, in engaging in any form of destructive activity. Additionally, building upon existing research on anomalies in digital consumer behavior, this paper explores the precautions that companies should or could undertake to mitigate potential risks. As one of the few, this research provides a comprehensive exploration of the multifaceted nature of the dark side of consumer behavior on oSNS within the context of dystopian discourse. The dimensions were identified through an extensive review of the literature, and the ones selected are most relevant to oSNS.

The prominence of dystopia in this research is rooted in Pantzar's (2000) definition of this concept as "a dystopia where individuals are enslaved to an entertainment machine, succumbing to computer dependency and the erosion of rational life" (p. 13). Considering the maladaptive behaviors exhibited by digital consumers on oSNS, which inherently seek to disrupt established norms, there exists a resemblance to the notion of dystopia. What is more, Podoshen et al. (2014) suggested that although there have been studies on utopia, marketing, and consumption in the last 20 years, there was a paucity of literature on consumption and dystopia. This paper aims to bridge this gap by establishing a connection between dystopia and consumption in the realm of oSNS, shedding light on the consumption patterns within these platforms.

DARK CONSTRUCTS OF SOCIAL MEDIA AND DYSTOPIA

Dystopia and Online Social Networks

Maclaran and Brown (2005) defined utopia as a liberating force that inspires a better future. Within the realm of shared consumption, utopia reflects consumers' desire for fulfillment and self-improvement, leading to social progress and a flourished sense of community (Kozinets et al., 2002). There is usually a utopian fire in all entertainment products to appeal to consumers (Jameson, 1979). As one of them, to succeed, online social networking services (oSNS) must ignite this utopian spirit as an immersive and engaging medium. Conversely, dystopia represents a society characterized by dehumanization and unpleasantness. Dystopic environments are marked by malice, fragmentation, irrationality, disturbance, and addictive elements (Surry and Farquhar, 1997; Zolfagharian and Yazdanparast, 2017; Tirole, 2021), envisioning a future where violence and malevolence prevail (Podoshen et al., 2014).

Dystopian determinists argue that technology is inherently dehumanizing and will ultimately lead to mankind's destruction (Surry and Farquhar, 1997). They perceive the idea of technological utopia as illusory, believing that it will inevitably give rise to social menaces (Rambe and Nel, 2015). With oSNS providing a platform that imposes constraints, controls, and constant surveillance (Dima-Laza, 2012), it becomes an ideal setting for technology dystopia. The potential disruptive effects caused by fragmentation, leading to an aggressive, irrational, and disturbing environment, along with perceived privacy violations, are clear indicators of the dystopian nature of oSNS (Rambe and Nel, 2015).

Kozinets et al.'s (2002) notion of consumers' desire to be part of narratives, engage, and fill gaps aligns closely with consumer behavior where consumers seek to participate in the product development process, engage with brands, and fill gaps in their beloved brands' stories in the digital world. However, some individuals disrupt these ties by spreading paranoia and contributing to an incoherent and fragmented society. Furthermore, oSNS, being the platforms where the stage for violence is easily set, provide an environment conducive to creating a dystopian atmosphere in the media.

In this theoretical exploration, I propose that social networks are fertile ground for the creation of a dystopian context. I aim to elucidate how this dystopian discourse manifests in oSNS by examining the elements of dystopia that are applicable to these platforms. I have observed that dystopian themes present in certain consumption contexts play a role among social media users. Sometimes voluntarily or involuntarily, consumers actively participate and contribute to the dystopian hyperreality within oSNS. Here I define dystopia as collective or individual malicious efforts within oSNS where chaos reigns, affecting individuals, network owners, and participating companies. In this context, chaos is the situation that occurs when various irrational and malevolent acts corrupt the system.

Fear of Missing Out, Impulsive and Compulsive Buying

Impulsive buying, compulsive consumption, and the fear of missing out (FOMO) contribute to the dark side of consumer behavior (Moschis, 2017). Decision-making with numerous influencers can have significant psychosocial and economic implications for consumers (Dhir et al., 2021). Although the online world offers seemingly infinite information, according to information processing theory, individuals' cognitive capacity is limited, and they must prioritize the information they need to process. Accordingly, the urgent need to keep up with what others are experiencing gives rise to FOMO -defined as "a pervasive apprehension that others may be enjoying rewarding experiences from which one is absent"

(Przybylski et al., 2013, p. 1841)-. This fear drives impulsive and compulsive buying behaviors as well since individuals strive not to miss out on any potential gains. Without alternative means to evaluate their abilities and opinions, individuals resort to social comparison with others, as proposed by social comparison theory (Festinger, 1954).

FOMO manifests in two dimensions related to impulsive and compulsive buying: continuous information seeking and a tendency to purchase for the best deals, even when the product is not an immediate necessity (Gabler et al., 2017). Online platforms, including social networks, offer full-price transparency and employ psychological tricks (e.g., limited availability, displaying the number of people viewing a product) to encourage consumers to buy at the lowest prices. In such cases, online purchases and consumption are intentionally influenced, leading to online shopping sprees (Wansink, 1994).

Sherman et al. (2016) suggest that messages from peers, such as posts showcasing newly purchased outfits, reduce cognitive control for the sake of social acceptance. Moreover, as the information processing theory suggests, in the context of preference fluency, people tend to prioritize information that is easier to process. Thus, an Instagram feed from family and friends becomes a trigger for impulsive and compulsive consumption, making interactions with loved ones along with social acceptance the primary causes of the dystopian environment created on oSNS (Cabral, 2011; Bright and Logan, 2018).

While FOMO may initially benefit brands, the resulting dystopia and consumer fatigue can cause individuals to abandon oSNS. Social media fatigue reduces consumers' mental energy to engage with branded content on oSNS (Cundari, 2015). Bright and Logan (2018) suggest that consumers initially subscribe to receive feeds from sites until navigating through daily content becomes burdensome. One solution could be implementing opt-in features on networks, allowing consumers to select which information, news, discounts, and special offers they receive, ensuring they do not miss out on anything important and processing only relevant information. By distributing content in manageable amounts and with careful frequency, oSNS can help satisfy consumers' information needs and reduce FOMO (Bright and Logan, 2018). Balancing the provision of up-to-date brand information and exclusive content to alleviate FOMO while avoiding social media fatigue presents a challenge for marketers. The discussion above leads to the following propositions;

Proposition 1. The pervasive influence of oSNS on consumers' FOMO exacerbates their compulsive consumption tendencies, leading to an overwhelming state of perpetual engagement.

Proposition 2. The carefully curated opt-in communities, providing concise yet tailored information and appropriately aligned advertisements adept at effectively alleviating consumer unease surrounding the FOMO on oSNS, staying in harmony with the customer and the brands, solve consumer discomfort regarding FOMO on oSNS.

Addictive Consumption, Peers, and Influencers

When used with self-control, online social networking sites (oSNS) can positively affect self-development. However, many of us struggle to maintain control over these platforms when we experience extreme flow and telepresence. Lin et al. (2019), in which they applied the uses and gratifications (U&G) theory to social media addiction, found that addictive behavior is associated with the gratifications sought from social media. Sands *et al.* (2020) stated that social media satisfies the need for affection and replaces attention from family and friends. It also serves as social compensation (Sands *et al.*, 2020). Particularly, young adults who feel lonely and seek reassurance, as a psychosocial factor, tend to spend more time on social media (Rom and Alfasi, 2014). As the time spent on social media increases, individuals receive more feedback, becoming aware of their worthiness in receiving attention and likes (Andangsari et al., 2013), which provides gratification. However, excessive social media consumption, whether in communication or gaming, isolates individuals from real life and disrupts natural social relations. This leads to unsatisfied desires and neglect of daily activities. Ultimately, social media becomes an escape from real-life problems and a tool for coping with negative emotions (Savci and Aysan, 2017), exacerbating the situation and resulting in addiction, a characteristic of dystopia. Additionally, as stated by Stimulus-Response Theory (SRT), certain environmental cues, such as feedback and likes, or triggers, such as social acceptance, can elicit strong desires, leading to repetitive and addictive consumption behaviors.

Social media addiction, including social media and social game addictions, is classified as a non-substance behavioral addiction and is considered a disorder (Kuss and Griffiths, 2011). Specifically, regarding social media, individuals' urgency to track their presence on the platform and engage in profile stalking are indicators of addiction (Sheth, 2018). Andreassen and Pallesen (2014, p. 4054) define oSNS addiction as "being overly concerned about social networks, driven by a strong motivation to log on to or use the network and to devote so much time and effort to it so that it impairs other social activities, studies/job, interpersonal relationships and/or psychological health and well-being." As dystopia calls for, individuals become dehumanized and dependent on oSNS. Addiction brings several disadvantages, such as salience (social media dominates users' behaviors), withdrawal (negative emotions when away from social media), conflict (social networking conflicts with other tasks), reinstatements, and relapse (inability to reduce social network use), tolerance (increased use for the thrill), and mood modification (mood changes through relief and thrill) (Turel et al., 2011).

The ubiquity of social media, its prevalence, and the potential for personalized marketing enable marketers to target addictive users, whose behavior is primarily driven by endorsements from influencers, celebrities, micro-celebrities, and virtual peers (Sherman et al., 2016). Sherman et al. (2016) demonstrated that when peers endorse promotional messages, users' cognitive controls are reduced, and they are driven by instant gratification to gain social acceptance within their peer group. They also noted that such users are prone to engage in compulsive buying. As stated by the Compulsive Buying Theory (CBT), compulsive buying behavior results in addictive consumption because of the individuals' need to cope with negative emotions, fill an emotional void, and seek pleasure.

According to a study by Sultan (2021), as users are more inclined to keep up with social media, they are more likely to develop social media addiction and have a greater tendency to self-disclose. As the strong inclination towards social media consumption triggers addiction, it also leads to impulsive and compulsive buying and self-disclosure, resulting in conspicuous consumption.

Marketing companies are aware of oSNS addiction and sometimes even encourage buying through influencers and micro-celebrities. For the well-being of the public, social media marketers have a responsibility to consider the broader impacts of their promotional strategies and take protective actions against companies that disseminate potentially addictive marketing content through influencers or micro-celebrities. Unless preventive actions are taken by social network owners, users susceptible to addiction become easy targets (Gainsbury et al., 2016) for marketers promoting cigarettes, alcohol, gambling, and even certain drugs on social media.

The discussion leads to the following proposition:

Proposition 3. The pervasive fear of missing out (FOMO) relentlessly fuels an addictive cycle of consumption within the realm of social media.

Proposition 4. The addictive consumption patterns established through prolonged exposure to social media platforms precipitate impulsive and compulsive buying behaviors.

Proposition 5. The act of self-disclosure on social media platforms serves as a catalyst for conspicuous consumption as individuals are propelled towards showcasing material possessions and engaging in extravagant consumption patterns to bolster their public image and gain social validation within the digital realm.

Value Co-Destruction

The service-dominant (S-D) logic emphasizes the co-creation of value through collaborative efforts between consumers and companies (Vargo and Lusch, 2008). Fournier and Avery (2011) assert that brands, to a significant extent, emerge as a result of conversations among consumers in social networks, where various stakeholders engage in negotiation. In the realm of oSNS, branding takes on an open-source nature (Fournier and Avery, 2011), with the co-construction of brands seen as narratives contributed by multiple individuals, each sharing their unique stories (Gensler et al., 2013).

This collective wisdom also gives rise to the phenomenon of value co-destruction. Plé and Chumpitaz Cáceres (2010) define value co-destruction as "an interactional process between service systems that results in a decline in at least one of the system's well-being" (p. 431). These systems can be individuals, brands, or organizations (Lund et al., 2020). Drawing on practice theory, Echeverri and Skalen (2011) propose that value co-destruction occurs when incongruent elements within practices clash (p. 368). In the context of brands, such incongruent elements manifest when two or more participants combine their resources to undermine or destroy brand value (Vafeas et al., 2016). Applied to the consumer market, misbehavior during online interactions, such as through negative product reviews or inadequate information, can create a dystopian environment (Vafeas et al., 2016). For example, users posting negative reviews on a company's oSNS page can harm the brand and disrupt the established order, aligning with the notion of dystopia. Likewise, consumers utilizing a social media brand page to share information about a competitor's deal can erode brand value or lead to "brand value diminution" (Lund et al., 2020, p. 1508).

It is evident that co-destruction arises from consumer empowerment through user-generated content (UGC) within oSNS. Despite its numerous benefits, UGC also exposes firms to risks as they relinquish control to the crowd. Moreover, individuals within the crowd, acting as powerful actors, share their brand stories, which can sometimes be intentionally or inadvertently unfavorable. Each participant becomes an instrument of destruction through negative comments, likes, shares, and conversational trails. Once the destructive process commences, it possesses the significant potential to influence others (Gatzweiler et al., 2017), resulting in a spiral of negativity (Nam et al., 2020). Destructive content may expose the brand to reputational risks (Gatzweiler et al., 2017). On the other hand, UGC can also facilitate value co-creation, which can coexist with value co-destruction within interactions (Plé and Chumpitaz Cáceres, 2010). For instance, a consumer sharing unfavorable information about a brand to enlighten other consumers and guide their purchasing decisions can harm the vendor but create value for other consumers (Plé and Chumpitaz Cáceres, 2010). This implies that co-destruction is not always intentional but can occur unintentionally (Plé and Chumpitaz Cáceres, 2010).

While digital marketers heavily rely on social media users to spread the word and promote their brand, it is crucial to recognize that the potential for co-destruction within oSNS poses a fundamental threat to branding efforts, directly impacting brand performance and viability. When co-destruction is set in motion, there is often limited recourse available. Therefore;

Proposition 6. Value co-destruction of a brand primarily occurs due to inadequate information and the widespread practice of incongruent elements on oSNS platforms, exacerbating its negative impact.

Proposition 7: Value co-destruction can be effectively mitigated by consistently supplying carefully crafted and accurate information about the brand's value to consumers on oSNS platforms, thereby fostering positive brand experiences and reducing the likelihood of detrimental effects.

Deceptive Advertising

Stimulating sales through deceptive advertisements on oSNS represents an unethical strategy employed by businesses to artificially boost product demand (Ukaegbu, 2020). This dystopian phenomenon, instigated by companies, engenders consumer misconduct and significantly influences the digital consumer buying process through the dissemination of misleading information. Misleading advertisements manifest in various forms, such as manipulated information content, presentation, and generation (Xiao and Benbasat, 2011), as well as inaccurate post-purchase brand use feedback (Aftab et al., 2020).

Pointed out by information manipulation theory (IMT), when lying to others, people play with or manipulate pertinent information in a variety of ways throughout their discourse. An undisclosed advertisement becomes deceptive when it becomes indistinguishable for a reasonable consumer to discern between unbiased information and meticulously crafted advertising (Gottfried, 2015). Deceptive advertising, as defined by Carson et al. (1985), encompasses disseminating disinformation that distorts consumers' beliefs about the advertised product. It fabricates an illusory world, captivating consumers' minds with fantastical notions about the product's quality and features (Clow and Baack, 2007). However, when confronted with the truth, the idealized image of the company shatters.

Research indicates that consumers who discover they have been deceived are inclined to sever ties with the brands, even those to which they were previously loyal, and engage in negative word-of-mouth, which can significantly damage a business's reputation (Nuseir, 2018; Modi and Sharma, 2021). Furthermore, consumers will likely switch to competing brands (Modi and Sharma, 2021). Moreover, a consumer who loses faith in advertisements becomes distrustful of even genuine ones in the same context, rendering them more susceptible to future deceptive advertising (Modi and Sharma, 2021; Pollay, 1986). Tragically, this mistrust stemming from deceptive advertisements creates a negative bias that extends to unrelated advertisements through defensive processing (Darke and Ritchie, 2007). Once consumers feel deceived, they lose trust in advertisers and carry this skepticism to other advertisements, suspecting unethical activities by various entities on oSNS. The persuasion knowledge model contends that as consumers learn, they develop awareness and knowledge of persuasive strategies employed by advertisers, and it affects their responses to advertisements and their ability to detect deception. Thus, deception proves detrimental to both consumers and companies.

If deceptive advertising on oSNS affects innocent retailers through the carryover effect, it becomes essential to prevent distrust and negative carryover toward other advertisements. Potential solutions include implementing strict regulations enforced by oSNS owners (Baccarella *et al.*, 2020), encouraging self-regulation among advertisers (Darke et al., 2010), providing explanations and apologies (Darke and Ritchie, 2007), and adopting a consumer-based approach by training consumers to identify deceptive tactics (Wilson et al., 2021). Furthermore, according to media richness theory, individuals exhibit higher accuracy in detecting deception in media formats that incorporate nonverbal cues (Daft and Lengel, 1986). By acquiring persuasion knowledge, learning effective resistance strategies, and penalizing misleading tactics, consumers can differentiate between genuine and fake advertisements (Eisend and Tarrahi, 2022).

Analytical tools with straightforward procedures can also aid in detecting deceptive advertising (Barbour and Gardner, 1982). While these solutions help uncover the detrimental effects of deception, they extend beyond the scope of innocent advertisers. To safeguard the innocent, customers can be encouraged to write reviews about products/services on oSNS and provide star ratings, thereby benefiting others. As reviews and ratings accumulate, the credibility of deceptive advertisements diminishes, as others have already compared the product's actual performance with the claims in the advertisement. Therefore, it is proposed that:

Proposition 8. Deceptive advertisement not only undermines consumer trust but also fosters a pervasive and deep-rooted negative bias towards all advertisements, regardless of their accuracy, relevance, and genuine intent.

Proposition 9. Strategically designed and executed ethical advertisements with compelling multimedia content serve as a potent source of competitive advantage while cultivating unwavering consumer loyalty.

Fabricated Stories and Fake Reviews

Once brands enter the realm of social media, consumers gain the power to reshape the narratives surrounding those brands to align with their own preferences (Kohli et al., 2015). Over time, these consumer-generated stories intertwine with the brand's identity, potentially distorting the brand's original image in a falsely positive or negative direction (Scarles, 2009). This fabrication of stories gives rise to a problem: the emergence of "pseudo-news" (Baccarella et al., 2018, p.435), which appears factually accurate but lacks a basis in truth. Pseudo-news takes the form of intentionally fabricated information (disinformation) or unintentional misrepresentation (misinformation) (Hannah et al., 2015), both of which create a distorted reality and disrupt the established order, leading to a dystopian environment.

One common manifestation of fabricated stories is the proliferation of fake brand reviews. As stated by information manipulation theory (McCornack, 1992), individuals or organizations manipulate information for their own benefit to shape perceptions, influence attitudes, and ultimately affect consumer behavior. On oSNS, individuals, competing merchants, or even visitors to collaborative review platforms may disseminate sensationalized negative reviews to undermine a brand's value (Wu et al., 2020).

Falsified reviews are not always negative; they can also be positive (Luca and Zervas, 2016), crafted to enhance a brand's reputation or promote it within the oSNS community. Regardless of their sentiment, fake reviews mislead consumers in their purchasing decisions, thereby impacting a company's sales figures, even its stock value (Zhuang et al., 2018). For instance, the New Balance company was falsely associated with being "the official brand of the Trump revolution" on social media, leading to opposition supporters burning their New Balance shoes (Gupta, 2016).

Fake reviews, regardless of their polarity, erode the information value, trustworthiness, and quality of online product reviews. They undermine the credibility and helpfulness of reviews, creating an information imbalance between merchants and customers. To safeguard the value of brands from diminishing, it is crucial to understand the underlying motivations driving the posting of fake reviews. Thakur et al. (2018) define these motivations as the pursuit of social status, the need for attention from customers, self-proclaimed brand managers, and disgruntled customers, all driven by the pursuit of rewards.

Distinguishing fake reviews from genuine ones relies on analyzing micro-linguistic characteristics, including constructs such as comprehensibility, exaggeration, negligence, and specificity (Banerjee and Chua, 2017). Additionally, various features such as structure and format, personal pronoun usage, information orientation, lexical richness, etc. contribute to identifying fake reviews, encompassing aspects of informativeness, readability, and subjectivity (Banerjee and Chua, 2017). Leveraging sophisticated IT design features, such as artificial intelligence (AI), can aid in reducing the visibility of fake reviews and detecting them before they gain widespread publicity. Therefore;

Proposition 10. Individuals actively engage in fabricating stories and posting fake reviews on oSNS platforms, driven by a diverse range of psychological motives.

Proposition 11. The way of presentation and distinct characteristics of fabricated stories and fake reviews enable both consumers and marketers to discern them from authentic ones, facilitating the identification and mitigation of misleading information on oSNS platforms, and empowering users to make more informed decisions based on genuine feedback.

Cyberbullying

Besides all merits of oSNS, they are the perfect mediums for the evil regarding bullying in the cyber world. The dystopian environment is mainly created by dehumanizing (Surry and Farquhar, 1997) the other side by bullying.

The malicious irrationally disturbs the system and causes chaos. As a combination of definitions, cyberbullying, in the literature, can be set as the use of technological means to threaten, hurt, insult, harm, or abuse others, "with two criteria: repetition – the hurtful behavior happens more than once, and power imbalance - it is difficult for the victim to defend himself or herself" (Smith, 2014; p.12; Juvonen and Gross, 2008; Slonje, Smith, and Frisén, 2013). It is a multi-dimensional construct including *harassment* -sending repeated offensive or malicious messages to an individual on oSNS-, *flaming* – online fight through emails, messaging, or social media accounts-, *exclusion* – intentionally leaving a person out of the group or ignoring the person-, *outing* -posting of private, sensitive or embarrassing information about someone without consent on oSNS-, *masquerading* -use of a fake identity to harass someone on a social network-, *frapping* -impersonating someone by logging into his/her social media account-, *trickery* -sharing a secret or embarrassing information on oSNS to gain the trust of others-, *trolling* – provoking a response by assaulting the other person on oSNS- and *catfishing* -stealing someone's identity to create a profile on oSNS for deceiving others- (Willard, 2007; Karspersky Lab, 2018; Kansara and Shekokar, 2015; Hassan et al., 2018). Any unwelcome advertisement or insulting or threatening messages sent to the individual's account and expressing support for the harasser on oSNS are considered as cyberbullying (Hang and Dahlan, 2019). In summary, it could be anything that is unwanted and harmful online interactions that make the person feel embarrassed or unsafe (McHugh et al., 2018).

Cyberbullying can occur via advertisement and text message on (e.g.) Facebook, Twitter, Instagram, or Snapchat; or via advertisement, picture, and video clip on (e.g.) YouTube, Pinterest, and Instagram, or in chat rooms on any website that the conversational trail is the aim; or through advertisement and instant messaging on (e.g.) Instagram and WhatsApp (Smith, Görzig, and Robinson, 2018). Any unwanted and/or irritating repetitive commercial advertisements (e.g., porn site advertisements to the teens) displayed to the person are cyberbullying. For example, the 'happy slapping'[1] fad around 2005 has been said to spread from advertisements. It is the anonymity of the oSNS users that puts the person (especially the teens) at risk for cyberbullying and, at the same time, protects the bullies (Barlett et al., 2016).

Other than educating the participants, which is the method that many colleagues in the literature propose, there are some precautions that the social media owner could take to prevent cyberbullying. First of all, it should be noted that one of the main reasons for cyberbullying on oSNS is the imbalance between the victim and the perpetrator through deindividualization and perceived accountability (Lowry,

Moody, and Chatterjee, 2017). There is evidence that the technology of the oSNS that is appropriately designed can inhibit and even prevent cyberbullying on the media (Lowry et al., 2013; Lowry, Moody, and Chatterjee, 2017). If it is possible through IT, and it seems so, by diminishing the power imbalance on oSNS, cyberbullying intention could be reduced, if not fully prevented.

As proposed by Lowry, Moody, and Chatterjee (2017, p.870), there are four IT artifacts that the social network owners must consider during IT design: "*monitoring awareness*-- recognition that one's activities are being tracked (Vance, Lowry, and Egget, 2015) -, *evaluation awareness*-- the users' knowledge that their actions are being logged and reviewed (Trinkle et al., 2014) -, *social presence awareness*-- the degree (to) which a person (is) perceived as real (Lambropoulos, Faulkner, and Culwin, 2012) -, and *identifiability* -the degree to which others know a person's online interactions (Lowry, Moody, and Galetta, 2013)-". It is also possible through technology to control the audience of the advertisements. In short, for a social network user, the ability to identify others as human beings, not as a part of the technology or an avatar, would help social network owners to lower their engagement in deviant activities. Therefore, informing the participants that these four factors are present in the network could be the first step in preventing cyberbullying.

Proposition 12. The dystopian environment created by a bully on oSNS can be discouraged/reduced by presenting to the participants the precautions taken (i.e., threatening) and making them aware that there is a human being on the other side through featured social network IT designs.

THEORETICAL AND PRACTICAL IMPLICATIONS

Implications for Theory and Agenda for Future Research

A report by European Commission (2018) recommended taking a multi-dimensional approach when responding to dark phenomena of social media. The report points out the complexity of these issues and suggests finding the answers to counteract unfavorable developments. In this study, the primary goal was to display the complexity to lead to an understanding of how social media can create undesirable outcomes in marketing.

To improve our understanding of the possible dark sides of social media, I identify, at the core level, how social media company owners, consumers, and companies that operate on social media contribute to the dystopian environment. Thus, the first contribution of this paper is to conceptualize the basic inclusions of the three parties that cause the darkness in oSNS. Although many can be counted among the bright and dark sides of oSNS, there are still limited studies. This study contributes to the literature by defining possible dark areas of oSNS to draw the attention of marketing academics to this crucial area for future studies.

To the best of my knowledge, it is the first time in the literature that the dark side of oSNS is examined from a marketing point of view. While this study contributes to extant theory, several areas deserve further attention in future research on the dark sides of oSNS. Future research agenda is as follows:

Addictive Consumption: Effect of Peers, Influencers, and Micro-Celebrities

- Inspecting the influence of others (e.g., peers, micro-celebrities, influencers) on creating the darkness.
- The ways to harness the power of consumers, content, micro-celebrities, and influencers to educate the consumers about the possibility of the negative effects of oSNS.
- Longitudinal studies to examine the long-term effects of peer influence, influencers, and micro-celebrities on addictive consumption behaviors.
- Exploring the underlying psychological, social, and cognitive mechanisms that mediate the influence of peers, influencers, and micro-celebrities.
- Investigating the potential harms associated with excessive and compulsive consumption behaviors driven by social influence.
- Evaluating intervention strategies (e.g., digital well-being tools, personalized feedback) aimed at addressing the dark side of addictive consumption through oSNS.

FOMO, Value Co-Destruction Through User-Generated Content (UGC)

- Looking into consumer buying habits and their relationship with the dark oSNS.
- Investigating the ways that the UGC contributes to the brand value co-destruction.
- Examining the possible ways to prevent value co-destruction on oSNS.
- Understanding how FOMO drives individuals towards excessive and compulsive engagement with social media platforms
- Examining negative effects caused by FOMO and value co-destruction through UGC on interpersonal relationships.
- Investigating the role of social network algorithms in exacerbating FOMO and value co-destruction.
- Conducting longitudinal studies on the effectiveness of interventions aimed at reducing FOMO and promoting healthier social media use.

Deceptive Advertising

- Exploring the effects of deceptive advertisements on consumer behavior and decision-making processes.
- Developing and evaluating strategies -through algorithms and artificial intelligence- to detect and prevent deceptive advertising on oSNS.
- Finding new ways, other than technical, that distinguish deceptive advertisements from genuine ones with the insight of marketers.
- Examining the psychological, cognitive, and emotional aspects that contribute to individuals' susceptibility to manipulation and deception.

- Investigating the effect of deception/disinformation/misinformation on consumers when the information comes from a trustworthy person on oSNS.
- Investigating the measures taken by platforms and marketers to detect, prevent, and mitigate falsified claims in deceptive advertisement practices.
- Examine the consequences of deceptive advertising for brand reputation and trust.
- Understanding the long-term effects of deceptive advertising on brand trust, loyalty, and customer relationships on oSNS.
- Investigating the use of dark patterns and manipulative design techniques in deceptive advertising on oSNS.
- Longitudinal studies to assess the long-term effects of exposure to deceptive advertising on oSNS.

Fabricated Stories and Fake Reviews

- Identifying the effect of fabricated stories and fake news on oSNS on consumer buying behavior.
- Investigating the motivations and underlying factors that drive individuals or groups to create and spread fabricated stories and fake reviews on oSNS.
- Investigating how these deceptive practices influence consumers' attitudes, beliefs, perceptions, and purchase decisions.
- Examining the effect of consumers' realization of fabricated stories and fake news on brand value diminution and brand reputation.
- Understanding how users perceive and respond to fabricated stories and fake reviews on social networks.
- Investigating the ways for consumers to identify and mitigate deceptive information and fake reviews.
- Exploring the use of artificial intelligence, natural language processing, and machine learning approaches to automatically identify suspicious content and distinguish it from genuine user-generated content.
- Examining the extent that the marketers can reduce the competing deceptive claims.

Cyberbullying

- Identifying the possible ways the participants can harm, insult, embarrass or abuse others on oSNS.
- Scrutinizing the contribution of each entity to the harm given to the vulnerable and influence on security and privacy on oSNS.
- Examining how preventive it is -regarding cyberbullying- to make the bully aware that there is a human being on the other side.

Others

- The contribution of platform characteristics to the dark side of the oSNS.
- Examining practical intervention activities to the harm given by the evil on oSNS.
- Identifying the emerging issues and concepts associated with the darkness on oSNS.
- Emerging issues that create new and more darkness on oSNS are caused by a dystopian environment.
- How to map a customer journey that keeps the customer away from the dark concepts on oSNS.
- Looking into the ways to develop metrics and scales for marketers to measure the dark sides of oSNS.
- How can newly developed technologies (e.g., AI-powered analysis tools) help us to detect and prevent unethical behaviors on oSNS
- Development of theories and models that can help to understand darkness on oSNS.

Implications for Practitioners

In previous studies and existing theories, scholars have focused on identifying various psycho-social effects associated with social media use (Salo et al., 2018). However, the specific marketing-induced consequences at the individual level remain largely unexplored (Salo et al., 2018). These negative outcomes can arise from the inherent characteristics of oSNS platforms and user activities. Consequently, practitioners such as platform owners and service designers face a significant challenge in identifying technological artifacts that can mitigate the emergence of a dystopic environment on oSNS.

Providing ethical and effective treatment to customers confers a competitive advantage upon firms (Aftab et al., 2020). Such practices contribute to the establishment and maintenance of a positive brand image and reputation in the minds of target markets, preventing customers from forming unrealistic expectations about product performance. Unethical behaviors, such as deceptive advertisements based on false claims or the dissemination of fabricated stories, can lead customers to discontinue product usage when their actual experiences fail to align with the promised benefits.

These propositions hold particular relevance for marketing professionals operating on oSNS platforms, as they need to comprehend and monitor potential consequences at the individual consumer level. They are also instrumental in guiding efforts within social media communities to minimize negative outcomes. Drawing inspiration from the honeycomb framework introduced by Kietzmann et al. (2011), Figure 1 illustrates the contributions of various stakeholders to the darker aspects of online social networking. This framework serves as a valuable tool for understanding and analyzing the causes and repercussions of the dark side within the oSNS landscape. Consequently, it lays the foundation for developing strategies that promote responsible, effective, trustworthy, and secure utilization and consumption of oSNS. Further academic research is necessary to assist practitioners in comprehending potential risks and devising measures to counteract them, ultimately transforming oSNS into reliable, honest, and impactful marketing platforms.

Figure 1. Comparing and contrasting the contributions of oSNS owner, oSNS user and collaborative company to the dark sides of oSNS

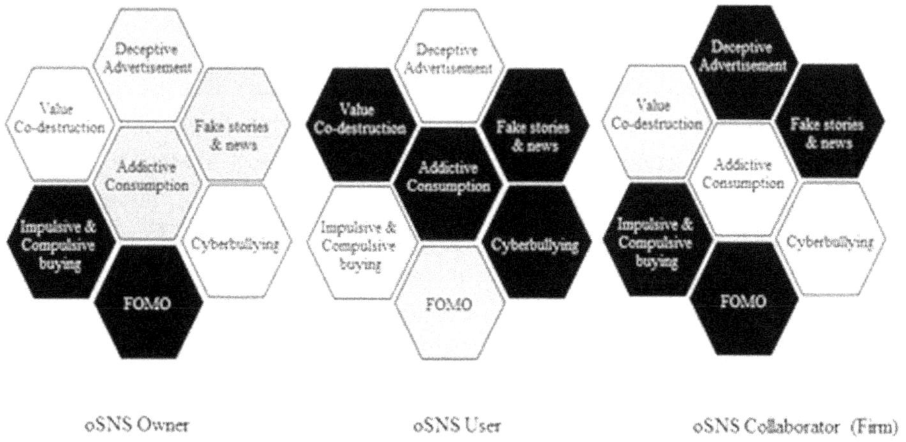

As put forward by the European Commission (EC) in 2018, the precautions to be taken are multi-dimensional. They can also guide marketing practitioners while they are forming their strategies. According to the report and the statements of this study, practitioners' efforts should be directed to;

The European Commission (EC) outlined comprehensive measures in 2018 to address the multifaceted challenges associated with the dark side of oSNS. Based on the report and the findings of this study, practitioners should focus their efforts on the following:

- enhance and encourage the transparency of the news shared and advertisements displayed on the oSNS, as they involve adequate data (EC, 2018)
- promote information literacy so that the individual consumer can recognize and counteract misinformation and disinformation (EC, 2018)
- encourage research on indicators and promote measures that can be implemented by oSNS owners to combat deceptive advertising and disinformation (EC, 2018)
- safeguard the presence of the brands on social media and take proactive steps to prevent value co-destruction caused by malicious actors.

In addition, oSNS stakeholders should adopt a collaborative approach, considering both the well-being of individual consumers and the long-term sustainability of the ecosystem. By applying knowledge and taking precautions against social toxins, the dystopian environment created by the dark aspects of oSNS can be effectively mitigated.

LIMITATIONS AND CONCLUSION

In conclusion, as researchers and practitioners of marketing, we still need to figure out the negative consequences that social media consumption brings about. There are ways to understand the cultural, societal, and consumer-related influences of the dark side of oSNS and the marketers that use these conceptions. The detrimental aspects of social media predominantly target vulnerable consumers, particularly young individuals. Thus, it is crucial to develop strategies for recognizing and mitigating unintentional or intentional dark marketing strategies on oSNS. This study is one of the first to describe the possible dark sides of oSNS that can lead to deception and consumer misbehavior, laying the groundwork for further investigation. Future studies can expand upon the concepts explored in this research, introduce new insights, or delve into different aspects of the phenomenon. Furthermore, the honeycomb framework can serve as a valuable tool for marketing practitioners and researchers, providing a multidimensional perspective for the development of related theories and models.

The implications advance research on the dark side of social media by identifying the multi-constructs and relating these to dystopia. The research is limited because it only pursues the marketing approach but does not dwell on the sociological or psychological constructs.

REFERENCES

Aftab, S., Mustafa, M. B., & Naqeeb, M. U. (2020). Impact of Unethical Advertisement and Brand Consumption on Consumer Buying Behavior *(p.30-53)*. *InTraders 2019: Academic studies in social, human and administrative sciences*. In Traders publishing. Hiper Yayın. İstanbul

Aghakhani, H., & Main, K. J. (2019). Can two negatives make a positive? Social exclusion prevents carryover effects from deceptive advertising. *Journal of Retailing and Consumer Services*, 47, 206–214. 10.1016/j.jretconser.2018.11.021

Andangsari, E., Gumilar, I., & Godwin, R. (2013). Social networking sites uses and psychological attachment need among Indonesian young adults population. *International Journal of Social Science Studies*, 1(2), 133–138. 10.11114/ijsss.v1i2.66

Andreassen, C. S., & Pallesen, S. (2014). Social network site addiction-an overview. *Current Pharmaceutical Design*, 20(25), 4053–4061. 10.2174/13816128113199990616240001298

Baccarella, C. V., Wagner, T. F., Kietzmann, J. H., & McCarthy, I. P. (2018). Social media? It's serious! Understanding the dark side of social media. *European Management Journal*, 36(4), 431–438. 10.1016/j.emj.2018.07.002

Banerjee, S., & Chua, A. Y. (2017). Theorizing the textual differences between authentic and fictitious reviews: Validation across positive, negative and moderate polarities. *Internet Research*, 27(2), 321–337. 10.1108/IntR-11-2015-0309

Barbour, F. L.II, & Gardner, D. (1982). Deceptive advertising: A practical approach to measurement. *Journal of Advertising*, 11(1), 21–30. 10.1080/00913367.1982.10672791

Barlett, C. P., Gentile, D. A., & Chew, C. (2016). Predicting cyberbullying from anonymity. *Psychology of Popular Media Culture*, 5(2), 171–180. 10.1037/ppm0000055

Block, J. J. (2008). Issues for DSM-V: Internet Addiction. *The American Journal of Psychiatry*, 165(3), 306–307. 10.1176/appi.ajp.2007.07101556183164277

Bright, L. F., & Logan, K. (2018). Is my fear of missing out (FOMO) causing fatigue? Advertising, social media fatigue, and the implications for consumers and brands. *Internet Research*, 28(5), 1213–1227. 10.1108/IntR-03-2017-0112

Cabral, J. (2011). Is generation Y addicted to social media? *The Elon Journal of Undergraduate Research in Communications*, 2(1), 5–14.

Carson, T. L., Wokutch, R. E., & Cox, J. E.Jr. (1985). An ethical analysis of deception in advertising. *Journal of Business Ethics*, 4(2), 93–104. 10.1007/BF00383562

Chan, T. K., Cheung, C. M., & Lee, Z. W. (2021). Cyberbullying on social networking sites: A literature review and future research directions. *Information & Management*, 58(2), 103411. 10.1016/j.im.2020.103411

Chatterjee, S., Goyal, D., Prakash, A., & Sharma, J. (2021). Exploring healthcare/health-product ecommerce satisfaction: A text mining and machine learning application. *Journal of Business Research*, 131, 815–825. 10.1016/j.jbusres.2020.10.043

Clow, K. E., & Baack, D. (Eds.). (2007). *Advertising design: Theoretical frameworks and types of appeals. In integrated advertising, promotion, and marketing communications* (3rd ed., pp. 171–186). Prentice Hall of India Pvt. Ltd.

Cundari, A. (2015). *Customer-Centric Marketing: Build Relationships, Create Advocates, and Influence your Consumers*. Amazon Digital Services, LLC. 10.1002/9781119154785

Daft, R. L., & Lengel, R. H. (1986). Organizational information requirements, media richness and structural design. *Management Science*, 32(5), 554–571. 10.1287/mnsc.32.5.554

Darke, P. R., Ashworth, L., & Main, K. J. (2010). Great expectations and broken promises: Misleading claims, product failure, expectancy disconfirmation and consumer distrust. *Journal of the Academy of Marketing Science*, 38(3), 347–362. 10.1007/s11747-009-0168-7

Darke, P. R., & Ritchie, R. J. (2007). The defensive consumer: Advertising deception, defensive processing, and distrust. *JMR, Journal of Marketing Research*, 44(1), 114–127. 10.1509/jmkr.44.1.114

Dima-Laza, S. (2012). Utopia versus dystopia—a perfect environment for a perfect existence. *2012 International Conference on Humanity, History and Society IPEDR*. IACSIT Press.

Duman, H., & Ozkara, B. Y. (2021). The impact of social identity on online game addiction: The mediating role of the fear of missing out (FoMO) and the moderating role of the need to belong. *Current Psychology (New Brunswick, N.J.)*, 40(9), 4571–4580. 10.1007/s12144-019-00392-w

Echeverri, P., & Skå°l'en, P. (2011). Co-Creation and Co-Destruction: A Practice-Theory Based Study of Interactive Value Formation. *Marketing Theory*, 11(3), 351–373. 10.1177/1470593111408181

Eisend, M., & Tarrahi, F. (2022). Persuasion knowledge in the marketplace: A meta-analysis. *Journal of Consumer Psychology*, 32(1), 3–22. 10.1002/jcpy.1258

Eroglu, Y. (2015). Interrelationship between attachment styles and Facebook addiction. *Journal of Education and Training Studies*, 4(1), 150–160. 10.11114/jets.v4i1.1081

European Commission. (2018). *Final report of the high level expert group on fake news and online disinformation*. EC. https://ec.europa.eu/digital-singlemarket/en/news/final-report-high-level-expert-group-fake-news-and-onlinedisinformation

Festinger, L. (1954). A theory of social comparison processes. *Human Relations*, 7(2), 117–140. 10.1177/001872675400700202

Fournier, S., & Avery, J. (2011). The uninvited brand. *Business Horizons*, 54(3), 193–207. 10.1016/j.bushor.2011.01.001

Gabler, C. B., Landers, V. M., & Reynolds, K. E. (2017). Purchase decision regret: Negative consequences of the steadily increasing discount strategy. *Journal of Business Research*, 76, 201–208. 10.1016/j.jbusres.2017.01.002

Gainsbury, S. M., King, D. L., Russell, A. M., Delfabbro, P., Derevensk, J., & Hing, N. (2016). Exposure to and Engagement with Gambling Marketing in Social Media: Reported Impacts on Moderate-Risk and Problem Gamblers. *Psychology of Addictive Behaviors*, 30(2), 270–276. 10.1037/adb000015626828642

Gatzweiler, A., Blazevic, V., & Piller, F. T. (2017). Dark side or bright light: Destructive and constructive deviant content in consumer ideation contests. *Journal of Product Innovation Management*, 34(6), 772–789. 10.1111/jpim.12369

Gensler, S., Völckner, F., Liu-Thompkins, Y., & Wiertz, C. (2013). Managing brands in the social media environment. *Journal of Interactive Marketing*, 27(4), 242–256. 10.1016/j.intmar.2013.09.004

Gottfried, R. A. (2015). Six ways this article is most definitely not an ad: Deceptive marketing and the need for clearly-defined disclosure rules in online native advertisement. *Loyola Consumer Law Review*, 27(3), 399–422.

Gupta, S. (2016). Trump supporters call to boycott Pepsi over comments the CEO never made. *CNN Money*. https://money.cnn.com/2016/11/16/news/companies/pepsi-fake-news-boycott-trump

Hang, O. C., & Dahlan, H. M. (2019, December). Cyberbullying lexicon for social media. In *2019 6th International Conference on Research and Innovation in Information Systems (ICRIIS)* (pp. 1-6). IEEE. 10.1109/ICRIIS48246.2019.9073679

Hannah, D. R., McCarthy, I. P., & Kietzmann, J. (2015). We're leaking, and everything's fine: How and why companies deliberately leak secrets. *Business Horizons*, 58(6), 659–667. 10.1016/j.bushor.2015.07.003

Harrigan, P., Coussement, K., Lancelot Miltgen, C., & Ranaweera, C. (2020). The future of technology in marketing; utopia or dystopia? *Journal of Marketing Management*, 36(3-4), 211–215. 10.1080/0267257X.2020.1744382

Hassan, S., Yacob, M. I., Nguyen, T., & Zambri, S. (2018). *Social media influencer and cyberbullying: A lesson learned from preliminary findings. Knowledge Management International Conference (KMICe)*, Miri Sarawak, Malaysia

Heth, J. N. (2018). How social media will impact marketing media. In *Social media marketing* (pp. 3-18). Palgrave Macmillan, Singapore.

Holden, C. (2001). 'Behavioral' addictions: Do they exist? *Science*, 294(5544), 980–982. 10.1126/science.294.5544.98011691967

Jameson, F. (1979). Reification and utopia in mass culture. *Social Text*, (1), 130–148. 10.2307/466409

Järvi, H., Kähkönen, A. K., & Torvinen, H. (2018). When value co-creation fails: Reasons that lead to value co-destruction. *Scandinavian Journal of Management*, 34(1), 63–77. 10.1016/j.scaman.2018.01.002

Juvonen, J., & Gross, E. F. (2008). Extending the school grounds?—Bullying experiences in cyberspace. *The Journal of School Health*, 78(9), 496–505. 10.1111/j.1746-1561.2008.00335.x18786042

Kansara, K. B., & Shekokar, N. M. (2015). A framework for cyberbullying detection in social network. *International Journal of Current Engineering and Technology*, 5(1), 494–498.

Karspersky Lab. (2018). *10 Forms of Cyberbullying*. https://kids.kaspersky.com/10-forms-of-cyberbullying/ (Accessed 17 April 2022)

Kietzmann, J. H., Hermkens, K., McCarthy, I. P., & Silvestre, B. S. (2011). Social media? Get serious! Understanding the functional building blocks of social media. *Business Horizons*, 54(3), 241–251. 10.1016/j.bushor.2011.01.005

Kohli, C., Suri, R., & Kapoor, A. (2015). Will social media kill branding? *Business Horizons*, 58(1), 35–44. 10.1016/j.bushor.2014.08.004

Kozinets, R. V., Sherry, J. F., DeBerry-Spence, B., Duhachek, A., Nuttavuthisit, K., & Storm, D. (2002). Themed flagship brand stores in the new millennium: Theory, practice, prospects. *Journal of Retailing*, 78(1), 17–29. 10.1016/S0022-4359(01)00063-X

Kuss, D. J., & Griffiths, M. D. (2011). Online social networking and addiction—A review of the psychological literature. *International Journal of Environmental Research and Public Health*, 8(9), 3528–3552. 10.3390/ijerph809352822016701

Lambropoulos, N., Faulkner, X., & Culwin, F. (2012). Supporting social awareness in collaborative e-learning. *British Journal of Educational Technology*, 43(2), 295–306. 10.1111/j.1467-8535.2011.01184.x

Lin, W. S., Chen, H. R., Lee, T. S. H., & Feng, J. Y. (2019). Role of social anxiety on high engagement and addictive behavior in the context of social networking sites. *Data Technologies and Applications*, 53(2), 156–170. 10.1108/DTA-09-2018-0076

Liu, Q., & Zhang, F. (2019). Study on the Influencing Factors of Mobile Users' Impulse Purchase Behavior in a Large Online Promotion Activity. [JECO]. *Journal of Electronic Commerce in Organizations*, 17(2), 88–101. 10.4018/JECO.2019040108

Lowry, P. B., Moody, G. D., & Chatterjee, S. (2017). Using IT design to prevent cyberbullying. *Journal of Management Information Systems*, 34(3), 863–901. 10.1080/07421222.2017.1373012

Lowry, P. B., Moody, G. D., Galletta, D. F., & Vance, A. (2013). The drivers in the use of online whistle-blowing reporting systems. *Journal of Management Information Systems*, 30(1), 153–190. 10.2753/MIS0742-1222300105

Luca, M., & Zervas, G. (2016). Fake it till you make it: Reputation, competition, and Yelp review fraud. *Management Science*, 62(12), 3412–3427. 10.1287/mnsc.2015.2304

Lund, N. F., Scarles, C., & Cohen, S. A. (2020). The brand value continuum: Countering co-destruction of destination branding in social media through storytelling. *Journal of Travel Research*, 59(8), 1506–1521. 10.1177/0047287519887234

Maclaran, P., & Brown, S. (2005). The center cannot hold: Consuming the utopian marketplace. *The Journal of Consumer Research*, 32(2), 311–323. 10.1086/432240

McHugh, B. C., Wisniewski, P., Rosson, M. B., & Carroll, J. M. (2018). When social media traumatizes teens: The roles of online risk exposure, coping, and post-traumatic stress. *Internet Research*, 28(5), 1169–1188. 10.1108/IntR-02-2017-0077

Mesch, G. S. (2018). Parent–child connections on social networking sites and cyberbullying. *Youth & Society*, 50(8), 1145–1162. 10.1177/0044118X16659685

Modi, V., & Sharma, P. (2021). Indian Customers' Perception & Reaction to Deceptive Advertisements of Hair Care Products. *Gap Interdisciplinarities-A Global Journal of Interdisciplinary Studies*, 4(1), 49–62.

Moschis, G. P. (2017). Research frontiers on the dark side of consumer behaviour: The case of materialism and compulsive buying. *Journal of Marketing Management*, 33(15-16), 1384–1401. 10.1080/0267257X.2017.1347341

Nam, K., Baker, J., Ahmad, N., & Goo, J. (2020). Dissatisfaction, disconfirmation, and distrust: An empirical examination of value co-destruction through negative electronic word-of-mouth (eWOM). *Information Systems Frontiers*, 22(1), 113–130. 10.1007/s10796-018-9849-4

Nuseir, M. T. (2018). Impact of misleading/false advertisement to consumer behaviour. *International Journal of Economics and Business Research*, 16(4), 453–465. 10.1504/IJEBR.2018.095343

Pantzar, M. (2000). Consumption as Work, Play, and Art: Representation of the Consumer in Future Scenarios. *Design Issues*, 16(3), 3–18. 10.1162/074793600052053298

Peeroo, S., Samy, M., & Jones, B. (2017). Facebook: A blessing or a curse for grocery stores? *International Journal of Retail & Distribution Management*, 45(12), 1242–1259. 10.1108/IJRDM-12-2016-0234

Plé, L. (2017). Why do we need research on value co-destruction? *Journal of Creating Value*, 3(2), 162–169. 10.1177/2394964317726451

Plé, L., & Chumpitaz Cáceres, R. (2010). Not always co-creation: Introducing interactional co-destruction of value in service-dominant logic. *Journal of Services Marketing*, 24(6), 430–437. 10.1108/08876041011072546

Podoshen, J. S., Venkatesh, V., & Jin, Z. (2014). Theoretical reflections on dystopian consumer culture: Black metal. *Marketing Theory*, 14(2), 207–227. 10.1177/1470593114523446

Pollay, R. W. (1986). The distorted mirror: Reflections on the unintended consequences of advertising. *Journal of Marketing*, 50(2), 18–36. 10.1177/002224298605000202

Przybylski, A., Murayama, K., DeHann, C. R., & Gladwell, V. (2013). Motivational, emotional, and behavioral correlates of fear of missing out. *Computers in Human Behavior*, 29(4), 1841–1848. 10.1016/j.chb.2013.02.014

Rambe, P., & Nel, L. (2015). Technological utopia, dystopia and ambivalence: Teaching with social media at a S outh A frican university. *British Journal of Educational Technology*, 46(3), 629–648. 10.1111/bjet.12159

Rao, G., & Madan, A. (2012). A study exploring the link between attachment styles and social networking habits of adolescents in urban Bangalore. *International Journal of Scientific and Research Publications*, 3(1), 1–12.

Rom, E., & Alfasi, Y. (2014). The role of adult attachment style in online social network affect, cognition, and behavior. *Journal of Psychology and Psychotherapy Research*, 1(1), 24–34. 10.12974/2313-1047.2014.01.01.3

Salo, J., Mäntymäki, M., & Islam, A. K. M. N. (2018). The dark side of social media—and Fifty Shades of Grey introduction to the special issue: The dark side of social media. *Internet Research*, 28(5), 1166–1168. 10.1108/IntR-10-2018-442

Savci, M., & Aysan, F. (2017). Technological addictions and social connectedness: Predictor effect of internet addiction, social media addiction, digital game addiction and smartphone addiction on social connectedness. *Dusunen Adam : Bakirkoy Ruh Ve Sinir Hastaliklari Hastanesi Yayin Organi*, 30(3), 202–216. 10.5350/DAJPN2017300304

Scarles, C. (2009). Becoming tourist: Renegotiating the visual in the tourist experience. *Environment and Planning. D, Society & Space*, 27(3), 465–488. 10.1068/d1707

Shen, Y., Zhang, S., & Xin, T. (2020). Extrinsic academic motivation and social media fatigue: Fear of missing out and problematic social media use as mediators. *Current Psychology (New Brunswick, N.J.)*, 1–7.

Sherman, L. E., Payton, A. A., Hernandez, L. M., Greenfield, P. M., & Dapretto, M. (2016). The Power of the Like in Adolescence: Effects of Peer Influence on Neural and Behavioral Responses to Social Media. *Psychological Science*, 27(7), 1027–1035. 10.1177/0956797616645673 27247125

Slonje, R., Smith, P. K., & Frisén, A. (2013). The nature of cyberbullying, and strategies for prevention. *Computers in Human Behavior*, 29(1), 26–32. 10.1016/j.chb.2012.05.024

Smith, P. K. (2014). *Understanding school bullying: Its nature & prevention strategies*. Sage. 10.4135/9781473906853

Smith, P. K., Görzig, A., & Robinson, S. (2018). Issues of crosscultural variations in cyber bullying across Europe and beyond. *Media@LSE Working Paper Series*. Published by Media@LSE, London School of Economics and Political Science ("LSE")

Sullivan, A. (2016), "I used to be a human being." *New York Magazine*. https://nymag.com/selectall/2016/09/andrew-sullivan-technology-almost-killed-me.html

Sultan, A. J. (2021). Fear of missing out and self-disclosure on social media: The paradox of tie strength and social media addiction among young users. *Young Consumers*, 22(4), 555–577. 10.1108/YC-10-2020-1233

Surry, D. W., & Farquhar, J. D. (1997). Diffusion theory and instructional technology. *Journal of Instructional Science and technology*, 2(1), 24-36.

Thakur, R., Hale, D., & Summey, J. H. (2018). What motivates consumers to partake in cyber shilling? *Journal of Marketing Theory and Practice*, 26(1-2), 181–195. 10.1080/10696679.2017.1389236

Tirole, J. (2021). Digital dystopia. *The American Economic Review*, 111(6), 2007–2048. 10.1257/aer.20201214

Trinkle, B. S., Crossler, R. E., & Warkentin, M. (2014). I'm game, are you? Reducing realworld security threats by managing employee activity in online social networks. *Journal of Information Systems*, 28(2), 307–327. 10.2308/isys-50776

Turel, O., Serenko, A., & Giles, P. (2011). Integrating technology addiction and use: An empirical investigation of online auction users. *Management Information Systems Quarterly*, 35(4), 1043–1062. 10.2307/41409972

Ukaegbu, R. C. (2020). Deceptive Advertising and Consumer Reaction: A Study of Delta Soap Advertisement. *OAlib*, 7(3), 1–7. 10.4236/oalib.1105865

Vafeas, M., Hughes, T., & Hilton, T. (2016). Antecedents to value diminution: A dyadic perspective. *Marketing Theory*, 16(4), 469–491. 10.1177/1470593116652005

Vance, A., Lowry, P. B., & Eggett, D. (2015). A new approach to the problem of access policy violations: Increasing perceptions of accountability through the user interface. *Management Information Systems Quarterly*, 39(2), 345–366. 10.25300/MISQ/2015/39.2.04

Vargo, S. L., & Lusch, R. F. (2008). Why "service"? *Journal of the Academy of Marketing Science*, 36(1), 25–38. 10.1007/s11747-007-0068-7

Wansink, B. (1994). The Dark Side of Consumer Behavior: Empirical Examinations of Impulsive and Compulsive Consumption. In Allen, C. T., & John, D. R. (Eds.), *NA - Advances in Consumer Research* (Vol. 21, p. 508). Association for Consumer Research.

Willard, C. E. (2007). *Cyberbullying and Cyberthreats: Responding to the Challenge of Online Social Aggression, Threats, and Distress* (2nd ed.). Research Publishers LLC, USA: Illinois.

Wilson, A. E., Darke, P. R., & Sengupta, J. (2021). Winning the Battle but Losing the War: Ironic Effects of Training Consumers to Detect Deceptive Advertising Tactics. *Journal of Business Ethics*, •••, 1–17.

Wu, Y., Ngai, E. W., Wu, P., & Wu, C. (2020). Fake online reviews: Literature review, synthesis, and directions for future research. *Decision Support Systems*, 132(113280), 1–15. 10.1016/j.dss.2020.113280

Xiao, B., & Benbasat, I. (2011). Product-related deception in e-commerce: A theoretical perspective. *Management Information Systems Quarterly*, 35(1), 169–195. 10.2307/23043494

Young, K. S. (2007). Cognitive Behavior Therapy with Internet Addicts: Treatment Outcomes and Implications. *Cyberpsychology & Behavior*, 10(5), 671–679. 10.1089/cpb.2007.997117927535

Zhuang, M., Cui, G., & Peng, L. (2018). Manufactured opinions: The effect of manipulating online product reviews. *Journal of Business Research*, 87, 24–35. 10.1016/j.jbusres.2018.02.016

Zolfagharian, M., & Yazdanparast, A. (2017). The dark side of consumer life in the age of virtual and mobile technology. *Journal of Marketing Management*, 33(15-16), 1304–1335. 10.1080/0267257X.2017.1369143

Zwass, V. (2021). Editor's Introduction. *International Journal of Electronic Commerce*, 25(2), 125–126. 10.1080/10864415.2021.1887693

KEY TERMS AND DEFINITIONS

Compulsive buying: Repeated purchasing behavior that becomes a primary response to negative emotions or events, providing relief from such feelings.

Cyberbullying: The use of technology to threaten, intimidate, embarrass, or target another person, done through online platforms or digital means.

Dystopia: A conceptualized state or society characterized by significant suffering or injustice.

Fear of Missing Out (FOMO): The sense of anxiety or concern about potentially missing out on information, events, experiences, or life choices that could enhance one's life.

Honeycomb model: A framework that delineates the fundamental forces influencing the social media ecosystem within which social media marketers, users, and platforms operate.

Impulsive buying: Unplanned purchasing driven by irrational decision-making.

Influencer: An individual who possesses the capacity to impact potential buyers' decisions regarding products or services by endorsing or recommending them on social media platforms.

User-generated Content (UGC): Content, including text, videos, images, reviews, etc., created by individuals rather than brands or official entities.

Utopia: A conceptualized ideal place or state where everything is perfect.

ENDNOTE

[1] Happy slapping was a fad in which one or more people attack a victim to record the assault, commonly with a smartphone (https://en.wikipedia.org/wiki/Happy_slapping).

Section 4
Artificial Intelligence (AI) and Media

Chapter 14
Visual Media in Light of the Challenges of Generative Artificial Intelligence in Egypt

Hanan Elshibiny
Cairo University, Egypt

ABSTRACT

The research focuses on the possible changes in the basic foundations of the media message industry in light of the data of artificial intelligence and its applications such as writing the media material, preparing its executive text and presenting it to the recipient from designing clips of images, designing graphics, and sound effects. It also highlights the importance of the tremendous development in aspects of artificial intelligence and its implications for developing the media message, and the performance of visual media in particular, and contributing to the creation of a specialized field in media forms. In light of the tremendous technical developments that have included the media, they are positive that contribute to advancing media progress or negative loses its value.

INTRODUCTION

Many international news agencies, press and television institutions have relied on the use of artificial intelligence models in performing their daily work by using algorithms to generate automatic news without human intervention, or relying on automated responses to the public through chatting via robots and verifying fake news, which has created Major changes in the rate of its daily production of media content and meeting the needs of an audience composed of millions of people whose connection to digital media is increasing day after day, and were not effective with traditional methods of publishing and distribution, especially on websites, social media networks and digital broadcasting platforms, and despite the fact that International media and social media networks have made great strides in shifting towards activating artificial intelligence in providing their digital services. However, the newly developed artificial intelligence systems are still in their early experimental stages in the Arab region. Automating the media sector is something in the near future, but media experts disagree about the ability of artificial intelligence. He must replace the journalist, as he is unable to interact live and directly, or collect

DOI: 10.4018/979-8-3693-3767-7.ch014

Copyright ©2024, IGI Global. Copying or distributing in print or electronic forms without written permission of IGI Global is prohibited.

information from sources, and even the issue of objective accuracy, disagreement still exists about the ability of intelligence to ensure adherence to professional values and ethics, and the press and media move the world and are the two sectors that are among the most technologically advanced in the world. The world, the news determines the priorities of dialogue and public debate and determines what problems should be focused on.

Therefore, it was understandable how Jeffrey Hinton (the godfather of artificial intelligence) would meet with Sam Altman, director of OpenAI, which launched "ChatGPT," with Elon Musk, Stephen Hawking, Bill Gates, and hundreds of experts, legislators, and technology industry people. In the world, parliaments, governments, regional, and international organizations, to warn us of the dangers of this intelligence, and the potential threat to human existence, and to demand the necessity of establishing controls and legislation, because artificial intelligence journalism is growing greatly in the world of journalism and media, and will lead to a radical change in the world of media, and this change It will necessarily affect producers, as well as consumers who follow media outlets, as society is looking forward to knowing the future of these media outlets in light of these developments, whether positive ones that contribute to advancing media progress or negative ones that cause the media to lose their value.

BACKGROUND

Previous studies and research address topics related to employing artificial intelligence in the media and other topics of Professionalism of content produced with artificial intelligence tools, it consists of two axes:

The First Axis: Employing Artificial Intelligence in the Media

In Al-Ghatrifi's study in (2023), he aimed to explore the weaknesses and defects that could result from the use of generative artificial intelligence tools in journalism. The study concluded that the risks touch the core of the professional standards of journalistic work, such as bias, misinformation, information fraud, and the irrational use of the technological tool in producing content and their effects. On quality and deceiving the public, as well as violations and impacts on employment and the future of work in media institutions, and that journalism is a creative profession and that a person cannot be replaced in it as long as he is armed with his basic skills and has the ability to rationally integrate generative artificial intelligence tools according to a safe vision of professional practice and the public's right to know about the mandatory standards and rules (Al-Ghatrifi, 2023).

The ethics governing journalistic work the Ismail's study in (2022), which aims to reveal journalists' trends towards using artificial intelligence in developing journalistic content in Egyptian newspapers and websites. This goal includes a set of sub-objectives, which are to identify the reality of employing artificial intelligence applications in developing newspapers and websites and to determine To know the extent of the success of employing artificial intelligence applications in developing newspapers and websites, to know the positive and negative effects of using artificial intelligence techniques in Egyptian newspapers and websites, to know the skills required to work in newspapers and websites that use artificial intelligence techniques, to monitor proposals to enhance the use of artificial intelligence techniques in Egyptian newspapers and websites, and to determine Challenges facing Egyptian newspapers and websites in using artificial intelligence techniques (Ismail, 2022).

Abdel-Gawad's study in (2021) also aimed to identify the trends of the Egyptian elite towards employing security media for artificial intelligence applications and its role in combating cybercrime, and to learn about their vision of the future role of this new method in supporting and enhancing cybersecurity in Egypt. The study reached an agreement among the elite to adopt Applications of artificial intelligence in its various forms and media arts when dealing with cybercrimes. According to the vision of the elite, it will take the lead in news materials, as it is based on monitoring and following up on facts and events from various means of communication. It sought to achieve a main goal, which is to identify how to apply robot journalism and its production mechanisms to the Cairo 24 news website, as it is the first Egyptian website to apply this model of artificial intelligence techniques, and to identify the benefit or value that it added to the site, and to reveal the new and practices that it imposed, And the nature of the relationship between robot journalism and human journalists. The study concluded the importance of applying robot journalism in Egyptian journalistic websites, due to its ability to produce and present journalistic content that is more distinctive than that provided by human journalists, and more credible than that among the public, and its impact. Positive impact on the professional and ethical dimensions of journalistic work) Gawad, 2021).

Miroshnichenko's study in (2020) aimed to answer the question: Will robots replace journalists? Based on a review of the current state of automated journalism and an analysis of common arguments about robots not being able to overcome humans in creative practices, the study indicates that readers sometimes cannot distinguish between news written by robots or humans and that the use of robots has shown great success (Miroshnichenko,2020), While the study by Morvik in (2020) aimed to characterize the application of algorithms at the Czech News Agency (CTK) and convert large data files into news texts, relying on the production of reports on trading results on the Prague Stock Exchange using artificial intelligence without human intervention for the Czech News Agency during the year 2019, and to compare production rates. Algorithms and the quality of journalistic content produced by humans versus algorithms, in addition to conducting a field study on journalists and acting economic editors. The results indicated that the financial situation in Czech newsrooms indicates the inevitability of relying on artificial intelligence in Czech journalism to continue its mission. Despite all of this, journalists expect that their roles will remain important, and they will work in conjunction with artificial intelligence techniques to produce better reports (Morvik, 2020).

The Second Axis: Professionalism of Content Produced With Artificial Intelligence Tools

On the other hand, the study by Sangwon et al. (2020) examined the driving forces in predicting the level of credibility on artificial intelligence (AI) news. Specially, this study unveils the effects of communicative capital, such as media use and public discussion, among audiences, as well as social capital, such as social trust, on AI news credibility. Data collected through a nationwide online survey reveals that media use through television, social network sites, and online news sites, as well as public discussion yielded a positive association with AI news credibility. Of particular interest is that social trust moderated the effect of public discussion on credibility, indicating that the relationship between discussion and credibility was even stronger for those who have a higher level of trust in others. Implications are further discussed (Sangwon, et. al. 2020).

The study by Shangon et al. (2020) also monitored the user experience of the interface design of a news robot that automatically produces news about the main events of the Winter Olympic Games in real time. It produces six types of news by combining two types of content (general/individual) and three styles (text only). (Text + image, text + image + audio), by applying it to 30 users. The results showed that users preferred individual news that relied on text, but they considered it less credible. The demo elements (audio and image) were also appreciated provided that their quality was guaranteed. The respondents appreciated the news stories presented via the news robot as realistic and accurate, but they are shallow and superficial in terms of the depth of the content (Shangon, et. al. 2020). The study by Graefe et al. (2020) was concluded through a meta-analysis of studies conducted on the credibility of artificial intelligence content by monitoring the available practical evidence about the readers' perception of its credibility, quality, and ease. Reading machine news, and the results showed that there are no fundamental differences in the public's perceived credibility of machine-written news except in relation to the perceived quality and the readership of human-written news (Graefe, et. al. 2020)

The TanDoc's et al. study in (2020) also monitored how automated journalism fits in with the traditional values of journalism and how it affects the public's perceptions of credibility, based on an experimental study which is the declared author: Man vs. Machine and Purpose vs. Lack of Objectivity, by applying it to 420 participants who were citizens of Singapore. The study did not find major differences in the perceived credibility of the source between content produced via algorithms, a human journalist, or a combination of both. The study also showed no differences in the credibility of the message. The study also found an effect of the interaction between the type of declared author and the objectivity of the news, when the article is submitted to be written by a human journalist. The credibility of the source and message remains stable regardless of whether the article is objective or subjective (TanDoc, et. al. 2020). While the study by Yanfang in (2019) showed that the audience failed to distinguish a newspaper article written by a robot and another by a journalist, as the respondents gave a similar assessment of the quality of the article without clarifying the name of the author, as both the audience and journalists gave higher grades to the article written by the robot, meaning that the audience gave higher grades to the content. Written through algorithms when they were informed that it was written by a robot, and the results showed that the evaluations of both the public and journalists were different when they were told that it was written by a journalist, but they gave lower marks to the work of the algorithm when they were informed that its author was a journalist, and the study confirmed the negative attitude of the public. Towards journalists' credibility and passion for new information technology service products in South Korea based on journalists' resistance to change and innovation and their bias (Yanfang, 2019).

MAIN FOCUS OF THE CHAPTER

1. Identifying the concept of artificial intelligence and the concepts associated with it, their current and future impacts, and the most important technological elements active in creating media content and its environment in the future.

2. Evaluating the role of artificial intelligence applications in developing an automated system that matches the performance of humans in the field of media by better understanding the communication between humans and machines that enables artificial intelligence tools to achieve a degree of interaction with others.
3. Revealing the future of the media and the most important positive and negative effects, and preparing for the changes that will occur in the media after the use of artificial intelligence.
4. Identify the most important opportunities and challenges facing the media industry in light of the development of these technologies.

RESEARCH PROBLEM

Some researchers see a threat to journalism and the media, as it is likely to lead to a further decline in the role of the human journalist in light of new policies for media institutions, but media experts disagree about the ability of artificial intelligence to replace the journalist, as it is unable to interact. Live and direct with the public, or collecting information from sources, and even the issue of objective accuracy, there is still disagreement about the ability of intelligence to include it. Are those working in the media sector in general waiting for a change in the basic foundations of making the media message? Such as: writing the material, preparing its executive text and presenting it to the recipient, designing the visual clips, choosing and designing the graphic and sound effects. In other words, will some methods disappear and be replaced by new ones in the way of editing, directing, presenting, preparing, and editing all the way to formulating the treatment in television programs or dramatic works or series and films, Despite the importance of digital technological transformations and the opportunities and competitive advantages they have provided in the spread of media content and the policies associated with it, there are many challenges imposed by these developments in artificial intelligence and digital transformations on the media environment in general, the most important of which is the form of the medium and the content in particular. With these advantages that resulted from the association of the term artificial intelligence with the media, society is now looking forward to knowing the future of these means in light of these developments, whether they are positive in advancing the wheel of media progress or negative in that the media loses its value.

THE ANALYSIS OF THE RESEARCH PROBLEM

The research problem can be analyzed by answering the flowing study questions:
1. What are the most important technological elements in the visual media content industry?
2. What are the most important positive and negative effects that will occur on visual media after the use of artificial intelligence?
3. What are the opportunities and challenges facing the visual media industry in light of the development of artificial intelligence technologies?
4. Is the media expected to distance itself and its tools from the tremendous technical developments taking place?
5. Does the impact of artificial intelligence and its elements in the media reinforce the idea of the impact of technology on professional values in media work?

Type and Method of Study

This research falls within exploratory studies, so the necessities of the research required the use of the descriptive method and the quantitative and qualitative methods.

Study Population and Sample

Study population: satellite television channels in Egypt and their social networking sites.

Research sample: The researcher met twenty 20 journalists working in newsrooms on satellite television channels and their affiliated social media sites.

Data Collection Tools

The researcher interviewed (20) workers in the creativity and innovation departments and newsrooms in the Arab and Egyptian channels located in Egypt.

THEORETICAL FRAMEWORK OF THE STUDY

First: The Unified Theory of Acceptance and Use of Technology

The scientist Davis is considered the true founder of the technology acceptance model in 1989, when he pointed out that users' lack of acceptance of working on information systems and technology is considered an important obstacle to the success of these systems. He also proved that understanding why people choose to accept or reject any technology is one of the biggest challenges for researchers in the field of information systems and technology. The technology acceptance model ranked first among the models that attempt to explain the success and failure of acceptance of information systems and technology, as this model was tested extensively and extensively experimentally. Which led to belief in its strength, credibility, and adoption by the academic community.

This theory aims to explain the intention and behavior of use. The theory uses behavioral intention as an indicator of the behavior of using technology. The theory suggests that expected performance, expected effort, and social influence directly affect the intention to use, and that the available facilities directly affect the behavior of use along with the intention. Use, as the technology acceptance model is one of the reliable models to explain the acceptance and use of information systems, and one of the most important basic characteristics of the unified theory and use of technology is the reactions of individuals towards the use of technology, which includes the factors of individuals adoption of technology, the independent variables, behavioral intention, the actual use of technology (variables dependent), the individual characteristics of technology users and (Intermediate variables), which assume that the relationship between expected performance, expected effort, social factors, and behavioral intention varies according to age and gender that the relationship between behavioral intention, expected effort, and social factors varies according to experience; There is a relationship between social influence and behavioral intention that varies according to the voluntariness of use. Finally, there is a relationship between use behavior and available facilities that varies according to age and experience (sumak, et.al. 2020).

The unified theory model of technology acceptance and use consists of four elements (Venkatesh, 2003):

- **Expected performance**

It means the degree to which individuals believe that their use of technology will lead to gains in job performance, and this can also be viewed as the perceived benefit from using technology, and this factor will be pivotal; Because if workers in the field of journalism and media believe that the ease of their use of digital applications such as social networking sites, Facebook, Twitter, and others, will help them improve their performance at work, such as conveying information faster than traditional means, which will benefit their job performance, and Johnny Han believes, Demographic factors have a major role in accepting technology as it is believed that the higher the educational level, there is a strong incentive to accept technology and use it in media work. It was also found that females are more opposed to accepting the use of modern technology in media work (Han, 2020).

- **Expected effort**

It means the ease of using technology. For example, journalists may compare the effort and time spent using digital applications to achieve a specific purpose, compared to other means, such as traditional media. This element is linked to the necessity of combining a group of factors, which include the pleasure expected from using technology, and confidence in using that technology. In media work, there is also the trend and determination of journalists and media workers towards accepting this technology and using it in their job tasks (Rebort, 2020).

- **Social factors**

It means to what extent individuals believe it is important that others believe they should use technology; this explains whether journalists expect others, such as bosses, colleagues, the public, and others, to appreciate their use of digital applications. In this context, Johnny Han pointed out that perceived social factors play a major role in workers' confidence in the technology that is used within the work environment (Han, 2018).

- **Facilities available**

It means the extent to which the individual believes that the infrastructure and technology necessary to support the technology exist in the individual or organization, and this variable relates to the availability of the necessary capabilities to use digital applications, such as the availability of knowledge, computers, smart phones, and Internet services, or the organization's permission to use social media during work, in addition to the four previous factors that constitute the elements. The basic constructivism of the theory, and there are other factors that have an indirect effect on the behavioral intention to use technology (AlSalhi, 2015), which are:

- Attitude toward using technology: What is meant is the user's reaction toward using the system and includes four factors: attitude toward behavior, internal motivation, influence toward use, and influence.
- System efficiency: This means the ability to complete the job using the system without the help of others.
- Anxiety: This means anxiety about using the system as a result of the fear of losing information or making a mistake when using the system.

Second: The theory of the spread of new ideas

The theory is based on how new ideas and innovations are accepted, how the public adopts and accepts them, and the stages through which they spread among people. The theory initially appeared at the hands of Jobohlin in 1975, who summarized his theory in four basic elements (Abdel Hamid, 1997):

- **New idea**: It is the idea that its owner believes that it is something new, unparalleled, and it does not matter much in the field of human behavior whether the idea is new or not. When measured by the period of time that elapses from the moment of its appearance or use, its newness to him is what determines the way he behaves towards it.
- **Idea transmission**: Diffusion is the process by which a new idea is broadcast, and it involves the emergence of a new idea from its source to those who use or adopt it. The basis of this process is human interaction through which a person transmits the new idea to another person.
- **The prevailing social system**: The social standards of the existing social organization affect the process of the spread of new ideas, and the social standard is the common behavioral pattern among members of a particular social organization. These patterns may be traditional that reduce the possibility of embracing new ideas or in their attitudes towards them because they may be modern. You are encouraged to follow these ideas, but not all new ideas are the same. One person may pass it on to another person only, while another person may spread it among a large group of people.
- **The period necessary for the transition:** The individual may hear of the new idea and may decide to use it after it has attracted his attention. Then he determines the extent of its benefit to him then he tries it out and then adopts it. What is meant by adoption here is the process that the individual goes through from hearing about the new idea until he embraces it, this process may pass. With five stages: awareness, interest, evaluation, attempt, and finally adoption.

DATA COLLECTION TOOLS

Note

It is the careful observation or listening of a specific phenomenon or a group of them, and the use of tools and methods that are consistent with its nature. It is the intentional systematic observation that directs attention, senses and mind to a particular phenomenon and events in order to realize the relationships and connections between them, as for how to use the note (Hussein, 2006):

- Accurate and clear definition of the objective of observation in accordance with the research objective.
- Determine the types of behavior to be observed procedurally.

The interview:

The interview is one of the scientific research methods widely used in order to obtain information related to people's conditions, tendencies, or trends. This tool is one of the most common methods for collecting primary data in the social sciences and media studies due to its diversity and multiplicity of forms, and it includes a set of open and closed questions that are specified and prepared in advance. Before implementing and conducting the interview, the researcher interviewed (20) journalists in the creativity and innovation departments and newsrooms in the Arab and Egyptian channels located in Egypt.

RESULTS

The First Topic: Employing Artificial Intelligence Applications in the Field of Media and Their Effects

Although the idea of relying on automated news formulation is not new, as machine learning algorithms are trained to take into account only variables that improve their predictive accuracy, on the data used, but at the same time they need to verify the possibility that automated journalism is biased in terms of the information content in Text, and knowledge of the mechanisms that allow human bias to influence automated journalism, even if the data that the system operates on is considered neutral, and the growth of the media information, public relations, media and entertainment software market is expected to occupy a large part of it (Leppänen, 2020):

- **Automated journalism**: which is known as automation or robot journalism, which relies on natural language generation algorithms that support it into news stories, whether texts, artificial intelligence applications for automatic data conversion, or images, videos, and data, and then distributing them across digital platforms. This technology has gained great importance with the increase in It was applied in many news agencies, newspapers, and websites, as it caused breakthroughs in news coverage of economic, sports, and weather topics, and in the publication of thousands of news stories. Media institutions also showed great efficiency in relying on automated news dissemination, such as the Associated Press, Reuters, Los Angeles Times, The Washington Post...and others.
- **Television production**: Artificial intelligence can also help in managing and organizing content efficiently. Artificial intelligence can help, which was a problem facing television workers due to the lack of metadata. Algorithms also help in spreading and improving the efficiency of delivery networks, which is a great advantage for operators. Pay TV who want to improve broadcast quality, where content producers compete to provide creative works that attract the audience, and to avoid duplication of content on the producer or broadcaster by understanding the audience's preferences and behavior through machine learning and predicting the videos that the audience is likely to watch (Yan, 2020).

In November (2018), the new Chinese news agency, Xinhua, launched what it said was a broadcaster working with artificial intelligence technology, and it was called the "composite broadcaster" because it relied on a technology that combined audio and video recording in real time through a virtual character who was able to read the news successfully, in a way that non-specialists could not detect as being different from the performance of a human broadcaster.

When this experiment was launched, many did not notice the seriousness of what was happening to human employment opportunities in the field of broadcasters work. Indeed, some specialists began to downplay the importance of this "hack" after they considered that what happened was nothing more than a "deceptive use", built on "technology". Teaching simple machines.

But "Xinhua" did not stop working. In March of (2019), it launched its developed model in this regard, when a "broadcaster" appeared on the screen and said that her name was "Shen Xiaoming," and she was nothing but a "robot," reflecting a full-fledged human image. In a pink suit, short hair, and elegant earrings, as I read news about the arrival of delegates to Beijing, to participate in an annual parliamentary meeting, "Xinhua" says that it is continuing with what it started, and that the automated broadcasters have become part of the production capabilities in its workplaces, and that they are doing great.

In a quote by the well-known English novelist Agatha Christie, who passed away in 1976, there is an important phrase in explaining the paths that humanity takes in approaching new inventions: She believed that "necessity is not the mother of invention as is commonly believed, but rather that invention stems directly from human laziness and their desire to save effort." When we examine Ms. Christie's statement, we will find that it may be appropriate to explain this overwhelming rush to develop artificial intelligence mechanisms from the perspective that they can simply accomplish tasks that humans do, more quickly, at a lower cost, with better accuracy, and without suffering.

NHK TV also developed an automated sound generation system, in a style similar to a professional broadcaster, by experimenting with automatic production in March 2019, including daily and weekly weather forecasts, temperature and rainfall, as well as using automated voiceover in live broadcasting of sports games, via a base. Data recorded with the names of players, results, elapsed times, standings and previous results through an automated audio system. The Rio de Janeiro Olympics and the Paralympics were used. Artificial intelligence techniques also provided the implementation of automated videos, as automated tools enable the analysis of the video content, selecting the most important excerpts contained in it, and preparing a video. Short compilation, which is what YouTube uses (Gunawardena, et. al. 2021).

Elaph electronic newspaper also adopted a "virtual" artificial intelligence broadcaster. To present the news, the "smart" broadcaster, Hala Al-Wardi, who describes herself as the "smart media face" emerging through advanced algorithms, appeared in an interview with the BBC NEWS Arabic channel, in which the virtual broadcaster said that she is "the daughter of tomorrow and the future" and is indispensable to the human element, which She was in an interview conducted by a human journalist from BBC Arabic with her, and the artificial intelligence broadcaster was more complete, more professional, and closer to human performance than her Chinese and Korean counterparts. The answers of the artificial colleague "Al-Wardi" were astonishingly precise and thoughtful. At least she did not make a single mistake. She used sound and generous language. She gave an excellent interview in which she admitted that "artificial intelligence is scary." However, she reassured "the doubters" by saying that she would not "You take the place of someone," and that the need for "human fingers on the computer" will continue to guarantee the presence of the human element in this industry (BBC NEWS, 2023).

- **Dealing with big data:** Artificial intelligence applications can save time and energy wasted on monitoring the system by performing databases, user experience, and log data and combining them in one data platform. The power of smart algorithms lies in their ability to handle very com-

plex situations by scanning big data, as Artificial intelligence algorithms can process databases that are unlimited in size, and determine their findings (Emelshtrich, 2018).
- **Social media networks and digital platforms**: As the use of social media has expanded and flourished at an increasing rate over the years, artificial intelligence through the algorithms used to recommend content on social media has become the subject of increasing scrutiny, as platforms such as Facebook, X, and YouTube use machine learning to suggest media content. By sampling and recommending ads that improve user interaction, American civil society organizations and researchers have expressed concerns that these algorithms will help spread misinformation and spread digital propaganda (Papadimitriou, 2016).

Digital broadcasting platforms and social networking sites also use advanced technologies in building digital platforms, so that the content changes with the change in consumer behavior, the way he searches and displays, the history of his data, and his interests as well. For example, Netflix focuses on displaying appropriate content to its viewers and building "recommendations" based on search behavior on its platform. Digital, Netflix indicates that it saves approximately one billion US dollars annually thanks to the ability of artificial intelligence technology to automate content flows and interaction with customers. Audience data can be transformed into effective campaigns to retain customers and personalize content to create a more personal relationship with viewers. CNN also uses a system... Automated boot chat to send a daily report to user accounts in Facebook Messenger about the most important events of interest to people based on their prior interests that are automatically recorded.

The development of artificial intelligence in visual media may have some negative effects, here are some examples of these effects (Kronke, 2020):

- **Manipulation of information**: Through artificial intelligence, images and videos can be elaborately manipulated, creating fake content that appears realistic, and this can be used to spread false news or create chaos and confusion.
- **Privacy and security:** Artificial intelligence may violate the privacy of individuals by tracking and analyzing photos and videos. It may also be used to penetrate security systems and manipulate sensitive information.
- **Discrimination and bias:** AI relies on input data to train it Therefore the use of AI in visual media may perpetuate and reinforce existing biases, which can negatively impact diversity and fair representation.
- **Job loss:** The application of artificial intelligence in visual media may reduce the need for human labor in some areas, and this may cause job loss and a negative impact on the economy.
- **Dependency on technology**: The increasing reliance on artificial intelligence in visual media may lead to society becoming dependent on technology, which will have a negative impact if intelligent systems stop working or malfunction.

There are also many positive effects of artificial intelligence in visual media. Here are some examples of these effects:

- **Improving content quality**: AI can improve the quality of photos and videos through image enhancement and automatic adjustment techniques that can improve contrast, clarity, colors and reduce noise which leading to a better visual experience for viewers.

- **Taking advantage of massive data**: Artificial intelligence has the ability to analyze and understand the vast data available in visual media. This data can be used to determine audience interests and understand viewer behavior, enabling media companies to provide personalized content and improve their strategies.
- **Improving the user experience**: Artificial intelligence can improve the user experience in visual media by providing personalized recommendations and diverse content, and smart systems can learn about viewers' preferences and provide relevant and personalized content that meets their individual needs.
- **Diagnosis and analysis**: Artificial intelligence can analyze images and videos quickly and accurately, and can be used to detect photography errors or analyze elements present in visual media. It can also be used to recognize people, places, objects, and other sights
- **Creativity and innovation**: Artificial intelligence can be used in visual media to produce creative and new content. Can develop innovative graphics and visual effects techniques, as well as generate artistic content and innovative designs.

The Second Topic: Visual Media and the Most Important Challenges of Artificial Intelligence

Today, the world is experiencing a digital revolution characterized by the spread of the Internet everywhere and the emergence of advanced and accurate sensors characterized by artificial intelligence and rapid electronic learning. "Robot journalism" is one of the most important tools and techniques of artificial intelligence and its uses in the field of media. It means collecting information about events and issues, classifying it, and writing it. In the form of news and reports and published in a completely automated way without human intervention (Caswell, Dörr, 2018).

With the multiple uses of "robot journalism" at the present time among news agencies and major newspapers, and their race to bring this technology into action, and to rely on it effectively, questions began to be raised about it. With regard to the challenges it imposes on the human element, and the extent to which a robot can replace the media professional, take over his job, and carry out his tasks, and the extent to which media professionals can develop their capabilities to keep pace with this development, especially with the multiplicity of capabilities of this technology, whose development does not seem to stop there, but There is no doubt that it will greatly affect the news process in all its aspects and stages (Frary, 2019).

Artificial intelligence is viewed from two angles: intelligence that imitates human intelligence and intelligence that imitates human behavior and actions. In the first case, artificial intelligence imitates humans, whether their acting or thinking, until reaching the level of complete similarity, while in the second case, artificial intelligence can oppose human behavior and do the right thing. Given his known experiences, this is what was indicated by many science fiction scenarios that include the rebellion of machines, starting with the movie Terminator (Badawy, 2020)

So artificial intelligence either plays the role of a human or surpasses humans as a human simulation or it performs as a "smarter" entity and surpasses humans. As an organism of the next evolutionary level, both "mimetic" and "paradoxical" approaches point to such scenarios in which AI replaces and then replaces humans, either by imitating or outperforming them, as inevitable. In light of this, scholars' discussions about this last point is in scientific contexts.

Given the reality, what the market needs and the industrial requirements for artificial intelligence, we find that there are industries that are mostly interested in the computational power of artificial intelligence, such as air traffic control or social media algorithms. In this case, it can be described as the predictive results of big data and their mathematical analysis. Artificial intelligence is considered an assistant to humans, which is a perspective Very narrow while there are at least three industries that seek, for very practical reasons, not only to develop better artificial intelligence but to completely replace humans with artificial intelligence (Miroshnichenko, 2020):

- **Military armies**: where intelligent war machines are expected to make human-like decisions immediately on the battlefield, which increases the efficiency of their performance while reducing human losses.
- **The sex industry:** Smart sex dolls are expected to completely replace sex partners and then perhaps even life partners for humans by simulating human sex.
- **The media**: where news writing algorithms ultimately aim to replace human journalists. The final stage of the idea of news writing algorithms is to write news instead of humans, in a much better, faster, cheaper, and more productive way.

At the present time the use of robot journalism in the field of media depends on the following (MarieAliman, Kester, 2020):

- Searching for and processing data as searching for and processing big data is considered one of the algorithms in journalism, as it helps journalists find linked data on a topic with ease.
- Identifying topics worthy of publication and follow-up, as algorithms, through their ability to analyze huge data and link it together are able to make quick and accurate decisions about news worthy and more deserving of publication at the present time than others by evaluating the public's interests and reactions to journalistic content.
- Supervising and purifying comments as algorithms are able to enhance and supervise online conversations to ensure they proceed correctly without deviating from the rules.
- News writing: Through algorithms collecting and comparing data, they can write ready-made journalistic texts without human intervention, and in doing so they use limited templates that were determined for them by the human element.

It is clear that artificial intelligence will play a major role in the future of news. The twenty-first century is undoubtedly the era of data journalism and automated journalism, and journalists themselves do not realize that they are helping to do this by entrusting all news production processes to machines, and over time their circle of influence will weaken, whether in selecting... Information and judging its suitability by publishing it or in producing it and delivering it to the public, in exchange for a noticeable expansion of machine influences, which may replace humans through modern algorithms that fully understand what the public needs, or more precisely, that direct their interests and control them to a large extent (Túñez-López, et. Al., 2018).

Media experts realize that the challenges of robot journalism lie in moving from machines programmed to act, and to machines that have the ability to determine how to act on every occasion, or more precisely to robots with autonomy and the ability to think and program their reactions. The future of robots with journalism is not related to Not only in producing and processing texts, but also reaching the extent of the human element's participation in prioritizing and determining them, thus creating several challenges facing those working in visual media, the most important of which are (Túñez-López,et.Al.,2020):

The First Challenge: Simulation, Collecting and Presenting Programs and News

A system equipped with artificial intelligence (AI) can create video clips that appear very realistic, in which versions of people from program presenters or news broadcasters can appear, speaking in their native languages or other languages and with the same original tone of voice while showing emotional expressions depending on the nature of the material or program they are presenting. Amendments will be made to everything that the actor, program presenter, or broadcaster does or says in the original video entered into the system to produce a new and modified video. Several tests will be conducted to compare its modern algorithm with its predecessor, which was concerned with manipulating images and videos, a large number of which large research sites on the Internet contributed in part to developing where attractive topics can be developed specifically designed to suit the interests of the audience, where the geographical area related to the scope of interest can be determined, and informational interview questions can be formulated to attract the attention of guests and the audience. Imagine yourself as a television interviewer conducting an interview and you will conduct an interview with a well-known person. You may enter brief information about this person, and because the interview a specific time determines the time for the interview, collecting statistics related to the topic and verifying the sources.

"When I started working in journalism there were actors reading the news and people accepted" that says Nick Newman, senior research associate at the Reuters Institute for the Study of Journalism at the University of Oxford, and a former BBC editor (BBC NEWS, 2014).

The fact that journalists don't always read the news means this attempt could work, Newman believes. It will only be useful for short newscasts, but he's not sure viewers will build an engaged relationship with an AI broadcaster. "For news programming, I think humanity will still be really important.

Challenge Two: New Colleagues

Robot journalism has faced some challenges from professional and ethical aspects. These challenges have been discovered at various levels that including the level of data search as well as the originality, objectivity, and level of transparency of the algorithms which used the methods of using data and the extent of misuse in addition to the level of values and logic included in the instructions. The first of these challenges was with regard to the validity of the information integrated into artificial intelligence software, whose truthfulness or falsity cannot be verified if the data provided in it are not digital, which leads to sometimes incorrect outputs Therefore robot journalism would violate the principles of copyright, especially since Artificial intelligence software can retrieve data from vast areas in a deliberate violation of the rights of the original sources of this data, which requires the media person to continue understanding and writing news materials in a humane manner with deep meaning, as well as continuing to verify the authenticity of the materials prepared by robots that providing logical explanations for them and linking them in Its correct context as is known the availability of a certain amount of confidence in media products at least, in terms of their credibility is an essential factor in the sustainability of journalism and its fulfillment of its basic mission, which is the reason for its existence but what generative artificial intelligence products do, especially in this regard, casts a dark shadow on the future of this profession and industry, by exporting more pressure on the accuracy factors trust in people who provide news has fallen to its lowest levels ever, according to a survey conducted by a polling company. Public Opinion Ipsos Only 42 percent of people in the UK trust TV news readers, down 16 percentage points in one year. Suspicion of news providers as monopolists of the truth has become an unusual modern phenomenon, as many choose to get their news instead through content creators or influencers while another team points out the need to study journalistic ethical standards that have not changed for a long time, and try to link them to software. With artificial intelligence to be compatible with the stipulated standards, especially since some of the data that is formulated by software can be filled with racial and sexual ideas and biases, according to the human programmer who entered the data into the artificial mind, whether intentionally or unintentionally, but is artificial intelligence capable of replicating Personal connection? "You will never have the same connection with an AI that you have with another human," admits Adam Maussan entrepreneur of an AI news TV startup However people will stop looking for neutrality. We don't "We do this because we think robots do a better job than humans. This is ridiculous."

Human intelligence possesses an advanced mixture of logical thinking skills, multiple deductions, a moral system, behavioral controls, awareness of good and evil tendencies diverse communication, feeling its differences, evaluating contextual problems and risks, perception and social interaction, intuition and interpretations, and observations, which are skills that artificial intelligence does not possess like the effectiveness of humans and media professionals are required to adapt their knowledge and skills to new concepts that are appropriate for the existence of robotic journalism in order to continue (Skynewsarabia,2015).

It can be said that within a few years, the virtual broadcaster will become part of the prevailing media work mechanisms in various countries of the world especially when small media companies with limited budgets will resort to this path, to reduce costs and avoid the obstacles of contracting with well-known human broadcasters with names and salaries. This will happen despite the great criticism aimed at employing a non-human broadcaster, considering that he lacks one of the most important components of the broadcaster's work that is the ability to communicate with the audience that achieve credibility and trust. Although the media audience's trust in human broadcasters is still declining in reliable opinion polls around the world, some researchers who specializing in media sociology still insist that the relationship that arises between the broadcaster and the audience members remain an important factor in building the desired trust as a segment of these individuals believes that the broadcaster is speaking to them in a personal capacity that he is participating with them in building their perceptions of events, taking positions, and forming opinions as we mentioned in the survey of the international research company "Ipsos," and the emergence Trust in people who present news through British media increased by 42%, a decline of 16 points in one year. This is a significant decline that reinforces doubts about the ability of these means to persuade, and opens the door for developers of virtual broadcasters to move forward with their new experiences.

However, the Egyptian media seems until this moment to be far from keeping pace with progress in the field of launching virtual broadcasters and although there are rare attempts in some secondary media organizations to use this technology, the largest sector of the main media institutions has not shown interest in engaging in this experiment perhaps the most important reason is This refers to the central and vital role played by the human broadcaster in the national media system which is a role that goes beyond the idea of reading the news, presenting the course of current events, or hosting relevant sources to explore their opinions, to providing opinion and advice to the public and providing "subjective" impressions and comments on Events, and despite the special nature of the national media, and the central role that is usually assigned to the broadcaster in his programs, news bulletins and entertainment products, the artificial broadcaster will certainly reach it when this happens, we will have to monitor the manifestations of this experience and see the amount of trust that the virtual broadcaster will have in exchange for what enjoyed by his human counterpart and there will be a fierce competition in a not-too-distant time between the human broadcaster and the virtual one, and among the elements of this competition elements such as confidence, attractiveness, interaction, personal charisma, professional mastery and cultural formation will emerge. The judge in this competition will be the audience and the hope is that the results will not be shocking or disappointing. Meanwhile, we can expect, in the near future, that our colleagues in the journalism and media profession will take the form of intelligent robots that will carry out various journalistic tasks more quickly than human beings.

The Third Challenge: Creating Stories and Videos for Characters

The program can be provided with the general idea (short story), the goal, and a description of the characters by age, educational attainment, characteristics, and way of thinking, and a description of the environment in which the characters of the work live, where the artificial intelligence elements will be able to reach a partial solution to the problem by using the idea of texts or scenarios to connect successive sentences. Imposing restrictions such as causal relationships and the way events occur.

Artificial intelligence elements have also developed a technology that can fabricate video clips that appear real to any person once only one photograph of him is available. This new technology, which is based on an experimental artificial intelligence system that has high technical capabilities has been employed in many of the matters that the media employs in its programs and news. And her other works as fake videos are expected to spread on social networking sites and some television channels.

Regarding the details of this technical and scientific achievement, researchers at the Samsung Center for Artificial Intelligence in Moscowa nd the Skolovo Institute of Technology in Moscow, presented a research paper containing preferable information about the project, and it was published on the famous arx IV website concerned with the latest technology achievements and research as they were able to move an image One or several images of people by training the artificial intelligence system on a set of video clips that include many celebrities so that it can learn the main points of the faces.

After that, the artificial intelligence system was able to combine several composite features with one or more images from a picture of a person to form a convincing video clip in the style of a talking head or even move the rest of the body's organs in a way that is closer to reality (Shamri, 2021).

Fourth Challenge: Deep Fakes

Deep fake software artificial intelligence technology produces lifelike but fake videos based on real people, has been used for comedic purposes (a Tom Cruise impersonation on TikTok) to cinematic purposes (such as a "non-aging" Luke Skywalker in... Planetary War film series) to artistic purposes (an unofficial musical collaboration between singers Drake and Weekend) to criminal purposes (identity theft, extortion) to anti-democratic purposes (spreading fake news).

It was named by this term because it combines "reality" and "fake" that is digital forgery of videos, the applications of which are known as deep fabrication which is the most prominent product of artificial intelligence as it has enabled the counterfeiting of audio and animated video clips of public, or perhaps unknown, figures which targets communities or individuals. On the other hand, the capabilities of digital verification programs to detect or deny the falsity of these clips are very limited (Abdel Hamid, 2020).

It seems that the most dangerous issue with those applications that have become used in all types of journalism fields is the existence of a real origin for the fake video that can be compared and presented clearly to indicate the fakery to prove the fakery and convince the recipient of it.

For this and other reasons, social media networks decided to send more potentially fabricated articles to third parties in order to investigate their credibility, and thus display the results of these parties under the original blog posts. To resolve this, social media networks must immediately begin relying on a developed mechanism. To monitor possible fabricated articles and figures and send them to fact-finding agencies. Indeed, testing of the new feature for verifying information has begun in the West.

The methods of exposure to media material through "traditional" and "new" media have changed significantly with the boom in the contributions of artificial intelligence to journalistic work. Among the evidence of this change is that many of the statements, photos, and videos, received through "social media" platforms in particular, have become replaced Greater doubt, and much of the correct information has become subject to discredit while some fabricated information has become more believable. These applications, which are being developed with passion, and their own systems are being developed very diligently, come up with something new every hour and increase their share in the production of media and creative content. Steadily and intensively to the point that some experts predicted that about 90 percent of the news and media products we consume will be the work of these machines within a few years.

Fifth Challenge: Augmented Reality

The term augmented reality means merging virtual information with the real world When a person uses this technology to look at the surrounding environment which is equipped with information that moves between it and integrates with the image that the person is looking at, technical development has greatly helped in the emergence of this technology In our hands and in our personal tools such as computers and mobile phones, it is the process of adding digital data, compiling it, visualizing it, and using digital methods to reflect the real reality of the environment surrounding a person. The augmented reality is used to combine digital content with the real world. It differs from virtual reality in that you will not need any headset, glasses, or any other device. All you need is the device's camera and the augmented reality application. Certainly these are factors that help in the presentation process to the recipient through the possibility of providing attractive elements so that the recipient lives as if he is part of the events he is witnessing, or that he is inside the scene experiencing the changes or they are coexisting within the exhibition hall (Moussa, Abdel Fattah, 2020).

Sixth Challenge: Material Technical Challenges

The problem of financing and the financial shortage in modern technology projects such as artificial intelligence applications, especially since most of the media and television channels have turned into companies, and the rapid and successive development in the technology of artificial intelligence applications and its models makes keeping up with it not easy, and other technological factors such as the efficiency of communication networks, And how easily it is available (AlRazek, 2022).

Seventh Challenge: Ethical and Social Challenges

Most of the challenges within the framework of ethical concerns imposed by artificial intelligence applications are as follows (Attia, 2019):

- Technological illiteracy in society and lack of awareness of artificial intelligence application technology.
- Artificial intelligence is a violation of the privacy of others, and may affect the level of human communication and interaction.
- Media professionals must realize that algorithms may be false or misleading, as they have been programmed by people who have their own biases, and logical models may lead to wrong conclusions. This means that media professionals will always have to verify the data and question the results.
- Some programs have become cheap and many media professionals can obtain them, and most journalists do not have the skills of programmers and data scientists.

Eighth Challenge: Intellectual Property Rights

Creators face many difficulties in maintaining the value of their works in the digital environment, in fact artificial intelligence may make it difficult for creators to maintain it as intellectual property rights are one of the main issues to think about when it comes to generative artificial intelligence.

If AI is used to produce works of art, literature, music, or any other type of work protected by intellectual property rights, it is important to determine who holds the intellectual property rights over these works.

In some legal systems, AI is considered a type of tool used by humans, and thus the human owner of the tool is considered the holder of the intellectual property rights. In this case the developer or company that developed the AI may be the legal owner of the works created by it.

On the media level quick action must be taken before these applications succeed in sending more journalists home, flooding the media field with misleading news, fake images and fabricated videos, stealing intellectual property rights, and undermining the world of journalism by stripping its products of the necessary minimum level of trust. Among these measures, the regulatory bodies regulating the media industry should strive to enact regulatory rules for the use of artificial intelligence products in journalistic work, and that self-regulatory bodies, unions, and press associations should add new parts to the media work manuals, codes of honor, and "codes" of practice. It specializes in dealing with the products of this intelligence. These legislative and regulatory approaches will not be complete except by adopting specific rules to protect intellectual property rights, and restraining the hands of these applications and those in charge of them from violating literary rights (Ismail, 2022).

The Third Section: Research Results and Discussion

The research results relate to an attempt to answer the questions in the section related to the methodological and theoretical framework of the research as well as the sub-questions that were prepared during the in-depth interview which are:

The first question: What benefit will the media get in developing form and content when they use artificial intelligence?

Sub-question: How successful is the use of artificial intelligence techniques in completing work? Are there benefits resulting from the data of this technology, or is it just a race to provide dazzling elements and nothing else?

Most Important Results

1. The respondents stressed that it is necessary to first acknowledge the pros and cons of the relationship between the generations of technologies and the mechanisms of media work, and that modern technology can be used to deceive people. However this does not negate its great contribution to serving people and facilitating many aspects of their lives, in addition to rapid and successive development. In visual AI techniques and models, which makes keeping up with them not easy.
2. The respondents indicated the ability of artificial intelligence technologies to simulate human behavior in carrying out many media tasks. This result confirms the importance of these technologies and the necessity of working to own and invest in them and benefit from the positives they achieve but under the supervision and follow-up of the human element.
3. The respondents indicated that the most prominent positive effects of modern technology is the role of artificial intelligence techniques in developing the content presented on television channels and that artificial intelligence plays a helpful role in developing the visual media landscape by giving media professionals greater speed in research and scrutiny that enabling them to do their job better.
4. The ability to accomplish this in record times and at a much lower financial cost than before the availability of artificial intelligence elements and their uses in the media sector.
5. The ability for the journalist to use machines in locations, situations, and times that a human journalist cannot do at the specified place and time.
6. It is necessary for the journalist to have a broad culture and high skills in order to maintain his position, job and superiority so that he remains the one who manages the automated journalist as an assistant in preparing the media material.

The second question: Is the media expected to distance itself, its audience, and its performance from the developments taking place in visual artificial intelligence technology?

Sub-question: Can the impact of lack of interaction and rapid response to developments imposed by artificial intelligence data on the media be limited?

Most Important Results

1. There are possibilities for a clash and incompatibility to emerge in the future between the intelligent product and the human product.

2. In light of the emergence of the Internet and satellite television channels, the ability of the media sector to adapt to changes and to change the way it interacts with the viewer has been demonstrated therefore all indicators indicate speed of adaptation and integration.
3. The emergence of many workers in the media sector calling for the necessity of preparing a plan towards transformation and interaction with elements of artificial intelligence.
4. The necessity of attracting and empowering creative talents and exploring the conditions of news and media institutions and the prospects for their development.
5. Paying attention to digital education, that is, spreading awareness and electronic culture in society among teachers, learners and parents.
6. Benefiting from countries experiences in the field of using artificial intelligence, as the exchange of experience enriches our experience

Question Three: Does the visible impact of artificial intelligence in the media reinforce the idea of the impact of modern technologies on professional values in media work?

Sub-question:

Will the new data related to artificial intelligence lead to fundamental changes in the journalistic process in terms of its structure, the roles that can be played and will it also affect the professional and ethical aspects that govern media work?

Most important results:
1. Researchers are aware of the concern that some people have regarding their work regarding the ethical impact that video and photo editing projects may have.
2. These technologies constitute a violation of the privacy of others and may affect the level of communication, interaction and humanity.
3. Human supervision is necessary in the use of artificial intelligence in the media and cannot be dispensed with.
4. Create new programs through which the media can discover videos, photos, and fabricated news.
5. In light of the close connection between communications technology and the communication process and their role in shaping a more secure future that ensures the ease of disseminating and receiving information and reduces the risks associated with it.
6. The current media landscape requires international entities to regulate the artificial intelligence sector in light of the spread of individuals and unknown parties spreading false information among the public using artificial intelligence techniques.
7. The necessity of having laws and legislation that regulate this stage in general to protect the human race and its rights from the behavior of artificial intelligence.

SOLUTIONS AND RECOMMENDATIONS

1- Holding intensive courses for workers in the visual media sector and specialists, preparing national human cadres and developing the infrastructure in a way that allows the development of these technologies and their applications which further improves the level of performance that using artificial intelligence techniques and its applications.
2- Holding intensive courses among workers in the university academic sector for professors, technicians, trainers and specialists which further improves the level of performance using artificial intelligence techniques and its applications. Media colleges and departments also have a responsibility to introduce media students to these techniques Therefore the provision of technical educational content must be expedited. It is commensurate with the size of the upcoming challenges for all students of media and communication faculties in Egyptian universities.
3- Expanding reliance on artificial intelligence applications in the Egyptian media and not limiting it to the content editing part to include data journalism, automatic correction and the detection of misleading information and fake news by subjecting them to analysis and comparison to prove their authenticity and verifying the credibility of the content in the various media to confront the fake news that It greatly harmed the credibility of content creators increased media production on the Internet and filtered trends on various search engines and social media sites.
4- Working to provide a legal and legislative framework that guarantees the regulation of the work of these modern technologies in a way that ensures that they do not deviate from legitimacy and any negative uses that may result from them may harm the Egyptian state in many aspects.

FUTURE RESEARCH DIRECTIONS

1- Conduct comparative studies between Egyptian, Arab and international visual media that use artificial intelligence.
2- Conduct an experimental study on the public to clarify the similarities and differences between outputs produced traditionally and those produced through artificial intelligence applications that are the positive and negative effects of that.

CONCLUSION

The rapid development of technology increases the need to carefully manage this nascent phase of artificial intelligence as our current responses will certainly influence its future course. There is still concern about artificial intelligence when it comes to adopting it in our daily work. There is an inherent discomfort in handling an inanimate object or in this case a software application that acts like a human. In addition artificial intelligence is more than any other technology, raises concerns about loss of function. Unlike other technologies, artificial intelligence applications, which are being developed with passion are also developing their own systems very diligently, It invents something new every hour and its share in the production of media and creative content increases steadily and intensely to the point that some experts expect that about 90 percent of the news and media products we consume will be the work of these machines within a few years.

Artificial intelligence is improving at record speed, we can benefit from the amazing unique and evolving manifestations of artificial intelligence but this good news is no longer able to withstand a set of bad news which surrounds the world of this intelligence and makes it a source of serious threat to the media because we cannot see its limits. Artificial intelligence has become a clear threat to the future of the journalist, the translator, the linguistic proofreader, the bulletin announcer, the program presenter, the dialogue facilitator and the article writer.

Artificial intelligence has become one of the most important headlines that appear in media products around the world today. It has also become linked to many aspects of our political, security, social, economic, health, and cultural lives. At every intersection between it and one of these fields, problems arise and risks are talked about.

The regulatory bodies regulating the media industry must strive to enact regulatory rules specifically for the use of artificial intelligence products in journalistic work and self-regulatory bodies, unions, and press associations that must add new sections to the media work manuals, codes of honor and "codes" of practice that specialize in dealing with all products of this intelligence. These legislative and regulatory approaches will not be complete except by adopting specific rules to protect intellectual property rights and restraining the hands of these applications that are in charge of them from violating literary rights.

It will be important for these regulatory and legislative approaches to include a clear and basic principle that obligates users of these applications in producing journalistic and creative materials spread across "media" of all kinds to place a mark through which every user understands that the product was prepared by artificial intelligence or with its assistance.

REFERENCES

Abdel Gawad, M. M. (2021). elite trends towards employing security media for artificial intelligence applications in combating cybercrimes. *Arab Journal of Media and Communication Research, Al-Ahram Canadian University, Egypt.*

Abdel Hamid, Amr. (2020). Employing artificial intelligence applications in producing media content and its relationship to its credibility among the Egyptian public. *Journal of Media Research, Al-Azhar University, Faculty of Mass Communication, Egypt.*

Abdel Hamid, M. (1997). *Theories of Influence.* Modern Egyptian library, Cairo, Egypt

Al-Ghatrifi, A. (2023). Digital Platforms and Transformations of the New Media Space. *Misr University Journal for Human Studies, Misr University of Science and Technology,.*

AlRazek, M. (2022). Artificial Intelligence Technologies in Media Reality and Future Developments. *Egyptian Journal of Media.*

AlSalhi, H. (2015). *Using interactive communication technology in practicing public relations activities in organizations operating in Yemen, Cairo University.* Faculty of Information.

Attia, B. (2019). the extent to which media professionals accept the use of artificial intelligence applications in the field of media, a survey study. *Egyptian Journal of Media Research, Faculty of mass communication.* Cairo University.

Badawy, M. (2020). Mechanisms for Implementing and Producing Robotic Journalism in Egypt in Light of the Use of Artificial Intelligence Tools. *Egyptian Journal of Media Research.*

Caswell, D., & Dörr, K. (2018). Automated Journalism Event driven narratives From simple descriptions to real stories. *Journalism Practice.* Advance online publication. 10.1080/17512786.2017.1320773

Changhoon, J. C., Lee, S., SoHyun, P., Kim, D., Song, J., Kim, D., Lee, J., & Suh, B. (2020). Understanding User Perception of Automated News Generation System. In *Proceedings of the.CHI'20, USA.*

Emelshtrich, L. N. (2018). *Robot Journalism: Can Human Journalism Survive?* World Scientific publishing.

Frary, M. (2019). The future is robotic: Would journalists have more time to investigate news stories if robots did the easy bits? *Index on Censorship*, 48(1), 8–10. 10.1177/0306422019842082

Graefe, A., & Bohlken, N. (2020). *Automated Journalism: A Meta-Analysis of Readers' Perceptions of Human-Written in Comparison to Automated News, Media and Communication.* Business Faculty, Macromedia University of Applied Sciences.

Gunawardena, P., Amila, O., Sudarshana, H., Nawaratne, R., Luhach, A. K., Alahakoon, D., Perera, A. S., Chitraranjan, C., Chilamkurti, N., & De Silva, D. (2021). Real-time automated video highlight generation with dual-stream hierarchical growing self-organizing maps. *Journal of Real-Time Image Processing*, 18(5), 1457–1475. 10.1007/s11554-020-00957-0

Han, J. (2020). *The Use of UTAUT and Post Acceptance Models to Investigate the Attitude towards a Telepresence Robot in an Educational Setting Robotics Sheffield Hallam University.*

Han, J.-H. (2018). UTAUT Model of Pre-service Teachers for Telepresence Robot, Assisted Learning. *J. Creat. Inf. Cult.*

Hussein, S. (2006). *Media Research.* World of Books, Cairo, Egypt.

Ismail, F. (2022). Journalists attitudes towards using artificial intelligence in developing journalistic content in Egyptian newspapers and websites. *Egyptian Journal of Public Opinion Research, Cairo University, of mass communication, Egypt.*

Krönke, C. (2020). Artificial Intelligence and Social Media. In Wischmeyer, T., & Rademacher, T. (Eds.), *Regulating Artificial Intelligence.* Springer. 10.1007/978-3-030-32361-5_7

Leppänen, L., Tuulonen, H., & Heikel, S. (2020). Automated Journalism as a Source of and a Diagnostic Device for Bias in Reporting [Issue.]. *Media and Communication,* 8(3), 39–49. 10.17645/mac.v8i3.3022

Miroshnichenko, A. (2019). *Robot Journalism, the Third Threat.* York-Ryerson Future Communications Conference, York University, USA.

Miroshnichenko, A. (2020). *AI to Bypass Creativity: Will Robots Replace Journalists?* Journal Information.

Moravec, V., MacKová, V., Sido, J., & Ekštein, K. (2020). *Communication Today.* Trnava Vol.

Moussa, I &, Abdel Fattah, A. (2020). Trends of journalists and leaders towards employing artificial intelligence techniques within newsrooms in Egyptian journalistic institutions, an applied study. *Egyptian Journal of Public Opinion Research.*

Papadimitriou, A. (2016). *The future of communication: Artificial intelligence and social network.* Media & Communication Studies.

Robert, L., Alahmad, R., Esterwood, C., Kim, S., & Zhang, Q. (2020). *Review of Personality in Human-Robot Interactions, Trends Inf.* Syst.

Sangwon, L. (2020). *Predicting AI News Credibility: Communicative or Social Capital or Both? Communication Studies.* Korea University.

Shamri, A. (2021). *Visual Media in Light of the Challenges of Artificial Intelligence.* University of Baghdad, College of Arts.

Sumak, B., Hericko, M., Pusnik, M., & Polančič, G. (2020). *Factors Affecting Acceptance and Use of Model: An Empirical Study Based on TAM, International Journal of Computing and Information.* Faculty of Electrical Engineering and Computer Science.

Tandoc, E., Edson, L., & Wu, S. (2020). *Man vs. Machine? The Impact of Algorithm Authorship on News Credibility, Digital Journalism.* Taylor & Francis.

Túñez-López, J.M., & Toural-Bran, C. (2018). Uso de bots y algoritmos para automatizar la redacción de noticias: Percepción y actitudes de los periodistas en España. *El Profesional de la Información.*

Túñez-López, J. M., Toural-Bran, C., & Frazão-Nogueira, A. G. (2020). *From Data Journalism to Robotic Journalism, The Automation of News Processing.* Journalistic Metamorphosis.

Venkatesh, V, Morris &all. (2003). The unified theory of acceptance and use of technology (UTAUT): A literature review. *Journal of Enterprise Information Management*.

Yan, D. (2020). *Robotic Cameraman for Augmented Reality based Broadcast and Demonstration*. University of Essex.

Yanfang, W. U. (2019). *Is Automated Journalistic Writing Less Biased? An Experimental Test of Auto-Written and Human-Written News Stories*. Journalism Practice University of Missouri.

KEY TERMS AND DEFINITIONS

Algorithms: Algorithms are named after the mathematician Muhammad bin Musa Al-Khwarizmi, meaning the code that a programmer writes and compiles to produce an executable unit. It includes a set of procedures arranged in a logical order and is implemented to reach a desired goal or outcome.

Augmented Reality: A technology that combines the real world with digital elements added to it. The experience of physical reality is enhanced and enhanced by adding digital elements such as images, text, 3D graphics, videos, and audio.

Automation or Robot Journalism: It is the use of robots and automated technologies to carry out journalism and publishing operations automatically, without human intervention. Robot journalism aims to improve the efficiency, speed of production of journalistic content, provide comprehensive and continuous coverage of events and news.

Generative Artificial Intelligence: A branch of artificial intelligence that focuses on creating systems and programs capable of generating new content in an intelligent and creative manner. Generative artificial intelligence aims to enable computer systems to produce outputs similar to those produced by humans, such as texts, images, sounds, and videos.

Simulation in the Media: It is the process of using technology and programs to create and generate media content that resembles or simulates reality in a realistic way.

Visual Media: A branch of media that aims to convey information, ideas, and messages using visual media such as motion pictures, films, television programs and series, television advertisements and promotional videos, and social media platforms .

Chapter 15
Artificial Intelligence in the Spanish Media:
New Uses and Tools in the Production and Distribution of Content

Marta Sánchez Esparza
http://orcid.org/0000-0001-6525-0148
UNIE Universidad, Spain

Santa Palella Stracuzzi
http://orcid.org/0000-0001-6610-7079
EAE Business School, Spain

ABSTRACT

In Spain, the media have been exploring artificial intelligence tools for some time. This study investigates which tools are used and in which processes, as well as their impact on the generation of content and the transformation of professional profiles. The methodology has a quantitative approach, through a survey of 35 journalists from the Association of Investigative Journalists (API), made up of media professionals from all over Spain. Among the main uses of AI are the processing and conversion of oral language into writing, the analysis of large amounts of data, the automation of tasks, and the relationship with audiences. A significant segment of respondents use AI tools in their work and believe that it will eventually be used for all automated tasks. However, most of them are not afraid of losing their jobs, as they value the importance of the human and creative component in their work performance.

INTRODUCTION

The arrival of Artificial Intelligence technologies in the media offers multiple benefits, such as the possibility of recommending content to users, automating journalists' tasks, improving audience interaction through chatbots, or verifying information (Rivas de Roca, 2021; Sánchez-Esparza et al., 2024). However, the implementation of these technologies faces issues ranging from economic cost to difficulties in hiring experts to develop AI solutions to internal attitudes of resistance to change (Fieiras et al., 2022). The presence of AI in journalism has sparked major debates about the extent of its adoption. Its

DOI: 10.4018/979-8-3693-3767-7.ch015

integration into content production and distribution processes has created new opportunities, but also drawbacks (Noain-Sánchez, 2022).

Among the benefits of AI in journalism is the ease of use of data, but there are also challenges such as the absence of technological infrastructures and qualified personnel and high costs, which hinder the implementation of AI in media organizations (De Lima & Salaverría, 2021). This research aims to address the impact that the arrival of AI is having on the work of journalists, through the study of a group of these professionals specialized in investigative journalism. The paper analyzes what tools are being used in the media in Spain, for what uses and what impact they are having on the transformation of content and professional profiles, as well as the perspectives of these professionals regarding the possibilities and risks derived from the implementation of these new technologies in the media.

The incorporation of AI in the media is part of the digital transformation processes experienced in the sector in recent decades. These processes are the result of the interaction between different forms of digital innovation that give rise to the emergence of new actors, structures, practices, and values. These elements, which replace and complement those that previously existed, are often accompanied by the emergence of new organizational forms, infrastructures, and institutional architectures (Hinings, Gegenhuber, & Greenwood, 2018). Digital transformation also implies a change in work methodologies and the establishment of new forms of relationships between the actors involved. It therefore involves a change in the production model that influences all the elements and activities involved in the value chain of a given product or service (Mergel, Edelmann, & Haug, 2019).

Nowadays, the digital transformation of the media involves a set of complex processes that must be approached in a strategic and comprehensive sense, since they affect both the structure of the content that is produced and distributed, and the relationship that the media themselves establish with their audiences (Sánchez, 2022). The growing prominence assumed by audiences in digital media has favored the transition from the production models typical of industrial environments, in which they remained unrelated to the development and production of the content they consumed, to digital environments, in which the boundaries between producers and consumers are increasingly blurred (Fernández, 2017).

In this context, the emergence of generative artificial intelligence tools raises the need to redefine the processes of production and distribution of news content. In fact, automation powered by generative AI allows media outlets to accelerate their production processes, freeing journalists from mechanical tasks, to focus on those that bring greater value to their work (Papadimitriou, 2016), automate the search and classification of information (Lemelshtrich, 2018) or combat disinformation more proactively and effectively (Flew et al., 2012).

In addition, technologies based on generative AI make it possible to analyze the behavior of audiences to offer personalized content to different users (Newman et. al, 2019). In this way, through the content recommendation systems currently used by news platforms, social networks, and streaming services, it is possible to adapt the user experience to their demands and needs, which favors a deeper and more meaningful connection with the content and with the medium itself.

However, these transformations are not without some important ethical challenges. The spread of fake news generated by algorithms and the risk of bias in content created by artificial intelligence systems are an obvious threat to the credibility of the media (Manfredi & Ufarte, 2020). In fact, as the use of these technologies becomes more widespread, it will become more important to establish a balanced relationship between human interaction and automation. Transparency in the implementation of these tools and collaboration between humans and machines will continue to be imperative to avoid bad practices and ensure the creation of relevant content for the audience. In this sense, collaboration between technologists, media professionals, and ethicists will be essential to shape a sustainable, innovative and user-centric digital media landscape.

The use of AI-based systems is causing a change in business models, and a significant transformation of the professional profiles that work in journalistic newsrooms. This change is manifested in the introduction of new roles, the demand for specialized skills, and the redefinition of some of the tasks that journalists have traditionally been performing. Thus, as a result of this transformation, opportunities have been created for professional profiles hitherto unrelated to this field, such as data engineers, experts in human-machine interaction, generative content writers, or editorial data analysts.

In fact, analogous to what has happened during other phases of digital transformation, the integration of generative AI into media not only redefines existing roles but also creates new possibilities for effective collaboration between artificial intelligence and human creativity.

BACKGROUND

The Implementation of AI Technologies in Media

In the media industry, AI creates significant changes and challenges. Some authors speak of a Fourth Industrial Revolution, driven by AI and automation, which is already transforming the way news and media content is produced, distributed, and consumed. This transformation raises questions about media accountability, the role of journalism, and freedom of expression (Vučković, 2023).

AI is currently used in the media to optimize and improve operations, such as data analysis and multimedia content generation (Sančanin & Penjisevic, 2022), and also to automate processes, including social media management, where algorithms can be trained to analyze users' actions, preferences, and reactions (Canavilhas, 2022; Jing, 2023). The implementation of AI on social media platforms is becoming inevitable, with applications including chatbots, which detect harmful behaviors, analyze data, and strategize (De Lima-Santos & Wilson, 2021). AI is also used in the news industry to disrupt traditional approaches, leveraging machine learning, planning, scheduling, and optimizing processes, which are increasingly developed (Eva, 2022). For professionals, the transformation experienced by the media means a liberation from routine tasks that allows them to produce higher-quality content. However, it also raises concerns about the growing reliance on technology platforms and the risk to editorial independence. Media workers perceive a threat to their jobs and a potential loss of their symbolic capital as intermediaries between reality and audiences (Koldobika, 2023).

For all of the above, the implementation of AI in the media poses social and epistemological challenges for journalists and the profession. In fact, there is a debate about the use of these technologies in the media within public institutions such as the European Union. Until now, regulatory frameworks related to AI rarely include the media; when they do, they address issues such as misinformation, data, AI literacy, diversity, plurality, and social responsibility (Porlezza, 2023). However, for the time being, policy documents adopted at the European level do not take into account the specificities of the sector (Pierson et al., 2023).

Meanwhile, artificial intelligence is revolutionizing the way media outlets operate and deliver content to their audiences. With the advancement of this technology, media has found new ways to collect, analyze, and present information in a more efficient and personalized way. Machine learning algorithms can analyze large amounts of information in a short amount of time, making it easier to identify patterns and trends in data. This has led to an improvement in the accuracy and speed of news delivery, allowing publishers to provide up-to-date and relevant information to their audience more quickly.

The arrival of AI in the media is not completely replacing human work, but for the time being, it complements it and streamlines certain processes. Media professionals play a crucial role in monitoring, making decisions, and ensuring the quality of AI-generated content. AI has the potential to help journalists craft new and original content, engage with audiences, verify online media content, and more, making media processes more efficient and impacting yet to be determined. Professionals face the forced challenge of adapting by learning artificial intelligence techniques, in a scenario full of questions about the performance of their functions. There are already numerous cases of synthetic media that generate their content completely automatically using algorithms, without the intervention of journalists (Ufarte-Ruiz et al., 2023). The algorithms used by these media simulate human behavior in the information process and learn from an initial set of data to produce and distribute artificial digital content with a realistic appearance and sound, including text, audio, and video. Through automated procedures, they generate personalized content and develop data verification processes. The algorithms thus allow media organizations to quickly select and receive topics in a fully customized way.

The Transformation of Journalism Thanks to Technology

The development of digital technologies has also driven a profound transformation of the profession of journalism, especially investigative journalism. The changes brought about by digitalization have provided journalists with new tools and platforms that simplify the exploration, analysis, and dissemination of information. These changes have impacted not only the methodologies used in their research, but also their scope, depth, and effectiveness.

The emergence of digital platforms has, first of all, made it easier for journalists from all over the world to cooperate in collaborative investigative projects, sharing resources and knowledge. This has led to research and collaborations between media outlets in different countries, broadening the scope and impact of the topics discussed. In addition, the use of digital tools has also helped citizens and organizations with very diverse profiles to support and disseminate the work of journalists, providing additional resources and giving greater scope to their investigations.

The Panama Papers represent an excellent example of this type of investigation. Following the leak of more than 11.5 million confidential documents from the law firm Mossack Fonseca, the International Consortium of Investigative Journalists (ICIJ) launched an exhaustive investigative process in 2015 involving more than 400 journalists from various media outlets around the world (López, 2018). After more than a year of research, in which digital technologies were instrumental in the acquisition, analysis, and processing of the leaked data, on April 3, 2016, the coordinated publication of the information by more than 109 media outlets from 76 different countries began. The revelations that emerged, in addition to having a major political impact at the global level, had a decisive influence on the promotion of legal measures aimed at combating tax avoidance and evasion at the international level (O'Donovan et al, 2019).

But in addition to facilitating collaboration among journalists, digital technologies have played a key role in the increasing democratization of access to information. Before the advent of digital systems, obtaining information involved a considerable investment of resources and often delivered unreliable results. In fact, in the context before the digital age, the success of investigative journalists depended to a large extent on their ability to obtain information from journalistic sources and to access leaks. Today, the abundance of information generated by digital systems allows for less mediated access to information, which translates into greater independence and the ability to conduct deeper and more complex investigations.

As a result of these transformations, digital technologies have opened up new opportunities for the creation of journalistic content. The growing trend towards the opening of data by public and private organizations or the emergence of tools and technologies that allow the extraction, processing and analysis of large data sets for informational purposes (Henninger, 2013, p. 158), have promoted the emergence of a new type of investigative journalism that, with a strong technological base, It uses data as a fundamental material for the construction of the informative story. This form of journalism, known as data journalism, has an eminently multidisciplinary character, integrating elements from the social sciences, statistical analysis, computer science, and information design (Fernández, 2017).

Currently, data journalists develop complex journalistic work in which they merge their ability to investigate with data analysis. Through interactive visualizations, mobile apps, and other forms of non-linear storytelling, data-driven stories offer an immersive user experience and a deeper understanding of the topics researched. Not only does this promote transparency and accountability, but it also stimulates public participation in the process of news discovery and dissemination.

In this context, generative AI tools can help journalists gather and process information at an unprecedented speed and scale. Through algorithms capable of automatically monitoring and extracting information from different sources (Hansen et al., 2017), AI not only allows journalists to collect more data but, above all, to process it and interpret its meaning more efficiently, quickly and accurately.

Some authors argue that the greatest short-term potential for AI in investigative journalism lies in data preparation tasks, such as extracting data from various documents and probabilistic linking records between databases (Stray, 2021).

THEORETICAL FRAMEWORK

Mission and History of Investigative Journalism

The Investigative Reporters and Editors (IRE) defined investigative journalism as the result of an original work of the journalist (as opposed to the result of investigations by the police, the courts, or other agencies), which deals with a topic of public relevance and importance to the audience, and which brought to light information that someone wanted to keep secret (Casal, 2007). The IRE was created in 1975 to promote investigative journalism in the United States. Through donations, he championed collective projects for the preparation of reports and research analysis and created a documentary collection with all the research works carried out in the history of this discipline.

Thus, investigative journalism seeks to uncover and expose hidden truths and hold those in power accountable for their actions. It plays a crucial role in providing the public with accurate and impartial information, promoting transparency and democracy. Through their investigations, investigative journalists strive to bring important issues to light, uncover corrupt practices, and shed light on social, political, and economic injustices. In doing so, they act as a control mechanism, ensuring that those in power are held accountable and that the public is informed and empowered to make decisions (Chen et al., 2021).

Investigative journalism emerged in the United States of America at the end of the 19th century and in the early years of the 20th century, thanks to the proliferation of a type of reporter eventually known as the 'Muckrakers', whose journalistic investigations led President Theodore Roosevelt himself to promote legislative measures to address some of the problems denounced. This type of journalism was consolidated in the following decades, experiencing a period of splendor around major scandals such as the Watergate case. The genre spread rapidly, and not just in the United States. In the 1990s, dozens of scandals were published in Britain and the rest of Europe, and according to authors such as Casal (2007), investigative journalism became an ideal for the profession, and the reporters who practiced it, a kind of heroes. For this reason, this group is of great interest when it comes to analyzing their degree of adaptation and use of new AI tools.

Artificial Intelligence (AI) and New Professional Profiles in the Media

Artificial Intelligence (AI) is the ability of a machine or computer system to simulate and perform tasks that would normally require human intelligence, such as logical reasoning, learning, and problem-solving (Morandín-Ahuerma, 2022). It is based on the use of algorithms and technologies that allow machines to develop certain skills and tasks autonomously or semi-autonomously.

As artificial intelligence improves, many processes are becoming more efficient and tasks that seem complicated today will be performed more quickly and accurately. This is why AI is reshaping professional profiles in the media industry. AI is expected to extend automated news to audio and video formats, change business models, and modify journalists' roles to focus on higher-value tasks (Túñez-López et al, 2021, Noain-Sánchez, 2022). The digital transformation of the media ecosystem requires new journalistic profiles with a combination of traditional journalistic knowledge and technological skills (García-Caballero, 2020).

AI can improve journalism by enabling faster breaking news and deeper analysis, emphasizing the need for editorial oversight when integrating AI into newsrooms (Marconi, 2020). Overall, AI is revolutionizing media professions, as it demands professionals to adapt to new roles and skills while also leveraging AI's capabilities to improve journalistic practices.

The media sector has undergone a profound restructuring due to the digital transformation of the media ecosystem, requiring new journalistic profiles with new skills and abilities (García-Caballero, 2020). New professional identities in the media are evolving in response to changes brought about by technology, the transformation of audiences, and the demands of the media environment. The emergence of non-media actors producing content and the decline in the audience interest in news are also determining factors in this transformation (Buck, 2014). These new identities must now be characterized by the ability to adapt to digital formats and tell stories in an engaging way on online platforms; multidisciplinarity; proficiency in the use of emerging technologies; the focus on the audience; data management skills; collaboration and teamwork and social media engagement and management, among other issues.

In this context, the arrival of AI in the media accelerates the transformation of journalists' professional profiles, moving to a less operational role, avoiding routines that can be imitated by machines and increasing cognitive contributions to news analysis and production (Túñez-López et al, 2021).

In this sense, some communication companies have already made forecasts about a foreseeable cast of new professional profiles that are expected to be incorporated in the coming years, as a result of the technological revolution generated by the irruption of digital and AI technologies.

At Radiotelevisión Española (RTVE), a state-owned public corporation with more than 6,500 employees, 45 new professional profiles have already been identified that could appear in the coming years due to the implementation of Artificial Intelligence technologies, especially in the areas of data and information collection, information processing and processing, and distribution and relationship with audiences. Among these new professional profiles, some stand out, such as automation editor, manager of editorial tools, ethical AI editor, or computational journalist (Sánchez-Esparza et al., 2024).

The implementation of Artificial Intelligence (AI) in the media industry brings benefits such as improving journalists' capabilities, saving time, and increasing productivity (Koldobica, 2023). However, challenges arise, such as the need to change mindsets, prioritize training on AI tools due to a lack of knowledge, and address ethical dilemmas arising from the integration of AI into newsrooms (Noain-Sánchez, 2022).

AI also presents obstacles related to media organizations' upholding editorial independence and the potential threat to journalists' jobs and symbolic capital (Abdulmajeed, 2023). In addition, AI systems can inadvertently perpetuate historical inaccuracies and biases, leading to discriminatory attitudes and behaviors in news content (Leiser, 2022). Overcoming these challenges requires a societal approach that takes into account the impact of AI on individuals, journalists, and the public, emphasizing the appropriate use of AI for the benefit of the profession and society (Tuñez-López et al., 2021).

OBJECTIVES

The aim of this research has been to analyze the use of AI tools and technologies in the Spanish media, through a specific professional group: investigative journalists integrated into the Association of Investigative Journalists (API).

To achieve this general objective, the following specific objectives were set and developed from the perspective of the investigative journalists integrated into the IPA of Spain:

- Explore the implementation of AI tools in the media, specifying the types, origin, uses, frequency and area of activity
- Describe the benefits, obstacles, and challenges of AI with respect to professional profiles.

RESEARCH METHODOLOGY AND APPROACH

An exploratory research with a quantitative approach was carried out, using a field research design with a descriptive cross-sectional approach. The study was conducted among journalists who are members of the Association of Investigative Journalists of Spain (API).

The research was divided into two stages: a thorough review of the literature that included the exploration of various documentary sources, such as Web of Science, Scopus, and Google Scholar, as well as the use of the SCISPACE platform to improve the search for scientific publications through the integration of artificial intelligence. The second stage consisted of fieldwork, which included data collection using a specific instrument and a descriptive analysis to examine the distribution of responses and the prevalence of opinions or behaviors among the IPA participants surveyed.

To carry out the study, the survey technique was used and a questionnaire was designed and administered to a representative sample of 35 IPA investigative journalists, selected from a total of 62 members, equivalent to 56% of the collective. According to the criteria established by Palella and Martins (2017), this sample size is considered sufficiently representative of the population.

The questionnaire consisted of 41 mixed questions, including dichotomous, multiple-choice, and open-ended answer options. The validity of the instrument was assessed through the judgment of three experts in research methodology, journalism and communication, and data engineering, whose suggestions for improvement were incorporated into the final version of the questionnaire.

In addition, Cronbach's alpha coefficient was calculated to evaluate the internal consistency of the instrument, obtaining a value of 0.736, which indicates a moderate to good consistency in the participants' responses, considered acceptable when exceeding the threshold of 0.7.

The study focused on two main variables with their respective indicators: the first variable was related to Artificial Intelligence (AI) technologies and professional profiles, addressing aspects such as the emergence of new profiles, substitute functions, job loss, and training in the use of AI. The second variable focused on the implementation of Artificial Intelligence Technologies, exploring aspects such as the types of technologies, their origin, uses, frequency, area of activity, implementation, benefits, and obstacles. The instrument was administered through the Google Forms tool directly in the web or mobile browser, and by sending the link to the 62 IPA journalists.

RESULTS AND DISCUSSION

Characteristics of the sample: The sample consists of journalists affiliated with the Spanish Association of Investigative Journalists (API), with a varied distribution of roles:

- One-third of respondents hold editorial roles, indicating a significant presence of this profile in the media organizations represented in the sample. In addition, a diversity of journalistic roles is observed among the respondents, including journalists, reporters, and directors, among others.
- In terms of the nature of the means of work, almost half of the respondents work in digital media, while the rest are distributed between written media, audiovisual media, and combinations of several media.

Regarding the perspectives of IPA investigative journalists on AI technologies, results were obtained on the implementation of AI technologies in terms of types, provenance, uses, frequency, and area of activity from the perspective of IPA members in Spain.

According to the figure below (1), nearly half of respondents (48.6%) mentioned that the AI-based technologies currently used include machine recognition, followed by 40% who mentioned machine translation (MT) and 45.7% who mentioned tools for SEO.

Artificial Intelligence in the Spanish Media

Figure 1. Types of AI-based technology used

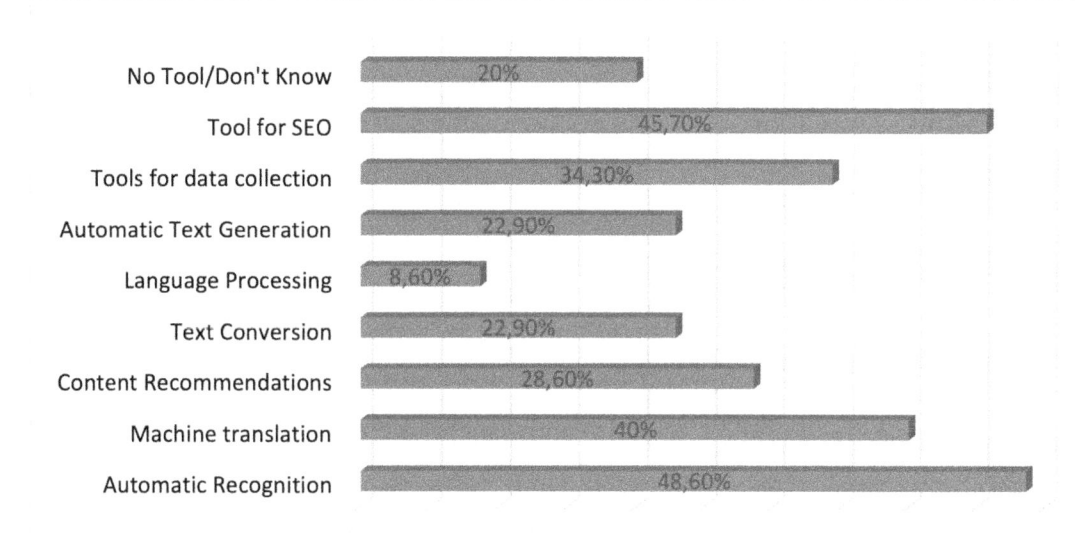

Technology	Percentage
No Tool/Don't Know	20%
Tool for SEO	45,70%
Tools for data collection	34,30%
Automatic Text Generation	22,90%
Language Processing	8,60%
Text Conversion	22,90%
Content Recommendations	28,60%
Machine translation	40%
Automatic Recognition	48,60%

(Survey results)

44.10% of IPA journalists use these tools sporadically, 35.30% regularly, and not at all 20% as shown in the following figure (2).

Figure 2. Frequency of use of AI tools

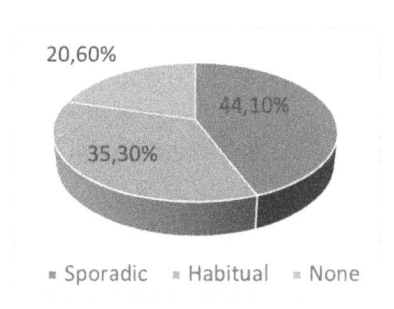

Category	Percentage
Sporadic	44,10%
Habitual	35,30%
None	20,60%

(Survey results)

Regarding the areas of activity where they use AI tools, 68.8% indicated their use in the collection of data and information, while 50% mentioned their application in the processing and treatment of data. In addition, 34% reported using these tools in distribution and interaction with audiences, as can be seen in the figure below (3).

Figure 3. Areas of activity where they use AI tools

- Data and Information Collection — 68,80%
- Processing and treatment — 50%
- Distribution and relationship with audiences — 34,40%
- No — 6,30%
- I don't know — 3,10%

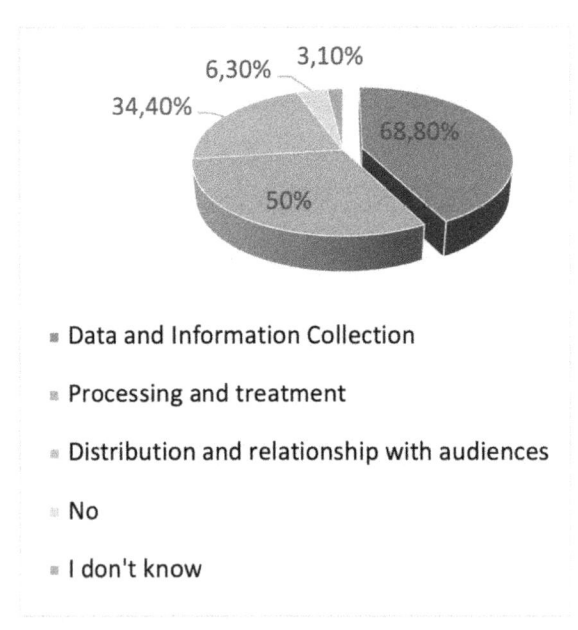

(Survey results)

A large majority, represented by 80%, perceive AI tools as beneficial for businesses and organizations. In addition, 77% believe that these tools also provide benefits at the individual level, in contrast to a small 11% who do not share this perception.

On the other hand, in relation to the main uses of AI, it is noteworthy that 54.8% of respondents pointed to the processing and conversion of oral language into written language as a key application. In addition, 42.8% mentioned the analysis of large amounts of data, while 45.7% highlighted the relevance of content recommendation. Likewise, 41% emphasized audience analysis and automatic text generation, while 25.8% highlighted the importance of search engine content optimization.

Participants agree that the implementation of AI tools will be beneficial for media organizations. It is emphasized that these tools can improve the efficiency and automation of tasks, leading to a more effective use of resources and the production of higher-quality content.

It is specifically mentioned that AI can streamline processes such as interview transcription, image generation, and video processing, resulting in reduced costs and increased productivity. In addition, it is highlighted that AI facilitates tedious or recurring tasks for journalists, thus improving their quality of work life and allowing them to spend more time on creative or analytical activities.

In addition to these benefits, it is highlighted that AI can contribute to the personalization and optimization of content, which allows you to more effectively reach specific audiences and improve interaction with them. It is also mentioned that it improves data processing and prediction, resulting in more informed and accurate decision-making.

Despite some concerns expressed about potential job losses or the quality of AI-generated content, most responses reflect a positive perception of the potential benefits of implementing AI tools in media organizations.

IPA journalists identify a number of obstacles and negative effects related to the implementation of AI in media organizations. 65.7% of respondents point out that there is concern about the possible generation of low-quality content, which could erode the reputation and credibility of these organizations. In addition, 57% express concern about the impact AI could have on existing jobs, which could lead to resistance to change and affect employee morale.

In addition, 54% of the participants mention possible cultural problems, such as fear or resistance to changes in job roles or in the way tasks are performed, while 51.4% highlight economic concerns due to the lack of investment needed to adopt these technologies. Implementing AI can require significant investment in infrastructure, training, and skills development, which is challenging, especially for smaller media organizations.

These obstacles are identified as major challenges that must be addressed with carefully planned strategies to achieve a successful implementation of AI tools in media organizations, as shown in Figure 4.

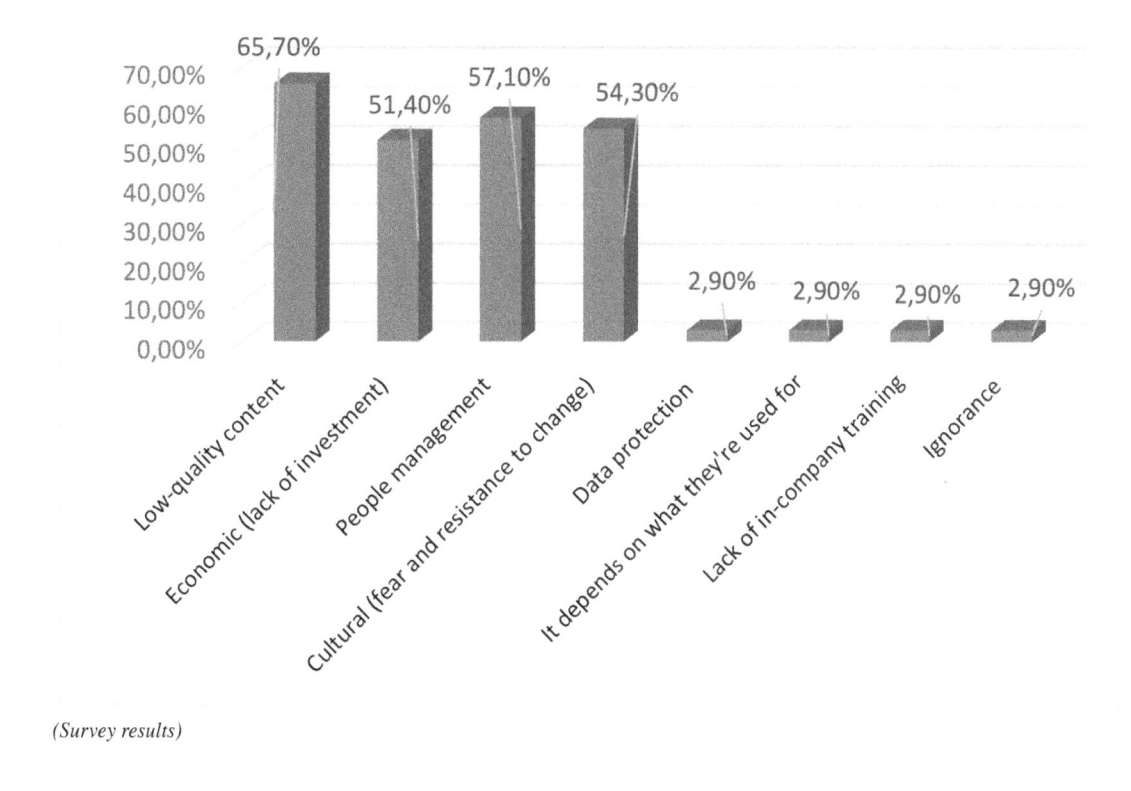

Figure 4. Obstacles in the implementation of AI tools in media organizations

(Survey results)

Artificial Intelligence and Jobs

In the companies where IPA members work, 100% of those surveyed stress that no professional profiles have disappeared and that no new profiles have appeared, although the early arrival of some is on the horizon. In terms of role replacement, 61.8% of respondents are of the opinion that AI could replace all functions related to automated tasks in their company. This reflects a widespread perception of the potential of AI technologies to automate routine and repetitive processes in the workplace.

On the other hand, 20.6% of respondents suggest that only some technical functions could be replaced by AI, while 17% say that all functions could be replaced except those that require a strategic and creative approach. This perspective highlights the importance of distinctive human skills, such as creativity, strategic decision-making, and adaptability, which can be difficult for AI to replicate, as indicated in Figure 5.

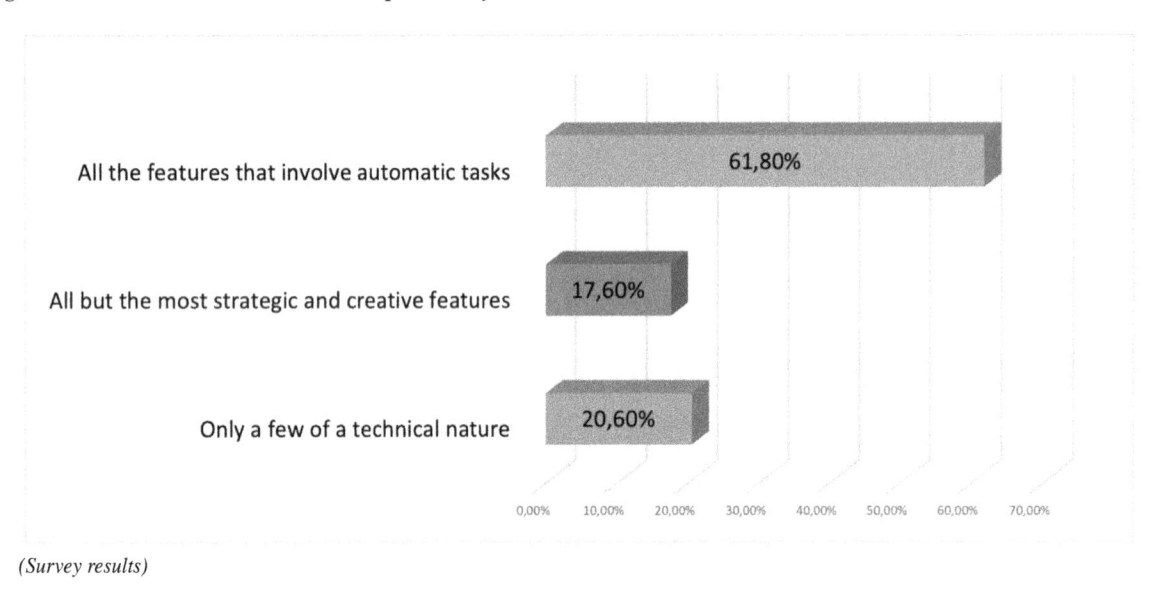

Figure 5. Functions that could be replaced by AI

Function	Percentage
All the features that involve automatic tasks	61,80%
All but the most strategic and creative features	17,60%
Only a few of a technical nature	20,60%

(Survey results)

91.4% of respondents do not feel fear of losing their jobs due to the implementation of AI. When asked why they did not have this fear, 62.07% highlighted that their work involves a fundamental human component, such as direct contact with sources, the ability to discover stories through conversations, and decision-making based on experience and human judgment.

20.69% highlighted the creative nature of their work, which they consider difficult to replicate by an AI, relying on the unique ability of human beings to generate original ideas and approaches. Meanwhile, 17.24% recognized the potential of AI as a useful tool to improve certain aspects of their work but emphasized that human intervention is still necessary to use it effectively and ensure the quality of the results, as shown in Figure 6.

Figure 6. Fear of losing a job

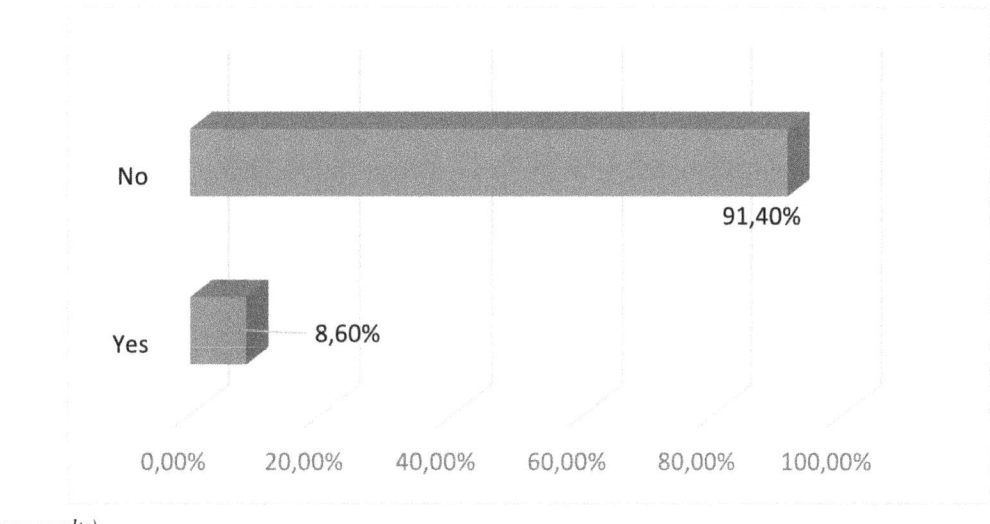

No — 91,40%
Yes — 8,60%

(Survey results)

Although AI could pose a threat to some jobs, it is recognized that there are aspects of human job roles that are difficult for AI to replicate, such as creativity, specialized knowledge, and a unique focus on problem-solving. Respondents show interest in developing skills that allow them to excel in areas where AI cannot yet fully match human capabilities, such as generating original content and a deep understanding of specific topics.

On the other hand, Figure 7 shows that 62.5% of respondents have made the decision to train and learn the use of tools in this area, while only 37.5% have not yet considered this option.

Figure 7. Decision to train or learn in the use of AI

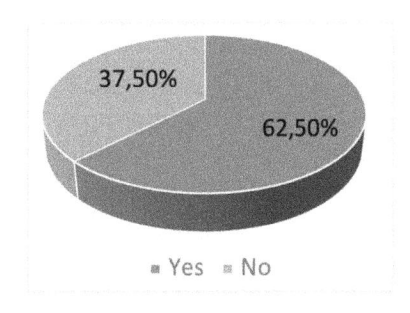

Yes — 62,50%
No — 37,50%

(Survey results)

Algorithms, Sensationalism, and Disinformation

The study addressed the perception that investigative journalists have about the impact of AI on the proliferation of certain content, driven by specific algorithms. One example is the fear that this technology will prioritize sensationalist content in the media, which are the ones that generate the most traffic on web pages. 82.4% think that AI will bring this type of content, which serves as click bait and generates greater business volume (Figure 8). In this same dynamic, algorithms could prioritize some content and make others disappear, according to 54.3% of respondents.

Figure 8. Will AI prioritize sensationalist content?

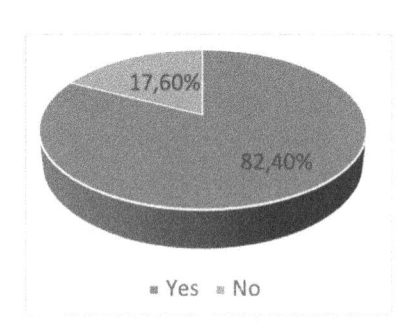

(Survey results)

80.4% of respondents say their companies are not using any AI tools to verify content suspected of being fake. However, 19.6% are. In these cases, natural language recognition technology and free tools from Google are used, as well as other generative AI tools such as ChatGPT. The latter is used at a particular level by the journalists surveyed.

All respondents believe that AI is contributing to the spread of fake content, especially through fake images and Deep fakes. The use of algorithms that serve to virtualize certain information also increases the impact of these falsehoods, according to the respondents.

Among the reasons given by journalists in relation to the proliferation of disinformation due to AI are the ease of creating false content either through the generation of text, images, videos or sounds, which may appear real and truthful to the public, and the increasing difficulty in distinguishing between true and false information. as they are contents with a very realistic appearance. Also the manipulation of images and sounds and the lack of verification and human control.

On the other hand, journalists also believe that the same technology serves to prevent the proliferation of false content (48.6%), or that it can sometimes be useful (31.4%), since many AI tools can be used to detect and verify hoaxes and Deep fakes more quickly and effectively. However, in 58.8% of cases, respondents' companies are not investing in AI tools to combat misinformation at the moment. On the other hand, 41.2% are already doing so (Figure 9).

Figure 9. Will AI prioritize sensationalist content?

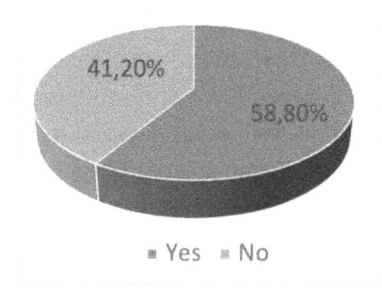

[Pie chart: Yes 58.80%, No 41.20%]

(Survey results)

The results obtained from the sample provide a comprehensive view of IPA journalists' perceptions, attitudes, and concerns regarding the integration of AI in the field of journalism. Despite the challenges and barriers identified, significant opportunities are recognized to improve the efficiency and quality of journalistic work through the responsible and effective application of AI.

Regarding the impact of AI on the professional profiles of investigative journalists, the results reveal that while there are concerns about the potential decline in content quality and the effects on existing jobs, the majority of respondents do not fear losing their jobs due to AI. This suggests confidence in unique human abilities to generate original ideas and make decisions based on experience and judgment. However, the importance of training and adaptation to new skills is recognized, reflecting an evolution in professional profiles towards less operational roles and more focused on higher-value tasks, as pointed out by Túñez-López et al. (2021).

In relation to the identification of benefits, problems, obstacles, and challenges for professional profiles, the sample reflects a generally positive perception of the potential benefits of AI, such as improving the effectiveness and streamlining of journalistic work. However, concerns about the potential reduction in content quality, impact on existing jobs, and ethical and training challenges are also highlighted. These findings are consistent with the idea that AI presents opportunities to improve journalists' capabilities, but it also poses challenges related to editorial independence, professional ethics, and the need to adapt to an ever-evolving work environment, as Koldobika (2023) and García-Caballero (2020) point out.

In summary, the results obtained from the sample offer a comprehensive view of how the implementation of AI is influencing the professional profiles of investigative journalists and the content disseminated by the media, highlighting both the potential benefits and the challenges and barriers that must be overcome to ensure a successful and sustainable integration of AI in the new journalism.

CONCLUSION AND RECOMMENDATIONS FOR THE FUTURE

The results of the research provide a detailed overview of the implementation of AI tools in the Spanish media, addressing aspects such as types, provenance, uses, frequency, and area of activity. It is observed that automatic speech recognition (ASR) and tools for data collection and/or processing are the technologies most commonly used by investigative journalists today.

The main use of these tools is the processing and conversion of oral language into writing, followed by content recommendation and analysis of large amounts of data. Although less frequent, automatic text generation, audience analysis, and search engine content optimization are also highlighted as important uses of AI in this area.

The implementation of AI tools in media organizations is a reality in the short term. The obstacles that journalists foresee in the process of implementing AI are the proliferation of low-quality and sensationalist content, job losses, as well as fear and resistance to change. For the time being, no new professional profiles associated with AI have appeared or disappeared, although the arrival of new functions and roles in the media is expected.

Regarding the influence of AI in the dissemination of false content, respondents believe that this technology contributes to the virtualization of these falsehoods and that the ease with which false images and Deep fakes are generated and the manipulation of content makes it increasingly difficult to differentiate between truth and lies. However, a significant percentage believe that AI could also play an important role in preventing the proliferation of this content.

In relation to new professional profiles, although a small percentage of respondents have experienced the emergence of new AI-associated profiles, there is an emerging trend towards the integration of technical and specialized roles in SEO with AI in media companies. However, the need to incorporate new AI-related professional profiles into work teams has not yet been seen, which can be attributed to a lack of understanding of its potential or a resistance to change.

Respondents show an awareness of the importance of adapting and being prepared for the changes that AI may bring to the job market. They highlight the need for training in AI and the acquisition of new skills and knowledge related to this technology, both to use it as a support tool in their current work and to explore opportunities in other fields. In short, the results reflect a view that recognizes the value of AI as a complement, but not a complete replacement, for human skills in journalism.

Looking to the future, it would be advisable to extend this type of research at the academic level to new professional groups, including other groups of diverse specialization within journalism, so that the results and findings are more conclusive. On a professional level, the reality of the growing use of AI in the media imposes transformation strategies on the companies themselves, which involve the requalification of professionals through training and preparation in new skills and the use of tools. It is also advisable to transform the mentality of the professionals themselves, to whom a decisive investment in technological training is recommended.

REFERENCES

Abdulmajeed, M., & Fahmy, N. (2023). Meta-analysis of AI Research in Journalism: Challenges, Opportunities and Future Research Agenda for Arab Journalism. In Musleh Al-Sartawi, A. M. A., Razzaque, A., & Kamal, M. M. (Eds.), *From the Internet of Things to the Internet of Ideas: The Role of Artificial Intelligence. EAMMIS 2022. Lecture Notes in Networks and Systems* (Vol. 557). Springer. 10.1007/978-3-031-17746-0_18

Buck, A. (2014). *Building professional identities through social media*. SPIR. https://spir.aoir.org/ojs/index.php/spir/article/view/8485

Canavilhas, J. (2022). Artificial Intelligence Applied to Journalism: Machine Translation and Content Recommendation in the "A European Perspective" (EBU) project. *Latin Journal of Social Communication*, (80), 24.

Casal, F. M. (2007). *Introduction to Contemporary Investigative Journalism in the U.S. Press. Doxa Communication Interdisciplinary Journal. Number 5*. CEU Ediciones.

Centre for Sociological Research (CIS). (2018). *Three main problems that currently exist in Spain*. CIS. http://www.cis.es/cis/export/sites/default/- Archivos/Indicadores/documentos_html/TresProblemas.html (24.10.2018)

Chen, Y., Li, M., Lu, G., Shen, H., & Zhou, J. (2021). Hydroxychloroquine/Chloroquine as Therapeutics for COVID-19: Truth under the Mystery. *International Journal of Biological Sciences*, 17(6), 1538–1546. 10.7150/ijbs.5954733907517

Porlezza, C. (2023) Promoting responsible AI: A European perspective on the governance of artificial intelligence in media and journalism. *Communications*, 48(3), 370–394. 10.1515/commun-2022-0091

De Lima-Santos, M.-F., & Cerón, W. (2022). Artificial Intelligence in News Media: Current Perceptions and Future Outlook. *Journalism and Media*, 3(1), 13–26. 10.3390/journalmedia3010002

De-Lima-Santos, M.F., Salaverría, R. (2021). *From Data Journalism to Artificial Intelligence: Challenges Faced by La Nación in Implementing Computer Vision in News Reporting*. 10.5294/pacla.2021.24.3.7

Díaz Güell, L. (2003). *Journalism and Investigative Journalists in Spain, 1975-2000: Contribution to Political, Legal, Economic and Social Change* [Doctoral dissertation, Complutense University of Madrid].

Eva, K. (2022). *Usage of artificial intelligence on social media in Europe*. Ad Alta., 10.33543/1202330333

Fernandez, A. (2017). *Hybrid Stories: The Role of Narrativity in the Visualization of Interactive Information* [PhD Thesis, Universidad Europea]. Abacus Repository https://193.147.239.238/handle/11268/6981

Fieiras-Ceide, C., Vaz-Álvarez, M., & Túñez-López, M. (2022). Artificial intelligence strategies in European public broadcasters: Uses, forecasts and future challenges. *El Profesional de la Información*, 31(5), e310518. 10.3145/epi.2022.sep.18

Flew, T., Spurgeon, C., Daniel, A., & Swift, A. (2012). The promise of computational journalism. *Journalism Practice*, 6(2), 157–171. 10.1080/17512786.2011.616655

García-Caballero, S. (2020). New professional profiles for the journalistic market. *Mediterranean Journal of Communication*, 11(1), 287–289. 10.14198/MEDCOM2020.11.1.15

Hansen, M., & Roca-Sales, M. (2017). *Artificial Intelligence: Practice and Implications for Journalism. Tow Center for Digital Journalism.* Columbia Journalism School, New York.

Henninger, M. (2013). *Data-driven journalism. Challenge and Change: Reassessing Journalism's Global Future.* Sydney, Australia: UTS ePRESS University of Technology. http://www.teccomstudies.com/index.php?journal=teccomstudies&page=article&op=view&path[]=148

Jessica, M. (2022, May 19). Kunert., Jannis, Frech., Michael, Brüggemann., Volker, Dr. Lilienthal., Wiebke, Loosen. (2022). How Investigative Journalists Around the World Adopt Innovative Digital Practices. *Journalism Studies*, 23(7), 761–780. 10.1080/1461670X.2022.2033636

Jing, H. (2023). The Rising Trend of Artificial Intelligence in Social Media. *Advances in Computer and Electrical Engineering book series.* 10.4018/978-1-6684-6937-8.ch003

Koldobika, MesoM. (2023). Without journalists, there is no journalism: the social dimension of generative artificial intelligence in the media. *Information Professional.* 10.3145/epi.2023.mar.27

Leiscr, M.R., (2022). *Bias, journalistic endeavors, and the risks of artificial intelligence.* Springer. 10.4337/9781839109973.00007

Lemelshtrich, N. (2018). Robot Journalism, Can Human Journalism Survive? Israel: Herzliya Interdisciplinary Center.

López López, P. J. (2018). Data Journalism in the Panama Papers. *TecCom Studies,* 7(1). http://www.teccomstudies.com/index.php?journal=teccomstudies&page=article&op=view&path%5b%5d=148

Manfredi, J. L., & Ufarte, M. J. (2020). Artificial intelligence and journalism: a tool against disinformation. *Revista CIDOB d'Afers Internacionals, 124*, 49–72. https://www.jstor.org/stable/26975708

Marconi, F. (2020). *Newsmakers: Artificial Intelligence and the Future of Journalism.* Columbia University Press., https://www.jstor.org/stable/10.7312/marc1913610.7312/marc19136

Marieke, M., & Hendriksen, A. (2023). The future of jobs: interviews with artificial intelligence.]10.22541/au.168599000.07517003/v1

Mergel, I., Edelmann, N., & Haug, N. (2019). Defining digital transformation: Results from expert interviews. *Government Information Quarterly, 36*(4). doi: https://doi.org/. giq.2019.06.00210.1016/j

Morandín-Ahuerma, F. (2022). What is Artificial Intelligence? *International Journal of Research Publication and Reviews*, 03(12), 1947–1951. 10.55248/gengpi.2022.31261

Noain Sánchez, A. (2022). Addressing the Impact of Artificial Intelligence on Journalism: The perception of experts, journalists and academics. *Communicatio Socialis*, 35(3), 105–121. 10.15581/003.35.3.105-121

O'Donovan, J., Wagner, H. F., & Zeume, S. (2019). The value of offshore secrets: Evidence from the Panama Papers. *Review of Financial Studies*, 32(11), 4117–4155. 10.1093/rfs/hhz017

Palella, S., & Martins, F. (2017). *Quantitative research methodology.* FEDEUPEL.

Papadimitriou, A. (2016). *The Future of Communication: Artificial Intelligence and Social Networks.* Media & Communication Studies. Mälmo University. http://bit.ly/379xa7O

Pierson, J., Kerr, A., Robinson, S. C., Fanni, R., Steinkogler, V. E., Milan, S., & Zampedri, G. (2023). Governing artificial intelligence in the media and communications sector. *Internet Policy Review*, 12(1). Advance online publication. 10.14763/2023.1.1683

Rivas-de-Roca, R. (2021). *Opportunities of robotization in local journalism: the case of 'Mittmedia.* Index Comunicación. 10.33732/ixc/11/02Oportu

Rubio Campaña, A. (2006). *Spanish journalists in the Rif War. The beginning of investigative journalism in Spain.* [Dissertation, Complutense University of Madrid].

Sančanin, B., & Penjisevic, A. (2022). Use of artificial intelligence for the generation of media content. *Social Informatics Journal*, 1(1), 1–7. 10.58898/sij.v1i1.01-07

Sánchez Esparza, M. (2015) *The journalistic construction of the story of corruption: analysis of the Malaya case.* [Dissertation, University of Málaga]. Institutional repository of the University of Málaga. https://riuma.uma.es/xmlui/handle/10630/8845

Sánchez Gonzales, H. (2022). Digital transformation and audience. Trends and use of artificial intelligence in fact-checking media. *Scopes: International Journal of Communication*, 56, 9–20.

Sanz, R. M., & Stolle, P. D. (2019). The practice of investigative journalism in Spain. The perception of your current state. *Revista Latina de Comunicación Social*, (74), 822–839.

Stray, J. (2021). Making artificial intelligence work for investigative journalism. *Algorithms, Automation, and News*, 97-118. 10.1080/21670811.2019.1630289

Tijeras, R. (2018). Investigative journalism in Spain. *Communication, 21*(9).

Túñez-López, J. M., Fieiras-Ceide, C., & Vaz-Álvarez, M. (2021). Impact of Artificial Intelligence on Journalism: Transformations in the company, products, contents and professional profile. *Communicatio Socialis*, 34(1), 177–193. 10.15581/003.34.1.177-193

Ufarte-Ruiz, M. J., Murcia-Verdú, F. J., & Túñez-López, J. M. (2023). *Use of artificial intelligence in synthetic media: first newsrooms without journalists.* Information Professional., 10.3145/epi.2023.mar.03

Vučković, J. (2023). *Artificial intelligence in the media. Comparative Legal Challenges in Contemporary Law - In memoriam Dr.* Stefan Andonović., 10.56461/ZR_23.SA.UPISP_JV

ADDITIONAL READING

Cerezo, P. (2022). *Deconstructing the media. How to adapt communication companies to the digital environment.* Almuzara.

Davenport, T. H., & Kirby, J. (2016). *Only humans need to apply: Winners and losers in the age of smart machines.* Harper Business.

Ghosh, M., & Thirugnanam, A. (2021). Introduction to Artificial Intelligence. In: Srinivasa, K.G., G. M., S., Sekhar, S.R.M. (eds) *Artificial Intelligence for Information Management: A Healthcare Perspective. Studies in Big Data.* Springer, Singapore. https://doi.org/10.1007/978-981-16-0415-7_2

Rogers, D. L. (2021). *Strategic Guide to Digital Transformation.* Ediciones Urano.

Russell, S., & Norvig, P. (2020). *Artificial intelligence: A modern approach* (4th ed.). Pearson.

Sierra, J., & Lavilla, D. (2024). *Digital Connections: The Communication Revolution in Contemporary Society.* McGraw-Hill.

KEY TERMS AND DEFINITIONS

Artificial Intelligence: Discipline of computer science that focuses on the design and management of technology capable of emulating human intelligence. This involves the creation of systems and algorithms that allow machines to perform tasks inherent to human intelligence, such as learning, reasoning, self-correcting, and making decisions autonomously.

Investigative Journalists: Professionals who uncover and expose relevant and hidden information that affects society. They are dedicated to investigating matters of importance that some people or organizations wish to keep secret. Their work, which is often prolonged over time, focuses on unraveling the truth and exposing corruption, abuse of power, and other problems. This type of journalism involves systematic, in-depth, and original research, and often involves intensive use of data and public records. Their goal is to inform the public and promote transparency and accountability.

Media: The main means of mass communication (broadcasting, publishing, and the internet) regarded collectively.

Professional Profiles: Professional profiles are ideal models of workers prepared to assume certain functions that are in demand within an organization, thanks to their qualifications and knowledge.

Technologies: The application of scientific knowledge for practical purposes, especially in industry. The term can also refer to the products resulting from these efforts, including both tangible tools such as utensils or machines, and intangible ones such as software.

AFTERWORD

The title of this book "Changing Global Media Landscapes: Convergence, Fragmentation, and Polarization" addresses the media problem from three perspectives: the message (content), the technology, and the consequences. Marshall McLuhan's arguments in his influential book "The Medium is the Message" published in 1967 are still relevant in the 21st century (McLuhan, 1967). McLuhan emphasized that the various media processes reshape and reconstruct the patterns of people's thinking, behaviors, and sociocultural environment (McLuhan, 1967). The chapters of this book offer a view of the history of communication and technology developments including artificial intelligence

I understand and appreciate the debates concerning the ideas introduced by McLuhan in his book. However, it is important to recognize that Marshall McLuhan foresaw a brighter future for media technology, a concept that aligns with what is described as today's "digital media". On the one side flow of information has expanded, and so have the carriers and channels for transferring the information. Conversely, the receivers are engulfed swimming in uncontrol waves of data and information leading to confusion, conflict, contradictions, fragmentation, and even polarization. Hence the audience began to question aspects of the content presented by digital and social media.

1. CREDIBILITY

In this volume, readers will be exposed to the concept of how traditional media turned into a tool for expressing the opinions of the ruling authority, governments, and politicians, while social media has become an instrument for ordinary citizens and the public to express their ideas and opinions. Media credibility is on the line.

2. CONFLICT

Media criticism and coverage of issues and the public debate on social media increase the possibility of creating a conflict because of the different framing processes, from the initial formation of frames to the subsequent development of news stories and reports. This complex interplay of political, cultural, social, and religious factors shapes and reshapes the narratives surrounding conflicts and their representation in the media.

3. FAIRNESS

The chapters in this book highlight that achieving fairness and objectivity in "frame balancing" is challenging. Dominant frames continue to focus on issues of identity, public opinion motivation, and maintaining a positive social context that sustains discord. This conclusion will be beneficial for readers and media professional

4. IDENTITY

The book delves into the issue of how media plays a role in enforcing and fracturing the identity of their audience. The individual's social and cultural identity can be made up of gender, class, age, race, ethnicity, sexual orientation, nationality, origin of nationality, and religion, with many of these identities intersecting (Luther et al, 2018, p. 2). Humans naturally have a desire to categorize. Exposure to media and information about shared identities can strengthen or even completely change people's perceptions. Marketing, advertisements, and artificial intelligence may play a role in this area as well.

5. PERCEPTION

Media presents to its audience a certain narrative with various images and social and cultural interpretations. In the process, it creates a certain perception of others. Some of the chapters in this book offer a roadmap for media organizations by examining the role of individual beliefs in shaping perceptions of the world and others. Globally, people consume messages of media and at the same time, they are consumed by the media.

6. SOCIAL MEDIA

There is a need for the government to sensitize the youth and the stakeholders on the efficient and effective use of social media to galvanize them to appropriately use technological innovation like social media responsibly for the transformation of society by the rule of law.

CONCLUSION

Contributing scholars in this book voiced their concerns about the technological imperative and the consideration of constant changes in technology and its impact on media, and the ethical imperative and the consideration of ethics in global, regional, and local interaction. People with a reasonable understanding of how media and social media work are the judges of what is true in a message or not. Just as the concept of media and media technology has evolved, so, too has the assessment of data and information attracted scholars to study and evaluate. The distribution and sharing of factual information is viewed as a basic responsibility of the media in democratic societies. Citizens have the right to know. Users of social media need facts and reliable information to express their opinions. An issue referred to in this book. Finally, media literacy as well as information and technology, become imperative to help distinguish between information and disinformation and to slow down polarization and division.

REFERENCES

Catherine, L. A. Luther; Lepre, Ringer. Carolyn; Clark, Neemah. (2018). *Diversity in US Mass Media*. Wiley Blackwell

McLuhan, M. (1967). *The Medium is the Message*. Bantam Books.

Compilation of References

Abdel Gawad, M. M. (2021). elite trends towards employing security media for artificial intelligence applications in combating cybercrimes. *Arab Journal of Media and Communication Research, Al-Ahram Canadian University, Egypt.*

Abdel Hamid, Amr. (2020). Employing artificial intelligence applications in producing media content and its relationship to its credibility among the Egyptian public. *Journal of Media Research, Al-Azhar University, Faculty of Mass Communication, Egypt.*

Abdel Hamid, M. (1997). *Theories of Influence.* Modern Egyptian library, Cairo, Egypt

Abdulmajeed, M., & Fahmy, N. (2023). Meta-analysis of AI Research in Journalism: Challenges, Opportunities and Future Research Agenda for Arab Journalism. In Musleh Al-Sartawi, A. M. A., Razzaque, A., & Kamal, M. M. (Eds.), *From the Internet of Things to the Internet of Ideas: The Role of Artificial Intelligence. EAMMIS 2022. Lecture Notes in Networks and Systems* (Vol. 557). Springer. 10.1007/978-3-031-17746-0_18

Academy of Nutrition and Dietetics. (2018). *Code of Ethics for the Nutrition and Dietetics Profession.* AND. https://www.eatrightpro.org/-/media/files/eatrightpro/practice/code-of-ethics/codeofethicshandout.pdf

Adam, B. S., & Gips, J. (2014). Tablets, touchscreens, and touchpads: How varying touch interfaces trigger psychological ownership and endowment. *Journal of Consumer Psychology*, 24(2), 226–233. 10.1016/j.jcps.2013.10.003

Adika, N. (2023). Social media usage trends in Africa: GeoPoll report. *Geopoll.* https://www.geopoll.com/blog/social-media-usage-trends-in-africa-geopoll- report/

Adisa, D. (2023, October 30). Everything you need to know about social media algorithms. *Sproutsocial.* https://sproutsocial.com/insights/social-media-algorithms/

Advertising Standards Authority. (2017). *Advice online. Children: Food.* ASA. https://www.asa.org.uk/advice-online/children-food.html

AfDB, OECD, UNDP, UNECA. (2012, May 28) African economic outlook 2012: Promoting youth employment. *African Economic Outlook/OECDiLibrary* OECD. /10.1787/aeo-2012-en

African Union. (2020, June). A *study on the roles of youth to peace and security in Africa: An Independent expert report by the peace and security council of the African Union.* AU. https://www.peaceau.org/uploads/a-study-on-the-roles-and-contributions-of-youth-to-peace-and-security-in-africa-17-sept-2020.pdf

Aftab, S., Mustafa, M. B., & Naqeeb, M. U. (2020). Impact of Unethical Advertisement and Brand Consumption on Consumer Buying Behavior *(p.30-53). InTraders 2019: Academic studies in social, human and administrative sciences.* In Traders publishing. Hiper Yayın. İstanbul

Aghakhani, H., & Main, K. J. (2019). Can two negatives make a positive? Social exclusion prevents carryover effects from deceptive advertising. *Journal of Retailing and Consumer Services*, 47, 206–214. 10.1016/j.jretconser.2018.11.021

Compilation of References

Aguinis, H., & Glavas, A. (2012). What we know and don't know about corporate social responsibility: A review and research agenda. *Journal of Management*, 38(4), 932–968. 10.1177/0149206311436079

Ahmed, S. T. (2020). Managing News Overload (MNO): The COVID-19 Infodemic. *Information (Basel)*, 11(8), 375–390. 10.3390/info11080375

Ahmed, S. T., & Roche, T. (2021). Making the connection: Examining the relationship between undergraduate students' digital and academic success in an English medium instruction (EMI) university. *Education and Information Technologies*, 26(1), 4601–4620. 10.1007/s10639-021-10443-0

Aïmeur, E., Amri, S., & Brassard, G. (2023). Fake news, disinformation and misinformation in social media: A review. *Social Network Analysis and Mining*, 13(1), 30. 10.1007/s13278-023-01028-536789378

Akpan, E. O. B., & Targema, T. S. (2022). Social media, mass mobilisation, and national development in Nigeria: Lessons from the #EndSARS protest. *ASEAN Journal of Community Engagement*. 2(6), 228 -243. https://scholarhub.ui.ac.id/cgi/viewcontent.cgi?article=1166&context=ajce

Aksak, E. O., Ferguson, M. A., & Duman, S. A. (2016). Corporate social responsibility and CSR fit as predictors of corporate reputation: A global perspective. *Public Relations Review*, 42(1), 79–81. 10.1016/j.pubrev.2015.11.004

Al Naqbi, N., Al Momani, N., & Davies, A. (2022, August 30). The Influence of social media on perceived levels of national security and crisis: A case study of youth in the United Arab Emirates. *Sustainability (Basel)*, 14(7), 10785. 10.3390/su141710785

Al-Ghatrifi, A. (2023). Digital Platforms and Transformations of the New Media Space. *Misr University Journal for Human Studies, Misr University of Science and Technology*,.

Al-Hooti, Z., Alawi, A. A., Ahmed, Z., & Al-Busaidi, T. (2024). Impact of social media marketing, innovation, and effective management on SMEs performance: A conceptual study. In *Communications in computer and information science* (pp. 222–232). Springer. 10.1007/978-3-031-50518-8_17

Alhouti, S., Johnson, C., & Holloway, B. (2016). Corporate social responsibility authenticity: Investigating its antecedents and outcomes. *Journal of Business Research*, 69(3), 1242–1249. 10.1016/j.jbusres.2015.09.007

Al-Obaidi, A. (20027). *Broadcast, Internet, and TV Media in the Arab World and Small Nations*. The Edwin Mellen Press, Lewiston.

Al-Obaidi, J. (2019). Information, Data, and Intelligence: Global Digital Media Polarization, Democratization, and Participation. In *Global Perspectives on Media, Politics, Immigration, Advertising, and Social Networking*. Cambridge Scholars Publishing.

AlRazek, M. (2022). Artificial Intelligence Technologies in Media Reality and Future Developments. *Egyptian Journal of Media*.

AlSalhi, H. (2015). *Using interactive communication technology in practicing public relations activities in organizations operating in Yemen, Cairo University*. Faculty of Information.

Ambrose, J. (2021, April 21). Ikea to invest £3.4bn in renewable energy by 2030. *The Guardian*. https://www.theguardian.com/business/2021/apr/21/ikea-to-invest-34bn-by-2030-in-renewable-energy

American Academy of Pediatrics. (2022). *Family Life/Power of Play*. AAP. https://www.healthychildren.org/English/family-life/Pages/default.aspx

American Dental Education Association. (2013). *The U.S. Department of Agriculture Issues Rule Banning Sugary Drinks and Snacks in Schools.* ADEA. https://www.adea.org/ADEA/Blogs/ADEA_State_Update/The_U_S__Department_of _Agriculture_Issues_Rule_Banning_Sugary_Drinks_and_Snacks_in_Schools.html

Amos, D. (2010). Confusion, contradiction, and irony: The Iraqi media in 2010. *Shorenstein Center Discussion Paper Series.*

Andangsari, E., Gumilar, I., & Godwin, R. (2013). Social networking sites uses and psychological attachment need among Indonesian young adults population. *International Journal of Social Science Studies*, 1(2), 133–138. 10.11114/ijsss.v1i2.66

Anderson, C. (2006). *The long tail: Why the future of business is selling less of more.* Hyperion. Britannica. https://www.britannica.com/topic/media-convergence

Andreassen, C. S., & Pallesen, S. (2014). Social network site addiction-an overview. *Current Pharmaceutical Design*, 20(25), 4053–4061. 10.2174/13816128113199990616240001298

Annis, W. (1939). The effect of editorial cartoons versus humorous cartoons upon the reader's editorial interpretation. *Journal of Educational Psychology*, 30(7), 513–518.

An, S., Jin, H. S., & Park, E. H. (2014). Children's advertising literacy for advergames: Perception of the game as advertising. *Journal of Advertising*, 43(1), 63–72. 10.1080/00913367.2013.795123

Appel, G., Grewal, L., Hadi, R., & Stephen, A. T. (2019). The future of social media in marketing. *Journal of the Academy of Marketing Science*, 48(1), 79–95. 10.1007/s11747-019-00695-132431463

Arnold, T. (2024, January 3). Resistance to same-sex blessings grows in Africa, but bishops are divided globally. *Catholic News Agency.* https://www.catholicnewsagency.com/news/256435/resistance-to-same-sex-blessings-grows-in-africa-but-bishops-are-divided-globally.

Arraf, J., & Lonsdorf, K. (2020). Iraqi security forces storm Tahrir Square, clash with protesters. *NPR News.*

Ashley, S. (2020). *News Literacy and Democracy.* Routledge.

Ashley, S., Craft, S., Maksl, A., Tully, M., & Vraga, E. K. (2022). Can news literacy help reduce belief in COVID misinformation? *Mass Communication & Society.*

Attar, R. W., Almusharraf, A., Alfawaz, A., & Hajli, N. (2022). New trends in e-commerce research: Linking social commerce and sharing commerce: A systematic literature review. *Sustainability (Basel)*, 14(23), 16024. 10.3390/su142316024

Attia, B. (2019). the extent to which media professionals accept the use of artificial intelligence applications in the field of media, a survey study. *Egyptian Journal of Media Research, Faculty of mass communication.* Cairo University.

Austin, L., & Gaither, B. (2018). Redefining fit: Examining CSR company-issue fit in stigmatized industries. *Journal of Brand Management*, 26(1), 9–20. 10.1057/s41262-018-0107-3

Babrow, A. S., & Mattson, M. (2003). Theorizing about health communication. In Thompson, T. L., Dorsey, A., Miller, K. I., & Parrott, R. (Eds.), *Handbook of health communication* (pp. 263–284). Lawrence Erlbaum Associates.

Baccarella, C. V., Wagner, T. F., Kietzmann, J. H., & McCarthy, I. P. (2018). Social media? It's serious! Understanding the dark side of social media. *European Management Journal*, 36(4), 431–438. 10.1016/j.emj.2018.07.002

Badawy, M. (2020). Mechanisms for Implementing and Producing Robotic Journalism in Egypt in Light of the Use of Artificial Intelligence Tools. *Egyptian Journal of Media Research.*

Ball-Rokeach, S. J. (1985). The origins of individual media-system preference: A sociological framework. *Communication Research*, 12(4), 485–510. 10.1177/009365085012004003

Ball-Rokeach, S. J., & DeFleur, M. L. (1976). A preference model of mass-media effects. *Communication Research*, 3(1), 3–21. 10.1177/009365027600300101

Bandura, A. (2012). Social cognitive theory. In Van Lange, P. A. M., Kruglanski, A. W., & Higgins, E. T. (Eds.), *Handbook of theories of social psychology* (pp. 349–373). Sage Publications. 10.4135/9781446249215.n18

Banerjee, S., & Chua, A. Y. (2017). Theorizing the textual differences between authentic and fictitious reviews: Validation across positive, negative and moderate polarities. *Internet Research*, 27(2), 321–337. 10.1108/IntR-11-2015-0309

Banning, S. A. (2007). Factors affecting the marketing of a public safety message: The third-person effect and uses and gratifications theory in public reaction to a crime reduction program. *Atlantic Journal of Communication*, 15(1), 1–18. 10.1080/15456870701212716

Barbour, F. L.II, & Gardner, D. (1982). Deceptive advertising: A practical approach to measurement. *Journal of Advertising*, 11(1), 21–30. 10.1080/00913367.1982.10672791

Barlett, C. P., Gentile, D. A., & Chew, C. (2016). Predicting cyberbullying from anonymity. *Psychology of Popular Media Culture*, 5(2), 171–180. 10.1037/ppm0000055

Barnett, M. L., Jermier, J. M., & Lafferty, B. A. (2006). Corporate reputation: The definitional landscape. *Corporate Reputation Review*, 9(1), 26–38. 10.1057/palgrave.crr.1550012

Barry, C. T., Berbano, M., Anderson, A., & Levy, S. (2024). Psychology TOK: Use of TikTok, mood, and self-perception in a sample of college students. *Journal of Technology in Behavioral Science*. 10.1007/s41347-024-00390-1

Bartholomé, G., Lecheler, S., & de Vreese, C. (2015). Manufacturing Conflict? How Journalists Intervene in the Conflict Frame Building Process. *The International Journal of Press/Politics*, 20(4), 438–457. 10.1177/1940161215595514

Bart, Y., Stephen, A. T., & Sarvary, M. (2014). Which products are best suited to mobile advertising? A field study of mobile display advertising effects on consumer attitudes and intentions. *JMR, Journal of Marketing Research*, 51(3), 270–285. 10.1509/jmr.13.0503

Bashar, A., Wasiq, M., Nyagadza, B., & Maziriri, E. T. (2024). Emerging trends in social media marketing: A retrospective review using data mining and bibliometric analysis. *Future Business Journal*, 10(1), 23. 10.1186/s43093-024-00308-6

Bates, R. H. (1983). Modernization, Ethnic Competition, and the Rationality of Politics in Contemporary Africa. *State versus Ethnic Claims: African Policy Dilemmas*. Westview Press.

Batrinca, B., & Treleaven, P. (2014). Social media analytics: A survey of techniques, tools and platforms. *AI & Society*, 30(1), 89–116. 10.1007/s00146-014-0549-4

Baumgartner, J. C. (2007). Humor and political communication: An extension and refinement of political humor typologies. *The Social Science Journal*, 44(1), 177–194.

Baxter, P., & Jack, S. (2008). Qualitative case study methodology: Study design and implementation for novice researchers. *The Qualitative Report*, 13(4), 544–559.

BBC News. (2018). *First ads banned under new junk food rules*. BBC News. https://www.bbc.com/news/uk-44706755

Becker, A. B. (2011). Laughing matters: Humor's role in persuasion and attitude change. *Human Communication Research*, 37(4), 566–591.

Béjot, M., & Doittau, B. (2004). Advertising to children in France. *Young Consumers*, 5(3), 69–72. 10.1108/17473610410814274

Belair-Gagnon, V. (2015). *Social media at BBC news: The re-making of crisis reporting*. Routledge. 10.4324/9781315742052

Bennett, W. L., Lawrence, R. G., & Livingston, S. (2008). *When the press fails: Political power and the news media from Iraq to Katrina*. University of Chicago Press.

Berrigan, F. J. (1979). *Community communications. The role of community media in development*. UNESCO.

Berrocal-Gonzalo, S., Zamora-Martínez, P., & González-Neira, A. (2023). Politainment on Twitter: Engagement in the Spanish Legislative Elections of April 2019. *Media and Communication*, 11(2), 163–175. 10.17645/mac.v11i2.6292

Besalú, R., & Pont-Sorribes, C. (2021). Credibility of digital political news in Spain: Comparison between traditional media and social media. *Social Sciences (Basel, Switzerland)*, 10(5), 170. 10.3390/socsci10050170

Bhat, A. (2024). Multistage sampling: Definitions, steps, applications +example. *QuestionPro* https://www.questionpro.com/blog/multistage-sampling-advantages-and-application/

Bhattacharya, C. B., Korschun, D., & Sen, S. (2009). Strengthening stakeholder–company relationships through mutually beneficial corporate social responsibility initiatives. *Journal of Business Ethics*, 85(2), 257–272. 10.1007/s10551-008-9730-3

Bhattacharya, C. B., & Sen, S. (2004). Doing better at doing good: When, why, and how consumers respond to corporate social initiatives. *California Management Review*, 47(1), 9–24. 10.2307/41166284

Bhattacharya, C. B., Sen, S., & Korschun, D. (2008). Using corporate social responsibility to win the war for talent. *MIT Sloan Management Review*, 49(2), 37–44.

Bik, H., & Goldstein, M. (2013). An introduction to social media for scientists. *PLoS Biology*, 11(4), e1001535. 10.1371/journal.pbio.100153523630451

Bimber, B. (1990). Karl Marx and the Three Faces of Technological Determinism. *Social Studies of Science*, 20(2), 333–351. https://www.jstor.org/stable/285094. 10.1177/030631290020002006

Birtchnell, T., Devinney, T. M., Auger, P., & Eckhardt, G. (2006). The other CSR. *Stanford Social Innovation Review*, 4(3), 30–37.

Block, J. J. (2008). Issues for DSM-V: Internet Addiction. *The American Journal of Psychiatry*, 165(3), 306–307. 10.1176/appi.ajp.2007.0710155618316427

Borah, P. (2016). *Media effects theory*. .10.1002/9781118541555.wbiepc156

Bostock, B. (2019). Iraq blacked out the internet for 70% of the country and blocked social media to quell deadly anti-corruption protests. *Business Insider*. <https://www.businessinsider.com/iraq-blocks-facebook-whatsapp-cuts-internet-protests-2019-10>

Boutilier, R. G., Thomson, I. H., & Geall, V. (2018). Greenwashing and the problem of legitimacy: Creating credibility in sustainability reporting. *Journal of Business Ethics*, 147(2), 349–362.

Boyd, D. (2014). *It's Complicated: The Social Lives of Networked Teens*. Yale University Press.

Boyland, E. J., & Whalen, R. (2015). Food advertising to children and its effects on diet: Review of recent prevalence and impact data. *Pediatric Diabetes*, 16(5), 331–337. 10.1111/pedi.1227825899654

Bracken, C. (2006). Perceived source credibility of local television news: The impact of television form and presence. *Journal of Broadcasting & Electronic Media*, 50(4), 723–741. 10.1207/s15506878jobem5004_9

Brammer, S., Jackson, G., & Matten, D. (2012). Corporate social responsibility and institutional theory: New perspectives on private governance. *Socio-economic Review*, 10(1), 3–28. 10.1093/ser/mwr030

Compilation of References

Brammer, S., & Millington, A. (2008). Does it pay to be different? An analysis of the relationship between corporate social and financial performance. *Strategic Management Journal*, 29(12), 1325–1343. 10.1002/smj.714

Brammer, S., Millington, A., & Rayton, B. (2007). The contribution of corporate social responsibility to organizational commitment. *International Journal of Human Resource Management*, 18(10), 1701–1719. 10.1080/09585190701570866

Brandt, J., Buckingham, K., Buntain, C., Anderson, W., Ray, S., Pool, J., & Ferrari, N. (2020). Identifying social media user demographics and topic diversity with computational social science: A case study of a major international policy forum. *Journal of Computational Social Science*, 3(1), 167–188. 10.1007/s42001-019-00061-9

Bright, L. F., & Logan, K. (2018). Is my fear of missing out (FOMO) causing fatigue? Advertising, social media fatigue, and the implications for consumers and brands. *Internet Research*, 28(5), 1213–1227. 10.1108/IntR-03-2017-0112

Brinkman, H. J. (1968). The effects of political cartoons on readers' responses to editorials. *Public Opinion Quarterly*, 32(3), 459–471.

Broadcasting Authority of Ireland. (2013). *Policy - BAI Children's Commercial Communication Code*. WHO. https://extranet.who.int/nutrition/gina/en/node/22970

Brooks, A. (2018, August 7). 7 Unexpected Ways Instagram Has Changed the World. *Social Media Today* https://www.socialmediatoday.com/news/7-unexpected-ways-instagram-has-changed-the-world/539032/

Brown, J. R., & Dant, R. P. (2013). The role of e-commerce in multi-channel marketing strategy. In *Progress in IS* (pp. 467–487). 10.1007/978-3-642-39747-9_20

Brubaker, J. (2008). The freedom to choose a personal agenda: Removing our reliance on the media agenda. *American Communication Journal, 10*(3). http://ac-journal.org/journal/pub/2008/fall%200820%20Defining%20Digital%20Freedom/ Article1.pdf

Brunk, K. H. (2010). Reputation building: Beyond our control? Inferences in consumers' ethical perception formation. *Journal of Consumer Behaviour*, 9(4), 275–292. 10.1002/cb.317

Buck, A. (2014). *Building professional identities through social media*. SPIR. https://spir.aoir.org/ojs/index.php/spir/article/view/8485

Burkhalter, J. N., Wood, N. T., & Tryce, S. A. (2014). Clear, conspicuous, and concise: Disclosures and Twitter word-of-mouth. *Business Horizons*, 57(3), 319–328. 10.1016/j.bushor.2014.02.001

Cabral, J. (2011). Is generation Y addicted to social media? *The Elon Journal of Undergraduate Research in Communications*, 2(1), 5–14.

Çakıcı, Z. (2023). Din, Kimlik ve Müzik: Genç Erkeklerin Müzik Dinleme Pratikleri Üzerine Nitel Bir Araştırma. *Etkileşim*, 6(11), 316–337. 10.32739/etkilesim.2023.6.11.199

Canadian Ad Standards. (2016). *About the Initiative*. Canadian Ad Standards. https://adstandards.ca/wp-content/uploads/2018/03/2016ComplianceReport-2.pdf

Canavilhas, J. (2022). Artificial Intelligence Applied to Journalism: Machine Translation and Content Recommendation in the "A European Perspective" (EBU) project. *Latin Journal of Social Communication*, (80), 24.

Carillo, K., Scornavacca, E., & Za, S. (2017). The role of media dependency in predicting continuance intention to use ubiquitous media systems. *Information & Management*, 54(3), 317–335. 10.1016/j.im.2016.09.002

Carroll, L. & Engel, S. (2021). Framing basic income in Australia: how the media is shaping the debate. *Australian Journal of Political Science, 56*, 410–427 10.1080/10361146.2021.1998344

Carroll, A. B. (1979). A three-dimensional conceptual model of corporate performance. *Academy of Management Review*, 4(4), 497–505. 10.2307/257850

Carroll, A. B. (1999). Corporate social responsibility: Evolution of a definitional construct. *Business & Society*, 38(3), 268–295. 10.1177/000765039903800303

Carson, T. L., Wokutch, R. E., & Cox, J. E.Jr. (1985). An ethical analysis of deception in advertising. *Journal of Business Ethics*, 4(2), 93–104. 10.1007/BF00383562

Caruana, R., & Chatzidakis, A. (2014). Consumer social responsibility (CnSR): Toward a multi-level, multi-agent conceptualization of the "other CSR". *Journal of Business Ethics*, 121(4), 577–592. 10.1007/s10551-013-1739-6

Casal, F. M. (2007). *Introduction to Contemporary Investigative Journalism in the U.S. Press. Doxa Communication Interdisciplinary Journal. Number 5*. CEU Ediciones.

Castelló, I., Morsing, M., & Schultz, F. (2013). Communicative dynamics and the polyphony of corporate social responsibility in the network society. *Journal of Business Ethics*, 118(4), 683–694. 10.1007/s10551-013-1954-1

Castillo-Esparcia, A., Caro-Castaño, L., & Almansa-Martínez, A. (2023, May 3). Evolution of digital activism on social media: Opportunities and challenges. *El Profesional de la Información*, 32(3), e320303. 10.3145/epi.2023.may.03

Caswell, D., & Dörr, K. (2018). Automated Journalism Event driven narratives From simple descriptions to real stories. *Journalism Practice*. Advance online publication. 10.1080/17512786.2017.1320773

CDP. (n.d.). *Carbon Disclosure Project (CDP)*. CDP. https://www.cdp.net/

Celebi, S. I. (2015). How do motives affect attitudes and behaviors toward internet advertising and Facebook advertising? *Computers in Human Behavior*, 51, 312–324. 10.1016/j.chb.2015.05.011

Centre for Sociological Research (CIS). (2018). *Three main problems that currently exist in Spain*. CIS. http://www.cis.es/cis/export/sites/default/- Archivos/Indicadores/documentos_html/TresProblemas.html (24.10.2018)

Cervi, L., Tejedor, S., & Blesa, F. G. (2023). TikTok and political communication: The latest frontier of politainment? A case study. *Media and Communication*, 11(2), 203–217. 10.17645/mac.v11i2.6390

Cervi, L., Tejedor, S., & Blesa, F. G. (2023). TikTok and the Peruvian presidential elections: A new frontier of politainment. *International Journal of Communication*, 17, 4595–4612.

Chaney, D. (1972). The Theory of 'Uses and Gratifications'. In: *Processes of Mass Communication. New Perspectives in Sociology*. Palgrave, London. 10.1007/978-1-349-00684-7_3

Changhoon, J. C., Lee, S., SoHyun, P., Kim, D., Song, J., Kim, D., Lee, J., & Suh, B. (2020). Understanding User Perception of Automated News Generation System. In *Proceedings of the.CHI'20, USA*.

Chan, M., Lee, F. L. F., & Chen, H.-T. (2021). Examining the Roles of Multi-Platform Social Media News Use, Engagement, and Connections with News Organizations and Journalists on News Literacy: A Comparison of Seven Democracies. *Digital Journalism (Abingdon, England)*, 9(5), 571–588. 10.1080/21670811.2021.1890168

Chan, T. K., Cheung, C. M., & Lee, Z. W. (2021). Cyberbullying on social networking sites: A literature review and future research directions. *Information & Management*, 58(2), 103411. 10.1016/j.im.2020.103411

Chatterjee, S., Goyal, D., Prakash, A., & Sharma, J. (2021). Exploring healthcare/health-product ecommerce satisfaction: A text mining and machine learning application. *Journal of Business Research*, 131, 815–825. 10.1016/j.jbusres.2020.10.043

Chaudary, S., Zahid, Z., Shahid, S., Khan, S. N., & Azar, S. (2016). Customer perception of CSR initiatives: Its antecedents and consequences. *Social Responsibility Journal*, 12(2), 263–279. 10.1108/SRJ-04-2015-0056

Chen, H. S. (2010). Towards green loyalty: Driving from green perceived value, green satisfaction, and green trust. *Sustainable Development (Bradford)*, 21(5), 294–308. 10.1002/sd.500

Chen, J., Zhang, Y., Han, C., Liu, L., Liao, M., & Fang, J. (2024). A comprehensive overview of micro-influencer marketing: Decoding the current landscape, impacts, and trends. *Behavioral Sciences (Basel, Switzerland)*, 14(3), 243. 10.3390/bs1403024338540546

Chen, Y., Li, M., Lu, G., Shen, H., & Zhou, J. (2021). Hydroxychloroquine/Chloroquine as Therapeutics for COVID-19: Truth under the Mystery. *International Journal of Biological Sciences*, 17(6), 1538–1546. 10.7150/ijbs.5954733907517

Chigbo, M. (2023, February 6). *Leveraging digital literacy for the economic empowerment of the urban poor in Southwestern Nigeria.* [Thesis, Bingham University, Karu, Nasarawa State, Nigeria]

Chigbo, M., & Okocha, D. O. (2023). A self-discourse narrative on survival of the media in Africa. *The NOUN Scholar Journal of Arts and Humanities.*, 3(1), 148–164.

Cho, Y. (2009). *New media uses and preference effect model: Exploring the relationship between new media use habit, preference relation, and possible outcomes* [Doctoral dissertation, Rutgers University-Graduate School-New Brunswick]

Chong, D., & Druckman, J. N. (2007). A Theory of Framing and Opinion Formation in Competitive Elite Environments. *Journal of Communication*, 57(1), 99–118. 10.1111/j.1460-2466.2006.00331.x

Chung, K. & Kim, J. (2021). Multi-modal emotion prediction system using convergence media and active contents. *Personal and Ubiquitous Computing (2023), 27,* 1245– 1255. 10.1007/s00779-021-01602-8

Çildan, M., Erdoğdu, M., & Demirhan, A. (2012). The impact of social media on political participation and political attitudes: The example of Turkey. [IJRTE]. *The International Journal of Research in Teacher Education*, 3(1), 61–78.

Cilliers, F. Q. (2013). The role and effect of social media in the workplace. *N. Ky. L. Rev.*, 40, 567.

Cioppi, M., Curina, I., Francioni, B., & Savelli, E. (2023). Digital transformation and marketing: A systematic and thematic literature review. *Italian Journal of Marketing*, 2023(2), 207–288. 10.1007/s43039-023-00067-2

Clow, K. E., & Baack, D. (Eds.). (2007). *Advertising design: Theoretical frameworks and types of appeals. In integrated advertising, promotion, and marketing communications* (3rd ed., pp. 171–186). Prentice Hall of India Pvt. Ltd.

Cohen, R., Newton-John, T., & Slater, A. (2017). The relationship between Facebook and Instagram appearance-focused activities and body image concerns in young women. *Body Image*, 23, 183–187. 10.1016/j.bodyim.2017.10.00229055773

Colle, R. (2003). Threads of development communication. In Servaes, J. (Ed.), *Approaches to development: studies on communication for development* (pp. 22–72). UNESCO.

Collier, P., & Hoeffler, A. (1998). On economic causes of civil war. *Oxford Economic Papers*, 50(4), 563–573. 10.1093/oep/50.4.563

Commey, G. (2020, February 10). *Impact of social media on African youth*. West African Civil Society Institute. https://wacsi.org/wp-content/uploads/2020/10/Impact-of-Social-Media-on-African-Youth.pdf

Cooke-Jackson, A. (2012). Review: Health Communication in the New Media Landscape (2009). *The Journal of Media Literacy Education*. 10.23860/jmle-4-1-10

Cornell, S. (2006). What does post-modern mean. *Summit Ministries*. https://www.summit.org/resources/articles/what-does-postmodern-mean/

Cosentino, C. (2022). Data fragmentation and data linking: A threat and an opportunity. *Harvard Data Science Review*. 10.1162/99608f92.946ef791

Crane, A. (2005). Meeting the ethical gaze: Challenges for orienting to the ethical market. In Harrison, R., Newholm, T., & Shaw, D. (Eds.), *The ethical consumer* (pp. 421–432). Sage. 10.4135/9781446211991.n15

Cremer, F., Sheehan, B., Fortmann, M., Kia, A. N., Mullins, M., Murphy, F., & Materne, S. (2022). Cyber risk and cybersecurity: A systematic review of data availability. *The Geneva Papers on Risk and Insurance. Issues and Practice*, 47(3), 698–736. 10.1057/s41288-022-00266-635194352

Creyer, E. H., & Ross, W. T. (1997). The influence of firm behavior on purchase intention: Do consumers really care about business ethics? *Journal of Consumer Marketing*, 14(6), 421–432. 10.1108/07363769710185999

Cundari, A. (2015). *Customer-Centric Marketing: Build Relationships, Create Advocates, and Influence your Consumers*. Amazon Digital Services, LLC. 10.1002/9781119154785

Daft, R. L., & Lengel, R. H. (1986). Organizational information requirements, media richness and structural design. *Management Science*, 32(5), 554–571. 10.1287/mnsc.32.5.554

Daineko, L., Гончарова, Н. В., Zaitseva, E., Гончарова, Н., & Dyachkova, I. A. (2023). Gamification in education: A literature review. In *Lecture notes in networks and systems* (pp. 319–343). Springer. 10.1007/978-3-031-48020-1_25

Dalgic, T., & Leeuw, M. (2014). Niche marketing revisited: Theoretical and practical issues. In *Developments in marketing science: Proceedings of the Academy of Marketing Science* (pp. 137–145). Springer. 10.1007/978-3-319-13159-7_32

Danielson, M., & Rolandsson, B. (2020). Staging authenticity: Personal and political projection in Swedish political entertainment television. *International Journal of Cultural Studies*, 23(5), 690–706.

Darke, P. R., Ashworth, L., & Main, K. J. (2010). Great expectations and broken promises: Misleading claims, product failure, expectancy disconfirmation and consumer distrust. *Journal of the Academy of Marketing Science*, 38(3), 347–362. 10.1007/s11747-009-0168-7

Darke, P. R., & Ritchie, R. J. (2007). The defensive consumer: Advertising deception, defensive processing, and distrust. *JMR, Journal of Marketing Research*, 44(1), 114–127. 10.1509/jmkr.44.1.114

Darlington, N. (2022, October 2022). *Blockchain for beginners: What is blockchain technology? A step-by-step guide*. Block Geeks. https://blockgeeks.com/guides/what-is-blockchain- technology/

Dave, A. (2011). Media Convergence: Different Views and Perspectives. *IMS Manthan*, VI(1), 170.

Davison, W. P. (1983). The Third-Person Effect in Communication. *Public Opinion Quarterly*, 47(1), 1–15. https://www.jstor.org/stable/2748702. 10.1086/268763

Davis, R. D., Kitch, S. W., & Kitch, W. (2018). Political jokes and the social cycle: How the era of the weblog remixed humor and news. *Journalism Studies*, 19(12), 1790–1807.

de Bruijn, A., Engels, R., Anderson, P., Bujalski, M., Gosselt, J., Schreckenberg, D., Wohtge, J., & de Leeuw, R. (2016). Exposure to online alcohol marketing and adolescents' drinking: A cross-sectional study in four European countries. *Alcohol and Alcoholism (Oxford, Oxfordshire)*, 51(5), 615–621. 10.1093/alcalc/agw02027151968

De Lima-Santos, M.-F., & Cerón, W. (2022). Artificial Intelligence in News Media: Current Perceptions and Future Outlook. *Journalism and Media*, 3(1), 13–26. 10.3390/journalmedia3010002

De Vreese. (2003, September). The spiral of cynicism reconsidered. *European Journal of Communication*. 10.1177/0267323105055259

Deane, F., Woolmer, E., Cao, S., & Tranter, K. (2023). Trade in the digital age: Agreements to mitigate fragmentation. *Asian Journal of International Law*, 14(1), 154–179. 10.1017/S204425132300036X

Dearling, W. J. (1998). *Communication and Democracy: Exploring the Intellectual Frontiers in Agenda-Setting Theory*. Mahwah, NJ: Lawrence Erlbaum Associates.

Deglise, C., Suggs, L. S., & Odermatt, P. (2012). Short message service (SMS) applications for disease prevention in developing countries. *Journal of Medical Internet Research*, 14(1), e3. 10.2196/jmir.182322262730

De-Lima-Santos, M.F., Salaverría, R. (2021). *From Data Journalism to Artificial Intelligence: Challenges Faced by La Nación in Implementing Computer Vision in News Reporting*. 10.5294/pacla.2021.24.3.7

Delmas, M., & Burbano, V. C. (2011). The drivers of greenwashing. *California Management Review*, 54(1), 64–87. 10.1525/cmr.2011.54.1.64

Deloitte. (2020). *#GetOutInFront - Global research report*. Deloitte..

Dennis, E. E., Martin, J. D., & Wood, R. (2019). *Media use in the Middle East: A six-nation survey*. Northwestern University Qatar.

Deuze, M. (2017). Politainment and the transformation of political communication. In Hartley, J., Steemers, J., & Deuze, M. (Eds.), *The Handbook of Global Media and Communication* (pp. 102–113). Wiley-Blackwell.

Díaz Güell, L. (2003). *Journalism and Investigative Journalists in Spain, 1975-2000: Contribution to Political, Legal, Economic and Social Change* [Doctoral dissertation, Complutense University of Madrid].

Diehl, S., Koinig, I., & Scheiber, R. (2022). *Cross-media advertising in times of changing media environments and media consumption patterns*. Springer eBooks. 10.1007/978-3-030-86680-8_11

Dillard, J. P., Hunter, J. E., & Burgoon, M. (1984). Sequential-request persuasive strategies: Meta-analysis of foot-in-the-door and door-in-the-face. *Human Communication Research*, 10(4), 461–488. 10.1111/j.1468-2958.1984.tb00028.x

Dima-Laza, S. (2012). Utopia versus dystopia—a perfect environment for a perfect existence. *2012 International Conference on Humanity, History and Society IPEDR*. IACSIT Press.

Dodd, S. (2016, April 1). Learning from HGTV: Media Convergence and Design Branding in America. *Design Issues*, 32(2), 53–63. 10.1162/DESI_a_00382

Dörner, A. (2001). *Politainment: Politics as part of the mediated event society*. Suhrkamp.

Dowling, G. R. (2006). *Creating corporate reputation: Identity, image, and performance*. Oxford University Press.

Dudovskiy, J. (2022, January). Multi-stage sampling. In *The Ultimate Guide to Writing a Dissertation in Business Studies: A step-by-step assistance* (6th ed.). Business Research Methodology. https://research-methodology.net/sampling-in- primary-data-collection/multi-stage-sampling/

Duman, H., & Ozkara, B. Y. (2021). The impact of social identity on online game addiction: The mediating role of the fear of missing out (FoMO) and the moderating role of the need to belong. *Current Psychology (New Brunswick, N.J.)*, 40(9), 4571–4580. 10.1007/s12144-019-00392-w

Du, S., Bhattacharya, C. B., & Sen, S. (2010). Maximizing business returns to corporate social responsibility (CSR): The role of CSR communication. *International Journal of Management Reviews*, 12(1), 8–19. 10.1111/j.1468-2370.2009.00276.x

Du, Z., Liu, J., & Wang, T. (2022). Augmented reality marketing: A systematic literature review and an agenda for future inquiry. *Frontiers in Psychology*, 13, 925963. 10.3389/fpsyg.2022.92596335783783

Dwivedi, Y. K., Ismagilova, E., Rana, N. P., & Raman, R. (2021). Social media adoption, usage and impact in business-to-business (B2B) context: A state-of-the-art literature review. *Information Systems Frontiers*, 25(3), 971–993. 10.1007/s10796-021-10106-y

Easterly, W., & Levine, R. (1997). Africa's growth tragedy: Policies and ethnic divisions. *The Quarterly Journal of Economics*, 112(4), 1203–1250. 10.1162/003355300555466

Echeverri, P., & Ska°l'en, P. (2011). Co-Creation and Co-Destruction: A Practice-Theory Based Study of Interactive Value Formation. *Marketing Theory*, 11(3), 351–373. 10.1177/1470593111408181

Edelman. (2023). *2023 Edelman Trust Barometer – Global report*. Edelman. https://www.edelman.com/trust/2023/trust-barometer

Edelman, M. W. (1985). The sea is so wide and my boat is so small: Problems facing Black children today. In McAdoo, H. P., & McAdoo, J. L. (Eds.), *Black children: Social, educational, and parental environments* (pp. 72–82). Sage Publications, Inc.

Edgerly, S. (2017). Seeking out and avoiding the news media: Young adults' proposed strategies for obtaining current events information. *Mass Communication & Society*, 20(3), 358–377. 10.1080/15205436.2016.1262424

Edosomwan, S., Prakasan, S. K., Kouame, D., Watson, J., & Seymour, T. (2011). The history of social media and its impact on business. *The Journal of Applied Management and Entrepreneurship*, 16(3), 79.

Eisend, M., & Tarrahi, F. (2021). Persuasion knowledge in the marketplace: A meta-analysis. *Journal of Consumer Psychology*, 32(1), 3–22. 10.1002/jcpy.1258

Ellen, P. S., Mohr, L. A., & Webb, D. J. (2000). Charitable programs and the retailer: Do they mix? *Journal of Retailing*, 76(3), 393–406. 10.1016/S0022-4359(00)00032-4

Emelshtrich, L. N. (2018). *Robot Journalism: Can Human Journalism Survive?* World Scientific publishing.

Engeln, R., Loach, R., Imundo, M. N., & Zola, A. (2020). Compared to Facebook, Instagram use causes more appearance comparison and lower body satisfaction in college women. *Body Image*, 34, 38–45. 10.1016/j.bodyim.2020.04.00732505866

Entman, R. (1993). Framing: Toward Clarification of a Fractured Paradigm. *Journal of Communication*, 43(4), 51–58. 10.1111/j.1460-2466.1993.tb01304.x

Eroglu, Y. (2015). Interrelationship between attachment styles and Facebook addiction. *Journal of Education and Training Studies*, 4(1), 150–160. 10.11114/jets.v4i1.1081

Essoungou, A. (2010, December). A social media boom begins in Africa. *Africa Renewal*. https://www.un.org/africarenewal/magazine/december-2010/social-media-boom-begins-africa

Euronews (2024). Which countries have banned TikTok and why? *Euronews.*

European Commission Press Release. (2024) *Commission opens proceedings against TikTok under the DSA regarding the launch of TikTok Lite in France and Spain, and communicates its intention to suspend the reward programme in the EU*. EC. https://ec.europa.eu/commission/presscorner/detail/en/ip_24_2227

European Commission. (2018). *Final report of the high level expert group on fake news and online disinformation.* EC. https://ec.europa.eu/digital-singlemarket/en/news/final-report-high-level-expert-group-fake-news-and-onlinedisinformation

European Parliament and the Council of the European Union. (2014). *Directive 2014/95/EU of the European Parliament and of the Council of 22 October 2014 amending Directive 2013/34/EU as regards disclosure of non-financial and diversity information by certain large undertakings and groups.* Europea. https://data.europa.eu/eli/dir/2014/95/oj

European Parliament and the Council of the European Union. (2019). *Regulation (EU) 2019/2088 of the European Parliament and of the Council of 27 November 2019 on sustainability-related disclosures in the financial services sector.* Europea. https://data.europa.eu/eli/reg/2019/2088/oj

European Parliament and the Council of the European Union. (2022). *Directive (EU) 2022/2464 of the European Parliament and of the Council of 14 December 2022 amending Regulation (EU) No 537/2014, Directive 2004/109/EC, Directive 2006/43/EC and Directive 2013/34/EU, as regards corporate sustainability reporting.* Europa. https://data.europa.eu/eli/dir/2022/2464/oj

Eva, K. (2022). *Usage of artificial intelligence on social media in Europe.* Ad Alta., 10.33543/1202330333

Ezaka, S. (2022, August). Postmodernism and Broadcasting in Nigeria. *International Journal of Innovative Science and Research Technology*, 7(8), 577. https://www.ijisrt.com/assets/upload/files/IJISRT22AUG063_(1).pdf

Eze, K. (2015, August 7 - 8). *Youth participation in governance in Africa* (Discussion paper). The Mandela Institute for Development Studies Youth Dialogue, Victoria Falls. Zimbabwe. file:///C:/Users/MAUREEN%20CHIGBO/Downloads/YOUTH_PARTICIPATION_IN_GOVERNANCE_IN_AFR.pdf

Fairtrade International. (n.d.). *Standards for businesses.* FTI. https://www.fairtrade.net/act/fairtrade-for-business

Falasca, K. (2014). Political News Journalism: Mediatization across Three News Reporting Contexts. *European Journal of Communication*, 29(5), 583–597. 10.1177/0267323114538853

Fardouly, J., Diedrichs, P. C., Vartanian, L. R., & Halliwell, E. (2015). Social comparisons on social media: The impact of Facebook on young women's body image concerns and mood. *Body Image*, 13, 38–45. 10.1016/j.bodyim.2014.12.00225615425

Faria. (2022) *Advertising worldwide, statistics and facts.* Statista. https://www.statista.com/topics/990/global-advertising-market/#topicOverview

Fatma, M., & Khan, I. (2020). An investigation of consumer evaluation of authenticity of their company's CSR engagement. *Total Quality Management & Business Excellence*. 10.1080/14783363.2020.1791068

Fearon, J. D., & Laitin, D. D. (2000). Violence and the Social Construction of Ethnic Identity. *International Organization*, 54(4), 4. 10.1162/002081800551398

Federal Trade Commission. (2013). *"Dot Com Disclosures" Guidance Updated to Address Current Online and Mobile Advertising Environment.* FTC. https://www.ftc.gov/news-events/news/press-releases/2013/03/ftc-staff-revises-online-advertising-disclosure-guidelines

Fedorikhin, A., & Cole, C. A. (2004). The effects of humor on memory: Constrained by the pun. *Journal of Memory and Language*, 50(4), 415–429.

Feezell, J. T. (2018). Agenda setting through social media: The importance of incidental news exposure and social filtering in the digital era. *Political Research Quarterly*, 71(2), 482–494. 10.1177/1065912917744895

Fernandez, A. (2017). *Hybrid Stories: The Role of Narrativity in the Visualization of Interactive Information* [PhD Thesis, Universidad Europea]. Abacus Repository https://193.147.239.238/handle/11268/6981

Festinger, L. (1954). A theory of social comparison processes. *Human Relations*, 7(2), 117–140. 10.1177/001872675400700202

Fieiras-Ceide, C., Vaz-Álvarez, M., & Túñez-López, M. (2022). Artificial intelligence strategies in European public broadcasters: Uses, forecasts and future challenges. *El Profesional de la Información*, 31(5), e310518. 10.3145/epi.2022.sep.18

Flew, T., Spurgeon, C., Daniel, A., & Swift, A. (2012). The promise of computational journalism. *Journalism Practice*, 6(2), 157–171. 10.1080/17512786.2011.616655

Fombrun, C. J. (1996). *Reputation: Realizing value from the corporate image*. Harvard Business School Press.

Fombrun, C. J., & Shanley, M. (1990). What's in a name? Reputation building and corporate strategy. *Academy of Management Journal*, 33(2), 233–258. 10.2307/256324

Fournier, S., & Avery, J. (2011). The uninvited brand. *Business Horizons*, 54(3), 193–207. 10.1016/j.bushor.2011.01.001

Francis. (2023). Declaration Fiducia Supplicans on the Pastoral Meaning of blessings. *Vatican*. https://www.vatican.va/roman_curia/congregations/cfaith/documents/ rc_ddf_doc_20231218_fiducia-supplicans_en.html

Frary, M. (2019). The future is robotic: Would journalists have more time to investigate news stories if robots did the easy bits? *Index on Censorship*, 48(1), 8–10. 10.1177/0306422019842082

Frei, N. K., Wyss, V., Gnach, A., & Weber, W. (2024). 'It's a matter of age': Four dimensions of youths' news consumption. *Journalism*, 25(1), 100–121. 10.1177/14648849221123385

Friant-Perrot, M., & Garde, A. (2022). The regulation of alcohol marketing in France: The Loi Evin at thirty. *The Journal of Law, Medicine & Ethics*, 50(2), 312–316. 10.1017/jme.2022.5735894563

FSC. (n.d.). *What is FSC?* FSC. https://www.fsc.org/en/what-is-fsc

Gabler, C. B., Landers, V. M., & Reynolds, K. E. (2017). Purchase decision regret: Negative consequences of the steadily increasing discount strategy. *Journal of Business Research*, 76, 201–208. 10.1016/j.jbusres.2017.01.002

Gainsbury, S. M., King, D. L., Russell, A. M., Delfabbro, P., Derevensk, J., & Hing, N. (2016). Exposure to and Engagement with Gambling Marketing in Social Media: Reported Impacts on Moderate-Risk and Problem Gamblers. *Psychology of Addictive Behaviors*, 30(2), 270–276. 10.1037/adb000015626828642

Galal, S. (2022, November 17). Social media in Africa – statistics and facts. *Statista*.https://www.statista.com/topics/9922/social-media-in-africa/#topicOverview

Galan, L., Osserman, J., Parker, T., & Taylor, M. (2021). *How Young People Consume News and The Implications for Mainstream Media (Flamingo Report)*. Oxford University Press.

Gallopel-Morvan, K., Spilka, S., Mutatayi, C., Rigaud, A., Lecas, F., & Beck, F. (2017). France's Evin law on the control of alcohol advertising: Content, effectiveness and limitations. *Addiction (Abingdon, England)*, 112(S1), 86–93. 10.1111/add.1343127188432

Gamper, M. (2022). Social Network Theories: An Overview. In Klärner, A., Gamper, M., Keim-Klärner, S., Moor, I., von der Lippe, H., & Vonneilich, N. (Eds.), *Social Networks and Health Inequalities*. Springer. 10.1007/978-3-030-97722-1_3

García-Caballero, S. (2020). New professional profiles for the journalistic market. *Mediterranean Journal of Communication*, 11(1), 287–289. 10.14198/MEDCOM2020.11.1.15

Compilation of References

Gatzweiler, A., Blazevic, V., & Piller, F. T. (2017). Dark side or bright light: Destructive and constructive deviant content in consumer ideation contests. *Journal of Product Innovation Management*, 34(6), 772–789. 10.1111/jpim.12369

Gavilan, D., Avello, M., & Abril, C. (2014). The mediating role of mental imagery in mobile advertising. *International Journal of Information Management*, 34(4), 457–464. 10.1016/j.ijinfomgt.2014.04.004

Gaziano & McGrath. (1986). Measuring the concept of credibility. *Journalism Quarterly, 63*(3), 451-462.

Gensler, S., Völckner, F., Liu-Thompkins, Y., & Wiertz, C. (2013). Managing brands in the social media environment. *Journal of Interactive Marketing*, 27(4), 242–256. 10.1016/j.intmar.2013.09.004

Gerson, J. (2020, October 7). Experts Explain Why Instagram's Effects on Mental Health Aren't All Bad. Bustle https://www.bustle.com/wellness/instagram-positive-effects-mental-health-experts

Ghai, S., Magis-Weinberg, L., Stoilova, M., Livingstone, S., & Orben, A. (2022, August). Social media and adolescent well-being in the global South. *Current Opinion in Psychology*, 46, 101318. 10.1016/j.copsyc.2022.10131835439684

Ghosh, T. (2016). Winning versus not losing: Exploring the effects of in-game advertising outcome on its effectiveness. *Journal of Interactive Marketing*, 36(1), 134–147. 10.1016/j.intmar.2016.05.003

Gilal, F. G., Paul, J., Gilal, N. G., & Gilal, R. G. (2021). Strategic CSR-brand fit and customers' brand passion: Theoretical extension and analysis. *Psychology and Marketing*, 38(5), 759–773. 10.1002/mar.21464

Gil-Ramírez, M., de Travesedo-Rojas, R. G., & Almansa-Martínez, A. (2019). Politainment and political personalisation. From television to YouTube. *Revista Latina de Comunicación Social*, 74, 1542–1564. 10.4185/RLCS-2019-1398

Glass, G. V. (1976). Primary, secondary, and meta-analysis of research. *Educational Researcher*, 5(10), 3–8. 10.2307/1174772

Goanta, C., & Ranchordas, S. (2019). The regulation of social media influencers: An introduction. *Social Science Research Network*. 10.2139/ssrn.3457197

Goffman, E. (1974). *Frame Analysis: An Essay on the Organization of Experience*. Harpor & Row.

Gómez-Rico, M., Collado, A. M., Vijande, M. L. S., Molina-Collado, M. V., & Imhoff, B. (2022). The role of novel instruments of brand communication and brand image in building consumers' brand preference and intention to visit wineries. *Current Psychology (New Brunswick, N.J.)*, 42(15), 12711–12727. 10.1007/s12144-021-02656-w35035183

Goodman, L. A. (1961). Snowball sampling. *Annals of Mathematical Statistics*, 32(1), 148–170. 10.1214/aoms/1177705148

Gottfried, R. A. (2015). Six ways this article is most definitely not an ad: Deceptive marketing and the need for clearly-defined disclosure rules in online native advertisement. *Loyola Consumer Law Review*, 27(3), 399–422.

Graber, D. (1981). Media agenda-setting in a presidential election: issues, images, and interest. New York (N.Y.): Praeger.

Graefe, A., & Bohlken, N. (2020). *Automated Journalism: A Meta-Analysis of Readers' Perceptions of Human-Written in Comparison to Automated News, Media and Communication*. Business Faculty, Macromedia University of Applied Sciences.

Greenwood, S. D., Sorenson, J., & Warner, B. R. (2016). Political satire and the politics of emotion. *The International Journal of Press/Politics*, 21(4), 458–478.

GRI. (n.d.). *About GRI*. GRI. https://www.globalreporting.org/standards/

Gross, K., & Brewer, P. R. (2007). Sore Losers: News Frames, Policy Debates, and Emotions. *The Harvard International Journal of Press/Politics*, 12(1), 122–133. 10.1177/1081180X06297231

Guanah, J. S., Obi, J., Egbra, O. S., & Akumabor, N. T. (2017, September). *Social media, youths and agricultural development social media, youths and agricultural development in the Niger Delta region of Nigeria.* Research Gate. https://www.researchgate.net/publication/342716459_Social_media_Youths_and_Agricultural_Development_Social_media_Youths_and_Agricultural_Development_in_the_Niger_Delta_Region_of_Nigeria

Gunawardena, P., Amila, O., Sudarshana, H., Nawaratne, R., Luhach, A. K., Alahakoon, D., Perera, A. S., Chitraranjan, C., Chilamkurti, N., & De Silva, D. (2021). Real-time automated video highlight generation with dual-stream hierarchical growing self-organizing maps. *Journal of Real-Time Image Processing*, 18(5), 1457–1475. 10.1007/s11554-020-00957-0

Gunther, A. C. (1992). Biased press or biased public? Attitudes toward media coverage of social groups. *Public Opinion Quarterly*, 56(2), 147–167. 10.1086/269308

Gupta, S. (2016). Trump supporters call to boycott Pepsi over comments the CEO never made. *CNN Money*. https://money.cnn.com/2016/11/16/news/companies/pepsi-fake-news-boycott-trump

Gupta, S., Jain, G., & Tiwari, A. A. (2021). Investigating the dynamics of polarization in online discourse during the COVID-19 pandemic. In *Lecture notes in computer science* (pp. 704–709). Springer. 10.1007/978-3-030-85447-8_58

Gyimah-Brempong, K., & Kimenyi, M. S. (2013, April). *Youth policy and the future of African development*. (African growth initiative working paper 9). African Growth Initiative at Brookings. https://www.brookings.edu/wp-content/uploads/2016/06/04_youth_policy_african_development_kimenyi.pdf

Han, J.-H. (2018). UTAUT Model of Pre-service Teachers for Telepresence Robot, Assisted Learning. *J. Creat. Inf. Cult.*

Hang, O. C., & Dahlan, H. M. (2019, December). Cyberbullying lexicon for social media. In *2019 6th International Conference on Research and Innovation in Information Systems (ICRIIS)* (pp. 1-6). IEEE. 10.1109/ICRIIS48246.2019.9073679

Hänggli, R., & Kriesi, H. (2012). Frame Construction and Frame Promotion (Strategic Framing Choices). *The American Behavioral Scientist*, 56(3), 260–278. 10.1177/0002764211426325

Han, J. (2020). *The Use of UTAUT and Post Acceptance Models to Investigate the Attitude towards a Telepresence Robot in an Educational Setting Robotics Sheffield Hallam University*.

Hannah, D. R., McCarthy, I. P., & Kietzmann, J. (2015). We're leaking, and everything's fine: How and why companies deliberately leak secrets. *Business Horizons*, 58(6), 659–667. 10.1016/j.bushor.2015.07.003

Hansen, M., & Roca-Sales, M. (2017). *Artificial Intelligence: Practice and Implications for Journalism. Tow Center for Digital Journalism*. Columbia Journalism School, New York.

Hariharasudan, A., Pandeeswari, D., & Hassan, A. (2022, March 16). Research Trends in Post Modernism: A Bibliometric Analysis. *World Journal of English Language*, 12(2), 148–149. 10.5430/wjel.v12n2p148

Harrigan, P., Coussement, K., Lancelot Miltgen, C., & Ranaweera, C. (2020). The future of technology in marketing; utopia or dystopia? *Journal of Marketing Management*, 36(3-4), 211–215. 10.1080/0267257X.2020.1744382

Harris, J. L., Pomeranz, J. L., Lobstein, T., & Brownell, K. D. (2009). A crisis in the marketplace: How food marketing contributes to childhood obesity and what can be done. *Annual Review of Public Health*, 30(1), 211–225. 10.1146/annurev.publhealth.031308.10030418976142

Haryani, S., & Motwani, B. (2015). Discriminant model for online viral marketing influencing consumers behavioural intention. *Pacific science review B: Humanities and social sciences,* 1(1), 49-56.

Hassan, S., Yacob, M. I., Nguyen, T., & Zambri, S. (2018). *Social media influencer and cyberbullying: A lesson learned from preliminary findings. Knowledge Management International Conference (KMICe)*, Miri Sarawak, Malaysia

Hayes, A. F. (2022). *Introduction to mediation, moderation, and conditional process analysis: A regression-based approach*. Guilford Publications.

Heiss, R., Bode, L., Adisuryo, Z. M., Brito, L., Cuadra, A., Gao, P., Han, Y., Hearst, M., Huang, K., Kinyua, A., Lin, T., Ma, Y., Manion, T. O., Roh, Y., Salazar, A., Yue, S., & Zhang, P. (2024). Debunking mental health misperceptions in short-form social media videos: An experimental test of scientific credibility cues. *Health Communication*, 1–13. 10.1080/10410236.2023.230120138389200

Hellmueller. (2012). *The credibility of credibility measures: A meta-analysis in leading communication journals, 1951 to 2011*. In WAPOR 65th Annual Conference, Hong Kong.

Helm, J. (2013). Ethical and legal issues related to blogging and social media. *Journal of the Academy of Nutrition and Dietetics*, 113(5), 688–690. 10.1016/j.jand.2013.02.008

Hennessy, B. (1970). A headnote on the existence and study of political attitudes. *Social Science Quarterly*, 463–476.

Henninger, M. (2013). *Data-driven journalism. Challenge and Change: Reassessing Journalism's Global Future*. Sydney, Australia: UTS ePRESS University of Technology. http://www.teccomstudies.com/index.php?journal=teccomstudies&page=article&op=view&path[]=148

Heth, J. N. (2018). How social media will impact marketing media. In *Social media marketing* (pp. 3-18). Palgrave Macmillan, Singapore.

Highfield, T. (2017). Networked humour: Understanding internet memes. In *Digital media, humor and identity* (pp. 59–77). Routledge.

Hobbs, R. (2013). Media literacy. In Lemish, D. (Ed.), *The Routledge International Handbook of Children, Adolescents and Media* (pp. 417–424). Routledge.

Hoeck, L., & Spann, M. (2020). An experimental analysis of the effectiveness of multi-screen advertising. *Journal of Interactive Marketing*, 50(1), 81–99. 10.1016/j.intmar.2020.01.002

Hoeffler, S., & Keller, K. L. (2002). Building brand equity through corporate societal marketing. *Journal of Public Policy & Marketing*, 21(1), 78–89. 10.1509/jppm.21.1.78.17600

Hoffmann, J., & Hawkins, V. (Eds.). (2015). *Communication and Peace: Mapping an emerging field* (1st ed.). Routledge., 10.4324/9781315773124

Holbert, R. L., & Young, D. G. (2012). *Exploring relations between political entertainment media and traditional political communication information outlets: A research agenda*. The International Encyclopedia of Media Studies. 10.1002/9781444361506.wbiems127

Holden, C. (2001). 'Behavioral' addictions: Do they exist? *Science*, 294(5544), 980–982. 10.1126/science.294.5544.98011691967

Hopkins, R. F. (1966). Christianity and sociopolitical change in sub-Saharan Africa. *Social Forces*, 44(4), 555–562. 10.2307/2575091

Horowitz, D. (1985). *Ethnic Groups in Conflict*. University of California Press.

Hossain, M. A. (2019). Effects of uses and gratifications on social media use. *PSU Research Review*, 3(1), 16–28. 10.1108/PRR-07-2018-0023

Hovland, C. I., Janis, I. L., & Kelley, H. H. (1953). *Communication and persuasion: Psychological studies of opinion change*. Yale University Press.

Hovland, I., Janis, L., & Kelley, H. (1953). *Communication and persuasion; Psychological studies of opinion change.* Yale University Press.

Hsu, M., Tien, S., Lin, H., & Chang, C. (2015). Understanding the roles of cultural differences and socioeconomic status in social media continuance intention. *Information Technology & People*, 28(1), 224–241. 10.1108/ITP-01-2014-0007

Hu, X. (2015). *Assessing source credibility on social media—An electronic word-of-mouth communication perspective.* [Doctoral Dissertation, Bowling Green State University].

Humphreys, L., Von Pape, T., & Karnowski, V. (2013). Evolving mobile media: Uses and conceptualizations of the mobile internet. *Journal of Computer-Mediated Communication*, 18(4), 491–507. 10.1111/jcc4.12019

Hunter, J. E., & Schmidt, F. L. (2004). Methods of meta-analysis: *Correcting errors and bias in research findings.Sage (Atlanta, Ga.).*

Huntington, S. P. (2000). *The clash of civilizations? In Culture and politics* (pp. 99-118). Palgrave Macmillan, New York.

Hussein, S. (2006). *Media Research.* World of Books, Cairo, Egypt.

Hu, Y. (2015). Health communication research in the digital age: A systematic review. *Journal of Communication in Healthcare*, 8(4), 260–288. 10.1080/17538068.2015.1107308

Hwang, K., & Zhang, Q. (2018). Influence of parasocial relationship between digital celebrities and their followers on followers' purchase and electronic word-of-mouth intentions, and persuasion knowledge. *Computers in Human Behavior*, 87, 155–173. 10.1016/j.chb.2018.05.029

Idris, I. (2020). *Responding to popular protests in the MENA region.*

Igwe, I. (2024). Minister petitions IGP, asks court to stop Niger mass wedding of 100 orphans. *Channels TV.* https://www.channelstv.com/2024/05/14/minister-petitions-igp- asks-court-to-stop-niger-mass-wedding-of-100-orphans/

IKEA. (2021a). *IKEA continues commitment to climate action by joining COP26 as a partner.* IKEA. https://www.ikea.com/us/en/newsroom/corporate-news/ikea-joins-cop26-as-a-partner

IKEA. (2021b). *Insights from new global study.* IKEA. https://about.ikea.com/en/newsroom/2021/10/25/globescan-study-2021

IKEA. (2022a). *Sustainability – caring for people and the planet.* IKEA. https://about.ikea.com/en/sustainability

IKEA. (2022b). *People & Planet Positive - IKEA sustainability strategy.* IKEA. https://ikea-sustainability-strategy

IKEA. (2022c). We want to make healthy and sustainable living affordable for everyone. IKEA. https://about.ikea.com/en/sustainability/healthy-and-sustainable-living

IKEA. (2022d). *IKEA Sustainability Report FY2022.* IKEA. https://https://ikea-sustainability-report-fy22

Ilicic, J., & Webster, C. (2014). Investigating consumer–brand relational authenticity. *Journal of Brand Management*, 21(4), 342–363. 10.1057/bm.2014.11

Imoh, G. O. (2013). Mass media and democratic consolidation in Africa: Problems, challenges and prospects. *New Media and Mass Communication.* 16, https://core.ac.uk/download/pdf/234652401.pdf

Interactive Advertising Bureau. (2011). *Self-Regulatory Program For Online Behavioral Advertising Factsheet.* IAB. https://www.iab.com/wp-content/uploads/2015/06/OBA_OneSheet_Final.pdf

Compilation of References

Interactive Advertising Bureau. (2011). *Self-Regulatory Program For Online Behavioral Advertising Factsheet*. IAB. OBA_OneSheet_Final.pdf (iab.com)

Irwin, H. (1989). Health communication: The research agenda. *Media International Australia*, 54(1), 32–40. 10.1177/1329878X8905400110

Islam, G. (2014). Social Identity Theory. In Teo, T. (Ed.), *Encyclopedia of Critical Psychology*. Springer. 10.1007/978-1-4614-5583-7_289

Ismail, F. (2022). Journalists attitudes towards using artificial intelligence in developing journalistic content in Egyptian newspapers and websites. *Egyptian Journal of Public Opinion Research, Cairo University, of mass communication, Egypt*.

ISO. (2018). *26000 Guidance on social responsibility*. ISO. https://www.iso.org/iso-26000-social-responsibility.html

Itzkowitz, A., Whitelaw, B., Donald, D., Montagu, G., Gilbert, J., Germuska, J., Lambertini, L., Fainman-Adelman, L., & Ha, T. (2023). *Next Gen News: Understanding the Audiences of 2030*. FT Strategies & Knight Lab.

Iyengar, S., & Simon, A. F. (2000). New perspectives and evidence on political communication and campaign effects. *Annual Review of Psychology*, 51(1), 149–169. 10.1146/annurev.psych.51.1.14910751968

Izquierdo-Yusta, A., Olarte-Pascual, C., & Reinares-Lara, E. (2015). Attitudes toward mobile advertising among users versus non-users of the mobile Internet. *Telematics and Informatics*, 32(2), 355–366. 10.1016/j.tele.2014.10.001

Jackson, D. (2011). Strategic Media, Cynical Public? Examining the Contingent Effects of Strategic News Frames on Political Cynicism in the United Kingdom. *The International Journal of Press/Politics*, 16(1), 157–175. 10.1177/1940161210381647

Jackson, G., Bartosch, J., Avetisyan, E., Kinderman, D., & Knudsen, J. S. (2020). Mandatory non-financial disclosure and its influence on CSR: An international comparison. *Journal of Business Ethics*, 162(2), 323–342. 10.1007/s10551-019-04200-0

Jain, S. (2024). An analysis of the influence of user generated content (UGC) on brand perception and consumer engagement in digital marketing strategies. *Social Science Research Network*. 10.2139/ssrn.4781464

Jameson, F. (1997). *Post modernism, or, the cultural logic of late capitalism*. Duke University Press Durham. https://is.muni.cz/el/fss/jaro2016/SOC757/um/61816962/Jameson_The_cultural_logic.pdf

Jameson, F. (1979). Reification and utopia in mass culture. *Social Text*, (1), 130–148. 10.2307/466409

Järvi, H., Kähkönen, A. K., & Torvinen, H. (2018). When value co-creation fails: Reasons that lead to value co-destruction. *Scandinavian Journal of Management*, 34(1), 63–77. 10.1016/j.scaman.2018.01.002

Jenkins, H. (2006). *Convergence Culture: Where Old and New Media Collide*. New York University Press.

Jernigan, D. H., Ross, C. S., Ostroff, J., McKnight-Eily, L. R., & Brewer, R. D. (2013). Youth exposure to alcohol advertising on television—25 markets, United States, 2010. *Morbidity and Mortality Weekly Report*, 62(44), 877. https://www.cdc.gov/mmwr/preview/mmwrhtml/mm6244a3.htm

Jessica, M. (2022, May 19). Kunert., Jannis, Frech., Michael, Brüggemann., Volker, Dr. Lilienthal., Wiebke, Loosen. (2022). How Investigative Journalists Around the World Adopt Innovative Digital Practices. *Journalism Studies*, 23(7), 761–780. 10.1080/1461670X.2022.2033636

Jha, A. K., & Verma, N. K. (2023). Social media platforms and user engagement: A multi-platform study on one-way firm sustainability communication. *Information Systems Frontiers*, 26(1), 177–194. 10.1007/s10796-023-10376-8

Jing, H. (2023). The Rising Trend of Artificial Intelligence in Social Media. *Advances in Computer and Electrical Engineering book series*. 10.4018/978-1-6684-6937-8.ch003

Johnston, H., & Noakes, J. A. (Eds.). (2005). *Frames of protest: Social movements and the framing perspective*. Rowman & Littlefield Publishers.

Joshi, Y., Lim, W. M., Jagani, K., & Kumar, S. (2023). Social media influencer marketing: Foundations, trends, and ways forward. *Electronic Commerce Research*. 10.1007/s10660-023-09719-z

July, D.L.B., DSA's. (2021). Flawed International Outlook: The Appeal of the Mass Party and its. *Contradictions*.

Juvonen, J., & Gross, E. F. (2008). Extending the school grounds?—Bullying experiences in cyberspace. *The Journal of School Health*, 78(9), 496–505. 10.1111/j.1746-1561.2008.00335.x18786042

Kagan, R. (2024). *Rebellion: How Antiliteralism is Tearing America Apart-Again*. Alfred A.

Kalyango, Y., & Adu-Kumi, B. (2013). Impact of social ledia on political mobilization in East and West Africa. *Global Media Journal*, 12(1).

Kansara, K. B., & Shekokar, N. M. (2015). A framework for cyberbullying detection in social network. *International Journal of Current Engineering and Technology*, 5(1), 494–498.

Kaplan, R. D. (1994). *The coming anarchy: how scarcity, crime, overpopulation, tribalism, and disease are rapidly destroying the social fabric of our planet*.

Kapoor, K. K., Tamilmani, K., Rana, N. P., Patil, P. P., Dwivedi, Y. K., & Nerur, S. P. (2017). Advances in social media research: Past, present and future. *Information Systems Frontiers*, 20(3), 531–558. 10.1007/s10796-017-9810-y

Karabulut, N., & Önder, Ç. H. (2017). Determining the factors affecting the voting preferences of young voters in the 2014 local elections. Bilge Adamlar / Wise Men, 16(58), 217-232.

Karpf, D., & Kreiss, D. (2016). The Role of Qualitative Methods in Political Communication Research: Past, Present, and Future. *Political Communication*, 33(3), 343–360.

Karspersky Lab. (2018). *10 Forms of Cyberbullying*. https://kids.kaspersky.com/10-forms-of-cyberbullying/ (Accessed 17 April 2022)

Kaufman, S., & Smith, J. (1999). Framing and reframing in land use change conflicts. *Journal of Architectural and Planning Research*, 16, 164–180.

Kaya, R., & Bayat, M. (2022). Çevrimiçi dünyada yükselen bir trend: Display (görüntülü) reklamlar. *Elektronik Sosyal Bilimler Dergisi*, 21(82), 759–770. 10.17755/esosder.1031584

Kayode, L., & Omar, B. (2020). Do social media matter: Examining social media use and youths' political particiaption during 2019 Nigeria general elections. *The Round Table: The Commonwealth Journal of International Affairs*.

Kellner, D. (2020). Jean Baudrillard. *The Stanford Encyclopedia of Philosophy*. https://plato.stanford.edu/archives/win2020/entries/baudrillard/>

Kemp, D., & Owen, J. R. (2013). Community relations and mining: Core to business but not "core business.". *Resources Policy*, 38(4), 523–531. 10.1016/j.resourpol.2013.08.003

Kent, M. L., & Taylor, M. (2016). From Homo economicus to Homo dialogicus: Rethinking social media use in CSR communication. *Public Relations Review*, 42(1), 60–67. 10.1016/j.pubrev.2015.11.003

Compilation of References

Kent, M. P., & Pauzé, E. (2018). The effectiveness of self-regulation in limiting the advertising of unhealthy foods and beverages on children's preferred websites in Canada. *Public Health Nutrition*, 21(9), 1608–1617. 10.1017/S136898001700417729433594

Kerlinger, F. N. (1986). *Foundations of Behavioral Research* (3rd ed.). Holt, Rinehart and Winston.

Khan, A., Rezaei, S., & Valaei, N. (2022). Social commerce advertising avoidance and shopping cart abandonment: A fs/QCA analysis of German consumers. *Journal of Retailing and Consumer Services*, 67, 102976. 10.1016/j.jretconser.2022.102976

Kietzmann, J. H., Hermkens, K., McCarthy, I. P., & Silvestre, B. S. (2011). Social media? Get serious! Understanding the functional building blocks of social media. *Business Horizons*, 54(3), 241–251. 10.1016/j.bushor.2011.01.005

Kim, J., & Kim, M. (2022). Rise of social media influencers as a new marketing channel: Focusing on the roles of psychological well-being and perceived social responsibility among consumers. *International Journal of Environmental Research and Public Health*, 19(4), 2362. 10.3390/ijerph1904236235206553

Kim, K. H. (2021). Digital and social media marketing in global business environment. *Journal of Business Research*, 131, 627–629. 10.1016/j.jbusres.2021.02.052

Kim, S., & Lee, H. (2019). The effect of CSR fit and CSR authenticity on the brand attitude. *Sustainability (Basel)*, 12(1), 275. 10.3390/su12010275

Kim, S., & Rim, H. (2024). The role of public skepticism and distrust in the process of CSR communication. *International Journal of Business Communication*, 61(2), 198–218. 10.1177/2329488419866888

Kim, Y., & Ferguson, M. A. (2019). Are high-fit CSR programs always better? The effects of corporate reputation and CSR fit on stakeholder responses. *Corporate Communications*, 24(3), 471–498. 10.1108/CCIJ-05-2018-0061

King, B. G. (2015). Reputation, risk, and anti-corporate activism: How social movements influence corporate outcomes. In L. Bosi, M. Giugni & K. Uba (2016), *The consequences of social movements* (pp. 215–236). Cambridge University Press.

Klinger, K., & Metag, J. (2021). Media efects in the context of environmental issues. In the *Handbook of International Ttrends in Environmental Communication*. Routledge. https://www.taylorfrancis.com/chapters/edit/10.4324/9780367275204-5/media- effects-context-environmental-issues-kira-klinger-julia-metag.

Knell, M. (2021). The digital revolution and digitalized network society. *Review of Evolutionary Political Economy*, 2(1), 9–25. 10.1007/s43253-021-00037-4

Kohli, C., Suri, R., & Kapoor, A. (2015). Will social media kill branding? *Business Horizons*, 58(1), 35–44. 10.1016/j.bushor.2014.08.004

Koldobika, MesoM. (2023). Without journalists, there is no journalism: the social dimension of generative artificial intelligence in the media. *Information Professional*. 10.3145/epi.2023.mar.27

Koob, C. (2021). Determinants of content marketing effectiveness: Conceptual framework and empirical findings from a managerial perspective. *PLoS One*, 16(4), e0249457. 10.1371/journal.pone.024945733793631

Koskei, M. K. (n.d.). *Post modernism and hyperreality*. Academa. https://www.academia.edu/10747720/POST_MODERNISM_AND_HYPERREA LITY_AND_THE_MEDIA?email_work_card=title

Kothari, C. R. (2004). *Research Methodology: Methods and Techniques* (2nd ed.). New Age International Publishers.

Kozinets, R. V., Sherry, J. F., DeBerry-Spence, B., Duhachek, A., Nuttavuthisit, K., & Storm, D. (2002). Themed flagship brand stores in the new millennium: Theory, practice, prospects. *Journal of Retailing*, 78(1), 17–29. 10.1016/S0022-4359(01)00063-X

Kreft, N. (2011). Comment on David Estlund. What good Is it?—Unrealistic political theory and the value of intellectual work. *Analyse & Kritik*, 33(2), 417–422. 10.1515/auk-2011-0205

Krishen, A. S., Dwivedi, Y. K., Bindu, N., & Kumar, K. S. (2021). A broad overview of interactive digital marketing: A bibliometric network analysis. *Journal of Business Research*, 131, 183–195. 10.1016/j.jbusres.2021.03.061

Krönke, C. (2020). Artificial Intelligence and Social Media. In Wischmeyer, T., & Rademacher, T. (Eds.), *Regulating Artificial Intelligence*. Springer. 10.1007/978-3-030-32361-5_7

Kuan, D., Hasan, N. A. M., Zawawi, J. W. M., & Abdullah, Z. (2021). Framing Theory Application in Public Relations: The Lack of Dynamic Framing Analysis in Competitive Context. *Media Watch*, 12(2), 333–351. 10.15655/mw_2021_v12i2_160155

Kumar, V., Choi, J., & Greene, M. (2016). Synergistic effects of social media and traditional marketing on brand sales: Capturing the time-varying effects. *Journal of the Academy of Marketing Science*, 45(2), 268–288. 10.1007/s11747-016-0484-7

Kuss, D. J., & Griffiths, M. D. (2011). Online social networking and addiction—A review of the psychological literature. *International Journal of Environmental Research and Public Health*, 8(9), 3528–3552. 10.3390/ijerph809352822016701

Lambropoulos, N., Faulkner, X., & Culwin, F. (2012). Supporting social awareness in collaborative e-learning. *British Journal of Educational Technology*, 43(2), 295–306. 10.1111/j.1467-8535.2011.01184.x

Larasati, Z. W., Yuda, T. K., & Syafa'at, A. R. (2022). The digital welfare state and the problem arising: An exploration and future research agenda. *The International Journal of Sociology and Social Policy*, 43(5/6), 537–549. 10.1108/IJSSP-05-2022-0122

Lazarsfeld, P., Berelson, B., & Gaudet, H. (1944). *The People's Choice: How the Voter Makes Up His Mind in a Presidential Campaign*. Duell, Sloane, and Pearce.

Lee, K. (2005). Global social change and health. In Lee, K., & Collin, J. (Eds.), *Global change and health* (pp. 13–27). Open University Press/McGraw-Hill Education.

Lee, M. Y., & Yeon, J. (2022). Humorous entertainment programs and political attitude change: The moderating role of political ideology. *Communication Studies*, 73(2), 257–275.

Leiser, M.R., (2022). *Bias, journalistic endeavors, and the risks of artificial intelligence*. Springer. 10.4337/9781839109973.00007

Lemelshtrich, N. (2018). Robot Journalism, Can Human Journalism Survive? Israel: Herzliya Interdisciplinary Center.

León-Flández, K., Rico-Gómez, A., Moya-Geromin, M. Á., Romero-Fernández, M., Bosqued-Estefania, M. J., Damian, J., López-Jurado, L., & Royo-Bordonada, M. Á. (2017). Evaluation of compliance with the Spanish Code of self-regulation of food and drinks advertising directed at children under the age of 12 years in Spain, 2012. *Public Health*, 150, 121–129. 10.1016/j.puhe.2017.05.01328675833

Leong, L. Y., Jaafar, N. I., & Ainin, S. (2018). The effects of Facebook browsing and usage intensity on impulse purchase in f-commerce. *Computers in Human Behavior*, 78, 160–173. 10.1016/j.chb.2017.09.033

Leppänen, L., Tuulonen, H., & Heikel, S. (2020). Automated Journalism as a Source of and a Diagnostic Device for Bias in Reporting [Issue.]. *Media and Communication*, 8(3), 39–49. 10.17645/mac.v8i3.3022

Leung, J., Schoultz, M., Chiu, V., Bonsaksen, T., Ruffolo, M., Thygesen, H., Price, D., & Geirdal, A. Ø. Concerns over the Spread of Misinformation and Fake News on Social Media—Challenges Amid the Coronavirus Pandemic. *Med. Sci. Forum, 4*, 39. 10.3390/ECERPH-3-09078

Levinson, A.R. (2016). Solidarity on Social Media. *Colum.Bus. L.Rev.,303.*

Levy, M. R., & Windahl, S. (1984). Audience activity and gratifications: A conceptual clarification and exploration. *Communication Research*, 11(1), 51–78. 10.1177/009365084011001003

Lewis, W. A. (1985). *Racial Conflict and Economic Development*. Harvard University Press. 10.4159/harvard.9780674424654

Li, C. H., Chan, O. L. K., Chow, Y. T., Zhang, X., Tong, P. S., Li, S. P., Ng, H. Y., & Keung, K. L. (2022). Evaluating the effectiveness of digital content marketing under mixed reality training platform on the online purchase intention. *Frontiers in Psychology*. 10.3389/fpsyg.2022.881019

Lilleker, D., & Cornfield, M. (2011). Politainment: The Use of Entertainment in Political Communication. In McNair, B. (Ed.), *The Routledge Handbook of Political Communication* (pp. 193–204). Routledge.

Lim, J. S., Ri, S. Y., Egan, B. D., & Biocca, F. A. (2015). The cross-platform synergies of digital video advertising: Implications for cross-media campaigns in television, Internet and mobile TV. *Computers in Human Behavior*, 48, 463–472. 10.1016/j.chb.2015.02.001

Lin, T. H., Chang, M.-C., Chang, C.-C., & Chou, Y.-H. (2022). Government-sponsored disinformation and the severity of respiratory infection epidemics including COVID-19: A global analysis, 2001-2020. *Social Science & Medicine*, 29, 114744. 10.1016/j.socscimed.2022.11474435124544

Lin, W. S., Chen, H. R., Lee, T. S. H., & Feng, J. Y. (2019). Role of social anxiety on high engagement and addictive behavior in the context of social networking sites. *Data Technologies and Applications*, 53(2), 156–170. 10.1108/DTA-09-2018-0076

Liu, Q., & Zhang, F. (2019). Study on the Influencing Factors of Mobile Users' Impulse Purchase Behavior in a Large Online Promotion Activity. [JECO]. *Journal of Electronic Commerce in Organizations*, 17(2), 88–101. 10.4018/JECO.2019040108

Liu, Y., & Gu, X. (2019). Media multitasking, attention, and comprehension: A deep investigation into fragmented reading. *Educational Technology Research and Development*, 68(1), 67–87. 10.1007/s11423-019-09667-2

López López, P. J. (2018). Data Journalism in the Panama Papers. *TecCom Studies, 7*(1). http://www.teccomstudies.com/index.php?journal=teccomstudies&page=article&op=view&path%5b%5d=148

Lops, P., Jannach, D., Musto, C., Bogers, T., & Koolen, M. (2019). Trends in content-based recommendation. *User Modeling and User-Adapted Interaction*, 29(2), 239–249. 10.1007/s11257-019-09231-w

Loveless, M. (2008). Media dependency: Mass media as sources of information in the democratizing countries of Central and Eastern Europe. *Democratization*, 15(1), 162–183. 10.1080/13510340701770030

Lovotti, C. and Proserpio, L. (2021). The October 2019 Protest Movement in Iraq. An Analysis of the'Early Moments of the Mobilization. *Partecipazione e conflict,14*(2) .644-662.

Lowry, P. B., Moody, G. D., & Chatterjee, S. (2017). Using IT design to prevent cyberbullying. *Journal of Management Information Systems*, 34(3), 863–901. 10.1080/07421222.2017.1373012

Lowry, P. B., Moody, G. D., Galletta, D. F., & Vance, A. (2013). The drivers in the use of online whistle-blowing reporting systems. *Journal of Management Information Systems*, 30(1), 153–190. 10.2753/MIS0742-1222300105

Luca, M., & Zervas, G. (2016). Fake it till you make it: Reputation, competition, and Yelp review fraud. *Management Science*, 62(12), 3412–3427. 10.1287/mnsc.2015.2304

Luedecke, G. & Boykoff, M. (2017, March 6). *Environment and the media*. Springer. .10.1002/9781118786352.wbieg0464

Lund, N. F., Scarles, C., & Cohen, S. A. (2020). The brand value continuum: Countering co-destruction of destination branding in social media through storytelling. *Journal of Travel Research*, 59(8), 1506–1521. 10.1177/0047287519887234

Luo, X., & Bhattacharya, C. B. (2006). Corporate social responsibility, customer satisfaction, and market value. *Journal of Marketing*, 70(4), 1–18. 10.1509/jmkg.70.4.001

Lupton, D. (1994). Toward the development of critical health communication praxis. *Health Communication*, 6(1), 55–67. 10.1207/s15327027hc0601_4

Luther, A. (2018). *Diversity in US Mass Media*. 2nd (ed). Wiley Blackwell.

Lynch, G. (2011). *I Say to You: Ethnic Politics and the Kalenjin in Kenya*. University of Chicago Press. 10.7208/chicago/9780226498096.001.0001

Maclaran, P., & Brown, S. (2005). The center cannot hold: Consuming the utopian marketplace. *The Journal of Consumer Research*, 32(2), 311–323. 10.1086/432240

Madden, M., Lenhart, A., & Fontaine, C. (2017). *How youth navigate the news landscape: recent qualitative research*. Knight Foundation.

Maheshwar, M. (2017). *Mass Media and Health Communication in India*.

Maignan, I., & Ferrell, O. C. (2004). Corporate social responsibility and marketing: An integrative framework. *Journal of the Academy of Marketing Science*, 32(1), 3–19. 10.1177/0092070303258971

Maksl, A., Ashley, S., & Craft, S. (2015). Measuring News Media Literacy. *The Journal of Media Literacy Education*, 6(3), 29–45.

Manfredi, J. L., & Ufarte, M. J. (2020). Artificial intelligence and journalism: a tool against disinformation. *Revista CIDOB d'Afers Internacionals, 124*, 49–72. https://www.jstor.org/stable/26975708

Marconi, F. (2020). *Newsmakers: Artificial Intelligence and the Future of Journalism*. Columbia University Press., https://www.jstor.org/stable/10.7312/marc19136 10.7312/marc19136

Margolis, J. D., & Walsh, J. P. (2003). Misery loves companies: Rethinking social initiatives by business. *Administrative Science Quarterly*, 48(2), 268–305. 10.2307/3556659

Marieke, M., & Hendriksen, A. (2023). The future of jobs: interviews with artificial intelligence.]10.22541/au.168599000.07517003/v1

Marketing Accountability Standards Board. (2018). *Common Language in Marketing Project Team, 2018. Display Advertising (Digital) Definition*. Marketing Dictionary. https://marketing-dictionary.org/d/display-advertising-digital/

Markiewicz, D. (1975). Humor as a form of persuasion: A study of some comic elements in political cartoons. *Communication Monographs*, 42(4), 315–326.

Compilation of References

Martinez-Caro, J., Aledo-Hernandez, A., Guillen-Perez, A., Sanchez-Iborra, R., & Cano, M. (2018). A comparative study of web content management systems. *Information (Basel)*, 9(2), 27. 10.3390/info9020027

Masullo, G. M., Brown, D. K., & Harlow, S. (2023). Shifting the protest paradigm? Legitimizing and humanizing protest coverage lead to more positive attitudes toward protest, mixed results on news credibility. *Journalism*, 0(0). 10.1177/14648849231200135

Matten, D., & Moon, J. (2008). "Implicit" and "explicit" CSR: A conceptual framework for a comparative understanding of corporate social responsibility. *Academy of Management Review*, 33(2), 404–424. 10.5465/amr.2008.31193458

McCombes, S. (2022). *Sampling Methods | Types, Techniques, & Examples*. Scribbr. https://www.scribbr.co.uk/research-methods/sampling/

McCombs, M., Shaw, L. D., & Weaver, D. (1997). *Communication and Democracy: Exploring the Intellectual Frontiers in Agenda-Setting Theory*. Mahwah, NJ: Lawrence Erlbaum Associates, 1997.

McCroskey, J. C., & Teven, J. J. (1999). Goodwill: A reexamination of the construct and its scale. *Communication Monographs*, 66(1), 90–103. 10.1080/03637759909376464

McGee, R., & Greenhalf, J. (2012, December 14). *Young citizens: Youth and participatory governance in Africa*. International Institute for Environment and Development. https://www.comminit.com/la/content/young-citizens-youth-and-participatory-governance-africa

McHugh, B. C., Wisniewski, P., Rosson, M. B., & Carroll, J. M. (2018). When social media traumatizes teens: The roles of online risk exposure, coping, and post-traumatic stress. *Internet Research*, 28(5), 1169–1188. 10.1108/IntR-02-2017-0077

McLeod, D. M., Kosicki, G. M., & McLeod, J. M. (2009). Political communication effects. In *J. Media effects: Advances in theory and research. 228–251*. Routledge.

McManus, J. H. (1994). *Market-driven Journalism: Let the Citizen Beware?* Sage.

McQuail, D. (2010). *McQuail's mass communication theory*. Sage. https://nibmehub.com/opac-service/pdf/read/McQuail's%20Mass%20communication%20theory.pdf

McQuail, D. (2010). *McQuail's mass communication theory*. Sage publications.

Mearsheimer, J. J. (2001). *The Tragedy of Great Power Politics*. W. W. Norton.

Media Foundation for West Africa. (2021, December 3). *The Gambian elections: the press, social Media and the newfound freedom*. MFWA. https://www.mfwa.org/the-gambian-elections-the-press-social-media-and-the-newfound-freedom/

Meenaghan, T. (2001). Understanding sponsorship effects. *Psychology and Marketing*, 18(2), 95–122. 10.1002/1520-6793(200102)18:2<95::AID-MAR1001>3.0.CO;2-H

Melki, J., Tamim, H., Hadid, D., Makki, M., El Amine, J., & Hitti, E. (2021). Mitigating infodemics: The relationship between news exposure and trust and belief in COVID-19 fake news and social media spreading. *PLoS One*, 16(6), 1–13. 10.1371/journal.pone.025283034086813

Mengü, Y., Sevi, B., Yegen, B. C., & Yilmaz, E. (2015). Usage of social media for political purposes during March 2014 local elections in Turkey. *Social Media + Society*, 1(2), 2056305115614241.

Meral, K. Z. (2021). Social media short video-sharing TikTok application and ethics: data privacy and addiction issues. In *Multidisciplinary approaches to ethics in the digital era* (pp. 147–165). IGI Global. 10.4018/978-1-7998-4117-3.ch010

Mergel, I., Edelmann, N., & Haug, N. (2019). Defining digital transformation: Results from expert interviews. *Government Information Quarterly*, *36*(4). doi: https://doi.org/. giq.2019.06.00210.1016/j

Meriç, E., & Çakıcı, Z. (2024). From TikTok Trends to Pandemic Essentials: A Comparative Analysis of the World Health Organization's Health Communication Strategies on TikTok. In *Transformed Communication Codes in the Mediated World: A Contemporary Perspective* (pp. 1-23). IGI Global.

Merriam-Webster. (2023). Social media. *Merriam-Webster.com dictionary*. https://www.merriam-webster.com/dictionary/social%20media

Mesch, G. S. (2018). Parent–child connections on social networking sites and cyberbullying. *Youth & Society*, *50*(8), 1145–1162. 10.1177/0044118X16659685

Messaoudi, F., & Loukili, M. (2024). E-commerce personalized recommendations: A deep neural collaborative filtering approach. *SN Operations Research Forum*, *5*(1). 10.1007/s43069-023-00286-5

Messner, M., & Distaso, M. W. (2008). The source cycle. *Journalism Studies*, *9*(3), 447–463. 10.1080/14616700801999287

Meyer, M., Adkins, V., Yuan, N., Weeks, H. M., Chang, Y. J., & Radesky, J. (2019). Advertising in young children's apps: A content analysis. *Journal of Developmental and Behavioral Pediatrics*, *40*(1), 32–39. 10.1097/DBP.0000000000000622 30371646

Mheidly, N., & Fares, J. (2020). Health communication research in the Arab world: A bibliometric analysis. *Integrated Healthcare Journal*, *2*, e000011. 37441309

Michelon, G., Pilonato, S., & Ricceri, F. (2015). CSR reporting practices and the quality of disclosure: An empirical analysis. *Critical Perspectives on Accounting*, *33*, 59–78. 10.1016/j.cpa.2014.10.003

Mills, C. W. (1956). *The power elite*. Oxford University Press.

Minor, D., & Morgan, J. (2011). CSR as reputation insurance: Primum non nocere. *California Management Review*, *53*(3), 40–59. 10.1525/cmr.2011.53.3.40

Miroshnichenko, A. (2019). *Robot Journalism, the Third Threat*. York-Ryerson Future Communications Conference, York University, USA.

Miroshnichenko, A. (2020). *AI to Bypass Creativity: Will Robots Replace Journalists?* Journal Information.

Mngusuul, U. B. (2015). Social media and the mobilization of youths for socio-political participation. *New Media and Mass Communication*, *42*. https://core.ac.uk/download/pdf/234652824.pdf

Modi, V., & Sharma, P. (2021). Indian Customers' Perception & Reaction to Deceptive Advertisements of Hair Care Products. *Gap Interdisciplinarities-A Global Journal of Interdisciplinary Studies*, *4*(1), 49–62.

Moon, J. (2014). *Corporate social responsibility: A very short introduction*. Oxford University Press. 10.1093/actrade/9780199671816.001.0001

Moorhead, S. A., Hazlett, D. E., Harrison, L., Carroll, J. K., Irwin, A., & Hoving, C. (2013). A new dimension of health care: Systematic review of the uses, benefits, and limitations of social media for health communication. *Journal of Medical Internet Research*, *15*(4), e85. 10.2196/jmir.1933 23615206

Morandín-Ahuerma, F. (2022). What is Artificial Intelligence? *International Journal of Research Publication and Reviews*, *03*(12), 1947–1951. 10.55248/gengpi.2022.31261

Moravec, V., MacKová, V., Sido, J., & Ekštein, K. (2020). *Communication Today*. Trnava Vol.

Compilation of References

Moreno, M., & Koff, R. (2015). 11. Media theories and the facebook influence model. In the *Psychology of Social Networking, 1*. https://doi.org/10.1515/9783110473780-01

Moreton, L., & Greenfield, S. (2022). University students' views on the impact of Instagram on mental wellbeing: A qualitative study. *BMC Psychology*, 10(1), 1–10. 10.1186/s40359-022-00743-635227331

Morgenthau, H. J. (1948). World politics in the mid-twentieth century. *The Review of Politics*, 10(2), 154–173. 10.1017/S0034670500042236

Moschis, G. P. (2017). Research frontiers on the dark side of consumer behaviour: The case of materialism and compulsive buying. *Journal of Marketing Management*, 33(15-16), 1384–1401. 10.1080/0267257X.2017.1347341

Mosseri, A. (2023). *Head of Instagram. During an episode of the "20VC" podcast*.

Moussa, I & Abdel Fattah, A. (2020). Trends of journalists and leaders towards employing artificial intelligence techniques within newsrooms in Egyptian journalistic institutions, an applied study. *Egyptian Journal of Public Opinion Research*.

Mudrack, P. (2007). Individual personality factors that affect normative beliefs about the rightness of corporate social responsibility. *Business & Society*, 46(1), 33–62. 10.1177/0007650306290312

Murphy, M., & Sashi, C. M. (2018). Communication, interactivity, and satisfaction in B2B relationships. *Industrial Marketing Management*, 68, 1–12. 10.1016/j.indmarman.2017.08.020

Musa, A. O. (2011). *The role of political, socio-economic factors and the media in Nigeria's Inter-religious conflict*. [Thesis, University of Liverpool]. https://livrepository.liverpool.ac.uk/5335/4/Musa_Ali_Oct2011_5335.pdf

Mwakideu, C. (2021, September 1). China's growing influence on Africa's media. *DW*. https://www.dw.com/en/experts-warn-of-chinas-growing-media-influence-in-africa/a-56385420

Nadel, S. F. (1956). Understanding primitive peoples. *Oceania*, 26(3), 159–173. 10.1002/j.1834-4461.1956.tb00676.x

Nam, K., Baker, J., Ahmad, N., & Goo, J. (2020). Dissatisfaction, disconfirmation, and distrust: An empirical examination of value co-destruction through negative electronic word-of-mouth (eWOM). *Information Systems Frontiers*, 22(1), 113–130. 10.1007/s10796-018-9849-4

Napoli, P. M. (2003). *Audience economics: Media institutions and the audience marketplace*. Columbia University Press.

Napoli, P. M. (2011). *Audience evolution: New technologies and the transformation of media audiences*. Columbia University Press.

National Bureau of Statistics-Nigeria. (2023). *Nigeria-human development indices general household survey 2017, first round*. National Bureau of Statistics. https://www.nigerianstat.gov.ng/nada/index.php/catalog/72

Nelson, K. A. (2004). Consumer decision making and image theory: Understanding value-laden decisions. *Journal of Consumer Psychology*, 14(1-2), 28–40. 10.1207/s15327663jcp1401&2_5

Netblocks. (2016). *Iraq shuts down the internet again as protests intensify*. Netblocks. https://netblocks.org/reports/iraq-shuts-down-internet-again-as-protests-intensify-Q8oOWz8n>

Neto, K. A., & Hernriques, M. H. (2022). Geoconservation in Africa: State of the art and future challenges. *Gondwana Research*, 110, 107–113. 10.1016/j.gr.2022.05.022

Nettelhorst, S. C., Jeter, W. K., Brannon, L. A., & Entringer, A. (2017). Can there be too much of a good thing? The effect of option number on cognitive effort toward online advertisements. *Computers in Human Behavior*, 75, 320–328. 10.1016/j.chb.2017.04.061

Newman, N., Fletcher, R., Eddy, K., Robertson, C. T., & Nielsen, R. K. (2023). *Digital News Report 2023*. Reuters Institute.

Newman, N., Fletcher, R., Robertson, C. T., Eddy, K., & Nielsen, R. K. (2022). *Digital Media Report 2022*. Reuters Institute.

Neyens, E., & Smits, T. (2017). Empty pledges: A content analysis of Belgian and Dutch child-targeting food websites. *International Journal of Health Promotion and Education*, 55(1), 42–52. 10.1080/14635240.2016.1218295

Neyens, E., Smits, T., & Boyland, E. (2017). Transferring game attitudes to the brand: Persuasion from age 6 to 14. *International Journal of Advertising*, 36(5), 724–742. 10.1080/02650487.2017.1349029

Nieland, J.-U. (2008). *Politainment*. The International Encyclopedia of Communication. 10.1002/9781405186407.wbiecp047

Noain Sánchez, A. (2022). Addressing the Impact of Artificial Intelligence on Journalism: The perception of experts, journalists and academics. *Communicatio Socialis*, 35(3), 105–121. 10.15581/003.35.3.105-121

Noakes, J. A., & Wilkins, K. G. (2002). Shifting frames of the Palestinian movement in US news. *Media Culture & Society*, 24(5), 649–671. 10.1177/016344370202400506

Norman, J., Kelly, B., McMahon, A. T., Boyland, E., Baur, L. A., Chapman, K., King, L., Hughes, C., & Bauman, A. (2018). Sustained impact of energy-dense TV and online food advertising on children's dietary intake: A within-subject, randomised, crossover, counter-balanced trial. *The International Journal of Behavioral Nutrition and Physical Activity*, 15(1), 1–11. 10.1186/s12966-018-0672-629650023

Number of global social network users 2017–2025. (2022, April 28). Statista. https://www.statista.com/statistics/278414/number-of-worldwide-social-network-users

Nuseir, M. T. (2018). Impact of misleading/false advertisement to consumer behaviour. *International Journal of Economics and Business Research*, 16(4), 453–465. 10.1504/IJEBR.2018.095343

Nwoye, K. O., & Okafor, G. O. (2014). New media and political mobilization in Africa: The Nigerian experience. *American Journal of Social Sciences.*, 2(2), 36–42.

Nyamnjoh, F. B. (2010). *Africa's media: Between professional ethics and cultural belonging*. Fredrich Ebert Stifung. https://library.fes.de/pdf-files/bueros/africa-media/07366.pdf

O'Connor, A., & Ihlen, Ø. (2018). Corporate social responsibility and rhetoric: Conceptualization, construction, and negotiation. In *The handbook of organizational rhetoric and communication* (pp. 401–415).

O'Donovan, J., Wagner, H. F., & Zeume, S. (2019). The value of offshore secrets: Evidence from the Panama Papers. *Review of Financial Studies*, 32(11), 4117–4155. 10.1093/rfs/hhz017

O'Regan, M. (2007). Explaining Media Frames of Contested Foreign Conflicts: Irish National "Opinion Leader" Newspapers. Frames of the Israeli-Palestinian Conflict (July 2000 to July 2004)'. *Networking Knowledge*, 1(2), 1–25. 10.31165/nk.2007.12.27

O'Shaughnessy, J., & O'Shaughnessy, N. J. (2002). Postmodernism and marketing: Separating the wheat from the chaff. *Journal of Macromarketing*. https://www.academia.edu/20497686/Postmodernism_and_Marketing_Separating_the_Wheat_from_the_Chaff?email_work_card=thumbnail

Oberschall, A. (1978). Theories of social conflict. *Annual Review of Sociology*, 4(1), 291–315. 10.1146/annurev.so.04.080178.001451

Obiora, C., Chiamogu, A. P., & Chiamogu, U. P. (2022). Social media regulation, freedom of expression and civic space in Nigeria: A study based on authoritarian mass communication. *Journal of Government and Political Issues*, 2(3), 126–136. https://papers.ssrn.com/sol3/papers.cfm?abstract_id=4448717. 10.53341/jgpi.v2i3.69

Odeh. S. (2019). *al-ilam al-araqi pen al-taghtiyya "al-babghaiya" lalaslata wagma fadaiyat (Iraqi media between "parrot" coverage of the authority and the repression of satellite channels)'*. Independent Arbaya.

Ofcom. (2022). News consumption in the UK: 2022. Ofcom.

Ogunnaike, J. (2024, January 21). Soyinka laments bastardisation of social media by Nigeria. *Vanguard*. https://www.vanguardngr.com/2024/01/soyinka-laments-bastardization-of-social- media-by-nigerians/#google_vignette

Okamgba, J. G. (2023). Nigeria has 740 operational broadcast stations, newly approved 67, says NBC. *Techeconomy*. https://techeconomy.ng/nigeria-has-740-operational- broadcast-stations-newly-approved-67-says-nbc/

Okocha, D. O., & Dapoet, B. A. (2022). *Social media and hashtag activism in Nigeria: A narrative review.*https://www.researchgate.net/publication/364910641_Social_Media_and_Hashtag Activism_in_Nigeria_A_Narrative_Review

Okocha, D. O., & Chigbo, M. (2023). Flattening the curve of fake news in the epoch of infodemic in Nigeria news media industry. *Journal of Communication and Media Technology*, 5(1).

Okoro, N., & Santas, T. (2017, February). An appraisal of the utilisation of social media for political communication in the 2011 Nigerian presidential election. *African Research Review.*, 11(1), 115. 10.4314/afrrev.v11i1.9

Olan, F., Jayawickrama, U., Arakpogun, E. O., Suklan, J., & Liu, S. (2024). Fake news on Social Media: The Impact on Society. *Information Systems Frontiers*, 26(2), 443–458. 10.1007/s10796-022-10242-z

Olaniran, B., & Williams, I. (2020). Social Media Effects: Hijacking Democracy and Civility in Civic Engagement. *Platforms, Protests, and the Challenge of Networked Democracy*, 77–94. 10.1007/978-3-030-36525-7_5

Oliveira, F., Santos, A., Aguiar, B., & Sousa, J. (2014). GameFoundry: Social gaming platform for digital marketing, user profiling and collective behavior. *Procedia: Social and Behavioral Sciences*, 148, 58–66. 10.1016/j.sbspro.2014.07.017

Oludele, S. M. (2020). Social change in contemporary Nigeria: A theoretical discourse. *RSC, 12*(1), https://www.fuds.si/wp- content/uploads/2020/09/solaja_mayowa_oludele_57-82.pdf

Olukoshi, A. (2004). Changing patterns of politics in Africa. *Cadernos De Estudos Africanos*. 15 - 38. 10.4000/cea.1045

Onuch, O., Mateo, E., & Waller, J. G. (2021). Mobilization, Mass Perceptions, and (Dis)information: "New" and "Old" Media Consumption Patterns and Protest. *Social Media + Society*, 7(2). 10.1177/2056305121999656

Orlitzky, M., Schmidt, F. L., & Rynes, S. L. (2003). Corporate social and financial performance: A meta-analysis. *Organization Studies*, 24(3), 403–441. 10.1177/0170840603024003910

Ostic, D., Qalati, S. A., Barbosa, B., Shah, S. M. M., Vela, E. G., Herzallah, A. M., & Liu, F. (2021). Effects of social media use on psychological well-being: A mediated model. *Frontiers in Psychology*, 12, 678766. 10.3389/fpsyg.2021.67876634234717

Otlan, Y., Kuzmina, Y., Rumiantseva, A., & Tertytchnaya, K. (2023). Authoritarian media and foreign protests: Evidence from a decade of Russian news. *Post-Soviet Affairs*, 39(6), 391–405. 10.1080/1060586X.2023.2264079

Ovuorie, T. (2022, April 1). Increased social media use puts African leaders on edge. *DW*. https://corporate.dw.com/en/increased-social-media-use-puts-african-leaders-on-edge/a-61303854

Palella, S., & Martins, F. (2017). *Quantitative research methodology*. FEDEUPEL.

Pallant, J. (2010). *SPSS survival manual: A step by step guide to data analysis using SPSS*. McGraw-Hill Education.

Pantzar, M. (2000). Consumption as Work, Play, and Art: Representation of the Consumer in Future Scenarios. *Design Issues*, 16(3), 3–18. 10.1162/07479360052053298

Papadimitriou, A. (2016). *The Future of Communication: Artificial Intelligence and Social Networks*. Media & Communication Studies. Mälmo University. http://bit.ly/379xa7O

Papadimitriou, A. (2016). *The future of communication: Artificial intelligence and social network*. Media & Communication Studies.

Park, C. S., & Kaye, B. K. (2021). What's This? Incidental Exposure to News on Social Media, 'News-Finds-Me' Perception, News Efficacy, and News Consumption. In Shen, F. (Ed.), *Social Media News and Its Impact* (pp. 73–97). Routledge. 10.4324/9781003179580-6

Parker, J. C., & Thorson, E. (Eds.). (2009). *Health communication in the new media landscape*. Springer Publishing Company.

Park, K. (2022). The mediating role of skepticism: How corporate social advocacy builds quality relationships with publics. *Journal of Marketing Communications*, 28(8), 821–839. 10.1080/13527266.2021.1964580

Pearce, S. C., & Rodgers, J. (2020). Social media as public journalism? Protest reporting in the digital era. *Sociology Compass*, 14(12), 1–14. 10.1111/soc4.12823

Pearson, N., Biddle, S. J., Griffiths, P., Sherar, L. B., McGeorge, S., & Haycraft, E. (2020). Reducing screen-time and unhealthy snacking in 9–11 year old children: The Kids FIRST pilot randomised controlled trial. *BMC Public Health*, 20(1), 1–14. 10.1186/s12889-020-8232-931996192

Peeroo, S., Samy, M., & Jones, B. (2017). Facebook: A blessing or a curse for grocery stores? *International Journal of Retail & Distribution Management*, 45(12), 1242–1259. 10.1108/IJRDM-12-2016-0234

Peloza, J., & Shang, J. (2011). How can corporate social responsibility activities create value for stakeholders? A systematic review. *Journal of the Academy of Marketing Science*, 39(1), 117–135. 10.1007/s11747-010-0213-6

Pennycook, G., Binnendyk, J., Newton, C., & Rand, D. G. (2021). A Practical Guide to Doing Behavioral Research on Fake News and Misinformation. *Collabra. Psychology*, 7(1), 25293. 10.1525/collabra.25293

Pierson, J., Kerr, A., Robinson, S. C., Fanni, R., Steinkogler, V. E., Milan, S., & Zampedri, G. (2023). Governing artificial intelligence in the media and communications sector. *Internet Policy Review*, 12(1). Advance online publication. 10.14763/2023.1.1683

Plé, L. (2017). Why do we need research on value co-destruction? *Journal of Creating Value*, 3(2), 162–169. 10.1177/2394964317726451

Plé, L., & Chumpitaz Cáceres, R. (2010). Not always co-creation: Introducing interactional co-destruction of value in service-dominant logic. *Journal of Services Marketing*, 24(6), 430–437. 10.1108/08876041011072546

Podoshen, J. S., Venkatesh, V., & Jin, Z. (2014). Theoretical reflections on dystopian consumer culture: Black metal. *Marketing Theory*, 14(2), 207–227. 10.1177/1470593114523446

Pollay, R. W. (1986). The distorted mirror: Reflections on the unintended consequences of advertising. *Journal of Marketing*, 50(2), 18–36. 10.1177/002224298605000202

Pollock, J., Borges, C., & Cook, P. (2020). *Judi*. Converging Innovations in Health Communication and Public Health The Vibrant Role of Social Capital.

Ponti, M., Bélanger, S., Grimes, R., Heard, J., Johnson, M., Moreau, E., & Williams, R. (2017). Screen time and young children: Promoting health and development in a digital world. *Paediatrics & Child Health*.29601064

Ponzi, L., Fombrun, C., & Gardberg, N. (2011). RepTrak Pulse: Conceptualizing and validating a short-form measure of corporate reputation. *Corporate Reputation Review*, 14(1), 15–35. 10.1057/crr.2011.5

Popkin, B. M. (2009). Global dimensions of sugary beverages and programmatic and policy solutions. *Official Journal of the International Chair on Cardio Metabolic Risk*, 2(2), 6–9.

Porlezza, C. (2023) Promoting responsible AI: A European perspective on the governance of artificial intelligence in media and journalism. *Communications*, 48(3), 370–394. 10.1515/commun-2022-0091

Porter, M. E., & Kramer, M. R. (2006). Strategy and society: The link between competitive advantage and corporate social responsibility. *Harvard Business Review*, 84(12), 78–92.17183795

Postelnicu, M. (2016). Two-step flow model of communication. *Encyclopedia Britannica*. https://www.britannica.com/topic/two-step-flow-model-of- communication.

Potter, W. J. (2004). Theory of media literacy: A cognitive approach. *Sage (Atlanta, Ga.)*. 10.4135/9781483328881

Priya, C. I., & Kesavraj, G. (2022). Social media—A key pathway to marketing analytics. In *Cognitive Science and Technology* (pp. 263–275). 10.1007/978-981-19-2350-0_26

Przybylski, A., Murayama, K., DeHann, C. R., & Gladwell, V. (2013). Motivational, emotional, and behavioral correlates of fear of missing out. *Computers in Human Behavior*, 29(4), 1841–1848. 10.1016/j.chb.2013.02.014

Rahman, B. H. (2014). Conditional influence of media: Media credibility and opinion formation. *Journal of Political Studies*, 21(1), 299.

Rambe, P., & Nel, L. (2015). Technological utopia, dystopia and ambivalence: Teaching with social media at a S outh A frican university. *British Journal of Educational Technology*, 46(3), 629–648. 10.1111/bjet.12159

Ramirez, I. (2024). What are some theories about human nature that you believe are true, compatible with scientific understanding, but difficult or impractical to prove? *Quora*https://www.quora.com/What-are-some-theories-about-human-nature-that-you-believe-are-true-compatible-with-scientific-understanding-but-difficult-or-impractical-to-prove

Rao, G., & Madan, A. (2012). A study exploring the link between attachment styles and social networking habits of adolescents in urban Bangalore. *International Journal of Scientific and Research Publications*, 3(1), 1–12.

Rasmussen, M. G. B., Pedersen, J., Olesen, L. G., Brage, S., Klakk, H., Kristensen, P. L., Brønd, J. C., & Grøntved, A. (2020). Short-term efficacy of reducing screen media use on physical activity, sleep, and physiological stress in families with children aged 4–14: Study protocol for the SCREENS randomized controlled trial. *BMC Public Health*, 20(1), 1–18. 10.1186/s12889-020-8458-632293374

Reese, E., Haden, C. A., Baker-Ward, L., Bauer, P., Fivush, R., & Ornstein, P. A. (2011). Coherence of Personal Narratives across the Lifespan: A Multidimensional Model and Coding Method. *Journal of cognition and development: official journal of the Cognitive Development Society*, 12(4), 424–462. 10.1080/15248372.2011.587854

Reichard, J. D. (2011). Demassifying Religion: Futurist Interpretations of American Socioeconomic and Religious Change. *International Review of Social Sciences and Humanities.*, 2(1), 222–229. https://www.academia.edu/2227219/Demassifying_Religion_Futurist_Interpretations_of_American_Socioeconomic_and_Religious_Change

Ren, P., Wang, Y., & Zhao, F. (2023). Re-understanding of data storytelling tools from a narrative perspective. *Visual Intelligence/Visual Intelligence*, 1(1). 10.1007/s44267-023-00011-0

Reuters. (2024). *EU opens formal investigation into TikTok over possible online content breaches*. Reuters. https://www.reuters.com/technology/eu-opens-formal-proceedings-against-tiktok-under-digital-services-act-2024-02-19/

Rifon, N. J., Choi, S. M., Trimble, C. S., & Li, H. (2004). Congruence effects in sponsorship: The mediating role of sponsor credibility and consumer attributions of sponsor motive. *Journal of Advertising*, 33(1), 30–42. 10.1080/00913367.2004.10639151

Ritter, T. (2020). Reclaiming or rebranding marketing: Implications beyond digital. *AMS Review*, 10(3–4), 311–314. 10.1007/s13162-020-00178-5

Rivas-de-Roca, R. (2021). *Opportunities of robotization in local journalism: the case of 'Mittmedia*. Index Comunicación. 10.33732/ixc/11/02Oportu

Robert, L., Alahmad, R., Esterwood, C., Kim, S., & Zhang, Q. (2020). *Review of Personality in Human-Robot Interactions, Trends Inf.* Syst.

Rogers, E. M., Singhal, A., & Quinlan, M. M. (2014). Diffusion of innovations. In *An integrated approach to communication theory and research* (pp. 432–448). Routledge.

Romani, S., Grappi, S., & Bagozzi, R. P. (2013). Explaining consumer reactions to corporate social responsibility: The role of gratitude and altruistic values. *Journal of Business Ethics*, 114(2), 193–206. 10.1007/s10551-012-1337-z

Rom, E., & Alfasi, Y. (2014). The role of adult attachment style in online social network affect, cognition, and behavior. *Journal of Psychology and Psychotherapy Research*, 1(1), 24–34. 10.12974/2313-1047.2014.01.01.3

Rosenberry, J., & Vicker, L. A.(2002). *Applied Mass Communication Theory: A Guide for Media Practitioners*. Pearson, Boston and New York.

Ross, K. (2016). *Politainment and the Rise of Celebrity Politicians*. Palgrave Macmillan.

Rotaru, I., Nitulescu, L., & Rudolf, C. (2010). The post-modern paradigm–a framework of today's media impact in cultural space. *Procedia: Social and Behavioral Sciences*, 5, 328–330. 10.1016/j.sbspro.2010.07.098

Rubio Campaña, A. (2006). *Spanish journalists in the Rif War. The beginning of investigative journalism in Spain*. [Dissertation, Complutense University of Madrid].

Runde, D. F., Savoy, C. M., & Staguhn, J. (2021, October 15). *China and SMEs in sub-Saharan Africa: A window of opportunity for United States*. Center for Strategic and International Studies. https://www.csis.org/analysis/china-and-smes-sub-saharan-africa-window-opportunity-united-states

Ryan, T., Allen, K., Gray, D. L. L., & McInerney, D. M. (2017). How social are social media? A review of online social behaviour and connectedness. *Journal of Relationships Research*, 8, e8. Advance online publication. 10.1017/jrr.2017.13

Sabherwal, R., Sabherwal, S., Havakhor, T., & Steelman, Z. R. (2019). How does strategic alignment affect firm performance? The roles of information technology investment and environmental uncertainty. *Management Information Systems Quarterly*, 43(2), 453–474. https://api.semanticscholar.org/CorpusID:167222033. 10.25300/MISQ/2019/13626

Safeer, A. A., He, Y., Lin, Y., Abrar, M., & Nawaz, Z. (2021). Impact of perceived brand authenticity on consumer behaviour: Evidence from generation Y an Asian perspective. *International Journal of Emerging Markets*, 18(3), 685–704. 10.1108/IJOEM-09-2020-1128

Salim, S.K. (2021). 5. Iraq: Media between Democratic Freedom and Security Pressures. *Arab media systems,3*.

Salminen, J., Mustak, M., Sufyan, M., & Jansen, B. J. (2023). How can algorithms help in segmenting users and customers? A systematic review and research agenda for algorithmic customer segmentation. *Journal of Marketing Analytics*, 11(4), 677–692. 10.1057/s41270-023-00235-5

Salo, J., Mäntymäki, M., & Islam, A. K. M. N. (2018). The dark side of social media—and Fifty Shades of Grey introduction to the special issue: The dark side of social media. *Internet Research*, 28(5), 1166–1168. 10.1108/IntR-10-2018-442

Salwen, M. B., & Matera, F. R. (1992). Public Salience of Foreign Nations. *The Journalism Quarterly*, 69(3), 623–632. 10.1177/107769909206900310

Sančanin, B., & Penjisevic, A. (2022). Use of artificial intelligence for the generation of media content. *Social Informatics Journal*, 1(1), 1–7. 10.58898/sij.v1i1.01-07

Sánchez Esparza, M. (2015) *The journalistic construction of the story of corruption: analysis of the Malaya case*. [Dissertation, University of Málaga]. Institutional repository of the University of Málaga. https://riuma.uma.es/xmlui/handle/10630/8845

Sánchez Gonzales, H. (2022). Digital transformation and audience. Trends and use of artificial intelligence in fact-checking media. *Scopes: International Journal of Communication*, 56, 9–20.

Sangwon, L. (2020). *Predicting AI News Credibility: Communicative or Social Capital or Both? Communication Studies*. Korea University.

Sanz, R. M., & Stolle, P. D. (2019). The practice of investigative journalism in Spain. The perception of your current state. *Revista Latina de Comunicación Social*, (74), 822–839.

Saqib, N. (2020). Positioning – A literature review. *PSU Research Review*, 5(2), 141–169. 10.1108/PRR-06-2019-0016

SASB. (n.d.). *About SASB*. SASB. https://www.sasb.org/about/

Sasu, D. D. (2022, November 15). Social media in Nigeria – statistics & facts. *Statista*. https://www.statista.com/topics/10117/social-media-in-nigeria/#topicOverview

Savci, M., & Aysan, F. (2017). Technological addictions and social connectedness: Predictor effect of internet addiction, social media addiction, digital game addiction and smartphone addiction on social connectedness. *Dusunen Adam : Bakirkoy Ruh Ve Sinir Hastaliklari Hastanesi Yayin Organi*, 30(3), 202–216. 10.5350/DAJPN2017300304

Saxton, G. D., & Wang, L. (2014). The social network effect: The determinants of giving through social media. *Nonprofit and Voluntary Sector Quarterly*, 43(5), 850–868. 10.1177/0899764013485159

Scarles, C. (2009). Becoming tourist: Renegotiating the visual in the tourist experience. *Environment and Planning. D, Society & Space*, 27(3), 465–488. 10.1068/d1707

Schäfer, M. (2011). *Bastard Culture!* How User Participation Transforms Cultural Production. 10.5117/9789089642561

Schäfer, S. (2023). Incidental news exposure in a digital media environment: A scoping review of recent research. *Annals of the International Communication Association*, 47(2), 242–260. 10.1080/23808985.2023.2169953

Schelling, T. C. (1963). War without Pain, and other Models. *World Politics*, 15(3), 465–487. 10.2307/2009474

Scheufele, D. (1999). Framing as a Theory of Media Effects. *Journal of Communication*, 49(1), 103–122. 10.1111/j.1460-2466.1999.tb02784.x

Scholz, R. W., & Tietje, O. (2002). *Embedded case study methods: Integrating quantitative and qualitative knowledge*. SAGE Publications. 10.4135/9781412984027

Schudson, M. (2001). The Objectivity Norm in American Journalism*. *Journalism*, 2(2), 149–170. 10.1177/146488490100200201

Schuler, D. A., & Cording, M. (2017). Corporate social responsibility. In Wright, P. M., & McMahan, G. M. (Eds.), *The Oxford handbook of strategic human resource management* (pp. 451–469). Oxford University Press.

Scott, S. D., Klassen, T. P., & Hartling, L. (2013). Social media use by health care professionals and trainees: A scoping review. *Academic Medicine*, 88(9), 1376–1383. 10.1097/ACM.0b013e31829eb91c23887004

Semetko, H. (2000). Framing European Politics: A Content Analysis of Press and Television News. *Journal of Communication, 50*(2), 93–109. doi:. 1460-2466.2000.tb02843.x.10.1111/j

Sen, S., Bhattacharya, C. B., & Korschun, D. (2006). The role of corporate social responsibility in strengthening multiple stakeholder relationships: A field experiment. *Journal of the Academy of Marketing Science*, 34(2), 158–166. 10.1177/0092070305284978

Seok Sohn, Y., Han, J. K., & Lee, S. H. (2012). Communication strategies for enhancing perceived fit in the CSR sponsorship context. *International Journal of Advertising*, 31(1), 133–146. 10.2501/IJA-31-1-133-146

Shah, S. S. A., & Khan, Z. (2021). Creating advocates: Understanding the roles of CSR and firm innovativeness. *Journal of Financial Services Marketing*, 26(2), 95–106. 10.1057/s41264-020-00084-8

Shamri, A. (2021). *Visual Media in Light of the Challenges of Artificial Intelligence*. University of Baghdad, College of Arts.

Sharma, A., Dwivedi, R., Mariani, M. M., & Islam, T. (2022). Investigating the effect of advertising irritation on digital advertising effectiveness: A moderated mediation model. *Technological Forecasting and Social Change*, 180, 121731. 10.1016/j.techfore.2022.121731

Shaw, E. F. (1979). Agenda-Setting and Mass Communication Theory. *Gazette (Leiden, Netherlands)*, 25(2), 96–105. 10.1177/001654927902500203

Shen, Y., Zhang, S., & Xin, T. (2020). Extrinsic academic motivation and social media fatigue: Fear of missing out and problematic social media use as mediators. *Current Psychology (New Brunswick, N.J.)*, 1–7.

Sherman, L. E., Payton, A. A., Hernandez, L. M., Greenfield, P. M., & Dapretto, M. (2016). The Power of the Like in Adolescence: Effects of Peer Influence on Neural and Behavioral Responses to Social Media. *Psychological Science*, 27(7), 1027–1035. 10.1177/0956797616645673 27247125

Shetu, S. N. (2023). Do user-generated content and micro-celebrity posts encourage generation Z users to search online shopping behaviour on social networking sites—The moderating role of sponsored ads? *Future Business Journal*, 9(1), 100. 10.1186/s43093-023-00276-3

Shifman, L., Thelwall, M., & Wilkerson, I. (2007). With a little help from my friends: A content analysis of the interaction between the UK Independence Party and its online supporters. *Sociological Research Online*, 12(6), 4.

Shin, D. (2024). Misinformation and Algorithmic Bias. In Smith, M. R. (Ed.), *Artificial Misinformation* (pp. 15–31). Palgrave Macmillan. 10.1007/978-3-031-52569-8_2

Short, R. (2021, June 22). How social media is empowering small business in Africa, *Genesis*. https://www.wathi.org/how-social-media-is-powering-small-business-in-africa-genesis-june-2021/

Silver, L., & Johnson, C. (2018, October 9). *Internet connectivity seen as having positive impact on life in sub-Saharan Africa*. Pew Research Center. https://www.pewresearch.org/global/2018/10/09/internet-connectivity-seen-as-having-positive-impact-on-life-in-sub-saharan-africa/

Simon, J. P. (2016). User-generated content – Users, a community of users and firms: Toward new sources of co-innovation? *Info*, 18(6), 4–25. 10.1108/info-04-2016-0015

Compilation of References

Singh, K. U., Kumar, A., Kumar, G., Choudhury, T., Singh, T., & Kotecha, K. (2024). Sentiment analysis in social media marketing: Leveraging natural language processing for customer insights. In *Lecture notes in networks and systems* (pp. 457–467). 10.1007/978-981-99-9489-2_40

Sîrbu, A., Pedreschi, D., Giannotti, F., & Kertész, J. (2019). Algorithmic bias amplifies opinion fragmentation and polarization: A bounded confidence model. *PLoS One*, 14(3), e0213246. 10.1371/journal.pone.021324630835742

Slonje, R., Smith, P. K., & Frisén, A. (2013). The nature of cyberbullying, and strategies for prevention. *Computers in Human Behavior*, 29(1), 26–32. 10.1016/j.chb.2012.05.024

Smith, P. K., Görzig, A., & Robinson, S. (2018). Issues of crosscultural variations in cyber bullying across Europe and beyond. *Media@LSE Working Paper Series*. Published by Media@LSE, London School of Economics and Political Science ("LSE")

Smith, A. R. (2014). *The politics of popular culture*. Routledge.

Smith, P. K. (2014). *Understanding school bullying: Its nature & prevention strategies*. Sage. 10.4135/9781473906853

Smith, R. A. (2017). *Audience segmentation techniques*. Oxford Research Encyclopedia of Communication. 10.1093/acrefore/9780190228613.013.321

Soares, C. D. M., & Jóia, L. A. (2015). The influence of social media on social movements: An exploratory conceptual model. In *Lecture notes in computer science* (pp. 27–38). Springer. 10.1007/978-3-319-22500-5_3

Song, B., & Tao, W. (2022). Unpack the relational and behavioral outcomes of internal CSR: Highlighting dialogic communication and managerial facilitation. *Public Relations Review*, 48(1), 102153. 10.1016/j.pubrev.2022.102153

Song, B., & Wen, T. J. (2019). Online corporate social responsibility communication strategies and stakeholder engagements: A comparison of controversial versus noncontroversial industries. *Corporate Social Responsibility and Environmental Management*, 27(2), 881–896. Advance online publication. 10.1002/csr.1852

Statista.com. (2020). *Number of internet and social media users worldwide as of July 2022*. Statista. https://www.statista.com/statistics/617136/digital-population-worldwide/#:~:text=As%20of%20April%202022%2C%20there,population%20were%20social%20media%20users

Statista.com. (2022). *Global advertising revenue 2014-2027*. Statista.com https://www.statista.com/statistics/236943/global-advertising-spending/

Statista.com. (2023). *Digital advertising worldwide - statistics & facts*. Statista. https://www.statista.com/outlook/dmo/digital-advertising/worldwide (May,2023).

Statista.com. (2023). *Mobile internet users worldwide*. Statista. https://www.statista.com/topics/779/mobile-internet/#topicOverview

Stephen, A. T. (2016). The role of digital and social media marketing in consumer behavior. *Current Opinion in Psychology*, 10, 17–21. 10.1016/j.copsyc.2015.10.016

Sternthal, B., & Craig, C. S. (1973). Humor in advertising. *Journal of Marketing*, 37(4), 12–18. 10.1177/002224297303700403

Stray, J. (2021). Making artificial intelligence work for investigative journalism. *Algorithms, Automation, and News*, 97-118. 10.1080/21670811.2019.1630289

Street, J. (2012). *Politainment: When politics and entertainment converge*. Rowman & Littlefield.

Strinati, D. (1995). *An introduction to theories of popular culture.* Routledge https://api.pageplace.de/preview/DT0400_9781134565085_A25033634/preview- 9781134565085_A25033634.pdf

Sullivan, A. (2016), "I used to be a human being." *New York Magazine.* https://nymag.com/selectall/2016/09/andrew-sullivan-technology-almost-killed-me.html

Sultan, A. J. (2021). Fear of missing out and self-disclosure on social media: The paradox of tie strength and social media addiction among young users. *Young Consumers,* 22(4), 555–577. 10.1108/YC-10-2020-1233

Sumak, B., Hericko, M., Pusnik, M., & Polančič, G. (2020). *Factors Affecting Acceptance and Use of Model: An Empirical Study Based on TAM, International Journal of Computing and Information.* Faculty of Electrical Engineering and Computer Science.

Sun, Y. (2008, April). On Behavioral component of the third-person effect. *Communication Research,* 35(2), 257–278. 10.1177/0093650207313167

Surry, D. W., & Farquhar, J. D. (1997). Diffusion theory and instructional technology. *Journal of Instructional Science and technology, 2*(1), 24-36.

Swart, J. (2021). Tactics of news literacy: How young people access, evaluate, and engage with news on social media. *New Media & Society,* 25(3), 505–521. 10.1177/14614448211011447

Szukits, Á., & Móricz, P. (2023). Towards data-driven decision making: The role of analytical culture and centralization efforts. *Review of Managerial Science.* 10.1007/s11846-023-00694-1

Taber, D. R., Chriqui, J. F., Vuillaume, R., Kelder, S. H., & Chaloupka, F. J. (2015). The association between state bans on soda only and adolescent substitution with other sugar-sweetened beverages: A cross-sectional study. *The International Journal of Behavioral Nutrition and Physical Activity,* 12(1), 1–9. 10.1186/1479-5868-12-S1-S726221969

Takens, J., van Atteveldt, W., van Hoof, A., & Kleinnijenhuis, J. (2013). Media Logic in Election Campaign Coverage. *European Journal of Communication,* 28(3), 277–293. 10.1177/0267323113478522

Takov, P., & Banlanjo, N. M. (2021). Postmodernism vis-a-vis African Traditional Cultures: Rethinking the Pathways to Authenticity. *Global Journal of Human-Social Science: Arts & Humanities-Psychology,* 21(2), 33. https://globaljournals.org/GJHSS_Volume21/5-Postmodernism-Vis-a-Vis- African.pdf

Tandoc, E., Edson, L., & Wu, S. (2020). *Man vs. Machine? The Impact of Algorithm Authorship on News Credibility, Digital Journalism.* Taylor & Francis.

Tang, M. J., & Chan, E. T. (2020). Social media: Influences and impacts on culture. In *Advances in intelligent systems and computing* (pp. 491–501). 10.1007/978-3-030-52249-0_33

Tariq, S., Tariq, A., Raweem, A., Tahira, H., Amjad, J., & Nauman, K. (2023). Impact of Social Media Advertisement on Customer Purchase Intention: A Sequential Mediation Analysis. *Abasyn University Journal of Social Sciences, 16*(1).

Tay, L. (2014). # LOLitics: Analyzing the role of humor in political participation. *The American Behavioral Scientist,* 58(5), 617–634.

Taylor, P. M. (1992). *War and the media: Propaganda and persuasion in the Gulf War.* Manchester University press.

Thakur, R., Hale, D., & Summey, J. H. (2018). What motivates consumers to partake in cyber shilling? *Journal of Marketing Theory and Practice,* 26(1-2), 181–195. 10.1080/10696679.2017.1389236

The Next Web (TNW). (2024). What it'd take for the EU to ban TikTok. *The Next Web.* https://thenextweb.com/news/would-eu-us-ban-tiktok

Compilation of References

Tiago, M. T. P. M. B., & Veríssimo, J. M. C. (2014). Digital marketing and social media: Why bother? *Business Horizons*, 57(6), 703–708. 10.1016/j.bushor.2014.07.002

Tijeras, R. (2018). Investigative journalism in Spain. *Communication, 21*(9).

Tilly, C. (1991, September). Domination, resistance, compliance... discourse. In *Sociological forum* (pp. 593–602). Eastern Sociological Society.

Tirole, J. (2021). Digital dystopia. *The American Economic Review*, 111(6), 2007–2048. 10.1257/aer.20201214

Trinkle, B. S., Crossler, R. E., & Warkentin, M. (2014). I'm game, are you? Reducing realworld security threats by managing employee activity in online social networks. *Journal of Information Systems*, 28(2), 307–327. 10.2308/isys-50776

Tully, M. (2021). Why News Literacy Matters. In Bélair-Gagnon, V., & Usher, N. (Eds.), *Journalism Research That Matters* (pp. 91–102). Oxford University Press.

Túñez-López, J. M., Fieiras-Ceide, C., & Vaz-Álvarez, M. (2021). Impact of Artificial Intelligence on Journalism: Transformations in the company, products, contents and professional profile. *Communicatio Socialis*, 34(1), 177–193. 10.15581/003.34.1.177-193

Túñez-López, J. M., Toural-Bran, C., & Frazão-Nogueira, A. G. (2020). *From Data Journalism to Robotic Journalism, The Automation of News Processing*. Journalistic Metamorphosis.

Túñez-López, J.M., & Toural-Bran, C. (2018). Uso de bots y algoritmos para automatizar la redacción de noticias: Percepción y actitudes de los periodistas en España. *El Profesional de la Información*.

Tung, N. (2020). A fragile inheritance. *VQR Online*.https://www.vqronline.org/photography/2020/09/fragile-inheritance

Turel, O., Serenko, A., & Giles, P. (2011). Integrating technology addiction and use: An empirical investigation of online auction users. *Management Information Systems Quarterly*, 35(4), 1043–1062. 10.2307/41409972

Turner, , Baker, R., & Kellner, F. (2018). Theoretical Literature Review: Tracing the Life Cycle of a Theory and Its Verified and Falsified Statement. *Human Resource Development Review*, 17(1), 34–61. 10.1177/1534484317749680

Ufarte-Ruiz, M. J., Murcia-Verdú, F. J., & Túñez-López, J. M. (2023). *Use of artificial intelligence in synthetic media: first newsrooms without journalists*. Information Professional., 10.3145/epi.2023.mar.03

Ugorji, L.I. & Ogun D. A. (2023, December 20) *Concerning fiducia supplicans: A declaration for the propagation of the faith on the pastoral meaning of blessings in the church*. A statement issued by the Catholic Bishops Conference of Nigeria.

Ukaegbu, R. C. (2020). Deceptive Advertising and Consumer Reaction: A Study of Delta Soap Advertisement. *OAlib*, 7(3), 1–7. 10.4236/oalib.1105865

Ullah, I., Borelli, R., & Kanhere, S. S. (2022). Privacy in targeted advertising on mobile devices: A survey. *International Journal of Information Security*, 22(3), 647–678. 10.1007/s10207-022-00655-x36589145

United Nations High Commissioner for Refugees. (2022). *Factsheet 4: Types of misinformation and disinformation*. UN. https://www.unhcr.org/innovation/wp- content/uploads/2022/02/Factsheet-4.pdf

United Nations. (2020). *World youth report 2020: Youth social entrepreneurship and the 2020 agenda*. UN-iLibrary. 10.18356/248b499b-en

United Nations. (n.d.). *Sustainable Development Goals*. UN. https://sdgs.un.org/goals

Vafeas, M., Hughes, T., & Hilton, T. (2016). Antecedents to value diminution: A dyadic perspective. *Marketing Theory*, 16(4), 469–491. 10.1177/1470593116652005

Valli, C., & Nai, A. (2023). Let me think about it: Cognitive elaboration and strategies of resistance to political persuasion. *Media Psychology*, 26(2), 89–112. 10.1080/15213269.2022.2098774

Van Bavel, J., Rathje, S., Harris, E., Robertson, C., & Sternisko, A. (2021). How social media shapes polarization. *Trends in Cognitive Sciences*, 25(11), 913–916. 10.1016/j.tics.2021.07.01334429255

Vance, A., Lowry, P. B., & Eggett, D. (2015). A new approach to the problem of access policy violations: Increasing perceptions of accountability through the user interface. *Management Information Systems Quarterly*, 39(2), 345–366. 10.25300/MISQ/2015/39.2.04

Vargo, S. L., & Lusch, R. F. (2008). Why "service"? *Journal of the Academy of Marketing Science*, 36(1), 25–38. 10.1007/s11747-007-0068-7

Vázquez-Herrero, J., Negreira-Rey, M.-C., & Sixto-García, J. (2022). Mind the Gap! Journalism on Social Media and News Consumption Among Young Audiences. *International Journal of Communication*, 16, 3822–3842.

Veeriah, J. (2021). Young Adult's ability to detect fake news and their new media literacy level in the wake of the COVD-19 pandemic. *Journal of Content. Community & Communication*, 13(7), 372–383.

Velte, A. (2018, March 1). Ethical challenges and current practices in activist social media archives. *The American Archivist*, 81(1), 112–134. 10.17723/0360-9081-81.1.112

Venkatesh, V, Morris &all. (2003). The unified theory of acceptance and use of technology (UTAUT): A literature review. *Journal of Enterprise Information Management*.

Verk, N., Golob, U., & Podnar, K. (2021). A dynamic review of the emergence of corporate social responsibility communication. *Journal of Business Ethics*, 168(3), 491–515. 10.1007/s10551-019-04232-6

Villaespesa, E., & Wowkowych, S. (2020). Ephemeral storytelling with social media: Snapchat and instagram stories at the Brooklyn Museum. *Social Media + Society*, 6(1), 205630511989877. 10.1177/2056305119898776

Viner, R., Davie, M., & Firth, A. (2019). *The health impacts of screen time: a guide for clinicians and parents*. Royal College of Paediatrics and Child Health. https://www.rcpch.ac.uk/sites/default/files/2018-12/rcpch_screen_time_guide_-_final.pdf

Vogel, D. (2005). Is there a market for virtue? The business case for corporate social responsibility. *California Management Review*, 47(4), 19–45.

Vraga, E. K., Tully, M., Maksl, A., Craft, S., & Ashley, S. (2021). Theorizing News Literacy Behaviors. *Communication Theory*, 31(1), 1–21. 10.1093/ct/qtaa005

Vučković, J. (2023). *Artificial intelligence in the media. Comparative Legal Challenges in Contemporary Law - In memoriam Dr.* Stefan Andonović., 10.56461/ZR_23.SA.UPISP_JV

Wainner, C. N. (2018). *Social media addiction and its implications for communication.*

Walker, C. E., Krumhuber, E. G., Dayan, S., & Furnham, A. (2021). Effectsofsocialmedia use on desire for cosmetic surgery among young women. Current Psychology, 40(7), 3355-3364. Tsesis,A.(2017).Terrorist speech on social media. *Vand.L.Rev.*, 70, 651.

Waltz, K. N. (1979). *Theory of International Politics*. Addison-Wesley Publishing Company.

Wansink, B. (1994). The Dark Side of Consumer Behavior: Empirical Examinations of Impulsive and Compulsive Consumption. In Allen, C. T., & John, D. R. (Eds.), *NA - Advances in Consumer Research* (Vol. 21, p. 508). Association for Consumer Research.

Webster, J. G.& Ksiazek, T. B. (2012). The Dynamics of Audience Fragmentation: Public Attention in an Age of Digital Media. *Journal of Communication*.

Webster, J. G., & Ksiazek, T. B. (2012). The dynamics of audience fragmentation: Public attention in an age of digital media. *Journal of Communication*, 62(1), 39–56. 10.1111/j.1460-2466.2011.01616.x

Weigelt, K., & Camerer, C. (1988). Reputation and corporate strategy: A review of recent theory and applications. *Strategic Management Journal*, 9(5), 443–454. 10.1002/smj.4250090505

Weimann, G. (2015). Communication, twostep flow of. In *International Encyclopedia of the Social & Behavioral Sciences* (Second Edition). 10.1016/B978-0-08-097086-8.95051-7

Wells, C., Spottswood, E. L., & Marsh, J. C. (2016). Is this the Onion? The humorous potential of internet journalism. *Communication Studies*, 67(5), 551–566.

WHO. (2023). *Infodemic*. WHO. https://www.who.int/health-topics/infodemic#tab=tab_1

Widaman, K. F., Early, D. R., & Conger, R. D. (2013). *Special populations*. In Oxford University Press eBooks. 10.1093/oxfordhb/9780199934874.013.0004

Wiederhold, B. K. (2018). The tenuous relationship between Instagram and teen self-identity. *Cyberpsychology, Behavior, and Social Networking*, 21(4), 215–216. 10.1089/cyber.2018.29108.bkw29624448

Wiederhold, B. K. (2019). Instagram: Becoming a worldwide problem? *Cyberpsychology, Behavior, and Social Networking*, 22(9), 567–568. 10.1089/cyber.2019.29160.bkw31526293

Wilcox, K., & Stephen, A. T. (2013). Are close friends the enemy? Online social networks, self-esteem, and self-control. *The Journal of Consumer Research*, 40(1), 90–103. 10.1086/668794

Willard, C. E. (2007). *Cyberbullying and Cyberthreats: Responding to the Challenge of Online Social Aggression, Threats, and Distress* (2nd ed.). Research Publishers LLC, USA: Illinois.

Williams, R. M.Jr. (1994). The sociology of ethnic conflicts: Comparative international perspectives. *Annual Review of Sociology*, 20(1), 49–79. 10.1146/annurev.so.20.080194.000405

Wilson, A. E., Darke, P. R., & Sengupta, J. (2021). Winning the Battle but Losing the War: Ironic Effects of Training Consumers to Detect Deceptive Advertising Tactics. *Journal of Business Ethics*, •••, 1–17.

Wilson, K., Fornasier, S., & White, K. M. (2010). Psychological predictors of young adults' use of social networking sites. *Cyberpsychology, Behavior, and Social Networking*, 13(2), 173–177. 10.1089/cyber.2009.009420528274

Wimmer, R. D., & Dominick, J. R. (2011). *Mass Media Research: An Introduction* (9th ed.). Wadsworth.

Winner, L. (2014). *Technologies as forms of life*. Palgrave Macmillan UK eBooks. 10.1057/9781137349088_4

Wolstein, J., & Babey, S. H. (2018). Sugary Beverage Consumption Among California Children and Adolescents. *Policy Brief (UCLA Center for Health Policy Research)*, 2018(2), 1–8.29999284

Wondolleck, J. M., Gray, B., & Bryan, T. (2003). Us versus them: How identities and characterizations influence conflict. *Environmental Practice*, 5(3), 207–213. 10.1017/S1466046603035592

Woods, H. C., & Scott, H. (2016). # Sleepyteens: Social media use in adolescence is associated with poor sleep quality, anxiety, depression and low self-esteem. *Journal of Adolescence*, 51(1), 41–49. 10.1016/j.adolescence.2016.05.00827294324

World Health Organization. (2022). *WHO European regional obesity report*. WHO. https://www.euro.who.int/en/publications/abstracts/who-european-regional-obesity-report-2022

Wright, R. R., Sandlin, J. A., & Burdick, J. (2023). What is critical media literacy in an age of disinformation? *New Directions for Adult and Continuing Education*, 178, 11–25.

Wu, Y., Ngai, E. W., Wu, P., & Wu, C. (2020). Fake online reviews: Literature review, synthesis, and directions for future research. *Decision Support Systems*, 132(113280), 1–15. 10.1016/j.dss.2020.113280

Xiao, B., & Benbasat, I. (2011). Product-related deception in e-commerce: A theoretical perspective. *Management Information Systems Quarterly*, 35(1), 169–195. 10.2307/23043494

Yan, D. (2020). *Robotic Cameraman for Augmented Reality based Broadcast and Demonstration*. University of Essex.

Yanfang, W. U. (2019). *Is Automated Journalistic Writing Less Biased? An Experimental Test of Auto-Written and Human-Written News Stories*. Journalism Practice University of Missouri.

Yan, N. (2021, June). Social media is redistributing power. *Open Journal of Social Sciences*, 9(6), 107–118. 10.4236/jss.2021.96010

Yarahmadi, F. (2020, January 6). *Multistage Sampling Technique and Estimating Sample Size for a Descriptive Study on Viewers' Perception of TV Commercials*. Sage Research Method. https://doi.org/10.4135/9781529713961

Yildiz, M. N., & Keengwe, J. (2015). *Handbook of Research on Media Literacy in the Digital Age*. IGI.

Yin, R. K. (2018). *Case study research and applications: Design and methods*. SAGE Publications.

Yioutas, J., & Segvic, I. (2003). Revisiting the Clinton/Lewinsky Scandal: The Convergence of Agenda Setting and Framing. September 2003. *Journalism & Mass Communication Quarterly*, 80(3), 567–588. 10.1177/107769900308000306

Young, D. G. (2006). "The Daily Show" and the reinvention of political journalism. *Political Science Quarterly*, 121(2), 293–319.

Young, K. S. (2007). Cognitive Behavior Therapy with Internet Addicts: Treatment Outcomes and Implications. *Cyberpsychology & Behavior*, 10(5), 671–679. 10.1089/cpb.2007.997117927535

Yousaf, M., Rahman, B. H., & Yousaf, Z. (2020). Constructing Reality: Framing of the Kashmir Conflict in Dictatorial and Democratic Regimes in the Pakistani English Press. *Media Watch*, 11(3), 401–415. 10.15655/mw_2020_v11i3_203045

Zakaria, F. (2024). *Age of Revolutions: Progress and Backlash from 1600 to the Present*. W.W. Norton & Company.

Zamora-Medina, R. (2023). Politainment as dance: visual storytelling on TikTok among Spanish political parties. In *Research Handbook on Visual Politics* (pp. 228–243). Edward Elgar Publishing. 10.4337/9781800376939.00025

Zamora-Medina, R. (2023). TikTok and its implications for politainment: An analysis of Spanish political parties. *Media Culture & Society*, 45(1), 142–160.

Zeng, J., Xing, Y., & Jin, C. (2023). The impact of VR/AR-based consumers' brand experience on consumer–Brand relationships. *Sustainability (Basel)*, 15(9), 7278. 10.3390/su15097278

Zhang, D., Morse, S., & Kambhampati, U. (2017). *Sustainable development and corporate social responsibility*. Routledge. 10.4324/9781315749495

Zhang, G. (2023). The influence of social media marketing on consumers' behaviour. *Advances in Economics. Management and Political Sciences*, 20(1), 119–124. 10.54254/2754-1169/20/20230181

Zhang, X., & Choi, J. (2022). The importance of social influencer-generated contents for user cognition and emotional attachment: An information relevance perspective. *Sustainability (Basel)*, 14(11), 6676. 10.3390/su14116676

Zhuang, M., Cui, G., & Peng, L. (2018). Manufactured opinions: The effect of manipulating online product reviews. *Journal of Business Research*, 87, 24–35. 10.1016/j.jbusres.2018.02.016

Ziakis, C., & Vlachopoulou, M. (2023). Artificial intelligence in digital marketing: Insights from a comprehensive review. *Information (Basel)*, 14(12), 664. 10.3390/info14120664

Zolfagharian, M., & Yazdanparast, A. (2017). The dark side of consumer life in the age of virtual and mobile technology. *Journal of Marketing Management*, 33(15-16), 1304–1335. 10.1080/0267257X.2017.1369143

Zwass, V. (2021). Editor's Introduction. *International Journal of Electronic Commerce*, 25(2), 125–126. 10.1080/10864415.2021.1887693

About the Contributors

Jabbar Al-Obaidi received his Ph.D. in Communication from the University of Michigan, Ann Arbor, a master's degree from Hartford University, and a bachelor's degree from Baghdad University. Currently, Professor Al-Obaidi is the Academic Director of International Student Recruitment and Global Partnerships, Academic Affairs. Dr. Al- Obaidi served as the academic director of Global Programs (2018-2023), the director of the Center of Middle East Studies (2011-2018) at Bridgewater State, the chairperson of the Department of Communication Studies (2005-2011), Acting Chair 2019-2020 and 2021-2022. Professor Al- Obaidi served as the co-academic director of the Mandela Washington Fellowship for Young African Leaders 2021-2023. Al-Obaidi served as the co-chair of NECHE Self-Study Steering Committee, Bridgewater State University 2021-2023. In addition to the U.S., Dr. Al-Obaidi taught in Iraq, Jordan, Yemen, the United Arab Emirates, and China. His research focuses on Middle Eastern media and socio-political and cultural issues, and he offers courses on intercultural communication, media ethics and law, and diversity in U.S. Media (race, class, and gender. Al-Obaidi produces and hosts a weekly TV program INFOCUS Bridgewater Cable TV. His latest co-edited book titled The Role of Educators as Agents and Conveyors for Positive Change in Global Education was published by IGI Global 2023. Al-Obaidi presented a research paper titled Agenda-Setting and Framing Theories: Perspectives on Digital and Social Media Fragmentation and Convergence to the Twenty-Seventh Annual Conference of the Arab-US Association for Communication Educators held at the University of Kuwait, Kuwait, October 2023. In 2022 Al-Obaidi published a chapter titled An Opinion: What the Qur'an Says That Disqualifies the Perspectives of Militant Radical Muslims in Islamophobia and Acts of Violence, (edit) Carolyn Turpin-Petrosino. Oxford University Press.

***

Nazlı Aytuna is a faculty member at Galatasaray University's Communication Department and serves as the Director of the Media Research Center. She holds a graduate degree in 'Communication, Technologies and Power' and a PhD in Political Science from Paris I Panthéon-Sorbonne. Prof. Aytuna teaches undergraduate and graduate courses in Persuasion Strategies, Theories of the Information Society, Social Psychology, and Lobbying. Her research focuses on the use of social media across different demographics, and she particularly examines various forms of communication in political persuasion. Actively conducts field studies and research on digital media literacy, aiming to bridge theoretical knowledge with practical applications. Her academic background and practical experiences enhance her understanding of communication dynamics, positively contributing to her field.

Zindan Çakıcı graduated summa cum laude from the Department of Public Relations and Publicity at Kadir Has University's Faculty of Communication in 2018. He completed his master's degree in Strategic Communication Management at Galatasaray University's Institute of Social Sciences in 2020. In 2024, Dr. Çakıcı earned his doctoral degree following the successful defense of his dissertation titled "Visual Representation of Irregular Migration in the Turkish Press: Afghan Migration After the Taliban Regime" at Galatasaray University's Institute of Social Sciences, Department of Media and Communication Studies. Throughout his academic career, Dr. Çakıcı has garnered acclaim, receiving a total of 9 awards from prestigious institutions such as KalDer, Tühid, TRT, and KKB for his outstanding contributions to the fields of communication and social responsibility. His scholarly interests encompass diverse areas, including migration studies and new media.

Maureen Chigbo, a PhD student at the Bingham University, Nigeria with focus on Communication for Development. She publishes Realnews, the pioneer Nigerian weekly investigative online news magazine. She was the first female general editor of Newswatch, a very influential weekly news magazine based in Lagos, Nigeria. Chigbo, the first female President of the Guild of Corporate Online Publishers (GOCOP), has been a practicing journalism for more than 30 years. Her professional goal is to promote peace, justice and equal opportunity for all in Nigeria through effective investigative journalism that will expose any form of injustice and corruption and facilitate political, socio-economic development in the country.

Elanor Colleoni, IULM University, Italy, is Assistant Professor of Corporate social evaluations and digitalization. Her research focuses on non-market strategies and audiences' judgements formation processes over socially (ir)-responsible organizational actions. Her research has been published in leading management and communication journals, such as Academy of Management Review, Academy of Management perspectives, Business & Society, Journal of Communication, among others.

About the Contributors

Chiara Esposito, IULM University Milan, Italy, graduated in Strategic communication at IULM University in November 2023 with a thesis on the reputational impact of CSR communication strategies. She currently works as engagement and D&I manager in a leading international company.

Shabnam Jahan has completed her Masters in Journalism Mass Communication from SRM University, Chennai. She has a total interning experience of 6 months and has previously interned at Asiana Times as a content writer and at The News Minute as a Graphic Designer. She is currently working as a Content Writer at Leisure Byte.

Tasnim Jahan is currently working as Assistant Professor at Ramaiah University of Applied Sciences and have previously worked a Teaching Assistant of Law at Symbiosis Law School, Hyderabad and as a Research Associate at National Law School, Bengaluru. She is also pursuing her PhD in Intellectual Property Rights from West Bengal National University of Juridical Sciences. Having profound interest in Academia and research, she has presented papers in various National and International Conferences and have few reputed publications under her name.

Vishnu Achutha Menon is an independent journalist, writer, researcher, and an Indian percussionist. He is a recipient of the Junior Scholarship the Ministry of Culture awarded. His research interests are film studies, verbal & nonverbal communication, south Asian performances, Natyasastra, media studies, media analysis techniques, Laban Movement Analysis, and Ethnomusicology.

Grazia Murtarelli, IULM University Milan, Italy, is Assistant Professor of Corporate Communication. Her research focuses on the analysis of online scenario and, more specifically, on the following issues: social media-based relationship management, online dialogue strategies, digital visual engagement processes and social media measurement and evaluation. She is Public Relations Student & Early Career Representative at International Communication Association. She is also a faculty affiliate of the Centre of Research for Strategic Communication at IULM University.

Haitham Numan is a professional pollster, public relations assistant professor, public opinion analyst, and a Ph.D. candidate in the philosophy of Middle Eastern politics at the Arab and Islamic Institute, Exeter University. He also serves as a national representative of Iraq at the World Association of Public Opinion Research (WAPOR). Beyond that, for 15 years, Haitham worked as a mass communication educator and survey researcher. His research interests include research methods, public opinion, political communication, and mass communication. He has published nearly 20 scientific research papers, including journal articles and books. Haitham Numan is also a Country Expert on the Digital Society Project as part of the NSF-funded project "Measuring Internet Politics".

Desmond Onyemechi Okocha, Ph.D., is an Associate Professor and Dean, Faculty of Communication and Media Studies, Bingham University, Nigeria, a Research Fellow at University of Religions and Denominations, Iran and Member of the Swiss-based International Panel on the Information Environment (IPIE). He was a Special Adviser on Digital Media and Strategic Communication to Abia State Governor, Nigeria from 2020-2023. He holds a Diploma in Media Studies from Ireland, Bachelor of Arts (BA) degree in Management from the United Kingdom, Master of Arts (MA) in Journalism and Mass Communication from Sikkim Manipal University, India and PhD in Journalism and Mass Communication from Nims University, Rajasthan, India. Besides, working and consulting for World Bank, Global Fund for Women and Open Society Initiative for West Africa (OSIWA) funded projects, he was the pioneer National Knowledge Management and Communication Coordinator for the International Fund for Agricultural Development (IFAD) funded Livelihood Improvement Family Enterprises in the Niger Delta, Nigeria. He has published over 130 articles in refereed journals and 3 edited books. His research interests are Digital Journalism, Media and Society, Emerging Media and Corporate Communication.

Alparslan Ergün Özkaya completed his undergraduate studies at Galatasaray University Faculty of Communication and Bordeaux-Montaigne University Institute of Information and Communication Sciences. He is currently pursuing a master's degree in Public Relations at Istanbul University. Since 2023, he has been working as a Research Assistant at Galatasaray University Faculty of Communication.

Santa Palella Stracuzzi, EAE Business School, Madrid. She has a PhD in Educational Sciences. Degree in Education, mention in Educational Administration. Master's degree and post-doctorate in Educational Sciences. She is the author of the book Methodology of Quantitative Research, which received the award for best book of the year 2024, currently in its fourth edition. Her lines of research are in the field of Management and Communication, Human Resources, Educational Innovation in Communication and New Technologies, Artificial Intelligence. He has taught subjects such as: Internal Communication, Institutional Image, External Promotion; Communication and Leadership, Leadership for Management, Leadership, Fundamentals of Human Resources, Work Life Cycle, Talent Management, Research Methodology, Epistemology, among others in different Universities in Venezuela and Spain.

About the Contributors

Stefania Romenti, IULM University Milan, Italy. Stefania Romenti is Full Professor of Strategic communication and PR. She is Director of the Executive Master in Corporate Public Relations and Adjunct Professor at IE Business School. She is Founder and Director of the Research Centre in Strategic Communication and Former President Elect of the European Association of Public Relations Education and Research Association. Her research focuses on strategic communication, corporate reputation, stakeholder management and engagement, dialogue, social media, measurement, and evaluation.

Ayşegül Sağkaya Güngör has a PhD degree on marketing. Her particular area of interest is branded entertainment like advergames and in-game advertisement, particularly their impact on online consumer behavior. Other research areas in her interest include consumer acceptance of technology, contemporary digital marketing methods and e-commerce. Currently she is lecturing in various universities on the subjects of e-commerce, e-business, digital marketing and marketing management.

Marta Sánchez Esparza is a journalist and PhD in Information Sciences from the University of Malaga. Professor at the Rey Juan Carlos University and the International Business University (UNIE). He has taught the subjects of Information Theory, Public Opinion, Media and Public Relations Planning. His areas of interest refer to the transformation of journalism in the digital age, the construction of public opinion, disinformation and hate speech, artificial intelligence and new technologies. He belongs to the High-Performance Research Group on Citizen Participation and Digital Literacy Possibilities (PARTICYPAD) of Rey Juan Carlos University. He is currently PI of the research project 'Artificial intelligence and new frontiers: the transformation of professional identities and narratives in communication companies', at the International Business University (UNIE).

Shashikant Saurav is an Assistant Professor of Law, currently working at Symbiosis Law School, Hyderabad. He takes lectures on the Law of Crimes, laws related to women, Property Laws, etc. Previously, he was an Assistant Professor of Law at the Indian Institute of Legal Studies. He graduated in law from Aligarh Muslim University in 2018 and completed his LLM from Central University of South Bihar in 2019. As a part of his master's program, he wrote his dissertation on "Efficacy of Rape laws in India - reckoning the Reforms under the criminal justice system". He qualified for Assistant Professor, UGC-NET (Law) in December 2019. He specialises in criminal laws, and his research area includes transgender rights, women's rights, gender neutrality, consumer protection, etc. He has participated in and presented papers at various national and international conferences and has a few reputed publications.

Surjit Singha is an academician with a broad spectrum of interests, including UN Sustainable Development Goals, Organizational Climate, Workforce Diversity, Organizational Culture, HRM, Marketing, Finance, IB, Global Business, Business, AI, Women Studies, and Cultural Studies. Currently a faculty member at Kristu Jayanti College, Dr. Surjit also serves as an Editor, reviewer, and author for prominent global publications and journals, including being on the Editorial review board of Information Resources Management Journal and a contributor to IGI Global. With over 13 years of experience in Administration, Teaching, and Research, Dr. Surjit is dedicated to imparting knowledge and guiding students in their research pursuits. As a research mentor, Dr. Surjit has nurtured young minds and fostered academic growth. Dr. Surjit has an impressive track record of over 75 publications, including articles, book chapters, and textbooks, holds two US Copyrights, and has successfully completed and published two fully funded minor research projects from Kristu Jayanti College.

P E Thomas has put in 34 years of service in teaching and research in the realm of Communication and Media Studies. His area of specialisation includes New Media and Information Society, Development Communication and Media in Conflict. He has been handling coursework in areas such as Print Journalism, Advertising, Print Production, New Media, and Film Studies.

Index

Symbols

5Cs 160, 161, 162, 163, 173, 174, 178

A

Africa 35, 56, 61, 63, 64, 65, 66, 72, 76, 78, 79, 179, 180, 181, 182, 183, 184, 186, 187, 188, 191, 192, 193, 194, 195, 196, 197, 198
Agenda-Setting Theory 1, 2, 4, 13, 62, 70, 72, 73, 74, 81, 192
Algorithms 91, 96, 97, 99, 104, 184, 195, 212, 244, 258, 260, 261, 266, 267, 268, 270, 271, 275, 282, 284, 285, 286, 287, 288, 296, 301, 302
Artificial Intelligence 7, 89, 97, 99, 106, 114, 191, 234, 242, 244, 245, 258, 259, 260, 261, 262, 266, 267, 268, 269, 270, 271, 272, 273, 274, 275, 276, 277, 278, 279, 280, 281, 282, 283, 284, 285, 286, 288, 289, 290, 293, 299, 300, 301, 302
Audience Engagement 92, 94, 95, 99, 106
Augmented Reality 89, 91, 96, 102, 156, 191, 274, 282
Automation 93, 266, 281, 282, 283, 284, 285, 289, 292, 301

B

Brand Visibility 96, 106

C

Communication Technologies 2, 14, 15, 160, 191
Communication Theory 14, 37, 53, 55, 62, 79, 81, 86, 104, 177
Conflicts 16, 17, 18, 19, 20, 21, 22, 23, 29, 30, 31, 32, 33, 36, 37, 131, 161, 172, 238
Consumer Activism 128, 129, 130, 136, 140, 141, 147
Consumers Behavior 111, 114, 121, 122
Content 1, 2, 3, 4, 5, 7, 10, 11, 12, 15, 16, 17, 19, 20, 21, 22, 32, 37, 40, 56, 57, 58, 59, 60, 61, 62, 63, 64, 66, 68, 71, 73, 74, 75, 76, 77, 80, 84, 85, 86, 87, 88, 89, 90, 91, 92, 93, 94, 95, 96, 97, 98, 99, 103, 104, 105, 106, 113, 116, 117, 118, 119, 123, 126, 141, 152, 155, 156, 160, 161, 162, 165, 168, 170, 171, 172, 173, 174, 177, 178, 179, 180, 184, 187, 190, 191, 193, 195, 196, 198, 200, 201, 205, 208, 211, 212, 215, 216, 219, 220, 221, 222, 223, 224, 225, 226, 227, 228, 232, 237, 238, 239, 240, 241, 244, 245, 251, 256, 258, 259, 260, 261, 262, 266, 267, 268, 269, 270, 272, 274, 276, 278, 279, 280, 281, 282, 283, 284, 285, 286, 287, 288, 289, 292, 293, 295, 296, 297, 298, 299, 301
Convergence 1, 2, 3, 4, 5, 10, 11, 12, 13, 14, 68, 84, 85, 87, 88, 89, 94, 95, 98, 100, 106, 149, 151, 152, 153, 154, 155, 156, 157, 174
Convergence Environment 1, 2
Corporate Reputation 128, 129, 130, 131, 132, 133, 134, 135, 136, 137, 138, 139, 140, 141, 142, 143, 145, 146, 147
Credibility Perceptions 42
CSR 128, 129, 130, 131, 132, 133, 134, 135, 136, 137, 138, 139, 140, 141, 142, 143, 144, 145, 146, 147, 148
CSR Communication 128, 129, 130, 131, 132, 133, 134, 135, 140, 141, 143, 145, 148
CSR Credibility 128, 130, 137, 138, 139, 140, 148
CSR Fit 139, 142, 145
Cultural Studies 230
Cyberbullying 113, 242, 243, 245, 249, 251, 252, 253, 254, 255, 256

D

Dark Side 234, 235, 236, 243, 244, 246, 247, 248, 249, 251, 253, 254, 255
Deceptive Advertising 240, 241, 244, 245, 247, 249, 255
Digital Activism 189, 190, 195
Digital Consumer 234, 235, 240
Digital Control 114, 115, 121
Digital Marketing 84, 85, 86, 87, 91, 92, 93, 98, 100, 103, 106, 108, 109, 110, 112, 113, 118, 119, 120, 122, 124, 125, 126, 211
Digital Media 2, 6, 7, 12, 13, 14, 85, 105, 106, 111, 112, 113, 129, 132, 149, 152, 160, 174, 177, 192, 202, 203, 211, 231, 258, 284, 285, 290
Disinformation Divide 199
Dispute 18, 20, 28, 29, 30, 31, 32, 33, 34, 184

E

Environment 1, 2, 3, 5, 11, 18, 55, 56, 58, 59, 61, 63, 65, 66, 67, 68, 69, 70, 72, 73, 75, 76, 79, 81, 84, 85, 87, 88, 89, 90, 97, 98, 99, 100, 117, 118, 125, 130, 132, 151, 155, 162, 163, 172, 173, 177, 188, 192, 193, 196, 210, 218, 234, 235, 236, 237, 239, 241, 242, 243, 246, 247, 250, 251, 254, 261, 262, 264, 273, 274, 275, 288, 297, 301

F

Fake Reviews 241, 242, 245
FOMO 88, 236, 237, 238, 244, 249, 250, 256
Fragmentation 1, 2, 3, 4, 5, 6, 11, 12, 14, 15, 84, 85, 87, 88, 90, 91, 92, 98, 100, 102, 105, 106, 135, 168, 192, 236
Framing 1, 2, 3, 4, 6, 7, 8, 9, 11, 12, 13, 14, 16, 17, 18, 19, 20, 21, 22, 24, 25, 27, 28, 30, 32, 33, 34, 35, 36, 37, 68, 75, 174

G

Gaziano 38, 42, 43, 52
Generative Artificial Intelligence 258, 259, 272, 275, 282, 284, 300
Global Media Landscape 100, 106, 174

H

Health Communication 103, 149, 150, 151, 152, 153, 154, 155, 156, 157, 231
Honeycomb Model 234, 256

I

Individual Beliefs 128, 129, 130, 133, 135, 136, 137, 138, 140, 141, 148
Investigative Journalists 283, 286, 287, 289, 290, 296, 297, 298, 299, 300, 302

J

Jobs 183, 283, 285, 289, 293, 294, 295, 297, 300

M

McGrath Credibility Scale 42, 43
Media 1, 2, 3, 4, 5, 6, 7, 8, 9, 10, 11, 12, 13, 14, 15, 16, 17, 18, 19, 20, 21, 22, 23, 35, 36, 37, 38, 39, 40, 41, 42, 43, 45, 46, 47, 48, 49, 50, 51, 52, 53, 54, 55, 56, 57, 58, 59, 60, 61, 62, 63, 64, 65, 66, 67, 68, 69, 70, 71, 72, 73, 74, 75, 76, 77, 78, 79, 80, 81, 82, 84, 85, 86, 87, 88, 89, 90, 91, 92, 93, 94, 95, 96, 97, 98, 99, 100, 101, 102, 103, 104, 105, 106, 107, 108, 109, 110, 111, 112, 113, 114, 115, 116, 117, 118, 119, 120, 123, 124, 125, 126, 127, 129, 130, 131, 132, 137, 141, 145, 148, 149, 150, 151, 152, 153, 154, 155, 156, 157, 158, 160, 161, 162, 163, 165, 166, 167, 168, 170, 172, 173, 174, 176, 177, 178, 179, 180, 181, 182, 183, 184, 185, 186, 187, 188, 189, 190, 191, 192, 193, 194, 195, 196, 197, 198, 199, 200, 201, 202, 203, 204, 205, 206, 208, 209, 210, 211, 212, 213, 214, 215, 216, 217, 218, 219, 220, 221, 222, 223, 224, 225, 226, 227, 228, 229, 230, 231, 232, 234, 235, 236, 237, 238, 239, 240, 241, 242, 243, 244, 246, 247, 248, 249, 250, 251, 252, 253, 254, 256, 258, 259, 260, 261, 262, 263, 264, 266, 267, 268, 269, 270, 271, 272, 273, 274, 275, 276, 277, 278, 279, 280, 281, 282, 283, 284, 285, 286, 288, 289, 290, 292, 293, 296, 297, 298, 299, 300, 301, 302
Media Effects 14, 52, 55, 57, 59, 61, 62, 63, 67, 68, 69, 70, 71, 72, 74, 75, 76, 77, 78, 79, 197
Media Preference 41, 42, 43, 50
Mental Health 90, 103, 200, 208, 214
Mobilizing 183, 194

N

New Colleagues 271
News Consumption 160, 161, 162, 164, 165, 166, 167, 168, 172, 173, 174, 176, 177, 178, 200, 201, 203, 212
News Literacy 160, 161, 162, 163, 176, 177, 178
News Literacy Behaviours 160, 161, 178

O

Online Social Networks 120, 236, 255

P

Peace 18, 20, 27, 28, 29, 30, 31, 33, 34, 35, 66, 182, 193, 195, 201
Polarization 3, 5, 6, 11, 13, 68, 84, 85, 87, 98, 100, 102, 105, 184, 198, 199, 201, 204, 209, 211, 214, 227
Political Attitude 41, 43, 231
Political Entertainment 217, 220, 223, 224, 225, 228, 230, 231, 232
Political Participation 20, 50, 187, 196, 216, 219, 222, 225, 227, 230, 232
Political Persuasion 215, 216, 217, 218, 219, 220, 221, 222, 223, 227, 228, 229, 232
Print Media 6, 19, 20, 22, 23, 200, 203
Professional Profiles 283, 284, 285, 288, 289, 290, 293, 297, 298, 300, 302

R

Regulations And Self-Regulation Rules 121
Revolution 6, 7, 11, 68, 87, 89, 103, 151, 182, 189, 200, 209, 241, 269, 285, 288, 302

S

Simulation 56, 57, 269, 271, 282
Social Media 1, 2, 3, 4, 5, 6, 7, 9, 10, 11, 12, 15, 17, 38, 39, 40, 41, 42, 43, 45, 46, 48, 49, 50, 51, 52, 53, 54, 57, 62, 63, 67, 84, 85, 86, 87, 88, 89, 90, 91, 93, 94, 95, 96, 97, 98, 99, 100, 101, 102, 103, 104, 105, 106, 108, 109, 110, 111, 114, 115, 117, 118, 120, 123, 124, 125, 126, 129, 131, 137, 141, 145, 148, 149, 150, 154, 157, 158, 161, 165, 166, 167, 170, 172, 174, 176, 177, 178, 179, 180, 181, 182, 183, 184, 185, 186, 187, 188, 189, 190, 191, 192, 193, 194, 195, 196, 197, 198, 199, 200, 201, 203, 204, 205, 206, 208, 209, 211, 212, 213, 214, 215, 216, 217, 218, 219, 220, 221, 222, 223, 224, 225, 226, 227, 228, 229, 230, 231, 232, 234, 235, 236, 237, 238, 239, 241, 242, 243, 244, 246, 247, 248, 249, 251, 252, 253, 254, 256, 258, 263, 264, 268, 270, 274, 278, 281, 282, 285, 288, 299, 300
Society 2, 3, 4, 5, 7, 36, 37, 42, 50, 54, 55, 56, 57, 58, 59, 61, 62, 63, 65, 66, 67, 68, 69, 70, 71, 72, 73, 74, 75, 76, 77, 86, 89, 96, 101, 103, 105, 113, 130, 131, 143, 146, 151, 161, 164, 173, 176, 177, 178, 179, 186, 187, 188, 189, 191, 192, 193, 194, 195, 198, 199, 201, 209, 210, 211, 214, 223, 225, 231, 232, 234, 236, 250, 253, 254, 256, 259, 262, 268, 275, 277, 289, 302
Socio-Political Change 179, 182, 183, 194
Spain 52, 112, 117, 118, 123, 127, 181, 283, 284, 289, 290, 299, 301
Sub-Saharan Africa 179, 180, 181, 182, 183, 184, 187, 191, 192, 193, 194, 196, 197, 198

T

Technologies 2, 11, 13, 14, 15, 64, 65, 82, 85, 86, 87, 92, 93, 97, 98, 99, 106, 123, 149, 150, 151, 152, 153, 155, 156, 158, 160, 161, 176, 181, 186, 191, 234, 246, 252, 262, 268, 276, 277, 278, 280, 282, 283, 284, 285, 286, 287, 288, 289, 290, 293, 294, 298, 302
Tools 5, 21, 90, 92, 96, 97, 98, 101, 104, 111, 150, 154, 186, 190, 198, 199, 209, 241, 244, 246, 259, 260, 262, 263, 265, 267, 269, 274, 280, 283, 284, 286, 287, 288, 289, 290, 291, 292, 293, 295, 296, 298, 302

U

Unethical Practice 108, 111, 112, 121

V

Value Co-Destruction 239, 240, 244, 247, 251, 253
Visual Media 258, 262, 268, 269, 271, 276, 278, 281, 282

Y

Young People 41, 111, 112, 113, 127, 160, 161, 162, 164, 176, 177, 178, 179, 180, 182, 183, 185, 186, 190, 191, 192, 193, 209, 219, 225, 230
Young Voters 215, 216, 217, 219, 223, 224, 226, 227, 228, 231
Youth 39, 56, 112, 114, 115, 118, 126, 176, 179, 180, 182, 183, 184, 185, 186, 187, 188, 189, 190, 191, 192, 193, 194, 195, 196, 198, 200, 208, 209, 217, 219, 220, 223, 233, 253
Youths 57, 176, 179, 180, 182, 183, 185, 186, 187, 188, 189, 191, 194, 196, 209, 217

Publishing Tomorrow's Research Today

Uncover Current Insights and Future Trends in Scientific, Technical, & Medical (STM) with IGI Global's Cutting-Edge Recommended Books

Print Only, E-Book Only, or Print + E-Book.
Order direct through IGI Global's Online Bookstore at www.igi-global.com or through your preferred provider.

Artificial Intelligence in the Age of Nanotechnology
ISBN: 9798369303689
© 2024; 299 pp.
List Price: US$ 300

Quantum Innovations at the Nexus of Biomedical Intelligence
ISBN: 9798369314791
© 2024; 287 pp.
List Price: US$ 330

Intelligent Engineering Applications and Applied Sciences for Sustainability
ISBN: 9798369300442
© 2023; 542 pp.
List Price: US$ 270

Exploring Ethical Dimensions of Environmental Sustainability and Use of AI
ISBN: 9798369308929
© 2024; 426 pp.
List Price: US$ 265

AI-Based Digital Health Communication for Securing Assistive Systems
ISBN: 9781668489383
© 2023; 299 pp.
List Price: US$ 325

Applications of Synthetic Biology in Health, Energy, and Environment
ISBN: 9781668465776
© 2023; 454 pp.
List Price: US$ 325

Do you want to stay current on the latest research trends, product announcements, news, and special offers?
Join IGI Global's mailing list to receive customized recommendations, exclusive discounts, and more.
Sign up at: www.igi-global.com/newsletters.

Scan the QR Code here to view more related titles in STM.

www.igi-global.com | Sign up at www.igi-global.com/newsletters | facebook.com/igiglobal | twitter.com/igiglobal | linkedin.com/igiglobal

Ensure Quality Research is Introduced to the Academic Community

Become a Reviewer for IGI Global Authored Book Projects

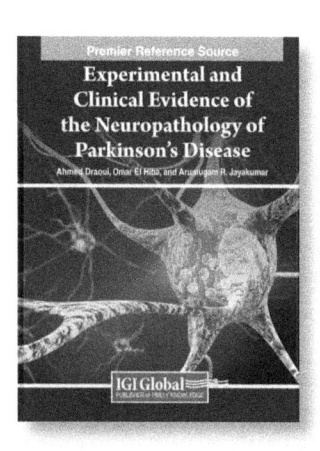

The overall success of an authored book project is dependent on quality and timely manuscript evaluations.

Applications and Inquiries may be sent to:
development@igi-global.com

Applicants must have a doctorate (or equivalent degree) as well as publishing, research, and reviewing experience. Authored Book Evaluators are appointed for one-year terms and are expected to complete at least three evaluations per term. Upon successful completion of this term, evaluators can be considered for an additional term.

If you have a colleague that may be interested in this opportunity, we encourage you to share this information with them.

IGI Global's Open Access Journal Program

Publishing Tomorrow's Research Today

Including Nearly 200 Peer-Reviewed, Gold (Full) Open Access Journals across IGI Global's Three Academic Subject Areas: Business & Management; Scientific, Technical, and Medical (STM); and Education

Consider Submitting Your Manuscript to One of These Nearly 200 Open Access Journals for to Increase Their Discoverability & Citation Impact

Web of Science Impact Factor	Journal
6.5	Journal of Organizational and End User Computing
4.7	Journal of Global Information Management
3.2	International Journal on Semantic Web and Information Systems
2.6	Journal of Database Management

Choosing IGI Global's Open Access Journal Program Can Greatly Increase the Reach of Your Research

Higher Usage
Open access papers are 2-3 times more likely to be read than non-open access papers.

Higher Download Rates
Open access papers benefit from 89% higher download rates than non-open access papers.

Higher Citation Rates
Open access papers are 47% more likely to be cited than non-open access papers.

Submitting an article to a journal offers an invaluable opportunity for you to share your work with the broader academic community, fostering knowledge dissemination and constructive feedback.

Submit an Article and Browse the IGI Global Call for Papers Pages

We can work with you to find the journal most well-suited for your next research manuscript. For open access publishing support, contact: journaleditor@igi-global.com

Publishing Tomorrow's Research Today
IGI Global
e-Book Collection

Including Essential Reference Books Within Three Fundamental Academic Areas

Business & Management
Scientific, Technical, & Medical (STM)
Education

- Acquisition options include Perpetual, Subscription, and Read & Publish
- No Additional Charge for Multi-User Licensing
- No Maintenance, Hosting, or Archiving Fees
- Continually Enhanced Accessibility Compliance Features (WCAG)

| Over **150,000+** Chapters | Contributions From **200,000+** Scholars Worldwide | More Than **1,000,000+** Citations | Majority of e-Books Indexed in Web of Science & Scopus | Consists of Tomorrow's Research Available Today! |

Recommended Titles from our e-Book Collection

Innovation Capabilities and Entrepreneurial Opportunities of Smart Working
ISBN: 9781799887973

Advanced Applications of Generative AI and Natural Language Processing Models
ISBN: 9798369305027

Using Influencer Marketing as a Digital Business Strategy
ISBN: 9798369305515

Human-Centered Approaches in Industry 5.0
ISBN: 9798369326473

Modeling and Monitoring Extreme Hydrometeorological Events
ISBN: 9781668487716

Data-Driven Intelligent Business Sustainability
ISBN: 9798369300497

Information Logistics for Organizational Empowerment and Effective Supply Chain Management
ISBN: 9798369301593

Data Envelopment Analysis (DEA) Methods for Maximizing Efficiency
ISBN: 9798369302552

Request More Information, or Recommend the IGI Global e-Book Collection to Your Institution's Librarian

For More Information or to Request a Free Trial, Contact IGI Global's e-Collections Team: eresources@igi-global.com | 1-866-342-6657 ext. 100 | 717-533-8845 ext. 100

Are You Ready to Publish Your Research?

IGI Global — Publishing Tomorrow's Research Today

IGI Global offers book authorship and editorship opportunities across three major subject areas, including Business, STM, and Education.

Benefits of Publishing with IGI Global:

- Free one-on-one editorial and promotional support.
- Expedited publishing timelines that can take your book from start to finish in less than one (1) year.
- Choose from a variety of formats, including Edited and Authored References, Handbooks of Research, Encyclopedias, and Research Insights.
- Utilize IGI Global's eEditorial Discovery® submission system in support of conducting the submission and double-blind peer review process.
- IGI Global maintains a strict adherence to ethical practices due in part to our full membership with the Committee on Publication Ethics (COPE).
- Indexing potential in prestigious indices such as Scopus®, Web of Science™, PsycINFO®, and ERIC – Education Resources Information Center.
- Ability to connect your ORCID iD to your IGI Global publications.
- Earn honorariums and royalties on your full book publications as well as complimentary content and exclusive discounts.

Join Your Colleagues from Prestigious Institutions, Including:

- Australian National University
- Massachusetts Institute of Technology
- Johns Hopkins University
- Tsinghua University
- Harvard University
- Columbia University in the City of New York

Learn More at: www.igi-global.com/publish

or Contact IGI Global's Aquisitions Team at: acquisition@igi-global.com

Individual Article & Chapter Downloads
US$ 37.50/each

Easily Identify, Acquire, and Utilize Published Peer-Reviewed Findings in Support of Your Current Research

- Browse Over **170,000+ Articles & Chapters**
- **Accurate & Advanced** Search
- Affordably Acquire **International Research**
- **Instantly Access** Your Content
- Benefit from the **InfoSci® Platform Features**

THE UNIVERSITY of NORTH CAROLINA at CHAPEL HILL

It really provides an excellent entry into the research literature of the field. It presents a manageable number of highly relevant sources on topics of interest to a wide range of researchers. The sources are scholarly, but also accessible to 'practitioners'.

- Ms. Lisa Stimatz, MLS, University of North Carolina at Chapel Hill, USA

Milton Keynes UK
Ingram Content Group UK Ltd.
UKHW010228300724
446304UK00005B/111